INDEX TO OBITUARY NOTICES IN THE RELIGIOUS HERALD RICHMOND, VIRGINIA 1828–1938

Prepared by
The Historical Records Survey
of Virginia
Division of Professional and
Service Projects
Works Projects Administration

Reprinted
Two Volumes in one

CLEARFIELD

Originally published
by
The Historical Records Survey of Virginia
Works Projects Administration
Richmond, Virginia, 1940

Reprinted, two volumes in one, for
Clearfield Company, Inc. by
Genealogical Publishing Co., Inc.
Baltimore, Maryland
1996, 2005

International Standard Book Number: 0-8063-4625-6

Made in the United States of America

INVENTORY OF CHURCH ARCHIVES

OF VIRGINIA

Prepared by

The Historical Records Survey of Virginia
Division of Professional and Service Projects
Work Projects Administration

Sponsored by

The Virginia Conservation Commission

GUIDE TO THE MANUSCRIPT COLLECTIONS OF THE
VIRGINIA BAPTIST HISTORICAL SOCIETY, SUPPLEMENT NO. 1
INDEX TO OBITUARY NOTICES IN THE RELIGIOUS HERALD
RICHMOND, VIRGINIA, 1828-1938

Richmond, Virginia
The Historical Records Survey of Virginia
December 1940

The Historical Records Survey Projects

Sargent B. Child, Director
Milton W. Blanton, Regional Supervisor
Kathleen Bruce, State Supervisor

Division of Professional and Service Projects

Florence Kerr, Assistant Commissioner
Blanche M. Ralston, Chief Regional Supervisor
Ella G. Agnew, State Director

WORK PROJECTS ADMINISTRATION

Howard O. Hunter, Acting Commissioner
F. H. Dryden, Regional Director
Russell S. Hummel, State Administrator

PREFACE

In January 1936, the Historical Records Survey, a nation-wide project of the Works Progress Administration, now the Work Projects Administration, was organized nationally. Dr. Luther H. Evans was appointed National Director of the Survey. In March 1936, the Survey began to function in Virginia as part of the Federal Writers' Project, of which Dr. H. J. Eckenrode was State Director, and Dr. Lester J. Cappon of the University of Virginia part-time Technical Assistant. In November 1936, when the Historical Records Survey became independent of the Federal Writers' Project, Dr. Cappon was appointed part-time State Director. At the same time Miss Elizabeth B. Parker, a former supervisor of the Survey, was appointed Assistant State Director. When Dr. Cappon resigned in June 1937, Miss Parker succeeded him as State Director. On September 5, 1939, the Historical Records Survey of Virginia became a State-wide non-Federal project with Miss Parker as State Supervisor.

Likewise in January 1936 the Survey of Federal Archives, a nationwide project of the Works Progress Administration, now the Work Projects Administration, was organized under the national directorship of Dr. Phillip M. Hamer, an official of the National Archives, Washington, D. C. In February 1936 work was started in Virginia with Mr. T. C. Durham as Regional Director. In September 1936, Dr. Kathleen Bruce was appointed Regional Director to succeed Mr. Durham. On August 1, 1937, the Survey of Federal Archives of Virginia became a State-wide non-Federal project, with Dr. Bruce as State Director.

On January 1, 1940, the two projects, the Survey of Federal Archives and the Historical Records Survey of Virginia, were consolidated by the Work Projects Administration to constitute a new Historical Records Survey project. Dr. Bruce was appointed State Supervisor and Miss Parker, Assistant State Supervisor. Miss Parker resigned from the Historical Records Survey on April 29, 1940.

By authority of the Presidential Letter, E-236, October 18, 1940, the Historical Records Survey is authorized to "conduct a survey and prepare for duplication inventories of all official records of the counties and of the Federal Government (except the Post Office) within the State; conduct a survey and prepare for duplication inventories of the records of the churches of all denominations within the State; and copy the imprints of all materials, printed before 1877 within the present boundaries of the United States, which are in the custody of all public, semi-public, and notable private libraries within the State." The ultimate objective is to make contributions of public value.

In conformity with the authorization, the Historical Records Survey of Virginia has in progress for publication inventories of the archives of Virginia counties and churches, and of all Federal agencies within the State except the Post Office. It also has under way a survey of American imprints prior to 1877. Under the direction of the Federal Government, the inventories are deposited with the appropriate agency.

THE INDEX TO OBITUARY NOTICES IN THE RELIGIOUS HERALD, RICHMOND, VIRGINIA, 1828-1938, originated as Supplement No. 1 to a volume planned by Miss Parker on the manuscripts and the printed materials of the Virginia Baptist Historical Society. An index such as this is not commonly undertaken by the Historical Records Survey projects. But the Religious Herald is a notable Baptist journal, and has performed, since it was first issued on January 11, 1828, a public service by publishing notices of deaths and marriages. To understand the full value of this public service, it should be noted that the official register of births, deaths, and marriages, required in every Virginia

Preface

parish during the colonial period, disappeared along with the State church which did not long survive the colony. No legal record of births and deaths was again required in Virginia until an act of the Virginia Assembly passed in 1853, effective January 1, 1854, ordered the commissioners of revenue to report on births and deaths to the clerk of each county court, and to the clerk of each corporation court in the Commonwealth. The Code of 1860 continued in substance the provisions of the Act of 1853. The maintenance of legal records was seriously affected by the War for Southern Independence. County archives in the path of the Confederate and Union armies suffered heavy losses. The registration of births and deaths was again required by the Code of 1873. Under the Code of 1887, each commissioner of revenue was instructed to make an annual registration of the births and deaths in his district. But on March 4, 1898, the General Assembly repealed the sections of the Code of 1887, which dealt with the registration of births and deaths, with a view, perhaps, to improving procedure. An act of 1912, effective March 12, 1912, made each justice of the peace a registrar responsible to the State Board of Health. As registrar, a justice's duty was to maintain a record of births and deaths for that portion of his magisterial district assigned him by the State Registrar. If there happened to be no justice in the area, or if a justice refused to act, the State Registrar appointed some other suitable person to perform the duty. THE INDEX TO OBITUARY NOTICES IN THE RELIGIOUS HERALD ... contains around 19,000 references. The great majority of them are to folk who were either members of or connected with the Baptist churches in Virginia. As is the case with thousands of other Virginians who died between 1827 and 1854, and 1897 and 1912, no public record exists of the deaths of these persons. And even though recorded in the archives of their churches, the individual records are difficult to reach. Moreover, not only county records but church records suffered in the upheaval of 1861-65. The contribution of the index, therefore, is to make available the wealth of information that lies buried in the four almost complete files of the Religious Herald, in the custody of the Virginia Baptist Historical Society at Richmond.

When Miss Elizabeth Coalter, joined the staff of the Historical Records Survey in April 1939, as supervisor of the Survey of Church Archives, the field work on the INDEX TO OBITUARY NOTICES ... had been started. The work has been checked, edited, and compiled in 1940 under Miss Coalter's supervision. A few departures have been made from the original procedure first established for this index. For instance, page numbers have been deleted. This has been done inasmuch as all issues of the Religious Herald do not have numbered pages, and confusion resulted when it was attempted to number them consecutively. In some years the issues were paged consecutively through the year; in other years each issue was paged individually. Most of the notices appear in the obituary column which is usually on the third, or fourth page of the issue. A few notices were printed as news items; others are resolutions of churches on the death of an individual. The symbol * is used to denote a name which has been found spelled differently in the same notice. For example, "SNEED, James A., s. of C. P. and Helen Winn SNEAD, Aug. 19, 1937." The same symbol is used also when there seems to be a typographical error in one or more entries as in "ABRAHAM, W. Y. (Mrs.), d. of Rev. A. Broadus, May 30, 1895 ... ABRAHAMS, W. Y. (Rev.), Nov. 19, 1903;" or when a name is spelled in an unusual manner as "WOOD, Emily E., d. of John and Cassandria Wood, Aug. 16, 1855." The place of death has been eliminated since it is not always clear where the individual died.

Preface

A companion volume, GUIDE TO THE MANUSCRIPT COLLECTIONS OF THE VIRGINIA BAPTIST HISTORICAL SOCIETY, SUPPLEMENT NO. 2, INDEX TO MARRIAGE NOTICES IN THE RELIGIOUS HERALD, RICHMOND, VIRGINIA, 1828-1938, is in progress. This volume was also planned by Miss Parker.

Kathleen Bruce

Kathleen Bruce
State Supervisor
Historical Records Survey of Virginia

Richmond, Virginia
December 17, 1940

ABBREVIATIONS

Capt.	Captain
Col.	Colonel
d. of	daughter of
Gen.	General
gr. d.	granddaughter
gr. s.	grandson
Lt.	Lieutenant
m.	married
Maj.	Major
s. of	son of
Sgt.	Sergeant
w. of	wife of

- A -

ABBITT
   Julian H. (Dr.), Feb. 14, 1907
   Mary Ann, w. of George Abbitt,
     Nov. 26, 1857
   R. W., Sept. 23, 1937
   Sally A. (Mrs.), July 21, 1892
   Sarah F., w. of Dr. W. H.
     Abbitt, June 3, 1897
   William B. (Dr.), Apr. 15,
     1858
   William Chatham, Mar. 23, 1916
   William H. (Dr.), Dec. 5. 1907
ABBOT
   Isaac Houghton, Dec. 27, 1877*
   Louisa F. T., w. of J. H.
     Abbot, Sept. 30, 1875
ABBOTT
   Daniel Lord, s. of Isaac H.
     Abbott, Aug. 9, 1860*
   Fannie Jane, w. of Daniel L.
     Abbott, Sept. 13, 1860
   James A., Aug. 4, 1938
   John, May 10, 1860
   Lucy (Mrs.), May 1, 1851
ABELL
   J. Ralls, s. of Rev. John S.
     Abell, Dec. 16, 1886*
   Susan D., w. of J. Rawls Abell,
     Aug. 20, 1903*
   Willie McLeod, s. of A. P.
     Abell, Dec. 29, 1864
ABERNATHY
   John Clayton, s. of John J.
     and Marietta Abernathy,
     May 28, 1885*
   Liles E., Apr. 6, 1843
   Thomas John, s. of J. Clayton
     and Imogen A. Abernathy,
     May 31, 1894
ABERNETHY
   John J., May 15, 1873*
ABRAHAM
   Elizabeth D., w. of Mordecai
     Abraham, Dec. 4, 1851
   H. L., Apr. 27, 1882
   Jesse A., Mar. 17, 1887
   John W., Jan. 1, 1880

   Mary, w. of Dr. Charles L.
     Abraham, Sept. 1, 1837
   Mordecai, Jr., s. of Morde-
     cai and Polly Abraham,
     Nov. 13, 1856
   Rosa Hilliard (Mrs.), June
     24, 1926
   W. Y. (Mrs.), d. of Rev.
     John A. Broadus, May 30,
     1895*
   Wickliffe Harrison, s. of
     W. Y. and Annie H. Abraham,
     Oct. 2, 1884*
   William F., Dec. 29, 1842
ABRAHAMS
   Grace Love, w. of St. George
     T. Abrahams, Oct. 28, 1937*
   Mary F., w. of Jesse A.
     Abrahams, June 28, 1888
   Polly, w. of Mordecai Abra-
     hams, Dec. 19, 1839
   W. Y. (Rev.), Nov. 19, 1903*
ABRAMS
   Grace, w. of Rev. St. George
     T. Abrams, Apr. 15, 1937*
   Mamie, July 29, 1920
ACKER
   Mary J. (Mrs.), Sept. 27,
     1934
ACKISS
   Caleb L., Feb. 21, 1884
ACREE
   Alex. S., Jan. 3, 1884
   Edward F., Jan. 5, 1905
   Edward S., Aug. 23, 1883
   Lucy Ellen, d. of Edward S.
     and Mary Susan Acree,
     Oct. 16, 1845
   Roland R. (Rev.), Nov. 21,
     1918
   Thomas (Mrs.), June 12, 1845
ADAIR
   Hugh T., Dec. 4, 1930
   Jane A., w. of James Adair,
     Apr. 9, 1863
ADAM
   Richard, Mar. 16, 1893

* Possible inaccuracy in name, or spelling, but given as printed

OBITUARY NOTICES IN THE RELIGIOUS HERALD WITH DATES OF PUBLICATION

Richard (Mrs.), Dec. 12, 1901; Mar. 20, 1902

ADAMS
Alex., Sept. 5, 1834*
Alice, d. of Joseph and Catharine E. Adams, July 18, 1907
Amanda J., w. of R. E. Adams, Mar. 11, 1920
Andrew Broadus, Apr. 21, 1892*
Ann, w. of Thomas Adams, Jan. 11, 1839
Apphia (Mrs.), June 25, 1830
Charles S. (Elder), Feb. 28, 1850
Cornelius Boardman, Sept. 20, 1860
Edward, May 10, 1855
Elizabeth, w. of James Adams, Jan. 14, 1841
Elizabeth, w. of Gustavus Adams, d. of William Pattie, Oct. 21, 1841
Elizabeth (Mrs.), Aug. 13, 1885
George, Apr. 24, 1856
George F. (Rev.), Apr. 26, 1877
Harriet, w. of Elder Charles Adams, July 14, 1870
J. M. (Mrs.), June 14, 1923
J. W., June 8, 1905
James M., Apr. 12, 1900
John Abram, Mar. 25, 1920
John David, Mar. 23, 1854
John G., Dec. 2, 1852
John R., June 16, 1887
Joseph, Sept. 4, 1884
Julia C., w. of Robert S. Adams, Sept. 11, 1862
Littleton F., s. of George Adams, Feb. 23, 1854
Louisa Marshall, d. of John G. and Lucy Adams, Aug. 3, 1848
Luny O., w. of J. G. Adams, Nov. 10, 1881*
Luther A., s. of Richard Adams, July 9, 1857
Martha P., w. of Richard Adams, Oct. 8, 1885
Mary, w. of Elder George F. Adams, Mar. 21, 1834
Mary A., w. of Capt. A. B. Adams, May 22, 1884
Mary Ann, w. of William C. Adams, Aug. 6, 1857
Mary Eliza, d. of Johnson and Laura A. Adams, July 14, 1853
Mary Leitch, d. of John S. Adams, Feb. 27, 1862
Priscilla L., Aug. 24, 1871
R. K., Apr. 22, 1869
Richard, Mar. 11, 1858
Richard E., Mar. 21, 1901
Robbie L., s. of R. S. Adams, Nov. 23, 1882
Robert Stribling, Feb. 18, 1904
S. J., Oct. 22, 1896
S. L. (Mrs.), Mar. 20, 1924
Sallie Wade (Mrs.), Jan. 31, 1935
Sarah L. B., w. of Rev. George F. Adams, Jan. 23, 1851
Susan A., w. of W. W. Adams, d. of Capt. W. Wilson, Mar. 13, 1862
Tabitha, Feb. 15, 1828
Turner, July 12, 1855
W. H., July 3, 1913
William, Nov. 20, 1873
William C., s. of Capt. F. M. Adams, Mar. 6, 1845
William F., s. of John G. and Lucy Adams, Mar. 6, 1845

ADCOCK
Frances, w. of Capt. William Adcock, d. of Mrs. Keziah Frayser, Apr. 24, 1835
William (Capt.), Mar. 27, 1835

ADDISON
Carmen Holloman (Mrs.), Jan. 20, 1927

ADEY

* Possible inaccuracy in name, or spelling, but given as printed

OBITUARY NOTICES IN THE RELIGIOUS HERALD WITH DATES OF PUBLICATION

Charles (Rev.), Jan. 20, 1927
Charles (Mrs.), Oct. 17, 1929
ADKERSON
　Mae, Dec. 25, 1924
ADKINS
　Alice L. (Mrs.), Mar. 3, 1927
　Amanda S. (Mrs.), June 30, 1887
　Andrew J., July 24, 1856
　Blanche Hill, d. of Daniel and Alice Adkins, Oct. 19, 1923
　Daniel, Mar. 14, 1878
　Daniel D., Nov. 29, 1928
　John D., Nov. 24, 1887
　Lena May, Aug. 17, 1933
　Mary (Mrs.), Sept. 19, 1861
　Mary (Mrs.), May 24, 1888
　Sidney Everett, s. of Daniel and Alice Adkins, Mar. 2, 1876
ADKISSON
　Mamie McDonald (Mrs.), Jan. 21, 1892
　Mary Sydnor (Mrs.), Jan. 21, 1892
　Minnie Brown, Aug. 17, 1933
AGEE
　Adalaide, w. of A. B. Agee, Mar. 18, 1882
　Ann E., w. of John R. Agee, Feb. 7, 1895
　Ann V., d. of John R. and Ann Eliza Agee, Mar. 5, 1863
　Eliza Van-Lew, d. of John R. and Ann E. Agee, Sept. 27, 1883
　Lelia Winfrey, w. of R. B. Agee, Feb. 12, 1931
　Lucy F., d. of John R. and Ann Eliza Agee, Mar. 5, 1863
　Mary M., w. of Samuel Agee, Nov. 4, 1847
　Peter I., s. of John R. and Ann Eliza Agee, Mar. 5, 1863
　Sallie, w. of J. Bushrod Agee, Apr. 26, 1900
　Sallie L., d. of John R. and Ann Eliza Agee, Mar. 5, 1863
　Sue Putney, w. of Luther R. Agee, Apr. 17, 1913

T. Mosely, July 6, 1876
Truman, Dec. 15, 1932
AGLIONBY
　Fanny, w. of Charles Aglionby, d. of Col. James Wood Walker, Oct. 9, 1902
　William Beall, Oct. 27, 1870
AGNEW
　James L., July 30, 1863
　P. C., w. of Dr. James A. Agnew, Jan. 2, 1873
AIKIN
　Ann (Mrs.), Feb. 7, 1850
AINSLIE
　Deborah, w. of Elder Peter Ainslie, Feb. 17, 1832
AIREY
　George W. (Dr.), Nov. 23, 1876
AKLES
　Louisa J., Oct. 8, 1857
ALDERSON
　Allen Lindsay, s. of Elder L. A. Alderson, Oct. 2, 1851
　Eliza Floyd, w. of Rev. Lewis A. Alderson, Mar. 4, 1909
　Floyd Powell, s. of Elder L. A. Alderson, Oct. 8, 1857
　George (Col.), Apr. 20, 1871
　Jennett C., w. of Col. George Alderson, July 31, 1835
　John, Jr. (Rev.), Mar. 27, Apr. 10, 1873
　John Marcus, Nov. 19, 1863
　Joseph, Aug. 14, 1845
　Judith (Mrs.), Aug. 30, 1839
　L. A. (Rev.), June 9, Aug. 25, 1881
　Martha Dorothy, d. of George N. Alderson, Jan. 4, 1839
　Martha Graham, w. of John D. Alderson, Apr. 16, 1891
　Mary, w. of Col. Joseph Alderson, Apr. 30, 1857
　Rufus D., Aug. 4, 1859

OBITUARY NOTICES IN THE RELIGIOUS HERALD WITH DATES OF PUBLICATION

Sabina Isabella, d. of Col.
George Alderson, Jan. 16,
1840
ALDHIZER
E. A. (Mrs.), Oct. 9, 1913
John, Nov. 9, 1848
Sarah A., July 19, 1855
ALDRIDGE
Mary E., Apr. 13, 1876
Virginia, Mar. 16, 1933
ALEXANDER
Bessie Lenard, d. of Thomas
B. and Eliza A. Alexander,
Feb. 22, 1872*
Brenda Blake, d. of W. W.
and E. W. Alexander, Mar.
31, 1892
Edmonia (Mrs.), Jan. 15, 1880
Emma Hughes (Mrs.), Apr. 12,
1923
John H., Feb. 18, Apr. 8,
1909
Martha (Mrs.), Sept. 5, 1850
Mary, d. of Col. Robert Alexander, Mar. 13, 1856
Mary E. (Mrs.), Mar. 31, 1887
Mary R., w. of Col. Robert
Alexander, Dec. 9, 1880
Purcell Jackson, s. of William
W. and Edith W. Alexander,
May 18, 1893
Rebecca Ann Wills, w. of James
Alexander, Apr. 1, 1880
Susan S. C. (Mrs.), Aug. 19, 1831
Thomas B., May 12, 1870
Thomas J., s. of Thomas B. and
Eliza A. Alexander, Feb. 22,
1872
William C., Oct. 17, 1850
William H. K., s. of Thomas
B. and Eliza A. Alexander,
Feb. 22, 1872
ALFORD
Henry (Rev.), Jan. 28, Feb. 2,
1871
ALLAN
Frances K., w. of John Allen,
Mar. 6, 1829
Lena, d. of James M. M. and
Lavenia Allan, Mar. 2, 1865

ALLCOTT
Norton Henry, s. of Philo.
and M. B. Allcott, Dec. 4,
1879*
ALLDREDGE
Barbara Taliaferro, w. of
Dr. Eugene P. Alldredge,
Mar. 5, 1936
ALLEGRE*
Anna, w. of William Allegre,
June 2, 1859
ALLEGREE*
A. E., Aug. 21, 1924
William, Apr. 12, 1833
ALLEN
Ada O., d. of Charles W.
and Catura Allen, Apr.
12, 1877
Addie Diggs, w. of Roland
D. Allen, Oct. 24, 1901
Alice (Mrs.), Feb. 27, 1913
Anne Price, w. of Capt.
Littleberry W. Allen,
Mar. 1, 1833
Damaris A., w. of James
Allen, Dec. 13, 1849
David, Dec. 6, 1860
Effie Bevil (Mrs.), Oct. 26,
1922
Eliza, w. of Simeon Allen,
June 21, 1883
Eliza K., d. of George E.
and Sarah A. Allen, Dec.
11, 1879
Elizabeth (Mrs.), July 7,
1853
Elizabeth (Mrs.), July 16,
1863
Elizabeth, w. of John Allen,
Mar. 18, 1875
Elizabeth T., d. of Mrs.
Judith Allen, Nov. 12,
1840*
Ellen C., d. of Mitchell F.
and Nancy Allen, July 28,
1881
Eudora Ann Jane, d. of
James M. Allen, Jan. 27,
1853
Frances, w. of Benjamin Allen,

* Possible inaccuracy in name, or spelling, but given as printed

OBITUARY NOTICES IN THE RELIGIOUS HERALD WITH DATES OF PUBLICATION

July 2, 1830
Frences Rebecca, d. of Jonathan Allen, Nov. 11, 1852
George H. (Mrs.), Aug. 31, 1848
George J., June 2, June 30, 1927
George N., s. of William I. and Margaret Dix Allen, June 13, 1901
H., Feb. 26, 1857
James M. (Capt.), Mar. 15, 1860
Joel (Rev.), Jan. 1, 1885
John Washington, s. of Robert and Eliza W. Allen, Dec. 25, 1862
Judith D. (Mrs.), Aug. 1, 1844
L. B., Feb. 16, 1933
L. W. (Rev.), Jan. 11, 18, 1872
L. W., Jr., s. of L. W. and Ann M. Allen, Dec. 31, 1857
Lucy J., w. of Rev. L. W. Allen, d. of James Long, Apr. 20, 1905
Maria L. (Mrs.), Dec. 18, 1856
Mary (Mrs.), Aug. 21, 1856
Mary (Mrs.), Apr. 19, 1894
Mary B., w. of William Austin Allen, Sept. 26, 1828
Mary E. (Mrs.), Jan. 25, 1844
Mary E., July 8, 1858
Mary Jane, Nov. 9, 1854
Nancy, Apr. 17, 1890
Nannie Thomas, w. of Rev. William E. Allen, Aug. 21, 1873
Richard (Rev.), Nov. 5, 1868
Robert Boyd, s. of C. E. and Panthea B. Allen, Jan. 19, 1860
Robert G., July 16, 1863
Robert S., Oct. 20, 1870
Sarah S., July 9, 1857
Selden W., s. of J. M. and Mary R. Allen, Aug. 11, 1859

Thomas Martin, s. of Elder L. W. and Ann M. Allen, Sept. 13, 1849
Virginia W., d. of Granville Allen, May 19, 1853
W. I., Apr. 20, 1922
Walter Kendall (Rev.), Jan. 7, 1926
Walter P., Oct. 23, 1851
William, s. of H. Allen, Jan. 4, 1839
William, May 25, 1843
William, Dec. 25, 1862
William, June 27, 1872

ALLENSWORTH
Mildred Oena, d. of William B. Allensworth, Apr. 3, 1884*

ALLEY
Lottie Christine, w. of Carroll O. Alley, Apr. 18, 1912

ALLGOOD
Peterson, May 7, 1874
Tabitha J. C., w. of Peterson Allgood, Feb. 27, 1840

ALLISON
Anna Carroll, d. of R. T. and L. J. Allison, Sept. 12, 1895
Edward R., Jan. 10, 1878
J. W. (Mrs.), d. of James Thomas, July 13, 1876
L. M., w. of Luther Allison, Mar. 3, 1898
Laura J., w. of Robert T. Allison, Aug. 27, 1874
Mary Alice, w. of O. B. Allison, Oct. 14, 1909
William Williamson, Feb. 17, 1927

ALLMOND*
Jane Allen, w. of A. D. Allmond, Feb. 18, 1892

ALLPORT
Mildred P., w. of John Allport, Sept. 27, 1888
Mollie Shuman (Mrs.), Mar. 21, 1907

* Possible inaccuracy in name, or spelling, but given as printed

OBITUARY NOTICES IN THE RELIGIOUS HERALD WITH DATES OF PUBLICATION

James Preston, June 13, 1872
ALMOND*
  Anne, Jan. 7, 1892
  Martha M., May 26, 1892
  Virginia, w. of Thomas M.
    Almond, d. of Rev. Andrew
    Broaddus, Mar. 24, 1870
  William Ambrose, Apr. 16, 1914
ALSOP
  Elijah L., s. of Dr. William
    S. and Lavinia Alsop, Aug.
    30, 1860
  John W., s. of Dr. William S.
    Alsop, Feb. 8, 1883
  Martha E., w. of S. S. Alsop,
    d. of Benjamin and Elizabeth
    L. Burnett, Oct. 2, 1879
ALVIS
  Bernard Lee, s. of R. H. and
    B. A. Alvis, Nov. 2, 1893
  J. W. (Elder), Jan. 28, 1858
  Kate C., d. of S. A. and K. C.
    Alvis, Jan. 11, 1900
  Nettie William, d. of William
    J. and Mary E. Alvis, Feb.
    24, 1887
  R. C. (Mrs.), Mar. 12, 1931
AMBROSE
  John Thomas, s. of Lorenzo
    and Malvina Ambrose, Oct. 29,
    1840
  Sarah (Mrs.), Jan. 15, 1925
AMES
  Ann, w. of John Ames, Feb. 16,
    1865
AMMEN
  Clinton Varner, s. of Michael
    S. and Henrietta R. Ammen,
    Sept. 18, 1862*
  Virginia, d. of Michael T.
    and Henrietta R. Ammen,
    Dec. 20, 1860
AMMONS
  Peter Taomas B., s. of Ballad
    Ammons, Aug. 10, 1848*
  R. Allen, Nov. 29, 1923
AMONETT*
  Frances (Mrs.), Aug. 6, 1863
  Nancy J. (Mrs.), Jan. 22, 1874
AMONETTE

William, Mar. 17, 1853
AMORY
  D., Aug. 5, 1858
  Edward V., s. of Thomas and
    Isabella Amory, Apr. 21,
    1864
  Elizabeth Ann, w. of Elder
    E. S. Amory, Nov. 9, 1843
  Martha, w. of E. S. Amory,
    Apr. 25, 1850
  Mollie E., d. of E. S. and
    Maria Amory, July 28, 1859
ANCELL
  Bettie E., w. of Capt. J. J.
    Ancell, Feb. 16, 1888
  Edward J., s. of William H.
    and Virginia Ancell, July
    29, 1858
ANDERSON
  Adelaide G., d. of Dr. M. A.
    and Ella K. Anderson,
    Aug. 11, 1859
  Ann (Mrs.), Dec. 26, 1850
  Ann Eliza (Mrs.), w. of Dr.
    J. M. Anderson, July 30,
    1830
  Ann R., w. of Dr. George L.
    Anderson, June 25, 1846
  Anna Mason, d. of Lieut.
    James A. and Sallie A.
    Anderson, Oct. 4, 1860
  Archibald (Dr.), July 25, 1867
  Benjamin (Mrs.), Jan. 23, 1851
  Benjamin, Jan. 1, 1863
  Callis, d. of M. G. and Jane
    L. Anderson, May 5, 1859
  Camillus C., Dec. 3, 1844
  Christina Belle, d. of Jeter
    Dandridge and M. D. Ander-
    son, Aug. 26, 1886
  Churchwell, Jr., s. of Church-
    well and Rebecca Anderson,
    Dec. 2, 1858
  E. G., May 26, 1887
  Edmund M., Jr., Aug. 4, 1864
  Eliza A., w. of M. M. Ander-
    son, Mar. 12, 1868
  Eliza I. (Mrs.), Sept. 8, 1842
  Elizabeth A., w. of Capt.
    William Anderson, July 16,

* Possible inaccuracy in name, or spelling, but given as printed

OBITUARY NOTICES IN THE RELIGIOUS HERALD WITH DATES OF PUBLICATION

1857
Elizabeth D., w. of John G. Anderson, Sept. 2, 1836
Ella, w. of Dr. Thomas B. Anderson, Oct. 29, 1868
Ella, July 20, 1893
Elsie Hendricks (Mrs.), Jan. 8, 1925
Emily H., w. of Edmund M. Anderson, Apr. 5, 1883
Ersa, s. of John A. and Ida E. Anderson, July 23, 1874
Eudora J., d. of John T. and Frances A. Anderson, Dec. 16, 1836
Euodia L., child of Thomas W. Anderson, June 17, 1847*
Frances Ann, w. of John T. Anderson, Nov. 19, 1868
Genet, Apr. 18, 1834*
Genet (Lieut.), Jan. 29, 1863
George, Oct. 12, 1848
Hallie A., d. of Dr. L. B. and E. T. Anderson, Apr. 2, 1896
Harriet, w. of Dr. Thomas B. Anderson, July 3, 1845
Harriet Anne, w. of M. D. Anderson, d. of Dr. Thomas B. Anderson, Dec. 23, 1897
Jane L., w. of E. O. Anderson, Dec. 31, 1885
Jesse, May 28, 1868
John, Sr., Jan. 4, 1866
John Henry, s. of William H. and Sarah Keesee Anderson, Aug. 5, 1897
John McL., July 15, 1880
John S. (Capt.), Jan. 29, 1863
John T., Jan. 1, 1863
John T., Dec. 29, 1864
Joseph Schoolfield, s. of M. M. Anderson, May 4, 1871
Kate Crane, Dec. 5, 1867
Lillian Martin, d. of Jeter Dandridge and M. D. Anderson, Aug. 11, 1887
Linnaeus B. (Rev.), June 18, 1903
Louisa, w. of Capt. Michael Anderson, Mar. 12, 1868

Lucy Calvert (Mrs.), d. of Thomas D. Toy, Aug. 23, 1883
Lucy Winston, June 18, 1896
M. M., m. first Eliza Ann Rudd, second, Marian Thompson, Oct. 18, 1894
Mamie W., Feb. 8, 1923
Maria, May 1, 1851
Maria D., w. of Genett Anderson, Dec. 25, 1879*
Martha (Mrs.), Nov. 20, 1829
Martin B., Mar. 6, 1890
Mary (Mrs.), Apr. 13, 1832
Mary (Mrs.), Oct. 23, 1884
Mary Rudd, d. of Mrs. John Anderson, Nov. 2, 1916*
Mary Elizabeth, d. of David J., Jr. and Sarah Anne Anderson, June 8, 1905
Mary Ella, d. of Reuben and Nancy Boatright, Sept. 25, 1924
Mary Judson, w. of L. G. Anderson, d. of J. G. and C. A. Miller, Mar. 30, 1882
Mary Louisa, w. of Michael Anderson, July 21, 1932
Mary Tiller (Mrs.), Feb. 18, Mar. 17, 1932
Mathew G., Nov. 11, 1880
Matthew P. (Dr.), May 29, 1845
Nannie B., w. of William L. Anderson, June 7, 1866
Nelson, Jan. 20, 1876
Patsy C., w. of Arch Anderson, d. of Capt. John Winston, Apr. 2, 1857
Patsy Tanner, Feb. 4, 1915
Pattie B., Mar. 16, 1911
Rebecca A., w. of William Anderson, Feb. 23, 1865
R. S., Sept. 12, 1889
Ruby, d. of Joel and Sallie Anderson, Mar. 31, 1892
Samuel L., Feb. 21, 1867
Sarah (Mrs.), Mar. 28, 1861
Sarah A., May 7, 1863
Sarah E., mother of Overton P. Anderson, Feb. 15, 1833

* Possible inaccuracy in name, or spelling, but given as printed

OBITUARY NOTICES IN THE RELIGIOUS HERALD WITH DATES OF PUBLICATION

Sarah Mildred, w. of W. A.
  Anderson, Oct. 6, 1921
Sidney, s. of Dr. L. B.
  Anderson, Dec. 8, 1898
Susan (Mrs.), June 23, 1842
T. B., July 20, 1899
T. Marion, Oct. 31, 1895
Theodore C., Mar. 13, 1913
Thomas, Sept. 24, 1846
Thomas B. (Dr.), Sept. 28, 1871
Thomas C., June 24, 1852
Thomas D., July 13, 1899
W. P., Apr. 8, 1897
W. S. (Mrs.), Nov. 30, 1922
Walter O., Jan. 19, 1865
Westworth, Mar. 22, 1923
William (Mrs.), Jan. 26, 1860
William A., Feb. 19, 1863
William G., Dec. 6, 1860
William Granville, Jan. 5, 1865
William Pitt, Apr. 29, 1897
Wilmoth S. (Mrs.), Sept. 16, 1937
ANDERTON
  Annie W. (Mrs.), June 16, 1892
  C. H. (Mrs.), d. of James C.
    Trice, Feb. 8, 1923
ANDREW*
  John F. (Rev.), Jan. 8, 1830
ANDREWS
  Andrew, Dec. 2, 1831
  Ann (Mrs.), June 9, 1842
  Ann Ellen (Mrs.), Mar. 5, 1865
  E. C. (Rev.), Dec. 16, 1937
  Ella M., Aug. 21, 1879
  Emma S., w. of John Andrews,
    Dec. 6, 1866
  J. E., Mar. 10, 1938
  James, Nov. 5, 1868
  James B., Sept. 26, 1895
  Lewis, July 22, 1858
  Lilian Broaddus, w. of M. W.
    Andrews, d. of James M.
    Broaddus, Sept. 16, 1915
  Mary S., w. of L. B. Andrews,
    Nov. 12, 1896
  Maud, d. of L. B. and Mary S.
    Andrews, Nov. 12, 1896
  Maud Elton, d. of Lewis H.
    and Alice B. Andrews,
    May 1, 1873
  Robert, June 8, 1843
  Sarah, w. of Lewis Andrews,
    Sept. 5, 1844
ANGELL
  Edith McLean (Mrs.), May 15, 1924
  Lionee, w. of Taylor Angell,
    Apr. 23, 1863
  Robert H., Nov. 16, 1933
  Susan Elva (Mrs.), July 29, 1937
  Thomas T., Jan. 14, 1932
ANGLE
  Lavinia Esther, w. of Caleb
    Angle, May 16, 1918
  Raymond Parker, s. of G. W.
    Angle, Apr. 26, 1906
ANNAN
  Nellie G., w. of William B.
    Annan, d. of Dr. William
    M. Dent, Dec. 24, 1885
ANSELL
  Hattie Loise, d. of William
    and Fannie Ansell, Mar. 7, 1889*
ANSLEY
  Mary, w. of F. W. Ansley,
    Jan. 4, 1906
ANTHONY
  Birdie, d. of P. and Alice
    Anthony, Apr. 28, 1887
  Charles Lewis (Rev.), Nov. 16, 1922
  John C., s. of Cornelius L.
    Anthony, Jan. 22, 1863
  Mary A. (Mrs.), May 18, 1871
  Sarah L., d. of Cornelius L.
    Anthony, Jan. 22, 1863
  William B., July 7, 1870
APLING
  Elizabeth, d. of Austin M.
    Apling, May 3, 1833
APPERSON
  Ann E., w. of James M. Apperson, Dec. 25, 1890
  Bessie Tinsley, w. of John
    M. Apperson, Mar. 18, 1920
  Braxton (Mrs.), May 21, 1925
  Charlie Willis, s. of Richard

* Possible inaccuracy in name, or spelling, but given as printed

OBITUARY NOTICES IN THE RELIGIOUS HERALD WITH DATES OF PUBLICATION

W. and Rachel A. Apperson, Sept. 6, 1860
Charlotte, d. of Richard W. and Rachel Apperson, Aug. 30, 1860
D. (Maj.), Sept. 11, 1879
E. C. (Mrs.), May 25, 1893
Eveline, Sept. 16, 1909
Martha Frances Glasscock, w. of William C. Apperson, Oct. 18, 1906
Sallie Manly, Oct. 9, 1879
William T., May 17, 1860

APPLEBERRY*
Benjamin A., s. of Capt. William Appleberry, Nov. 19, 1846
George F., s. of Capt. William and Judith Appleberry, Apr. 9, 1863
Judith, w. of William Appleberry, May 17, 1855
Sallie N., w. of D. J. Appleberry, Aug. 3, 1871
William J., s. of William Appleberry, Dec. 15, 1859

APPLEBURY*
Absalom W., s. of William Applebury, May 3, 1855
William, July 15, 1858

APPLER
Mary A., w. of Jacob E. Appler, Mar. 4, 1852

APPLETON
George D. (Mrs.), July 25, 1889

ARCHER
Anna E. (Mrs.), July 28, 1887
Mary Jane, Apr. 10, 1835
Nannie Irving, July 30, 1874
Robert P. (Dr.), Aug. 21, 1829
William, May 12, 1864

ARDIS
Hattie L., w. of Col. C. H. Ardis, Jan. 31, 1889

ARENDALL
Lee, s. of Jake Arendall, Jan. 15, 1925

ARGABRITE
G. W. (Rev.), Apr. 16, 1931

ARMENTROUT
Walter E., s. of W. S. Armentrout, Aug. 2, 1923

ARMES
Tommie R., Jan. 2, 1919

ARMISTEAD
Lula E., d. of William A. Armistead, Oct. 11, 1888
Mary Jane (Mrs.), Jan. 28, 1831
Moss William, Oct. 17, 1878

ARMITAGE
Thomas (Rev.), Jan. 30, 1896

ARMSTRONG
Albert G., Oct. 6, 1859
Ann (Mrs.), Jan. 25, 1872
Annis Bell, adopted d. of Mr. and Mrs. Armstrong, June 8, 1871
David Thompson, June 7, 1894
Emma A., d. of Price O. T. and Sarah F. Armstrong, July 8, 1858
Frances (Mrs.), d. of Rev. Thomas Courtney, July 7, 1859
J. G. (Rev.), Feb. 26, 1891
James Curtis, s. of W. Cowan and Esse E. Armstrong, Nov. 20, 1879*
John Edward (Mrs.), Feb. 22, 1934
Mary Susan, Oct. 24, 1901
Sarah F., w. of Price O. T. Armstrong, July 8, 1858
Virginia T., w. of J. E. Armstrong, Oct. 14, 1880

ARNEST
Gertrude T., w. of Thomas M. Arnest, d. of Gen. R. L. T. Beale, May 7, 1914

ARNOLD
Lucy Jane, d. of Col. William A. Arnold, Mar. 23, 1854
Mary (Mrs.), Feb. 18, 1847
Mary Susan, d. of Col. William A. Arnold, Mar. 8,

* Possible inaccuracy in name, or spelling, but given as printed

OBITUARY NOTICES IN THE RELIGIOUS HERALD WITH DATES OF PUBLICATION

1855
Oland, s. of R. B. and Lucy
  G. Arnold, Oct. 15, 1891
Sarah A., w. of James Arnold,
  Jan. 14, 1847
ARNOTT
  William (Rev.), July 1, 1875
ARRINGTON
  A. J., May 27, 1858
  James R., Sept. 4, 1913
ARTHUR
  Adeline, w. of Lewis Arthur,
    Aug. 4, 1887
  Austin J. (Rev.), Sept. 29,
    1932; Feb. 2, 1933
  James S., Apr. 29, 1847
  Mattie F. (Mrs.), mother of
    Rev. Howard L. Arthur,
    July 21, 1938
  N. B. (Mrs.), Oct. 3, 1861
ASH
  Lucy Marion, Sept. 4, 1924
  Rebecca, w. of Caleb Ash,
    Jan. 27, 1832
ASHBROOK
  Edna, w. of Thomas Ashbrook,
    Mar. 28, 1844
ASHBURN
  Allan A., Feb. 17, 1927
  Henry, Sept. 11, 1913
  Joseph P., July 31, 1879
  Judith, w. of Peter Ashburn,
    Feb. 16, 1922
  Lucy Ann, w. of William L.
    Ashburn, Apr. 7, 1921
ASHBY
  John A., June 26, 1890
ASHER
  Elizabeth (Mrs.), Sept. 3,
    1874
ASHLEY
  Thomas, Sept. 20, 1866
ASHMUN
  J. (Rev.), Sept. 5, 1828
ASHTON
  J. B., May 23, 1828
  William (Rev.), Sept. 2, 1836
ASKEW
  Sally, Jan. 5, 1860
ASTON

Bettin A., d. of John R.
  Aston, Sept. 20, 1855
William, Sept. 17, 1863
ATHEY
  Emma, w. of Rev. Samuel
    Athey, Feb. 14, 1924
  Genevieve, d. of Rev.
    Samuel Athey, Feb. 2,
    1899
  Samuel M. (Rev.), Nov. 23,
    Dec. 28, 1922
ATKINS
  A. C., w. of Rev. Samuel
    J. Atkins, May 1, 1902
  Ann Waller, w. of Tom At-
    kins, Apr. 10, 1919
  Anthonette, d. of Frank A.
    Atkins, July 8, 1897
  Archie Gibbs, Jr., Nov. 20,
    1924
  Banie W., d. of Andrew J.
    Atkins, Aug. 20, 1891
  Elizabeth Archer (Mrs.),
    June 19, 1924
  Eoline, d. of Hiram H. At-
    kins, July 17, 1902
  Frances C. (Mrs.), Mar. 22,
    1894
  J. O., Sept. 8, 1910
  Joseph, Dec. 11, 1862
  Lucian M., Aug. 30, 1928
  Mary A. (Mrs.), May 7, 1891
  Mary M., w. of Joseph Atkins,
    Apr. 28, 1864
  Nancy (Mrs.), Jan. 18, 1877
  Patrick Henry, s. of James
    Atkins, Dec. 21, 1871
  R. V., Feb. 13, 1918
  S. J. (Rev.), July 3, 1890
  William, s. of Col. W. T.
    Atkins, Jan. 15, 1891
ATKINSON
  Anne, w. of Elder Joseph W.
    Atkinson, July 20, 1854
  Benjamin E., Apr. 8, 1847
  Elizabeth, w. of George W.
    Atkinson, Nov. 12, 1830
  Elizabeth, d. of Milton P.
    Atkinson, July 1, 1847
  George W., Jan. 26, 1860

OBITUARY NOTICES IN THE RELIGIOUS HERALD WITH DATES OF PUBLICATION

Jennie (Mrs.), Aug. 7, 1873
Mary E., w. of John S. Atkinson, Aug. 6, 1840
Mary Elizabeth, d. of Col. John S. Atkinson, Nov. 17, 1842
Mary M., Oct. 9, 1862
Nancy, Feb. 3, 1842
Robert W., Mar. 3, 1921
Thomas (Rev.), Jan. 13, 1881
Winifred, w. of Charles Atkinson, Mar. 17, 1859
ATTKINSON*
  Elkanah B., Sept. 8, 1898
ATTKISSON
  Elmira, Oct. 3, 1895
  Mary Cleveland, d. of S. D. and Susie C. Attkisson, Feb. 9, 1888
ATWELL
  Lulie H., s. of Sam L. and Ella Atwell, Feb. 28, 1884*
  Samuel, May 24, 1860
ATWOOD
  John Randolph, Jr., s. of J. R. and Florence Atwood, Apr. 22, 1897
AUSTIN
  Ann, d. of Dr. William W. Austin, May 17, 1833
  Ann, Sept. 29, 1842
  Eliza Jane, d. of G. B. and J. Austin, Jan. 18, 1855
  Emily Semple (Mrs.), d. of Thomas Pescud Chisman, Sept. 25, 1924
  I. T. (Rev.), Dec. 22, 1892
  Locky, w. of Dr. William W. Austin, May 17, 1833
  Nancy, w. of Capt. William Smith Austin, Oct. 4, 1849
AVANT*
  Mary A. E., w. of James Avant, d. of John and Lucy Campbell, Oct. 21, 1852
AVENT
  Bettie, d. of Tamlin Avent, Mar. 10, 1853
  Tamlin, Apr. 8, 1875
AVERETT
  E. B. (Dr.), s. of Dr. Thomas H. Averett, Apr. 1, 1858
  John T., Feb. 24, Mar. 10, 1898
  W. P., Apr. 28, 1927
AVERY
  John P., May 12, 1870
AYER
  Roberta C., w. of Dr. L. M. Ayer, d. of Rev. Addison Hall, Feb. 22, 1883
AYLETT
  Emily (Mrs.), d. of Patrick Henry, Nov. 3, 1842
  Mary Lee, d. of William and Helen Moren Aylett, Aug. 13, 1874
AYLOR
  Aylette W., s. of W. J. Aylor, Apr. 4, 1889
  Irene N., w. of Robert H. Aylor, June 5, 1873
  John P., June 3, 1886
AYRES
  Catherine, w. of O. S. Ayres, June 27, 1867
  Eugene Edmond, Sept. 9, 1920
  Hannah Laura, w. of George M. Ayres, Mar. 5, 1936
  James E., July 20, 1911
  Myrtle, May 21, 1863
  Rosa, w. of James D. Ayres, July 1, 1909

* Possible inaccuracy in name, or spelling, but given as printed

- B -

BABB
W. H., Nov. 5, 1908
BABCOCK
Charles Lemuel, Feb. 11, 1915
Rufus (Rev.), May 20, June 10, 1875
BABER
Bettie S., Apr. 23, 1863
Edward (Col.), Nov. 29, 1860
Edward Jefferson, s. of Robert H. and Frances Lee Baber, Jan. 6, 1876
Edward W., s. of Col. Edward Baber, Feb. 28, 1855
G. W., Apr. 26, 1877
John S., Jan. 30, 1890
Lou T. (Mrs.), Dec. 20, 1883
Nannie, Jan. 17, 1929
Porter, Mar. 18, 1847
BACON
A. S., Oct. 29, 1891
J. S. (Rev.), Nov. 18, Dec. 9, 1869; Feb. 10, 1870
Martha, d. of Allen Bacon, Aug. 16, 1855
BACOT
Emily Leslie, w. of Samuel Bacot, Mar. 4, 1869
BADGER
Elvira, d. of George Badger, July 2, 1830
BADKINS
Bettie, w. of George W. Badkins, June 14, 1860
BAGBY
Alfred (Dr.), Apr. 8, 1926
Anderson, June 6, 1929
Andrew H., s. of Richard H. and Ann E. Bagby, Jan. 5, 1843
Ann Elizabeth (Mrs.), Mar. 15, 1894
Daniel, Aug. 24, 1843
Dorothy, w. of Richard Bagby, July 26, 1849
Harry Boyce, s. of Rev. H. A. Bagby, July 2, 1891
Mary Jane, w. of Rev. B. Bagby, d. of Maj. Benjamin and Dorothy Cleiuverius, Aug. 7, 1856
Sarah Jane Pollard, w. of Rev. Alfred Bagby, Feb. 2, 1888
Elizabeth, w. of John Bagby, Oct. 14, 1836
Elizabeth (Mrs.), Mar. 14, 1872
George Franklin (Mrs.), Feb. 4, 1915
George Poindexter, June 7, 1934
H. A. (Mrs.), Feb. 11, 1937
Harriet Brumley, d. of Thomas J. Bagby, May 25, 1854
James D., Jan. 1, 1885
John (Dr.), s. of Rev. Richard Hugh Bagby, Feb. 2, 1905
John James, Jan. 23, 1919
John R. (Dr.), Feb. 25, Mar. 18, Apr. 22, 1915
John R. (Maj.), Mar. 27, Apr. 3, 1890
Juliet, d. of Rev. A. Bagby, Oct. 12, and 26, 1876
Lucy Fleet, w. of Dr. John Bagby, Jan. 29, Apr. 9, 1885
Luther, Aug. 30, 1934
Marius T., s. of Rev. G. F. Bagby, Nov. 18, 1875
Martha, w. of James D. Bagby, Apr. 2, 1885
Mary A., w. of Travis Bagby, Oct. 29, 1874
Mary Etta, Mar. 22, 1855
Pattis M., May 29, 1924
R. H. (Rev.), Nov. 3 and 17, Dec. 1 and 8, 1870; Apr. 20 and 27, May 4, June 1, Nov. 10 and 17, 1871

OBITUARY NOTICES IN THE RELIGIOUS HERALD WITH DATES OF PUBLICATION

Richard Hugh, s. of Dr. Alfred Bagby, Jan. 17, 1929
Sue Etta, Sept. 27, 1923
Thomas P. (Mrs.), June 8, 1922
Travis, Mar. 14, 1850
William F. (Mrs.), July 21, 1921

BAGGARLY
C. M. (Dr.), Sept. 14, 1911

BAGWELL
Bena M., d. of W. H. H. and N. A. Bagwell, Dec. 13, 1900
R. W. (Rev.), May 21, June 18, 1936
Rose Dix (Mrs.), Oct. 13, 1898
W. H. H. (Mrs.), Oct. 7, 1926

BAILES*
M. G., May 26, 1887

BAILEY
A. C., w. of Andrew Bailey, Sr., Mar. 20, Nov. 21, 1872
A. M., May 8, June 5, 1879
Agnes A., w. of Elder William O. Bailey, Feb. 24, 1853
Agnes R., w. of M. S. Bailey, Aug. 14, 1902
Amanda C., w. of Abraham Bailey, Mar. 20, 1873
Andrew, Nov. 18, 1852
Andrew, Nov. 21, 1872
Ann E., Feb. 11, 1869
C. T. (Dr.), June 13, 1895
Calphurnia Atkisson, w. of E. C. Bailey, Aug. 25, 1887
Caroline, w. of Leighton W. Bailey, June 3, 1852
Chiles Hackett, s. of Aminadab M. and Mary C. Bailey, May 6, 1858
Clarence Lee, s. of Luther R. and Mary E. Bailey, Apr. 6, 1882
E. B., May 12, 1910
Edmund, Apr. 29, 1847
Edward P. (Col.), Dec. 25, 1890
Eliza B., w. of John W. Bailey, July 11, 1844
Elizabeth, w. of Terrisha Bailey, Nov. 18, 1841
Elizabeth, w. of D. M. Bailey, May 6, 1909
Elizabeth Mary, w. of George Bailey, May 19, 1887
Emma, w. of John H. Bailey, Jan. 16, 1873
Emory L., Jan. 3, 1907
Everett B., May 19, 1910
Frances R. (Mrs.), Jan. 26, 1843
Francis Monroe, s. of Cadmus L. and Elizabeth E. Bailey, Oct. 9, 1862
George, Aug. 4, 1887
George H., Oct. 1, 1896
George W., Oct. 23, 1862
George W. (Sgt.), Jan. 12, 1865
J. C. (Rev.), Dec. 29, 1881
J. M., Mar. 29, 1928
James F., Jan. 8, 1880
James Peyton, Jan. 1, 1852
James W., Mar. 21, 1907
John A., Mar. 6, 1913
John A. (Mrs.), Dec. 14, 1922
John D., Feb. 13, 1868
Jonathan, Nov. 21, 1844
Joseph E., s. of Rev. J. C. Bailey, May 18, 1871
Joseph H., Apr. 26, 1894
Leila Ada, d. of C. H. and M. J. Bailey, July 11, 1872
Lilian Boaze, w. of J. A. Bailey, July 28, 1927
Lycurgus H., s. of James F. and Clementine W. Bailey, Dec. 10, 1863
Martha Margaret, w. of Aminadab M. Bailey, d. of Mrs. Elizabeth W. Coleman, Oct. 13, 1837
Mary C., w. of A. M. Bailey, Feb. 21, 1889
Mary Hunter, d. of A. M. and Mary C. Bailey, June 19, 1851
Melvina P., June 13, 1872
Nancy, July 13, 1854
Nancy C., w. of William E. Bailey, Feb. 17, 1837

* Possible inaccuracy in name, or, spelling, but given as printed

OBITUARY NOTICES IN THE RELIGIOUS HERALD WITH DATES OF PUBLICATION

Nettie, w. of W. T. Bailey, d. of N. B. and Amanda M. Jones, May 4, 1882
Newton Howard, s. of A. M. and M. C. Bailey, June 27, 1844
P. R., s. of A. Bailey, Sr., June 8, 1843
Philip, Oct. 10, 1834
Robert Ryland, s. of Rev. Josiah Bailey, Aug. 7, 1862
Samuel, Sept. 9, 1836
Sarah Cooper, w. of Rev. J. C. Bailey, Feb. 12, 1885
Sarah W., w. of Jonathan Bailey, Dec. 5, 1878
Susan, w. of William E. Bailey, Aug. 31, 1871
T. N. (Mrs.), Apr. 16, 1925
Terrisha, Jan. 16, 1868
Thomas (Mrs.), Nov. 27, 1930
W. E., s. of Elder Josiah C. Bailey, Mar. 9, 1905
W. T., Aug. 26, 1886
William Edward, s. of Rev. J. C. Bailey, May 18, 1905
William St. George, s. of J. F. and C. W. Bailey, May 5, 1864

BAILY*
Elizabeth (Mrs.), Oct. 3, 1828
William (Capt.), Sept. 19, 1828

BAIN
Emma Crismond, w. of Jesse C. Bain, May 1, 1879
Mattie B., Apr. 26, 1906

BAIRD
Gladys, d. of J. M. Baird, July 9, 1914

BAKER
A. B. (Capt.), Sept. 18, 1879
A. W., Sept. 7, 1933
Agnes, w. of Elder Joseph Baker, Sept. 3, 1840
Catharine, w. of Rev. Joseph Baker, Oct. 27, 1870
Charles E., Mar. 12, 1857
Charlotte Anne (Mrs.), June 1, 1922
Cora Maude, Oct. 14, 1920
Elijah Witt, s. of John Brown and Elizabeth Baker, Oct. 22, 1863
Elizabeth, Jan. 21, 1847
Elizabeth A. (Mrs.), Jan. 28, 1869
Ellis T., Nov. 5, 1903
Elvira Susan, d. of Isaac Baker, Oct. 16, 1851
Ernest Frazer, s. of Ernest and Lucy Frazer Baker, Apr. 5, 1900
F. W., Apr. 16, 1914
Frederick, Sept. 2, 1831
Henry C., Mar. 4, 1875
Joel, Jan. 25, 1833
John Brown, Oct. 22, 1863
John Edward, s. of John B. Baker, Oct. 22, 1863
John W., Nov. 15, 1860
Joseph (Elder), Mar. 13, 1856
Joseph S. (Rev.), Aug. 9, Sept. 6, 1877
Judith T., d. of Albert Durrett, Oct. 8, 1857*
Kate L. (Mrs.), May 28, 1885
Louise Camson (Mrs.), July 14, 1904
Mary Ann, Jan. 23, 1851
Mary J., Oct. 31, 1907
Mattie F., Dec. 29, 1887
Nolia, w. of W. A. Baker, Apr. 15, 1920
Oliver, June 23, Sept. 1, 1921
Polly (Mrs.), Nov. 17, 1927
Sallie A., w. of Rev. F. M. Baker, d. of S. S. McGruder, May 28, 1868
Samuel, s. of Capt. Andrew Baker, Aug. 9, 1866
Sarah, July 27, 1832
Sarah R., w. of Thomas Baker, Dec. 30, 1836
Scott, Dec. 3, 1846
Thomas W., Mar. 25, 1920
Virginia, w. of H. L. Baker, Apr. 19, 1855
W. T., Sept. 4, 1924
W. W., Mar. 3, 1927

* Possible inaccuracy in name, or spelling, but given as printed

OBITUARY NOTICES IN THE RELIGIOUS HERALD WITH DATES OF PUBLICATION

William P., Jan. 10, 1861
William Thomas, s. of William
  B. and Macca Baker, Jan. 8,
  1857
BALDERSON
  Frances, w. of William Balderson, Oct. 1, 1846
  Mollie, w. of Bob Balderson, Feb. 24, 1921
  R. W., May 30, 1861
  William, Sr., June 29, 1854
BALDOCK
  W. H., May 24, 1917
BALDWIN
  A. W., July 2, 1936
  Agnes, d. of Elder A. A. Baldwin, July 16, 1863
  Charles I., Sept. 21, 1871
  George W., Mar. 24, 1864
  Josephine, d. of Rev. Archibald A. and Mary M. Baldwin, Oct. 16, 1856
  Martha Hanna, d. of Rev. Archibald A. and Mary M. Baldwin, Oct. 16, 1856
  Mary, w. of Thomas Baldwin, Mar. 4, 1858
  N. C. (Rev.), Feb. 26, 1903
  Nancy, w. of Rev. Noah C. Baldwin, Nov. 30, 1854
  Thomas J., Mar. 19, 1885
  William A., June 15, 1876
BALFOUR
  John O. (Dr.), Aug. 3, 1843
  Regina, w. of Dr. John O. Balfour, Aug. 3, 1843
BALL
  Ann C., w. of W. N. Ball, Mar. 29, 1855
  Austin, Aug. 22, 1844
  Bettie Land, d. of Dr. James E. and A. F. V. Ball, Sept. 15, 1859
  Cordelia, d. of W. N. and Ann C. Ball, May 26, 1853
  Dandridge, s. of Samuel Ball, Feb. 2, 1871
  Elizabeth, w. of Thomas Ball, July 31, 1829
  Emily H., w. of Philip A. Ball,
    May 13, 1869
  I. D. (Mrs.), mother of Rev. W. L. Ball, Sept. 19, 1907
  Isham, Oct. 25, 1860
  Jane C., w. of Isham Ball, Feb. 29, 1844
  Maria M. (Mrs.), Nov. 16, 1832
  Ritchie, s. of Carter Ball, Aug. 12, 1852
  Roberta (Mrs.), Apr. 5, 1928
  Walter Melvin, s. of John and Mary Ball, June 12, 1890
  William, Jan. 24, 1834
BALLARD
  Lucy Burnley, w. of Thomas Ballard, d. of James Duke, Nov. 30, 1871
  Mary, d. of J. J. Ballard, Jan. 19, 1922
  Sarah A., w. of John J. Ballard, Sept. 20, 1865
  Thomas, Jan. 30, 1879
  Walter Evans, s. of Henry C. and Sallie P. Ballard, Jan. 26, 1865
  William G., Oct. 13, 1892
BALLEW*
  John Thomas, s. of Rev. Benjamin Ballew, Dec. 22, 1910
BALLOW*
  Edward Bransford (Mrs.), Jan. 20, Feb. 3, 1916
  Judy, Aug. 10, 1882
  William Montgomery (Dr.), Oct. 13, 1853
BALLOWE*
  Anne Maria, d. of David N. and Eliza Ann Ballowe, May 5, 1853
  David N., Oct. 15, 1863
  Mary (Mrs.), Apr. 5, 1860
BANDY
  Minnie Lou, d. of I. T. and Sallie J. Bandy, Aug. 5, 1875
  Nannie, d. of Isaac T. Bandy, Nov. 24, 1887
BANE
  Allen, June 20, 1878

* Possible inaccuracy in name, or spelling, but given as printed

OBITUARY NOTICES IN THE RELIGIOUS HERALD WITH DATES OF PUBLICATION

Anna, w. of Jesse Bane, June 11, 1868
J. H. (Mrs.), Dec. 22, 1921
James E., Jan. 20, May 19, 1887
Jesse, July 1, 1875
Jessie, d. of John and Elizabeth E. Bane, Dec. 18, 1862
John William, s. of Haven and Louisa Bane, Mar. 1, 1860
Joseph R., s. of J. H. and E. E. Bane, June 28, 1888
Mary A., Nov. 20, 1873
Nancy, d. of Jesse Bane, Jan. 22, 1857
Sarah, d. of Jesse Bane, Jan. 22, 1857

BANES*
C. H. (Col.), Jan. 21, 1897

BANKS
Ann (Mrs.), Nov. 18, 1869
Anna Virginia, d. of William Banks, Apr. 2, 1874
Edwin (Maj.), s. of Dr. R. G. Banks, Oct. 24, 1867
Matilda E., w. of Dr. R. G. Banks, May 7, 1846
Ralph, Aug. 13, 1830
Richard G. (Dr.), Nov. 18, Dec. 23, 1869; Jan. 6, 1870
William H., Mar. 20, 1884

BANTON
Julia Ann, w. of Edmond Banton, Apr. 21, 1927

BAPTIST
E. G. (Rev.), s. of Rev. Edward Baptist, Feb. 6, 1896
E. L. (Mrs.), Apr. 20, 1911
E. L. (Rev.), s. of Richard Harwood and Sallie Goode Baptist, Apr. 16, 1914
Edward (Rev.), s. of William Glanville and Mary Langston Baptist, June 4, 1863
John G. (Col.), Feb. 17, 1837
Noel Wryothesley, s. of Rev. E. G. and Sarah A. Baptist, Jan. 22, 1880
Powhatan D., child of Rev. E. G. Baptist, Mar. 17, 1864

William H., Oct. 2, 1829

BARBEE
James Madison, May 9, 1938

BARBER
May Briggs, w. of Robert Bruce Barber, Mar. 6, 1919
Samuel B. (Rev.), Dec. 22, 1881
Sarah, w. of Silas Barber, July 16, 1857
William N., Dec. 18, 1862

BARBOUR
Alice H., w. of Willard Barbour, d. of Joseph and Araminta Goode Hutson, Jan. 31, 1895
Bessie K., July 19, 1923
J. W. (Mrs.), Sept. 15, 1921
John William (Rev.), m. first Martha Dawson, second Fannie West, Nov. 19, 1931
Margaret R., Oct. 23, 1930
Philip P. (Judge), Mar. 4, 1841
S. H., Mar. 7, 1907

BARDEN
A. L., Apr. 15, Dec. 20, 1920
Charlie, May 12, 1927
Curry W., s. of Willie S. and Bettie F. Barden, May 21, 1885
Frances N., w. of T. W. Barden, Oct. 19, 1899
H. K., Apr. 17, 1930
John W. (Mrs.), Apr. 4, 1929
Thomas Williams, June 27, 1907

BARFOOT
Emmie L. (Mrs.), Mar. 22, 1934

BARGAMIN
Mary J., w. of George Bargamin, Apr. 14, 1904
Mary Manson, d. of Paul and Laura Bargamin, July 25, 1878

BARGER
M. E. (Mrs.), June 3, 1926

BARGLEBAUGH
Rebecca A. (Mrs.), Mar. 22, 1877

BARHAM

* Possible inaccuracy in name, or spelling, but given as printed

OBITUARY NOTICES IN THE RELIGIOUS HERALD WITH DATES OF PUBLICATION

Hannah S. (Mrs.), May 1, 1930
Virginia A. (Mrs.), Apr. 14,
  1910
W. R. (Mrs.), Jan. 9, 1913
BARKER
  Ann E. (Mrs.), Nov. 11, 1897
  Colista Ann, w. of William N.
    Barker, Aug. 29, 1861
  D. A. (Mrs.), May 28, 1903
  Dolly B., mother of Rev. F. M.
    Barker, Aug. 2, 1860
  Elizabeth, w. of Maj. Benjamin
    B. R. Barker, Sept. 1, 1837
  Etta, w. of Dr. W. C. Barker,
    d. of Col. Charles Jones
    Mar. 1, 1900
  Francis M. (Rev.), Nov. 19,
    Dec. 24, 1863; Mar. 24, 1864
  Hattie, d. of J. P. Barker,
    July 18, 1889
  Isabella R., w. of Rev. J. G.
    Barker, Apr. 17, 1845
  Jesse B., May 28, 1914
  John A. (Mrs.), July 30, 1925
  John Alexander (Rev.), Mar. 1,
    Mar. 22, 1923
  Maynard, Oct. 6, 1938
  Oscar Bayne, Sept. 9, Oct. 21,
    1937
  Robert Armistead, s. of Rev.
    F. M. and D. A. Barker,
    Nov. 6, 1862
  Sophronia C., w. of N. B. Barker, d. of Rev. John Davis,
    Nov. 6, 1856
  William Carey (Dr.), Mar. 26,
    1931
  William Carey, III, Apr. 11,
    1935
BARKLEY
  Paul, Dec. 14, 1899
  W. D., s. of Rev. J. G. and
    L. T. Barkley, Sept. 19,
    1889
BARKSDALE
  Albert W. (Rev.), June 6,
    Aug. 15, 1878
  Hallie Craddock, w. of Judge
    W. R. Barksdale, May 3, May
    10, 1900

  Harriot T. (Mrs.), June 13,
    1828
  James H., s. of Hudson
    Barksdale, June 9, 1837
  Jonathan, Nov. 4, 1852
  Judith A. (Mrs.), Feb. 13,
    Feb. 27, 1902
  Lillian Haymes (Mrs.), Mar.
    17, 1938
  Martha C. Dunkum (Mrs.),
    Sept. 28, 1899
  Robert, Aug. 7, 1856
  Susan (Mrs.), Mar. 28, 1889
  W. R. (Judge), Apr. 23, 1925
BARLOW
  Anna (Mrs.), Jan. 24, 1834
  Edmund Lacy, Nov. 14, 1929
  John W., Oct. 13, 1898
  Lucy P. (Mrs.), July 1, 1886
  Maggie W., d. of T. J. and
    Annie M. Barlow, Oct. 30,
    1873
  Margaret N., w. of John H.
    Barlow, Aug. 13, 1863
  R. J., Dec. 22, 1927
  Richard Carson, Sept. 13,
    1928
BARNES
  Bettie A. Morris, w. of Andrew J. Barnes, Jan. 27,
    1881
  C. S. W. (Mrs.), d. of John
    A. and Rachael Brown, June
    21, 1917
  E. Holmes (Mrs.), Feb. 5,
    1857
  Elenor W., d. of Francis
    Barnes, Mar. 3, 1842*
  Eliza B. (Mrs.), Nov. 26,
    1885
  Emma G. (Mrs.), Apr. 8, 1880
  F. C., w. of Rev. James H.
    Barnes, July 28, 1921
  Francis (Capt.), May 27,
    1852
  H. J., Dec. 3, 1874
  J. H., Jr., s. of Rev. J. H.
    and Mary Florence Barnes,
    Mar. 31, 1887
  J. H. (Mrs.), May 26, 1921

* Possible inaccuracy in name, or spelling, but given as printed

OBITUARY NOTICES IN THE RELIGIOUS HERALD WITH DATES OF PUBLICATION

Jacob F., June 3, 1875
James, Mar. 28, 1872
James H., Mar. 16, 1893
James H., s. of William H.
  and Lucy Saunders Barnes
  June 3, July 1, 1909
Joseph, July 12, 1855
Laura King (Mrs.), June 15,
  1933
Lucy A., w. of John B. Barnes,
  May 22, 1890
Lucy Ann, Mar. 9, 1848
Lucy Araminta, d. of Andrew J.
  and Bettie A. Barnes, Dec.
  25, 1879
Lucy B., w. of Francis Barnes,
  July 29, 1869
Lucy Saunders, w. of William
  H. Barnes, Sr., Apr. 9, 1885
Martha Jane, w. of A. Barnes
  June 15, 1854
Mary, w. of George M. Barnes,
  Dec. 4, 1856
Mary Elizabeth, d. of William
  C. and Lydia Ann Barnes,
  June 26, 1856
Mastin, s. of Pleasant Barnes,
  July 29, 1909
Nancy A., w. of F. G. Barnes,
  May 8, 1851
R. B. (Mrs.), Apr. 18, 1912
Richard Tillman, Sept. 13,
  1928
Robert Andrew, s. of Andrew J.
  and Bettie A. Barnes, Jan.
  13, 1876
Rosa Ann, d. of William C. and
  Lydia Ann Barnes, June 26,
  1856
Samuel B. (Rev.), Dec. 24, 1931
Susan J. (Mrs.), d. of Capt.
  Y. Richards, May 2, 1867
Virginia, Feb. 3, 1870
W. H., Apr. 24, 1930
Willie, s. of A. J. Barnes,
  Jan. 30, 1890
William H., Sr., Feb. 5, 1874
Winifred Hutson, d. of William
  H. and Bettie Barnes, July
  22, 1886

BARNETT
  Betsy (Mrs.), Jan. 9, 1873
  Elizabeth, w. of Neill Barnett,
    June 9, 1870
  Fannie D., w. of J. L. Barnett,
    May 29, 1873
  J. E., June 8, 1922
  John D., Sept. 6, 1877
  John H. (Mrs.), Nov. 25, 1909
  Nancy, Feb. 11, 1875
  Neill, June 26, 1873
  W. S., Mar. 6, 1902
BARNHARDT
  Grace Bass, w. of J. A. Barn-
    hardt, d. of H. C. Bass,
    Nov. 13, Nov. 20, 1924
  J. A. (Rev.), Feb. 16 and 23,
    Apr. 20, 1922
BARNS
  Elizabeth (Mrs.), Sept. 22,
    1859
  Hannah McConnell, d. of Fran-
    cis J. and Araminta S. Barns,
    June 15, 1848
  Luther (Maj.), June 25, 1830
  Mary Gill, d. of Francis J.
    and Araminta S. Barns, Nov.
    2, 1848
BARNUM
  Elizabeth S., w. of Zorah
    Barnum, Mar. 25, 1841
BARR
  John, June 13, 1861
  W. D. (Rev.), Nov. 17, 1921
BARRECK*
  Julius C., Sept. 19, 1872
BARRET
  John, s. of William O. and
    Mary Barret, May 21, 1863
BARRETT
  Catharine R. (Mrs.), July 16,
    1830
  George, July 22, 1852
  Lewis Armistead, s. of R. C.
    Barrett, Sept. 11, 1873
  W. B., Dec. 19, 1929
BARRICK*
  Julia E., w. of W. E. Barrick,
    Nov. 8, 1877
BARRON

* Possible inaccuracy in name, or spelling, but given as printed

OBITUARY NOTICES IN THE RELIGIOUS HERALD WITH DATES OF PUBLICATION

A. C. (Dr.), Aug. 31, 1905
Cassie Mason, d. of Rev. A. C.
    Barron, June 17, 1875
BARROW
    H. P., Mar. 18, 1897
BARROWS*
    C. E. (Rev.), Jan. 10, 1884
BARTLETT
    James Robert, s. of Eleazer
    Bartlett, Nov. 25, 1852
BARTON
    Georgia Harris, d. of Dr. A.
        J. Barton, July 13, 1899
    Mary M., w. of Samuel O. Barton, May 17, 1883
    William S. (Judge), Jan. 20, 1898
BASHAW
    Holeman, Jan. 5, 1865.
    Lucius Winn, s. of Thomas F.
        and Elizabeth D. Bashaw,
        Sept. 18, 1862
BASKERVILLE
    Bernard, s. of George S. and
        Sarah Baskerville, Oct. 8, 1885
    Mildred (Mrs.), July 23, 1857
BASKET*
    Doratha A. (Mrs.), Mar. 28, 1867*
    Martha Jane, w. of Henry Basket, May 26, 1842
BASKETS*
    Sarah B., Dec. 11, 1873
BASKETT*
    Abraham, Oct. 18, 1839
    William (Elder), Feb. 1, 1828
BASKETTE*
    Frances D., w. of Abram Baskette, July 13, 1848
BASS
    Ann, w. of John Bass, Mar. 15, 1839
    Bettie Bruce (Mrs.), Jan. 29, 1920
    Bettie Rudd, w. of William E.
        Bass, Mar. 13, 1913
    Daniel, June 19, 1835
    Dutoy, Oct. 15, 1868
    Eveline, July 12, 1860

G. Adolphus (Lieut.), July 23, 1863
George, Mar. 22, 1855
Helen, Aug. 11, 1892
J. H. (Rev.), Aug. 7, Sept. 25, 1930
James Thomas, Jan. 20, 1938
Judith Ann, w. of Collin
    Bass, Oct. 23, 1835
Judith Frances, d. of Robert
    and Martha Bass, Aug. 29, 1834
Judith H., w. of James H.
    Bass, June 25, 1840
Laura O., d. of Silas C.
    Bass, Mar. 23, 1871
M. Helen, d. of Thomas R.
    Bass, May 11, 1893
Martha A., w. of Egbert Bass,
    d. of William Wilkinson,
    Oct. 8, 1863
Martha E., w. of Robert Bass,
    Jan. 23, 1851
Mary Ann, w. of Elam Bass,
    d. of Richard Oliver, May 13, 1869
Mary L. (Mrs.), Aug. 7, 1856
Mattie Maie (Mrs.), d. of
    D. T. McDowell, Mar. 25, 1926
Rebecca, w. of James H. Bass,
    Sept. 20, 1855.
Richard, Aug. 17, 1838
Robert E. (Mrs.), July 14, 1921
S. A. (Rev.), Sept. 29, 1921
Sallie (Mrs.), Dec. 20, 1928
Sarah, Jan. 3, 1867
Sarah P. (Mrs.), Aug. 14, 1879
W. E., Dec. 2, 1926
William, July 5, 1839
William J., s. of Susan Bass,
    Apr. 30, 1863
BATES
    James T., Oct. 31, 1872
    K. J., w. of Thomas Beverley
        Bates, Mar. 3, 1910
    Mollie Todd (Mrs.), Oct. 17, 1929

* Possible inaccuracy in name, or spelling, but given as printed

OBITUARY NOTICES IN THE RELIGIOUS HERALD WITH DATES OF PUBLICATION

Paulina, May 3, 1906
Rosalie Lumpkin (Mrs.), Feb. 24, Mar. 9, 1916
Thomas Beverly, July 19, 1883
Thomas J. (Dr.), June 27, 1895
Thomas J., Jr., July 13, 1876

BATTAILE
Addie M., w. of Henry Battaile, d. of George S. and Mary J. Rogers, July 21, 1881
Benjamin R., Sept. 13, 1883
Francis W., June 13, 1872
Lawrence, s. of Francis Battaile, Dec. 24, 1868
William (Col.), June 12, 1873

BATTEN
David D., Sept. 29, 1921
Kate, w. of Richard M. Batten, Mar. 3, 1881
Sallie E. (Mrs.), Aug. 15, 1935

BATTLE
Florence B., d. of Gen. Cullen A. and Georgia F. Battle, Sept. 28, 1882

BATTLEY*
Catherine Lavinia (Mrs.), Apr. 18, 1867

BAUGH
Amanda C. (Mrs.) Oct. 2, 1873
Eva May, d. of J. B. and Bettie A. Baugh, Sept. 22, 1870
Harvie Linwood, s. of R. A. Baugh, Feb. 5, 1874
John (Dr.), Apr. 29, 1858
Lucy Ann, w. of J. J. Baugh, July 19, 1860
M. E., w. of Arthur C. Baugh, d. of Dr. W. B. Daniel, Nov. 29, 1906; May 23, 1907
William F., s. of Dr. John M. Baugh, July 7, Sept. 1, 1910

BAUGHAN
M. A. (Mrs.), w. of M. W. Baughan, July 28, 1898

BAWEN
Peter B. (Dr.), July 19, 1860

BAXTER
Maria, w. of Thomas Baxter, June 28, 1839

Sydney, Dec. 18, 1879

BAYLISS
Charles F., Dec. 7, 1899
J. Henry, s. of Silas P. and Betty Ann Bayliss, July 31, 1856
Mildred Jane, w. of Charles F. Bayliss, Jan. 31, 1907

BAYLOR
Annie E., w. of Dr. R. H. Baylor, Aug. 10, 1893
Ellen Amelia, Aug. 30, 1849
George D. (Dr.), May 11, 1848
George R., May 9, 1878
Lula, w. of Rev. W. H. Baylor, d. of J. M. Gills, Oct. 20, 1892
Maria, d. of John Baylor, Apr. 4, 1850
Ola Alice, d. of Dr. R. H. Baylor, Feb. 12, 1874
Rosa H. (Mrs.), Mar. 11, 1926

BAYNE
Amanda C., w. of William Bayne, Oct. 3, 1878
Delia Elizabeth Rust, w. of Lawrence P. Bayne, d. of Dr. Bushrod and Margaret Carr Rust, June 23, 1898
Emily C., w. of Washington Bayne, May 26, 1892
Fannie L., w. of Patterson Bayne, July 15, 1880
Georgie C., w. of Patterson Bayne, Jr., Mar. 20, 1884
Latham S., s. of Patterson and Maria Louise Bayne, Aug. 29, 1861
Lawrence P., Feb. 12, 1885
M. S., Sept. 15, 1938
Patterson, Nov. 29, 1900
Washington, Oct. 23, 1873
William, Mar. 31, 1898

BAYNHAM
Virginia, w. of Dr. William Baynham, Mar. 10, 1853
William Armistead (Rev.), July 14, 1887

* Possible inaccuracy in name, or spelling, but given as printed

OBITUARY NOTICES IN THE RELIGIOUS HERALD WITH DATES OF PUBLICATION

BEACH
  Lucy M., July 23, 1891
  Richard D., Sept. 13, 1860
BEADLES
  children of William W.
  Beadles, Aug. 6, 1830
  Andrew F., Oct. 12, 1848
  Benjamin Wharton, s. of Lucy W. and John Beadles, Sept. 24, 1846
  Bettie (Mrs.), Aug. 30, 1928
  Elizabeth W., w. of W. W. Beadles, Feb. 17, 1876
  J. M. (Rev.), Sept. 21, 1922
  John, Apr. 20, 1848
  John, Aug. 28, 1856
  Marcellus W., May 22, 1862
  S. A. E., w. of A. J. Beadles, May 7, 1868
  Susan (Mrs.), May 6, 1841
  Tamasia A., d. of William W. Beadles, Feb. 11, 1858
  Willie, Sept. 26, 1867
BEAHM
  Eliza E., Oct. 14, 1886
BEAL*
  Lelia T., Sept. 10, 1896
BEALE
  Annye, Dec. 4, 1924
  Bartley, s. of Bartley J. Beale, Mar. 7, 1889
  Eula J., w. of B. J. Beale, May 31, 1888
  Frank B., Aug. 13, 1908
  George E., Aug. 15, 1918
  George W. (Dr.), July 21, Aug. 11, 1921
  Joseph Marvin, s. of George E. and Belle Daniel Beale, July 14, 1887
  Lucy M., w. of Richard L. T. Beale, Feb. 1, 1894
  Mary A., w. of Dr. George W. Beale, Nov. 23, 1933
  Mary S. (Mrs.), Dec. 6, 1883
  R. L. T. (Gen.), Apr. 27, 1893
  Richard L., Feb. 16, Mar. 1, 1928
  Rosa H., Nov. 23, 1933
  W. M. (Mrs.), May 15, 1913

BEAMAN
  S. F. (Mrs.), Aug. 5, 1869
BEAN
  Opie, Jr., Oct. 28, 1836
BEAR
  Eliza S. (Mrs.), d. of Robert S. Gaines, June 13, 1907
BEASELEY*
  Charles F., Aug. 13, 1868
BEASLEY
  Charles, Sept. 19, 1834
  Ellen V. Sorrell (Mrs.), Oct. 11, 1894
  George (Mrs.), Apr. 14, 1898
  Harry, s. of T. W. and E. L. Beasley, Dec. 25, 1889
  John P., s. of J. P. and Marie F. Beasley, July 30, 1857
  Marian B., Oct. 18, 1877
  Martha (Mrs.), Jan. 13, 1837
  Martha Jane, w. of H. L. Beasley, May 19, 1859
  Thomas W., Sept. 25, 1879
  Thomas Rial, s. of Rial and Nanny Beasley, May 8, 1862
BEATON
  E. B. (Mrs.), Dec. 30, 1915
  Edgar Badger, Jr., Oct. 5, 1876
BEATTIE
  Cassander A., s. of Rev. W. Q. and A. E. Beattie, Oct. 14, 1880
BEAUCHAMP
  Pauline W., w. of Joseph H. Beauchamp, July 19, 1883
BEAZELEY*
  Susanna B., w. of Capt. J. Beazeley, Apr. 20, 1848
BEAZLEY
  Charles L., Sept. 30, 1852
  Elizabeth C. (Mrs.), June 29, 1848
  Henry (Mrs.), Dec. 14, 1905
  India (Mrs.), Nov. 12, 1931
  Isabella H., d. of Charles Beazley, Dec. 3, 1857
  James M., Oct. 8, 1857
  Lucy A., w. of John P. Beazley,

* Possible inaccuracy in name, or spelling, but given as printed

OBITUARY NOTICES IN THE RELIGIOUS HERALD WITH DATES OF PUBLICATION

Apr. 1, 1852
Mary, w. of James Beazley,
Sept. 2, 1852
Mary B., w. of James M. Beazley, Sept. 8, 1853
Virginia H., w. of J. O. Beazley, Nov. 25, 1880
W. O. (Rev.), Oct. 31, Nov. 28, 1918
William S., s. of William and Susan Beazley, Apr. 26, 1855
Zenada, w. of H. L. Beazley, Feb. 1, 1906
BECK
Eveline, w. of Capt. James R. Beck, June 24, 1869
Octavia, w. of Rev. A. J. Beck, d. of Rev. E. W. Warren, Mar. 8, 1877
BECKER
Cornelia A. (Mrs.), d. of Mrs. M. A. Gates, Sept. 6, 1888
BECKETT
George H., s. of Dr. H. C. Beckett, Apr. 12, 1906
BECKHAM*
Hannah, d. of Thomas Beckham, Nov. 4, 1847
Rebecca (Mrs.), Feb. 26, 1852
BECKLEHAMMER
Mary, Aug. 19, 1858
BECKLEY
J. R. (Mrs.), Sept. 29, 1927
BECKNER
Albert Sidney, Nov. 17, 1898
Elizabeth F., w. of John S. Beckner, Jan. 13, 1870
BECKWITH
Jeannette I. Cridlin, w. of Newton Beckwith, June 17, 1886
BEEBE
Samuel (Rev.), Apr. 18, 1834
BEECH*
William B., Jan. 21, 1858
BELBRO*
William P., May 7, 1874
BELCHER
Thomas, Mar. 17, 1853
William B. (Elder), Jan. 17, 1861

BELFIELD
Alexander Opsley, s. of Dr. Alexander and Fanny A. Belfield, May 8, 1862
John Henry, s. of Richard and Mary F. Belfield, Nov. 15, 1855
R. Sydnor, July 2, 1936
J. Ruth E., d. of Col. John W. Belfield, May 6, 1858
William Hugh, s. of Richard and Mary F. Belfield, Nov. 15, 1855
BELL
A. H., Mar. 24, 1881
Ada C., w. of Rev. T. P. Bell, Feb. 16, Mar. 16, 1893
Alfred Parkes, s. of A. T. Bell, Feb. 5, 1931
Alice Hendren, w. of A. T. Bell, d. of Jeremiah Hendren, Aug. 10, 1899
Annie P. (Mrs.), Feb. 25, 1926
Anson B., s. of Binns Bell, July 22, 1847
Baily Thomas (Mrs.), Sept. 18, 1919
Carrie J., d. of George Bell, Aug. 5, 1858
Catherine (Mrs.), Apr. 21, 1859
Edward Land, s. of Dr. James E. and A. F. V. Bell, Jan. 17, 1856
Elizabeth H., w. of Savage Bell, Dec. 1, 1859
Elizabeth P., w. of George Bell, Aug. 2, 1900
Elizabeth Warren, w. of N. P. Bell, d. of Rev. Patrick Warren, July 8, 1926
Ernestine, d. of Dr. James E. and A. F. Bell, Aug. 20, 1868
George, Mar. 18, 1897
Hellen, d. of Elder William Bell, July 20, 1854
James Barkley, Dec. 29, 1932
John, Sept. 15, 1869

* Possible inaccuracy in name, or spelling, but given as printed

OBITUARY NOTICES IN THE RELIGIOUS HERALD WITH DATES OF PUBLICATION

    Joseph, s. of Wilton A. and
      Bettie H. Bell, Nov. 6,
      1884
    Joseph C., Mar. 20, 1924
    Malvina, w. of Edward Bell,
      Apr. 18, 1850
    Mary Annie Sadler, w. of J. B.
      Bell, Sept. 14, 1922
    Mary C. (Mrs.), June 14, 1894
    Mattie E., June 7, 1934
    Sallie E., Dec. 13, 1860
    Sallie G., d. of George Bell,
      Mar. 11, 1852
    Savage, Sept. 26, 1867
    Susan F. W., w. of John D. Bell,
      Feb. 22, 1855
    T. P. (Dr.), Oct. 5, 1916
    Thomas G. (Capt.), Feb. 27,
      1862
    W. T., Apr. 10, 1884
    William (Rev.), May 15, 1835
    William, May 21, 1857
BELLAMY
    Eliza Ellington, w. of Henry
      Washington Bellamy, Mar. 3
      and 24, 1938
    Henry Washington, Nov. 28, 1929
BELLWOOD
    Atlanta (Mrs.), Feb. 27, 1930
    Ralph (Rev.), Apr. 30, 1931
BELT
    Demetria, d. of Humphrey Belt,
      May 11, 1832
BELVIN
    Bertha May (Mrs.), d. of B. J.
      Perdue, Dec. 5, 1907
    John A., Aug. 19, 1880
BENDALL
    Mary, w. of Capt. I. Bendall,
      May 18, 1838
BENEDICT
    David (Rev.), Dec. 17, 1874;
      Feb. 25, 1875
BENN
    Nancy (Mrs.), July 11, 1889
BENNETT
    Ann L. (Mrs.), Aug. 26, 1875
    Frances, w. of Elder A. H.
      Bennett, Sept. 20, 1860
    J. W. (Mrs.), Apr. 21, 1921

    John (Rev.), Oct. 22, Nov. 12,
      1874
    Lucy D., d. of Maj. John
      Bennett, Aug. 27, 1868
    Mark (Elder), Aug. 26, 1875
    Mary Amos, w. of John I.
      Bennett, Dec. 19, 1895
    Samuel C., s. of Rev. A. H.
      Bennett, Aug. 20, 1896
    W. D. (Judge), Feb. 13, 1890
    William Oliver, Aug. 20, 1914
BENSON
    Mary Jane, Dec. 31, 1857
BENTLY*
    Mable, w. of J. L. Bently,
      Feb. 20, 1919
BENTLEY
    John G., Apr. 9, 1891
    Lucy, w. of Col. William
      Bentley, Dec. 25, 1851
    Nannie C., d. of John G.
      Bentley, July 5, 1860
BENTON
    William C. (Mrs.), July 11,
      1935
BERG
    John (Rev.), May 29, June 12,
      1873
BERKLEY
    Frank P. (Rev.), May 13,
      June 10, Aug. 12, 1920
    Frank P. (Mrs.), Feb. 23, 1933
BERLETT*
    Susanna (Mrs.), Feb. 14, 1834
BERNARD*
    Martha, w. of John Bernard,
      Oct. 19, 1854
BERNERD*
    Catherine, w. of Joseph Bern-
      erd, Oct. 16, 1856
BERREY*
    Thomas J., Aug. 17, 1922
BERRY
    Ann (Mrs.), Sept. 17, 1840
    Francis L. (Mrs.), Jan. 14,
      1847
    Isabella T. (Mrs.), Jan. 25,
      1900
    J. W., Mar. 26, 1908
    Martha E., d. of John and Mary

* Possible inaccuracy in name, or spelling, but given as printed

OBITUARY NOTICES IN THE RELIGIOUS HERALD WITH DATES OF PUBLICATION

E. Berry, Apr. 24, 1873
Mary Ann Mildred, w. of Finney
  J. Berry, d. of John Croxty
  and Sally Ann Green, June
  30, 1904
Mary F., w. of T. F. Berry.
  July 5, 1923
Nancy, Mar. 29, 1860
Rebecca, d. of T. F. Berry,
  July 5, 1923
BERRYMAN
  Fleming W., Jan. 13, 1842
  John J., Dec. 22, 1892
  Sophia (Mrs.), Apr. 24, 1856
  William J., Oct. 29, 1846
  William J., Jan. 11, 1883
BERSCH
  Jennie D., w. of John C.
    Bersch, Mar. 5, 1914
  Lynwood, July 23, 1925
BEST
  Edwin, Dec. 9, 1852
BETHEL
  A. F., Mar. 31, 1870
  Eloisa (Mrs.), May 19, 1881
BETHUNE
  Mary, d. of Andrew and Mary
    Bethune, June 28, 1883
BETTERTON
  Charlotte C., Nov. 21, 1872
  Sarah C. (Mrs.), Mar. 12, 1925
  Sue L., w. of William J. Betterton, Oct. 3, 1867
  Thomas, Apr. 24, 1862
BETTS
  Elisha (Capt.), Nov. 7, 1872
  Elisha, Mar. 9, 1911
  George W. (Sgt.), June 4, 1863
  J. T. (Rev.), July 25, 1935
  Julia Basye, Feb. 14, 1884
  Mary E., w. of A. D. Betts, d.
    of A. M. and Sophia York
    Davis, Sept. 25, 1879
  Parthenia, w. of Capt. Elisha
    Betts, June 25, 1854
  Sallie McG., d. of Elisha and
    Lucy B. Betts, Oct. 18, 1877
  Sarah (Mrs.), Mar. 26, 1857
  Sarah E. (Mrs.), Mar. 17, 1910
  Tenie (Mrs.), w. of E. R. Betts,
    June 3, 1880
  William Spencer (Capt.)
    Oct. 31, 1901
BEVERLEY
  Adrianna L., w. of James G.
    Beverley, d. of Dr. A. J.
    Shymanski, Jan. 29, Mar. 12,
    1857
BEVINS
  Elizabeth, w. of James Bevins,
    Mar. 13, 1862
  Floyd J., s. of J. C. Bevins,
    Mar. 13, 1862
BIBB
  Cary, Aug. 26, 1880
  Charles, father of Rev. M.
    Bibb, Mar. 26, 1885
  Elizabeth, w. of Benjamin
    Bibb, Feb. 6, 1840
  Elizabeth, w. of Charles Bibb,
    Aug. 26, 1880
  Elizabeth (Mrs.), May 29, 1863
  Emmet C., s. of W. E. and Kate
    Bibb, Aug. 19, 1880
  F. S. (Lieut.), June 25, July
    16, 1863
  Fleming (Capt.), Aug. 20, 1863
  Frances G. (Mrs.), July 6,
    1843
  Frances Hendrick, w. of Robert
    C. Bibb, June 29, 1848
  Georgie T., w. of William G.
    Bibb, Jr., Dec. 9, 1886
  Harriet, w. of Rev. Martin
    Bibb, July 3, 1845
  J. R. (Mrs.), Sept. 16, 1909
  L. J. (Mrs.), Apr. 19, 1894
  Lucretia (Mrs.), June 26,
    1890
  Martin (Rev.), Jan. 19, 1893
  Mary Ann (Mrs.), Dec. 14, 1838
  N. W. (Mrs.), w. of Capt.
    Fleming Bibb, Aug. 29, 1872
  Nancy, Jan. 22, 1846
  Permelia, w. of Robert P. Bibb,
    Mar. 12, 1874
  R. C., Feb. 4, 1864
  Rachel (Mrs.), Aug. 28, 1835
  Sabra J., w. of W. F. Bibb,
    Feb. 17, 1881

OBITUARY NOTICES IN THE RELIGIOUS HERALD WITH DATES OF PUBLICATION

Sarah, w. of William A. Bibb,
   Dec. 16, 1869
Susan A., w. of Benjamin
   Bibb, Feb. 6, 1845
Ward E., Mar. 31, 1938
BICE*
   Delia Virginia, w. of T. P.
   Bice, d. of J. M. and Elizabeth Headers, Mar. 4, 1926
BICKERS
   Ann, w. of Abner Bickers,
   May 30, 1861
   Carrie Willie, Sept. 22, 1870
   Martha Ann (Mrs.), July 9, 1874
   Martha Hill (Mrs.), d. of J. M.
   Duncan, Feb. 27, 1913
   Temperance Ann, w. of T. O.
   Bickers, d. of James Edward
   Smith, Sept. 3, 1896
   Thomas Henry, s. of T. O. and
   Temperance Bickers, July 28,
   1870*
   Thomas Oliver, Aug. 9, 1928
   Walter, s. of J. O. and Temperance A. Bickers, July 6, 1882
BICKFORD
   Celia Ann, w. of Rev. M. L.
   Bickford, July 24, 1856
   Martin L. (Rev.), May 4, 1876
BICKLY*
   Humphrey (Capt.), May 29, 1879
BIDGOOD
   Elizabeth S., w. of C. E.
   Bidgood, Nov. 14, 1867
   Horace, Feb. 25, 1892
   James, Apr. 18, 1850
   John T., Apr. 2, 1874
   Martha Sumner, w. of C. E.
   Bidgood, Apr. 23, 1896
   Mary Ann, w. of James C. Bidgood, Mar. 14, 1861
   Nathaniel, Dec. 6, 1883
   Priscilla B., w. of James C.
   Bidgood, July 11, 1895
   Willis D., June 11, 1846
   Willis, D., s. of John T. Bidgood, Mar. 24, 1898
BIGELOW
   William M., Nov. 3, 10, and
   17, 1892

   Woodbury B., Oct. 1, 1888
BIGGERS
   Mabel Lynch, Mar. 15, 1894
   Mary, Mar. 26, 1830
   Sallie Chunn, w. of A. F.
   Biggers, Mar. 22, 1923
BIGGS
   C. R. (Rev.), Sept. 3, 1857
   Joseph T., Mar. 3, 1892
   Walter S., s. of Joseph J.
   Biggs, Sept. 13, 1877
BILBRO
   Benjamin, Jan. 2, 1856
   Jane, w. of John Bilbro,
   Mar. 26, 1863
   John, Nov. 12, 1830
BILLINGSLEY
   Mary, w. of Joseph A.
   Billingsley, Oct. 10, 1850
   Sarah, w. of Elder John A.
   Billingsley, Apr. 14, 1842
BILLUPS
   L. W., July 27, 1893
BINFORD
   Anna M. (Mrs.), Sept. 1,
   1938
   Frances A. T., Apr. 16,
   1830
   Lucy C. (Mrs.), July 23, 1868
   Lucy S., w. of Joseph Binford,
   Mar. 4, 1926
   Martha Ann, Sept. 26, 1861
   Martha M., w. of Rev. Thomas
   Binford, Mar. 19, 1868
   Mary A., w. of Rev. Thomas
   Binford, Feb. 24, 1859
   Mary Alice, d. of R. E. Binford, Aug. 13, 1885
   Robert E., s. of Rev. Thomas
   Binford, July 2, 1896
   Thomas (Elder), May 14, 1874
   Thomas Fillmore, s. of William
   A. and Lucy Columbia Binford, June 26, 1851
   Thomas Judson, s. of Rev.
   Thomas Binford, Apr. 24,
   1856
   Willie A., Apr. 17, 1884
BINGHAM
   James W., Dec. 9, 1937

* Possible inaccuracy in name, or spelling, but given as printed

OBITUARY NOTICES IN THE RELIGIOUS HERALD WITH DATES OF PUBLICATION

BINNS
   child of Robert T. and Mary
     Vaiden Binns, Aug. 10, 1854
   Estelle Folkes, w. of C. R.
     Binns, Mar. 27, 1930
   Octavia Elizabeth, d. of
     William E. and Lucy C. Binns,
     Dec. 25, 1879
   Sarah, w. of C. J. Binns,
     July 23, 1863

BIRD
   Emily J., Feb. 14, 1878
   Emma C., w. of Spottswood
     Bird, d. of Alexander Dudley,
     May 15, 1890
   Frances A., w. of William A.
     Bird, Mar. 8, 1860
   Jennie Roy, d. of William Bird
     Feb. 4, 1869
   John (Rev.), Sept. 2, 1858
   John, s. of William and Frances
     Bird, Nov. 21, 1844
   Katherine Harwood (Mrs.), d.
     of Col. Archibald Roane Har-
     wood, May 9, 1901
   Mary Elizabeth, d. of Philemon
     and Elizabeth Bird, Nov. 21,
     1839
   Richard, July 28, 1881
   Robert, s. of William and
     Frances Bird, Nov. 21, 1844
   Samuel Harwood, s. of Spotts-
     wood and Emma C. Bird, Dec.
     30, 1886

BIRDSONG
   B. Thomas, Mar. 2, 1893
   Benjamin R., Apr. 12, 1906
   Harriet (Mrs.), Sept. 15, 1881
   Nathaniel B., Feb. 10, 1848
   Sarah H. (Mrs.), June 27, 1872

BISCOE
   Catharine, w. of William Bis-
     coe, Dec. 26, 1850
   Lula, d. of A. W. and Susie
     Biscoe, Jan. 3, 1895
   Henry L., Sept. 2, 1847
   Susie (Mrs.), June 24, 1897

BISE*
   T. P. (Mrs.), Mar. 25, 1926

BISHOP
   Elijah, Nov. 27, 1862
   Elisha, Oct. 28, 1886
   James (Elder), Nov. 27, 1862
   John B., s. of William and
     Ann Bishop, June 10, 1858
   Lavinia H. (Mrs.), d. of
     Robert Clark, Oct. 28,
     1886
   Nathan (Dr.), Aug. 19 and 26,
     1830
   Polly, w. of Elder James
     Bishop, June 27, 1878
   Susan L. (Mrs.), May 1, June
     3, 1902
   William (Mrs.), d. of Charles
     Lucas, Feb. 22, 1923

BISPHAM
   Alice Emma, Dec. 16, 1875
   Martha, w. of John F. Bispham,
     July 28, 1870

BITTING
   Caroline Shaddinger, w. of
     Rev. C. C. Bitting, Aug.
     24, 1916
   W. C. (Dr.), Feb. 5, 1931

BITTLE
   Alice V., d. of George Bittle,
     Aug. 15, 1901

BLACK
   Gabriella, w. of Nicholas M.
     Black, d. of James C. Gen-
     try, Apr. 29, 1875

BLACKBURN
   Absalom, Dec. 18, 1879
   Eudora A., w. of Robert L.
     Blackburn, Apr. 28, 1859
   Helen S. (Mrs.), Mar. 17,
     1921

BLACKWELL
   Ann, w. of Col. Samuel Black-
     well, June 27, 1850
   Calvin S. (Rev.), June 7,
     1923
   Eleanor V. (Mrs.), Sept. 6,
     1934
   George Herbert, s. of John
     W. Blackwell, Feb. 3, 1870
   Hiram Harding, Aug. 11, 1921
   Lucy H. (Mrs.), d. of Spencer
     Betts, Feb. 27, 1868

* Possible inaccuracy in name, or spelling, but given as printed

OBITUARY NOTICES IN THE RELIGIOUS HERALD WITH DATES OF PUBLICATION

Nancy (Mrs.), Feb. 23, 1843
Samuel (Col.), June 9, 1837
Sarah Kate, d. of J. W. Blackwell, Feb. 3, 1870
Virginia, w. of William Blackwell, Mar. 14, 1867
William, June 24, 1869
BLAIN*
   Kate, d. of Dr. H. L. Blain, Apr. 15, 1869
BLANE*
   Jane A., Dec. 7, 1871
BLAIR
   D. A. (Elder), Aug. 11, 1864
   J. E., Sept. 19, 1929
   Joseph D. (Mrs.), d. of Dr. Richard White, Mar. 30, 1893
   Lucy S., Sept. 20, 1860
   Walton M., s. of Dr. H. L. Blair, Nov. 1, 1860
   William (Elder), July 17, 1873
   William C. (Rev.), Aug. 21, 1930
BLAKE
   A., d. of Lewis Blake, Jr., Sept. 2, 1858
   Ann, w. of John B. Blake, Oct. 10, 1844
   Cicero, Nov. 18, 1875
   Fleming, Oct. 13, 1853
   John B., Jan. 21, 1869
   Margaret, w. of John L., Feb. 23, 1854
   Preston (Dr.), Sept. 8, 1927
   Sarah, w. of W. C. Blake, Feb. 23, 1854
   Sarah P., w. of Thomas J. Blake, Feb. 21, 1861
BLAKEY
   Fanny Roane, d. of J. A. and Lucy E. Blakey, Nov. 3 and 10, 1870
   James A., Mar. 15, 1877
   James R., Jan. 18, 1872
   Lucy Ellen, d. of Mrs. Lucy E. Blakey, May 30, 1878
   Mary Ann, w. of J. D. Blakey, d. of John McMullen, Jan. 8, 1880
   Rosilia Elizabeth Frances Ann, d. of Mrs. E. A. Blakey, Mar. 30, 1854
BLAND
   Elizabeth (Mrs.), July 9, 1840
   Elizabeth, w. of Claiborne Bland, June 21, 1849
   Harriet, w. of Absalom Bland, Aug. 13, 1857
   Josephine E., w. of Rev. W. S. Bland, Aug. 4, 1898
   M. A., w. of Col. Robert Bland, Apr. 23, 1863
   Mary Ann, d. of Mrs. Ann R. Bland, Apr. 30, 1863
   W. S. (Rev.), s. of John and Elizabeth C. Bland, Nov. 23, 1876
BLANK*
   Howell, s. of Henry S. and Beulah Blank, Dec. 16, 1886
   Sallie P. (Mrs.), Dec. 19, 1889
   William T., Apr. 26, 1877
BLANKS*
   Fannie, d. of James M. and Julia F. Blanks, Feb. 8, 1855
   Julia F. (Mrs.), d. of Josiah Dabbs, May 20, July 29, 1909
   Willie D., s. of W. D. Blanks, Dec. 3, 1896
   William Dabbs, Feb. 24, 1921
BLANTON
   Anderson, Apr. 22, 1852
   Martha Frances, w. of Thomas M. Blanton, May 4, 1899
   Mary Ann Elizabeth, w. of E. A. Blanton, Aug. 29, 1901
   Mollie B. (Mrs.), Aug. 11, 1887
   Susan S., w. of Joseph Blanton, Aug. 28, 1856
BLAYDES
   Caroline R., Oct. 16, 1879

* Possible inaccuracy in name, or spelling, but given as printed

OBITUARY NOTICES IN THE RELIGIOUS HERALD WITH DATES OF PUBLICATION

John C., Oct. 18, 1860
Ora W., Jan. 4, 1883
Polly B., Sept. 26, 1867
BLEDSOE
Aaron, Jan. 7, 1858
Aaron, Jr., June 18, 1891
Julia F., w. of Dr. P. Bledsoe, July 22 and 29, 1875
Mahala, w. of Aaron Bledsoe, July 15, 1858
Margaret (Mrs.), July 3, 1890
Mary J., July 27, 1876
Sarah Price, Mar. 24, 1881
Thomas, s. of Dr. R. G. Bledsoe, Jan. 13, 1921
BLICK
E. H. H. (Col.), Nov. 29, 1877
Edward Curry, s. of Dr. J. A. and Rosa Blick, Feb. 2, 1888
BLOCK
Susan T., w. of George S. Block, Apr. 4, 1907
Henry, Jan. 21, Mar. 11, 1886
BLOOMER
Annie, w. of Albert Bloomer, d. of Maj. John D. Hardgrove, Oct. 26, 1871
Charles C., s. of Albert and Annie Bloomer, Oct. 26, 1871
BLOUNT*
William B., May 16, 1828
BLOWE
Elizabeth M., Sept. 10, 1868
BLOXOM
David F., July 24, 1930
David T., Nov. 26, 1914
John M., Sr., Nov. 1, 1917
Roxie A. (Mrs.), Sept. 28, 1933
BLUNDON
Henry, Jan. 21, 1915
James, s. of Henry and Margaret F. Blundon, Nov. 3, 1853
William, Oct. 8, Nov. 12, 1936
BLUNT
Elizabeth D., w. of Francis Blunt, Aug. 2, 1855
Lee, s. of John H. and Sarah F. Blunt, Jan. 26, 1865

Lelia Ellen, d. of William B. and Sarah E. Blunt, Jan. 3, 1895
Mary C., w. of Lewis T. Blunt, Dec. 25, 1879
Mary E., w. of William A. Blunt, Oct. 28, 1858
Tabitha F., w. of Thompson Blunt, Jan. 16, 1835
BLYTHE
Eveline R., Dec. 29, 1892
BOARD
C. A. (Dr.), Mar. 24, 1910
BOATRIGHT*
Elizabeth L., w. of Thomas Boatright, d. of Capt. William and Elizabeth Anderson, Oct. 25, 1860
Jonas, Mar. 16, 1871
BOATWRIGHT
Annie Elizabeth (Mrs.), Aug. 30, 1934
Annie J. (Mrs.), Sept. 20, 1906
Ellen, w. of P. P. Boatwright, Feb. 2, 1928
Fred W., Jr., s. of F. W. Boatwright, Jan. 12, 1905
Hopsy, w. of Josiah A. Boatwright, Apr. 1, 1869
John G. (Dr.), Jan. 29, 1874
Louisa J., d. of James A. Boatwright, Feb. 21, 1867
Lucy, w. of Reuben Boatwright, Nov. 18, 1841
Nancy F., w. of Rev. Reuben Boatwright, Feb. 10, 1898
P. P., Apr. 10, 1930
R. B. (Mrs.), Apr. 8, 1926
Reuben, Sr., Apr. 16, 1840
Reuben Baker (Rev.), July 31, 1913
Theodore, June 4, 1891
W. L. (Mrs.), Feb. 22, 1923
W. Leake, June 15, 1922
William P., Nov. 27, 1873
William Thomas, s. of Walter L. and Mary A. Boatwright, July 30, 1885

* Possible inaccuracy in name, or spelling, but given as printed

OBITUARY NOTICES IN THE RELIGIOUS HERALD WITH DATES OF PUBLICATION

BOBBITT
   Fannie A. (Mrs.), Jan. 31, 1895
   M. L., Aug. 20, 1891
   Milton, June 9, 1853
BOGERT
   (Mrs.) mother of Lillie Bogert, June 26, 1930
   Thomas Scott, s. of George W. and Hibernia C. Bogert, Aug. 13, 1874
BOGGS
   Hugh C. (Rev.), Sept. 19, 1828
BOHANNAN*
   Alex. S., May 22, 1829
BOHANNEN*
   Thomas, Sept. 26, 1828
BOHANNON*
   William A., Oct. 10, 1861
BOLDING
   Archibald, s. of Thomas Bolding, May 28, 1857
   James, s. of Thomas Bolding, Dec. 3, 1857
BOLDRIDGE
   Agnes (Mrs.), Mar. 26, 1914
   William Franklin, May 27, 1909
BOLEY
   Benjamin F., Feb. 8, 1877
   Isabella, w. of Benjamin Boley, Apr. 13, 1843
BOLTON
   A. D. (Rev.), June 24, 1875
   A. H., Sept. 28, 1933
   Annie M., June 1, 1882
   Mary Ann (Mrs.), May 21, 1868
BOLLING
   Ann W. (Mrs.), Nov. 18, 1836
   Blair (Capt.), Aug. 9, 1839
BOLEN
   Elizabeth (Mrs.), Mar. 1, 1900
BOMAR
   James, Apr. 8, 1875
BOND
   Emma Nance, w. of Pleasant Bond, Oct. 5, 1905
   Isaac, May 7, 1868
   Sylvester, June 26, 1913
BONDURANT
   William B., Mar. 5, 1863
BONIC
   Ara, w. of R. A. Bonic, d. of Capt. H. W. Tyler, Mar. 30, 1871
BONIWELL
   Ann, w. of William Boniwell May 27, 1869
BONNEY
   C. L. (Mrs.), May 28, 1908
   Edson, June 27, 1889
   John, Apr. 24, 1873
   Mary E., Feb. 9, 1888
   Polly (Mrs.), Sept. 1, 1859
BOOKER
   Ada Fannie, d. of E. C. Booker, Jan. 11, Feb. 1, 1906
   Adelaide Willet, w. of Robert Booker, Sept. 16, 1920
   Bettie, w. of Dr. E. D. Booker, d. of Thomas Eubank, July 19, 1900
   David E., Aug. 19, 1886
   E. C., m. Sallie Eubank, Oct. 21, 1915
   E. D. (Dr.), Mar. 31, 1898
   Eliza Nash, w. of Rev. George E. Booker, d. of Isaac Burkholder, Oct. 15, 1868
   Ella G. (Mrs.), July 28, 1870
   Fannie, Nov. 22, 1894
   Frederick Marshall, s. of J. E. Booker, Apr. 8, 1880
   James, June 14, 1923
   John, Mar. 30, 1865
   John Edward, Nov. 29, 1900
   Lizzie Scott, d. of F. A. Booker, Sept. 9, 1875
   Lucinda Oglesby, w. of Rev. Richard Edward Booker, Sept. 19, 1929
   Martha, w. of Richard Booker, May 11, 1838
   Martha, Jan. 22, 1857
   Richard Edward, Sept. 6, 1900
   Sallie (Mrs.), Apr. 13, 1922
   Sallie Love (Mrs.), June 7, 1934

* Possible inaccuracy in name, or spelling, but given as printed

OBITUARY NOTICES IN THE RELIGIOUS HERALD WITH DATES OF PUBLICATION

William (Dr.), Jan. 15, 1857
BOOKHART
  Kate, d. of Dr. S. W. and Cynthia Bookhart, Mar. 5, 1874
BOONE
  Maggie Corbitt (Mrs.), Nov. 18, 1897
BOOTAN*
  Ann P., w. of John Bootan, d. of Col. Robert Hill, Apr. 25, 1872
BOOTEN*
  Sinclair, Dec. 12, 1839
  Willie, June 16, 1932
BOOTON*
  E. T. (Judge), Nov. 16, Dec. 7, 1905
  Jessie O., w. of Maj. Daniel F. Booten, Mar. 2, 1882
  Lizzie Slaughter, d. of Edwin and Judith Booton, July 7, 1859
  William S., s. of Sinclair Booton, Apr. 28, 1864
BOOTH*
  Charles G., s. of Joseph and Lucy A. Booth, May 15, 1869
  George G., Sept. 27, 1906
  John C., July 23, 1839
  John S., Nov. 7, 1867
  Walter T., July 8, 1909
  William P., Dec. 9, 1869
BOOTHE*
  Agnes (Mrs.), July 27, 1933
  Charles Edward, Mar. 7, 1918
  Dorothy, w. of John H. Boothe, d. of Burwell Branch, Aug. 23, 1888
  William H., June 16, 1910
BOOTWRIGHT
  John C., s. of William and Ann Bootwright, Aug. 23, 1839
  Sarah, w. of William Bootwright, Apr. 15, 1831
BOOZE
  C. J. (Mrs.), Mar. 3, 1921
  Sallie, w. of Gilbert C. Booze, May 6, 1920

BORDEN
  Mattie, Dec. 21, 1871
BORUM
  Adaline, w. of James H. Borum, July 11, 1867
  Edward C., Jan. 27, 1859
  Harriet Almira, d. of Joseph H. and Ann C. Borum, Jan. 28, 1847
  James T., Oct. 10, 1907
  James, Sr. (Rev.), July 6, 1843
  Joseph Witt, Apr. 20, 1922
  Rosa F., w. of J. W. Borum, Aug. 11, 1910
  S. R. (Mrs.), Dec. 24, 1868
  Sarah Catherine, Dec. 29, 1859
BOSHER
  Ann (Mrs.), Jan. 1, 1830
  E. J. (Capt.), Apr. 8, 1915
  Elizabeth B., w. of Robert H. Bosher, July 8, 1880
  Robert H., Dec. 24, 1885
  Robert S., Jan. 21, 1904
  Sarah L., d. of John and Jane Bosher, Sept. 20, 1860
BOSTICK
  Paul Isaiah, Apr. 18, May 9, 1912
BOSTON
  Annie, w. of Frank R. Boston, d. of I. Chase Schoolfield, May 21, 1885
  Frank R., Aug. 19 and 31, 1911
  Margaret, w. of Capt. R. H. Boston, Aug. 6, 1863
  Mary, w. of Rev. S. C. Boston, Apr. 22, 1869
  Peggie F., d. of Capt. R. H. Boston, May 13, 1852
  S. C., June 30, 1887
BOSWEL*
  John Walter, June 20, 1935
BOSWELL
  Charlie Howard, s. of W. N. and M. W. Boswell, July 17, 1873
  Elizabeth B. (Mrs.), Jan. 27, 1876

* Possible inaccuracy in name, or spelling, but given as printed

OBITUARY NOTICES IN THE RELIGIOUS HERALD WITH DATES OF PUBLICATION

Mary L., July 14, 1921
Thomas, Apr. 13, 1833
BOTTOM
  Elizabeth (Mrs.), June 24, 1841
  Elizabeth, w. of James Bottom, June 11, 1846
BOTTS
  Andrew L., Jan. 31, 1929
  Catharine, w. of D. W. Botts, Dec. 31, 1885
  Cora E., w. of A. T. Botts, Nov. 16 and 30, 1933
  Daniel W., July 29, 1897
  Lewis C., June 4, 1885
  Sallie, d. of Daniel Botts, Jan. 10, 1856
  William F., June 9, 1887
BOUGHAN
  Lucy Maranda, d. of J. T. and Sarah E. Boughan, Jan. 3, 1861
  Julia (Mrs.), Feb. 1, 1839
BOUGHTON
  Leah A., June 3, 1869
BOUIC
  David H., Apr. 12, 1900
BOULWARE
  Ann T., w. of Dr. Boulware, Mar. 19, 1874
  Aubin L., June 17, 1897
  Ewel, Apr. 5, 1860
  Gray, Mar. 5, 1857
  Gray, s. of Gray and Milly S. G. Boulware, Nov. 24, 1859
  Gemie, child of James and Caroline Boulware, Feb. 29, 1872
  John, Sept. 25, Oct. 9, 1829
  Lee, Nov. 1, 1839
  Lucy, w. of Mark Boulware, Apr. 22, 1852
  Mark, Oct. 22, 1846
  Mark, s. of M. L. and Rosina Boulware, Apr. 12, 1855
  Martha G., Jan. 10, 1850
  Mary, w. of William Boulware, Dec. 16, 1852
  Mary C. (Mrs.), Dec. 29, 1881
  Mary L., w. of Richard S. Boulware, May 5, 1859
  Mary S., w. of Richard S. Boulware, June 16, 1859
  Muscoe, Oct. 26, 1843
  Virginia L., w. of Gray Boulware, Jr., May 10, 1849
  William (Dr.), Feb. 11, 1875
BOURN
  Frances A., Dec. 6, 1860
  Mary Metz, gr. d. of Thomas Newman, Nov. 24, 1842
BOURNE
  Fannie A., w. of J. A. Bourne, Nov. 4, 1869
  Mary F. (Mrs.), May 13, 1897
  William, Feb. 27, 1851
BOUSH
  C., w. of Charles Boush, Mar. 12, 1840
BOUTWELL
  Catherine H., Mar. 20, 1873
BOWDEN
  Alexina Frances, w. of John Thomas Bowden, Feb. 13, 1918
BOWE
  Bruce, Apr. 19, 1923
  Emma Lewis, d. of N. W. Bowe, Oct. 18, 1906
  Marietta W., w. of Thomas C. Bowe, July 1, 1858
  N. W., Mar. 19, 1914
BOWEN
  Alexina Fletcher (Mrs.), Apr. 19, 1923
  Eliza F., w. of Dr. George M. Bowen, d. of James M. Bowen, Mar. 4, 1858
  Fannie, d. of George M. and Eliza F. Bowen, Sept. 24, 1857
  Margaret H. (Mrs.), Sept. 3, 1931
  Mollie, May 6, 1875
  Sallie F., Nov. 1, 1877
  Thomas Peter, s. of Dr. Peter B. and Emily M. A. Bowen, Feb. 23, 1843
  William A., Feb. 22, 1866
  William P., Feb. 27, 1879
BOWER

OBITUARY NOTICES IN THE RELIGIOUS HERALD WITH DATES OF PUBLICATION

George W. (Rev.), Apr. 9, 1885

BOWERS
Carr (Dr.), May 16, 1861
Eliza (Mrs.), Mar. 13, 1873
Elizabeth Ann, d. of Charles Bowers, Sept. 2, 1852
Frances (Mrs.), Aug. 19, 1847
Harvie M., Aug. 8, 1889
Helen E., w. of Marcus Bowers, d. of T. B. Dorset, Aug. 22, 1867
Mary Bettie, d. of John E. and Mary F. Bowers, Feb. 22, 1855
Mary Jane, w. of James Bowers, d. of W. Priddy, Sept. 16, 1836
Sanford, July 7, 1842
Willie Douglas, child of William S. and Emily R. Bowers, Sept. 11, 1873
William E., Apr. 4, 1828

BOWIE
Ann, w. of George Bowie, Sept. 14, 1893
Ann H. (Mrs.), d. of Charles T. Jesse, July 1, 1858
Edwin, Jan. 9, 1919
Sallie, w. of Charles Bowie, d. of W. I. Jones, Sept. 9, 1875
Sallie Broaddus, d. of Aubrey Bowie, Aug. 2, 1917
Walter, Sept. 22, 1853
Walter (Capt.), Dec. 20, 1900; Jan. 17, 1901
William M., Sept. 4, 1856

BOWIS
J. A. (Mrs.), Sept. 2, 1858

BOWLES
A. E., w. of James E. Bowles, Mar. 18, 1852
Ann, w. of Jesse Bowles, Jan. 18, 1894
Anderson G., s. of William B. Bowles, Apr. 13, 1839
Benjamin, Sr., July 30, Oct. 15, 1857
Betsey (Mrs.), Jan. 24, 1834
Betsy Ann, d. of William B. and Susan Bowles, Aug. 8, 1834
G. C., s. of H. T. Bowles Nov. 20, 1873
Charles K., May 24, 1860
D. W. K. (Judge), Sept. 10, 1885
Eliza, w. of Dr. Bowles, d. of Philip Pleasants, June 27, July 4, 1828
Elizabeth Ann, Apr. 2, 1830
Elizabeth J., w. of Benjamin F. Bowles, Feb. 23, 1854
Elizabeth T., w. of William B. Bowles, May 17, 1894
Fannie Knight, d. of C. K. Bowles, May 13 and 27, 1926
Florence Braham (Mrs.), Apr. 19, 1934
Frances, w. of Benjamin Bowles, Mar. 13, 1851
Francis P., s. of Pleasant and Page Bowles, Sept. 2, 1841
George S., Feb. 27, 1862
Jane, Jan. 20, 1887
Jane S. E., July 16, 1908
Jesse, July 12, 1877
John S. (Maj.), Nov. 3, 1904
Kate P., d. of John P. Bowles, Apr. 11, 1872
Lily Holland Sadler, w. of W. A. Bowles, Sept. 11, 1913
Lucy (Mrs.), July 22, 1847
Mary A., w. of Judge D.W.K. Bowles, d. of Col. George W. Richardson, Nov. 20, 1879
Matilda, w. of Benjamin Bowles, Jr., Dec. 30, 1847
Matilda, w. of William Bowles, d. of Frank and Susan Waldrop, Nov. 19, 1914
Mattie, d. of S. T. Bowles, Feb. 26, 1903
Mattie (Mrs.), June 11, 1925
Mattie Fleet (Mrs.), Apr. 26,

OBITUARY NOTICES IN THE RELIGIOUS HERALD WITH DATES OF PUBLICATION

1928; Apr. 24, 1930
Memora Montague, d. of Mrs.
Martha J. Bowles, Dec. 25,
1873
Myrtland, child of John W.
Bowles, Nov. 20, 1873
Nathaniel H., s. of Samuel
G. and Pamelia Bowles, Oct.
28, 1880
Pleasant, Jan. 29, 1874
Rosa Bryant, d. of W. J. and
L. J. Bowles, Oct. 4, 1888
Sallie A., w. of John S.
Bowles, June 6, 1881
Virginia, d. of Robert S. and
Virginia A. Bowles, Jan. 30,
1879
William, s. of Samuel T. and
Mattie F. Bowles, July 7,
1892
Willie W., d. of Maj. John S.
Bowles, May 21, 1874
BOWLING
R. B., Jan. 20, 1927
R. Bruce (Mrs.), Dec. 2, 1920
BOWMAN
Laura Alice, d. of W. L. Bowman, July 24, 1873
Nathalie B., May 3, 1923
R. C. (Mrs.), Jan. 25, 1894
Robert, July 5, 1855
BOWYER
Adam Joseph, Mar. 24, 1864
Charles, Oct. 3, 1872
Hattie Price, w. of George O.
Bowyer, Jan. 7, 1904
James T., s. of Houston Bowyer, Mar. 13, 1913
BOXLEY
Albert, Sept. 1, 1842
Annie L., w. of James C.
Boxley, July 3, 1890
D. V., w. of Joseph C. Boxley,
d. of Joseph Vaughan, Aug.
3, 1905
Fenton Bruce Mansfield, w. of
Dr. James G. Boxley, June 29,
1899
George, May 1, 1844
Helen, w. of William C. Boxley,
Feb. 4, 1897
J. C., Sept. 26, 1872
James Colby, s. of J. Joseph
and Roberta L. Boxley,
June 29, 1876
James Garland (Dr.), June 24,
1920
John Joseph, Apr. 29, 1915
Joseph C., Sept. 5, 1872
Lucy D., w. of Isaac G. Boxley, June 12, 1879
Mary Harris, w. of Frank
Boxley, July 29, 1920
Pallison, Sept. 29, 1859
Sallie, d. of Joseph and
Kate Collins Boxley, Feb.
15, 1872
BOYCE
Elizabeth F., Dec. 12, 1935
James P. (Mrs.), w. of Rev.
James P. Boyce, d. of Dr.
Fielding Ficklen, May 31, 1894
BOYD
Andrew L., June 24, 1886
Frances L., w. of George W.
Boyd, d. of Laban Palmer,
Aug. 7, 1862
George W., Jan. 30, 1890
Willie Washington, s. of Edwin and Martha Boyd, Jan.
31, 1850
BOYER
Mable, Mar. 10, 1932
Victoria T. (Mrs.), Nov. 14,
1889
BOYKIN
John (Maj.), July 22, 1858
Martha A., w. of John P.
Boykin, July 4, 1878
Mary L., d. of J. T. and Ada
W. Boykin, May 20, 1886
Mary Louisa, Nov. 17, 1859
BOZEMAN
Margaret, w. of James Bozeman,
d. of Lawrence and Sarah
Trant, Dec. 1, 1864
Mary Ella, w. of Rev. J. W.
Bozeman, d. of Jesse Snead,
Sept. 19, 1872
BRABHAM

OBITUARY NOTICES IN THE RELIGIOUS HERALD WITH DATES OF PUBLICATION:

Mary Etcher, May 27, 1915
BRACY
   Penina (Mrs.), Feb. 1, 1844
BRADBY
   W. A., Aug. 11, 1927
BRADFORD
   Anna, sister of Rev. George Bradford, Aug. 26, 1886
   Elizabeth, w. of Thomas H. Bradford, Oct. 15, 1874
   Elizabeth M., w. of Elder George Bradford, Mar. 9, 1843
   Enoch, Mar. 29, 1877
   Esther, w. of Nathaniel J. Bradford, Feb. 7, 1867
   Randolph (Dr.), June 25, 1868
BRADLEY
   Ann Eliza, Mar. 24, 1910
   Charles E., s. of William and Anna Bradley, Sept. 4, 1851
   Columbus C., May 3, 1900
   David, Dec. 22, 1881
   Ellen Brown, w. of George Y. Bradley, Feb. 14, 1850
   Frances E., w. of Thornton Bradley, Aug. 3, 1848
   George A., Jan. 12, 1928
   Henry H., Jan. 17, 1889
   Irving, s. of William W. and A. M. Bradley, Oct. 4, 1860
   James H., June 10, 1869
   James Murphy, s. of C. C. Bradley, Feb. 26, 1874
   John Lamb, Jan. 22, 1885
   Margaret, w. of Henry Bradley, Nov. 6, 1884
   Margaret D. (Mrs.), Aug. 17, 1854
   Mary Eliza, w. of George Y. Bradley, Apr. 4, 1907
   Mary F., w. of R. A. Bradley, Jan. 15, 1852
   Pleasant, Apr. 28, 1857
   Reuben, Mar. 17, 1892
   Theodoric Salley, child of Winfree and Sarah Ann Bradley, June 16, 1853
   Thomas, Dec. 3, 1846
   W. L., Jan. 30, 1896
   William C., s. of H. H. and Margaret M. Bradley, Nov. 10, 1864
BRADSHAW
   A. G., Apr. 21, 1927
   A. Q. (Mrs.), Mar. 30, 1905
   C. R., Oct. 31, 1912
   Elizabeth Scott, w. of Daniel Bradshaw, Jan. 26, 1882
   Flavius Josephus, s. of Uriah H. Bradshaw, Aug. 3, 1838
   Hannah, w. of Solomon Bradshaw, Apr. 11, 1889
   Hunter Adderson, s. of J. D. and E. T. Bradshaw, Apr. 17, 1884
   J. S. (Mrs.), May 10, 1928
   John, Jan. 25, 1923
   Joseph D., Mar. 21, 1901
   Joshua, Dec. 4, 1902
   Lena Thomas, w. of J. D. Bradshaw, Jan. 25, 1894
   Lucinda Coleman, d. of Mrs. Rody A. Bradshaw, Feb. 7, 1856
   Lucy A., w. of Willis Bradshaw, d. of James M. McCenny, Jan. 17, 1861
   Mary R., w. of James B. Bradshaw, Nov. 28, 1872
   Pattie Eley (Mrs.), Nov. 7 and 21, 1918
   R. B. (Mrs.), Jan. 1892
   Richard W., July 21, 1892
   Robert Milton, Sept. 28, 1882
   Russell, s. of J. D. and E. T. Bradshaw, Oct. 13, 1887
   Sidney Ernest (Dr.), Oct. 6, 1938
BRAGG
   Catharine (Mrs.), Jan. 6, 1842
   James B. Taylor, s. of John and Elizabeth Bragg, Feb. 9, 1865
   James M., May 5, 1859
   Joseph Samuel, s. of James E. and Julia Bragg, Mar. 22,

OBITUARY NOTICES IN THE RELIGIOUS HERALD WITH DATES OF PUBLICATION

BRAGG
  Mary E., d. of James R.
    Bragg, Mar. 13, 1884
  Nancy, w. of Thomas Bragg,
    Oct. 22, 1863
  Robert Milton, Sept. 5, 1895
  Rosa, d. of R. M. and Frances
    Bragg, Aug. 26, 1880
  Sarah Elizabeth, d. of John
    and Elizabeth Bragg, Aug.
    4, 1842
  Sarah Frances, w. of R. M.
    Bragg, May 21, 1891
  Willie D., s. of James E. and
    Julia Bragg, Mar. 8 and 22,
    1860
BRAIDFOOT
  Sophia (Mrs.), Mar. 3, 1859
BRAILSFORD
  Annie Roberta, d. of Maj. E. D.
    and Lummie Brailsford,
    Sept. 15, 1870
BRAMBLITT
  Mildred, w. of Eleanor Bramb-
    litt, Aug. 5, 1858*
BRAME
  Elizabeth, w. of John T. Brame,
    Sept. 9, 1875
  Lilly, w. of John Brame, d.
    of Capt. Frank Hester,
    Sept. 20, 1866
  S. Bettie, d. of John Brame,
    Oct. 16, 1873
BRAMHAM
  Fanny, July 10, 1851
  Horace (Dr.), May 30, 1834
  Mason S., Feb. 15, 1917
BRANCH
  Bolling (Maj.), Nov. 6, 1829
  Charles Y., Oct. 2, 1890
  E. W., Aug. 21, 1862
  Elizabeth (Mrs.), Apr. 22,
    1841
  Etta O., w. of R. A. Branch,
    Jan. 26, 1882
  Letcher Alexander, May 5,
    1881
  Thermuthis, d. of Mrs. S. J.
    Branch, Feb. 5, 1863
BRAND
  W. W. (Capt.), Aug. 6, 1914
BRANDER
  James, Feb. 27, 1829
BRANDRICK
  Florence, d. of John And
    Lucy Brandrick, Nov. 23,
    1893
BRANHAM
  Ludlow, s. of Marmaduke
    Branham, Aug. 2, 1839
BRANSCOMB
  George L., Dec. 31, 1840
BRANSFORD
  Owen C. (Col.), Dec. 3,
    1863
  Salina (Mrs.), w. of John
    Bransford, Dec. 7, 1832
BRANSON
  Belle, w. of John H. Bran-
    son, d. of J. M. Evans,
    May 22, 1884
BRANTLY
  W. T. (Mrs.), w. of Rev.
    W. T. Brantly, Aug. 24,
    1933
  William T. (Rev.), Mar. 9,
    1882
  William Tomlinson (Dr.),
    May 22, 1845
BRANTON
  John S., Feb. 13, 1873
BRAXTON
  Augustine, Aug. 2, 1860
  Dorothea Ann, w. of Augus-
    tine M. Braxton, June 9,
    1837
  Hester Van Bidder, May 25,
    1848
  Louisa U., Apr. 26, 1855
  Maria G., w. of Rev. T. C.
    Braxton, Oct. 21, Dec. 2,
    1858
  Martha Elizabeth, d. of
    Robert C. Braxton, Apr.
    23, 1863
  Robert C., July 6, 1882
  Thomas, June 11, 1840
  Thomas C. (Rev.), Aug. 20,
    1846
BRAY

---

* Possible inaccuracy in name, or spelling, but given as printed

OBITUARY NOTICES IN THE RELIGIOUS HERALD WITH DATES OF PUBLICATION

Elizabeth B., w. of George
 C. Bray, d. of George K.
 Robinson, July 19, 1855
John (Mrs.), Aug. 18, 1881
John E., May 28, 1885
Mary E., Oct. 31, 1878
May, Sept. 14, 1916
W. S. (Mrs.), June 29, 1922

BRAZIL
 William R., July 25, 1912

BREED
 Joseph B. (Rev.), Dec. 18, 1890

BREEDEN
 James O., Sept. 3, 1846
 John Burton, s. of Judith
  Ann Breeden, May 13, 1847
 W. H., Jan. 5, 1928

BREEDLOVE
 Robert A., Feb. 4, 1892
 Rosa Virginia, Sept. 14, 1848

BREEZE
 William T. (Sgt.), May 21, 1863

BRENT
 Alice (Mrs.), Sept. 20, 1855
 Emily A., w. of Charles J.
  Brent, Apr. 8, 1858
 Juliet P., w. of Fayette Brent,
  d. of Amos Johnson, July 11, 1889
 Sarah N., Aug. 31, 1843
 Ulla B., d. of London N. and
  Mary L. Brent, Mar. 8, 1855

BRETT
 W. T., June 25, 1914
 W. T. (Mrs.), Feb. 4 and 11, 1909

BREWER
 Eliza (Mrs.), Apr. 11, 1918
 Elizabeth, w. of Samuel Brewer,
  Nov. 7, 1844
 Elizabeth Williams, w. of John
  M. Brewer, Sept. 23, 1860
 Jesse Thomas, d. of John B.
  Brewer, Jan. 2, 1919
 John B., June 27, 1929
 Peter, Sept. 10, 1891

Samuel, Feb. 14, 1856
William Hunter, June 5, 1873
William S., Dec. 9, 1886

BRICKER
 J. Frank (Mrs.), July 28, 1932
 W. E., Feb. 3, 1927

BRICKHOUSE
 Mary Egerton, w. of Elder
  L. C. Brickhouse, Apr. 2, 1896
 R. E. (Mrs.), Dec. 30, 1926

BRIDGEFORTH
 Mary Ellen, w. of W. H.
  Bridgeforth, d. of John
  D. Powell, Dec. 24, 1885

BRIDGER
 Mattie F. (Mrs.), Mar. 3, 1881

BRIDGEWATER
 Mary W. (Mrs.), Nov. 9, 1848
 Nathaniel, Nov. 9, 1848

BRIDWELL
 Joseph, Sept. 6, 1849

BRIGGS
 George, June 10, 1841
 James, July 4, 1828
 Lucy (Mrs.), July 24, 1890
 Marion T., w. of Rev. John
  E. Briggs, July 1, 1926
 R. (Dr.), Nov. 16, 1858
 Thomas W., Jan. 4, 1849

BRIGHTWELL
 Jason, Mar. 13, 1829
 Jesse J., s. of William J.
  and Berta V. Brightwell,
  Nov. 12, 1885
 R. H. (Lieut.), Aug. 29, 1861
 Sarah E., w. of John T.
  Brightwell, Dec. 19, 1867

BRINSON
 H. F. (Mrs.), d. of R. P.
  Wilson, July 4, 1912

BRISTOW
 A. L., Mar. 19, 1874
 Ann Jane, June 19, 1862
 Anna Louella, d. of Rev.
  J. B. and N. R. Bristow,

OBITUARY NOTICES IN THE RELIGIOUS HERALD WITH DATES OF PUBLICATION

July 24, 1879
Bennie Ailsworth, s. of Fuller and Emma Bristow, May 4, 1899
Bettie F., Feb. 19, 1863
E. W., w. of A. L. Bristow, Apr. 20, 1876
Eugenia E., w. of James S. Bristow, Apr. 7, 1859
F. A., Dec. 14, 1911; Mar. 7, 1912
Fannie Kent, May 21, 1863
Fannie Rosaline, Nov. 1, 1866
Frances, w. of Lewis S. Bristow, Mar. 21, 1844
Isaac Addison, s. of Rev. J. B. and N. R. Bristow, Oct. 9, 1879
Jane, w. of Lewis L. Bristow, Oct. 14, 1852
L. C. (Judge), Dec. 3, 1896
Lelia W., w. of R. S. Bristow, d. of J. B. Faulkner, Aug. 2, Sept. 6, 1894
Lewis S., Sr., Apr. 20, 1871
Lucy Beulah, d. of L. W. Bristow, Dec. 7, 1871
Maggie, w. of Dr. Lewis M. Bristow, July 13, 1876
Mary, w. of William C. Bristow, Nov. 29, 1860
Mary (Mrs.), Mar. 15, 1883
Mary Ann, w. of John P. Bristow, June 29, 1876
Mary Frances, d. of W. C. and Maria Bristow, Feb. 5, 1874
Mary W., d. of O. K. Bristow, Apr. 8, 1858
Obediah R., June 19, 1862
Octavia (Mrs.), May 13, 1875
Olive, Aug. 26, 1926
Philip C., Feb. 19, 1863
Robert S., Sept. 16, 1926
Weston (Rev.), Mar. 20, June 26, 1919
Zachary W., Feb. 6, 1873
BRITE
   D. P. Apr. 4, 1872
BRITT
   Adolia, child of Rev. W. L. Britt, July 4, 1901
   Gertrude Burnette, w. of Rev. Walter L. Britt, Apr. 21. and 28, 1927
   I. T. (Col.), July 14, 1887
   Ida H. (Mrs.), May 19, 1938
   Walter Lee (Rev.), Mar. 15, 1934
   William Edward, s. of Edward and Ida Britt, Dec. 22, 1887
BRITTAIN
   Eliza Elliotte, d. of Samuel and Louisa Brittain, Aug. 13, 1840
   Louisa P., w. of Samuel Brittain, Sept. 17, 1840
BRITTLEBANK
   Martha Whaley (Mrs.), June 2, 1881
BRITTON
   George W. C., s. of L. F. and Virginia S. Britton, June 9, 1858
   Elvira W., w. of John J. Britton, Nov. 13, 1845
   Emily A. E., d. of John J. and Elvira W. Britton, Oct. 31, 1850
   John J., Sept. 9, 1841
   Lucy R., w. of Bishop John Britton, July 15, 1847
   Mary J. (Mrs.), June 21, 1928
   Mollie P., Feb. 23, 1893
   R. O. (Col.), June 16, 1859
   W. N. (Rev.), Feb. 16, 1928
   William C., Nov. 11, 1886
BROADDUS
   Albert G., Apr. 14, 1870
   Alexander Woodford, Mar. 6, 1884
   Alice R., w. of Dr. C. C. Broaddus, Dec. 30, 1886
   Andrew (Rev.), Mar. 12, 1868
   Andrew, s. of Andrew and Carrie Broaddus, June 19, 1890
   Andrew, June 30, 1898
   Andrew (Dr.), Apr. 26, 1900

OBITUARY NOTICES IN THE RELIGIOUS HERALD WITH DATES OF PUBLICATION

Andrew, III, Nov. 4, 1926
Annie, d. of Mrs. Annie E.
  Broaddus, June 17, 1897
Caroline W., w. of Rev. A.
  Broaddus, Aug. 26, 1852
Carrie, w. of Rev. A. Broaddus,
  Jr., d. of Dr. Fred W. and
  Caroline D. Powers, July 23,
  1891
Carrie, d. of Rev. Andrew
  Broaddus, July 12 and 26,
  Aug. 2, 1923
Catharine, w. of John Broaddus,
  July 15, 1852
Charles Werner, s. of Jinifer
  and Anita Broaddus, Feb. 11,
  1904
Columbia, child of Rev. A.
  Broaddus, Dec. 20, 1860
E. E., w. of J. W. Broaddus,
  Mar. 18, 1869
Edwin, Aug. 11, 1881
Eliza, w. of Edwin Broaddus,
  d. of Philip Montague, Aug.
  11, 1881
Elizabeth (Mrs.), July 22,
  1847
Ella Clyde (Mrs.), Sept. 20,
  1883
Ellen Odessa, d. of George W.
  and Elizabeth Broaddus, June
  15, 1899
Ella Hampton, d. of John E.
  Broaddus, Mar. 29, 1923
Emma Florentine, Dec. 22,
  1881
Eugene L. (Dr.), May 8, 1862
Fannie E., w. of John W. Broad-
  dus, June 26, 1856
Frances Ann, w. of Albert G.
  Broaddus, Mar. 16, 1843
Hallie, d. of Rev. Julian
  Broaddus, May 25, 1916
Hallie L. (Mrs.), Apr. 17,
  1890
Harriet, w. of John Broaddus,
  Oct. 3, 1850
Harvey N., July 20, 1871
Ida Gayle (Mrs.), d. of A. P. and
  A. F. Rowe, Sept. 28, 1893

J. B. (Mrs.), Apr. 14, 1921
James H., Sept. 3, 1868
James J., Feb. 11, 1858
James Mordecai, Aug. 4,
  1892
Jane R., w. of James J.
  Broaddus, Jan. 25, 1844
John, Apr. 17, 1884
John B., Sept. 16, 1836
John R., June 1, 1905
Joseph D., s. of Elder
  Mordecai W. Broaddus,
  July 3, 1845
Julian, June 14, 1917
Kate Garnett (Mrs.), Sept.
  16, 1926
Laura T. (Mrs.), d. of
  Nathaniel Motley, Aug. 27,
  1863
Lily, d. of Andrew Broaddus,
  Sept. 2, 1920
Louisa R., d. of William
  P. Broaddus, Aug. 2, 1849
Lucy Ann (Mrs.), d. of Rev.
  Robert Baylor Semple,
  Jan. 5, 1882
Lucy Christiana, w. of Wil-
  liam W. Broaddus, d. of Na-
  thaniel Motley, Oct. 1, 1896
Luther (Rev.), s. of Dr.
  Andrew Broaddus, Nov. 5
  and 19, 1885
M. E. (Rev.), Dec. 31, 1931
M. Ellen, w. of R. F. Broad-
  dus, July 25, 1901
Maria Louisa, d. of John A.
  Broaddus, Aug. 2, 1860
Martha, w. of Mordecai Broad-
  dus, Feb. 25, 1841
Martha Jane, w. of Rev. A.
  Broaddus, Sr., Mar. 22,
  1894
Mary Ann, w. of Rev. William
  Broaddus, Oct. 10, 1850
Mary Todd DAVIES, w. of Dr.
  Julian Broaddus, May 25,
  1905
Maurice E., Jr., s. of Dr.
  M. E. Broaddus, Dec. 11,
  1902

OBITUARY NOTICES IN THE RELIGIOUS HERALD WITH DATES OF PUBLICATION

Millicent C., w. of James M. Broaddus, d. of Charles W. and Susan Cole Jones, Apr. 18, 1918
Mordecai, Jan. 27, 1837
Mordecai R., June 16, 1859
Mordecai W., Dec. 10, 1840
Mordecai W., s. of John E. Broaddus, Feb. 18, 1886
Morris, s. of William W. Broaddus, July 16, 1896
Myrtle, d. of Mrs. Annie E. Broaddus, June 17, 1897
Nancy, w. of Albert G. Broaddus, May 22, 1862
Nina M. M., d. of Robert and Ellen Broaddus, Feb. 15, 1868
Ophelia, w. of James H. Broaddus, Oct. 28, 1858
Power, s. of A., Jr., and Carrie Broaddus, Sept. 22, 1881
Reuben, Apr. 12, 1833
Richard F., May 31, 1866
Richard Franklin, Sept. 23, 1926
Robert F., Nov. 6, 1884
Robert Semple, July 20, 1893
Robinette, w. of C. C. Broaddus, Nov. 24, 1887
Roland F., Dec. 31, 1914
Sallie M. (Mrs.), Feb. 20, 1902
Sarah Ann, w. of Mordecai R. Broaddus, Oct. 13, 1887
Sarah Jane, w. of E. Samuel Broaddus, June 24, 1841
Somerville, w. of Maj. Edmund Broaddus, June 14, 1877
Susie S., Sept. 23, 1886
T. Nash (Dr.), Oct. 17, 1918
Thomas, Apr. 22, 1869
Thomas M., Nov. 6, 1884
W. R., Sr. (Mrs.), Feb. 14, 1935
William F. (Dr.), Sept. 14 and 21, 1876
William H., Dec. 3, 1844
William J., Oct. 29, 1874
William L. (Dr.), s. of Rev. Andrew and Caroline Broaddus, Jan. 15 and 22, Feb. 19, 1914
William Lee (Mrs.), d. of Dr. John Muscoe and Ann Hancock Garnett, Dec. 16, 1926
William T., Sept. 26, 1867

BROADHEAD
Nancy (Sister), Sept. 8, 1870

BROADUS*
C. C., May 25, 1922
C. L. (Capt.), Sept. 24, 1896
Eliza, d. of Dr. John A. Broadus, Oct. 15, 1931
Elizabeth Susan, w. of James G. Broadus, July 30, 1863
Ellinor, w. of James M. Broadus, Aug. 2, 1839
James Henry, s. of James G. Broadus, Nov. 23, 1848
James Madison, July 29, 1880
John A. (Dr.), Mar. 21, Apr. 4, 1895
Maria C., w. of Rev. John A. Broadus, Nov. 26, 1857
Mary Catharine, w. of James Madison Broadus, May 7, 1908
Nellie, d. of J. A. and C. E. Broadus, July 5, 1866
Reubenella, d. of Dr. John A. Broadus, Mar. 18, 1920
Rosalie M., d. of J. Madison Broadus, June 7, 1934
T. A., Oct. 13, 1910
Thomas S., Jan. 26, 1865

BROADWELL
Freeman, Jan. 9, 1873
Mary, d. of Freeman Broadwell, Jan. 9, 1873

BROCK
Almira C., w. of Robert K. Brock, June 5 and 12, 1835
Emuella Augustine, d. of Robert K. and Elizabeth Brock, Sept. 21, 1838
Henry, July 26, 1843
Lelia Minton, w. of Dr. Leslie

* Possible inaccuracy in name, or spelling, but given as printed

OBITUARY NOTICES IN THE RELIGIOUS HERALD WITH DATES OF PUBLICATION

Claudius Brock, June 18, 1936
BROCKENBROUGH
  John A., Sept. 12, 1935
BROCKMAN
  Ann Eliza, w. of Elder Joshua L. Brockman, Nov. 3, 1853
  Bettie Tyree (Mrs.), Jan. 16, 1930
  Charles C., Mar. 16, 1854
  Charles L., s. of A. T. and Alice Brockman, Feb. 18, 1897
  Frances A. (Mrs.), Sept. 25, 1890
  J. L. (Elder), Sept. 4, 1856
  Joshua L., Oct. 1, 1885
  Lindsey E., Sept. 6, 1860
  Page, d. of Allie T. and Alice Brockman, Oct. 17, 1889
  Sally C., w. of F. D. Brockman, Apr. 3, 1845
BRODERS
  Douglas, Nov. 3, 1932
BRODIE
  Robert, Jan. 30, 1873
BRONAUGH
  David, May 12, 1853
BROOCKE
  Susan, w. of Philip E. Broocke, Dec. 24, 1857*
BROOCKES
  Catherine (Mrs.), Aug. 18, 1881
BROOCKS
  Josie E., w. of Edwin S. Broocks, Mar. 21, 1861
  Silas Hubbard, s. of Travis and Elizabeth Broocks, June 12, 1890
BROOKE
  Bettie White, w. of Philip Edward Brooke, Nov. 17, 1904*
  Dicey, Oct. 6, 1853
  Elizabeth W., w. of Philip E. Brooke, Oct. 27, 1904
  Humphrey, July 7, 1842
  Maria Whiting, w. of William T. Brooke, Nov. 9, 1854
  William Beale, June 5, 1845
  William L., father of Rev. C. W. Brooke, Dec. 29, 1904
  William T., Aug. 25, 1859
BROOKES
  Fielding, Oct. 23, 1829
  Jane C., w. of T. J. Brookes, Oct. 22, 1885
BROOKING
  Amanda M., w. of Charles R. Brooking, Dec. 29, 1842
  Ezekiel W., June 19, Nov. 6, 1913
  Hattie Belle, d. of Robert and Belle Brooking, Aug. 3, 1882
  Mary L., w. of E. W. Brooking, Dec. 15, 1892
  Mildred, w. of Robert Upsher Brooking, Apr. 10, 1862
  Robert W., Feb. 3, 1870
  Thomas A., Nov. 6, 1862
BROOKS
  (Mrs.), mother of Dr. John W. Brooks, June 28, 1888
  Alice Easley, w. of J. D. Brooks, d. of Charles Easley, Aug. 22, 1901
  Ann, w. of Philip E. Brooks, May 23, 1844*
  Ann Hasseltine, w. of E. C. Brooks, July 24, 1890
  Bettie M. (Mrs.), Apr. 1, 1926
  Henry N., s. of William and Mary E. Brooks, Dec. 14, 1865
  I. E. (Mrs.), Nov. 25, 1858
  Josiah, June 11, 1840
  Mary Ann, d. of James D. and Mary P. Brooks, Jan. 21 and 28, 1858
  Mary E., w. of Crawford F. Brooks, d. of Charles T. and E. F. Myers, Nov. 12, 1874
  Olivia, w. of F. T. Brooks, Jan. 30, 1879

* Possible inaccuracy in name, or spelling, but given as printed

OBITUARY NOTICES IN THE RELIGIOUS HERALD WITH DATES OF PUBLICATION

Roxie, (Mrs.), Dec. 25, 1902
R. J. (Sgt. and Mrs.), Aug. 18, 1910
S. P., June 18, 1931
Sallie A. (Mrs.), July 31, 1879
Sarah A., w. of James F. Brooks, Feb. 25, 1858
Sarah F., w. of James Brooks, July 6, 1882
Sidney Lewis, Oct. 27, 1927
William, Mar. 4, 1880
William, Dec. 25, 1884
William J., s. of Richardson J. Brooks, Feb. 9, 1865
Zachariah, Mar. 29, 1860
BROTHERTON
  Margaret Alice (Mrs.), Apr. 13, 1882
BROUGH
  Courtney, Dec. 4, 1845
BROUN
  Sallie Fleming, w. of William LeRoy Brown, Dec. 20, 1883
BROUNER
  Jacob (Elder), Sept. 28, 1848
BROWN
  A. (Maj.), Sept. 23, 1858
  A. E. (Rev.), June 12, 1924
  Abram Burwell (Dr.), Dec. 17 and 31, 1885
  Adaline, d. of William Brown, July 26, 1906
  Alexander Carson, Feb. 16, 1928
  Andrew J., s. of Armstead Brown, Dec. 1, 1859*
  Ann Hasseltine Judson, d. of Ann A. and William Brown, Mar. 15, 1839
  Annie Carlton, w. of Thomas Hite Brown, Apr. 5, 1900
  Archee, Dec. 20, 1866
  B. F., Apr. 29, 1926
  Bessye, Mar. 28, 1935
  Betty, Sept. 6, 1928
  Booth (Col.), July 25, 1850
  C. C. (Dr.), June 16, 1921

  Catharine (Mrs.), July 31, 1890
  Catherine G. (Mrs.), July 17, 1879
  Chancellor N. (Rev.), Dec. 3, 1936
  Clifford, s. of C. M. Brown, July 20, 1916
  Clifford M., Feb. 7, 1929
  Coleman, Feb. 24, 1887
  Corrie E., w. of Rev. C. C. Brown, Feb. 20, 1879
  Daniel, Oct. 28, 1847
  Daniel A., June 7, 1900
  David, June 26, 1879
  Deborah A., w. of Robert A. Brown, July 26, 1855
  E. E., w. of A. Brown, July 5, 1866
  E. L., w. of Enoch J. Brown, Dec. 30, 1852
  Edward Burwell, Apr. 30, 1891
  Elizabeth, d. of Thomas Brown, Feb. 20, 1862
  Emily, May 7, 1891
  Eusebia Neville, w. of James F. Brown, d. of J. Hill Lipscomb, Feb. 10, 1848
  Fanny Lavinia, w. of J. B. Brown, Nov. 5, 1868
  Fannie M. (Mrs.), Jan. 24, 1878
  Fielding, Jan. 26, 1843
  Frances (Mrs.), Mar. 24, 1842
  George P., Oct. 20, 1837
  George W. (Mrs.), Apr. 4, 1912
  Harrie, s. of Thomas H. and Annie W. Brown, Mar. 26, 1874
  Ida, Sept. 19, 1872
  J. A. (Dr.), Sept. 14, 1916
  J. W. (Mrs.), Sept. 24, 1936
  James A., July 2, 1896
  James D. (Rev.), Dec. 25, 1890
  James E., Dec. 16, 1909
  James S., May 22, 1879

* Possible inaccuracy in name, or spelling, but given as printed

-42-

OBITUARY NOTICES IN THE RELIGIOUS HERALD WITH DATES OF PUBLICATION

John B., Aug. 14, 1856
John S., s. of John G. D. Brown, Oct. 18, 1866
John S., Aug. 10, 1882
John W. (Rev.), May 19, 1881
Joseph (Capt.), Dec. 23, 1880
Joseph P., m. Mary Elizabeth Harwood, Sept. 27, 1894
Judith, Mar. 29, 1833
Louisiana Cole, d. of John D. Brown, Oct. 10, 1834
Lucy, w. of Capt. Joseph Brown, Aug. 3, 1871
Lucy Jarratt, w. of Rev. James L. Brown, d. of Jesse Jarratt, Apr. 7 and 14, 1910
Luther W., Aug. 12, 1926
M. A., w. of Coleman Brown, d. of James Crigler, Aug. 5, 1886
M. G., s. of Russel H. Brown, Feb. 26, 1857
Margaret A., d. of Martin Brown, Nov. 18, 1847
Maria F. (Mrs.), Apr. 17, 1856
Martha, w. of Nelson Brown, Dec. 28, 1832
Martha Virginia, d. of John B. and Lucy C. Brown, Aug. 14, 1856
Martin, Dec. 1, 1864
Mary (Mrs.), May 15, 1851
Mary (Mrs.), Feb. 1, 1855
Mary, w. of Bently Brown, d. of Austin Sandridge, Feb. 26, 1857
Mary A., w. of N. M. Brown, July 28, 1859
Mary A. M. (Mrs.), Mar. 11, 1847
Mary Ann (Mrs.), July 16 1857
Mary Ann Russel, w. of Armistead Brown, Sept. 9, 1852
Mary Cathran (Mrs.), Nov. 8, 1906
Mary Elizabeth, May 22, 1924
Mary F., w. of Rev. Thomas

Brown, Nov. 3, 1859
Mary Y., w. of William Brown, Mar. 27, 1884
Mattie E., d. of William H. Brown, Oct. 17, 1867
Mildred (Mrs.), June 3, 1858
Mildred Hattie, w. of A. Beale Brown, d. of James and Mary Garlic Semple, Feb. 1, 1906
Mollie Bruce, w. of Rev. Wade Bickers Brown, d. of Rev. Silas Bruce, Sept. 13, 1923
Nellie, d. of T. H. and Annie W. Brown, Aug. 4, 1864
P. (Elder), Mar. 19, 1891
Pamela Yancey, w. of Joseph D. Brown, Apr. 29, 1915
Ralph, Aug. 27, 1863
Russell H., Nov. 19, 1863
Sallie, d. of Edwin Brown, Jan. 18, 1849
Sallie (Mrs.), Jan. 27, 1876
Sallie F., May 28, 1885
Samuel (Rev.), Dec. 8, 1881
Samuel F., Dec. 5, 1935
Sarah A. (Mrs.), June 19, July 31, 1890
Sarah B. W., w. of Benjamin Brown, Jan. 11, 1839
Sarah H., w. of Thomas Brown, Aug. 23, 1855
Sarah Hannorah, d. of J. B. and Lucy C. Brown, Dec. 15, 1842
Sarah L., d. of Russell H. Brown, Apr. 23, 1863
Sue W., w. of Edward J. Brown, d. of Capt. William Peters, July 26, 1860
Susan, Feb. 16, 1893
Susan Coons (Mrs.), Jan. 26, Feb. 16, 1893
Susan H., Apr. 10, 1890
Susie F., Apr. 16, 1925
T. C., Feb. 7, 1878
Tarleton W., Feb. 10, 1870

OBITUARY NOTICES IN THE RELIGIOUS HERALD WITH DATES OF PUBLICATION

Thomas, May 30, 1867
Virginia (Mrs.), Jan. 16, 1913
William, Mar. 3, 1921
William Horatio, Feb. 19, 1880
Willie, child of John W. and Margaret Brown, Aug. 21, 1862
BROWNE
  C. T. (Rev.), May 17, 1883
  Martha Broadus, w. of T. E. Browne, d. of Rev. John Micou Farrar, Aug. 23, 1917
  Sallie, Jan. 16, 1908
  Sallie E., d. of Ethelred Browne, May 2, 1861
BROWNING
  Charles William, Feb. 25, 1926
  Hannah, w. of Francis Browning, June 23, 1837
  Harry E., Dec. 11, 1930
  Inez (Mrs.), Mar. 3, 1927
  J. F. (Mrs.), Feb. 26, 1857
  John D. (Capt.), Jan. 30, 1845
  John H., Mar. 31, 1842
  John Isaiah, Feb. 20, 1873
  Maria L., w. of Capt. James H. Browning, Apr. 8, 1875
  Robert, Sept. 25, 1851
BROWNLEY
  Kate Davis (Mrs.), Oct. 11, 1934
  Mary C. (Mrs.), Mar. 3, 1881
BROWNRIGG
  Thomas, s. of Richard and Sarah Campbell Brownrigg, Jan. 18 and 25, 1828
BRUCE
  Ann (Mrs.), w. of Joel Bruce, Aug. 20, 1846
  Anselina, w. of Landon Bruce, d. of Levi Wood, Aug. 29, 1872
  Betsie, d. of George A. and Sarah A. S. Bruce, Sept. 1, 1870
  Cecil Bracy, s. of James L. and Mattie Bruce, July 23, 1891
  Eugenia, July 11, 1889
  J. C., Nov. 30, Dec. 7, 1911
  James A., July 27, 1871
  James Clifton, May 16, 1907
  James W., May 16, 1907
  Joel, May 8, 1835
  John L., May 1, 1851
  Lucy Brooks (Mrs.), May 8, 1930
  Martha (Mrs.), May 14, 1830
  Martha S., w. of George A. Bruce, Feb. 10, 1910
  Mary Cornelia, d. of Samuel and Elizabeth Bruce, Aug. 3, 1832
  Mary W., w. of Reuben Bruce, Aug. 10, 1882
  Missouri (Mrs.), Apr. 6, 1882
  Richard H., Aug. 25, 1938
  Sallie F., d. of George A. Bruce, Apr. 24, 1873
  Sarah A. S., w. of George A. Bruce, d. of Thomas and Elizabeth Gayle, Sept. 1, 1870
  Silas (Rev.), Nov. 13 and 27, 1884
  Tennie, w. of Rev. Silas Bruce, Apr. 3 and 10, 1902
  Thomas Hester, s. of Samuel and Betsy Ann Bruce, Sept. 16, Dec. 16, 1920
BRUICE*
  James, Sr., Feb. 16, 1893
BRUMLEY
  Mary Frances, w. of Joseph Brumley, d. of Andrew Motley, Aug. 5, 1841
  Robert, May 12, 1859
BRUMMALL
  Josiah B., Nov. 13, 1879
  Lavinia, Mar. 23, 1871
  Maria (Mrs.), Oct. 18, 1888
  Rosalie, Dec. 11, 1879
BRYAN
  E. (Mrs.), Nov. 13, 1829
  George, Mar. 6, 1930

* Possible inaccuracy in name, or spelling, but given as printed

OBITUARY NOTICES IN THE RELIGIOUS HERALD WITH DATES OF PUBLICATION

Mary E., w. of John Bryan,
  d. of Elam and Elizabeth
  Blankenship, May 23, 1867
BRYANT
  Ambrose Booton, June 18, 1914
  Annie G. (Mrs.), May 12, 1921
  Emma H., w. of Edward Bryant,
    Oct. 9, 1879
  Fannie, Feb. 22, 1855
  Jennetta T. (Mrs.), Oct. 25,
    1849
  John M., s. of J. W. and
    Catharine Bryant, Oct. 26,
    1871
  Lucie E., d. of A. J. and
    Zenobia Bryant, Feb. 10,
    1898
  Maria F., w. of Alex
    Bryant, May 13, 1847
  Mary E. Z. (Mrs.), June 19,
    1890
  Zenobia B., w. of A. J.
    Bryant, d. of Dr. William
    R. Putney, Jan. 29, 1891
BRYCE
  Archibald, Aug. 27, 1846
  Mildred Chewning, w. of Benja-
    min F. Bryce, Apr. 3, 1884
BRYDIE
  Robert B., Aug. 13, 1885
BUCHANAN
  Abbie E., w. of Dr. James
    Buchanan, Apr. 24, 1924
  Alice (Mrs.), Mar. 4, 1920
  Annie Gaulding (Mrs.), Sept.
    28, 1922
  James, Apr. 12, 1860
  James, Oct. 22, 1931
  H. L. (Mrs.), Jan. 22, 1931
  Mary A., Mar. 11, 1858
BUCK
  Andrew S., Oct. 24, 1828
  Benjamin V., May 31, 1855
  Bettie, w. of Walter L. Buck,
    Sept. 29, 1859
  Eliza T., w. of John S. Buck,
    Sept. 23, 1858
  Elizabeth, w. of John S. Buck,
    Sept. 7, 1832
  Walter L., s. of John S. Buck,
    Jan. 10, 1861
  William C. (Elder), June 13,
    1872
BUCKLAND
  R. J. W. (Rev.), Mar. 1,
    1877
BUCKLES
  W. N. (Rev.), Feb. 13, 1908
BUCKNELL
  Margaret Crozer (Mrs.), Apr.
    21, 1870
BUCKNER
  Ann Hawes (Mrs.), Apr. 14,
    1861
  Catharine, w. of Richard
    Buckner, Dec. 28, 1850
  H. F. (Dr.), Dec. 28, 1882
  Judith (Mrs.), d. of Gray
    Boulware, Jan. 9, 1851
  Mary C. (Mrs.), May 30, 1889
  R. (Col.), Oct. 26, 1843
  Sarah Catherine Ashby, w. of
    Richard H. Buckner, Oct. 1,
    1896
  X. X. (Rev.), Feb. 1, 1872
BUDD
  Allen Watson, July 2, 1925
  Joseph S., Aug. 4, 1887
BUDWELL
  Mary B., d. of S. M. and
    J. B. Budwell, Oct. 15,
    1857
  Sallie Massie, w. of J. B.
    Budwell, Aug. 27, 1868
BULLARD
  Keziah, w. of Capt. R. W.
    Bullard, May 6, 1847
  Mildred S., Sept. 29, 1881
BULLIFANT
  Leutida (Mrs.), July 8, 1875
BULLINGTON
  John W., Mar. 19, 1857
  Maia, w. of Josiah Bulling-
    ton, Mar. 3, 1870
  Marinda Jane, d. of Harwood
    and Sarah Bullington, Nov.
    16, 1838
  Richard, Sept. 29, 1837
BULLOCK
  Ann, Feb. 14, 1856

-45-

OBITUARY NOTICES IN THE RELIGIOUS HERALD WITH DATES OF PUBLICATION

Ann, w. of Joseph Bullock,
   June 18, 1863
David, Sept. 21, 1838
Jane, Sept. 21, 1838
Laura Alphra, d. of S. B. and
   Louisa W. Bullock, July 3,
   1862
Malinda, Aug. 17, 1854
Nancy, Feb. 14, 1856
S. Wise, Jan. 13, 1881
Sarah Eliza, d. of Dr. Robert
   and Ann Bullock, May 11,
   1854
Thomas, July 30, 1857
BUMPASS
   William, July 7, 1837
BUNBURY
   A. J., Sept. 11, 1856
BUNCH
   Isaac Carl, July 15, 1915
BUNDICK
   Flora Bloxom (Mrs.), Feb.
   26, 1920
   George Clinton (Rev.), Aug.
   15, 1935
   Grace, d. of John A. and
   Annie W. Bundick, Apr. 2,
   1908
   John H., s. of John and Alice
   E. Bundick, Aug. 24, 1876
   Mary A., Jan. 20, 1848
BUNDY
   Stephen J., July 27, 1922
BUNN
   John T., Feb. 14, 1895
BUOY
   Mary Elizabeth, d. of T. M.
   Buoy, Aug. 21, 1902
BUNTIN*
   Mattie Jordan, w. of William
   Henry Buntin, Oct. 4, 1883
BUNTING
   Elizabeth, w. of George Young
   Bunting, Aug. 21, 1879
BURCH
   Demetria Ann, d. of Samuel
   S. and Catharine W. Burch,
   Jan. 11, 1855
   George F., s. of John N. and
   Isabella C. Burch, Aug. 17,
   1893
James Henry, July 12, 1877
Jane (Mrs.), July 18, 1844
Judson Kerfoot, s. of Julian
   Burch, July 29, 1915
Kate C. (Mrs.), July 17,
   1924
Mary Ella, June 2, 1859
Sarah W., w. of James H.
   Burch, June 19, 1856
BURDETT*
   Virginia M., w. of Joseph
   G. Burdett, Jan. 27,
   1881
BURDETTE
   James A., May 23, 1907
   Robert J. (Dr.), Dec. 10 and
   31, 1914
BURFOOT
   A. M. (Rev.), Dec. 31, 1931
   J. D., Nov. 12, 1936
   Mary Ann, w. of Thomas M.
   Burfoot, Apr. 16, 1840
   Mary Awilda, d. of Charles
   and Henrietta L. Burfoot,
   July 24, 1845
   Mary Awilda Claiborne, d. of
   Charles T. and Henrietta L.
   Burfoot, Aug. 11, 1853
   Thomas E., s. of Lawson Bur-
   foot, Dec. 6, 1833
BURFORD
   Augustus A., June 27, 1850
   Lucy L. (Mrs.), Nov. 8,
   1888
   Powhatan S., Nov. 12, 1908
BURFORT
   V. O. (Mrs.), July 23, 1908
BURGER
   David W., Feb. 20, 1890
BURGESS
   Alelia Ruth, d. of William
   J. Burgess, May 20, 1920
   Annie, d. of Charles T.
   Burgess, Aug. 10, 1876
   Charles T., Jr., Aug. 10,
   1876
   Elizabeth, w. of E. Burgess,
   Jan. 23, 1873
   Eula, Sept. 29, 1881

* Possible inaccuracy in name, or spelling, but given as printed

OBITUARY NOTICES IN THE RELIGIOUS HERALD WITH DATES OF PUBLICATION

Frances (Mrs.), Jan. 1, 1852
BURK*
   Emily Amanda, d. of William
     H. and Elmira C. W. Burk,
     Nov. 20, 1879
BURKE
   Bettie DeJarnette, w. of
     George W. Burke, Dec. 11,
     1930
   Clyde Carpenter, Mar. 3, 1938
   Dorothea, w. of George Burke,
     d. of Col. John Washington,
     Feb. 15, 1849
   Elizabeth J., d. of James
     Burke, Dec. 25, 1845
   Mary Evalyn, w. of Lucius C.
     Burke, d. of Rev. John O.
     Turpin, Apr. 10, 1924
   Mary L., May 7, 1857
   R. F., June 5, 1924
   Sarah W., d. of Robert Burke,
     Aug. 26, 1886
   Thomas H., Mar. 27, 1829
BURKHOLDER
   Catharine, Apr. 1, 1880
   William H., July 31, 1862
BURKS
   David, Sr., Apr. 11, 1828
   Maria Louisa, w. of William
     L. Burks, d. of Dr. R. A.
     Sale, Aug. 23, 1866
   Ora Mable, May 8, 1884
   Robert S. (Col.), Sept. 23,
     1886
BURN
   Jane A., w. of Henry C. Burn,
     July 31, 1873
BURNETT
   Elizabeth (Mrs.), Apr. 16,
     1840
   Henry C., Feb. 20, 1902
   John N. (Col.), Aug. 5, 1852
   Mary Caldwell, w. of Henry C.
     Burnett, Sept. 21, 1882
   Mary E., w. of Samuel H.
     Burnett, Mar. 17, 1870
   N. C. (Rev.), Feb. 26, 1920
   William J., s. of Joshua and
     Ann E. F. Burnett, Jan.
     12, 1843

   William Richard, s. of Robert
     Burnett, Oct. 18, 1860
BURNLEY
   Abner, Apr. 11, 1844
   Amanda T., d. of Henry M.
     Burnley, Dec. 16, 1841
   Caleb, May 7, 1863
   Edwin, July 16, 1868
   Hardin, Nov. 12, 1868
   Hardin (Dr.), Oct. 18, 1894
   Hardina M., d. of Col. Har-
     din Burnley, Apr. 18,
     1834
   Lou Temple, d. of Dr. H.
     and B. D. Burnley, Nov.
     11, 1880
   Mary Parke, June 20, July
     18, 1907
   Susan Temple, w. of Edwin
     Burnley, d. of Maj. Joseph
     Gwathmey, Aug. 10, 1838
   Susan Temple, June 23, 1870
   Zacheriah, Dec. 4, 1845
BURNLY*
   Henry M., June 29, 1848
BURNS
   D. E. (Rev.), Dec. 8, 1870
   Frances (Mrs.), June 7, 1855
   Margaret R., w. of Peter
     Burns, Dec. 13, 1877
   Peter, June 27, 1850
BURR
   David I., July 20, 1838
BURRELL
   C. Edward (Dr.), Apr. 14,
     1929
BURRESS
   Jane, w. of Peter L. Burress,
     Jan. 11, 1872
   Mary D., d. of Harris Bur-
     ress, Aug. 29, 1828
   Mary E., w. of William D.
     Burress, Dec. 14, 1854
   May Claggett, d. of J. E.
     Burress, Nov. 6, 1873
   Peter L., Feb. 23, 1882
BURRISS
   R. H. (Rev.), Jan. 5, 1928
BURROUGHS
   James, Aug. 22, 1861

* Possible inaccuracy in name, or spelling, but given as printed

OBITUARY NOTICES IN THE RELIGIOUS HERALD WITH DATES OF PUBLICATION

Maud J., May 6, 1937
Sallie A. (Mrs.), Sept. 8, 1927
Samuel, Mar. 25, 1852
Thomas J., Dec. 18, 1879
BURROWS
　Adaline, w. of Dr. J. L. Burrows, Aug. 27, 1874
　J. Lansing (Dr.), Jan. 12 and 26, 1893
　Lansing (Dr.), Nov. 20, 1919
BURRUSS
　children of C. D. Burruss, Feb. 22, 1835
　Ann E. (Mrs.), Apr. 4, 1878
　Catharine E., w. of Josiah Burruss, d. of William S. Ryland, Sept. 18, 1884
　Charles Pinckney, Apr. 30, 1885
　Ellette W., Mar. 22, 1877
　Georgia T., d. of E. W. Burruss, Apr. 3, 1862
　Jefferson, July 4, 1844
　John, July 3, 1879
　Josiah, May 8 and 22, 1884
　Kate V. (Mrs.), w. of C. P. Burruss, d. of Charles Gennet, Feb. 25, 1897
　Louisa R., w. of Richard H. Burruss, Sept. 25, 1845
　Lucy C., w. of Charles Burruss, Dec. 3, 1840
　Lucy J. (Mrs.), May 24, 1860
　Margaret, w. of John Burruss, Oct. 9, 1835
　Mary A., w. of William M. Burruss, Apr. 6, 1916
　Mary Ann, d. of Patrick H. and Martha Burruss, Aug. 27, 1857
　Mary Ann, d. of Paul and Mary Burruss, Sept. 13, 1860
　Mattie G., d. of P. and M. Burruss, July 11, 1867
　Nannie, d. of Josiah Burruss, Nov. 27, 1873
　Priscilla M., w. of John Burruss, Oct. 29, 1846
　Rachel, May 9, 1867
　Sally T. WORTHAM, w. of H. Burruss, Mar. 27, 1862
　Sarah Ellen, d. of Paul W. G. and Mary I. Burruss, June 2, 1853
　Sarah M., w. of John P. Burruss, Apr. 3, 1890
　Thomas R. (Mrs.), Aug. 5, 1880
　Warren Brickell, Mar. 6, 1873
BURSON
　Susanna, w. of Z. L. Burson, Feb. 14, 1856
BURT
　Bettie Bailey (Mrs.), Aug. 5, 1897
　George E., Oct. 8, 1903
　Jane, Oct. 11, 1888
　Monroe, Feb. 9, 1911
　Nicholas, July 19, 1888
　Sarah, Mar. 11, 1875
BURTIS
　Peter T., Dec. 26, 1901
BURTON
　Addison, Mar. 14, 1878
　Amanda W., w. of Hudson Burton, July 26, 1860
　Benjamin, May 3, 1860
　Benjamin Theodore, s. of Mary Burton, Oct. 10, 1850
　Carrie Hamlet, d. of Rev. R. and E. R. Burton, July 24, 1873
　Daniel W., Apr. 28, 1864
　Eliza H. S. (Mrs.), Jan. 1, 1863
　Ella, Sept. 11, 1930
　George W., May 20, 1897
　Henry T., s. of Mrs. Peter Burton, Mar. 30, 1865
　James F., July 2, 1885
　John, Jan. 2, 1822
　John, Mar. 23, 1871
　John M., s. of John M. and Frances C. Burton, July 23, 1857
　John R., s. of Thomas and Mary L. Burton, July 7,

OBITUARY NOTICES IN THE RELIGIOUS HERALD WITH DATES OF PUBLICATION

1859
John Y., Jan. 26, 1871
Julianna, w. of Maj. William Burton, Nov. 19, 1846
Laura J. (Mrs.), Nov. 24, 1884
Margaret A., Apr. 16, 1857
Morgia A., w. of R. M. Burton, d. of John R. Erambeat, Dec. 23, 1875
Petronilla F., Mar. 13, 1879
R. (Rev.), June 12, 1829
R. S. (Mrs.), July 23, 1891
Reuben (Capt.), Aug. 21, 1829
Roberta Shuck, w. of Marion Burton, d. of Carter Mahon, Apr. 30, 1863
Sarah E., Nov. 7, 1907
Susan E., d. of Allen Burton, Sept. 22, 1859
Susan F., Feb. 1, 1855
Tina (Mrs.), Oct. 8, 1931
Thomas J., Aug. 4, 1881
Tyree G., Oct. 28, 1852

BURWELL
George Washington (Dr.), Sept. 4, 1873
Panthea E., w. of Capt. John R. S. Burwell, Sept. 25, 1851
William Armistead, s. of Lewis and Sallie E. Burwell, Apr. 4, 1867

BUSH
P. W., May 2, 1918
Sarah A., Mar. 10, 1864
Thomas J., Jan. 18, 1866
Urbane, Oct. 13, 1859

BUSKEY
William J., June 8, Aug. 10, 1916

BUSTARD
James G., s. of James and Margaret C. Bustard, June 13, 1889

BUTCHER
Rebecca Sands (Mrs.), Jan. 27, 1859

BUTLER
Betsey (Mrs.), Apr. 26, 1923
Cherry F., Dec. 22, 1887
Fanny H., w. of J. R. Butler, July 18, 1867
James M., Apr. 13, 1838
John, Dec. 18, 1829
John, Dec. 23, 1852
Lucy, Feb. 5, 1880
Martha, July 21, 1859
Mary E. (Mrs.), July 23, 1891
Mary J., w. of Jesse T. Butler, Apr. 4, 1889
Mattie, child of James R. and Fannie H. Butler, July 9, 1863
Nellie, d. of Rev. John M. Butler, June 19, 1879
Thomas, May 8, 1856
Thomas H., July 9, 1874
W. A. (Mrs.), June 15, 1922

BUTTERWORTH
Annie Belle, w. of Emmett Butterworth, d. of W. B. and M. A. Smithson, Oct. 17, 1901

BUTTON
Duncan Young, s. of John Y. and Maud A. Button, Aug. 31, 1899
Frank M., Feb. 15, 1906
James M., Feb. 20, 1868
Jane (Mrs.), Mar. 23, 1893
Joseph W., July 27, 1871
Mary Ella, July 22, 1920
Mary James (Mrs.), May 20, 1926

BUXTON
Ruby, May 5, 1927

BYBEE
Ellen, Mar. 27, 1902
George (Mrs.), June 27, 1901

BYERLY
Maria Angus, w. of John L. Byerly, Mar. 12, 1863

OBITUARY NOTICES IN THE RELIGIOUS HERALD WITH DATES OF PUBLICATION

BYERS
   James M., Mar. 20, 1873
BYRD
   Colwell P., Dec. 10, 1914;
      Apr. 8, 1915
   Richard E., Oct. 29, 1925

BYRNE
   Henry Milton, s. of H. M.
      and E. F. Byrne, July
      16, 1925
BYWATERS
   B. F., Mar. 8, 1923

C

CABANIS
Lucy Carter, Apr. 29, 1915

CABANISS
Ellen, w. of William H. Cabaniss, Jan. 9, 1873
William H., Feb. 13, 1868

CABELL
Adelaide W., w. of Dr. A. J. Cabell, Apr. 12, 1906
Clara Hawes, w. of Frederick Mortimer, Mar. 7, 1901
Mary E., Nov. 3, 1904
Mary Spigener (Mrs.), w. of Dr. William Craghead Cabell, d. of Col. Isaac Hughes and Catharine Spigener Watson, Nov. 11, 1920

CALDER
Virginia (Mrs.), July 6, 1871

CALDWELL
J. Randolph, Aug. 23, 1923
Mary, d. of Oites Caldwell, Oct. 31, 1918
Richard, Jan. 17, 1878
Susan (Mrs.), Feb. 20, 1913

CALHOUN
Nathan, July 7, 1870

CALLAHAN
Hattie Spake (Mrs.), May 19, 1921
John S., Feb. 16, 1838

CALLAND
Elizabeth, w. of Samuel Calland, Feb. 22, 1828

CALLAWAY
B. M. (Dr.), Oct. 2, 1902
Charlotte E., d. of Capt. Robert and Elizabeth Callaway, Apr. 2, 1857
Fielding B., s. of Capt. James F. Callaway, July 11, 1861
Mary, w. of Capt. J. F. Callaway, July 8, 1852

CALLCOTE
A. D. (Lt. Col.), Oct. 1, 1863; Feb. 25, 1864
Harriet J., w. of Alexander Callcote, Aug. 16, 1860

CALLENDINE
M. B., June 28, 1883

CALLIS
Charles R., Mar. 9, 1933
George, Sept. 29, 1927
Nancy, Mar. 9, 1848
W. Eugene, Dec. 28, 1933

CALLISON
Simpson Grant (Rev.), Jan. 9, 1930

CALWELL
J. N. (Mrs.), Feb. 22, 1923

CALLOWAY
Ann J. (Mrs.), Jan. 30, 1896
Joseph, Jan. 25, 1839

CALVERT
Mary Wade (Mrs.), w. of Ralls Calvert, Jan. 12, 1843

CALVIN
John, June 27, 1828

CAMDEN
Elwain McKinney, s. of R. W. Camden, Nov. 28, 1918
Gilbert Crews, s. of R. W. Camden, Aug. 7, 1913
Horsley, Mar. 7, 1929
Jane (Mrs.), May 27, 1858
Sarah, w. of John F. Camden, Mar. 29, 1855
Sterling E. (Dr.), Dec. 24, 1857
Willie Campbell, w. of Horsley Barnes Camden, July 25, 1935

CAMERON
Ella Mae Orndoff (Mrs.), Jan. 21, 1926

CAMMACK

-51-

OBITUARY NOTICES IN THE RELIGIOUS HERALD WITH DATES OF PUBLICATION

  G. W., Oct. 10, 1878
  J. C., Jan. 16, 1873
  Jane (Mrs.), w. of John
    C. Cammack, May 28, 1874
  Kate Lester, d. of John Chue,
    and Jane Cammack, Feb. 22,
    1849
  Mary J., May 4, 1916
CAMP
  Andrew Jackson, Jan. 23, 1919
  Ella Virginia, w. of P. D.
    Camp, Sept. 15, 22
    and 29, Oct. 20, 1938
  Frances V. (Mrs.), May 2,
    1867
  James Leonidas, Jan. 28,
    Feb. 18 and 25, 1926
  Mary A., w. of John W., Dec.
    13, 1849
  Paul D., Feb. 14 and 21,
    1924
  Robert, s. of J. L. Camp,
    Jan. 30, 1913
  William S., Aug. 27, 1857
CAMPBELL
  Alexander, Mar. 22, 1866
  Amanda M., w. of Joseph W.
    Campbell, Feb. 25, 1875
  Arthur W., May 13, 1852
  Bettie M. (Mrs.), Aug. 9,
    1906
  Carroll Venable, s. of Hugh
    Campbell, Aug. 20, 1925
  D. R. (Rev.), Nov. 16, 1865
  Elizabeth Ann (Mrs.), Oct.
    23, 1829
  Emily D. (Mrs.), Apr. 18,
    1878
  J. P. (Rev.), Sept. 13, 1906
  Jeannette R. R. w. of
    William Campbell, d. of Dr.
    James H. Latane, Feb.
    5, 1880
  Joseph, April 2, 1885
  Joseph W., Feb. 25, 1875
  Josephine, d. of Alexander
    and Betty Campbell, Sept.
    27, 1855
  Mary (Mrs.), Mar. 1, 1877
  Mary E. (Mrs.), w. of Achilles
    Campbell, Apr. 27, 1832
  Mary Elizabeth, w. of
    James W. Campbell, Oct.
    25, 1906
  Mary Elizabeth, d. of
    William Campbell, Oct.
    26, 1838
  Mary Fleet, d. of William
    and Sally E. Campbell,
    Sept. 3, 1863
  Matthew T., Oct. 17, 1895
  Mary Hill, w. of Hugh Campbell, July 8, 1841
  Mittie Jane, w. of Joseph
    S. Campbell, d. of Rev.
    Z. L. Burson, Nov. 27, 1873
  Mollie E., d. of Rev. Newton
    and Laura W. Campbell, June
    26, 1879
  Otera A., w. of Hugh Campbell,
    Jan. 12, 1854
  Priscilla, w. of William Campbell, d. of Capt. Robert
    Courtney, Aug. 3, 1843
  R. P. H., Apr. 30, 1863
  Robert (Rev.), Oct. 30, 1845
  Robert Courtney, Nov. 5, 1931
  Robert L., Feb. 2, 1888
  S. E. H. (Mrs.), Oct. 15,
    1891
  S. E. H., Feb. 11, 1892
  Sallie Elizabeth, w. of William
    Hugh Campbell and d. of John
    D. G. Brown, May 7, 1908
  Sally Brown, d. of Hugh Campbell, Oct. 12, 1854
  Virginia, w. of Richard Campbell, d. of Thomas Broaddus,
    Feb. 23, 1865
  William, Nov. 30, 1843
  William, July 16, Oct. 8,
    1925
  William R., s. of Joseph N.
    Campbell, Oct. 25, 1860
  William S., Dec. 11, 1879
CANADA
  Henry C., Jan. 16, 1879
  Martha W. (Mrs.), Jan. 26, 1882
  William F., April 25, 1850
  Willie H., Dec. 4, 1879

OBITUARY NOTICES IN THE RELIGIOUS HERALD WITH DATES OF PUBLICATION

CANFIELD
  John Sedin, May 21, 1885
CANNON
  John H. (Mrs.), June 26, 1902
CANNY
  Mary Jarvis (Mrs.), Aug. 17, 1922
CANTOR
  Reuben, July 4, 1828
CAPELL
  John R., Nov. 24, 1887
CAPPS
  Nancy J., Feb. 9, 1888
CARDEN
  David P., July 24, 1873
  E. (Mrs.), Jan. 2, 1868
  Isabella Ann, w. of G. Henry Carden, Apr. 14, 1881
CARDLE
  Sarah (Mrs.), June 23, 1921
CARDWELL
  Edna J. (Mrs.), Dec. 4, 1873
  Mary L., w. of George Cardwell, Mar. 28, 1861
  Melvina B. (Mrs.), Feb. 7, 1907
CAREY
  Callie, w. of William Carey, d. of John Marshall, July 16, 1925
  E. A., May 14, 1863
  John, June 22, 1843
CARIER
  T. Eldridge, Mar. 25, 1909
CARLETON
  Bennie, s. of Mrs. Bettie H. Carleton, and gr.s. of Rev. R. H. Bagby, May 15, 1873
  Eliza (Mrs.), Nov. 11, 1920
CARLTON
  Alexander, Mar. 27, 1862
  Alice, June 6, 1861
  Benoni, Jr., Aug. 20, 1868
  Broaddus O., s. of Alfred F. Carlton, Oct. 1, 1936
  Ellis M., June 28, 1934
  Frances (Mrs.), Dec. 16, 1852
  Henry, Sept. 26, 1828
  J. F., Mar. 9, 1838
  Jane E., July 12, 1849
  Jane W. (Mrs.), Oct. 22, 1840
  Joseph K., May 22, 1930
  Julia Ann (Mrs.), Apr. 12, 1855
  Julian, s. of Alexander and Virginia Carlton, Mar. 31, 1859
  Martha H., w. of B. Carlton, d. of John Bagby, Jan. 10, 1866
  Victoria (Mrs.), Apr. 4, 1872
CARMEN
  W. E. (Mrs.), July 7, 1921
CARMINE
  Anna (Mrs.), June 25, 1936
CARNEAL
  George Trice, s. of James M. Carneal, Mar. 23, 1871
  James D., Jan. 16, 1936
  Josephine (Mrs.), w. of L. J. Carneal, d. of Joseph Mosby, Nov. 3 and 17, 1870
  Mary E., w. of J. W. Carneal d. of Rev. James D. Wright Aug. 10, 1871
  W. L., May 17, July 26, 1923
CARNEFEX
  Joel, May 21, 1908
CARNEFIX
  E. M., Mar. 17, 1887
  Georgie, s. of J. W. F. and S. A. Carnefix, Mar. 3, 1881
CARNEY
  Christiana, w. of James H. Carney, Oct. 6, 1853
  Emily J. (Mrs.), Apr. 13, 1893
  James, Mar. 30, 1871
  James H., May 18, 1854
  Martha A., w. of Stephen Carney, Aug. 5, 1858
  Rice H., May 1, 1856
  Richard, Sept. 22, 1842
  Richard E., July 28, 1898

OBITUARY NOTICES IN THE RELIGIOUS HERALD WITH DATES OF PUBLICATION

Wright B. Sr. (Mrs.), Mar. 11, 1926
CAROLL
　Booker, July 22, 1831
CARPENTER
　Anne, w. of John Carpenter, Jan. 1, 1852
　Catherine V. (Mrs.), June 9, 1904
　Charles W., Mar. 27, 1829
　Elvira H., w. of A. H. Carpenter, Jan. 20, 1887
　Florence Anna, d. of Robert C. and Jane F. Carpenter, July 20, 1871
　Garland M., Dec. 27, 1855
　Hester Booton, Mar. 3, 1927
　J. C., Nov. 10, 1910
　J. T. (Rev.), Sept. 2, 1897
　James Alexander, s. of James D. and Sarah Carpenter, Dec. 13, 1849
　James C., Apr. 1, 1880
　James P., July 26, 1877
　Jane F., w. of R. C. Carpenter, Feb. 22, 1883
　Jennie F., Sept. 29, 1892
　Jenny C., Dec. 25, 1856
　John, Aug. 18, 1853
　Joseph (Mrs.), Jan. 4, 1855
　Junie Moss, s. of C. A. and Cornelia Carpenter, Dec. 25, 1890
　Louisianna, d. of Richard Carpenter, Nov. 8, 1860
　Lydia Ann, Oct. 11, 1888
　Margaret Ellen, w. of Caius M. Carpenter, May 6, 1909
　Maria L. J., d. of Mrs. G. Carpenter, May 31, 1849
　Mary E. (Mrs.), w. of James C. Carpenter, Mar. 13, 1845
　Patsey, w. of Pleasants Carpenter, July 27, 1854
　Philenia, Mar. 13, 1829
　Phoebe U., w. of William Carpenter, Jr., Jan. 28, 1847
　Richard Cote, Mar. 3, 1892
　Sarah, w. of Thomas Carpenter, Aug. 21, 1879
　Sarah J., w. of William J. Carpenter, Aug. 18, 1853
　Susan, w. of William Carpenter, Jr., July 4, 1844
　Susan, w. of James Carpenter, Aug. 5, 1868
　Waller, July 23, 1874
　William, July 12, 1855
　William H. (Dr.), Jan. 22, 1931
　William W., Jan. 4, 1866
CARR
　Alice S., w. of Charles Carr, June 16, 1837
　Bernard, June 5, 1851
　Catherine (Mrs.), Oct. 12, 1871
　Emily A. (Mrs.), Feb. 1, 1877
　H. Virginia (Mrs.), Dec. 1, 1910
　Holland, Oct. 8, 1885
　J. O., Nov. 29, 1934
　John O., Sept. 8 and 22, 1864
　John R., Mar. 25, 1920
　Malissa (Mrs.), Oct. 2, 1873
　Mary (Mrs.), Apr. 11, 1889
　Mary Susan (Mrs.), w. of Thomas O., Dec. 31, 1885
　Sally (Mrs.), w. of John, Oct. 12, 1854
　Thomas O., Jr., May 29, 1863
　Thomas O., Feb. 8, 1894
　William C. (Lt.), Oct. 2, 1862
CARRADUS
　Catherine B. (Mrs.), Apr. 10, 1835
CARRAWAY
　S. F. B. (Mrs.), Nov. 9, 1871
　Willie, July 26, 1877
CARRICK
　Lucy Jane (Mrs.), Nov. 1, 1877
　Mary Eliza, d. of William Carrick, Aug. 19, 1875
CARRINGTON
　A. M. (Mrs.), Dec. 25, 1890
　Codrington, Apr. 14, 1952
　Emma, w. of H. C. Carrington, Feb. 2, 1893

OBITUARY NOTICES IN THE RELIGIOUS HERALD WITH DATES OF PUBLICATION

Emma Dove, d. of Emma and H. C. Carrington, Feb. 2, 1893
Robert Bernard, Mar. 13, 1919

CARROLL
Arianna V. (Mrs.), Oct. 28, 1920
B. H. (Dr.), Nov. 19, 1914
Eugene, s. of Rev. John L. Carroll, Mar. 1, 1906
J. M. (Dr.), Jan. 29, 1931
John L. (Rev.), July 4, 1895
Nancy, w. of Booker Carroll, July 14, 1859
Nannie Mitchell, d. of Rev. J. L. and S. M. Carroll, Oct. 30, 1873
Sarah Ginzzelle, d. of Rev. John L. and S. M. Carroll, Aug. 16, 1877

CARRUTHERS
James (Maj.), June 27, 1828

CARSON
Martha, w. of Capt. Simon Carson, June 5, 1851
Mary Elizabeth, d. of W. B. and Mary G. Carson, Feb. 22, 1877
Mary Griffith, w. of W. B. Carson, d. of Stephen Griffith, July 12, 1877

CARSWELL
Lunie Varner, d. of Rev. E. R. Carswell, Jr., Oct. 22, 1874

CARTER
A. G., w. of Robert S. Carter, d. of A. P. Woodson, Feb. 12, 1857
Alexander, s. of John F. Carter, April 6, 1854
Alexina Thomas, d. of Theodore F. and Mary E. Carter, Dec. 10, 1868
Andrew, Mar. 21, 1929
Andrew C., s. of Moses Carter, Feb. 5, 1857
Andrew C., s. of Mary A. Carter, July 22, 1858
Ann O. (Mrs.), Mar. 3, 1864
Ann R., w. of B. H. Carter, May 23, 1889
Anne, w. of Capt. J. Carter, d. of Rev. Joel Hubbard, Aug. 13, 1874
Annie C., Feb. 22, 1934
Barney H., June 30, 1910
Clare Carpenter, Nov. 17, 1921
China, Feb. 15, 1855
Cynthia, Oct. 26, 1916
E. L. (Mrs.), Nov. 9, 1893
Elizabeth P., d. of Daniel and Ann Carter, Jan. 31, 1850
Ella Winston, w. of N. M. Carter, d. of George E. and Eloisa Farley, Oct. 13, 1910
Emma C. (Mrs.), d. of Henry Coleman, June 10, 1909
Emma S. (Mrs.), d. of Rev. John Fox, Dec. 9, 1926
Frances J., d. of Thomas Carter, May 21, 1885
Frances Marian, d. of Sherwood Carter, July 28, 1859
Franklin G., s. of James Carter, Apr. 26, 1860
Gabriel, July 22, 1875
Henry L., Feb. 15, 1844
Hill (Capt.), May 27, 1875
J. H., July 2, 1925
J. Selden, Jan. 2, 1936
J. W. (Dr.), Oct. 31, 1907
James H., Feb. 20, 1908
James L., Feb. 11, 1864
James R., Apr. 23, 1931
John (Elder), Dec. 18, 1845
John Augustus, s. of John T. and Virginia E. Carter, Dec. 10, 1846
John G. (Rev.), May 12, 1859
Joseph R., Aug. 25, 1870
Landon, Jr., s. of Landon Carter, May 29, 1829
Lemuel Baker, s. of S. R. and Lizzie Wooding Carter,

OBITUARY NOTICES IN THE RELIGIOUS HERALD WITH DATES OF PUBLICATION

Mar. 2, 1905
Lizzie Wooding (Mrs.),
  Apr. 1, 1920
Louise Josephine, Sept. 7,
  1922
Lucy, May 5, 1837
Lutilda, w. of Rev. Dr.
  John Carter, May 5, 1881
Margaret R., w. of Thomas
  Carter, Apr. 24, 1862
Maria F., w. of Samuel S.
  Carter, d. of David J.
  Saunders, May 31, 1883
Martha A., w. of P. B. Carter,
  July 18, 1889
Mary, w. of Henry Carter,
  Jan. 8, 1863
Mary Ann, d. of William A.
  and Caroline M. Carter,
  Sept. 25, 1851
Mary Bradley, w. of James
  H. Carter, Feb. 8, 1912
Matthew W., July 24, 1890
Miles, s. of Elder John
  Carter, Sr., Apr. 10,
  1845
Mollie R. (Mrs.), Mar.
  19, 1931
Nancy (Mrs.), Sept. 27, 1866
Nancy C., Sept 6, 1833
Nancy R., d. of Thomas Carter
  May 3, 1860
Norveta Blanche, d. of
  Miskel A. and Mary Jane
  Garter, Dec. 4, 1890
Onie M., Feb. 3, 1898
Philip Henry, s. of Dr. John
  G. and L. L. Carter, Nov.
  2, 1838
R. W., Aug. 13, 1925
Raleigh Williamson, Oct.
  22, 1891
Rebecca M., d. of Calvin P.
  and Mollie Carter, July
  19, 1894
Richard, Apr. 22, 1915
Richard H., s. of William
  L. Carter, Feb. 29, 1872
Robert W., Sept. 18, 1873
S. G., Dec. 28, 1911

Samuel, s. of Mrs. A. O. Carter,
  May 15, 1862
Susan F. (Mrs.), Oct. 14, 1875
Theoderick B., Feb. 3, 1859
Thomas, s. of China Carter,
  Feb. 5, 1856
Thomas, s. of Thomas and Margaret Carter, Sept. 16, 1847
Thomas L., May 23, 1935
Thomasia T., Oct. 8, 1874
Virginia E., w. of John Carter,
  Apr. 10, 1856
William, Sept. 27, 1860
William E., s. of Elias J.
  Carter, Apr. 11, 1861
William H., Feb. 12, 1857
William H., s. of Thomas
  Carter, Feb. 17, 1876
William M., Jan. 25, 1849
William S., Dec. 23, 1869
William Thomas, Aug. 23, 1923
CARWILE
  Mamie Daniel, Mar. 15, Nov.
    15, 1928
  Mary A., w. of Z. W. Carwile,
    May 25, 1876
CARTWRIGHT
  John, Apr. 20, 1911
  Mary L. (Mrs.), Jan. 29, 1914
CARVER
  Frances A. (Mrs.), Dec. 15,
    1898
  Martha C., d. of Lucy and
    Reuben Carver, Oct. 16, 1856
  Matilda A., d. of Lucy and
    Reuben Carver, Oct. 16, 1856
  Mildred C., d. of Lucy and
    Reuben Carver, Oct. 16, 1856
  Sally A., w. of Col. D. C.
    Carver, d. of William Payne,
    Apr. 30, May 29, 1863
  William, s. of Lucy and Reuben
    Carver, Oct. 16, 1856
CARY
  Albert, Oct. 11, 1877
  Betty Willis (Mrs.), Apr.
    15, 1847
  John B., Jr., s. of John B.
    Cary, Aug. 30, 1860
  John B. (Col.), Jan. 20, 1898

OBITUARY NOTICES IN THE RELIGIOUS HERALD WITH DATES OF PUBLICATION

Mathew, Oct. 4, 1839
Rhoda, w. of Peter M. Cary,
  Sept. 12, 1872
CASE
  C., Mar. 23, 1899
  Virginia Phillips, w. of
    Catlin Case, Mar. 9,
    1916
CASEY
  Alaric H., Nov. 13, 1884
  Vergil S., Apr. 14, 1881
CASH
  Abner Conway, s. of A. B.
    Cash, May 26, 1887
  Lucy E., w of Joseph Cash,
    Oct. 16, 1879
  W. R. (Mrs.), Feb. 19, 1903
CASON
  Catharine (Mrs.), May 29,
    1851
  Edward (Mrs.), Sept. 7, 1848
  Edward (Capt.), Feb. 14, 1850
  Isaac, Feb. 16, 1882
  Isaac G., July 28, 1881
  Isaac Graves, May 22, 1884
  John L., Aug. 19, 1847
  Maria E., Jan. 10, 1901
  Nancy, w. of Benjamin
    Cason, Oct. 10 and 17,
    1878
CASSEDY
  Pattie Parrish (Mrs.), Feb.
    20, 1930
CASTON
  Lucy H. (Mrs.), d. of
    Nathaniel P. Mimms, May
    11, 1871
CASWELL
  Alex. (Dr.), Jan. 18, 1877
CATE
  Rebecca Luada, d. of Gideon
    Cate, Sept. 10, 1863
CATHER
  Willella, d. of William
    Cather, Feb. 11, 1869
CATHON
  Esther, w. of James Cathon,
    Feb. 22, 1900
CATLETT
  Bettie G., Aug. 18, 1859

  Elizabeth, w. of William
    S. Catlett, June 19,
    1856
  John, s. of Patrick R.
    and Elizabeth F. Catlett,
    Jan. 10, 1861
  Margaret M., d. of Patrick R.
    and Elizabeth F. Catlett,
    Jan. 10, 1861
  Sarah S. (Mrs.), Sept. 1,
    1842
  Thomas L., Sept. 25, 1879
  William, July 24, 1845
  William, June 5, July 24,
    1845
CATRON
  Harriet J., Aug. 16, 1877
CATTERTON
  (Mrs.), Jan. 27, 1916
CAULDWELL
  Ebenezer, July 1, 1875
CAUTHORN
  Annie E., d. of Richard
    and Fannie E. Cauthorn,
    Aug. 28, 1879
  Duncan Shepherd, s. of M.
    C. and A. W. Cauthorn,
    July 22, 1880
  Elizabeth, May 6, 1880
  Ethelbert G., May 5, 1853
  Frances Elizabeth, d. of
    Mrs. Leah A. Cauthorn,
    Jan. 8, 1857
  Harriet B., w. of Godfrey
    Cauthorn, Sept. 25, 1845
  Lizzie, d. of A. W. and
    Carrie A. Cauthorn, Oct.
    11, 1883
  M. E. Tyler, d. of R. F. T.
    and Frances Cauthorn,
    May 30, 1861
  Maria, w. of Leroy Cauthorn,
    Jan. 25, 1844
  R. F. T., Dec. 21, 1882
CAVADA
  William, Apr. 29, 1841
CAVE
  Ella Andrews (Mrs.), May 5,
    1921
CAWTHORN

OBITUARY NOTICES IN THE RELIGIOUS HERALD WITH DATES OF PUBLICATION

Elvira A. (Mrs.), d. of
Thomas Thornhill, Nov.
12, 1857
Joel T., s. of Rev. John
Cawthorn, Dec. 30, 1920;
Feb. 10, 1921
John Lewis, s. of T. B. and
M. B. Cawthorn, Feb. 20,
1862

CHADICK
James, Apr. 3, 1851

CHADOIN
Lewis (Rev.), Apr. 16,
1874

CHAFFIN
G. A., Oct. 1, 1857
Martha (Mrs.), Oct. 2,
1835
Sarah M., w. of William T.
Chaffin, Dec. 5, 1872

CHALKLEY
Carrie Bitting (Mrs.),
Aug. 8, 1895
Edna, July 1, 1897
H. K, Jan. 16, 1919
Ibra P., child of P. A.
Chalkley, Jan. 28, 1875
Ida Mae (Mrs.), Mar. 17,
1932
Mary W. (Mrs.), Mar. 29,
1923
O. H., May 3, 1883
P. A., July 30, 1885
Percy, s. of G. P. Chalkley,
Dec. 9, 1886

CHALKLY
R. B., July 19, 1855

CHALTON
G. T., May 11, 1899

CHAMBERLAIN
Cornelia, w. of James L.
Chamberlain, Feb. 25,
1858
Fanny L. (Mrs.), Jan.
24, 1861
Sarah Elizabeth, w. of Capt.
S. Chamberlain, Sept. 30,
1841

CHAMBERLAYNE
William (Gen.), Sept. 16, 1836

CHAMBERS
Allie E. (Mrs.), Mar. 25,
1926
C. D., Nov. 21, 1935
Eulalia Rudd, d. of J. S. and
E. D. Chambers, Jan. 21,
1915
George, Mar. 2, Apr. 27, 1862
Julia Trainham, w. of R. E.
Chambers, Sept. 13 and 27,
Oct. 18 and 25, 1917
R. E. (Mrs.), May 25, 1905
R. E. (Rev.), July 28, 1932

CHAMBLIN
Charles Isaac, s. of Mason and
Dewanna Chamblin, Mar. 3,
1859
Clayton, s. of James H. Chamb-
lin, July 17, 1862
Peyton W., s. of Mason and
Dewanna Chamblin, Dec. 29,
1859

CHAMBLISS
Anna Lee, d. of Mrs. J. R.
Chambliss, Jr., Oct. 14,
1875
Bessie T., d. of Rev. J. A.
Chambliss, July 10, 1873
Elizabeth Rives, d. of Col.
J. R. Chambliss, Nov. 7,
1850
Jane Gordon, w. of John Chamb-
liss, Aug. 29, 1834
Judith, w. of Elder Mathew
Chambliss, Mar. 10, 1853
John A. (Dr.), Oct. 12, 1916
John R. (Col.), gr.s. of Rev.
Nathaniel Chambliss, Apr.
29, June 3, 1875
Joseph Ellerbil, s. of Rev.
J. E. and L. Chambliss,
Mar. 19, 1868
Louisa, d. of Col. John R.
Chambliss, May 20, 1847
Lucile, d. of Rev. J. A.
Chambliss, Oct. 29, 1874
Nathanael (Elder), Jan. 11,
1828
Thomas Atkinson, May 19, 1881

CHANCELLOR

OBITUARY NOTICES IN THE RELIGIOUS HERALD WITH DATES OF PUBLICATION

Ann, w. of George Chancellor, Jan. 31, 1861
Elizabeth, Feb. 1, 1849
John, Mar. 4, 1858
CHANCY
Geroge W., Feb. 28, 1855
Emily, w. of George W. Chancy, Jan. 10, 1856
Maria Perrington, d. of George W. and Emily Chancy, Nov. 26, 1846
Mary Ann, d. of George W. and Emily Chancy, Nov. 26, 1846
CHANDLER
Addie, d. of Bolling and Mary J. Chandler, Jan. 27, 1881
Ann Elizabeth, Mar. 12, 1863
Annie, d. of Oliver W. and Sarah E. Chandler, Aug. 22, 1861
Annie Hatchett (Mrs.), Apr. 24, 1884
Daniel J., Aug. 15, 1867
Frederick H. H., s. of Elder H. J. and M. A. G. Chandler, Nov. 25, 1858
J. A. C. (Dr.), June 7, 1934
J. E., w. of S. T. Chandler, Aug. 22, 1889
J. E., Aug. 30, 1934
J. Thomas, May 29, 1863
John C., s. of R. T. Chandler, Aug. 17, 1871
John Y., Feb. 8, 1883
Lenore Burton, w. of Dr. J. A. C. Chandler, Sept. 9, 1920
Martha F., Sept. 29, 1881
Mollie E., Oct. 13, 1881
Nancy, w. of Rufus Chandler, Feb. 5, 1857
Olive, w. of Joseph C. Chandler, Dec. 7, 1832
Robert Archer, Nov. 1, 1855
William Randolph, s. of Capt. Thomas T. Chandler, Dec. 1, 1853
Rufus (Elder), Aug. 4, 1837
Edwina, w. of Thomas T. Chandler, July 28, 1853
CHANEY
L. F., June 6, 1878
Polina, w. of W. C. Chaney, May 18, 1882
CHANNELL
C. C., Jan. 23, 1902
CHANY
William, Dec. 31, 1857
CHAPEL
Ann J., d. of Charles E. and Ann B. Chapel, Nov. 14, 1844
CHAPELL
Joseph R., Sept. 11, 1884
CHAPIN
C. V., w. of Herman L. Chapin, May 18, 1893
Hannah, d. of Rev. Stephen Chapin, Sept. 4, 1856
Heman L., Mar. 12, 1868
Mary E., d. of Rev. Dr. Stephen Chapin, May 1, 1873
Stephen (Rev.), Oct. 30, 1845
Stephen (Mrs.), July 27, 1854
CHAPLAIN
Sarah A., w. of T. C. Chaplain, Sept. 3, 1857
CHAPLIN
Charles Carroll (Dr.), Nov. 13, 1884
Charles Green, July 21, 1864
Harriet Elizabeth (Mrs.), Feb. 27, 1919
Lucie Exall, w. of Dr. C. C. Chaplin, Mar. 7, 1901
Willie Exall, s. of C. C. and Lucy Chaplin, July 21, 1864
CHAPMAN
Alex (Mrs.), Mar. 14, 1929
Ann (Mrs.), Aug. 21, 1902
Bettie, d. of James and Ann Chapman, Jan. 29, 1863
Bettie J., d. of Thomas W. Chapman, Nov. 22, 1860
Edmund G., June 28, 1888
Jane, Dec. 6, 1855
Jane B. (Mrs.), June 9, 1837
Kate, w. of James Chapman, d.

OBITUARY NOTICES IN THE RELIGIOUS HERALD WITH DATES OF PUBLICATION

of G. M. Bohannon, July 10, 1884
Katie L., d. of S. F. and Rebecca E. Chapman, Mar. 23, 1876
Margaret (Mrs.), July 9, 1908
Martha L. B., d. of Edmund G. Chapman, Mar. 4, 1852
Philip P., s. of George M. Chapman, June 7, 1839
Rebecca Elgin, w. of Rev. S. F. Chapman, Dec. 20, 1900
Roberta, d. of John W. Chapman, Jan. 15, 1880
Samuel F., s. of S. F. and Rebecca E. Chapman, Sept. 30, 1875
Samuel Foker, July 3, 1919
Samuel W., Jan. 30, 1868
Virginia M., w. of Bernard T. Chapman, July 6, 1882
William, Jan. 23, 1868
William A., father of Rev. Samuel Chapman, Jan. 16, 1873
William W., Feb. 5, 1874

CHAPPALL
Hiram, Aug. 19, 1841

CHAPPEL
Robert A., Feb. 19, 1863

CHAPPELL
A. B., Dec. 27, 1877
Adela Richards, d. of Sandy and Ann J. Owen, w. of Walter B. Chappell, Dec. 21, 1898
Ann B., w. of C. E. Chappell, Apr. 27, 1843
Anna Wood REMINGTON (Mrs.), July 3, 1879
Andrew Wood, s. of A. F. and Anna W. Chappell, Nov. 20, 1879
E. T., Sr., June 28, July 12, 1894
Hiram P., s. of Charles E. and Ann B. Chappell, Sept.
15, 1842
Mary Emma, d. of J. O. Chappell, Dec. 8, 1921
Mercedes, d. of R. W. and Lucy A. Chappell, Sept. 17, 1885
Nannie, w. of Junius Chappell, Nov. 1, 1877
Pamelia (Mrs.), Feb. 12, 1852
R. W., July 24, Aug. 14, 1902
Sue Atkinson (Mrs.), Sept. 15, 1881
Thomas J., Nov. 24, 1881
William E., Apr. 4, 1901

CHARLES
Hannah, July 23, 1908

CHARLTON
Frances, Jan. 2, 1870
Maury L., s. of J. J. and S. L. Charlton, June 14, 1894
W. R., s. of Walter R. and Fannie A. Charlton, July 28, 1870

CHARNOCK
Charles Ryland, Oct. 8 and 15, 1931

CHART
Adam, Jan. 5, 1838

CHARTERS
James P., Jan. 21, 1886
Susan Philips, w. of James P. Charters, Sept. 17, 1885

CHARTTERS
Evelyn Wortley, d. of Rev. Howard W. and M. C. Montague, Aug. 5, 1893

CHASE
Daniel, Aug. 15, 1872

CHASTAIN
William Whitsitt, July 3, 1890

CHATHAM
Mary E., w. of Col. Thomas Chatham, Nov. 25, 1880

CHAUDOIN
Elizabeth M., d. of Elder

OBITUARY NOTICES IN THE RELIGIOUS HERALD WITH DATES OF PUBLICATION

Lewis Chaudoin, Jan 20, 1848
Jane E., w. of Lewis Chaudoin, Jr., Feb. 10, 1842
Kittie M., Oct. 8, 1874
Lewis (Elder), Apr. 10, 1845
M. A., w. of Lewis Chaudoin, May 18, 1832
Virginia, Apr. 23, 1863

CHEATHAM
Frank (Mrs.), June 1, 1922
Indiana J., w. of William Cheatham, d. of Col. Samuel Hancock, Feb. 15, 1855
James H., Mar. 10, 1853
James T., Dec. 25, 1924
Lillius, s. of Abijah and Mary W. Cheatham, Apr. 2, 1863
Louise, Apr. 16, 1925
Martha, w. of Col. Z. E. Cheatham, Apr. 10, 1856
Martha F., w. of Madison Cheatham, d. of Thomas Gregory, Sept. 16, 1852
Martha P., d. of Thomas Cheatham, Aug. 3, 1832
Mary, d. of Abijah and Mary W. Cheatham, Dec. 20, 1860
Mary Woodson (Mrs.), d. of Col. Woodson W. Hancock, Dec. 9, 1875
Obedience, w. of R. M. Cheatham, Oct. 14, 1880
Virginia T., d. of Silas and Eliza Cheatham, Dec. 30, 1847
William Lee, s. of Dr. T. J. Cheatham, Sept. 24, 1885

CHEATWOOD
Jane W. (Mrs.), Mar. 3, 1860

CHELF
Charles Fielding, Feb. 11, 1926
Loula, July 15, 1936

P. E., May 11, 1922

CHENAULT
David A., Sept. 3, 1885

CHENERY
James G., Feb. 14, 1867

CHERNAULT
Jimmie, s. of Richard Chernault, Jan. 25, 1877

CHESLEY
Bessie, Mar. 9, 1922
Mary Susan, w. of Henry G. Chesley, d. of Robert W. and Frances P. Ferneyhough, Feb. 12, 1914

CHESTERMAN
Elizabeth (Mrs.), Jan. 26, 1865

CHEWNING
A. J. (Mrs.), Apr. 7, 1927
A. J., Oct. 17, Dec. 19, 1929
Benjamin, Nov. 23, 1893
Bettie F., w. of N. S. Chewning, d. of David S. and Sabina Cox, Mar. 19, 1874
Clementina, w. of William B. Chewning, May 4, 1876
E. W., w. of E. A. Chewning, Oct. 13, 1910
Edward Baptist, s. of Herbert and Nicy Chewning, June 11, 1840
Elizabeth Elba, w. of Reuben Chewning, June 19, 1902
George, s. of Capt. Reuben Chewning, Aug. 8, 1901
Fannie S., w. of Melvin M. Chewning, Nov. 24, 1887
Hulda Maria, w. of O. L. Chewning, Aug. 1, 1844
John Joseph, s. of William R. and Clementina Chewning, Apr. 9, 1863
Louisa, w. of Reuben Chewning, Aug. 28, 1856
Mary S., d. of Kelles Chewning, Mar. 9, 1875
Oscar F., s. of William H. Chewning, Sept. 27, 1894
Reuben (Capt.), July 28, 1837

OBITUARY NOTICES IN THE RELIGIOUS HERALD WITH DATES OF PUBLICATION

Reuben T., Jan. 30, 1896
William B., Feb. 22, 1833
Z. W. (Mrs.), Apr. 29, 1937
CHICK
Eugene Augustus, Sept. 28, 1899
William H., June 30, 1904
CHIDESTER
Katharine Harrison, d. of Holdridge and Hannah Walker Chidester, Nov. 28, 1895
CHILD
Julia (Mrs.), Feb. 4, 1858
CHILDERS
Joseph R., s. of Nathaniel Childers, Oct. 26, 1832
Sally H., w. of Nathaniel Childers, Dec. 26, 1834
W. W., s. of J. B. Childers, Sept. 28, 1876
CHILDRESS
Ann E., w. of Luther D. Childress, Dec. 2, 1897
Annie B., Oct. 9, 1890
Benjamin, s. of Capt. Leonard H. Childress, Mar. 23, 1838
Cornelia Jane, w. of William T. J. Childress, Feb. 12, 1920
J. Clifton, Feb. 4, 1886
Jack, s. of J. W. and J. B. Childress, Sept. 17, 1885
L. A. Alderson, child of Capt. Leonard and Caroline Childress, Feb. 6, 1845
Leonard H. (Capt.), Feb. 2, 1843
Lettie Rives, d. of Dr. A. W. and Bettie Childress, Mar. 4, 1858; Sept. 13, 1860
Lucie A., June 30, 1898
Mary (Mrs.), Nov. 7, 1867
Nettie (Mrs.), Dec. 29, 1927
Nettie Dobyns, w. of B. F. Childress, Aug. 3, 1916
Sophronia Elisa, w. of Clifton Childress, Oct. 4, 1900
William J., Feb. 12, 1920
Willie A. Alvis (Mrs.), Mar. 4, 1926
CHILES
Lucy F., w. of Thomas Chiles, Feb. 3, 1859
Mary (Mrs.), d. of David Lipscomb, June 14, 1839
Mary H., w. of John B. Chiles, June 2, 1859
Nancy, July 16, 1868
Samuel, Nov. 9, 1848
Susan R., w. of Fendall Chiles, Sept. 30, 1869
Thomas G., May 8, 1851
William Andrew, s. of Elliot Chiles, July 17, 1851
CHILTON
Fannie (Mrs.), July 16, 1931
John J., Dec. 8, 1881
John Poindexter, Aug. 13, 1868
Mary E., w. of George Chilton, d. of John Ball, July 19, 1855
Merry, Aug. 10, 1905
William, June 15, July 27, 1922
CHINA
John, June 27, 1872
CHINN
Eliza Clay, w. of Dr. John W. Chinn, d. of George S. Kerfoot, Sept. 28, 1854
CHISHOLM
A. E. (Mrs.), May 27, 1886
E. V., Feb. 22, 1894
William, May 11, 1854
CHITTUM
J. Douglas, Feb. 5, 1925
CHITWOOD
Joseph K., Apr. 10, 1884
CHRISTIAN
Albert Thornhill, s. of David A. and Mary Agnes Christian, Dec. 27, 1888
Ann F. (Mrs.), Oct. 9, 1862
Bettie, w. of James H. Christian, Sept. 2, 1886
Caroline L., July 16, 1857

OBITUARY NOTICES IN THE RELIGIOUS HERALD WITH DATES OF PUBLICATION

E. D., Jan. 19, 1899
Edmund, May 25, 1848
Elizabeth, w. of Rev. R. A.
  Christian, Feb. 25, 1875
James, Apr. 11, 1850
James H. (Rev.), Mar. 20,
  1873
Lewis, s. of Edward and Ellen
  Christian, June 24, 1869
Mattie Olivia, d. of James
  L. Christian and Sallie C.
  Christian, July 1, 1880
Mercer W., July 22, 1937
Susan B., w. of James H.
  Christian, June 25, 1857
Susan M., Apr. 26, 1888
Thomas, Jan. 15, 1891
Thomas A., Mar. 22, 1923
William C., Dec. 12, 1844
William Steptoe (Dr.), Dec.
  29, 1910
CHRISTMAS
  Maud, d. of J. W. and M. S.
  Christmas, Feb. 15, 1877
CHRISTOPHER
  William C., Apr. 11, 1867
CHURCHILL
  Charles S., June 25, 1857
  Sarah, w. of Charles Churchill,
  Apr. 7, 1842
CHURN
  Nathaniel J., Aug. 23, 1928
CLAIBORNE
  Mary Anne, d. of Charles B.
  Claiborne, Jan. 12, 1860
CLANTON
  Elizabeth (Mrs.), Aug. 2,
  1839
CLARK
  A. V., w. of E. J. T. Clark,
  Oct. 11, 1906
  Benjamin F., s. of Rev. John
  Clark, Aug. 22, 1834
  Clemenza, July 21, 1881
  Cleveland (Maj.), Dec. 19,
  1935
  Daniel B., s. of Mrs. Martha
  Clark, Dec. 18, 1829
  Edward, s. of Mrs. Martha
  Clark, Dec. 18, 1829

Edward T., Apr. 29, 1897
Eliza J., June 15, 1832
Elizabeth, w. of Thomas Clark,
  Dec. 28, 1838
Elizabeth, w. of Spencer Clark,
  Feb. 7, 1856
Elizabeth (Mrs.), Nov. 26,
  1885
Elizabeth Ann, w. of John
  Cornelius Clark, d. of
  Edward and Elizabeth Topp-
  ing, June 21, 1900
Elizabeth P., Mar. 11, 1852
Euline Revere (Mrs.), Dec. 20,
  1923; May 15, 1924
F. C. (Rev.), June 13, 20,
  and 27, 1889
Florence Wilburn (Mrs.), Oct.
  15, 1914
George W. (Dr.), July 24,
  1930
Henry T. (Rev.), s. of Rev.
  W. Thorburn Clark, Nov. 30,
  1916
James, Oct. 3, 1850
James H., father of J. G. Clark,
  May 4, 1876
Jennie Hume, w. of James
  G. Clark, d. of Rev. Thomas
  Hume, Sr., Nov. 29, 1866
John (Rev.), May 30, 1844
John M. (Capt.), Jan. 16,
  1845
John S., Mar. 13, 1829
John T., Nov. 20, 1924
Lucretia E. (Mrs.), Aug. 8,
  1872
Lucy, w. of Rev. John Clark,
  Feb. 28, 1856
Martha J. (Mrs.), July 17,
  1902
Mary F., w. of R. L. Clark,
  Dec. 28, 1905
Narcissus, w. of William E.
  Clark, May 31, 1877
Percy B., s. of William B. and
  Carrie G. Clark, Aug. 20,
  1896
Peter Henry, s. of James J.
  and Lucinda Clark, Feb. 5,

OBITUARY NOTICES IN THE RELIGIOUS HERALD WITH DATES OF PUBLICATION

1863
Phebe Ann, d. of Mrs. Martha
  Clark, Dec. 18, 1829
Robert A., June 10, 1841
Susan Elizabeth (Mrs.), Aug.
  16, 1860
Thomas, Feb. 8, 1877
Virginia, Nov. 10, 1842
Virginia B., w. of Walter G.
  Clark, Dec. 24, 1857
William C., Apr. 10, 1862
William L., May 19, 1921
CLARKE
  Adam (Rev.), Oct. 26, 1832
  Almoran Salle, Mar. 3,
    1864
  Ambrose W., Aug. 31, 1843
  Ann J. (Mrs.), Feb. 21,
    1895
  Annie Winkler (Mrs.), Dec.
    22, 1938
  Araminta, w. of John Clarke,
    June 20, 1895
  Asa, Apr. 27, 1893
  Augustus B., June 25, 1938
  Carroll Havelock, s. of Maj.
    Charles H. and Cassandria
    A. Clarke, Nov. 23, 1865*
  Cassandra, w. of Maj. Hammet
    Clarke, Apr. 11, 1872
  Christopher, Mar. 13, 1851
  Claybrook, s. of F. C. and
    M. E. Clarke, Sept. 26,
    1878
  Daniel, Dec. 5, 1828
  Dinah, w. of Charles Clarke,
    July 22, 1852
  Edwin L., Sept. 7, 1893
  Emma B., w. of A. B. Clarke,
    Mar. 3, 1927
  G. Harvey, Nov. 5, 1931
  Henry J., Aug. 25, 1864
  James W., s. of Zaccheus
    and Hester A. Clarke,
    Sept. 24, 1885
  Jane (Mrs.), Jan. 2, 1840
  Jesse Frayser, June 11, 1874
  John E., s. of Zaccheus and
    Hester A. Clarke, Sept.
    24, 1885

John Stanley, s. of A. B.
  Clarke, Aug. 2, 1877
Joseph William, Sept. 27,
  1906
Kesiah, s. of Jesse F.
  Clark, July 29, 1847
Lelia T., w. of A. B. Clarke,
  Jan. 12, 1905
Lemuel Leonard, June 19,
  1930
Littleberry, Jan. 21, 1841
Martha B., w. of N. Clarke,
  June 24, 1869
Martha E., w. of Rev. Francis
  C. Clarke, Sept. 20, 1906
Mary (Mrs.), May 28, 1868
Mary Jane, d. of Junius A.
  and Callie S. Clarke, Sept.
  25, 1862
Mattie L., d. of Zacheus and
  Hester Clarke, Mar. 22,
  May 31, 1888*
Nancy, Feb. 3, 1842
Nancy, w. of Asa Clarke,
  July 5, 1883
Nathan Bell, July 31, 1884
Rebecca Bell, d. of Nathan B.
  Clarke, Sept. 9, 1852
Robert J., Feb. 20, 1845
Robert Waddy, s. of E. M. D.
  and Amanda M. Clarke, Sept.
  20, 1860
Sophia (Mrs.), May 11, 1843
Spencer Woodson, s. of Junius
  and Callie S. Clarke, Nov.
  26, 1863
Thomas, Nov. 14, 1828
Veturia A. (Mrs.), Oct. 24,
  1872
W. Meade (Rev.), May 7, 1914
Wade N., Oct. 1, 1874
Wilson Bell, s. of N. B. and
  Martha Clarke, Jan. 31,
  1850
CLARKSON
  Ann Rebecca, w. of James L.
    Clarkson, Sept. 22, 1870
  Elizabeth, w. of James Clark-
    son, Mar. 2, 1854
  George B., Feb. 1, 1872

* Possible inaccuracy in name, or spelling but given as printed

OBITUARY NOTICES IN THE RELIGIOUS HERALD WITH DATES OF PUBLICATION

John H., Feb. 5, 1880
Mary (Mrs.), Mar. 1, 1866
Mary E., d. of John Clarkson, Dec. 12, 1834
Mildred A. M. (Mrs.), May 13, 1897
Thomas Stonewall Jackson, s. of John H. and Sallie Clarkson, Feb. 4, 1869

CLARY
Amos (Rev.), Sept. 15, Nov. 17, 1938

CLASH
Percy, Oct. 11, 1883

CLAUD
Elizabeth (Mrs.), Sept. 27, 1860
Fannie Hancock (Mrs.), d. of George B. Hancock, Oct. 15, 1896

CLAUGHTON
Lizzie E., July 25, 1918

CLAY
Alice, d. of C. H. A. Clay, Apr. 16, 1874
Ann, w. of Matthew Clay, July 7, 1837
Eleazar (Rev.), May 13, 1836
Henry M., Aug. 31, 1854
James L., Feb. 28, 1924
M. Alice, d. of C. H. A. and Mary E. Clay, May 14, 1874
Matthew, Mar. 3, 1853
Phinemas, Apr. 12, 1855

CLAYBROOK
Catharine, w. of Chastain Claybrook, Oct. 11, 1849
Charlotte (Mrs.), Sept. 11, 1884
F. W. (Rev.), Aug. 20, Oct. 8, 1914
Mary Franklin, w. of Rev. F. W. Claybrook, d. of B. F. Dew, May 24, 1894
Nannie Garnett, w. of Rev. Fred W. Claybrook, Dec. 14, 1922
Richard, Dec. 19, 1834

Sally M., Nov. 29, 1849

CLAYTON
Ann Eliza (Mrs.), Apr. 29, 1841
Charles (Mrs.), Apr. 15, 1937
Clara A., w. of John Clayton, Nov. 26, 1840
George W., Jan. 8, 1863
Harriet L., w. of John Clayton, Dec. 1, 1837
J. H. N. (Mrs.), d. of John and Frances Baylor, July 2, 1863
Lucy R., w. of James W. Clayton, d. of John and Harriet S. Clayton, Oct. 13, 1881
Mary, w. of Charles Clayton, d. of Spencer T. and Elizabeth Hancock, Dec. 25, 1890

CLEATON
Pattie D., w. of William L. Cleaton, Feb. 16, 1893
Thomas J., Mar. 11, 1915

CLEAVELAND
Elizabeth, w. of Jeremiah Cleaveland, Dec. 1, 1837
Frances, w. of Elder Porter Cleaveland, Sept. 22, 1842
James F., s. of Jeremiah and Susan Cleaveland, May 31, 1866
Mary, d. of Jeremiah Cleaveland, Feb. 25, 1841

CLEGG
Hilary, Sept. 17, 1863

CLEMANS
Elizabeth (Mrs.), Sept. 30, 1831

CLEMENT
Clara Churn, w. of Rev. Charles Clement, Apr. 7, 1927
James T., Apr. 22, 1858
Lucy C. (Mrs.), July 5, 1860
Mary Walker, d. of Harris

OBITUARY NOTICES IN THE RELIGIOUS HERALD WITH DATES OF PUBLICATION

K. Clements, Mar. 18, 1852
Stephen (Capt.), Jan. 22, 1857
Susan LeGrand, d. of Capt. Lafayette W. and Phoebe C. Clement, Nov. 15, 1860
CLEMENTS
Charles, July 13, 1848
Claiborne, June 23, 1859
Frances Ann, d. of James T. Clements, Nov. 23, 1848
J. J., Sept. 24, 1896
Margaret (Mrs.), July 14, 1842
R. Leonard, Nov. 8, 1928
Richard Powell, Mar. 30, 1893
S. A., w. of Maj. W. R. E. Clements, Oct. 31, 1850
Sallie Ann, d. of Harris K. Clements, Dec. 25, 1856
Sarah (Mrs.), Apr. 25, 1867
William J., May 14, 1863
CLEMONS
A. E. (Mrs.), d. of Floyd C. and E. J. Moring, Aug. 13, 1891
CLEVELAND
Annie V., Feb. 8, 1917
George B., Dec. 22, 1932
Jeremiah, May 31, 1866
Maria B. (Mrs.), Sept. 24, 1868
Mary Catherine, d. of Nathaniel M. and Matilda W. Cleveland, June 7, 1860
Mary E. (Mrs.), d. of Col. Joseph S. Perkins, Apr. 16, 1903
Nathaniel M., Sept. 22, 1864
P. (Rev.), July 8, 1875
Richard M., Nov. 24, 1887
Samuel Woodward, May 5, 1892
Sarah H., w. of William Cleveland, Apr. 17, 1862
Susan M., w. of Jeremiah Cleveland, May 30, 1872
CLIFT
Mary E., w. of Albert Clift, Mar. 20, 1884

CLIFTON
Nellie, d. of J. C. and M. J. Clifton, Oct. 23, 1873
CLINGENPUL
Kyle, Apr. 10, 1862
CLOPTON
Abner W., Feb. 2, 1882
Agness Ophelia, d. of William and Celina Clopton, July 5, 1833
Ann Brumley, d. of William H. Clopton, Dec. 26, 1844
Edwin J., Sr., Mar. 10, 1853
Ellen Hill, w. of William E. Clopton, Feb. 24, 1887
Fannie, Aug. 18, 1910
James (Elder), June 20, 1850
John C., Apr. 6, 1871
Martha, w. of Rev. James Clopton, Feb. 1, 1849
S. C. (Elder), Oct. 28, 1847
Samuel C. (Rev.), May 25, June 1 and 15, 1905
Waldegrave (Dr.), Nov. 30, 1832
William A. S., s. of Rev. James C. Clopton, Oct. 1, 1863
William E. (Rev.), July 13, 1848
William E., Feb. 24, 1887
William H., Apr. 13, 1876
Willie B., s. of William E. and Ellen H. Clopton, Aug. 15, 1878
CLORE
Ida, w. of James H. Clore, June 27, 1912
Sallie K., d. of William Henry and Louisa E. Clore, June 18, 1857
CLOUGH
Tommie O., s. of Samuel Clough, July 12, 1877
CLUVERIUS
Courtney (Mrs.), Mar. 13, 1856
John T., s. of Beverly and Mary

OBITUARY NOTICES IN THE RELIGIOUS HERALD WITH DATES OF PUBLICATION

A. Cluverius, May 2, 1861
Joseph A., Aug. 21, 1851
W. B. (Mrs.), May 30, 1889
William Thomas, s. of Beverly
 W. and Mary Cluverius,
 Mar. 21, 1861
CLYNE
 M. A., w. of John W. Clyne,
  June 16, 1870
COAKLEY
 Andrew J., s. of William B.
  Coakley, Oct. 14, 1886
 Daniel (Mrs.), Oct. 20, 1853
 Daniel, Sr., July 4, 1889
 Daniel, Jan. 13, 1921
 Elizabeth, w. of Daniel Coakley, Nov. 10 and 17, 1853
 Nancy, w. of Daniel Coakley,
  Oct. 22, 1846
COATES
 Elizabeth (Mrs.), Apr. 29,
  1852
 Elizabeth (Mrs.), Mar. 16,
  1893
 Evelina A., w. of Dr. Stapleton Coates, June 23, 1881
 James, July 2, 1863
 John A., Oct. 26, 1882
 Mary, w. of James Coates,
  May 20, 1886
 R. D., Feb. 15, 1934
 Rebecca D., Feb. 14, 1935
 Robert Alexander, Mar. 12,
  1925
COATS
 H. C., Nov. 30, 1916
COBB
 Alma B., d. of William L.
  and B. C. Cobb, May 15,
  1873
 Emma Lewis, d. of Mr. and
  Mrs. W. L. Cobb, Oct. 27,
  1892
 George M., Aug. 18, 1898
 Hardy (Rev.), Feb. 15, 1833
 James E., Mar. 15, 1877
 Kilby F., Nov. 22, 1883
 Leah B. (Mrs.), Oct. 14, 1886
 Lelia Reese, w. of J. T.
  Cobb, Mar. 28, Apr. 11, 1901

 Margaret (Mrs.), May 6, 1897
 Maria L., w. of J. E. Cobb,
  Sr., Aug. 5, 1897
 R. T., June 17, 1875
 Virginia G. (Mrs.), June
  26, 1919
 W. L., Sept. 9, 1909
 W. L. (Mrs.), Feb. 4, 1926
 William Lewis, s. of W. L.
  and Bettie Cobb, Aug. 1,
  1878
COBBS
 Bettie P., Apr. 5, 1894
 James S., Aug. 13, 1885
 James S., Sept. 8 and 15,
  1892
 John J., Nov. 4, 1869
 Louisa Banks, w. of W. W. Cobbs,
  Sept. 25, Oct. 21, 1884
 Minerva A., w. of R. T. Cobbs,
  Nov. 8, 1860
COBEY
 Elizabeth Winter (Mrs.),
  Nov. 3, 1837
COBURN
 F. M. (Mrs.), May 18, 1922
COCHRAN
 Catharine (Mrs.), d. of William
  Johnson, Aug. 11, 1910
COCKE
 Lucien H. (Mrs.), d. of
  Frank H. Smith, Apr. 13,
  1899
 Charles H., s. of Dr. Charles
  L. Cocke, May 10 and 17,
  1900
 Charles Lewis, May 9, 1901
 Charles Lewis, s. of C. H.
  Cocke, gr.s. of Dr. Charles
  L. Cocke, Sept. 26, 1907
 Cornelia, w. of Col. Robert
  Cocke, d. of Cornelius
  and Mary Hubbard, Sept. 15,
  1881
 Harriet (Mrs.), Aug. 26, 1886
 John F. (Capt.), Feb. 21,
  1856
 John Flemming, Nov. 19, 1857
 Marian Bayne, d. of Charles
  H. and E. R. Cocke, Apr. 5,

OBITUARY NOTICES IN THE RELIGIOUS HERALD WITH DATES OF PUBLICATION

1883
Mary, w. of Chastain Cocke, Apr. 24, 1873
Mary E., w. of John S. Cocke, gr.d. of Reuben Nuckols, July 8, Aug. 19, 1852
Mary S., w. of Pettus M. Cocke, July 10, 1851
Sallie Lewis, d. of Dr. Charles L. Cocke, Aug. 2, 1900
Sarah, w. of John Cocke, May 31, 1833
Susanna Virginia (Mrs.), Mar. 1, 1906
William Roland (Judge), Apr. 8, May 20, 1875

COFER
Alonzo M., s. of James H. L. Cofer, Aug. 5, 1880
Annie Gwathney, Oct. 4, 1934
Emma Virginia, d. of Isaac and Sarah Cofer, Aug. 8, 1878
Joseph (Elder), Jan. 25, 1839
Lelia Read (Mrs.), June 24, 1937
Maggie, d. of Junius O. Cofer, Nov. 17, 1881
Mollie E., w. of Andrew J. Cofer, Mar. 22, 1923
Nathan P., July 30, Dec. 3, 1914
Paul Ashton, Apr. 3, 1919
Thomas Ashton, s. of Abner B. and Sue Cofer, May 2, 1878

COFFIN
John G., Sept. 10, 1868

COFFMAN
Catharine (Mrs.), Jan. 13, 1853
Enoch, Sept. 27, 1860
Kate (Mrs.), Apr. 19, 1928

COGBILL
Emma F., w. of David Cogbill, d. of P. A. Hatcher, Jan. 22, 1863

COGHILL
Ann, w. of L. A. Coghill, Mar. 22, 1877
B. C., June 10, 1880
Bettie K. (Mrs.), June 12, 1924
Edward Ruthven, Dec. 24, 1925
Elizabeth (Mrs.), Jan. 24, 1850
Emma T., d. of Lawrence A. and Ann E. Coghill, Apr. 23, 1857
James L., Oct. 16, 1862
James T., s. of J. W. and E. Coghill, Feb. 23, 1888
John Waller, s. of Benjamin Coleman Coghill, Jan. 25, 1923
L. A., Dec. 1, 1892
Millicent, w. of B. C. Coghill, Apr. 5, 1833
Mollie R. (Mrs.), June 17, 1920
Richard Parker, s. of William Newton Coghill, Nov. 7, 1878
Rosa Campbell, d. of T. D. and M. R. Coghill, Sept. 27, 1894
T. D. (Maj.), Apr. 30, 1925
William Henry, s. of J. H. and Sarah P. Coghill, July 27, 1848
William Newton, June 24, 1869
Willie, child of William N. and Lizzie J. Coghill, Jan. 19, 1860

COHEN
A. D. (Rev.), May 25, 1905

COHRON
Cordelia Weller (Mrs.), Jan. 15, 1925
Cornelius H., Sept. 29, 1921

COKE
Rebecca, d. of Mrs. Rebecca Coke, June 29, 1848

OBITUARY NOTICES IN THE RELIGIOUS HERALD WITH DATES OF PUBLICATION

Rebecca, w. of John Coke,
  July 20, 1848
Richard, Sr., Oct. 17, 1844
COKER
  Hannah Lide (Mrs.), June
    7, 1900
COLBERT
  G. N. (Judge), Dec. 7, 1876
  H. B., w. of Judge N. M.
    Colbert, Sept. 8, 1921
  Mary Lucy, d. of Judge G. N.
    Colbert, Jan. 15, 1880
  W. S., Feb. 4, 1886
COLE
  Andrew Patterson (Judge),
    Oct. 8, 1917
  Catharine, w. of W. A.
    Cole, Aug. 13, 1885
  Cornelia Boatwright (Mrs.),
    Aug. 27, 1931
  Edward Dorsey (Col.), Sept.
    27, 1917
  G. H. (Rev.), May 28, 1903
  Hannah M., w. of Micajah B.
    Cole, Mar. 31, 1853
  Henrietta, d. of James S.
    and Elizabeth A. Cole,
    Feb. 1, 1855
  Henry Clay, May 23, 1929
  J. T., Sept. 14, 1882
  James S., Dec. 22, 1870
  Jesse, s. of Ben W. Cole,
    Sept. 17, 1891
  John Wesley, Aug. 18, 1932
  Martha D. (Mrs.), Jan. 4,
    1844
  Nancy R. (Mrs.), d. of John
    Broaddus, Apr. 16, 1863
  Robert W. (Rev.), Oct. 1 and
    22, 1868
  Stockton Wharton (Rev.),
    Jan. 17 and 31, 1929
  Susan, w. of John Cole, Mar.
    26, 1840
COLEBRIN
  Mary A., w. of Robert P.
    Colebrin, d. of Rev. J.
    S. Wharton, Dec. 25, 1890
COLEMAN
  A. E. (Mrs.), Mar. 5, 1908

Ada Eliza, w. of John L.
  Coleman, Jr., d. of Whited
  M. and Mary H. Coleman,
  Feb. 21, 1884
Ann (Mrs.), May 14, 1857
Arabella, w. of John Cole-
  man, Aug. 9, 1877
Aylett B., s. of John J.
  Coleman, Jan. 12, 1865
Bessie, d. of W. E. and
  Bessie Johnson Coleman,
  June 26, 1890
Bessie D., d. of Rev. James
  D. and H. Coleman, Dec.
  22, 1859
Bettie F., w. of David M.
  Coleman, d. of Robert M.
  Moore, Aug. 11, Sept. 8,
  1864
Channing Moore, Feb. 27,
  1890
Daniel, s. of Henry R. and
  Emma C. Coleman, Mar. 29,
  1860
Daniel L., July 17, 1845
Dorothy, w. of Dr. Hawes N.
  Coleman, Mar. 3, 1842
Eliza, w. of William Cole-
  man, d. of Charles Mosley,
  Apr. 29, 1869
Elizabeth P. F., w. of James
  S. Coleman, Oct. 18, 1849
Elizabeth W. (Mrs.), May 18,
  1854
Emma, May 17, 1883
Gulielmus, Nov. 6, 1856
H. A., Feb. 19, 1903
Hawes, Mar. 4, 1831
Hawes, Jan. 21, 1841
Hawes, s. of Dr. H. N. and
  Sallie A. E. Coleman, Aug.
  22, 1861
Huldah DeJarnette, w. of Rev.
  James D. Coleman, July 19,
  1894
J. M. (Mrs.), d. of James John-
  son, Dec. 14, 1905
J. P., Sept. 30, 1858
James D. (Rev.), Dec. 5 and 12,
  1878; Jan. 30, 1879

OBITUARY NOTICES IN THE RELIGIOUS HERALD WITH DATES OF PUBLICATION

James M. (Dr.), Feb. 8, Mar. 15, 1934
Jean Denham, d. of Rev. J. M. Coleman, Sept. 9, 1909
Jemima (Mrs.), Apr. 3, 1835
John, Mar. 17, 1892
John Daniel, s. of George William Coleman, Feb. 22, Apr. 5, 1923
John O., s. of John Coleman, Sept. 24, 1885
Josiah R., May 18, 1893
L. M. (Lt.Col.), Apr. 2, 1863
Lucy Ann (Mrs.), Aug. 29, 1834
Lyttleton Goodwin (Dr.), Nov. 20, 1829
Marcia, d. of Mrs. Ann W. Coleman, Aug. 22, 1834
Maria Edmonia, d. of Capt. John Coleman, Jan. 21, 1841
Martha, w. of Col. Daniel Coleman, May 26, 1842
Mary, w. of Richard L. Coleman, Mar. 18, 1880
Mary G., w. of Dr. Hawes N. Coleman, Sept. 6, 1855
Mary M., w. of John Daniel Coleman, Mar. 30, 1911
Matilda, w. of Robert Coleman, June 5, 1873
Nancy W., w. of Henry C. Coleman, Feb. 7, 1850
Pryor, s. of Dr. H. N. and Sallie A. E. Coleman, Aug. 22, 1861
R. G. (Elder), Nov. 26, 1840
Reuben Lindsay, s. of Thomas Coleman, Mar. 31, 1892
Richard L., Jan. 3, 1850
Robert, May 11, 1854
Robert T. (Dr.), Mar. 27, 1884
Ruffin H., Feb. 24, 1887
Sallie, d. of John Coleman, May 3, 1866
Sallie A. E., w. of Dr. H. N. Coleman, Jr., Aug. 22, 1861
Sarah, w. of James Coleman, Jan. 3, 1895
Sarah Ann, d. of Capt. John Coleman, Aug. 21, 1851
Sarah N., w. of John H. Coleman, Feb. 4, 1864
Thomas, Feb. 5, 1852
Thomas B., Jr., Apr. 1, 1831
Thomas D., s. of Daniel L. Coleman, Oct. 10, 1872
Tyree Witt, s. of George William Coleman, May 20, 1875
W. R. (Mrs.), Oct. 2, 1924
William J. (Dr.), Nov. 11, 1920
William M., July 11, 1889

COLGATE
Samuel, Apr. 29, 1897

COLLAWN
William, May 31, 1855

COLLEY
John James, s. of Charles T. and Frances Colley, Apr. 24, 1862
Matthew E., s. of Mrs. Ann F. Colley, Apr. 11, 1872
Nannie M., w. of Thomas H. Colley, Apr. 10, 1884
Oscar James, s. of Rufus J. and Martha J. Colley, Apr. 24, 1862
Rufus, Jan. 22, 1903

COLLIE
Malinda, d. of Carter Collie, May 9, 1861

COLLIER
Alice S., d. of M. W. Collier, July 11, 1872
C. W. (Rev.), Aug. 20, Sept. 10, 1914
C. W. (Mrs.), w. of Rev. C. W. Collier, Nov. 19 and 26, 1936
Carrie S., Aug. 9, 1877
George W. (Elder), May 12, 1837

OBITUARY NOTICES IN THE RELIGIOUS HERALD WITH DATES OF PUBLICATION

Jane (Mrs.), May 13, 1831
Mark W., Sept. 25, 1884
Martha A., Sept. 25, 1884
Mary L. (Mrs.), May 5, 1910
Robert R., s. of Robert W.
  and Mary L. Collier, Mar.
  15, 1883
Sallie, w. of Elder George
  W. Collier, Mar. 1, 1866
COLLINGS
  Elizabeth (Mrs.), Jan. 13,
  1921
COLLINS
  Annie (Mrs.), Sept. 16, 1920
  Caroline C., w. of Rev. N.
    G. Collins, July 23, 1846
  Catharine, w. of Rev. E.
    Collins, Jan. 9, 1851
  Catharine N., w. of John O.
    Collins, Jan. 25, 1883
  Elizabeth (Mrs.), Mar. 14,
    1878
  Elizabeth, w. of J. B.
    Collins, Mar. 27, 1902
  Frank, July 7, 1921
  George Robert, Aug. 22,
    1918
  Harry, s. of G. W. and Annie
    C. Collins, Feb. 3, 1887
  J. B., Feb. 23, 1928
  J. Johnson, gr.s. of Col.
    V. Johnson, Feb. 15, 1849
  J. Maxie, July 17, 1873
  James R., July 25, 1901
COMEGYS
  Joseph Hawkins, s. of Dr. J. M.
    and Kate Comegys,
    Oct. 18, 1866
  Sallie Electa, d. of Dr.
    Comegys, Oct. 3, 1867
COMER
  Florence, Dec. 4, 1890
  Maggie, w. of James M. Comer, June 1, 1876
  Mahone, Dec. 4, 1890
  Samuel, May 6, 1886
COMPTON
  Eliza D., w. of James R.
    Compton, Mar. 4, 1880
CONDREY

John A., Feb. 8, 1934
Susan O., d. of Robert Y.
  Condrey, Sept. 7, 1848
Willie, s. of Julius and
  Aurelia Condrey, Oct. 16,
  1890
CONDUIT
  Thomas (Rev.), Oct. 28,
  1836
CONE
  Dorastus, Sept. 24, 1885
  George W., Nov. 2, 1911
CONLY
  S. W., Apr. 2, 1896
CONNALLY
  Fanny L., w. of Thomas D.
    Connally, d. of Rev. John
    Kerr, Aug. 14, 1845
CONNELLY
  George Matthew, June 13,
    1935
  Louise Jones, w. of J. B.
    Connelly, Apr. 15, 1926
  May E. (Mrs.), May 13,
    1926
  Patrick H., Mar. 1, 1860
CONNER
  Champ C. (Rev.), s. of
    John Conner, Apr. 1, 1875
  Elizabeth W., Mar. 14,
    1861
CONOLLEY
  John, Feb. 27, 1851
CONWAY
  Edward Henry, Apr. 20, 1871
  Frank Brooke, s. of L. B.
    and Bettie J. Conway,
    June 27, 1878
  John Blair, s. of L. B.
    and B. J. Conway, Jan.
    22, 1863
  Lilly Cardwell, w. of A. C.
    Conway, d. of G. Y. and
    V. A. Cardwell, Sept. 3
    and 24, 1891
  Sallie B., May 22, 1879
  Sarah B., Feb. 14, 1856
COOK
  Ada F. (Mrs.), Apr. 28,
    1938

OBITUARY NOTICES IN THE RELIGIOUS HERALD WITH DATES OF PUBLICATION

Ambrose, Mar. 18, 1847
Ann K. (Mrs.), Dec. 14, 1838
Blanch Moseley, w. of John S. Cook, June 13, 1901
Emily Virginia, d. of J. Cook, Oct. 29, 1857
Fortunatus Sydnor, s. of William F. Cook, Aug. 4, 1864
George F. (Rev.), Oct. 6, Nov. 10, 1932
George W., Jan. 30, 1908
James Burton (Rev.), Apr. 20, June 8, 1922
Jane, w. of Josiah Cook, July 8, 1875
Jane M., w. of William B. Cook, Jan. 29, 1874
Jeremiah (Mrs.), Jan. 2, 1851
Jeremiah, Apr. 5, 1888
John Earnest (Rev.), Jan. 14, 1926
John L., Apr. 29, 1836
Louisa L. (Mrs.), d. of Daniel S. and Maria Carr Kerfoot, Apr. 15, 1915
M. E., w. of William F. Cook, May 19, 1881
Mildred Barker (Mrs.), May 2, 1929
Rebecca Clyde, w. of T. A. Cook, June 17, 1880
Richard B. (Rev.), June 1, 1916
Sarah, Mar. 8, 1894
Susanna, w. of Ambrose Cook, Oct. 30, 1845
COOKE
Andrew J., s. of Andrew B. Cooke, Apr. 11, 1850
Ann J., May 14, 1840
Annie M. A. (Mrs.), May 23, 1867
B. F., July 26, 1900
Benjamin Pendleton, June 21, July 12, 1849
Bertha A., Oct. 4, 1888
Carroll Eyster, s. of William H. and Sallie E. Cooke, Jan. 2, 1873
Champe G., Aug. 28, 1862
Charles H., Mar. 1, 1906
E. C. (Mrs.), Feb. 12, 1885
Ella Josephine, d. of James M. Cooke, Oct. 24, 1867
George H. (Dr.), June 27, 1929
Giles, May 13, 1847
Jane F., Mar. 10, 1842
John Esten, Oct. 7, 1886
John T., Mar. 27, 1845
Joseph, s. of Andrew Cooke, Dec. 27, 1883
Maria (Mrs.), June 3, 1920
Mary Alice, d. of Benjamin and Ella Cooke, Nov. 8, 1855
Nancy, w. of John Cooke, Sept. 17, 1857
Sarah D. (Mrs.), Dec. 25, 1879
Thomas (Rev.), May 7, 1863
William O., s. of Capt. William C. Cooke, June 1, 1854
COONES
William, Mar. 31, 1842
COONS
Andrew Jackson, Oct. 17, 1929
Dillard, Apr. 27, 1838
E. S., w. of William Coons, June 3, 1869
Eugene Mirril, s. of Col. R. and Eudoxy Coons, July 30, 1846
James William, June 10, 1852
Nannie Mason, w. of George Dallas Coons, May 14, 1903
COOPER
Fleet (Rev.), Feb. 22, 1828
Frances, w. of John Cooper, Nov. 12, 1857
J. W. (Rev.), Dec. 7, 1922
Leroy, Apr. 1, 1858
Lollie Shaw, Feb. 6, 1873
Sarah Frances, w. of Dr. C. S. Cooper, May 30, 1878
Sollie Shaw, s. of Wise A.

OBITUARY NOTICES IN THE RELIGIOUS HERALD WITH DATES OF PUBLICATION

and Asenath N. Cooper,
Mar. 6, 1873
W. L., Aug. 10, 1922
Walker, s. of Marcus Cooper,
Dec. 2, 1875
William D. (Dr.), Nov. 18,
1897
COORPENDER
William Fenner, Apr. 8,
1880
COPENHAVER
M. B., Aug. 20, 1863
Sarah Ann, w. of William C.
Copenhaver, Nov. 29,
1860
COPES
James, Apr. 26, 1877
CORBETT
George T., Apr. 27, 1911
CORBIN
Lemuel A., May 23, 1907
Sallie Hill, Mar. 25, 1915
Sallie V. (Mrs.), Oct. 22,
1925
Sarah, w. of Armistead Corbin, June 8, 1843
CORBITT
C. L. (Rev.), Oct. 18, 1934
James M., Oct. 31, 1901
Martha A., w. of James M.
Corbitt, Sept. 10, 1891
Samuel, May 9, 1878
W. C., May 4, 1922
CORDER
Fannie M., Aug. 1, 1872
Sarah A. (Mrs.), Mar. 4,
1897
Thomas P., June 12, 1890
CORE
Mary, w. of W. T. Core, d.
of John W. and Mary Cutherfell, Aug. 16, 1894
COREY
Harry S. (Dr.), Dec. 19,
1929
CORNELIUS
Rachel, w. of Rev. Samuel
Cornelius, d. of William
Booth, May 23, 1850
S. (Rev.), Aug. 4, 1870

CORNELL
A. B. (Mrs.), May 30, 1895
Ezra, Jan. 7, 1875
CORNETT
Henrietta, w. of Jeremiah
Cornett, Aug. 14, 1845
CORNWELL
Ruth (Mrs.), June 6, 1907
William, May 2, 1861
CORR
Ann Elizabeth, d. of Paul
and Frances Watlington,
Feb. 3, 1898
Betsy, Oct. 8, 1857
Ella Ballad, w. of Robert
R. Corr, Feb. 18, 1926
Emma Basye, w. of Rev. H.
L. Corr, Nov. 25, 1937;
Jan. 27, Feb. 24, 1938
H. W., Sept. 21, 1893
Jesse L., s. of Levi P.
Corr, Aug. 7, 1884
Levi P., Oct. 21, 1897
Mary Catherine (Mrs.), Jan.
2, 1913
Mildred, w. of Thomas Corr,
Apr. 16, 1857
P. W. (Rev.), Mar. 5, 1931
Roberta, Mar. 9, 1838
William E., Oct. 30, 1930
William H., s. of Levi P.
and Ann E. Corr, Dec. 30,
1880
CORRON
Charles David, s. of Rev. J. P.
Corron, Apr. 7, 1859
James William, s. of Rev. J.
P. Corron, Mar. 3, 1859
John T., s. of Rev. J. P.
and Elizabeth Corron, June
5, 1862
CORTHORN
Edmond H., Aug. 28, 1862
COSBY
Amelia D. (Mrs.), Aug. 18,
1842
Anthony M. (Lt.), May 21,
1863
B. F., Nov. 25, 1920
Eliza Frances, w. of Dr.

OBITUARY NOTICES IN THE RELIGIOUS HERALD WITH DATES OF PUBLICATION

William H. Cosby, Dec. 21, 1848
Elizabeth (Mrs.), Dec. 18, 1879
Henry, Oct. 29, 1874
Ira L., July 12, 1934
John H., June 4, 1863
Joseph H. (Rev.), Mar. 7, 1935
Leeland, Apr. 19, May 17, 1900
Lenorah, d. of Mrs. Caroline Cosby, Aug. 14, 1851
Lucilla (Mrs.), Oct. 25, 1888
Martha S., w. of James E. Cosby, July 19, 1860
Mary S., w. of Rev. B. E. Cosby, Mar. 17, 1870
Mattie, Apr. 20, 1922
Mildred S., d. of Capt. E. E. and Ann Cosby, Aug. 27, 1874
P. G., Sr., Feb. 1, 1923
R. A., w. of J. N. Cosby, Oct. 18, 1894
COSTEN
　Elizabeth Lynch (Mrs.), Apr. 22, 1920
COSTIN
　Vashti, Aug. 26, 1880
COTE
　W. N. (Rev.), May 3, 1877
COTTEN
　Mary Agnes (Mrs.), Sept. 30, 1875
　William H., Oct. 5, 1882
COTTINGHAM
　George, Apr. 1, 1915
　Henry, Mar. 13, 1879
COTTON
　Lucy (Mrs.), June 22, 1848
COTTRELL
　Joseph F., Mar. 31, 1887
　Sarah Ann, w. of Hollin Cottrell, Jan. 8, 1836
　William, Jan. 19, 1838
COUCH
　Ann (Mrs.), Feb. 13, 1829

　Elizabeth, Oct. 7, 1852
　Lucy A., w. of William T. Couch, Sept. 21, 1876
　Sarah A., w. of Samuel P. Couch, d. of C. H. Pettus, Aug. 10, 1871
　William S. (Dr.), s. of John Couch, Feb. 18, 1858
　William T., Mar. 19, 1868
　William Walker, June 28, 1917
COUGHLIN
　Elvira V., w. of Daniel Coughlin, d. of John N. Doggett, May 20, 1886
COULLING
　Annie (Mrs.), w. of Rev. D. Coulling, Apr. 5, 1860
　George Parker, s. of Elder David and Annie W. Coulling, July 7, 1859
COUNCIL
　Georgie C., w. of Rev. J. C. Council, Sept. 17, 1908
　Godwin, Aug. 5, 1841
　P., w. of Goodwin Council Feb. 26, 1857
　Roberta Bennett, d. of J. C. and Mary E. Council, Dec. 10, 1868
　Sarah A., w. of Rev. James G. Council, Sept. 23, 1869
　V. H. (Rev.), Jan. 9, 1936
COUNCILL
　C. H., Jan. 3, 1895
　J. Calvin (Col.), Feb. 18, 1904
　Martha A., Jan. 9, 1908
　Mary Susan, w. of Charles H. Councill, Oct. 22, 1868
　Robert Crawford, s. of Rev. J. G. Councill, Nov. 4, 1869
　Virginia, w. of Charles H. Councill, d. of John W. and Arinthia Goffigon, Feb. 4, 1892
COUNCILLE
　Richard C., Dec. 22, 1910
COURSEY

OBITUARY NOTICES IN THE RELIGIOUS HERALD WITH DATES OF PUBLICATION

Rachel, w. of Thomas
Coursey, Jan. 19, 1871
COURTNEY
Dorothy S., w. of Joseph
Courtney, Sept. 20,
1839
Franklin, s. of William P.
Courtney, Nov. 26, 1868
James Mortimer, s. of
James W. Courtney, Jan.
18, 1855
James Whitaker, Feb. 22,
1894
Joseph C., Mar. 30, 1899
Lavinia Campbell, d. of T.
L. and Mrs. S. W. Courtney,
July 19, 1860
Lawrence Straughan, July
23, 1891
Margaret E., d. of James
and Maria Courtney, Jan.
19, 1860
Maria G., w. of James W.
Courtney, Feb. 2, 1899
Martha (Mrs.), Feb. 29,
1844
Martha E., w. of William P.
Courtney, Feb. 27, 1879
Mary Beale, w. of P. C.
Courtney, Nov. 3, 1898
Mary C., May 15, 1829
May C., d. of James W. and
Maria G. Courtney, Jan.
22, 1863
Pocahontas, d. of R. M.
Courtney, Feb. 5, 1885
Priscilla, w. of Robert
Courtney, Nov. 5, 1840
R. Mortimer, Jan. 30, 1908
Robert (Capt.), Mar. 18,
1852
Sallie Ann, w. of L. S.
Courtney, July 16, 1908
Sally Browne, w. of Theodore
Courtney, d. of Capt.
Thomas and Sarah B. Haynes,
June 3, 1909
Sarah, w. of Robert Courtney,
July 19, 1860
William Hugh, Mar. 20, 1862

COUSINS
Charles L., Mar. 19, 1936
Richard Henry, June 6, July
18, 1828
Susan P., w. of L. A.
Cousins, d. of Thomas
Thornhill, Nov. 12, 1857
COVINGTON
Hannah L., d. of Richard and
Emily Covington, Oct. 19,
1843
John Austin, s. of W. G.
and L. E. Covington, Mar.
18, 1880
Lily (Mrs.), July 20, 1933
Lucy, d. of John A. and Ida
Covington, Oct. 24, 1878
Mollie Sue, d. of Joseph
and Susan C. Covington,
May 29, 1873
Virginia Bagby (Mrs.), Oct.
26, 1922
William Wallis, s. of John
Covington, Jan. 2, 1851
COWARDIN
(Mrs.), d. of Col. T. J.
Evans, Feb. 25, 1886
O. B. (Col.), July 12, 1900
COWHERD
Bettie S., d. of Dr. Colby
Cowherd, Feb. 15, 1872
Charles S., May 8, 1862
Colby (Dr.), Feb. 25, 1897
Earnest, s. of M. D. and
Addie H. Cowherd, Feb. 5,
1891
Frances, w. of Reuben Cow-
herd, Oct. 22, 1846
Jonathan T., Jan. 9, 1873
Lula, d. of J. and Phillippa
Cowherd, July 26, Aug. 9,
1877
Martha D., Aug. 6, 1857
Sarah A. E. (Mrs.), July 3,
1890
Walter, s. of E. F. and Mrs.
Cowherd, Dec. 9, 1875
William, Mar. 3, 1870
COWLES
Washington (Col.), Mar. 17,

OBITUARY NOTICES IN THE RELIGIOUS HERALD WITH DATES OF PUBLICATION

1853
COWLING
Matilda, w. of Willis Cowling, Aug. 8, 1828
Willis, Aug. 22, 1828
COX
A. B., July 7, 1927
Alice T., w. of Powhatan Cox, July 19, 1900
Alpheus (Dr.), July 14, 1887
Andrew, s. of Jacob Cox, Jan. 30, 1902
Barbara A. (Mrs.), July 8, 1875
Breckenridge, Mar. 12, 1891
Brickhouse Bell, Mar. 1, 1894
C. C. (Rev.), Nov. 3, 1904
Calhoun, s. of Dr. R. H. and Ann E. Cox, Aug. 25, 1853
Caroline M., w. of John F. Cox, Oct. 22, 1846
Catharine M., w. of James L. Cox, Oct. 27, 1870
Charles E., Aug. 7, 1862
D. (Mrs.), July 12, 1839
Eliza Ann, w. of George H. Cox, Aug. 25, 1859
Elizabeth, Nov. 21, 1895
Fannie E., w. of Walter M. Cox, Oct. 20, 1870
George, July 3, 1845
Henry A., Sept. 14, 1882
Henry Nelson, Nov. 20, 1879
J. J., June 25, 1885
J. Edward (Dr.), s. of George W. Cox, Sept. 23, 1920
James William, s. of Dr. R. H. and Sarah A. E. Cox, Sept. 8, 1853
John F., Oct. 1, 1863
John Pollard, s. of Millard F. Cox, July 10, 1913
Josephine (Mrs.), Feb. 25, 1926
Junius, s. of Dr. R. H. and Ann E. Cox, Aug. 25, 1853
Junius E., Oct. 31, 1929
Lillian L., d. of Elijah D. and S. M. Cox, Oct. 12, 1899
Loulie, w. of J. Robert Cox, Mar. 2, 1893
Lucy J., w. of Benjamin H. Cox, d. of Joseph F. Spencer, Oct. 8, 1857
M. D., w. of B. F. Cox, d. of William B. and Sarah Bruce Estis, July 10, 1913
Martha, d. of J. B. and R. L. Cox, Aug. 16, 1894
Mary L., w. of G. W. Cox, Dec. 26, 1844
Matilda Smith, w. of Richard Cox, Mar. 29, 1894
Mattie D., May 27, 1920
Powhatan, Sept. 30, 1926
Rhoda, w. of Abraham Cox, Oct. 11, 1877
Richard, Mar. 8, 1894
Richard W., Nov. 16, 1899
Roberta Lee (Mrs.), Sept. 24, 1903
Rosalie Edgeworth, d. of Robert H. Cox, Sept. 16, 1847
Sallie U., Aug. 27, 1908
Washington, s. of William Cox, Nov. 12, 1863
CRADDOCK
Bettie S. (Mrs.), d. of Rev. B. Phillips, Apr. 26, 1866
Charles, Jr., (Rev.), Jan. 11, 1866
Elizabeth, Feb. 11, 1858
Fanny Y., w. of Dr. Charles Craddock, Jan. 15, 1885
James, Feb. 1, 1855
John W., Aug. 21, 1884
Kate A., w. of J. A. Craddock, Aug. 23, 1883
Mary F., d. of John B. Craddock, Feb. 23, 1854
Mary Louisa, Nov. 4, 1852
CRAFT

OBITUARY NOTICES IN THE RELIGIOUS HERALD WITH DATES OF PUBLICATION

Abram (Rev.), Mar. 2, 1905
Elivira Elizabeth, d. of Samuel and M. J. Craft, Nov. 22, 1860
Lucy L. (Mrs.), Feb. 6, 1890
Susan P., w. of Rev. J. B. Craft, May 7, 1914

CRAFTON
John J., Dec. 16, 1841
Lucy Ann, w. of Thomas B. Crafton, Nov. 19, 1849
William T., s. of Thomas A. and Lucy B. Crafton, July 12, 1894

CRAIG
John W. (Rev.), Apr. 20, 1933
Kennerly, July 2, 1874
Mary Jane (Mrs.), June 2, 1892
W. C., Dec. 28, 1916

CRAIN
Nancy, w. of Maj. James Crain, June 27, 1844
Rebecca B., d. of Maj. James Crain, July 1, 1841
Robert Bailey, s. of Bailey and Huldah Crain, July 11, 1850
Virginia Catherine, d. of James Crain, Mar. 17, 1837
William T. (Dr.), s. of James Crain, Sept. 2, 1836

CRALLE
Bettie (Mrs.), Apr. 2, 1925
Dorins G., June 7, 1849
Margaret S., w. of R. R. Cralle, Feb. 13, 1868
Susan B. (Mrs.), Sept. 29, 1897

CRANDALL
David Wilbur (Rev.), July 30, 1830
Ida C., w. of Floyd Crandall, d. of Chauncey Meade, Sept. 6, 1888

CRANDOL
Amanda, w. of Rev. William A. Crandol, June 5, 1873
Martha M., Jan. 1, 1857
Susan, w. of Richard Crandol, Oct. 18, 1839

CRANE
child of Thomas R. Crane, June 27, 1850
Alcesta Flora, w. of Rev. William Carey Crane, Sept. 3, 1840
Catharine Ann, child of William Crane, Aug. 19, 1831
Cephas (Rev.), Feb. 8, 1917
David Roper, s. of James C. Crane, July 19, 1855
Fuller, Jan. 15, 1885
Henry Richmond, s. of Henry R. and Clara M. Crane, Mar. 8, 1888
James Taylor, s. of James Crane, Oct. 6, 1853
Jane Louisa, w. of Rev. W. Carey Crane, Dec. 29, 1842; Jan. 12, 1843
Joseph Steel, s. of James C. Crane, Aug. 10, 1832
Lydia, w. of William Crane, Oct. 1 and 8, 1830
Robert Semple, s. of James C. Crane, Mar. 24, 1853
Ward, s. of William Crane, Apr. 27, 1832
William, Apr. 4, 1867
William Carey (Dr.), Mar. 12 and 19, 1885
William Woolfolk, Mar. 4, 1897
Zachary Taylor, s. of Thomas J. Crane, Aug. 5, 1847

CRANK
George H., Feb. 28, 1889
Victoria A., d. of G. H. and E. W. Crank, Aug. 8, 1878

CRAVEN
Jane Carey, June 21, 1883

CRAWFORD
Anderson, Feb. 4, 1909
Andrew, Nov. 1, 1839

OBITUARY NOTICES IN THE RELIGIOUS HERALD WITH DATES OF PUBLICATION

Corinne, d. of Wynn and
Bettie L. Crawford, Aug.
1, 1895
N. M. (Dr.), Nov. 16, 1871
Neeson, Aug. 20, 1891
Peter, Aug. 14, 1873
Sallie R. (Mrs.), Mar.
26, 1868
Sarah W., w. of John B.
Crawford, Nov. 26,
1863
Susan D., w. of John B.
Crawford, Sept. 3,
1857
William, Apr. 12, 1860
CREASY
Charles Elmore, s. of Jacob
and Frances A. Creasy, Feb.
12, 1880
CREATH
A. Blanche, d. of A. F.
and L. J. Creath, June
12, 1890
Andrew Fuller, Oct. 20,
1938
C. W., w. of Rev. S. A.
Creath, d. of Henry E.
Scott, Oct. 12, 1876
Frances A., w. of Rev. J.
W. Creath, Feb. 28, 1856
J. W., Dec. 20, 1894
J. W. D. (Rev.), Jan. 19,
1882
Joseph Warner Dossey, Sept.
8, Dec. 1, 1881
Lewis H., Oct. 30, 1913
Lucretia (Mrs.), June 30,
1853
Melancthon L. (Rev.), Oct.
8, 1846
Mary Coleman, w. of Rev.
Thomas B. Creath, Nov.
5, 1903
Samuel C., s. of Rev. T. B.
Creath, Nov. 28, 1867
Samuel W. W., s. of Rev. J.
W. D. and Frances Creath,
Apr. 13, 1848
Thomas B., Jr., Aug. 7, 1862
Thomas B. (Rev.), Dec. 1 and
29, 1892
William J., s. of Rev. T.
B. Creath, Aug. 7, 1862
CREBBS
John Will, Feb. 23, 1893
John William, s. of J. C.
and Ann E. Crebbs, Jan.
26, Feb. 23, 1893
CREEDIE
Lena Bettie (Mrs.), Apr.
21, 1921
CREEL
Mary A. B. (Mrs.), d. of
John S. Whitescarver,
Sept. 23, 1880
CRENSHAW
Ada, d. of Mrs. A. T. Crenshaw, Nov. 11, 1915
Anna Katharine, d. of Peyton Crenshaw, Jan. 13,
1927
Charles T., s. of S. D.
Crenshaw, Apr. 3, 1829
Ella Wilson, d. of Leroy
A. and Sarah B. Crenshaw,
Sept. 10, 1857
Harriet A., d. of R. R. and
Mary E. A. Crenshaw, May
21, 1863
James H., s. of Spottswood
H. and Sarah A. Crenshaw,
June 1, 1854
Lizzie, d. of John and Sarah
Crenshaw, Mar. 10, 1859
Mary A. (Mrs.), Oct. 20,
1892
Olivia E., w. of Edwin P. Crenshaw, d. of Col. John S.
Stubblefield, July 10,
1879
Ophelia (Mrs.), Dec. 9,
1915
William, Sept. 22, 1881
CREW
Elizabeth L., June 8, 1848
Polly (Mrs.), Oct. 5, 1832
CREWS
Amanda (Mrs.), Sept. 2,
1852
Ann R. (Mrs.), Apr. 1, 1858

OBITUARY NOTICES IN THE RELIGIOUS HERALD WITH DATES OF PUBLICATION

Beverley D. (Mrs.), July
  9, Aug. 13, 1891
Fannie W., w. of John B.
  Crews, Aug. 7, 1856
Hiram G. (Rev.), June 7,
  July 19, 1917
J. W. P., Apr. 10, 1884
Jesse C., May 21, 1863
Joseph B., Dec. 29, 1864
Lucy Ann, July 4, 1929
Louisa, w. of William
  Crews, d. of Capt. Thomas
  Wooding, Dec. 3, 1857
Maggie Judson, d. of John
  J. and Mary A. Crews,
  Dec. 24, 1868
Mary Wilson (Mrs.), Apr.
  25, 1907
Melchisedec, Mar. 28, 1878
Nannie Friend, w. of Rev.
  H. G. Crews, Mar. 19,
  May 28, 1885
Sarah W., w. of Isaac S.
  Crews, Feb. 4, 1858
CRIDLIN
  Emma Haseltine, w. of Rev.
    R. W. Cridlin, Apr. 19,
    May 24, 1906
  Lewis Macon, s. of James A.
    and Sarah T. Cridlin,
    Mar. 19, 1891
  Mollie E., w. of Rev. R.
    W. Cridlin, d. of Thomas
    V. Burgess, Dec. 5,
    1867
  R. W. (Rev.), Sept. 25,
    1913
CRIGLER
  Ann E. (Mrs.), Dec. 16,
    1886
  Catharine, w. of William
    Crigler, June 27, 1850
  Christopher, Jan. 6, 1859
  E. Roberta, d. of Roberts
    and Anna Crigler, Sept. 2,
    1875
  Ethel Burroughs (Mrs.), d.
    of Dr. J. B. Burroughs,
    Aug. 8, 1901
  G. R., Apr. 26, 1900

George R., Aug. 9, 1900
Henry T., Jan. 28, 1904
Lucy E., Oct. 18, 1866
Mary E. PARR, w. of William
  G. Crigler, Feb. 2, 1905
William, Apr. 19, 1855
William C., Mar. 17, 1859
CRISMOND
  Horace F., Jan. 22, 1903
  Margaret Gravatt, Feb. 19,
    1920
CRISS
  M. (Mrs.), July 15, 1886
  Mary Isabella (Mrs.), Nov.
    11, 1886
CRITCHER
  Parke Florence, Jan. 21,
    1875
CRITTENDEN
  Addison Hall (Lt.), s. of
    George W. Crittenden, gr.s.
    of Elder Addison Hall,
    Nov. 5, 1863
  Andrew J. (Dr.), Dec. 18,
    1856
  Andrewella J., d. of Dr.
    Andrew J. Crittenden, May
    27, 1858
  C. B. (Mrs.), May 21, 1868
  C. C., Apr. 30, 1903
  George W., Mar. 8, 1849
  Henry A. (Mrs.), Apr. 10,
    1890
  James S., s. of Samuel S.
    and Catharine Crittenden,
    Apr. 12, 1877
  John Lewis, July 13, 1905
  Lewellyn (Lt.), Sept. 4,
    1862
  Margaret Spratly, w. of
    James C. Crittenden, June
    12, Aug. 7, 1845
  Maria U., w. of James C.
    Crittenden, May 12, 1853
  Mary A., Dec. 25, 1890
  Mary Y., d. of Mrs. Catherine
    B. Crittenden, May 15,
    1835
  R. H. (Rev.), June 18, 1874
  Susan C., w. of Major George

OBITURAY NOTICES IN THE RELIGIOUS HERALD WITH DATES OF PUBLICATION

W. Crittenden, d. of Elder
Addison Hall, Oct. 16,
1845
Susan J., w. of John L.
Crittenden, Mar. 28, 1901
William, Nov. 23, 1854
Zachariah, Sept. 8, 1842
CROFT
Sallie, July 19, 1855
CRONIN
Clementine B., d. of Henry
R. and Mary A. Cronin,
Nov. 5, 1857
CROOKS
Joseph B., Dec. 24, 1863
CROPP
Lucy T., w. of Warner Lewis
Cropp, Jan. 1, 1857
Maria L. (Mrs.), Dec. 20,
1906
CROSS
Abraham, May 28, 1830
Annie M., w. of Rev. Israel
Cross, Dec. 9, 1880
Hardy (Col.), Jan. 6, 1859
J. Henry, Oct. 8, 1908
Lillian (Mrs.), Jan. 30,
1936
Mary Ann, w. of Col. Hardy
Cross, Apr. 6, 1838
CROSSFIELD
William, Sept. 1, 1859
CROSWELL
George W., May 10, 1928
Virginia, w. of William Crosswell, May 6, 1847
CROUCH
(Mrs.), May 6, 1909
Eleanor, Jan. 5, 1865
Nettie E., w. of George W.
Crouch, Jan. 2, 1879
Nettie Mercer, d. of George
W. Crouch, Dec. 4, 1879
Virginia, w. of Dr. John G.
Crouch, Mar. 4, 1831
William M., June 12, 1924
CROUSE
Ann E., May 21, 1846
Mary Jane, d. of John and Mary
Crouse, Apr. 25, 1850

CROW
John, Jr., July 21, 1892
Polley (Mrs.), July 11, 1861
CROWDER
B. A., w. of William J.
Crowder, Oct. 18, 1860
Bell A., d. of W. J. Crowder,
Sr., Aug. 6, 1896
Elizabeth, d. of Meredith
Crowder, Nov. 5, 1846
Herbert T., s. of William
P. Crowder, Aug. 31, 1871
Hosea (Rev.), Dec. 22, 1887;
Mar. 22, 1888
Ira H. (Mrs.), Aug. 5, 1920
J. L., Aug. 17, 1905
Martha, w. of Merideth Crowder, Sept. 29, 1837
Mary J., w. of William P.
Crowder, Apr. 24, 1873
Minnie B., d. of N. A. Crowder, Sept. 20, 1888
Sallie, Sept. 16, 1909;
Sept. 29, 1910
T. C., Sept. 1, 8 and 15,
1921
Virginia Thomas, d. of Thomas
W. Crowder, Sept. 16,
1875
William Edward Berkeley, s.
of Thomas W. and Mollie
E. Crowder, May 1, 1879
William P., Oct. 2, 1879
CROWTHER
Lucy J., w. of Harry Crowther,
Feb. 20, 1873
CROXTON
C., Oct. 7, 1858
Carter, May 29, 1845
Frances, w. of Carter Croxton, Dec. 13, 1849
CROZER
Abby C. (Mrs.), July 24,
1890
John P., Dec. 23, 1926
Samuel H., July 14, 1910
CRUDUPP
Fay (Mrs.), Oct. 13, 1898
CRUIKSHANK
C. R. (Rev.), Feb. 5, Oct.

OBITUARY NOTICES IN THE RELIGIOUS HERALD WITH DATES OF PUBLICATION

29, 1931
CRUIKSHANKS
Willie Simms, w. of Rev.
C. R. Cruikshanks, d.
of William James Walton,
Dec. 10, 1891
CRUMLEY
Sarah Louisa, w. of Harmon
Crumley, June 15, 1922
CRUMP
Benjamin T., Mar. 10, 1910
Charles Wallace, s. of George
Parke and Robinett W.
Crump, Mar. 15, 1894
Cornelius S., Apr. 19, 1855
Frances V., w. of W. B.
Crump, July 25, 1867
George Park, July 1, 1880
George Wilton, Jan. 5, 1899
James M., Dec. 13, 1849
Jeremiah Jeter, s. of
George P. and R. W.
Crump, Mar. 15, 1894
John Louis, s. of Mrs.
Matilda H. Crump, Dec.
22, 1859
Josephine Matilda, d. of
Mrs. Matilda Crump, Oct.
11, 1855
Maria, July 23, 1840
Mary Louise, d. of James D.
and Nannie A. Crump, Mar.
4, 1880
Rena R. (Mrs.), Apr. 14,
1892
Robert H., June 30, 1904
Sarah E., w. of E. M. Crump,
Aug. 27, 1874
Sarah E. (Mrs.), Feb. 18,
1909
CRUTCHER
John R., Feb. 5, 1836
Minerva, Aug. 2, 1860
CRUTCHFIELD
E. W., Feb. 18, 1897
Francis Edwin, s. of Andrew
F. and Sarah Crutchfield,
June 28, 1849
John Jeter (Justice), Nov.
25, 1920

L. E., w. of B. H. Crutch-
field, Feb. 18, 1897
Nancy G. W., w. of Robert
Crutchfield, May 19, 1842
Sarah W. A., Dec. 31, 1840
CRUTE
Christopher C., Feb. 11,
1864
Robert C., Aug. 6, 1936
CRYMES
Emma, d. of Leonard and
Susan Crymes, May 3, 1860
Marion Lambert, s. of Thomas
and Laura V. Crymes, Oct.
10, 1872
S. M. V., w. of Leonard Crymes,
July 25, 1867
Vivien, Apr. 9, 1908
CULLEN
Charles R. (Dr.), Apr. 13,
1899
Eliza T. (Mrs.), July 28,
1859
CULPEPER
Bessie, d. of A. F. and Mary
H. Culpeper, Nov. 18, 1875
Elizabeth G. Charles, w. of
John G. Culpeper, Nov. 6,
1873
John (Elder), Mar. 4, 1841
John (Rev.), Apr. 3, Dec. 18,
1873
Kate Estelle, d. of Benjamin
F. and Octavia E. Culpeper,
Sept. 30, 1869
CUMMINGS
Andrew Jackson (Rev.), Oct.
17, 1918
CUMMINS
Bishop, July 6, 1876
CUNDIFF
Edwin Dunaway, Aug. 17, 1933
H. F., Apr. 28, 1831
J. W., July 15, 1926
CUNLIFF
Susan G., w. of Edwin Cunliff,
Jan. 3, 1861
CUNNINGHAM
Agnes, d. of Capt. and Mrs.
Frank W. Cunningham, Sept.

OBITUARY NOTICES IN THE RELIGIOUS HERALD WITH DATES OF PUBLICATION

15, 1898
J. A. (Mrs.), d. of J. R.
  Tunstall, July 18,
  1901
Laura Perkins, d. of William
  H. and A. E. Cunningham,
  Nov. 6, 1879
Louisa H., Mar. 3, 1859
Mollie F., d. of Randolph
  Cunningham, Sept. 25,
  1862
Virginia, w. of Capt. Thomas
  Cunningham, Sept. 6, 1883
William, Mar. 7, 1867
CURIETT
  Susan Chilton (Mrs.), Feb.
  23, 1933
CURLING
  G. L., Dec. 16, 1926
CURRELL
  Maria F. (Mrs.), Oct. 9,
  1858
CURRIE
  Cordelia C., w. of A. H.
  Currie, Nov. 28, 1850
CURRY
  J. L. M. (Dr.), Feb. 19,
  1903
  J. L. M. (Mrs.), d. of
  James Thomas, Jr., May
  28, 1903
  Willie Whiting, s. of Rev.
  J. H. Curry, Feb. 11, 1875
CURTIS
  Charlie, s. of W. O. Curtis,
  July 14, 1910
  Elizabeth, w. of Thomas Cary
  Curtis, June 18, 1846
  Julia A. (Mrs.), Sept. 3,
  1863
  M. A., w. of E. Curtis, Dec.
  6, 1855
  Mary, w. of Thomas Curtis,
  Jan. 12, 1854
  Mary L. (Mrs.), Mar. 5, 1830
  Thomas (Elder), Nov. 19, 1840
  Thomas F. (Rev.), Sept. 19,
  1872
  William (Rev.), Dec. 11,
  1873
CUSHING
  Mary Ann, Jan. 10, 1856
CUSHMAN
  Mary Elizabeth, d. of Rev.
  A. G. Cushman, Sept. 8,
  1842
CUTCHIN
  Annie E., Oct. 8, 1925
  J. Frank, Nov. 20, 1919
  Jemima, w. of Joseph J.
  Cutchin, Mar. 8, 1888
  Mildred A. (Mrs.), Jan. 8,
  1891
  William Henry, July 21, 1892
CUTHBERT
  Julia E., w. of Rev. James
  H. Cuthbert, Nov. 19,
  1885
CUTTING
  S. S., (Rev.), Feb. 16, 1882

- D -

DABBS
  Frances (Mrs.), Apr. 7, 1842
  George J. Apr. 11, 1889
  Joseph, June 5, 1873
  Joseph Alexander, s. of
    Josiah Dabbs, Feb. 3, 1842
  Josiah, Apr. 10, 1862

DABNEY
  Alfred B., s. of W. W. Dabney,
    Sept. 14, 1882
  B. W., Feb. 13, 1829
  Cornelius, July 28, 1837
  Cornelius, July 13, 1843
  Cornelius, Dec. 14, 1871
  Cornelius, s. of W. W. Dabney,
    Apr. 23, 1874
  Cornelius, S. of Cornelius
    and Mary Nicol Dabney,
    Apr. 2, 1896
  Edward N., July 21, 1864
  Elizabeth T., May 1, 1845
  Eula Lyle, d. of J. R.
    Dabney, June 17, 1909
  Frederick A. (Mrs.), Dec. 1,
    1921
  George E., Mar. 19, 1868
  Hannah Temple, d. of W. W.
    and Martha Ann Dabney,
    Oct. 13, 1870
  John C. (Mrs.), Feb. 8, 1923
  John W., Sept. 26, 1850
  Lucy Jane Frances, w. of
    James W. Dabney, d. of
    Josiah and Anna Kidd
    Pace, Mar. 20, 1913
  M. E., w. of R. D. Dabney,
    July 9, 1874
  Martha Ann, w. of W. W. Dabney,
    Feb. 4, 1886
  Martha Norvell, w. of Beverly
    Dabney, July 3, 1890
  Martha W., w. of Frederick N.
    Dabney, Sept. 3, 1874
  Mary Eliza, d. of Mordecai B.
    and Martha P. Dabney, Dec.
    28, 1843
  Nelson, s. of Edward N.
    Dabney, Dec. 2, 1852
  Patsey, May 31, 1855
  Richard, Aug. 9, 1860
  Salada (Mrs.), Mar. 16,
    1911
  Samuel Loving, Dec. 30,
    1909
  Sarah Ann, d. of Sarah F.
    Dabney, July 26, 1855
  Sarah Frances, w. of J. L.
    Dabney, June 28, 1855
  Susan, w. of Capt. Richard
    Dabney, Sept. 23, 1847
  Thomas J., s. of Benjamin
    Dabney Jr., May 18, 1854
  William, Dec. 5, 1829
  William, June 8, 1848
  William Winston, s. of
    William and Martha Ann
    Dabney, Mar. 31, 1842
  William Winston, Mar. 20,
    1890

DADE
  Mary R., w. of Albert G.
    Dade, Apr. 28, 1904
  William A. G., Oct. 23,
    1829

DAGG
  J. L. (Dr.), July 31, 1884

DALBY
  Drunett C., d. of John C.
    and Mary A. Dalby, July
    22, 1875
  Ida E. FACE (Mrs.), Feb.
    27, 1902
  Jane M., w. of William T.
    Dalby, Aug. 20, 1868
  W. M. R. H. G., Aug. 12,
    1880

DALTON
  Addie S., w. of James D.
    Dalton, d. of J. J. Muse,
    Dec. 20, 1883
  Annie Ruby, d. of James D.
    and Addie S. Dalton, Feb.
    7, 1878
  Bettie, w. w. of Joseph Dalton

OBITUARY NOTICES IN THE RELIGIOUS HERALD WITH DATES OF PUBLICATION

June 15, 1905
H. P. (Rev.), Apr. 20, 1922
Julian Muse, s. of J. D. and
  Addie S. Dalton, June 24,
  1875
DAMERON
  Calvin Peyton, s. of Walter C.
    and Rosa May Dameron, June 17,
    1909
  Emma F., d. of J. M. Dameron,
    Dec. 13, 1883
  J. M., Dec. 13, 1883
DANCE
  Mary P. (Mrs.), Mar. 23, 1876
  William S., Mar. 4, 1858
DANDRIDGE
  Alphonso M. s. of S. M. Dan-
    dridge, Oct. 19, 1854
  Archibald L., Nov. 2, 1838
  B. C., June 18, 1896
  Harriet S. w. of William G.
    Dandridge, Jan. 19, 1888
  Jane F. (Mrs.), Apr. 10, 1862
  Julius B., May 2, 1828
  Laura E., w. of Bolting S.
    Dandridge, Sept. 9, 1836
  Richard A., Apr. 11, 1850
  Robert F. (Dr.), Feb. 27,
    1829
  Spotswood A., s. of Spotswood
    M. and Jane F. Dandridge,
    Apr. 23, 1840*
  Spottswood Montgomery, Nov. 8,
    1849*
  William Archibald, s. of
    Spottswood M. and Jane F.
    Dandridge, July 24, 1835*
  William G., s. of William G.
    and Harriet S. Dandridge, Feb.
    7, 1878
DANFORTH
  Frances, w. of Joseph Danforth,
    Oct. 17, 1834
  John B. (Col.), July 8, 1875
DANIEL
  (Mrs.), mother of Dr. Charles
    W. Daniel, June 7, 1934
  Abraham, Apr. 21, 1864
  Amanda M. (Mrs.), Nov. 11,
    1909
  Ann, w. of Capt. Peter M.
    Daniel, Sept. 10, 1840
  Ann Eliza, w. of William
    B. Daniel, Mar. 3, 1864
  Ann Moncure, Nov. 22, 1849
  Bettie B. (Mrs.), Dec. 27,
    1923
  Charlie, s. of R. A. and
    Pattie M. Daniel, July
    30, 1885
  Elizabeth (Mrs.), mother of
    Mickelborough Daniel,
    May 16, 1850
  Ellen M., w. of William M.
    Daniel, June 17, 1897
  Henry, s. of H. M. and Cassie
    Daniel, Jan. 9, 1873
  Henry M., Dec. 3, 1844
  J. R. (Rev.), Feb. 7, 1924
  J. T., Oct. 17, 1935
  Josie, s. of W. A. and
    Matilda Daniel, Nov. 17,
    1881
  Leonard, Sept. 20, 1855
  Lucy A., d. of William A.
    and Matilda Daniel, Jan. 9,
    1873
  Marian Bruce, w. of Raleigh
    T. Daniel, d. of Charles G.
    Snead, Feb. 28, 1901
  Martha J., w. of Dr. William
    B. Daniel, Aug. 26, 1927
  Mary, w. of Robert Daniel,
    June 3, 1841
  Mary George, w. of John T.
    Daniel, Apr. 18, 1889
  Matilda, w. of J. W. Daniel,
    Aug. 11, 1853
  Mildred (Mrs.), Nov. 10,
    1937
  Polly, w. of Leonard Daniel,
    Sept. 20, 1855
  R. T., Aug. 23, 1877
  Robert, Jan. 25, 1883
  Robert (Maj.), Dec. 28, 1888
  Sarah T., Nov. 30, 1843
  Silas W., July 25, 1850
  William A., s. of Robert
    Daniel, June 11, 1863
  William A., Apr. 14, 1892

* Possible inaccuracy in name, or spelling, but given as printed

OBITUARY NOTICES IN THE RELIGIOUS HERALD WITH DATES OF PUBLICATION

William B. (Dr.), July 28, 1921
William Henry, Aug. 21, 1851
William M., Aug. 21, 1862
William Thomas, s. of William B. and Martha A. Daniel, June 19, 1851

DANIELS
   Maitland George, s. of Rev. G. M. Daniels, Jan. 12, 1899

DANNER
   Martha Jane, d. of Jacob S. Danner, Mar. 27, 1862

DANNE
   Mary Eliza, Aug. 30, 1923
   Willie, Feb. 6, 1908

DANTON
   Emma, w. of T. Danton, Aug. 26, 1858

DARBY
   Elizabeth (Mrs.), Sept. 1, 1842

DARDEN
   Annie, Sept. 13, 1917
   Jacob, (Elder), Sept. 11, 1829
   Martha F. (Mrs.), Feb. 13, 1918
   Mildred Louisa, Dec. 3, 1908
   Rufus Edward, Mar. 24, Apr. 14, 1910

DARGAN
   Edwin C. (Rev.), Jan. 15, 1931
   Ethel Forrester, d. of Dr. E. C. Dargan, Nov. 28, 1901
   Jane L., w. of Rev. J. O. B. Dargan, d. of Hugh Lide, Apr. 29, 1886
   John Herbert, s. of Rev. Edwin C. Dargan, Dec. 30, 1880

DARGON
   Lucien B., s. of Dr. T. A. Dargon, Oct. 20, 1870

DARRACOTT
   B. F., Jan. 6, 1859

DASORY
   Celia W., w. of Anthony Dasory, Oct. 27, 1837

DAUGHERTY
   Thomas J., Dec. 19, 1834

DAUGHTERY
   J. E., May 9, 1918

DAUGHTREY
   Alfred L., s. of Jacob K. Daughtrey, Apr. 20, 1854
   D. P., s. of Rev. Jacob K. Daughtrey, May 30, 1918
   J. K. P. (Mrs.), Jan. 7, 1937
   Jacob K., Nov. 26, 1868
   Robert C., Oct. 28, 1920

DAUGHTRY
   A. J., Mar. 26, 1931
   H. M. (Mrs.), May 15, 1919
   Nancy, w. of Rev. Jacob K. Daughtry, Apr. 22, 1875
   Virginia Wood, w. of D. P. Daughtry, Apr. 12, 1877
   W. B. (Rev.), Jan. 22, Apr. 23, 1914
   W. T., Feb. 14, 1907
   William H. (Dr.), Jan. 17, 1901

DAVENPORT
   Charles R., Mar. 21, 1867
   Edward, Aug. 12, 1831
   John, Mar. 19, 1830
   Julius T., (Elder), May 20, 1875
   Lucie B. (Mrs.), d. of Henry W. Quarels, Feb. 18, 1858
   Margaret (Mrs.), July 17, 1829
   Robert D., Jan. 4, 1849
   Willie R., s. of Mrs. F. G. R. Davenport, Aug. 16, 1855

DAVID
   Bessie, d. of Rev. W. J. and Wannie Bland David, Mar. 3, 1881
   Willie J., Jr., s. of W. J. David, Sept. 23, 1886

DAVIDSON

-85-

OBITUARY NOTICES IN THE RELIGIOUS HERALD WITH DATES OF PUBLICATION

A. F. (Rev.), Aug. 23, 1900
Archie A., Jan. 27, 1853
Carrie B., Oct. 26, 1899
Cridilla S., w. of William
  S. Davidson, Mar. 31, 1921
Dillie, Jan. 20, 1921
E. M. (Sister), May 16, 1889
Elizabeth, w. of A. A. David-
  son, July 30, 1857
Elizabeth Diuguid, w. of Rev.
  J. C. Davidson, Mar. 22,
  1923
Emily M., Mar. 15, 1917
Frances, w. of Samuel David-
  son, Mar. 22, 1860
Jennie J., w. of Rev. A. F.
  Davidson, Apr. 12, 1900
John A. (Rev.), s. of Rev.
  Samuel Davidson, Aug. 31,
  1832
Joseph Edward, s. of George
  W. and Martha A. Williamson
  Davidson, May 14, 1914
Judson Carey, (Rev.), May 7,
  Oct. 29, 1914
Lucy, (Mrs.), Apr. 1, 1841
Luray, s. of Elder Samuel
  Davidson, Nov. 25, 1841
Olivia C., w. of Rev. A. F.
  Davidson, Mar. 4, 1869
Reuben, Sept. 17, 1846
Thomas Osborne, Mar. 14,
  1929
Virginia Archer, d. of
  William B. and Mary P.
  Davidson, Nov. 5, 1868
William (Rev.), May 30, 1844
William S., June 24, 1897
William W., Sept. 14, 1838

DAVIES
  Mildred, Mar. 18, 1847
  Susan, w. of Landon Davies,
  d. of Col. B. Todd, Oct.
  31, 1867
  Susan Clements, w. of Landon
  L. Davies, d. of Col. John
  and Juliet Jeffries Pollard,
  Jan. 19, 1911

DAVIS
  Abram W., May 7, 1857
  Alice, July 14, 1881
  Ann O., w. of William W.
  Davis, Jan. 17, 1867
  Anna, d. of George W. Davis,
  June 13, 1901
  Anna F., w. of George S.
  Davis, Sept. 29, 1892
  Annie (Mrs.), Feb. 6, 1919
  B. C., Aug. 4, 1927
  C. C. (Rev.), Apr. 22,
  1926
  C. C., May 15, 1930
  C. H., Apr. 15, 1858
  Caroline D., d. of Rev.
  Thomas Pettus, Mar. 11,
  1886
  Catharine, w. of Abram W.
  Davis, May 7, 1857
  Charles H., July 27, 1922
  Columbia P., Dec. 6, 1860
  Cornelius H. (Dr.), s. of
  A. W. and Julia F. Davis,
  Nov. 11, 1920
  Decatur O., Oct. 19, 1911
  Delight T., d. of Dr. H.
  Wythe and M. E. Davis,
  Feb. 13, 1879
  Edmonia R., w. of W. T.
  Davis, Nov. 30, 1916
  Elizabeth B., w. of Richard
  A. Davis, Sr., Apr. 30,
  1868
  Elizabeth G., w. of Thomas
  Davis, Apr. 9, 1863
  Elizabeth H., w. of Col.
  J. Lucius Davis, d. of
  John C. Pick, July 2,
  1857
  Elizabeth W., w. of William
  T. Davis, Nov. 13, 1884
  Fannie Hitt (Mrs.), Nov.
  4, 1920
  Fielden C., s. of John
  Davis, Mar. 21, 1861
  Frances, w. of Richard Davis,
  Oct. 29, 1846
  G. R., Mar. 30, 1843
  George S., Sept. 26, Oct.
  3, 1918
  George Thomas, June 3, 1937

OBITUARY NOTICES IN THE RELIGIOUS HERALD WITH DATES OF PUBLICATION

Hardin, Nov. 14, 1850
Henry E. (Rev.), Nov. 30, 1865
J. A. (Rev.), Nov. 19, 1903
J. D. SEARS (Mrs.), Feb. 12, 1925
J. J., Dec. 22, 1887
Jackson, June 2, 1898
James A., Oct. 18, 1877
James Hervey, Oct. 10, 1867
James Rawlin, Oct. 30, 1862
Jane E. (Mrs.), Mar. 21, 1907
Jane S., w. of John S. Davis, Apr. 19, 1833
Jefferson, Dec. 12, 1889
Jefferson (Mrs.), Oct. 25, 1906
John (Rev.), July 2, 1846
John (Elder), Jan. 8, 1852
John F., Oct. 23, 1924
John W., s. of I. W. Davis, Feb. 11, 1897
John W. (Dr.), Nov. 17, 1927
John W., Feb. 26, 1931
Joseph C., Feb. 14, 1907
Judith Noel, Jan. 21, 1869
Laura Alice, d. of W. W. and Anne O. Davis, Apr. 3, 1862
Lewellyn Catesby, s. of Col. J. Lucius Davis, Feb. 12, 1863
Lillie (Mrs.), May 10, 1928
Llewellyn (Mrs.), Dec. 13, 1883
Lucy (Mrs.), July 7, 1898
Lucy A., Aug. 26, 1886
Malissa Belle, d. of James M. and S. A. Davis, July 3, 1890
Marie E. (Mrs.), Dec. 25, 1890
Martha E., w. of Rev. James A. Davis, Apr. 17, 1862
Martha E., d. of M. M. and Lucy E. Davis, May 25, 1871
Martha R., w. of Miles Davis, July 11, 1872
Mary, w. of Dr. Marion Davis, Jan. 13, 1870
Mary, w. of Dr. H. Wythe Davis, Aug. 30, 1900
Mary A., w. of G. L. Davis d. of Joseph and Ann Williams Davis, June 1, 1876
Mary A. (Mrs.), Jan. 23, 1890
Mary Ann (Mrs.), Mar. 13, 1851
Mary C. (Mrs.), Aug. 29, 1828
Mary Ellen, Dec. 22, 1887
Mary Frances, d. of Alfred C. Davis, Feb. 28, 1861
Mary Jane, w. of William Davis, June 21, 1860
Mary Louisa, Feb. 22, 1894
Matthew J., Dec. 27, 1855
Matthew Moyle, May 21, 1914
May, d. of George F. Davis, Oct. 13, 1870
McKensie, May 5, 1870
N. K. (Mrs.), Mar. 26, 1914
Nancy, w. of M. J. Davis, May 7, 1840
Nancy, w. of Stephen Davis, Mar. 17, 1853
Nancy N., w. of Matthias J. Davis, Oct. 22, 1846
Nannie E., July 1, 1926
Nannie Moore, Mar. 14, Apr. 18, 1929
Nora Bell, d. of Rev. J. A. Davis, Aug. 21, 1862
Olivia, June 2, 1892
P. H. (Mrs.), Sept. 14, 1882
Polly, sister of Wilson Davis, May 7, 1857
Richard A., Apr. 30, 1868
Robert, gr. s. of Abram W. and Catherine Davis, May 7, 1857
Robert C., Aug. 15, 1834
Robert Catesby, s. of J. Lucius and E. Harriet Davis, Mar. 20, 1856
Robert Christopher, s. of J. Lucius and E. Harriet Davis, July 17, 1856
Robert W., s. of Henry E. Davis, May 6, 1852

OBITUARY NOTICES IN THE RELIGIOUS HERALD WITH DATES OF PUBLICATION

Robert W., Dec. 29, 1864
Ruby Margaret, d. of John J. and Rebecca Davis, Mar. 2, 1893
Sallie (Mrs.), June 27, 1878
Sallie A., w. of Rev. H. E. Davis, Aug. 26, 1860
Sallie E., Mar. 1, 1860
Sally, July 21, 1859
Samuel, June 4, 1874
Sarah, w. of John Davis, Sept. 29, 1881
Sarah Alice, w. of D. O. Davis, d. of William Tyree, June 21, 1900
Sarah D., w. of Maj. Davis, June 20, July 11, 1844
Sarah E. (Mrs.), Sept. 11, 1879
Sarah Isabella, d. of William W. and Ann O. Davis, Sept. 22, 1864
Sarah R., w. of John T. Davis, d. of Lewis Chandoin, Apr. 22, 1869
Septimus, s. of J. Lucius and Elizabeth H. Davis, May 12, 1853
Shelton, May 31, 1860
Susan Jeffries, w. of Rev. J. A. Davis, Sept. 20, 1906
Susannah R. (Mrs.), mother of John C. Watkins, Mar. 2, 1899
W. H., Feb. 27, 1908
Wallis, child of Middleton M. and Lucy E. Davis, May 25, 1871
William, Sept. 14, 1882
William C., June 25, 1868
William D. (Dr.), s. of Elder John Davis, July 29, 1858
William Russell, Mar. 27, 1930
William Weaver, Feb. 18, 1897
Willie H., s. of Allen and Sarah Davis, June 16, 1881
Willie Johnson, w. of Thomas Davis, Feb. 21, 1929
Wirt E., Nov. 5, 1885; Mar. 11, 1886

DAVISON
Byrdie Bell, July 11, 1889

DAVISSON
Bettie, d. of Theodore N. and Sallie Davisson, Oct. 30, 1862
Sallie Rodgers (Mrs.), Mar. 14, 1895

DAWE
P. W. (Mrs.), d. of Capt. J. S. Pickett, Apr. 16, 1846

DAWSON
Cornelius G., Feb. 24, 1853
Helen Frances, d. of Edward Binford Dawson, Oct. 12, 1922
Leroy F. (Elder), Sept. 20, 1860
Lewis A., Oct. 31, 1844
Martin (Elder), June 19, 1873
William H., Sept. 8, 1887

DAY
Casandra, Feb. 3, 1848*
Catharine, May 16, 1828
Joana, Oct. 27, 1859
Julia Ann, May 10, 1860
Katie, d. of John H. and Emma Day, May 7, 1885
Lucy (Mrs.), Apr. 23, 1830
Mary A., w. of Judge Joseph Day, Aug. 13, 1903
Susan (Mrs.), Feb. 9, 1854
William H., May 21, 1863

DEACON
Mary A. (Mrs.), Mar. 6, 1879

DEADY
Anna Elizabeth, d. of William J. Deady, July 10, 1862

DEALE
W. H., Nov. 30, Dec. 28, 1916

DEANE
Francis H. (Dr.), Jan. 27, 1870

DEANS
Elizabeth A. (Mrs.), July 27,

---

* Possible inaccuracy in name, or spelling, but given as printed

OBITUARY NOTICES IN THE RELIGIOUS HERALD WITH DATES OF PUBLICATION

27, 1893
Elizabeth Mary (Mrs.), July 8, 1875
Elizabeth Mary, sister of Rev. Joseph F. Deans, Nov. 5, 1891
Erma Saunders (Mrs.), Apr. 28, 1932
Irma Wise, d. of Rev. Joseph Franklin and Mrs. Lightfoot Poindexter Deans, June 18, 1896
Joseph Douglas, s. of Rev. J. F. and Lighttie Deans, Dec. 24, 1885
Joseph Franklin (Rev.), Feb. 12 and 26, Mar. 5, 1903
L. L., w. of J. F. Deans, Jan. 7 and 28, 1937
Richard, Mar. 29, 1855
Willie Lightfoot, s. of Rev. Joseph F. Deans, July 20, 1882

DEATHERAGE
Catharine (Mrs.), June 28, 1860
George (Capt.), May 23, 1834
Thomas, Apr. 22, 1886

DEATLY
Lucy, w. of James Deatly, Sr., Aug. 4, 1837

DEATON
William S., Feb. 27, 1862

DECK
Fannie C., w. of D. M. Deck, Feb. 4, 1892

DECKER
Walter John, Dec. 6, 1928

DECORMIS
Joseph, Sr., Apr. 11, June 6, 1844
Joseph, Nov. 18, 1847
Susan, w. of Joseph Decormis, June 4, 1846

DEERING
Clarence, June 13, 1907

DeHART
J. H., Apr. 11, 1861

DEITRICK
A. P., Jan. 30, 1879
Bettie Mills, d. of William A. and Mary L. Deitrick, May 25, 1870
Evelina Anville, d. of Jacob L. and Pattie E. Deitrick, Oct. 15, 1863
Sallie A., w. of Capt. William A. Deitrick, Nov. 12, 1874
Sallie W., d. of William Deitrick, Jan. 6, 1859
William A. (Capt.), May 10, 1866

DEJARNATTE**
J. C. (Mrs.), d. of Alexander Herndon, June 18, 1896

DeJARNATTE
J. Elliotte, s. of James C. and Lucy M. DeJarnatte, Oct. 17, 1912
William Y., Dec. 17, 1840

DeJARNETT*
Daniel, Nov. 7, 1850

DEJARNETTE**
Elizabeth (Mrs.), Dec. 24, 1863
Huldah (Mrs.), Aug. 22, 1860
Nannie C., May 14, 1857

DeJARNETTE
Cora (Mrs.), d. of Rev. M. T. Sumner, Jan. 14, 1869
James C., June 25, 1931
James D., Apr. 26, 1894
Lucy Lee, d. of James C. and Lucy Mary Herndon DeJarnette, June 13, 1918
Sallie Lewis, d. of Elliot DeJarnette, Dec. 30, 1847

DEJERNATT*
Martha, w. of John Dejernatt, Sept. 23, 1836**

DELAND
D. B. (Judge), Jan. 2, 1873

DELANEY
Mary Biglow, w. of Chester H. Delaney, June 8, 1905

DELAPLANE
Mildred (Mrs.), May 22, 1902

DELK
B. Hardy, Mar. 17, 1921
Lizzie Maie, Feb. 24, 1921

* Possible inaccuracy in name, or spelling, but given as printed
** Spelled with a small j

OBITUARY NOTICES IN THE RELIGIOUS HERALD WITH DATES OF PUBLICATION

DeMENT
  Byron Hoover, Mar. 30, Apr. 6, 1933
DEMPSEY
  Absalom Cornelius (Rev.), July 11 and 18, 1872
  Elizabeth, w. of Rev. Absalom Dempsey, May 1, 1873
  Perlina W., d. of Wilson M. and Perlina Dempsey, Aug. 27, 1863*
  Sallie, d. of Wilson M. and Paulina Dempsey, Apr. 14, 1859
DENNING
  M. Virginia (Mrs.), d. of Thomas G. Bell, Dec. 20, 1877
DENNIS
  William J., Jan. 29, 1863
DENNISSON
  B. F., Jan. 1, 1903
DENNY
  Mattie Mosely, d. of R. S. and Otera F. Denny, June 3, 1880
DENSON
  James F., Apr. 21, 1870
DENTON
  Allen, Aug. 20, 1857
DEPRIEST
  Virginia Ann, d. of William F. and Ann P. Depriest, Apr. 6, 1848
DERIEUX
  Annie L., d. of Rollo Derieux, Jan. 11, 1906
  Lucy Ann, w. of Alfred Derieux, Apr. 12, 1855
  Virginia F., mother of Dr. W. T. Derieux, Sept. 22, Oct. 27, 1910
  W. T. (Dr.), Mar. 10, 1938
DERRING
  Ollie Guy, July 13, 1911
DESPER
  Wanda Grover Cleveland, d. of James and Penelope Desper, June 25, 1885
DEVIER
  Bettie A., d. of Giles Devier, July 17, 1873
  Lelia, d. of Giles and Kitty Devier, June 26, 1873
DEVIN
  James, Sept. 14, 1854
DEW
  Anna Maria, d. of Benjamin F. and Mary S. Dew, Oct. 26, 1854
  B. F., Nov. 8, 1877
  Catharine, d. of John W. and Catharine Dew, July 14, 1842
  Catharine, w. of John W. Dew, Mar. 7, 1844
  Ellen, w. of William Dew, d. of William D. Gresham, Jan. 25, 1872
  Fanny Susan, w. of B. F. Dew, Nov. 15, 1855
  Franklin, Oct. 28, 1880
  John, s. of John W. and Catharine Dew, July 14, 1842
  Juliet T., w. of Roderick Dew, d. of Rev. Thomas B. Evans and sister of Judge A. B. Evans, Feb. 23, 1893
  Lucy, w. of Thomas Dew, Dec. 3, 1857
  Lucy A., d. of Mrs. Elizabeth Dejarnette, Nov. 12, Dec. 24, 1863
  Mary Emma, d. of Roderick and Juliet T. Dew, Nov. 17, 1870
  Roderick Jr., s. of Roderick and Juliet Dew, Nov. 17, 1870
  Roderick, Dec. 9, 1880
  Sallie Browne, d. of Roderick Dew, Mar. 3, 1932
  Thomas (Capt.), May 24, 1849
  W. D., Mar. 1, 1934
DEWEES
  Mary (Mrs.), Aug. 11, 1842
DEWRY
  Washington Randolph, s. of Robert W. and Annie Dewry, Nov. 30, 1871
DEY
  Frances Lee, May 30, 1907
  George W. (Mrs.), w. of G. W.

---

* Possible inaccuracy in name, or spelling, but given as printed

OBITUARY NOTICES IN THE RELIGIOUS HERALD WIYH DATES OF PUBLICATION

Dey, Nov. 26, 1908; Jan. 21, 1909
George Walters, June 18, 1925
DIBRELL
L. (Dr.), s. of C. L. and Mary Dibrell, Feb. 3, 1848
DICK
Sarah L., Feb. 13, 1873
DICKENS
Charles, Jan. 27, 1859
DICKENSON
Clementine (Mrs.), May 9, 1861
David V. (Col.), Nov. 12, 1885
James, May 18, 1882
Ralph, Sept. 29, 1870
DICKERSON
A. M. (Mrs.), Feb. 25, 1904
Abbigail C., w. of Thomas Dickerson, Nov. 2, 1854
Agnes S. (Mrs.), Oct. 11, 1923
Carl Henry, Oct. 15, 1925
Christianna, w. of Elder C. Dickerson, Jan. 14, 1858
George Winston, s. of Jacob W. and Catherine Dickerson, Aug. 27, 1857
James T., Jr., s. of James T. Dickerson, Aug. 4, 1910
Joseph W., May 20, 1886
Lucy, w. of John F. Dickerson, May 21, 1908
William, May 14, 1863
Willie Ersa, s. of William A. and Sarah R. Dickerson, Jan. 30, 1879
DICKEY
John Roby (Dr.), Oct. 25, Nov. 22, 1923
DICKINSON
A. E. (Mrs.), Sept. 2, 1897
A. E. (Dr.), Nov. 22 and 29, 1906
Alfred Ernest, s. of Rev. A. E. and Fannie E. Dickinson, Nov. 16, 1865
Ann (Mrs.), July 13, 1843
Ann E., d. of Theuston Dickinson, Mar. 26, 1857

C. R. (Dr.), July 29, Sept. 16, 1880
Charles Grandison, Apr. 24, 1884
Charlotte, w. of J. J. Dickinson, Aug. 10, 1848
Corinne, w. of Rev. Jeter G. Dickinson, July 13, 1899
Crispin (Dr.), Dec. 6, 1888
Elizabeth W., w. of J. S. Dickinson, Aug. 31, 1876
Emily Frances, d. of Ralph N. and Lina M. Dickinson, Oct. 15, 1898
Eugene, Aug. 27, 1908
Fannie E., w. of Rev. A. E. Dickinson, d. of Rev. James B. Taylor, Oct. 30, 1879
Frances, w. of Charles Dickinson, Mar. 25, 1841
Frances Ann, w. of Ralph Dickinson, Feb. 22, 1866
Francis Gray, s. of James Gray and Elizabeth Cave Dickinson, Feb. 4, 1904
Frank P. (Dr.), Mar. 14, 1935
Griffith, Mar. 29, 1839
Hugh M., Nov. 29, 1888
James S., Sept. 29, 1859
James T. (Dr.), May 2, 1929
Jane, w. of Robert W. Dickinson, May 12, 1842
Janie Prichard, d. of Dr. A. E. Dickinson, May 2 and 16, 1918
Jennie, w. of C. G. Dickinson, Apr. 21, 1881
John J., May 27, 1852
Julia W., Oct. 9, 1924
Leonard Mansfield, s. of Ralph N. and Luia E. Dickinson, Sept. 28, 1876
Loomis Look, s. of Dr. S. W. Dickinson, May 4, June 8, 1882
Lou C. (Mrs.), Sept. 16, 1897
Lucy, w. of Dr. C. R. Dickinson, Sept. 29, 1859
Margaret, w. of Theuston Dickinson, Feb. 24, 1859
Mary, d. of Rev. A. E. and Fannie E. Dickinson, Sept.

OBITUARY NOTICES IN THE RELIGIOUS HERALD WITH DATES OF PUBLICATION

23, 1875
Mary F., w. of James
 Dickinson, Mar. 24, 1864
Mary Fannie, d. of Rev. A. E.
 and Fannie E. Dickinson,
 Aug. 23, 1860
Mary Williams, w. of L. R.
 Dickinson, d. of Rev. J. B.
 Taylor, June 27, 1907
Minnie Goodwin (Mrs,), Jan.
 15, 1914
Nancy, w. of Thomas Dickinson,
 Oct. 1, 1840
Nancy, w. of John Dickinson,
 July 31, 1862
Necayah, w. of Dr. W. P.
 Dickinson, d. of Capt. P.
 O. Lipscomb, July 30, 1857
Patsie Quarles, d. of Ralph
 Dickinson, Dec. 1, 1853
Ralph N., May 3, 1900
Ralph Q., Mar. 22, 1877
Roy C., s. of Mrs. Kate
 Dickinson, June 3, 1909
S. T. (Dr.), s. of W. W.
 Dickinson, Nov. 2, 1905
S. W. (Dr.), Nov. 10, 1932
Sallie Archer, Nov. 11, 1886
Sally Jane, d. of Hiram B.
 Dickinson, July 22, 1847
V. H. (Mrs.), Jan. 14, 1904
Virginia C., d. of W. C. and
 V. H. Dickinson, Mar. 13, 1884
W. P., Feb. 6, 1896
William A., s. of Rev. C.
 Dickinson, Jan. 28, 1858
William Gustavus, s. of Hiram
 D. and Sally H. Dickinson,
 July 3, 1845
DICKSON
 Nancy, w. of Capt. Samuel
 Dickson, Jan. 29, 1845
DIDLAKE
 Henry, Oct. 18, 1877
DIGGES
 Thomas A., Apr. 20, 1882
DIGGS
 Elizabeth P., w. of John Diggs,
 Mar. 2, 1854
Ella Samuel, w. of R. D. Diggs,
 July 6, 1899
Emma Jane, d. of Samuel L. and
 Mary F. Diggs, Dec. 25, 1873
Fannie Foster, d. of Rev.
 Isaac and Ann E. Diggs, Feb.
 4, 1864
Harriet Muse, d. of Rev. Isaac
 and Ann E. Diggs, Feb. 4,
 1864
Isaac (Elder), Aug. 7, Sept.
 4, 1873
Isaac, Dec. 21, 1922
John, May 7, 1863
Kate S., d. of Elder Isaac
 Diggs, July 15, 1858
Robert Dudley, Mar. 29, 1928
Sue Fleet, d. of Rev. Isaac
 Diggs, Sept. 21, 1876
Thomas, Aug. 31, 1843
Thomas Jackson, s. of Rev.
 Isaac and Ann E. Diggs, Feb.
 4, 1864
DIKE
 Anna E., May 21, 1857
DILL
 Amanda J., w. of J. M. Dill,
 Dec. 4, 1873
J. M., Dec. 5, 1907
William M., Jan. 19, 1871
DILLARD
 Anna, d. of James T. Dillard,
 Oct. 8, 1863
Annie Lee (Mrs.), Sept. 13,
 1923
Annie S., d. of John J. and
 Sallie C. Dillard, Aug. 6,
 1891
Dewetta Henry Minor (Mrs.),
 Oct. 7, 1920
Edward Farmer (Rev.), Nov.
 24, Dec. 29, 1898
Emily T. (Mrs.), Oct. 14,
 1880
Hardenia, Apr. 11, 1912
Jacob, Feb. 24, 1887
James, Feb. 4, 1892
James M., Feb. 6, 1894
John T., s. of James T.
 Dillard, Oct. 8, 1863
Martha A., w. of James T.

OBITUARY NOTICES IN THE RELIGIOUS HERALD WITH DATES OF PUBLICATION

Oct. 8, 1863
Mary C., Jan. 1, 1852
Mary Ellen (Mrs.), d. of D. M.
  G. Fauntleroy, Oct. 8, 1863
Mary Walker, May 3, 1906
Mattie, d. of Robert F.
  Dillard, Mar. 16, 1876
Nannie, Mar. 14, 1907
Stephen H., Jan. 9, 1829
W. F., Apr. 8, 1926
DIMNE
  Agnes N., Jan. 16, 1873
  Ira L., July 22, 1886
DIMURE
  Maria, w. of William Dimure,
    Aug. 16, 1894
DISHMAN
  Ann, w. of James Dishman,
    Mar. 17 and 31, 1859
  James W., Jan. 23, 1913
DIUGUID
  George A., Jr., May 3, 1934
  Laughton, June 22, 1905
DIVERS
  Francis, Sept. 27, 1839
DIX
  Levin W., s. of William A.
    and Elizabeth Dix, Mar.
    19, 1840
  Mary C., w. of Rev. Revin
    Dix, Nov. 23, 1848
  Nancy, Oct. 8, 1925
  Peggy (Mrs.), Feb. 3, 1921
DIXON
  Charles B., July 26, 1923
  Charles M., June 10, 1937
  Fannie, Mar. 5, 1936
  Linda Hayes, w. of William
    P. Dixon, Oct. 23, 1902
  Mary P., w. of Capt. William Dixon, May 23, 1849
  Mary W. (Mrs.), July 26, 1833
  N. A. (Mrs.), Jan. 23, 1890
  Thomas Henry, s. of William N.
    and M. A. Dixon, Dec. 18, 1856
DOAN
  James Randolph (Rev.), Sept.
    28, 1922
DOBBS
  C. E. W. (Rev.), Oct. 5, 1916

Martha, Oct. 4, 1900
DOBIE
  Ann L., w. of R. L. Dobie,
    Aug. 22, 1861
  Ethel, d. of Richard L. and
    Millie P. Dobie, Jan. 1,
    1885
  Gracie Hood, Jan. 19, 1911
  Harry Lundy, s. of R. M. and
    Sallie L. Dobie, June 8, 1882
  Indiana Broughton, w. of R. L.
    Dobie, d. of W. D. Taylor,
    July 2, 1874
  Janie G., w. of R. L. Dobie,
    d. of Capt. W. E. Proctor,
    June 27, 1895
  R. L., May 16, 1895
  R. L., Apr. 14, 1904
DOBSON
  Ann Elizabeth, d. of John T.
    and Sarah G. Dobson, Oct.
    19, 1854
  R. S. (Dr.), Mar. 23, 1882
DOBYNS
  George H., Feb. 21, 1895
  Leroy W., May 18, 1871
  Thomas, Nov. 27, 1845
  Venagus A., w. of Leroy W.
    Dobyns, Aug. 17, 1843
DODD
  Charles Hastings, Aug. 31,
    Oct. 12, 1933
  Helen Scott, d. of John B.
    and Bettie Dodd, June 11,
    1863
  L. Ashton, Aug. 20, 1936
  Pauline (Mrs.), Aug. 1, 1929
  Rosie (Sister), June 20, 1872
  Sallie Nash (Mrs.), Jan. 31,
    1935
DODGE
  Edward Brown, s. of Rev. Henry
    W. Dodge, Mar. 17, 1853
  Mary, d. of Henry W. Dodge,
    July 10, 1851
  Henry W. (Rev.), June 22, 1899
DODSON
  Ann, w. of James Dodson, Apr.
    16, 1857
  Beverly S., July 31, 1930

OBITUARY NOTICES IN THE RELIGIOUS HERALD WITH DATES OF PUBLICATION

Elias, Jan. 4, 1883
Elias (Rev.), Dec. 8, 1898
Emma F., Jan. 12, 1928
Joseph H., Nov. 5, 1885
Lucy A., w. of W. W. Dodson,
   July 20, 1871
P. H., Nov. 24, 1927
DOFFERMYERE
   J. N. (Mrs.), July 13, 1922
DOGAN
   R. J. (Rev.), May 31, Jan. 26,
   1928
DOGGETT
   D. S. (Rev.), Nov. 4, 1880
   Martha G., w. of Henry
   Doggett, Apr. 16, 1857
DOLD
   Ethel Hayes (Mrs.), w. of
   A. I. Dold, d. of O. J.
   and Anna Hayes, Aug. 8, 1901
DOLES
   Jacqueline Batten (Mrs.),
   Oct. 5, 1933
DOLIN
   James, Sept. 25, 1873
   Susan, d. of Thomas Dolin,
   Aug. 16, 1855
DOLL
   J. Whitefield, child of Elder
   John A. Doll, Feb. 11, 1858
   John A. (Rev.), Mar. 26, 1896
   William P., s. of Elder John A.
   and Sarah A. Doll, Apr. 11,
   1861
DOLLINS
   Henry, s. of John Dollins,
   Mar. 8, 1894
DONIPHAN
   Joseph (Judge), June 5,
   1873
DONNAHAW
   Ella F., d. of Richard H.
   and Anna Cloudis Donnahaw,
   Mar. 14, 1935
DONNELLY
   Estelle Gill, w. of Rev. C.
   Shirley Donnelly, Jan. 3,
   1929
DONOVAN
   Newton (Mrs.), Mar. 13, 1913

DOOLEY
   Thomas (Rev.), Aug. 29,
   1901
DOORES
   Elizabeth, w. of Edwin
   Doores, d. of J. S.
   Munroe, Feb. 10, 1848
DORAN
   Susan Covington (Mrs.),
   Dec. 3, 1925
DORMON
   Linda Glenn, Apr. 20, 1911
DORNEY
   Sylvester, Oct. 5, 1893
DORSET
   Julia, Jan. 8, 1891
   Margaret (Mrs.), Mar. 3,
   1864
   Mary, Nov. 29, 1866
   Victoria, w. of W. C.
   Dorset, Oct. 5, 1899
   William M. (Dr.), Apr. 18,
   1872
DORSETT
   Catharine (Mrs.), Nov. 15,
   1849
   Elizabeth (Mrs.), Apr. 23,
   1830
   Emma E., w. of Dr. J. L.
   Dorsett, d. of C. E. Chapell, Oct. 5, 1854
DORSEY
   S. C. (Rev.), Apr. 7, Aug.
   11, 1898
DOSS
   Luther S., June 6, 1929
   Overstreet, Apr. 30, 1863
DOTEY
   Martha E. FEATHERSTON (Mrs.),
   Apr. 18, 1878
DOUGHTY
   Mabel Mercer (Mrs.),
   Apr. 4, 1929
DOUGLASS
   Elizabeth, w. of Richard Douglass, Mar. 3,
   1853
DOUTHAT
   Robert, May 23, 1828
DOVE

OBITUARY NOTICES IN THE RELIGIOUS HERALD WITH DATES OF PUBLICATION

J. T., June 5, 1902
DOW
    Lorenzo, Feb. 14, 1834
DOWDY
    Emma (Mrs.), Feb. 6, 1919
    Emmett G., Mar. 17, 1898
    John T. (Capt.), July 27, 1882
    William S., June 17, 1880
DOWELL
    Jesse, Mar. 12, 1868
DOWNER
    Larkin, Jan. 21, 1841
    Lucy M. (Mrs.), Feb. 23, 1907
    W. W., Jan. 20, 1921
DOWNES
    Alice Simkins, w. of Thomas H. Downes, May 24, 1928
    Edward Preston, Jan. 21, 1875
DOWNEY
    John, June 22, 1832
    John Tucker, s. of Rev. J. W. Downey, Jan. 11, 1912
DOWNING
    Eliza N., w. of Robert E. Downing, Apr. 30, 1840
    Elizabeth (Mrs.), May 11, 1838
    Julian E., Oct. 5, 1922
    Mary A. (Mrs.), d. of Rev. William H. Kirk, Nov. 14, 1889
    Mary B. (Mrs.), d. of Col. Thomas D. Eubank, May 6, 1897
    Samuel (Col.), Apr. 12, 1839
DOWNMAN
    Joseph H. (Dr.), Jan. 28, 1831
DOWNS
    Betsy (Mrs.), June 18, 1857
DOX
    Mary Ann, d. of H. M. and Ella Dox, Feb. 7, 1861
DOYLE
    George, Oct. 7, 1858
    John, Apr. 3, 1829
    Sallie E. (Mrs.), Apr. 8, May 20, 1909
    William, Jan. 31, 1895
DOZIER
    Wilson B., Apr. 27, 1854

DRAKE
    Elmina, w. of G. W. Drake, d. of John Wood, Apr. 16, 1874
    Francis O., Nov. 26, 1846
    Francis T., Mar. 5, 1891
    Grandison Werter, s. of William Bell and Sarah Ball Drake, gr.s. of Isham Ball, Mar. 8, 1917
    John A. (Mrs.), Sept. 19, 1918
    R. A., Sept. 9, 1897
    Samuel W., Oct. 15, 1846
    William M., June 25, 1885
DRAPER
    Robert O. May 1, 1862
DRAYTON
    Alfred L., Feb. 20, 1862
DREWRY
    Henry, Oct. 10, 1828
    Mamie Crews, w. of Dr. David Barnes Drewry, May 23, 1901
    Robert Hudgins, s. of Robert W. and Annie Drewry, Jan. 12, 1865
DRINKARD
    Alfred Washington, July 20, 1933
    Amanda (Mrs.), Sept. 24, 1885
    Lucy (Mrs.), June 4, 1908
    Martha Jane, Feb. 15, 1934
    Mary, w. of William Drinkard, Jan. 17, Apr. 18, 1889
    William F. (Capt.), July 14, 1898
DRISCOLL
    H. S. (Rev.), Nov. 20, 1930
DRUIN
    Samuel, Mar. 10, 1842
DRUMHELLER
    Henry Austin, Feb. 23, 1928
DRUMMOND
    Eleshea Ann, w. of John R. Drummond, Nov. 19, 1874
    John R., July 13, 1882
    Louis D., Aug. 21, 1879
    Mary, w. of William C. Drummond, Feb. 17, 1832
    R. H., Mar. 9, 1922
DRURY
    Walter G., Jan. 6, 1881

OBITUARY NOTICES IN THE RELIGIOUS HERALD WITH DATES OF PUBLICATION

DUANE
  Buena Vista (Mrs.), Jan. 15, 1880
  Dennis, s. of J. C. Duane,
    Oct. 15, 1896
DUCKWILER
  Joseph, Mar. 8, 1877
DUDLEY
  E. E. (Dr.), Mar. 22, Apr. 12,
    1934
  Ella, Aug. 31, 1871
  Emmette Edgar, Jr., May 17,
    July 26, 1923
  Gerald Owen, s. of Rev. E. E.
    Dudley, Aug. 20, 1925
  H. M. (Judge), Sept. 26, 1907
  Henrietta G., w. of Capt.
    Griffin G. Dudley, Mar. 17,
    1842
  Lysander, Sept. 17, 1874
  Martha, w. of Alex Dudley,
    July 5, 1866
  Peyton G., Mar. 5, 1874
  R. M. (Dr.), Jan. 12, 1893
  Robert S., Apr. 2, 1891
  William T., July 14, 1887
DUER
  Steppie, w. of Capt. Rufus
    Duer, d. of Maj. Fitzhugh,
    Jan. 28, 1875
DUERSON
  Henry, July 10, 1879
  Maria, w. of Joseph Duerson,
    Jr., Aug. 16, 1839
  Mary Ellen, d. of F. L. and
    M. E. Duerson, Aug. 20, 1891
  Virgil O., s. of E. V. and
    S. G. Duerson, Aug. 14, 1890
  W. H. (Mrs.), Dec. 1, 1921
DUFREE
  Elizabeth C., w. of D. R.
    Dufree, d. of James Bosum,
    June 4, 1857
DUGGAN
  Janie Prichard, w. of Dr.
    James Reynolds Duggan, d.
    of Rev. John Lamb and Jane
    Elizabeth Taylor Prichard,
    Aug. 25, 1938
DUGGER
  Adelaid G., w. of Daniel
    Dugger, June 19, 1930
  Bettie E. MASON, w. of A. T.
    Dugger, July 15, 1886
  Lucy, d. of A. T. and Eliza-
    beth Dugger, Sept. 4, 1879
DUGGINS
  Indiana H., w. of William F.
    Duggins, Nov. 15, 1894
  William F., Jr., Nov. 15, 1894
DUKE
  Ann C., w. of Alfred Duke, May
    22, 1856
  Ann Elizabeth, w. of Jabez F.
    Duke, d. of William G.
    Walton, Feb. 17, 1921
  Ann O., w. of Thomas Duke,
    May 25, 1843
  Archibald B. (Capt.), Jan.
    23, 1845
  Bettie A., May 27, Oct. 21,
    1926
  Burnie, Jan. 27, 1832
  Claude Walter (Rev.),
    Sept. 10 and 17, Oct. 1,
    1936
  Edmund W., Sept. 10, 1863
  Elizabeth Southard, w. of T.
    H. Duke, Feb. 18, 1937
  Francis J., Jan. 4, 1906
  Frank W., Sept. 3, 1925
  James (Mrs.), Mar. 7, 1834
  James A. (Capt.), Mar. 26,
    1891
  John B. (Dr.), s. of Burnly Duke,
    Dec. 28, 1832
  Laura J., w. of Philip St.
    John Duke, d. of Josephus
    Gregory, Sept. 20, 1877
  Mary C., d. of Edmond and
    Susan Duke, Oct. 18, 1839
  Philip St. J., May 23, 1929
  Richard S., Jan. 6, 1848
  Sallie L., w. of Abram Duke,
    Dec. 8, 1921
  Susan E., w. of Edmond Duke,
    Sept. 10, 1863
  Thomas H., Feb. 18, 1937
  Victoria E., d. of Edmond W.
    and Susan Duke, Jan. 1, 1863
  Virginia A. (Mrs.), Feb. 27,

OBITUARY NOTICES IN THE RELIGIOUS HERALD WITH DATES OF PUBLICATION

1890
William, Feb. 23, 1854
William B., s. of Edmund Duke,
   Nov. 6, 1873
DULANEY
   William (Col.), Sept. 30, 1841
DULIN
   Amanda Washington, w. of B. P.
      Dulin, Apr. 14, 1892
   B. P. (Rev.), May 2, 1895
   Edward Judson, s. of Rev. B. P.
      Dulin, Nov. 15, 1877
   Martha Ann, Aug. 7, 1856
   Matilda M., w. of Burr P. Dulin,
      Nov. 18, 1841
   Roberta (Mrs.), Sept. 15, 1921
DULING
   Catherine G., Mar. 22, 1860
   Elizabeth Carey, w. of Rev.
      W. B. Duling, Apr. 4, 1929
   William Brooke, Nov. 19, 1931
DULTON
   Frances (Mrs.), Aug. 3, 1854
DUNAWAY
   A. B. (Mrs.), Apr. 27, 1916
   Alice Chilton, d. of Rev. J.
      Manning Dunaway, May 24,
      1906
   Ann Maria, w. of Dr. Thomas
      S. Dunaway, Feb. 23, 1899
   Anna C. (Mrs.), Apr. 5, 1888
   Clara Belle, d. of Beverly R.
      and Maria Dunaway, Mar. 1,
      1888
   Elizabeth J., w. of Dr. A. B.
      Dunaway, Apr. 13, 1916
   Felecia T., w. of Col. Thomas
      S. Dunaway, Sept. 16, 1852
   J. Manning (Rev.), Apr. 13,
      1922
   John, Dec. 15, 1898
   Martha Ellen, w. of Rev. A.
      B. Dunaway, May 12, 1881
   Mary (Mrs.), July 27, 1882
   Millie E., d. of Rawleigh
      Dunaway, Mar. 16, 1848
   Nannie Pollard, d. of Dr.
      W. F. Dunaway, Jan. 31,
      Feb. 7, Mar. 7, 1918
   Raleigh, Apr. 14, 1881

   Rawleigh, Sr., Feb. 17, Mar. 9,
      1848
   Sophronia, Sept. 12, 1844
   Susan S., Sept. 12, 1844
   Thomas S. (Col.), Mar. 21,
      1844
   Thomas S. (Rev.), Dec. 2 and
      9, 1915
   Thomas S., Feb. 25, 1932
   Urbane Brett, s. of R. Dun-
      away, Sr., Feb. 23, 1843
   Walter R., Sept. 12, 1844
   Walter Raleigh, s. of Raleigh
      and Anna C. Dunaway, Nov. 8,
      1849
   Wayland F. (Dr.), June 29, July
      6, 1916
   Wayland F. (Mrs.), w. of Dr.
      W. F. Dunaway, Nov. 21, 1918
DUNCAN
   A. G., Mar. 24, 1921
   Anna Laura, d. of John R. and
      Blanche Duncan, Aug. 6, 1896
   Annie Leitch, w. of Charles B.
      Duncan. d. of Capt. Asa
      Holland, Dec. 11, 1919
   Benjamin Harrison, Jan. 24,
      1895
   Ella G., d. of Robert and Mary
      L. Duncan, Nov. 24, 1859
   Emily (Mrs.), Mar. 20, 1890
   Fannie C., d. of James M.
      Duncan, Oct. 3, 1895
   G. C. (Rev.), Oct. 12, 1933
   Hansford Dade (Rev.), June 17,
      1875
   Harriet Duncan, w. of Elder
      Louis Duncan, Apr. 8, 1852
   Helen, d. of Charles B. and
      Ann L. Duncan, Mar. 4, 1897
   Ira W., Feb. 23, 1905
   J. A. (Dr.), Sept. 27, 1877
   James Madison, May 24, June
      7, 1894
   John H., Oct. 24, 1878
   Margaret A., d. of Mrs. Ann
      L. Duncan, Mar. 27, 1845
   Margaret C., July 18, 1918
   Martha, d. of John R. and
      Rachel Duncan, July 27, 1871

OBITUARY NOTICES IN THE RELIGIOUS HERALD WITH DATES OF PUBLICATION

Mary, d. of John R. and Rachael
  Duncan, June 24, 1858*
Mary Catherine, June 18, 1925
Mattie E., w. of H. S. Duncan,
  Feb. 6, 1902
Mildred C. (Mrs.), Apr. 25, 1861
Rachel, w. of John R. Duncan,
  July 27, 1871
Sallie F., w. of Capt. William
  E. Duncan, June 2, 1921
Wesley Leland (Rev.), Apr.
  15, 1886
William (Elder), Nov. 19, 1846
William E. (Capt.), May 30, 1912
DUNCANSON
  James W. (Dr.), Dec. 17, 1857
  Lucie K., Aug. 22, 1872
DUNFORD
  P. W., Apr. 3, 1890
DUNKUM
  M. E. (Mrs.), Jan. 26, 1888
  William (Rev.), July 9, 1846
DUNLAP
  Sallie G. (Mrs.), Feb. 13, 1919
DUNLAVEY
  Mary B., w. of Robert W.
    Dunlavey, Mar. 21, 1861
  Otheella, d. of George T. and
    Caroline Dunlavey, Sept. 5,
    1861*
  Robert W., Dec. 2, 1875
DUNLAVY
  Charles H., Jr., s. of Charles
    H. and Susan Dunlavy, May
    31, 1860
  Susan L., w. of John H.
    Dunlavy, July 23, 1868
  William, Nov. 11, 1841
DUNMAN
  Catharine (Mrs.), July 6, 1882
DUNN
  America (Mrs.), July 16, 1914
  Caroline (Mrs.), July 24, 1829
  Dorothy Ann (Mrs.), Feb. 24, 1910
  George Henry, May 27, 1897
  George W., s. of Wilson Dunn,
    May 29, 1862
  H. W., Mar. 14, 1929
  Hattie L., w. of W. B. Dunn,
    Feb. 21, 1889

Opal Alene, May 19, 1938
Rebecca, w. of Thomas R. Dunn,
  Jan. 13, 1832
Rosa V., d. of W. B. Dunn,
  Dec. 20, 1888
Samuel, Sept. 27, 1833
Sarah, w. of Thomas B. Dunn,
  Mar. 5, 1846
DUNNAVANT
  J. L., Apr. 22, 1915
  Lucinda H., w. of Leroy C.
    Dunnavant, July 23, 1908
DUNNEVANT
  Martha R., w. of Samuel A.
    Dunnevant, Apr. 15, 1858
DUNNINGTON
  Louisa F., July 18, 1878
DUNSTAN
  L. J., Aug. 7, 1930
DUNTON
  Christopher S., Jan. 24, 1907
  Elizabeth, w. of William Dun-
    ton, June 13, 1844
  Emma, Nov. 25, 1920
  Ida (Mrs.), Oct. 1, 1925
  Sallie E. (Mrs.), d. of Will-
    iam J. Fatherly, May 13, 1915
  William Thomas, Feb. 11, 1909
Du-PRIEST
  Indiana Roberta, Feb. 28, 1855
DURFEY
  William Addison, June 17, 1880
DURHAM
  Mary A., w. of William F.
    Durham, Aug. 22, 1878
DURRETT
  Frances (Mrs.), Apr. 28, 1864
  Henry, Apr. 28, 1853
  Mary Flippo, w. of Lawrence B.
    Durrett, d. of T. J. Flippo,
    Jan. 2, 1919
  Mildred, d. of John J. Durrett,
    Feb. 11, 1892
  Susan E., w. of John J. Dur-
    rett, Oct. 16, 1862
DUSCH
  Andrew, Aug. 18, 1921
DuVAL
  Lucie, w. of Miles P.
    DuVal, d. of W. W. T.

* Possible inaccuracy in name, or spelling, but given as printed

OBITUARY NOTICES IN THE RELIGIOUS HERALD WITH DATES OF PUBLICATION

and Lucie O. Cogbill, Sept. 25, 1890
Mattie, w. of B. J. DuVal, Dec. 10, 1891
R. K. (Dr.), May 12, 1898
Sarah B. (Mrs.), Dec. 9, 1886
William H., Nov. 9, 1843

DUVAL
Catharine B., w. of William J. Duval, Apr. 15, 1847
Edwin J., Aug. 6, 1896
Elisha, Jan. 29, 1874
Elizabeth M., w. of Samuel S. Duval, Mar. 5, 1857
Jennie E., d. of N. H. Duval, June 24, 1869
Joseph, Mar. 7, 1850
Leila O. (Mrs.), Aug. 13, 1896
Lucy, w. of Stephen Duval, Jan. 19, 1843
Mary (Mrs.), Feb. 5, 1874
Miles, May 25, 1876
Mollie A., w. of Dr. R. K. Duval, Dec. 16, 1886
Rhoda W. HALSEY, w. of Edward J. Duval, Nov. 2 and 9, 1893
Robert Cammack, Nov. 26, 1931
Stephen, Aug. 15, 1850
Virginia Ann (Mrs.), Oct. 28, 1841
William (Rev.), Apr. 4, 1850
Willie E. (Mrs.), d. of William Johnson, May 22, 1851

DUVALL
Cornelia, w. of William J. Duvall, Jr., Oct. 26, 1882
Mary L. (Mrs.), Sept. 6, 1849

DYER
Jonathan, Mar. 27, 1829

DYSON
Ann E., Nov. 18, 1875
E. A., w. of Charles T. Dyson, Dec. 15, 1892

- E -

EACHES
  Owen Philip (Dr.), Mar. 6, 1930
EAGER
  George B. (Dr.), Mar. 28, 1929
  John H. (Rev.), May 19, 1938
EANES
  Catherine M., Sept. 19, 1872
  Edward T., July 28, Sept. 29, 1927
  J. B., Oct. 9, 1930
  Otelia, Oct. 30, 1913
EARLE
  Bayliss, Mar. 18, 1869
  Helen Augusta, d. of Rev. T. J. and E. J. Earle, Dec. 19, 1878
  Mable Turner, w. of Rev. J. H. Earle, Mar. 11, 1909
EARLY
  Eliza A., Nov. 20, 1924
  [John](Bishop)**, Nov. 13, 1873
  N. B., May 1, 1902
  Patsy N., w. of Col. Richard Early, Mar. 16, 1876
  Richard (Col.), May 3, 1888
  S. Paschal, s. of Col. R. Early, Dec. 31, 1857
  Samuel P., Jan. 14, 1858
  T. Whitefield, May 24, 1888
EARNEST
  Agnes L., w. of G. L. Earnest, Apr. 2, 1885
  Charles Whitlock, Oct. 26, 1843
  George L., Jr., Nov. 25, 1880
  Lucy Ann, Oct. 26, 1843
  Mary Elizabeth, Oct. 26, 1843
EARP
  William Thomas, Jan. 31, 1929
EASLEY
  Charles Bruce, Dec. 5, 1889
  John W. (Dr.), Nov. 30, 1899
  M. B. (Mrs.), Nov. 2, 1911
  Robert C., Apr. 22, 1926
  William S., Mar. 8, 1860
EASON
  George W., Sept. 24, 1914
  Virginia (Mrs.), May 23, 1929
EAST
  Ann E., d. of Isaac East, Nov. 7, 1850
  Annie M., w. of Edward L. East, Sept. 9, 1880
  Annie Noell, d. of R. A. and Linnie East, Mar. 24, 1881*
  Elizabeth, w. of Isaac East, July 13, 1848
  Florence O., Sept. 13, 1934
  Grace E. M., Dec. 26, 1918
  John J., May 13, 1915
  John W., Apr. 21, 1927
  Laura A. (Mrs.), Sept. 24, 1863
  Mary (Mrs.), Oct. 22, 1863
  Mary E., w. of J. F. East, d. of William T. Bell, Mar. 21, 1889
  R. A., Jan. 15, 1931
  R. W. (Rev.), July 5 and 12, 1866
  William T., Apr. 19, 1923
EASTE
  Mary P., w. of T. Easte, Sept. 17, 1857
EASTHAM
  David (Mrs.), Sept. 20, 1860
  Rachel (Mrs.), d. of Meekins Carr, July 23, 1846
  William Byrd, s. of Albert G. Eastham, Apr. 11, 1867
EASTIN
  Nancy (Mrs.), w. of Rev. Stephen Eastin, July 26, 1877
  Sarah, w. of Elder Stephen Eastin, Aug. 25, 1842
  Stephen (Rev.), Mar. 17, 1870

* Possible inaccuracy in name, or spelling, but given as printed
** Methodist Episcopal Church, South

OBITUARY NOTICES IN THE RELIGIOUS HERALD WITH DATES OF PUBLICATION

EASTWOOD
  M. D. (Mrs.), Nov. 14, 1901
  Sarah Anne, w. of Edward
    Eastwood, Feb. 6, 1908
  William Sutherland, Mar. 29,
    1928
EATON
  George W. (Dr.), Aug. 15,
    1872
  J. M., Dec. 5, 1907
  Lewright Boardman, s. of
    J. R. Eaton, Apr. 12,
    1877
  Martin, Feb. 1, 1839
  T. T. (Rev.), Apr. 28, 1881
  T. T. (Rev.), July 4, 1907
ECHOLS
  Floyd Leslie (Dr.), Feb. 8,
    1934
  Judy, w. of Jacob Echols,
    Jan. 23, 1873
EDDINS
  Elizabeth Jane, Feb. 23,
    1843
  Margaret, w. of Capt.
    Theophilus Eddins, June
    29, 1848
  Iverson Thornton, Oct. 12,
    1899
  Sarah H., w. of William
    Eddins, Oct. 16, 1835
EDENTON
  M. L. M., Jan. 20, 1887
EDGE
  Annie Dunkum, d. of Philip
    Edge, Apr. 24, 1851
  Annie S., w. of Philip
    Edge, Sept. 26, 1850
  Atwell, May 6, 1880*
  Benjamin, s. of Atwell
    Edge, Dec. 18, 1862*
  Eliza, w. of Atwell Edge,
    June 15, 1871*
  Elizabeth B., w. of Philip
    Edge, Aug. 21, 1856
  Emma, d. of Philip Edge,
    Jan. 16, 1873
  John B., Sept. 2, 1886
  Philip, Dec. 6, 1863
EDLOE
  Elizabeth, w. of William P.
    Edloe, Nov. 18, 1869
EDMONDS
  A. E. Stewart, w. of William
    Edmonds, Nov. 6, 1873
  Carl B., Oct. 27, 1927
  Elizabeth M., d. of Col. Eli-
    as Edmonds, Dec. 17, 1830
  George Clifford, s. of Wil-
    liam C. Edmonds, Aug. 11,
    1870
  H. J. (Dr.), Jan. 3, Feb. 14,
    1935
  J. C. (Mrs.), Mar. 28, 1929
  Ralph (Col.), May 22, 1851
  Richard H., Oct. 9, 1930
  Robert, Mar. 12, 1868
  William R., Jan. 15, 1920
EDMONDSON
  Charlotte T., d. of Joseph N.
    and Elizabeth Edmondson,
    Sept. 2, 1841
  Hallie J., w. of Samuel R.
    Edmondson, Nov. 26, 1857
  Lettie, d. of Samuel R. Edmond-
    son, Dec. 29, 1859
  William A., Sept. 6, 1849
  J. W.(Mrs.), Apr. 10 and 17,1919
  Letitia, Mar. 5, 1846
EDMONSTON
  Martha S., w. of G. W.
    Edmonston, July 27, 1899
EDMUNDS
  Elizabeth S. (Mrs.), May 22,
    1930
  John W., Nov. 19, 1914
  Sallie G. (Mrs.), d. of Thomas
    and Nannie Coleman Edmunds,
    May 31, 1906
EDWARDS
  A. F. (Capt.), Oct. 8,
    1885
  Albriston, July 29, 1915
  Allen, Mar. 28, 1872
  Annie (Mrs.), Apr. 8, 1920
  Blanche (Mrs.), Feb. 24, 1921
  Brice William, Feb. 18, 1909
  Charlie Bruce, Dec. 26, 1889
  Decatur (Rev.), Dec. 29, 1921
  Dianah (Mrs.), May 11, 1882

* Possible inaccuracy in name, or spelling, but given as printed

-101-

OBITUARY NOTICES IN THE RELIGIOUS HERALD WITH DATES OF PUBLICATION

Eliza, w. of H. H. F. Edwards, Aug. 3, 1854
Elizabeth Ann, w. of John Edwards, June 19, 1835
Ellen M., mother of Rev. J. Hartwell Edwards, Aug. 7, 1902
Gilliam, Sept. 4, 1884
J. A. B., July 3, 1930
James C., June 20, 1834
John E. (Rev.), Apr. 16, 1891
Jordan, May 28, 1874
Kate Watson (Mrs.), July 14, 1932
Lena Landon, Nov. 9, 1922
Lucy B. (Mrs.), Dec. 21, 1882
Lula G. (Mrs.), Nov. 24, Dec. 8, 1881
Margaret D., d. of Hiram G. and Elizabeth M. Edwards, Mar. 7, 1834
Martha, w. of Elisha B. Edwards, Dec. 7, 1854
Mattie (Mrs.), Sept. 18, 1919
Octavia (Mrs.), Apr. 28, 1927
R. M., Aug. 28, 1902
Rachel D., July 16, 1891
Richard D., s. of John and Elizabeth Edwards, Sept. 19, 1834
Richard (Rev.), May 2 and 23, 1907
Sallie (Mrs.), June 20, 1889
Sarah, w. of John Edwards Oct. 12, 1882
Sarah Virginia, w. of John A. Edwards, d. of Poindexter W. Mosby, Apr. 4, 1867
Sylvanus, s. of John and Rachel Edwards, June 2, 1842
Thomas Albert, Mar. 14, 1918
W. W. (Rev.), Mar. 4, 1926
EFFORD
John S., Aug. 22, 1929

J. W. (Sgt.), June 25, 1863
EGGLESTON
Elvira (Mrs.), Sept. 19, 1878
Emma J., w. of Robert J. Eggleston, Oct. 1, 1868
Emmeline B. (Mrs.), Mar. 22, 1894
Helen M., w. of Edward W. Eggleston, d. of Richard and Martha B. Eggleston, Feb. 22, 1900
J. E., May 21, 1874
J. R., Aug. 23, 1866
Judith C. (Mrs.), Apr. 28, 1859
Matthew J., Oct. 25, 1839
Nannie Carter FOX (Mrs.), w. of R. S. Eggleston, Aug. 21 and 28, Sept. 25, 1919
Nannie Morris, Aug. 18, 1853
Richard Isham, s. of James R. and E. B. Eggleston, Oct. 15, 1846
William Edwin, Nov. 12, 1863
EGGLISTON
Eliza T., w. of George P. Eggliston, d. of Nathan Barnett, Feb. 12, 1857
ELAM
Elizabeth, w. of James Elam, Nov. 22, 1855
Ida, d. of Mrs. E. P. Elam, Oct. 23, 1862
India E. (Mrs.), Nov. 29, 1834
Ira D., s. of John G. Elam, Mar. 26, 1891
J. D., Apr. 1, 1937
J. W., Aug. 27, 1857
James, Mar. 27, 1845
John G., Mar. 12, 1914
Lizzie Blackwell, w. of J. H. Elam, d. of William C. Hamlin, July 20, 1911
Mary (Mrs.), May 18, 1838
Mary J., w. of John G. Elam, Sept. 30, 1897
Mary S., w. of Robert S. Elam, May 29, 1862
Nannie (Mrs.), Oct. 9, 1902
Richard, Nov. 9, 1843

OBITUARY NOTICES IN THE RELIGIOUS HERALD WITH DATES OF PUBLICATION

Ruby, Jan. 12, 1911
Sallie Palmer, w. of Thomas B. Elam, Nov. 16, 1922
Sophia Jane Hurndon, w. of W. A. Elam, Mar. 21, 1907*
W. A., Apr. 22, 1915
Wesley Osburn, s. of Thomas D. Elam, Oct. 5, 1905
William Henry, Aug. 22, 1929
William S., Sept. 13, 1883
Willie Alfred, s. of John T. Elam, May 1, 1873
ELDER
  Martha D., w. of John W. Elder, Dec. 8, 1904
ELDRIDGE
  Rebecca, w. of Richard Eldridge, Feb. 25, 1869
  William, s. of Robert and Rebecca Eldridge, Aug. 19, 1847
ELEY
  Benjamin, Mar. 28, 1872
  Eugene S., Mar. 20, 1930
  Frank Hutson, s. of Julius F. and Mary C. Eley, Sept. 6, 1877
ELGIN
  G. H. (Rev.), May 22, 1890
ELISON
  H., Apr. 29, 1841
ELITON
  Fleming, June 25, 1863
ELLER
  N. B., June 17, 1926
ELLERBE
  Eddie, s. of M. F. and A. Ellerbe, July 22, 1875
  George Wilmot, s. of M. F. and A. Ellerbe, July 11, 1872
ELLETT
  Annie Walden, d. of William T. and Evelyn T. Ellett, Dec. 26, 1889
  Benjamin Dabney, s. of William C. Ellett, Sept. 19, 1834
  Elihu, Mar. 31, 1892
  Fannie Baylor, d. of James D. and Mary Agnes Ellett, Feb. 20, 1896
  Frances K. (Mrs.), Oct. 7, 1852
  Josiah C., s. of James A. Ellett, July 8, 1858
  Mary Agnes, w. of James D. Ellett, d. of Temple Ellett, July 14, 1853
  Obedience F., w. of Robert Ellett, Jan. 28, 1864
  T. H., Jan. 1 and 22, 1914
ELLINGTON
  Nettie Moore, w. of Charles Ellington, Nov. 23, 1916
ELLIOT
  Temple, Oct. 5, 1832
  William H., Feb. 28, 1889
ELLIOTT
  Alice Turpin, w. of S. A. Elliott, Aug. 5, 1915
  Annie E., w. of Charles H. Elliott, Mar. 26, 1891
  Cora, Apr. 7, 1927
  Dorothy (Mrs.), Jan. 14, 1847
  Jesse Allen, s. of Andrew and Louisa Elliott, Mar. 10, 1864
  Marietta V. (Mrs.), May 24, 1917
  May, Aug. 5, 1920
  Mollie S., d. of Andrew and Louisa Elliott, Mar. 10, 1864
  Sallie G., w. of Joseph Elliott, Aug. 9, 1888
  Samuel A., Nov. 18, 1915
  Sarah Allen, d. of Andrew Elliott, May 7, 1863
  Sarah R. (Mrs.), Nov. 13, 1856
  Virginia C., w. of W. H. Elliott, Jan. 15, 1885
  Wyatt Moseley, s. of Gen. Wyatt M. Elliott, June 8, 1882
ELLIOTTE
  Hassie, Nov. 2, 1905
ELLIS
  Alberta Anne, d. of Joseph H. Chappell, Mar. 6, 1913
  Constance, d. of Rev. Hugh A. Ellis, Dec. 6, 1928
  Frances Louisa (Mrs.), June

* Possible inaccuracy in name, or spelling, but given as printed

OBITUARY NOTICES IN THE RELIGIOUS HERALD WITH DATES OF PUBLICATION

17, 1831
Frank M. (Rev.), July 1
  and 29, 1897
Jane G., w. of Charles
  Ellis, Oct. 1, 1896
John C., Aug. 30, 1833
John Smith, Dec. 18, 1845
Judith H., w. of William B.
  Ellis, Feb. 28, 1850
Lucy, Jan. 24, 1856
M. R. (Mrs.), May 24, 1928
M. Rea, May 26, 1927
Martha (Mrs.), May 22, 1856
Mary Ann, w. of William Ellis,
  Sept. 19, 1834
Mary C., w. of James H.
  Ellis, June 25, 1840
Mary M., w. of John Ellis,
  Mar. 30, 1843
Mildred, w. of William
  Ellis, Apr. 3, 1862
Nannette, d. of Harvey S.
  and Nettie Ryland Ellis,
  July 19, 1894
Paul E., Feb. 5, 1925
Percy T., s. of J. T. Ellis,
  Oct. 11, 1900
Rebecca J., w. of George W.
  Ellis, Sept. 3, 1846
S. G., Mar. 11, 1886
W. J., Mar. 3, 1927
ELLISON
  C. L. May 5, 1881
  James, May 31, 1883
  John J., July 25, 1878
  John W., Mar. 16, 1916
  Joseph, Nov. 12, 1840
  Martha B. (Mrs.), d. of Stephen Pleasants, Oct. 4, 1888
  Rosa B., w. of Charles E.
    Ellison, Feb. 21, 1895
  Sallie E., w. of Dr. L. A.
    Ellison, d. of Peter F.
    and Caroline E. Archer,
    Mar. 13, 1879
  Susan (Mrs.), June 4, 1908
ELLISS
  Lucy Frances, d. of John E.
    Elliss, Oct. 4, 1860
  Mary, w. of J. E. Elliss,
    Feb. 23, 1860
ELLYSON
  Bettie, Apr. 27, 1922
  Delaware B., Sept. 3, 1863
  H. K. (Mrs.), d. of Luther
    Barnes, July 22, 1886
  H. K., May 14, 1891
  Henry Keeling, Dec. 4, 11, and
    18, 1890
  J. Taylor, Mar. 27, 1919
  J. Taylor (Mrs.), Apr. 25,
    1935
  Mary E., w. of Rev. O. Ellyson,
    Oct. 2, 1902
  Susanna (Mrs.), July 26, 1863
  Theodore, Feb. 27, 1919
  William, Dec. 4, 1919
ELMORE
  Elizabeth, w. of Peter Elmore,
    July 25, 1867
  John Morris, s. of J. Henry
    Elmore, Feb. 11, 1869
  Lucretia (Mrs.), d. of
    Ellison Ellis, Sept. 7, 1871
  Susan, w. of Charles W. Elmore,
    June 26, 1879
  William, July 12, 1877
ELSOM
  Anna L. SHEPARD (Mrs.),
    Nov. 18, 1915
  Evelina T., w. of Nelson
    Elsom, d. of Reuben and
    Elizabeth Herndon, Apr. 17,
    1856
  N. W., Dec. 9, 1886
ELSWICK
  Addie B. (Mrs.), Aug. 11,
    1921
ELSWORTH
  Leighton, s. of John C. and
    Pattie E. Minnix Elsworth,
    Dec. 17, 1908
EMBREY
  R. W., Nov. 11, 1915
EMERSON
  Jonathan, July 10, 1829
ENGLAND
  Lavinia (Mrs.), Dec. 11, 1851
ENGLISH
  Alta, d. of W. N. English,

OBITUARY NOTICES IN THE RELIGIOUS HERALD WITH DATES OF PUBLICATION

Oct. 23, 1915
Emily E., w. of William
 English, Mar. 10, 1870
John, May 1, 1844
Julia A. (Mrs.), Aug. 11,
 1927
Matilda, W. of Thomas
 English, d. of Elder Corey,
 Apr. 11, 1867
Thomas, Feb. 5, 1863
William, June 24, 1869
ENOS
 Bettie, Feb. 1, 1877
ENROUGHTY
 Betty (Mrs.), Aug. 17, 1893
ENSWILER
 Glen, Dec. 1, 1921
EPES
 Elizabeth, w. of Jerome P.
 Epes, d. of William Morris,
 Jan. 19, 1888
 Martha C. (Mrs.), June 4,
 1885
EPLING
 Isaac, June 26, 1879
 James H., Mar. 31, 1887
EPPERLY
 I. L., Mar. 17, 1938
EPPERSON
 J. (Mrs.), Sept. 11, 1851
 Joseph, Oct. 8, 1863
EPPES
 George Davis, s. of George
 F. and Laura M. Eppes
 July 24, 1878
 H. J., Nov. 21, 1918
 John Temple, s. of George F.
 and Laura M. Eppes, Oct.
 16, 1890
 Laura M., w. of George F.
 Eppes, Dec. 6, 1900
EPPLING
 Philip, May 10, 1855
EPPS
 Elizabeth, Mar. 14, 1854
 Mary Price (Mrs.), Sept.
 24, 1891
 Scianna, w. of Benjamin H.
 Epps, Mar. 4, 1869
ERNY

Bettie Ann, w. of Frederick
 Erny, Dec. 23, 1852
ERWIN
 Emma C., Feb. 23, 1882
ESKEW
 William J., Jan. 22, 1903
ESTES
 Andrew Broaddus (Rev.),
 Apr. 2, 1835
 Anna C., w. of Rev. Andrew
 Broaddus Estes, d. of Thomas
 and Phoebe Lawton Willingham,
 Feb. 25, 1909
 David R. (Mrs.), d. of James
 W. Cook, Mar. 6, 1913
 Elizabeth, w. of Joel Estes,
 Apr. 6, 1854
 Elliot (Rev.), July 19, 1849
 Emma Cornelia, d. of Capt.
 Benjamin Estes, May 15, 1873
 Julia Ann, June 19, 1873
 Lucy Ann, July 15, 1897
 Samuel, s. of Rev. A. B. and
 Annie C. Estes, Mar. 5,
 1874
 Sarah Jane, June 19, 1873
 Walter (Mrs.), Feb. 3, 1927
ESTEY
 Jacob, Apr. 24, 1890
ESTIS
 C. R., Jan. 22, 1903
 Frederick, s. of Samuel Estis,
 Feb. 26, 1852
 William B., Apr. 20, 1899
ETHEREGE
 Caleb, Apr. 4, 1872
ETHERIDGE
 Dora L., Dec. 10, 1891
 Isaiah, Nov. 26, 1885
 Mary E. (Mrs.), Feb. 12, 1920
 Thomas L., Nov. 12, 1885
ETTER
 Andrew Jackson, Dec. 3, 1863
 James J. (Sgt.), Dec. 11, 1862
EUBANK
 Alexander E. (Rev.), Oct. 22,
 1903
 C. L. (Rev.), Sept. 24, 1936
 Carrie, d. of Alexander and
 Emma Eubank, Oct. 8, 1863

OBITUARY NOTICES IN THE RELIGIOUS HERALD WITH DATES OF PUBLICATION

Cornelia E., w. of James
  A. Eubank, Jan. 31, 1878
Edmonia E., w. of Joseph C.
  Eubank, Jan. 13, 1848
Ellen Ficklin, d. of Dr.
  Thomas D. and Virginia
  Eubank, Apr. 18, 1901
Fanny B., w. of Warner
  Eubank, Nov. 15, 1849
G. F., Feb. 10, 1921
George D. (Rev.), Oct. 14,
  1937
Giles I., July 8, 1920
J. H., Jan. 4, 1912
J. Rebecca, w. of James
  Eubank, Nov. 20, 1879
J. W. (Mrs.), June 14, 1917
James, Oct. 31, 1850
James. s. of Richard Eubank,
  Aug. 12, 1858
James Archer, Feb. 6, 1896
James T. (Rev.), Aug. 28,
  Sept. 11, 1930
John S., s. of Warner and
  Emma Eubank, Sept. 22, 1881
John T., Jan. 29, 1863
John T., July 11, 1889
John Y., July 28, 1859
Julia HAYNIE (Mrs.), May 28,
  1885
Kitty (Mrs.), July 31, 1873
M. Maria, w. of G. G. Eubank,
  d. of Col. Samuel Downing,
  July 21, 1864
Martha, w. of Johnson Eubank,
  May 1, 1879
Mary E. D., d. of Johnson and
  Patsey Eubank, June 26,
  1879
Mary Jane, Oct. 13, 1842
Nettie Scott (Mrs.), Feb.
  18, 1937
Patsey, d. of Richard Eubank,
  Aug. 12, 1858
Philip, Apr. 27, 1848
Philip C., June 13, 1907
Richard (Rev.), Jan. 24, 1856
Robert Pollard, June 14, 1923
Roxy Ada, d. of Marius F. and
  Roxy E. Eubank, Nov. 15,
  1888
Susan, w. of Richard Eubank,
  Nov. 20, 1856
Thomas, s. of P. C. and F. M.
  Eubank, Sept. 4, 1873
Thomas D., Apr. 21, May 5,
  1864
Thomas Jackson, Feb. 21, Apr.
  24, 1924
Virginia (Mrs.), d. of Col.
  Thomas S. and Felicia T.
  Dunaway, Aug. 1, 1907
Virginia Clay, w. of James H.
  Eubank, May 26, 1910
William, s. of Richard and
  Susan Eubank, Aug. 12, 1858
Wirt Henry, Apr. 18, 1878
EUDAILEY
  David, July 15, 1920
  Florence, d. of David Eudailey,
    Aug. 15, 1889
  James (Mr. & Mrs.), Aug. 2, 1860
  Moses, Jan. 28, 1864
  Sarah (Mrs.), June 11, 1874
  J. P. (Mrs.), Feb. 22, 1923
EUDAILY
  John, Jan. 14, 1897
  Samuel P., Aug. 20, 1863
EURE
  Mattie L., d. of J. H. and
    Margaret L. Eure, Mar.
    5, 1874
  Peter, Feb. 8, 1872
EUSTACE
  Martha J., w. of John H.
    Eustace, d. of Dr. William
    Wardlaw, May 23, 1828
EVANS
  Alice Dew, Feb. 14, 1907
  Andrew Browne (Judge), s.
    of Rev. T. B. Evans, June
    6, 1912; Jan. 23, 1913
  Bettie, w. of T. B. Evans,
    Apr. 13, 1899
  Elizabeth M., w. of Thomas
    B. Evans, Aug. 20, 1896
  Eva, d. of A. B. and C. A.
    Evans, May 20, 1875
  G. H., July 10, 1913
  George H. (Mrs.), May 13,

OBITUARY NOTICES IN THE RELIGIOUS HERALD WITH DATES OF PUBLICATION

1897
James B., Oct. 30, 1862
James B., Feb. 13, 1879
John Dew, s. of A. B. and
  C. A. Evans, May 20, 1875
John M., June 4, July 2, 1891
John Madison, s. of Tipton B.
  Evans, June 11, 1891
Lizzie T., d. of Rev. Thomas
  B. Evans, Oct. 8, 1925
Mary, May 4, 1838
Mary E., w. of A. B. Evans,
  Jan. 13, 1859
Mary E., Apr. 4, 1895
Mary Floyd, d. of McDonald
  Evans, Feb. 25, 1897
McDonald, Nov. 19, 1925
Nettie Hoskins, d. of W. T.
  Evans, Mar. 11, Apr. 1,
  1909
Olivia, June 5, July 3,
  1845
Pattie A., Oct. 1, 1914
Sarah E., w. of Thomas B.
  Evans, Dec. 2, 1836
Sarah Jane (Mrs.), July 3,
  1856
Sarah W., w. of Thomas B.
  Evans, July 5, 1833
Susan, w. of Rev. W. L. T.
  Evans, d. of N. S. Bulloch,
  Feb. 15, 1866
Susan A. (Mrs.), Oct. 28,
  1886
Thomas B. (Rev.), Aug. 19 and
  26, Sept. 9, 1875
Thomas B. (Mrs.), Apr. 25, 1929
W. C., Dec. 1, 1864
W. T., Feb. 5, 1931
Willie D., s. of Rev. Thomas
  D. Evans, Apr. 6, 1871
EVARTS
  Jeremiah, May 27, 1831
EVERHART
  Belle (Mrs.), June 24, 1915
EVERETT
  C. D. (Dr.), Feb. 8, 1877
  Kate A., d. of Charles D.
    Everett, Aug. 31, 1871
  Mary Coleman, June 2, 1932
EVERTS
  W. W. (Rev.), Oct. 2, 1890
EWELL
  Benjamin S. (Col.), June 28,
    1894
  Sarah, w. of Edward H. Ewell,
    Mar. 1, 1849
EWING
  John, Sept. 25, 1829
EXALL
  Angeline, w. of Rev. George G.
    Exall, July 25, 1901
  Araminta Alletta, w. of Henry
    Exall, d. of Col. William
    Patterson, Oct. 11, 1883
  Charles H., Feb. 20, 1879
  Ellen, d. of John and Lucy
    Exall, Sept. 4, 1835
  George G. (Rev.), m. Angeline
    E. Pierce, Jan. 26, 1899
  John, s. of John and Susan
    Exall, Mar. 1, 1833
  John, Dec. 26, 1850
  Lucy B., w. of John Exall,
    July 26, 1833
  Mary Ellen, d. of John and
    Susan Exall, Mar. 1, 1833
  Susan (Mrs.), May 6, 1875
  Thomas Hume, s. of George G.
    and Angeline E. P. Exall,
    Nov. 17, 1859
EZELL
  Maggie, d. of L. C. and M. S.
    Ezell, Sept. 25, 1879

- F -

FACER
Ellen, w. of Rev. Thomas H. Facer, Oct. 20, 1859

FAISON
Alline Ashton, d. of A. W. and Lucy A. Faison, Aug. 27, 1874
Fannie J., Mar. 14, 1929
R. H. (Mrs.), Apr. 1, 1937

FALLIN
Minnie Kirk, d. of J. Brooks and Annie A. Fallin, Sept. 20, 1888

FALLS
Benjamin, Mar. 28, 1872

FANT
Ann, w. of John P. Fant, Feb. 24, 1859
Mildred (Mrs.), July 1, 1886

FARINHOLT
Elizabeth, w. of A. G. Farinholt, June 17, 1880

FARIS
Abraham, July 4, 1929
Anna Cushing, d. of J. J. and A. E. V. Faris, Aug. 7, 1856
Belle, w. of John B. Faris, Aug. 27, 1891
Bettie R. (Mrs.), Jan. 9, 1930
Charlie, s. of Abram and Bettie Faris, Sept. 12, 1889
E. M. (Mrs.), July 16, 1896
James, Jan. 28, 1875
John N., June 18, 1908
Sarah, Dec. 30, 1886
Susan Ann (Mrs.), Apr. 3, 1856
Thomas, Aug. 22, 1828

FARISH
Annie R., d. of James W. and Mary E. Farish, Jan. 24, 1873
Clementina (Mrs.), Dec. 20, 1877
Martha Z., w. of Andrew J. Farish, Feb. 9, 1865
Mary K., w. of John D. Farish, Apr. 1, 1858
Millicent W., w. of Rev. William P. Farish, Apr. 21, 1870
Sarah E., w. of Charles T. Farish, Dec. 16, 1858
Mary Eleanor, d. of Benjamin Farish, Aug. 5, 1836
Eveline, w. of Benjamin Farish, June 21, 1839

FARLEY
Ernst W., Oct. 20, Nov. 10, 1938
George E., Mar. 2, 1839
Julia O. (Mrs.), July 16, 1874
Lalla Rookh, d. of William and Julia Farley, Oct. 9, 1851
William, July 30, 1846

FARMER
A., June 24, 1858
Byrd, Dec. 2, 1847
Charles W., June 19, 1890
Elizabeth (Mrs.), Mar. 30, 1843
J. S., Mar. 3, Dec. 22, 1938
James, s. of Meredith and Sarah Farmer, Dec. 2, 1858
Jones H., Feb. 16, 1928
Martha F., Oct. 17, 1861
Mary C., d. of Nicholas Farmer, Oct. 24, 1867
Mary Jane (Mrs.), Mar. 2, 1865
Mary W., w. of Byrd Farmer, Mar. 9, 1838
Myrtle Hart (Mrs.), Mar. 4, 1920
Virginia E. (Mrs.), Mar. 30, 1911
Willis H., s. of James H. and Minerva Farmer, Dec. 2, 1858

FARQUHARSON
James (Rev.), Mar. 11, 1858

FARRAR
Annie C., w. of Rev. J. M. Farrar, Oct. 7, 1897
Baker, June 4, 1863
Catharine, May 16, 1889
Charles Wesley, s. of A. W. and M. J. Farrar, Sept. 26, 1878
David S., Oct. 22, 1868
Edwin, Mar. 27, 1856

OBITUARY NOTICES IN THE RELIGIOUS HERALD WITH DATES OF PUBLICATION

Elizabeth, w. of Stephen
  Farrar, May 10, 1860
Elizabeth Leigh, d. of W. B.
  Farrar, Oct. 19, 1876
Garland, Apr. 6, 1882
George Foster, July 9, 1908
John, Mar. 1, 1849
John, Jan. 13, 1859
John B., Dec. 18, 1879
John B. (Mrs.), d. of James Norvell, Aug. 19, 1886
John Heth, s. of John and
  Sarah Maria Farrar,
  Aug. 5, 1841
Joseph C. (Dr.), Sept. 26, 1878
Martha, June 13, 1844
Martha, w. of Baker Farrar
  and d. of Obediah Jenkins,
  June 4, 1863
Mary, Mar. 23, 1843
Matthew, June 13, 1844
Roberta, d. of John and Sarah
  Maria Farrar, Mar. 5, 1846
Stephen, Sept. 7, 1838
Susan A., Mar. 18, 1869
Susannah, w. of Peter F.
  Farrar, Mar. 13, 1845
FARISS
  Elizabeth A., w. of James
    Fariss, d. of Joseph Jenkins, Sept. 4, 1873
  Frances, w. of James Fariss,
    Jan. 27, 1853
  M. Pocahontas, d. of J. C.
    Stratton, w. of W. W.
    Fariss, Aug. 11, 1892
FARRIS
  E. H., Jan. 22, 1865
FARRISH
  M. E. (Rev.), June 23, 1910
  William (Dr.), Jan. 13, 1848
FARROW
  D. T. C., Feb. 1, 1912
  Pleasant, Aug. 22, 1861
FARSON
  Samuel, Mar. 6, 1924
FARY
  Robert Raikes, s. of George
    F. and Martha J. Fary,
    Dec. 16, 1886

FATHERLY
  Almedia Virginia (Mrs.)
    July 15, 1920
  Jennie, Feb. 4, 1937
  Mary S. (Mrs.), Feb. 3, 1921
FAUCETT
  Sarah, w. of John R. Faucett,
    Dec. 31, 1885
FAUDREE
  Mary E., d. of Joseph and Mary
    E. Faudree, Feb. 3, 1859
FAULCON
  John (Rev.), Oct. 2, 1829
FAULCONER
  Joseph A., Aug. 1, 1878
  Lillie Reynolds, w. of James
    W. Faulconer, Apr. 13, 1933
  Mira E., w. of James A. Faulconer, Sept. 14, 1854
FAULKCONER
  Catherine E., w. of William
    Faulkconer, May 27, 1858
FAULKNER
  B. G., Aug. 7, 1862
  Etta Lee, d. of Pleasant E. and
    Frances A. Faulkner, May 12.
    and 19, 1898
  Frances, w. of Pleasant Faulkner,
    Sept. 21, 1893
  George P., Feb. 19, 1931
  John, Jan. 31, 1867
  John K. (Rev.), Aug. 7, 1913
  Joseph, May 19, 1853
  Lizzie, d. of Rev. J. K. and
    Victoria Faulkner, Feb. 1, 1866
  Mattie A., w. of T. J. Faulkner
    Jan. 16, 1890
  Susan, w. of Capt. John Faulkner,
    Mar. 5, 1840
  Victoria Chandler, w. of J. K.
    Faulkner, May 10, 1900
  William J., s. of Henry J.
    Faulkner, Aug. 20, 1868
FAUNT-LEROY*
  Ella, d. of Dr. P. G. and F.
    E. Faunt-LeRoy, May 9, 1889
FAUNT-LE-ROY*
  A. M., Apr. 11, 1895
  Thomas Waring, Oct. 19, 1876
FAUNT LE ROY*

* Possible inaccuracy in name, or spelling, but given as printed

OBITUARY NOTICES IN THE RELIGIOUS HERALD WITH DATES OF PUBLICATION

Thomas W. L., Jan. 27, 1887
FAUNTLEROY*
A. M. (Mrs.), Mar. 2, 1899
Clare, d. of Thomas Fauntleroy, Jan. 24, 1884
Frances Ann, w. of Thomas W. L. Fauntleroy, Mar. 13, 1862
Isabella E., w. of Dr. Robert B. Fauntleroy, April 8, 1858
John Henry Lynch, s. of Thomas Fauntleroy, Jan. 24, 1884
John S., s. of Mrs. Ann W. Fauntleroy, Feb. 7, 1901
Juliet M., w. of T. W. Fauntleroy, Nov. 26, 1857
Mattie Kate, d. of Dr. Samuel G. Fauntleroy, Nov. 22, Dec. 20, 1906
Moore Govan, s. of Robert P. W. Fauntleroy, Nov. 26, 1863
Robert, Nov. 16, 1852
S. Griffin (Dr.), July 20, 1871
S. Griffin (Dr.), Mar. 9, 1899
Sally, w. of Samuel G. Fauntleroy, Dec. 3, 1840
Susan G. (Mrs.), June 21, 1906
Thomas (Col.), Apr. 13, 1911
FAVIER
M. P., w. of V. A. Favier, Dec. 15, 1887
FEAMSTER
Mary Martha, May 12, 1837
Patsey Alderson (Mrs.), Sept. 10, 1885
FEASTER
Thomas Lyles, s. of J. C. and S. L. Feaster, Dec. 30, 1886
FEATHERS
Mahala A., d. of William Feathers, Mar. 5, 1863
FEATHERSTON
Amanda Melvina F., w. of W. B. Featherston, Nov. 12, 1857
Charles H., Nov. 19, 1863

Elizabeth S., w. of Charles H. Featherston, June 22, 1848
Susanna, w. of Montgomery Featherston, Dec. 10, 1840
William Booker, Apr. 18, 1878
FEAZEL
J. L., May 13, 1858
FELIX
J. D., s. of Dr. Joseph S. Felix, Sept. 10, 1903
Joseph S. (Rev.), Dec. 24, 1903
FELLER
Annie B., w. of Rev. L. P. Feller, June 20, 1867
FELLERS
Cassie R., w. of Capt. William Fellers, Aug. 13, 1868
Lewis P. (Rev.), July 20, 1882
FENDLEY
Harriet Virginia, d. of Thomas Fendley, Aug. 9, 1849
FENNELL
Benjamin (Dr.), s. of Capt. Isham Fennell, Aug. 4, 1864
FENTRESS
Elizabeth T., June 4, 1863
Josephine, June 15, 1893
Lizzie (Mrs.), Feb. 17, 1927
W. H., May 3, 1923
FENWICK
William, Feb. 13, 1829
FER
Eugene Adolph, Oct. 16, 1845
FERGUSON
A. C., May 26, 1904
Elizabeth, w. of Robert Ferguson, Aug. 25, 1842
H. A. K., Mar. 27, 1884
Henry Grady (Rev.), Jan. 17, 1901
James P. (Lt.), Nov. 6, Dec. 11, 1862
John, Feb. 18, 1858
Judith (Mrs.), Apr. 1, 1852
Mary Ann (Mrs.), w. of Frederick Ferguson, July 31, 1829
Mary Ethel, d. of Welton L. Ferguson, Sept. 3, 1903
Mary La Prade, Oct. 17, 1861
Virginia M. (Mrs.), Mar. 14,

* Possible inaccuracy in name, or spelling, but given as printed

OBITUARY NOTICES IN THE RELIGIOUS HERALD WITH DATES OF PUBLICATION

1929
William J., Sept. 24, 1925
William T., s. of Sidney M.
  Ferguson, Feb. 28, 1861
Williamson M. (Rev.), Dec.
  29, 1864
FERGUSSON
  Blanche Griffin, Oct. 16,
    1924
  Elizabeth Gertrude (Mrs.),
    Aug. 23, 1934
FERNEYHOUGH
  F. Polexinia, w. of R. W.
    Ferneyhough, Mar. 26,
    1885
  John R., Feb. 3, 1927
FERREBEE
  J. B. (Rev.), July 23, 1936
FERRELL
  Bedford B., s. of Rev. James
    B. Ferrell, Dec. 31, 1846
  James B. (Rev.), Aug. 30, 1849
  John W., Jan. 5, 1865
  Martha, w. of Rev. James B.
    Ferrell, Oct. 16, 1845
  P. W., Dec. 24, 1914
  Rawley W., Sept. 18, 1862
  Rebecca, w. of Thomas Ferrell,
    d. of Robert and Amy
    Stinson, Feb. 11, 1892
  Robert Lee, s. of E. and M.
    E. Ferrell, Jan. 25, 1877
  William J., Feb. 27, 1862
FERRIS
  Eugene, Oct. 24, 1878
  S. B. MICOU, w. of Eugene
    Ferris, Oct. 26, 1882
FEUDGE
  Daisie May, d. of Mrs. Fannie
    Roper Feudge, June 28,
    1894
  Rosie Belle, d. of Col. S.
    S, and Mrs. Fannie R.
    Feudge, June 8, 1871
FEWELL
  Ann E., w. of John R. Fewell,
    Feb. 6, 1873
FICKLEN*
  Fielding (Dr.), June 24, 1869
  Frances, w. of George Ficklen,
    Nov. 18, 1841
  George, Oct. 28, 1852
  Louisa V., d. of George Ficklen, Jan. 19, 1843
  Sarah Ann, d. of George Ficklen, Jan. 30, 1840
FICKLIN*
  Benjamin (Elder), Jan. 19,
    1865; July 31, 1873
  Ellen, w. of Benjamin Ficklin, Dec. 10, 1857
  Euphrasia, w. of Thomas D.
    Ficklin, May 14, 1857
  Evelina, w. of George Ficklin, Feb. 11, 1847
  Frances (Mrs.), June 20,
    1844
  John Slaughter, s. of Slaughter, and Caroline Ficklin,
    Sept. 18, 1862
FIDLER
  Sarah, w. of William Fidler,
    Jan. 11, 1844
FIELD
  Annie Powell, d. of James
    G. and F. Ella Field,
    Feb. 26, 1863
  George Harris, Mar. 18, 1937
  Louisa W., w. of William M.
    Field, June 13, 1889
  Margaret Cornelia, d. of
    James G. and F. Ella Field,
    Nov. 5, 1859
  Richard (Dr.), May 29, 1829
  Thomas W., June 1, 1871
FIELDING
  Ann, Oct. 12, 1848
  Betsy (Mrs.), Aug. 28, 1856
  Eliza M., Oct. 23, 1851
  William, Apr. 16, 1857
FIELDS
  J. Cam (Mrs.), Oct. 27, 1932
  M. F. (Mrs.), May 13, 1926
FIFE
  Beverly S., s. of Robert S.
    Fife, Mar. 17, 1837
  Howell, s. of Herndon and
    Sallie Fife, Nov. 4, 1869
  James (Rev.), Oct. 12 and 19,
    1876

* Possible inaccuracy in name, or spelling but given as printed

OBITUARY NOTICES IN THE RELIGIOUS HERALD WITH DATES OF PUBLICATION

James D., Jr., s. of James
and Katherine Reynolds
Fife, Oct. 8, 1908
Robert Herndon, Feb. 12,
1920
FIGG
Benjamin, June 14, 1839
FIGNER
Alphonso, Aug. 4, 1864
FILES
Rachel J. B., w. of Thomas
Files, Mar. 5, 1874
FINCH
Adoniram J., s. of Col.
John F. and Frances Finch,
Nov. 11, 1841
George E., Apr. 25, 1872
George F., s. of Col. John
F. Finch, Oct. 10, 1850
Martha L., w. of William
T. Z. Finch, Feb. 25,
1869
Mary A. (Mrs.), Mar. 4, 1852
Pleasant, Nov. 24, 1859
Sallie A., June 21, 1860
Sallie J., d. of John Weaver,
Sept. 27, 1877
Sarah W. (Mrs.), May 1, 1856
William L., Mar. 22, 1849
FINKS
James, Mar. 25, Apr. 8,
1852
James Fisher (Capt.), May
20, 1886
Mary (Mrs.), Sept. 28, 1871
Mary Duane, June 21, 1860
Sarah Cornelia, d. of M. F.
and Susan W. Finks, Sept.
18, Nov. 6, 1862
FINNELL
Luther Rice, Mar. 27, 1884
FINNEY
C. A., Dec. 27, 1923
Jane, w. of Alphonso Finney,
d. of Elder William Bell,
Jan. 29, 1846
FISHBACK
Frederick (Col.), Jan. 25,
1849
Martin, Feb. 24, 1842

Sophia Ann, w. of Col.
Fred Fishback, Mar. 4,
1875
FISHBURN
Junius M., Apr. 1, 1858
FISHER
(Sister), July 19, 1855
Anna Star, d. of Rev.
William Fisher, Jan. 11,
1923
Bettie D., d. of John W.
Fisher, Jan. 14, 1858
C. F., June 13, 1861
Cora R., d. of David R. and
Martha A. Fisher, Nov. 19,
1857
E. (Mrs.), Feb. 26, 1857
Eloise DICKINSON (Mrs.), Sept.
29, 1892
Frederick E., Mar. 17, 1921
John M., Feb. 26, 1857
John M., June 14, 1860
Jonas, July 10, 1890
Lewis, June 8, 1843
Lola, d. of Sam Fisher,
Oct. 14, 1909
Mandaville B., Apr. 11,
1878
Manie S., Nov. 27, 1884*
Mannie S., Oct. 16, 1884*
Margaret Baptist, d. of
Christopher F. and Sarah
V. Fisher, Feb. 1, 1855
Matilda Lotz, w. of Rev.
William Fisher, Mar.
30, 1899
Sarah V., w. of Capt. C.
F. Fisher, Oct. 30, 1873
W. C., Mar. 16, 1865
W. F. (Rev.), Mar. 6 and
27, 1930
William (Rev.), July 21, 1898
William J., s. of John
Fisher, Mar. 29, 1855
William M. (Rev.), Oct. 24,
1867
FISK
Pliny A. M. (Rev.), Feb. 29, 1828
FITCH
Jane, w. of Samuel Fitch,

* Possible inaccuracy in name, or spelling, but given as printed

OBITUARY NOTICES IN THE RELIGIOUS HERALD WITH DATES OF PUBLICATION

May 23, 1844
FITCHER
  Henrietta, w. of Rev. W.
    L. Fitcher, Mar. 7,
    1889
  Isaac Cobb, s. of Rev. W.
    L. and Mrs. Etta H.
    Fitcher, Sept. 14, 1871
  Nannie May, d. of Rev. W.
    L., Nov. 8, 1877
  Susie Zeigler (Mrs.), d.
    of Harry Sylvester Zeigler,
    July 20, 1911
FITCHETT
  Adaline, Mar. 6, 1873
  Anna, Sept. 2, 1920
  William Polk, Dec. 5, 1839
FITE
  Marion Fletcher, w. of James
    W. Fite, May 19, 1927
FITZ
  Irma Lee, d. of Mrs. J.
    Fitz, Aug. 8, 1912
  J. M. (Capt.), Mar. 16,
    1899
  James Lindsey, Jr., Mar.
    23, 1916
  Marie Estelle, w. of J. W.
    Fitz, d. of Thomas Sher-
    man, Apr. 8, 1875
  William W., Aug. 19, 1886
FITZGERALD
  A. E., w. of W. M. Fitz-
    gerald, Mar. 29, 1894
  Emily (Mrs.), July 19, 1888
  Emma, July 10, 1890
  James B., Aug. 11, 1892
  Jeremiah G., Oct. 8, 1857
  John E., s. of John W.
    Fitzgerald, Sept. 17,
    1891
  John W., Aug. 28, 1924
  Mary, d. of J. M. Fitz-
    gerald, Sept. 3, 1914
  Martha S., w. of John W.
    Fitzgerald, Mar. 13,
    1913
  McDowell, Jan. 2, 1919
  Mildred, July 14, 1853
  Nettie Clyde, d. of Samuel
    and Henrietta Fitzgerald,
    Oct. 11, 1888
  Sallie, d. of Samuel and
    Henrietta Fitzgerald,
    Sept. 27, 1877
  Samuel, May 29, 1862
  Thomas, June 23, 1892
  William, July 26, 1866
FITZHUGH
  Annie, d. of Dr. P. and G.
    Fitzhugh, Feb. 20, 1868
  Elizabeth G., w. of L. H.
    Fitzhugh, Jan. 30, 1851
  Helen M., d. of P. H. and
    Mary S. Fitzhugh, Sept.
    10, 1857
  Kate Payne, June 4, 1925
  Mary Steptoe, w. of Maj.
    Patrick H. Fitzhugh, d. of
    Dr. R. A. Christian,
    Apr. 23, 1896
  Patsy, w. of Robert Fitz-
    hugh, Dec. 1, 1870
  Philip Aylett, s. of Philip
    A. and Georgiana Fitzhugh,
    Apr. 21, 1853
  Sarah J. (Mrs.), d. of Lud-
    well Lee Luckett, Feb. 12,
    Mar. 5, 1914
  William H., May 28, 1830
FITZPATRICK
  Mittie L. (Mrs.), May 31, 1888
  William, Feb. 13, 1842
FIVASH
  Sarah (Mrs.), Aug. 5, 1836
FLAGG
  Eleazer Fletcher, Sept. 9,
    1831
  Ella W., w. of Lt. George
    H. Flagg, Aug. 4, 1864
FLANAGAN
  Alice, w. of James M. Flana-
    gan, Jan. 14, 1932
  Jane, Apr. 20, 1876
FLANNAGAN
  Lillie Kent (Mrs.), w. of
    W. R. Flannagan, June 29,
    July 6, 1933
  Mary, w. of James Flannagan,
    Mar. 13, 1851

OBITUARY NOTICES IN THE RELIGIOUS HERALD WITH DATES OF PUBLICATION

Sarah C., w. of William Flannagan, Apr. 22, 1858

FLEET
Alexander (Col.), Oct. 4 and 11, 1877
Alexander (Rev.), Oct. 10, 1912
Alexander Frederick (Col.), Sept. 14, 1911
Alma Lyne, d. of Thomas M. and Luella B. Fleet, Feb. 7, 1878
Ann Elizabeth, w. of Alexander Washington Fleet, July 28, 1904
Annie, d. of W. C. and Lucy D. Fleet, Nov. 6, 1873
Benjamin (Mrs.), w. of Dr. Benjamin Fleet, Jan. 18, 1900
Bessie P., Dec. 1, 1904
Betsy, w. of Col. Alexander Fleet, July 8, 1841
Beulah Pearle, d. of W. C. and J. Belle Fleet, Mar. 18, 1886*
Catharine Peachy, d. of James Robert Fleet, Apr. 22, 1852
Charles H., Nov. 19, 1846
Christopher B. (Dr.), Dec. 18, 1845
Elizabeth M. G., w. of William T. Fleet, d. of Col. Christopher Tompkins, Nov. 20, 1856
Florence, Feb. 5, 1903
H. M., Jr., s. of H. M. Fleet, July 25, 1907
H. M., Feb. 16, Mar. 15, 1928
H. McKim, May 10, 1928
Henry A., May 26, 1938
James David Crane, s. of Capt. W. C. and Belle Crane Fleet, Feb. 23, 1899
James Robert, Jr., s. of Capt. James Robert and Martha Ryland Fleet, Mar. 17, 1904
James W. (Judge), Nov. 24, 1927; Feb. 9, 1928
John A., s. of Dr. C. B. Fleet, Nov. 14, 1912
Josie (Mrs.), Mar. 27, 1924
Lucy D., w. of Capt. William C. Fleet, Dec. 25, 1873
M. Lou, Jan. 17, 1918
Maggie Ryland, d. of James R. and Reubie P. Fleet, Mar. 13, 1879
Maria Susan, w. of Dr. William T. Fleet, d. of Richard and Dorothy Bagby, June 21, 1906
Mary Ann, w. of Dr. C. Fleet, Nov. 14, 1828
Mary Catherine, d. of Col. Alexander Fleet, Mar. 7, 1861
Mary F., Nov. 12, 1925
William Craig, s. of Chapin Southwood Fleet, Mar. 26, 1891
William Hamilton, Apr. 22, 1920
William Jeffreys, s. of Rev. Alexander Fleet, July 25, 1901
William T. (Dr.), July 13, Aug. 3, 1899

FLEETWOOD
Sallie B., w. of P. Fleetwood, Dec. 6, 1888

FLEISHER
Hannah (Mrs.), May 14, 1830

FLEMING
Catharine M., d. of Anthony and Ann Fleming, July 28, 1853
Esther, Sept. 4, 1873
George (Dr.), Aug. 30, 1883
Z. T., May 30, 1912

FLEMMING
John, May 27, 1841
Lee (Mrs.), May 13, 1920
Maria A., Nov. 24, 1887
Mary O., w. of Dr. George Flemming, Oct. 29, 1868
Roxana, w. of Dr. Flemming, Aug. 17, 1843

* Possible inaccuracy in name, or spelling, but given as printed

OBITUARY NOTICES IN THE RELIGIOUS HERALD WITH DATES OF PUBLICATION

Willie T., s. of Dr. George Flemming, Dec. 18, 1862

FLESHOOD
Lee, Mar. 22, 1928

FLESHMAN
Ann (Mrs.), July 20, 1876

FLETCHER
Alvin, s. of Cyrus T. Fletcher, Jan. 8, 1891
Amanda (Mrs.), Sept. 18, 1873
Bettie W., w. of Robert W. Fletcher, July 5, 1860
Cyrus H., Dec. 14, 1905
Ella, Feb. 24, 1876
Eliza (Mrs.), July 27, 1893
Elizabeth Q., w. of John Fletcher, Sept. 7, 1848
Isham, July 14, 1859
Jefferson Paul, s. of Jefferson and Mary Jane Fletcher, Mar. 4, 1869
Josephine, Oct. 18, 1928
Julia, d. of Mrs. Eliza Fletcher, Oct. 27, 1881
Mary, w. of James Fletcher, Sept. 16, 1858
Mary Sue, w. of Cyrus H. Fletcher, Dec. 14, 1905
Robert, May 18, 1911
Sarah, d. of James Fletcher, Oct. 13, 1853
Tacie, w. of Robert Fletcher, d. of Thomas Glascock, Aug. 22, 1878
Virginia, Sept. 25, 1879

FLINCH
Flora Boyd, Oct. 22, 1885

FLIPPO
Ada H. (Mrs.), Apr. 9, 1936
Elmira, w. of Jefferson Flippo, Jan. 26, 1893
Fannie Augusta, d. of Oscar Farish and Roxie Flippo, Oct. 22, 1857
Frances C., w. of Joseph P. Flippo, Nov. 30, 1838
Gideon, May 28, 1903
J. A. (Dr.), Apr. 9 and 23, 1896
J. B., May 31, 1888
Joseph, May 10, 1860
Joseph P., June 28, 1877
Mary Ann, d. of Joseph and Mary Ann Flippo, Apr. 22, 1858
O. F. (Dr.), Aug. 9, 1906
Rachel T., w. of William E. Flippo, Mar. 16, 1876
Sammie, s. of E. I. and Annie E. Flippo, Sept. 15, 1892
Sarah J., w. of Gideon Flippo, Mar. 10, 1859
William, May 10, 1860

FLORA
Mary Onley (Mrs.), Oct. 31, 1929

FLOURNOY
Bertha James, d. of James F. and Lucy A. Flournoy, Nov. 12, 1908
Daniel H., Aug. 11, 1881
Francis (Capt.), May 3, 1883
James Francis, Dec. 24, 1936
Mary King, July 26, 1877

FLOYD
Fluvanna P., w. of John H. Floyd, Feb. 25, 1904
Gideon, June 3, 1847
John E., June 24, 1920
M. B. (Mrs.), Feb. 24, 1887
Robert S., s. of Stephen and Julia A. Floyd, Oct. 12, 1854
Stephen, Dec. 4, 1856
Susan, w. of John T. Floyd, Feb. 24, 1853
Susan E., d. of Stephen and Julia A. Floyd, Oct. 12, 1854

FLYNT
Lydia, w. of Thomas Flynt, Mar. 28, 1878

FOGG
Eliza T., Apr. 20, 1871
Lewis B., July 2, 1840
Saburnia E., w. of Lewis L.

OBITUARY NOTICES IN THE RELIGIOUS HERALD WITH DATES OF PUBLICATION

Fogg, Jan. 24, 1850
FOLEY
   Ann E. (Mrs.), July 20, 1876
   Sally, Apr. 25, 1850
   William E., June 25, 1858
FOLK
   Edgar Estes (Rev.), Apr. 5, 1900
FOLKES
   Eda Montague, w. of Rev. R. A. Folkes, d. of Dr. Lewis B. Montague, Mar. 11, 1920
   R. A. (Rev.), May 5, 1932
   Robert A., Jr., s. of R. A. Folkes, Apr. 26, 1894
FOLLIARD
   Eugene, s. of John Paul and Susan Walden Folliard, Nov. 12, 1931
FOLWELL
   Nannie H., d. of G. R. and L. A. Folwell, Dec. 6, 1866
FOMAN
   Missouria M. (Mrs.), Sept. 11, 1879
FONES
   Eliza Virginia (Mrs.), Apr. 13, 1933
   Elizabeth (Mrs.), Feb. 25, 1875
   George W., May 21, 1863
   H. H. (Mrs.), w. of Rev. H. H. Fones, d. of John Pullen, Apr. 19, 1917
   H. H. (Rev.), July 6, 1922
   R. A., Mar. 16, 1876
FONTAINE
   Edmond D., s. of Mrs. Mary O. Fontaine, Oct. 11, Nov. 15, 1855
   Mary Burrows (Mrs.), w. of Col. William Fontaine, May 26, 1887
   Patrick Henry (Rev.), Apr. 8, May 6, 1915
   Willie Spottswood, s. of Col. W. W. and Mary B. Fontaine,

Aug. 13, 1863
FOOTE
   Mary Ann, w. of James H. Foote, d. of Dr. F. Williams, June 5, 1856
FORBES
   Johnson G., Apr. 13, 1922
   Margaret Ann, w. of William Forbes, Apr. 26, 1900
   Reed (Mrs.), Nov. 8, 1928
   Sarah Louise, w. of A. William Forbes, Aug. 14, 1851
   W. S. (Mrs.), Jan. 15, 1914
   W. S., Aug. 14, 1930
FORCE
   W. Q., Jan. 13, Dec. 23, 1880
FORD
   A. A., s. of W. R. and M. W. Ford, Nov. 5, 1908
   A. B. (Mrs.), nee Taylor, Nov. 17, 1904
   Bettie Owen, d. of Elder Reuben Ford, Feb. 27, 1851
   Calvin, Sept. 8, 1887
   Caroline (Mrs.), d. of Rev. John Woolridge, Feb. 16, 1860
   E. D., July 28, 1881
   Edward Jeter, s. of Elder Reuben Ford, Feb. 20, 1851
   Eliza C. (Mrs.), Jan. 30, 1851
   Elizabeth, d. of W. L. Ford, Mar. 11, 1909
   Elizabeth (Mrs.), Feb. 16, 1860
   Frances, Sept. 23, 1858
   Frances P., July 8, 1858
   James A., Jan. 19, 1896
   John Culvrain, Sept. 25, 1890
   Joseph Thornton, Dec. 18, 1930
   Julia Ann, w. of Matthew W. Ford, Sept. 21, 1843
   Lee W., Jan. 11, 1906
   Lelia White, d. of John R. Ford, July 31, 1862
   Leonora C., Apr. 12, 1855
   Linda Walker, d. of J. M. and Mary J. Ford, Oct. 12, 1854
   Margaret Ariadne, Apr. 21, 1927

OBITUARY NOTICES IN THE RELIGIOUS HERALD WITH DATES OF PUBLICATION

Martha Ann, d. of James M.
Ford, Dec. 3, 1840
Martha Ann Lewis, w. of
James Ford, June 23, 1837
Mary J. (Mrs.), Mar. 16, 1854
Olivia W. (Mrs.), Dec. 29, 1887
Pamelia M., d. of Macon and
E. C. Ford, Nov. 27, 1873
Polly (Mrs.), w. of William A.
Ford, July 22, 1831
Sallie C., d. of John R. and
Susan Ford, Sept. 25, 1862
Susan A., w. of Mathew W.
Ford, Apr. 13, 1848
Thomas H., May 31, 1860
Virginia Elizabeth, w. of
Matthew W. Ford, d. of
Rev. Henry W. Watkins,
July 19, 1855
Walthall W., s. of Matthew
W. and Virginia Ford,
Nov. 6, 1851
William B., June 23, 1892
FORE
P. W. (Mrs.), June 14, 1888
Paul, Sept. 3, 1857
Rosa Gertrude, d. of Paul
E. Fore, Feb. 2, 1871
Virginia Ann, d. of Stephen C.
and Harriet J. Fore, Dec.
20, 1860
William A., July 21, 1859
Willie E., s. of Tracy R.
Fore, Dec. 20, 1883
FORESTER
T. B. (Rev.), Dec. 6, 1931
FORLOINE
Mary J., Oct. 1, 1857
FORLOINES
James Warsaw, s. of T. W.
and E. A. Forloines,
Dec. 25, 1873
FORMAN
Willie C. A., s. of Martha
A. Forman, Sept. 10, 1863
FORREST
R. H. (Mrs.), Jan. 14,
Feb. 11, 1926
Spencer H., Mar. 29, 1894
FORRESTER

Bessie Dargan, w. of Rev.
E. J. Forrester, d. of Dr.
J. O. B. Durgan, Dec. 6,
1883; Jan. 3, 1884
William L., Mar. 6, 1835
FORSEE
David N., Sept. 11, 1862
George F., May 15, 1913
FORSYTH
Robert W. (Rev.), Mar. 2,
1911
FORTUNE
William B., Aug. 13, 1863
FOSQUE
Polly, July 9, 1885
FOSTER
A. T. (Dr.), Dec. 16, 1858
Agnes N. Harvey, w. of
John N. Foster, Oct. 12,
1911
Ann M., w. of Joseph Foster,
Dec. 22, 1859
Anna, w. of Peter Foster,
Nov. 11, 1897
Charles (Capt.), June 13,
1828
Charles H., Aug. 3, 1916
Clement R., Oct. 14, 1858
Eldridge Marcellus (Mrs.),
Jan. 15, 1925
Elizabeth (Mrs.), Sept. 2,
1836
Fannie, w. of Rev. L. S.
Foster, d. of Charles
Merrick, July 22, 1875
George, Mar. 9, 1871
George, Mar. 13, 1884
George Singleton, Feb. 8,
1839
George W., June 25, 1857
James, s. of Thomas K.
and Mary E. Foster,
Dec. 14, 1838
James A., May 3, 1883;
Mar. 13, 1884
Lyle, Aug. 15, 1861
Lyle, Feb. 13, 1862
Martha, w. of J. A. Foster,
May 5, 1864
Mary R., w. of Larkin Foster,

OBITUARY NOTICES IN THE RELIGIOUS HERALD WITH DATES OF PUBLICATION

Oct. 11, 1860
Mary W. (Mrs.), Jan. 4, 1858
Mary Willie, d. of J. W. and Agnes W. Foster, Oct. 25, 1866
Mattie Virginia, d. of Joel C. Foster, Jan. 24, 1867
Nannie Daniel, w. of William Mynn Thorton Foster, Aug. 19, 1937
S. E., w. of Robert L. Foster, Mar. 11, 1875
Sarah, w. of George Foster, Sept. 30, 1858
Thomas K., Jan. 18, 1877
W. M., Feb. 11, 1926
FOULKES
Mary (Mrs.), Oct. 28, 1858
FOUNTAIN
Andrew, s. of James and Bettie Fountain, Dec. 16, 1886
Charles D., s. of William S. and Sarah S. Fountain, Sept. 4, 1856
FOUSHEE
William T., Feb. 2, 1860
FOUTS
John, Mar. 5, 1863
William, Mar. 5, 1863
FOWLER
Elizabeth, w. of J. C. L. Fowler, May 12, 1859
Magdalene S. (Mrs.), Mar. 15, 1839
FOWLES
Elizabeth, w. of Maj. Henry Fowles, Nov. 26, 1846
Martha Catherine (Mrs.), July 13, 1933
FOWLKES
Ada Gray, w. of W. Y. Fowlkes, Apr. 14, 1892
Edward Fuqua, s. of Robert and Sarah Fowlkes, June 21, 1866
Elizabeth Dickinson, Feb. 11, 1915
Ella (Mrs.), Mar. 7, 1895

Henry Meriwether, Dec. 29, 1897
Lizzie Clark, d. of Henry Meriwether and Jane Clark Fowlkes, Jan. 27, 1898
Martha A., w. of Paschal J. Fowlkes, May 22, 1919
Martha M. (Mrs.), Aug. 8, 1834
Mattie (Mrs.), Sept. 27, 1923
Paschal J., Nov. 2 and 16, 1882
Thomas C., June 21, 1923
FOX
Ann C., w. of Robert J. Fox, Apr. 24, 1873
Benjamin Franklin, Apr. 19, 1894
Carolina F., d. of John Claud, w. of Ezekiel Fox, Dec. 16, 1880
Edward, Oct. 23, 1835
Edward Campbell (Capt.), Aug. 11, 1864
Eliza, d. of Dr. William H. and Sallie G. Fox, Dec. 11, 1862
Eliza H., w. of Rev. Thomas H. Fox, d. of Rev. Peter Nelson, Nov. 22, 1855
Elizabeth (Mrs.), Apr. 2, 1840
Elizabeth, w. of Elder Joseph H. Fox, Nov. 17, 1859
Elvira H. (Mrs.), Sept. 6, 1855
Fannie B., w. of B. F. Fox, d. of John Powell, Mar. 20, 1890
Frances A., w. of Rev. Lilburn L. Fox. d. of Mrs. Louisa Chewning, June 1, 1843
George Carlton, s. of Dr. William and Sallie G. Fox, Aug. 21, 1862
George H., Oct. 19, 1871
James, Oct. 1, 1840
Jane, w. of Elder Thomas Fox, Jan. 23, 1851
Jennie, w. of Thomas H. Fox, Jr.,

OBITUARY NOTICES IN THE RELIGIOUS HERALD WITH DATES OF PUBLICATION

Mar. 30, 1865
John N. (Rev.), Feb. 28, 1884
John Powell, Sept. 2, 1937
Joseph, Mar. 25, 1831
Joseph, June 16, 1837
Joseph H. (Mrs.), Feb. 19, 1920
Joseph M., s. of Rev. John N. Fox, July 21, 1870
Katie Ryland, d. of Rev. Joseph H. Fox, Aug. 5, 1886
L. L. (Rev.), June 11, 1885
Laura Ratcliffe (Mrs.), Mar. 29, 1923
Lawrence N., Mar. 3, 1932
Louise Waller, d. of Laura Ratcliffe and W. C. Fox, Nov. 3, 1898
Martha, w. of Thomas P. Fox, Sept. 16, 1847
Martha A., Jan. 23, 1851
Mary, w. of James Fox, Dec. 21, 1865
Mary Ann, Apr. 29, 1909
Mary E., May 7, 1874
Mary Jane, w. of Thomas H. Fox, Jr., d. of Capt. William Williamson, Feb. 9, 1865
Mary Jane, w. of Ezekiel Fox, d. of Joseph Prince, Feb. 9, 1871
Meredith (Dr.), Feb. 28, 1850
Newton Smith, s. of John N. Fox, July 20, 1838
R. A. (Elder), Nov. 21, 1901
Robert C., July 23, 1891
Robert H., Nov. 16, 1871
Sallie, w. of James Fox, Mar. 22, 1866
Sallie, w. of Dr. W. H. Fox, June 2, 1910
Schooler, s. of Dr. W. H. Fox, Jan. 17, 1929
Susan Ryland (Mrs.), Jan. 22, 1920
Susan Y. (Mrs.), Mar. 14, 1844
Thomas (Elder), Dec. 18, 1835
Thomas Frank, Oct. 4 and 11; 1923
Thomas H. (Rev.), Nov. 30, 1865; Apr. 19, 1866
Thomas J., s. of Ezekiel Fox, June 30, 1910
W. H. (Dr.), Jan. 1, 1903
Walker Lyle, s. of John N. and Elizabeth G. Fox, Sept. 16, 1915
William Henry, Aug. 28, 1845

FRANCIS
Emma Ann, d. of Wilson and Mary Francis, Sept. 27, 1853
Jane M. (Mrs.), Dec. 29, 1859
John B., Sept. 3, 1846

FRANCISCO
Peter, Jan. 21, 1830

FRANK
William B., Dec. 18, 1884

FRANKLIN
Carolyn, d. of James H. Franklin, Oct. 8, 1936
Delia A., w. of A. Franklin, May 11, 1848
Edwin W., May 11, 1854
Elizabeth C. (Mrs.), Aug. 6, 1936
Evelina Ann (Mrs.), Aug. 5, 1847
Frances, w. of Robert Franklin, Jan. 31, 1834
J. H. (Mrs.), Feb. 15 and 22, Mar. 21, 1912
John J., Apr. 26, 1849
John Mack (Rev.), Jan. 20, 1938
Joseph, Sept. 10, 1857
Mary (Mrs.), May 27, 1858
Mary A., w. of Benjamin Franklin, Mar. 29, 1860
Mattie Fitzgerald (Mrs.), Feb. 12, 1925

OBITUARY NOTICES IN THE RELIGIOUS HERALD WITH DATES OF PUBLICATION

Mollie Burruss (Mrs.), Feb. 20, 1919
Nancy, Jan. 5, 1865
Sam, Sept. 22, 1921
W. D., Nov. 17, 1938
FRANKLYN
   John J., Apr. 26, 1849
FRANKS
   Washington, July 28, 1859
FRAVEL
   W. A. (Mrs.), Apr. 8 and 29, 1926
FRAY
   Eliza J., w. of John Fray, Jr., Dec. 20, 1860
   Emma R., w. of William H. Fray, d. of Henry and Elizabeth Roberts Crigler Miller, Mar. 10, 1921
   Henry Dutton, s. of W. H. and E. R. Fray, Nov. 3, 1881
   Mattie, w. of Albert Fray, Feb. 23, 1905
   Robert B., May 20, 1858
FRAYSER
   Elizabeth, Oct. 10, 1872
   Francis, May 13, 1836
   Frank P., Apr. 21, 1870
   Harriet, w. of Simon Frayser, Nov. 5, 1840*
   Indiana Lyon, w. of Lewis H. Frayser, Feb. 25, 1864
   Joshua, Jan. 18, 1839
   Maggie Mitchell, w. of J. Willie Frayser, Oct. 30, 1879
   Martha, July 12, 1860
   Mary, w. of Philip Frayser, Jan. 27, 1837
   Philip, July 2, 1840
   Simon, Jr., May 14, 1840*
FRAYZER
   Mildred Ann, d. of Simon and Harriet L. Frayzer, Nov. 25, 1831*
FRAZER
   Ann, w. of W. S. Frazer, May 31, 1877
   David McCoy, Apr. 29, 1926
   Herndon, Jr., Jan. 25, 1877
   Herndon (Rev.), July 26, 1877
   Hulda, w. of Elder Herndon Frazer, May 22, 1845
   John, Jan. 15, 1903
   John Decker (Dr.), Feb. 12, 1914
   Lucinda D., w. of W. T. B. Frazer, Dec. 17, 1891
   M. C. (Rev.), July 10, 1913
   Nannie, d. of John and Susie Frazer, Jan. 30, 1879
   Samuel D., s. of David M. and E. Irene Frazer, Feb. 21, 1901
   Sarah G., w. of John Frazer, July 9, 1857
   Susan Morton, w. of John Frazer, May 6, 1926
   William S., Feb. 9, 1860
   William T., Aug. 14, 1902
FRAZIER
   Edward Thomas, s. of W. R. Frazier, Sept. 1, 1910
   Keziah (Mrs.), Jan. 18, 1855
   Mildred H., d. of Caleb and Obedience Frazier, Aug. 14, 1851
   S. T. (Mrs.), Jan. 26, 1928
   Simon, Dec. 26, 1834*
FREAM
   Richard, Mar. 14, 1878
FRED
   Sallie Rogers, w. of Frank L. Fred, Dec. 22, 1870
FREEMAN
   Elizabeth A. (Mrs.), June 14, 1923
   Emily, Nov. 27, 1902
   Frances S., w. of Rev. Zenas Freeman, Apr. 27, June 15, 1838
   G. H., Mar. 5, Apr. 2, 1857
   Rosa, w. of John W. Freeman, Sept. 11, 1924
   W. B. (Gen.), Mar. 7, Feb. 14 and 28, 1935

* Possible inaccuracy in name, or spelling, but given as printed

OBITUARY NOTICES IN THE RELIGIOUS HERALD WITH DATES OF PUBLICATION

Walker B. (Mrs.), June 10, 1909
William, Mar. 29, 1860

FRENCH
(Rev.), Nov. 28, 1839
Edward Brown, s. of John W. and Judith F. French, Sept. 25, 1873
George B., Mar. 28, 1889
Henley Chapman, July 3, 1890
J. P., May 11, 1843
Mary Virginia, d. of John W. and Judith F. French, Sept. 17, 1863
Mattie C., w. of T. J. French, d. of Z. P. Armstrong, Jan. 12, 1882
Sarah, w. of Hugh French, Dec. 12, 1839

FRETWELL
Jane (Mrs.), Dec. 20, 1855

FRICKER
Fannie Eugenia, w. of James Fricker, d. of A. F. and M. A. Bannon, Dec. 23, 1886

FRIEND
Kate H. (Mrs.), Feb. 8, 1866
Martha Amelia, d. of Edward O. Friend, July 16, 1846

FRISTOE
Ashby Jackson (Dr.), Jan. 27, 1938
E. T., Aug. 4, 1892
Milton T., Mar. 22, 1877
William S. (Lt.), May 14, 1863

FRITTS
Cora Garrett (Mrs.), Jan. 5, 1933

FRIZZELL
Georgie M., w. of W. B. Frizzell, Apr. 19, 1923

FRONTZMAN
Lizzie, Jan. 27, 1859
Sallie M., Jan. 27, 1859

FROST
J. M. (Dr.), Nov. 16, 1916

FRY
C. F. (Mrs.), Nov. 6, 1884
Elizabeth (Mrs.), Apr. 11, 1844

FULCHER
Jane, w. of Philip Fulcher, Mar. 18, 1836
Mary Elizabeth, w. of W. J. Fulcher, May 20, 1886
William H. (Col.), Apr. 23, 1840

FULLER
Frank H. (Rev.), Nov. 28, Dec. 5, 1929
Richard (Dr.), Oct. 26, Nov. 2, 1876
Richard (Rev.), July 24, 1879
Robert W. (Rev.), June 24, 1880
S. T., July 30, Aug. 27, Sept. 17, 1891
Susan E., w. of Robert Fuller, d. of J. J. T. and Mary Townsend Pope, Jan. 4, 1906

FULTZ
David (Judge), Sept. 2, 1886

FUNK
Alberta, Oct. 26, 1922
John, Apr. 23, 1914
John S., Feb. 8, Mar. 22, 1917
R. H., Nov. 17, 1927
Solomon, June 24, July 1, 1880

FUQUA
Aram, Aug. 7, 1873*
C. C. (Mrs.), Nov. 19, 1925
E. T., w. of J. T. Fuqua, July 11, 1867
Edward B., Feb. 23, 1882
Elizabeth C., w. of Abram Fuqua, Oct. 26, 1854
George W., June 20, 1895
James B., s. of John Fuqua, Oct. 27, 1853
Samuel M., June 14, 1888
Tyree C., Nov. 19, 1863

FURBUSH
T. J., s. of C. H. Furbush, Mar. 17, 1898

FURCRON

* Possible inaccuracy in name, or spelling, but given as printed

OBITUARY NOTICES IN THE RELIGIOUS HERALD WITH DATES OF PUBLICATION

Mary C. (Mrs.). Dec. 9, 1852
Rosa Ann, d. of William A. and Mary C. Furcron, Aug. 15, 1850
FURGERSON
Reuben P., Nov. 26, 1868
FURGUSON
Lavinia F., w. of F. M. Furguson, Sept. 9, 1852

FURMAN
James Clement, May 14, 1891
Benjamin Porter, s. of R. Furman, Feb. 3, 1876
FUSSELL
John W. (Rev.), Nov. 12, 1863
Maria E. (Mrs.), d. of John Gathright, Sept. 22, Oct. 20, 1932

G

GAAR
    Ann, w. of Willis Gaar, Aug. 31, 1882
    M. H., May 11, 1893
    Mary H. (Mrs.), July 5, 1866

GABRIEL
    Samuel Willis, Nov. 12, 1936

GAILLARD
    Charles Washington (Rev.), Jan. 6, 1876

GAINES
    Edwin R., Jan. 27, 1876
    Elizabeth (Mrs.), Mar. 24, 1837
    Helen Jeanette, w. of Dr. John M. Gaines, Jan. 21 and 28, 1869
    Janet Harris, Oct. 6 and 13, 1932
    Lucius (Capt.), Jan. 14, 1864
    Mary A. C., w. of Richard Gaines, June 15, 1871
    Susie M., d. of E. R. and Mary S. Gaines, Sept. 14, 1876
    W. A. (Rev.), father of Prof. R. E. Gaines, June 1, 1916
    William H., June 14, 1860

GAINS
    Harry P., Jan. 30, 1890

GALE
    Mollie C. (Mrs.), Nov. 13, 1890
    J. S. (Mrs.), Jan. 20, Feb. 17, 1921
    John Samuel, Oct. 25, 1917
    William, Dec. 3, 1857

GALLASPIE
    Clinton (Mrs.), Feb. 24, 1927

GALPIN
    Eastman J., Jan. 22, 1925
    T. M. (Dr.), July 3, 1930

GALT
    Rosanna, w. of William Galt Jr., May 2, 1828

GAMBRELL
    J. B. (Mrs.), Jan. 26, 1911
    James Bruton, s. of Joel Bruton and Jane Elvira Gambrell, June 16, 1921

GAMMELL
    William, Aug. 11, 1842

GANNAWAY
    John L., Jan. 22, 1863
    Judith, w. of Theodorick C. Gannaway, Oct. 19, 1871*
    Maria E. (Mrs.), Oct. 22, 1874
    Theodoric C., Oct. 22, 1863*
    William G., Mar. 31, 1859

GANO
    Stephen (Rev.), Aug. 29, Oct. 3, 1828

GANT
    John, July 31, 1845

GARBER
    Fred H., Sr., May 22, 1924

GARCIN
    Margaret, w. of Ramon Garcin, mother of Dr. Ramon D. Garcin, July 23, 1914
    Ramon Edward, s. of Dr. Ramon D. Garcin, Aug. 4, 1898

GARDEEN
    Ann Eliza, w. of Dr. John Gardeen, June 28, 1888

GARDEN
    John B. (Dr.), June 1, 1876

GARDNER
    A. L., Nov. 30, 1933
    Amanda H. (Mrs.), w. of Col. A. B. Gardner, d. of Elder T. Bowles, Apr. 18, 1844
    Ann, w. of William Gardner, Aug. 22, 1850
    Ann. E., w. of Ezra Gardner, Nov. 17, 1904
    Anna Mary, d. of Thomas H. and Sarah Gardner, Jan. 18, 1849
    Blanche Ormond, d. of John B. and Sarah J. Gardner, Feb. 4, 1869

* Possible inaccuracy in name, or spelling, but given as printed

OBITUARY NOTICES IN THE RELIGIOUS HERALD WITH DATES OF PUBLICATION

Charles S. (Mrs.), June 18, 1914
Charles T. (Lt.), s. of Prof. Charles S. Gardner, Aug. 29, 1918
Claude Martin, June 19, 1924
Elizabeth, w. of Miles H. Gardner, Apr. 27, 1848
Elizabeth, w. of William Gardner, Sept. 2, 1869
Elizabeth H., d. of Miles H. and Elizabeth Gardner, Oct. 13, 1837
John, s. of William Gardner, Mar. 15, 1835
Louisa, w. of Rev. R. T. Gardner, July 7, 1853
Mary Ann, w. of George Gardner, May 31, 1849
Samuel, Sr., Sept. 17, 1840
Sterling, Feb. 28, 1878
Sylvany (Rev.), July 16, 1874

GARFIELD
James A. (President), Sept. 22, 1881

GARLAND
Cora Linda, d. of A. B. Garland, Apr. 28, 1859
Kate A., d. of Maj. A. B. Garland, Feb. 29, 1872
Luceneth (Mrs.), Jan. 20, 1898
Malvina, Feb. 1, 1883
Mary (Mrs.), Dec. 3, 1863
Robert, Mar. 7, 1861
R. D., Feb. 12 and 19, 1931
R. M., July 1, 1880
Samuel Iveson (Capt.), s. of Maj. A. B. Garland, May 29, 1863

GARLICK
Edward, s. of Dr. J. R. Garlick, June 18, 1903
John W. (Dr.), July 5, 1866
Lizzie, w. of Dr. John Garlick, d. of James Robert and Martha J. Fleet, July 7, 1881
Mildred C., Jan. 21, 1875
Sophia L., w. of Dr. John W. Garlick, July 3, 1856
William Lucke, Jan. 25, 1923

GARNER
A. W. (Mrs.), Sept. 14, 1916
James B., Jan. 7, 1869
Margaret Jane, w. of Conrad Garner, Feb. 12, 1903

GARNETT
Absalom G., s. of Rev. James Garnett, Feb. 27, 1896
Albert Elgin, s. of William A. Garnett, Nov. 18, 1875
Alice M., d. of James and Mary Garnett, Feb. 1, 1872
Ann E., w. of Joel Garnett, Mar. 30, 1905
Ann Elizabeth, d. of James Garnett Jr., Sept. 12, 1850
Ann Elizabeth, Apr. 14, 1892
Ann Maria, w. of Col. R. M. Garnett, Aug. 15, 1828
Bessie Allen, d. of Muscoe H. Garnett, Nov. 5, 1896
Bettie Allen (Mrs.), Sept. 11, 1902
Bettie S., d. of James and Mary Garnett, Feb. 1, 1872
Columbia, s. of James and Mary Garnett, Feb. 1, 1872
Franklin Edmond, s. of James Garnett Jr., Oct. 23, 1913
George, s. of Austin and Emily Garnett, July 9, 1896
George McAdams, s. of Muscoe H. Garnett, Aug. 19, 1886
George Whitfield, Aug. 10, 1876
Helen Mary, w. of Robert Edward Garnett, d. of James Garnett, Jr., Oct. 11, 1888
James (Rev.), July 22, Sept. 2, 1875
James T., Oct. 8, 1857
Jemmy M., d. of James and Mary Garnett, Feb. 1, 1872
Jerry C., Jan. 21, 1909
Joel, July 19, Aug. 16 and 23, 1888
John Muscoe (Dr.), Apr. 9, Sept. 17, 1885
John Muscoe, s. of Dr. John

OBITUARY NOTICES IN THE RELIGIOUS HERALD WITH DATES OF PUBLICATION

Muscoe Garnett, Nov. 24, 1932
John O., Dec. 23, 1858
John Roane (Dr.), Jan. 8, 1885
Joshua A., s. of Mrs. Frances B. Garnett, Feb. 1, 1839
Laura L., Oct. 18, 1917
Lucy Ann, w. of Reuben Garnett, June 19, 1835
Lulu, d. of Mary Garnett, Mar. 8, 1877
Marcia, d. of Joel and Ann Garnett, Mar. 31, Feb. 24, 1887
Martha T. H., Dec. 22, 1837
Mary C., w. of Absalom Garnett, Oct. 21, 1875
Mary Fogg (Mrs.), June 4, 1931
Mary (Molly), w. of Reuben Garnett, Sept. 27, 1839
Mary I. (Mrs.), d. of George B. P. Bowis, June 30, 1853
Mary Strickler, w. of J. Muscoe Garnett, Mar. 8, 1877
Mary T., d. of Rev. Garnett, June 15, 1843
Mary T., w. of James Garnett Jr., d. of Capt. Isaac Willis, May 27, 1869
Mattie E., d. of Thomas and Lucy H. Garnett, June 4, 1857
McCann, s. of James and Mary Garnett, Feb. 1, 1872
Mildred, June 23, 1837
Nannie, Nov. 10, Dec. 1, 1927
Priscilla B., w. of Dr. John M. Garnett, May 11, 1843
R. Calvin, Jan. 29, 1874
Reuben Hancock, Feb. 2, Mar. 23, 1893
Reuben M. (Col.), Mar. 25, 1847
Reuben Meriwether, Aug. 21 and 28, 1902
Rhenvernia, d. of James and Mary Garnett, Feb. 1, 1872
Rivington, s. of James and Mary Garnett, Feb. 1, 1872

Sallie Park, May 2, 1895
Salina Duane, d. of William J. and Mary E. Garnett, Feb. 5, 1863
Sarah Cornelia, w. of Franklin E. Garnett, d. of William Early, Sept. 24, 1874
Tabitha, Feb. 12, 1880
Tabitha Ann, d. of Elder James Garnett, June 7, 1900
Thomas Everett, Nov. 30, 1922
Tillie Baker, d. of George Whitfield and Mary L. Garnett, July 28, Aug. 11, 1887
W. B., Dec. 20, 1888
William Albert, May 3, 1883
Willie T., s. of James and Mary Garnett, Feb. 1, 1872

GARRETT
A. B., Dec. 25, 1924
Alfred (Mrs.), w. of Rev. Alfred Garrett, d. of Mrs. H. M. Borum, Oct. 27, 1904
Alice, d. of Silas S. Garrett, Aug. 8, 1878
Ann Roy (Mrs.), Mar. 21, 1861
Ann Timson (Mrs.), June 23, 1853
Cincinnatus, s. of William W. and Ann R. Garrett, June 8, 1848
Clara, w. of William Garrett, May 10, 1833
Elizabeth, w. of John Garrett, Dec. 25, 1851
Harrison W., Feb. 2, 1854
Jacob, June 3, 1875
Jacob W., s. of Jacob Garrett, Feb. 27, 1862
John Bunyan, s. of E. J. and F. F. Garrett, Nov. 13, 1856
John S., Mar. 26, 1868
Kate, Dec. 20, 1917
Lucy E., d. of Robert S. and Ann Garrett, Oct. 13, 1842
Mary, w. of Edward Garrett, Nov. 11, 1841
R. S., Nov. 5, 1857
R. T., Dec. 16, 1886
Rebecca, w. of John D. Garrett,

OBITUARY NOTICES IN THE RELIGIOUS HERALD WITH DATES OF PUBLICATION

Jan. 20, 1842
Richard Baynham (Rev.), Aug. 10, 1922
Richard H., Feb. 7, 1878
Robert Baynham (Dr.), Oct. 12, 1922
Robert W., s. of Jacob Garrett, Feb. 27, 1862
Sally Betty, d. of Richard Garrett, Sept. 24, 1857
Samuel M., s. of Robert S. and Ann Garrett, Oct. 13, 1842
Silas S., Aug. 8, 1878
Susan, w. of William N. Garrett, July 21, 1837
W. L., Jan. 19, 1905
William E., Aug. 19, 1915

GARRISON
Catharine (Mrs.), Nov. 17, 1837
Margaret Ann, w. of Thomas C. Garrison, Oct. 8, 1885
Reuben R., Jan. 30, 1930

GARTHRIGHT
Benjamin Watkins, July 5, 1923
Ella (Mrs.), Mar. 3, 1927
Mariah F., w. of Oliver Garthright, Nov. 29, 1877
Mollie, w. of Philip Garthright, Sept. 10, 1885
Oliver, Apr. 24, 1902
William Carter, May 31, 1866

GARTHWRIGHT
Willie, s. of W. C. and A. S. Garthwright, May 12, 1864

GARTON
Elizabeth, Aug. 28, 1902

GARY
H. B., Oct. 4, 1888
James, Sept. 20, 1839
John, Apr. 9, July 9, 1857
L. Eddie, s. of M. E. and B. F. Gary, Nov. 15, 1888
Luther M., s. of H. B. and Mary S. Gary, July 4, 1867
M. W. (Gen.), Apr. 14, 1881
Martha, w. of Thomas Gary, June 28, 1860

Mary (Mrs.), Jan. 27, 1837
Mary A., d. of William M. and Maria Gary, Oct. 24, 1844
Mary C. (Mrs.), Jan. 4, 1866
Mary Gertrude, d. of J. Emmet and Emmie G. Gary, Oct. 4, 1898
Rosa Graves, w. of Robert A. Gary, Feb. 5, 1880
S. M. G. (Col.), Jan. 13, 1887

GASKINS
Alice P., d. of Thomas Gaskins, Feb. 9, July 13, 1838
Ann, w. of Capt. R. J. Gaskins, Nov. 16, 1843
Henry W., June 22, 1838
John Eustace, Jan. 23, 1835
Mary A., w. of Richard S. Gaskins, d. of Capt. James Gatewood, July 24, 1856
Richard H. (Capt.), June 24, 1841
Thomas (Col.), Mar. 11, 1869
William Harrison, s. of Dr. Fuller Gaskins, Aug. 6, 1885
William M. (Rev.), July 27, 1848

GATES
Bettie Curtis, w. of William Beverly Gates, Aug. 22, 1861
Beverly Harvie, s. of William B. and Bettie C. Gates, Sept. 25, 1856
Carrie (Mrs.), Feb. 6, 1902
Edwin Lee, Sr., May 20, 1937
Ella E., Aug. 13, 1896
Francis W., s. of James R. Gates, Aug. 24, 1832
James C., Mar. 7, 1872
James Wilson, s. of Charles J. Gates, Nov. 4, 1886
John Lee, Dec. 16, 1886
Judith, w. of Joseph R. Gates, Mar. 24, 1859
Mollie, d. of B. W. Gates, Nov. 12, 1863
Sallie E., d. of Isaac and Phoebe Robertson, Jan. 3, 1895

OBITUARY NOTICES IN THE RELIGIOUS HERALD WITH DATES OF PUBLICATION

William E., Jan. 23, 1919
GATEWOOD
  Amanda (Mrs.); Jan. 31, 1929
  Ann, w. of Travis Gatewood,
    May 29, 1845
  Chancy, Feb. 29, 1844
  Chaney, Aug. 19, 1852
  D. A. (Mrs.), nee Partlow,
    Feb. 28, 1895
  Edith A. (Mrs.), July 4,
    1878
  Elizabeth, w. of Chaney
    Gatewood, Aug. 6, 1830
  Elizabeth (Mrs.), Mar. 10,
    1853
  Frances H., w. of L. B.
    Gatewood, Oct. 2, 1873
  Julia A., July 18, 1895
  Lewis Lunsford, Aug. 26, 1841
  Malinda, w. of Wyatt Gate-
    wood, June 5, 1862
  Marshall Pendleton, May 3,
    1928
  Minnie Pearl, d. of M. P.
    Gatewood, Jan. 16, 1919
  Nancy M. (Mrs.), Feb. 1, 1866
  Philip, Mar. 9, 1876
  Robert, Apr. 10 and 17, 1884
  Sarah E., Jan. 13, 1859
  T. B. (Rev.), July 24, 1913
GATH
  Martha (Mrs.), Nov. 5, 1874
GATHRIGHT
  Bettie H. (Mrs.), Dec. 10,
    1868
  C. C., Mar. 6, 1884
  L. J., Mar. 25, 1926
  Sallie Hunter, Apr. 27, 1854
GATHWRIGHT
  Louisa, Jan. 25, 1839
GATLAND
  Enid, d. of A. H. and Vic-
    toria Gatland, July 9, 1896
GAULDIN*
  Mary V., d. of R. L. Gauldin,
    Sept. 24, 1857
GAULDING
  Ella G., d. of D. E. Gauld-
    ing, Nov. 7, 1867
GAW
  E. Wirt, w. of Dr. Gaw,
    d. of Rev. George F.
    Williams, Oct. 12, 1916
  Sarah C. (Mrs.), July 25, 1901
GAY
  C. Ann S., d. of Neil B. and
    Martha Gay, May 27, 1909
  M. T. (Dr.), Jan. 18, 1900
  S. S., June 24, 1920
  William, Feb. 17, 1853
  William, Mar. 16, 1893
GAYLE
  (Sister), June 7, 1860
  Alberta, w. of John T. Gayle,
    Aug. 2, 1900
  Elizabeth, w. of Thomas Gayle,
    Feb. 20, 1868
  Josiah P., Oct. 7, 1875
  Josiah P., s. of M. J. and
    Virginia A. Gayle, June 28,
    1888
  Josiah P., Feb. 2, 1905
  Mary C., w. of Josiah P.
    Gayle, d. of Mordecai Broad-
    dus, Apr. 24, 1873
  Robert, Sr., June 11, 1857
  Seth, July 17, 1924
  Virginia, d. of M. J. and Vir-
    ginia Gayle, Apr. 20, 1876
GEARHEART
  F. W. (Mrs.), Jan. 27, Feb.
    3, 1921
GEISLER
  Jacob Morell, May 21, 1931
GELLATLY
  W. A., Feb. 11, 1885
GELLISPIE
  Daniel S., Apr. 18, 1901
  Maria H. (Mrs.), Mar. 27,
    1902
GENNETT
  John, June 10, 1852
GENT
  Lucinda Routh, w. of Capt.
    J. C. Gent, d. of Rev. Asa
    Routh, Feb. 1, 1917
GENTRY
  Alice C., d. of John R. and
    Mary J. Gentry, Nov. 20,
    1856

* Possible inaccuracy in name, or spelling, but given as printed

OBITUARY NOTICES IN THE RELIGIOUS HERALD WITH DATES OF PUBLICATION

Benajah, Dec. 17, 1830
Edwin, Mar. 31, 1892
Emma E., d. of A. H. Gentry,
  Oct. 21, 1886
Maria F., d. of Robert
  Gentry, July 23, 1857
Mary H., w. of Robert
  Gentry, Oct. 1, 1874
Newton V., Jan. 19, 1888
Robert, Feb. 19, 1880
Sarah (Mrs.), Oct. 21, 1875
William Andrews, s. of M. G.
  and Julia Ann Gentry,
  Dec. 4, 1845
GEOHEGAN
  Elizabeth Frances Ellen, d.
    of Charles and Elizabeth
    Geohegan, Jan. 27, 1832
GEORGE
  Angeline M., June 26, 1851
  Bezaleel, Jan. 28, 1897
  Cumberland (Elder), Dec. 17,
    1863; Dec. 21, 1865
  Elizabeth, d. of Reuben
    George, June 29, 1848
  Enoch, Sept. 5, 1828
  Franklin (Dr.), Jan. 27, 1898
  James (Dr.), Nov. 18, 1926
  James (Mrs.), w. of Dr. James
    George, Dec. 5, 1929
  Lawson, Aug. 1, 1844
  Sallie T. (Mrs.), Oct. 16,
    1890
  W. H., Mar. 8, 1900
  William (Mrs.), d. of Joseph
    P. Flippo, Oct. 18, 1889
  Z. Jeter (Elder), Apr. 29,
    June 17, 1858
  Zamoth, May 26, 1859
GERRELL
  Mary T. (Mrs.), Sept. 21, 1893
GESSFORD
  Clarence I., Jan. 6, 1927
GIANNINI
  Gaetano, Dec. 24, 1874; Jan.
    14, Mar. 25, 1875
GIBBON
  James (Maj.), July 3, 1835
GIBBS
  Frances (Mrs.), Mar. 4, 1831

  Lucy (Mrs.), Apr. 1, 1847
  Matilda (Mrs.), Apr. 16, 1925
  Peter E., Mar. 9, 1899
  S. A. (Mrs.), w. of P. E.
    Gibbs, Aug. 16, 1888
  Sarah A. E., Aug. 2, 1860
  Sarah E. (Mrs.), June 8, 1882
  W. H. (Mrs.), Dec. 22, 1938
GIBSON
  Ann, w. of Nelson N. Gibson,
    Dec. 24, 1846
  Ann, w. of Capt. Albert G.
    Gibson, Dec. 22, 1859
  Bettie F. SYDNOR (Mrs.),
    May 17, 1923
  C. M. (Mrs.), Aug. 16, 1894
  Charles M., Jan. 9, 1873
  Edwin E., Dec. 4, 1851
  Elizabeth (Mrs.), d. of
    W. C. Stout, May 4, 1916
  Joseph A., Aug. 8, 1907
  Lelia A. (Mrs.), June 13, 1895
  Lucy A., d. of Thomas G. Gib-
    son, Jan. 18, 1855
  Martha Dandridge, d. of Col.
    J. C. Gibson, May 20, 1847
  Mary Melvina, d. of Dr. Samuel
    C. Gibson, July 21, 1853
  Nancy J. (Mrs.), May 5, 1881
  Rebecca (Mrs.), d. of Joseph
    Jackson, Apr. 12, 1866
  Samuel Blair, Sept. 26, 1907
GILBERT
  Dollie, Jan. 20, Feb. 3,
    1927
  Ella, d. of George Gilbert,
    Apr. 20, 1871
  Estella, May 23, 1918
  George W., Mar. 11, 1875
  Hiram F. (Rev.), Dec. 26,
    1929; Jan. 16, 1930
  John, July 28, 1837
  John Cornelius, s. of George
    M. and Emma J. Gilbert,
    Mar. 4, 1869
  M. A. (Mrs.), May 22, 1884
  Mary Eliza, d. of George M.
    and Emma J. Gilbert,
    Mar. 4, 1869
  Samuel G. (Mrs.), d. of Capt.

OBITUARY NOTICES IN THE RELIGIOUS HERALD WITH DATES OF PUBLICATION

Campbell, Aug. 24, 1832
William, Aug. 16, 1906
Willie, Mar. 21, 1912
GILES
  G. O. (Dr.), Mar. 24, 1938
  George W., Jan. 21, 1937
  Jennie, w. of J. S. Giles, May 1, 1879
  John T., Apr. 13, 1933
  Stephen J., s. of James W. and Ann C. Giles, Aug. 6, 1857
  William B., former Governor of Virginia, Dec. 10, 1830
GILL
  Alma Gertrude, d. of R. S. and N. E. Gill, June 21, 1883
  Charles W., Sept. 15, 1887
  Emmett C., Feb. 27, 1936
  Gladys Lynn, d. of Emmett C. Gill, Nov. 7, 1918
  James Edward, Dec. 28, 1911
  Laura R. (Mrs.), d. of Rev. Alexander H. Bennett, Feb. 19, 1920
  Lucy Moncure, w. of T. B. Gill, June 16, 1927
  Mary Virginia, d. of Joseph and Mary H. Gill, Sept. 20, 1833
  Nancy, w. of Matthew Gill, Apr. 15, 1858
  William Spencer, July 20, 1905
GILLASPIE
  Elijah, Nov. 29, 1894
  Mary F., May 9, 1901
GILLASPIEY
  Nancy C., Oct. 9, 1862
GILLESPIE
  Docia, July 27, 1871
GILLETT
  Susan, Apr. 26, 1923
GILLETTE
  A. D. (Dr.), Oct. 5, 1882
  Margaret Smith (Mrs.), Dec. 26, 1912
GILLIAM
  Alice D., d. of Capt. John J. Gilliam, Sept. 17, 1857
  Ann Olivia, w. of John W. Gilliam, June 29, 1899
  Burnedette, d. of W. C. Gilliam, Oct. 3, 1901
  Clementine, d. of Wilson Gilliam, Feb. 23, 1860
  Edward G., June 23, 1892
  Eliza B., w. of Dr. Glover D. Gilliam, Feb. 19, 1885
  Emma P., w. of Edward G. Gilliam, d. of Cornelius Gilbert, Sept. 15, 1881
  Fannie Diuguied (Mrs.), Sept. 27, 1923
  Fannie Lee, Jan. 16, 1890
  Frank Hatchett, s. of J. J. Gilliam, June 6, 1929
  Glover D. (Dr.), Oct. 21, 1852
  Isham, Jan. 26, 1860
  James, July 30, 1857
  James H., Feb. 15, 1934
  James R., Mar. 6, 1856
  Jane Hamlet, w. of Walter Flood Gilliam, d. of Armistead and Sarah O. Hamlet, Aug. 3, 1916
  John Madison, Sept. 30, 1909; May 30, 1912
  Joseph Daniel, Jan. 2, 1879
  Josie Douglas, d. of Mr. and Mrs. J. W. Gilliam, Feb. 9, 1899
  Julia A., w. of E. Gilliam, Aug. 14, 1902
  M. A., w. of H. E. Gilliam, Aug. 22, 1889
  Mary H., w. of Capt. R. H. Gilliam, d. of John D. Priddy, Dec. 31, 1885
  Mary Jane, d. of James R. and Martha Whitehead Gilliam, May 30, 1912
  Martha C., mother of Dr. Francis B. Gilliam, Nov. 21 and 28, 1844
  Moses, Jan. 13, 1881
  Nannie Elma, d. of Edward and Judith C. Gilliam, Nov. 26, 1868

OBITUARY NOTICES IN THE RELIGIOUS HERALD WITH DATES OF PUBLICATION

Rice H., Dec. 29, 1859
S. Addie (Mrs.), May 24, 1888
Samuel R., s. of Overton T. Gilliam, Mar. 8, 1860
Sophia P., w. of Elder William T. Gilliam, Nov. 16, 1865
T. W., May 13, 1924
Thomas West, July 10, 1924
Walter Flood, Mar. 11, 1926
William A. (Capt.), s. of Rev. William T. Gilliam, Jan. 28, 1864
William A. (Dr.), Apr. 26, 1866
Wilson, Aug. 9, 1860
GILLILAND
  George W., Dec. 31, 1891
GILLISPIE
  William A. (Dr.), Feb. 4, 1875
GILLS
  Archibald, Aug. 4, 1870
  Cornelia Bertha, d. of Joseph A. and Kate A. Gills, Mar. 27, 1884
  E. E., Oct. 5, 1922
  Elizabeth (Mrs.), May 30, 1861
  Elizabeth C., d. of W. P. and E. P. Gill, May 8, 1884
  G. Dabney, Feb. 16, Mar. 16, 1893
  Julian Braxton, Oct. 21, 1920
  Lottie E. (Mrs.), Mar. 24, 1932
  Lucy Madison, d. of Robert F. Gills, Dec. 24, 1863
  Mary Susan, w. of William H. Gills, Dec. 30, 1909
  William, Aug. 23, 1883
GILMAN
  Fannie Bell, d. of William P. and Mary E. Gilman, Nov. 29, 1860
  Frances A., d. of Eliza P. Gilman, Dec. 31, 1840
  Maria E., w. of William P. Gilman, Apr. 4, 1867
GILMER
  B. H. (Dr.), Sept. 14, 1922

GILLUM
  Marie Dunkin, w. of John Gillum, May 23, 1918
  T. O. (Mrs.), May 6, 1937
GILOBERT
  Mattie, w. of W. P. Gilobert Apr. 28, 1887
GIMBERT
  Allan, May 31, 1923
GITT
  W. R. (Elder), Feb. 12, 1874
GIVENS
  Nashwell Taylor, May 4, 1905
GLASCOCK
  Bedford, s. of Thomas Glascock, Feb. 21, 1929
  Caroline E., w. of Thomas G. Glascock, July 9, 1857
  Helen, w. of John S. Glascock, Jan. 24, 1918
  Ida, w. of Bedford Glascock, Aug. 1, 1878
  Lucy Mildred, July 26, 1923
GLASS
  John B., s. of Rev. John S. Glass, July 29, 1858
  John S. (Rev.), Aug. 24, 1899
  Nancy, w. of Capt. Willis Glass, Apr. 26, 1855
  Pamelia, w. of David Glass, d. of Samuel and Letitia Wharton, Mar. 9, 1899
  Sarah, w. of James Glass, June 3, 1836
  Susan C., w. of J. Carter Glass June 25, 1903
GLASSELL
  Andrew M. (Dr.), July 19, 1888
GLASSFORD
  Cerelia Jane (Mrs.), d. of James Clingan, Feb. 9, 1871
GLAZEBROOK
  Lucy (Mrs.), May 1, 1873
GLEASON
  Maggie A., w. of H. M. Gleason, July 21, 1881
  Robert E. (Rev.), Aug. 7, 1902
GLENN
  D. A. (Rev.), June 12, 1930
  Florence Bowling, d. of Capt.

OBITUARY NOTICES IN THE RELIGIOUS HERALD WITH DATES OF PUBLICATION

Alonzo M. Glenn, Aug.
  6, 1885
James Richard, Mar. 20, 1924
Susanna (Mrs.), Dec. 17, 1830
William Thomas, s. of William
  and Jane Glenn, Feb. 1,
  1833
GLINN
  Emma, w. of G. R. Glinn,
    Sept. 11, 1890
  Laura B., w. of Peter D.
    Glinn, July 1, 1886
GLOVER
  Prudy, w. of A. J. Glover,
    d. of George Campbell,
    July 1, 1875
GOAD
  James M., Feb. 5, 1874
  Levi J., June 13 and 20,
    1861
GODDIN
  Alice, d. of John T. and
    Lizzie Goddin, June 10,
    1880
  James A., Feb. 1, 1872
  James Avery, s. of James H.
    and Mary T. Goddin, July
    20, 1876
  James H., Apr. 28, 1887
  Thomas Hammer, May 5, 1853
  Virgia, d. of James H. and
    Mary T. Goddin, July 20,
    1876
  Wellington, Dec. 16, 1886
GODFREY
  Nancy, w. of William Godfrey,
    Sr., Jan. 29, 1852
  William, Sr., May 11, 1854
GODSEY
  D. W., Apr. 28, 1921
  Edna J., d. of James B. and
    Kate Godsey, July 25, 1901
  Emolyn Nelson, d. of James
    and Ella Godsey, Dec. 18,
    1879
  J. B., May 16, 1918
  James Madison, July 29, 1909
  Martha A., May 14, 1874
  Mary E., w. of Daniel L.
    Godsey, Oct. 27, 1859

William D., s. of Daniel L.
  and Mary E. Godsey, Oct.
  27, 1859
GODWIN
  Anna W. (Mrs.), Mar. 27, 1924
  George A., s. of Mills B. and
    Lydia Crane Godwin, Apr. 20,
    1871
  Logan, s. of R. H. W. Godwin,
    Feb. 4, 1864
  Thomas C., May 10, 1839
GOFF
  John, July 6, 1854
  Lulie Foster, w. of T. L.
    Goff, d. of Thaddeus and
    Louise Foster, Jan. 16, 1890
GOFFIGON
  Arinthia (Mrs.), Feb. 4, 1892
  L. H. (Mrs.), Apr. 27, 1933
GOGGIN
  Elizabeth J., w. of Rev. T. C.
    Goggin, Nov. 5, 1874
  Polly, w. of Pleasant Goggin,
    d. of Rev. William Leftwich,
    Mar. 30, 1854
  Stephen, Mar. 14, 1872
GOHAGAN
  Fanney, d. of J. A. and A. F.
    Gohagan, May 12, 1853
GOLD
  Thomas D., Dec. 16, 1915
  Thomas E., Mar. 14, 1878
GOLDSMITH
  L. B. (Mrs.), Sept. 17, 1896
GOOCH
  Charles D., Mar. 17, 1927
  Maggie W., w. of Willis
    Gooch, d. of Capt. W. W.
    Wood, Mar. 7, 1867
  Mary, w. of Overton Gooch,
    Oct. 31, 1828
  Nannie D., w. of C. D.
    Gooch, May 10, 1923
  Richard Barnes, June 19, 1851
  Stephen, Feb. 27, 1840
  Stephen Oscar, s. of Edwin O.
    Gooch, Aug. 30, Nov. 15,
    1860
  Thomas, July 24, 1851
  William T., Nov. 6, 1851

OBITUARY NOTICES IN THE RELIGIOUS HERALD WITH DATES OF PUBLICATION

GOOD
  John S., Jan 25, 1872
  Mary E., w. of John S. Good, Jan. 25, 1872
GOODALL
  John H., s. of Elder Cincinnatus and Charlotte E. Goodall, Dec. 8, 1859
  Lucy B., Sept. 2, 1836
GOODCHILD
  Frank M. (Dr.), Mar. 15, 1928
GOODE
  Ann T. (Mrs.), Aug. 5, 1841
  Anna Lewis, w. of Walthall C. Goode, Jan. 28, 1875
  Benjamin E. (Elder), June 21, 1849
  Cyrus Vernon, s. of James B. and Judith A. Goode, June 3, 1869
  Damaris M., w. of D. B. Goode, June 15, 1854
  Daniel Benjamin, Mar. 4, 1920
  David M. (Capt.), Aug. 23, Oct. 25, 1883
  E. Branch, Apr. 20, 1882
  Ellis, s. of James B. and Judith A. Goode, Sept. 26, 1918; Aug. 11, 1921
  Emily Elizabeth, d. of Rev. John K. and Laura Goode, Nov. 12, 1908
  Eudora V., d. of Richard and Mary A. P. Goode, Sept. 10, 1846
  Frances W., June 5, 1856
  George H. (Mrs.), Nov. 7, 1912
  Harriet M., w. of John B. Goode, Feb. 6, 1851
  Hattie, d. of James B. and Judith A. Goode, June 3, 1869
  Jane E., w. of David Goode, d. of Henry Tate, Mar. 31, 1853
  John, Sr., Aug. 22, 1850
  Joseph, Dec. 15, 1870
  Joseph Benjamin, s. of James B. and Judith A. Goode, June 3, 1869
  Judith (Mrs.), July 26, 1860
  Louisa W., d. of Daniel B. and Damaus M. Goode, Mar. 30, 1838
  Mack, Oct. 3, 1850
  Martha Elizabeth, w. of Samuel Pleasants Goode, Sept. 13, 1900
  Martha J., w. of H. F. Goode, d. of Rev. William Hankins, June 12, 1873
  Mary A. P. w. of Richard Goode, Dec. 12, 1867
  Mary Jane, w. of David Goode, Aug. 19, 1897
  Mary W., w. of William Goode, Jr., July 26, 1849
  Maude, d. of W. O. and E. J. Goode, Aug. 23, 1888
  Mollie Bagwell, w. of Richard W. Goode, d. of W. H. H. Bagwell, Nov. 15, 1894
  Mollie Watkins, d. of David and Mary J. Goode, May 12, 1864
  Olia, w. of J. T. Goode, Apr. 3, 1919
  Phoebe A., w. of Samuel Goode, Dec. 9, 1852
  R. L. (Mrs.), Nov. 8, 1934
  Richard, July 23, Aug. 13, 1857
  Robbie, s. of Silas and Jennie Goode, Mar. 1, 1877
  Sallie Browne, d. of Silas and Jennie Goode, Mar. 1, 1877
  Sally, w. of Mack Goode, May 18, 1832
  Samuel P., Apr. 18, 1872
  Sarah Ann, w. of Joseph Goode, May 25, 1843
  Sarah E., w. of John Richard Goode, Aug. 17, 1871
  Shelbourne S., Sept. 29, 1881
  T. H., s. of J. B. Goode, May 24, 1883
  Thomas F. (Col.), s. of Dr. Thomas Goode, Jan. 12, 1905
  Virgie, d. of S. S. and Jennie Goode, June 1, 1876

OBITUARY NOTICES IN THE RELIGIOUS HERALD WITH DATES OF PUBLICATION

Walthall C., Aug. 4, 1870
William (Maj.), Dec. 18, 1845
William R., s. of John B. and Harriet M. Goode, Mar. 30, 1843

GOODIN
Martha, w. of Cornelius Goodin, d. of Berry Luckado, June 11, 1863

GOODLOE
Ann, w. of John H. Goodloe, Nov. 29, 1860
Archibald Lewis, m. Bettie M. Hill, May 26, 1904
B. H., Sept. 2, 1875
Eddie C. (Mrs.), July 7, Aug. 11, 1881
Elizabeth, w. of Simon P. Goodloe, May 23, 1872
John H., Jan. 7, 1897
Mary Eliza, w. of George P. Goodloe, Sept. 8, 1875
Mary L., May 30, 1861
Nellie J., w. of Spotswood H. Goodloe, d. of Capt. William P. Jarman, Sept. 6 and 13, 1866*
Sym B., June 5, 1845*

GOODLOW
Richard Fuller, s. of William and M. L. Goodlow, Mar. 4, 1869

GOODMAN
Amanda M. F., w. of John N. Goodman, Jan. 15 and 29, 1846
Angelia E., Oct. 23, 1862
Ann Eliza, w. of Elder J. W. Goodman, July 21, 1842
Hugh F. (Mrs.), June 3 and 17, 1920
J. T., Feb. 13, 1840
James Henry, s. of James and Eliza Goodman, Apr. 1, 1841
Joseph W., Oct. 9, 1862
Keziah, w. of C. G. Goodman, Aug. 14, 1862
Madrid Barnly, s. of Joseph and Amanda Goodman, Dec. 29, 1842

Manoah, s. of Augustus Goodman, Oct. 25, 1833
Manoah S., s. of Charles G. Goodman, Apr. 24, 1862
Mary F. (Mrs.), Nov. 3, 1881
Merryweather (Mrs.), Nov. 5, 1885
Nannie J. (Mrs.), Oct. 5, 1876
Octavia Gray (Mrs.), June 16, 1938
Richie J. (Rev.), Aug. 29, 1918
Sarah E. (Mrs.), Jan. 30, 1851
Susannah W., w. of Joseph Goodman, Apr. 22, 1858

GOODRICH
D. (Mrs.), Nov. 11, 1880
Lucy Ann, w. of Charles Goodrich, Oct. 16, 1845
Sarah, w. of E. L. Goodrich, May 5, 1881

GOODSON
Nicholas, July 20, 1843

GOODWIN
Adeline, w. of James H. Goodwin, Mar. 10, 1870
Annie E., d. of James A. Goodwin, Feb. 11, 1875
Archibald T., Jan. 29, 1846
Candace, w. of Archibald T. Goodwin, Apr. 22, 1847
Caroline Decker (Mrs.), May 21, July 16, 1925
Charles E., s. of Charles E. and Isabella Goodwin, Sept. 11, 1853
E. P. (Dr.), Sept. 30, 1869
Edward P., s. of James W. and Eliza Goodwin, Aug. 29, 1850
Elizabeth, w. of Hugh Goodwin, Apr. 6, 1832
Elizabeth G. (Mrs.), Sept. 27, 1877
Emily Frances (Mrs.), May 1, 1913
Frances A., w. of Peter Goodwin, d. of Rev. S. Woolfolk, May 14, 1863
Hugh, Jan. 23, 1845

* Possible inaccuracy in name, or spelling, but given as printed

-133-

OBITUARY NOTICES IN THE RELIGIOUS HERALD WITH DATES OF PUBLICATION

John, s. of Dr. William Goodwin, May 7, 1863
Juliet S. (Mrs.), d. of George H. Crank, Jan. 30, 1890
Mary, w. of Harwood Goodwin, Feb. 15, 1849
Mary E., Dec. 25, 1890
Mary Jane, d. of Archibald and Elizabeth Goodwin, Jan. 15, 1846
Nicy Ann, w. of Hugh Goodwin, July 26, Sept. 20, 1849
Nora M., w. of James H. Goodwin, June 7, 1883
Philip E. W. (Mrs.), d. of J. F. Flournoy, Oct. 10, 1912
Robert, Aug. 2, 1849
Susie B. (Mrs.), Feb. 28, 1918
Thomas Littleton, s. of Dr. John M. Goodwin, July 9, 1863
Weir Randolph, Aug. 11, 1910
William (Dr.), May 7, 1863

GOODWYN
Ada Byron, d. of James M. and Celia Goodwyn, Feb. 9, 1843
Fannie, d. of John B. and Julia A. Goodwyn, Mar. 24, 1864
Lizzie D., d. of Mrs. Mary F. Goodwyn, June 17, 1875

GOOLSBY
Georgianna Nicholas, d. of Thomas and Martha Goolsby, Apr. 15, 1841
John A., Feb. 4, 1892
M. V. (Mrs.), Sept. 11, 1890
Martha Ann, w. of John A. Goolsby, Feb. 27, 1879
Mary Marshall, d. of Thomas Goolsby, Sept. 7, 1838
Mollie (Mrs.), Apr. 24, 1919

GORDEN*
Katie A., w. of Caleb W. Gorden, d. of A. J. and Rebecca Ansell Gorden, Jan. 31, 1889

GORDON
A. J. Nov. 25, 1880; Jan. 6, 1881

Annie Foreman (Mrs.), July 28, 1927
Chalmers (Mrs.), July 5, 1934
Edward H., Jan. 30, 1851
Edward Harrison, s. of John A. Gordon, Oct. 26, 1871
Elizabeth F., w. of Bernard M. Gordon, July 6, 1848
Hannah Frazer, Jan. 12, 1865
Hannah, d. of Elder John C. Gordon, May 11, 1848
Jane E. L., w. of John A. Gordon, July 28, 1859
Jane Lewis, d. of Joseph H. and Hannah E. Gordon, June 7, 1900
John Addison, s. of Elder John C. Gordon, June 14, 1883
John Churchill (Elder), May 11, 1848
John Palmer, Sept. 1, 1938
Joseph A., Aug. 27, Sept. 10, 1891
Joseph H., Nov. 8, 1877
Joseph H., Sept. 17, 1891; Jan. 7, 1892
Lizzie Clifton, Jan. 8, 1903
Louisiana, w. of John N. Gordon, Dec. 4, 1884
Lucy, w. of Elder John G. Gordon, Mar. 23, 1838
Lucy H., w. of A. J. Gordon, d. of Larkin Willis, Dec. 9, 1875
Luther L., s. of Katie and Caleb Gordon, Feb. 6, 1890
Margaret (Mrs.), May 25, 1905
Marshall, Sept. 29, 1859
Mary Harris (Mrs.), Oct. 3, 1912
Nannie Judson, May 13, 1897
Rachel R., w. of James E. Gordon, d. of Clif and Mildred Harvey, July 13, 1899
Roxie B., w. of J. R. Gordon, d. of H. A. Boyd, Aug. 15, 1918
Susan Ann F., d. of Elder Robert Gordon, Oct. 14, 1836

* Possible inaccuracy in name, or spelling, but given as printed

OBITUARY NOTICES IN THE RELIGIOUS HERALD WITH DATES OF PUBLICATION

Theresa Willis, d. of Joseph H. and Hannah E. Gordon, May 22, 1913
Thomas Herndon, s. of Joseph and Hannah E. Gordon, Apr. 25, 1912
William H., Jan. 31, 1879

GORE
Julia L., d. of Elder D. N. and Sarah A. Gore, Mar. 16, 1876
Percy C., Feb. 5, 1903
Sidney S., July 12, 1906

GORNTO
Mattie, Nov. 25, 1886

GORRELL
Benjamin H., June 9 and 16, 1898
Charles Benjamin, s. of Dr. J. Hendren Gorrell, May 27, 1915
Jennie S., w. of B. H. Gorrell, Aug. 26, 1875
Joseph, May 6, 1847
Lelia Chandler, d. of B. H. and Jennie S. Gorrell, Aug. 13, 1868
Lida Burns, d. of B. H. and J. S. Gorrell, Sept. 14, 1871
Mary B., d. of B. H. and Mary J. Gorrell, Dec. 19, 1878

GOSS
Jesse Hamilton (Rev.), Apr. 26, May 24, 1839
John (Elder), Feb. 6, 1873

GOUGH
George E., Oct. 10, 1901
Henry, May 14, 1931
Nora E., Feb. 24, Mar. 16, 1916
W. R. (Mrs.), July 9, 1936

GOULD
E. B., w. of Dr. James B. Gould, Oct. 7, 1875

GOULDEN
J. R., May 1, 1902

GOULDER
M. Bettie, July 8, 1897

GOULDIN
John S., Dec. 23, 1847
Rebecca M., w. of John W. Gouldin, Sept. 29, 1859
Virginia M., d. of John Gouldin, Sept. 7, 1843

GOULDMAN
Albert Payne, Aug. 2, 1900
Henrietta, Jan. 15, 1914
Maria E. (Mrs.), Mar. 17, 1910
Sue, Jan. 14, 1932
Virginia E., d. of A. P. and M. E. Gouldman, July 29, 1858
Walter, Dec. 7, 1871

GOVAN
Anna Maria Tupper, w. of James Govan, May 13, 1875
Martha Margaret, d. of James and Lucy Garnett Govan, Oct. 9, 1851
Mary, d. of James and Anna Maria Tupper Govan, May 13, 1875

GOVERN
Charles C. (Rev.), Oct. 17, 1834

GRACE
Ellen Lovell (Mrs.), June 8, July 6, 1905

GRADY
Frank T. (Dr.), Oct. 11, 1860
Maria Virginia, d. of Dr. T. T. and Jane Grady, Mar. 7, 1850

GRAHAM
Jane W., w. of John Graham, July 17, 1856
John Newton, s. of John N. Graham, Nov. 8, 1866
Joseph B., July 23, 1903
S. H., Feb. 24, Mar. 24, 1898
Sarah, w. of David Graham, Mar. 21, 1878

GRANBERRY
Laura, d. of S. S. Granberry, Apr. 19, 1883

GRANT
James H., Feb. 8, 1849
Mary, July 4, 1828
U. S. (Gen.), July 30,

OBITUARY NOTICES IN THE RELIGIOUS HERALD WITH DATES OF PUBLICATION

1885
GRANTLAND
  Ann, w. of John B. Grantland, Aug. 20, 1830
  J. B., Oct. 6, 1842
GRAVATH
  William I., Sept. 22, 1921
GRAVATT
  Bettie A., w. of George Gravatt, d. of John Broaddus Sept. 18, 1902
  Ellis, Oct. 15, 1863
  Frances, w. of William Gravatt, Jan. 21, 1858
  George, Aug. 14, 1890
  George Jenifer, s. of George W. and Bettie A. Gravatt, Oct. 10, 1872
  George W., Apr. 23, 1863
  Lucy, Aug. 21, 1856
  Margaret Ellis (Mrs.), Dec. 27, 1900
  Nannie, d. of Robert and Lucy Gravatt, Oct. 23, 1862
GRAVELY
  Julia C., w. of Benjamin F. Gravely, d. of John W. and Nancy Thomas, June 7, 1900
GRAVES
  A. M. (Mrs.), Mar. 31, 1938
  A. W. (Rev.), Mar. 21, Apr. 11, 1929
  Amanda M., w. of Isaac L. Graves, July 20, 1871
  Ann Melissa, d. of Dr. R. H. and Ann J. Graves, June 14, 1877
  Bettie Lelia, d. of Dr. and Lucy Graves, July 16, 1863
  C. O. (Mrs.), Dec. 30, 1926
  Catharine S., w. of Jeremiah W. Graves, June 25, 1840
  Charley W., s. of Richard P. and Lucy F. Graves, Aug. 17, 1854
  Edwin Walker, s. of James W. and Sarah Jane Graves, Oct. 12, 1854
  Elizabeth M., d. of Isaac Graves, July 31, 1845
  Fannie, w. of Lewis Graves, Sept. 28, 1882
  Fenton Dutton, s. of Rev. Alvan W. and Donnie A. Graves, Aug. 7, 1884
  Frances, Apr. 21, 1881
  Harriet, w. of William Graves, July 16, 1846
  Hugh Curran, s. of Lewis Graves, Feb. 1, 1849
  Isaac, Sept. 25, 1845
  J. E. (Mrs.), Feb. 3, 1921
  J. W., June 5, 1884
  James W., Dec. 18, 1856
  Jane, Mar. 2, 1876
  John (Capt.), Jan. 26, 1843
  John R., Jan. 27, 1837
  Lewis, June 11 and 18, 1868
  Lucy F., w. of Capt. Richard P. Graves, Sept. 6, 1877
  Lucy M., w. of Asa W. Graves, Jan. 10, 1867
  Mary Ann, d. of Col. Thomas Graves, July 7, 1837
  Mary G., w. of William H. Graves, June 7, 1883
  Mary J. CRUMP, w. of Elijah Graves, Apr. 18, 1878
  Nancy (Mrs.), Aug. 26, 1858
  R. H. (Rev.), June 6, 1912
  R. M., May 7, 1874
  Rachel Angelina, d. of William Graves, Aug. 24, 1832
  Robert H., Dec. 3, 1863
  Rosewell Hobart (Rev.), Jan. 20, 1876
  Rufus E., July 6, 1922
  Sarah C., d. of Matthew Graves, Sept. 2, 1836
  Sarah J., w. of C. H. Graves, May 26, 1887
  Susan, d. of William Graves, Nov. 15, 1855
  Thomas (Mrs.), Oct. 26, 1838
  W. F. (Maj.), July 9, 1923
  William Preston, Apr. 10, 1890
GRAVETT
  Charlie T., s. of J. S.

OBITUARY NOTICES IN THE RELIGIOUS HERALD WITH DATES OF PUBLICATION

Gravett, Mar. 9, 1922
GRAY
  Alice, Dec. 6, 1388
  Alphonso A., Dec. 17, 1908
  Amey, w. of George P. Gray, June 23, 1842
  Belle B. (Mrs.), Sept. 8, 1927
  Emily Anderson, Mar. 29, 1855
  Gabriel, July 8, 1852
  Ida F., w. of Andrew J. Gray, June 30, 1887
  Jane R., May 24, 1860
  John L., s. of Dr. William A. Gray, June 12, 1873
  Laurence, s. of John and Bettie Gray, Jan. 2, 1873
  Lucy Steptoe (Mrs.), Dec. 19, 1935
  Lucy Susan (Mrs.), Nov. 11, 1897
  Margaret (Mrs.), Oct. 27, 1837
  Maria S. (Mrs.), Feb. 18, 1831
  Martha Wilson, d. of Capt. G. Gray, Jan. 25, 1849
  Mary (Mrs.), Aug. 26, 1920
  Richard W., s. of Dr. N. B. Gray, Sept. 30, 1858
  Sallie Terrell, w. of Alphonso A. Gray, Mar. 15, 1866
  William A. (Dr.), Mar. 7, 1889
  William Brooks (Dr.), s. of Dr. Alfred Gray, Dec. 8, 1904
GRAYBILL
  Ora Brugh (Mrs.), Mar. 13, 1924
GRAYSON
  George, s. of William D. and Mary F. Grayson, Mar. 20, 1862
  Mary, w. of William D. Grayson, Nov. 8, 1900
GREEN
  Benjamin, Jan. 28, 1864
  Bernard R., s. of J. T. Green, Feb. 19, 1920
  David, June 4, 1846
  Elizabeth (Mrs.), Jan. 13, 1853
  Elizabeth Ann, w. of Capt. Alden Green, Nov. 22, 1849
  Finnella M., Sept. 24, 1857
  Frances E., w. of J. Beverly Green, d. of Major Thomas Dabney, Feb. 25, 1869
  George, Oct. 21, 1852
  George Henry, Dec. 7, 1854
  Jane, w. of Robert Green, Apr. 18, 1867
  John P. (Rev.), June 1, 1933
  Lester, Aug. 31, 1933
  Letitia (Mrs.), Jan. 16, 1873
  Lucy (Mrs.), d. of Col. William Edwards, Mar. 29, 1855
  Lucy Y., w. of Charles T. Green, Nov. 25, 1875
  Martha (Mrs.), July 9, 1891
  Olivia Alma Spilman, w. of Charles Brimer Green, Apr. 5, 1888
  Philip, Feb. 16, 1871
  Richard P., Nov. 20, 1829
  Richard W., Oct. 15, 1863
  Robert W., Oct. 15, 1863
  Sophia, w. of Thomas P. Green, Nov. 4, 1841
  T. P. (Elder), Sept. 28, 1843
  Theophilus F., May 1, 1862
  Thomas Madison (Rev.), Feb. 12, 1925
  Virginia May (Mrs.), Mar. 23, 1893
  William F., Nov. 27, 1845
  William P., Sept. 13, 1860
GREENE
  Charles Edward, s. of W. E. and Sallie E. Greene, Aug. 26, 1880
  George W. (Rev.), Jan. 18, 1912
  Martha Ann, w. of Edward Greene, June 11, 1896
  Sallie Rebecca, d. of Edward

OBITUARY NOTICES IN THE RELIGIOUS HERALD WITH DATES OF PUBLICATION

and Martha Ann Greene,
  Sept. 29, 1881
Samuel Harrison (Dr.), Nov.
  4, 1920
Samuel S., Sept. 3, 1896
GREENHOW
  Frances B. (Mrs.), Jan. 16,
    1840
  James W., Dec. 23, 1852
GREENLAW
  Sally R. (Mrs.), Mar. 16, 1838
  William, June 2, 1837
GREENSTREET
  John, Sept. 18, 1873
GREENWAY
  Nellie Timberlake, w. of
    J. R. Greenway, d. of J.
    Massie Smith, Jan. 25,
    Apr. 19, May 10, 1894
GREENWOOD
  Darinda A., w. of William B.
    Greenwood, Mar. 8, 1860
  Nancy, w. of R. H. Greenwood,
    Aug. 8, 1878
  R. H., June 19, 1902
GREER
  Olga McGinnis, Oct. 12, 1922
  T. W. (Rev.), Feb. 1, 1900
  Will (Mrs.), Sept. 28, 1922
GREGG
  Amanda, d. of Decatur P. and
    Mary D. Gregg, Sept. 15,
    1842
GREGORY
  Alice J., w. of E. S. Gregory,
    July 4, 1872
  Amy M., d. of William H. and
    Sue A. Gregory, Oct. 9,
    1873
  Anna M., w. of William A.
    Gregory, Oct. 11, 1855
  Della S. (Mrs.), Mar. 26,
    1914
  E. N., Sr., Apr. 21, 1927
  Elizabeth, w. of John
    Gregory, Mar. 17, 1837
  Elizabeth A. (Mrs.), Mar. 17,
    1864
  Elizabeth R., w. of Dr. William W. Gregory, July 18,
    1844
  Ernest T. (Rev.), Apr. 14,
    1904
  Eva May, d. of George T.
    Gregory, Nov. 3, 1881
  Fendall, May 17, 1877
  George T. (Mrs.), July 19,
    1923
  Ida B., d. of Nelson Gregory,
    Feb. 28, 1867
  J. L., Dec. 25, 1890
  Jane W., w. of Dr. John W.
    Gregory, Oct. 11, 1833
  John Madison (Capt.), Jan.
    14, 1864
  John T., June 25, 1857
  Josephus, July 1, 1880
  Judith C. (Mrs.), May 14,
    1868
  Kate Davenport (Mrs.), June
    25, 1931
  Laura Alma, d. of Edwin S.
    and Rosa H. Gregory, Dec.
    11, 1873
  Laura Smelling (Mrs.), Mar.
    15, 1934
  Lettey, w. of Robert Gregory,
    Aug. 15, 1844
  M. A. (Mrs.), July 19, 1888
  Mamie Lee, d. of Charlie and
    Della Gregory, Aug. 22,
    1889
  Martha J. (Mrs.), Oct. 23,
    1856
  Mary, w. of Fendall Gregory,
    May 24, 1839
  Mary E. A., w. of Richard H.
    Gregory, Feb. 11, 1847
  Nelson, May 23, 1861
  O. F. (Rev.), Jan. 16, Apr.
    10, 1919
  Olinthus (Dr.), Apr. 8, 1841
  Polly, w. of Capt. John Gregory, July 12, 1849
  Richard, Jan. 2, 1845
  Richard A., Aug. 21, 1835
  Richard Thomas, s. of Richard
    A. and Elizabeth A. Gregory,
    Feb. 28, 1850
  Robert S., Apr. 21, 1853

OBITUARY NOTICES IN THE RELIGIOUS HERALD WITH DATES OF PUBLICATION

Rosa May, d. of Dr. John E. and E. C. Gregory, Feb. 10, 1887
Rosena Harriet (Mrs.), Oct. 8, 1914
Susan, w. of Rev. James Gregory, Feb. 1, 1855
T. S., July 22, 1858
Thomas, Apr. 13, 1843
Thomas, s. of Dr. William W. Gregory, July 18, 1844
Thomas, Mar. 20, 1856
William D., May 20, 1858
William H. (Maj.), May 8, 1829
William H., Feb. 28, 1884

GRESHAM

Ada, Mar. 18, 1897
Adelaide, w. of Thomas J. Gresham, Dec. 24, 1863
Albert G., Sept. 12, 1861
Alice Cannada (Mrs.), Apr. 6, 1916
Ann C., w. of B. F. Gresham, Dec. 3, 1857
Belle Maury, d. of E. J. and Fanny W. Gresham, Apr. 23, 1885
Bunnie, d. of Mrs. Edward Gresham, Oct. 30, 1873
Catherine T. (Mrs.), Oct. 5, 1905
Charles A., Sept. 24, 1846
Eddie W., s. of Rev. Edward Gresham, Feb. 4, 1886
Edward (Rev.), Apr. 24, 1873
Edward, s. of Dr. Philip and May Gresham, Sept. 14, 1899
Elijah, May 12, 1859
Fenelon, s. of Dr. Charles Gresham, Nov. 18, 1858
Frederick, s. of John N. and Hannah E. Gresham, Nov. 20, 1856
Gennett (Mrs.), July 4, 1867
George S., Nov. 25, 1880
George Thomas, Dec. 11, 1924
Hannah E., w. of John N. Gresham, d. of John Bagby, Sept. 13, 1883
Isabella, w. of Rev. Edward Gresham, Oct. 22, 1891
J. R., Aug. 29, 1918
John N., Aug. 28, 1884
Julia, Apr. 29, 1920
Junius S., s. of B. F. Gresham Oct. 25, 1883
Killie A., w. of Samuel Gresham, d. of Raleigh Dunaway, Feb. 23, 1888
Lucy T., Nov. 12, 1868
M. Ellie, d. of John H. and M. E. Gresham, July 15, 1869
Maria Josephine, w. of Edwin Gresham, Dec. 4, 1856
Martha Anna, w. of Richard T. A. Gresham, Oct. 11, 1849
Mary Alice, w. of B. F. Gresham, Oct. 2, 1884
Mary E., w. of Albert G. Gresham, Dec. 25, 1862
Mary M., w. of E. J. Gresham, July 27, 1871
Mary Page, d. of E. J. Gresham, Oct. 21, 1880
Mary S., d. of B. F. and Mary S. Gresham, Oct. 25, 1883
Mary Susan, Aug. 18, 1853
May, w. of Dr. Philip Gresham, June 6, 1907
May Ruth, d. of Clarence and Alice S. Gresham, Dec. 25, 1890
Mollie E., d of Sylvanus Gresham, Feb. 18, 1886
Nanny, d. of William and Harriet N. Gresham, Sept. 20, 1860
Philip (Dr.), May 11, 1882
R. S. (Mrs.), Mar. 9, 1933
R. T. A., Feb. 3, 1876
Ruby McCombs, d. of Clarence and Alice Gresham, Dec. 25, 1890
S. S., Jr., Jan. 28, 1886
S. S., Mar. 26, Apr. 9, 1891
Samuel Dec. 25, 1845
Samuel, June 12, 1873
Susannah (Mrs.), Oct. 1, 1868

OBITUARY NOTICES IN THE RELIGIOUS HERALD WITH DATES OF PUBLICATION

W. W., Nov. 2, 1933
William D., s. of Thomas
  Gresham, July 31, 1884
GRESSITT
  Frances, w. of Mordecai
    Gressitt, Sept. 23,
    1841
  Ida Lyell, w. of John
    M. Gressitt, Nov. 16,
    1933.
  John M., June 7, 1928
  Lola, d. of W. M. and
    Eliza Gressitt, Nov. 25,
    1880
GRIEVE
  William, Aug. 12, 1875
GRIFFIN
  Benjamin, Dec. 26, 1844
  Bettie, June 25, 1896
  John T., May 6, 1920
  Julia A. (Mrs.), May 10,
    1928
  Mary V. (Mrs.), May 8, 1902
  Miles V., Apr. 23, 1896
  Nannie, d. of Maj. John.
    Boykin, Aug. 24,
    1916
  Nathaniel, Nov. 4, 1886
  R. H., Nov. 11, 1858
  Virginia, mother of K. R.
    Griffin, Mar. 3, 1881
  Virginia Ann, w. of Nathaniel
    Griffin, Feb. 14, 1901
  Virginia J., d. of Nathaniel
    Griffin, June 29, 1899
  William H., Aug. 21, 1856
GRIFFITH
  Arthur Fleet, s. of Rev.
    Richard H. and Mary H.
    Griffith, Mar. 19, 1874
  Ida May, d. of Rev. Richard
    H. Griffith, Nov. 7, 1867
  James M., Sept. 1, 1910
  Jemima A., Jan. 2, 1873
  Joseph T., Mar. 23, 1911
GRIGG
  Jacob (Elder), Oct. 9, 1835
  Thomas Edward, July 13, 1933
GRIGGS
  Jeremiah (Col.), July 20,
    1871
  Lucy, May 7, 1885
  Willie, s. of Walter S.
    Griggs, Mar. 25, 1875
GRIGSBY
  James W., Feb. 23, 1893
GRIM
  Nina (Mrs.), d. of Mrs. W.
    A. Read, Jan. 1, 1931
GRIMES
  Johnnie Peyton, s. of J. Lee
    and Jennie M. Grimes, May
    14, 1874
GRIMSLEY
  A. M. (Rev.), father of Rev.
    M. R. Grimsley, May 3 and
    31, 1894
  Addie Walton, d. of Rev.
    Simeon U. and Sallie A.
    Grimsley, Oct. 30, 1879
  Milton R. (Rev.), Aug. 10,
    1899
  Robbie Holman, s. of Rev.
    Simeon U. and Sallie A.
    Grimsley, Oct. 30, 1879
  Sallie A., w. of Rev. S. U.
    Grimsley, Feb. 14 and 21,
    1924
  Simeon U., Dec. 20, 1906
  Thomas F. (Rev.), s. of Rev.
    Barnett Grimsley, Mar. 13
    and 20, 1913
  William L.J., s. of Rev. S.
    U. and S. A. Grimsley, Apr.
    14, 1898
GRIMSTEAD
  Mary C. (Mrs.), d. of Columbus
    and Sophia Ansell, Dec. 1,
    1910
GRINSTEAD
  John, Dec. 9, 1841
  Martha A. (Mrs.), June 14,
    1888
  Sarah E., w. of Richard Grinstead, d. of Stephen and
    Mary Pettus, Nov. 23, 1876
GRIZZARD
  Benjamin Harrison, s. of C.
    P. Grizzard, Apr. 8, 1897
  Cader Powell, s. of Richard L.

OBITUARY NOTICES IN THE RELIGIOUS HERALD WITH DATES OF PUBLICATION

and Mattie Grizzard, Feb. 10, 1921
Eugene Harris, Apr. 28, 1927
J. W., Mar. 10, 1921
Mary Mondell (Mrs.), Mar. 22, 1923
R. W. (Rev.), Nov. 5, 1936
Roger Wallace, s. of Cader and Ruth Grizzard, Aug. 20, 1891
Wilma Beaton, d. of E. H. Grizzard, Sept. 8, 1898

GROOME
Juliette FLEET, w. of William H. Groome, Mar. 7, 1912
Lafayette F., s. of William W. and Harriet J. Groome, Dec. 3, 1863
Minnie Logan, d. of William H. and Juliet C. Groome, June 30, 1892

GROVE
Elizabeth Bell (Mrs.), June 20, 1935

GRUBB
Mary Griffith (Mrs.), Feb. 5, 1925

GRUBBS
Annie Winn, d. of Edward A. and Sarah Ann Grubbs, July 2, 1863
Bernice, d. of Reuben E. and Cornelius Grubbs, Apr. 9, 1896
Elizabeth, w. of Hardin Grubbs, Jan. 8, 1857
John S., Dec. 9, 1852
Olander, s. of Hardin Grubbs, Jan. 8, 1857
Peter W., Apr. 2, 1885
Robert, s. of Edward A. and Sarah Ann Grubbs, July 2, 1863
Susan, w. of Anderson Grubbs, June 25, 1846
Thomas C., s. of Edwin and Elizabeth Grubbs, Oct. 22, 1863
Walter W., s. of Edward A. and Sarah Ann Grubbs, July 2, 1863
William Washington, s. of Peter W. and Ann Grubbs, Oct. 5, 1838

GUARD
Jane J., w. of Robert C. Guard, d. of Richard Waggoner, Apr. 30, 1857

GUINN
J. H., Aug. 31, 1933

GUNN
Burwell, May 24, 1855
J. Marger, May 22, 1879
Margaret A., w. of James M. Gunn, Sept. 22 and 29, 1859
Martha J., w. of James F. Gunn, Mar. 12, 1863
Mary Ann, w. of William F. Gunn, Mar. 10, 1870
William F., Aug. 25, 1853

GUNNEL
Alexander, Jan. 26, 1893
Lucy J. (Mrs.), Jan. 26, 1893

GUNTER
Bessie E., d. of Judge B. T. Gunter, July 11 and 25, 1901
Ellen F., w. of Col. B. T. Gunter, Dec. 5, 1878
Joseph, Dec. 24, 1840
Mary (Mrs.), Sept. 8, 1853
Mary T., July 28, 1837

GUTERAGE
Mary, Sept. 4, 1856

GUTHRIE
A. S., Dec. 25, 1902
Julia Ann, w. of Richard Thomas Guthrie, Dec. 6, 1860
Mary (Mrs.), Feb. 10, 1837
Mary J., Feb. 14, Apr. 24, 1924
Samuel, s. of Mrs. Matilda Guthrie, Dec. 10, 1863
William, Oct. 21, 1886
Willie Joseph Decator, s. of William B. and Susan E. Guthrie, Nov. 22, 1860

GUTRIDGE

OBITUARY NOTICES IN THE RELIGIOUS HERALD WITH DATES OF PUBLICATION

Lucy, d. of R. S. Gutridge, Nov. 3, 1859

GUY

Hannah, w. of Warner W. Guy, Mar. 5, 1840
Jane P., w. of George T. Guy, Apr. 27, 1843
Nancy, Mar. 10, 1837
Rebecca (Mrs.), d. of Richard M. Crandol, Nov. 1, 1860

GWALTNEY

Benjamin (Col.), May 11, 1843
Harriet Ryland (Mrs.), Nov. 30, 1922
James M., Sept. 18, 1890
John R., s. of Elder J. L. Gwaltney, Dec. 18, 1862
Joseph G. B., May 10, 1855
Louisa F., w. of Rev. L. R. Gwaltney, d. of A. A. Davidson, Oct. 17, 1861
Martha Brundell, w. of Rev. James L. Gwaltney, May 21, 1868
Mary, w. of Elder James Gwaltney, Dec. 21, 1832
Mary, d. of W. D. P. and Mary A. Gwaltney, Feb. 23, 1854
Mary Emily Beal, w. of Willis Reuben Gwaltney, Apr. 26, 1923
Thomas Ryland, Nov. 1, 1923; Jan. 31, 1924
Virginia (Mrs.), Apr. 23, 1896

GWATHMEY

Alfred Brooke, Feb. 11, 1892
Amanda B. (Mrs.), July 23, Sept. 3, 1868
Ann, w. of Richard Gwathmey, Apr. 21, 1837
Annie B., w. of A. B. Gwathmey, d. of James M. Binford, Jan. 5, 1888
Ann Maud, d. of Alfred B. Gwathmey, Feb. 23, 1888
Bettie B., d. of Dr. William Gwathmey, May 27, 1897

Caroline (Mrs.), Mar. 3 and 31, 1921
Charles Brown, s. of Robert Temple Gwathmey, Aug. 16, Sept. 20, 1894
Cora Leed, d. of Lewellyn T. and Sue W. Gwathmey, May 29, 1863
Edward Garlick, Feb. 19, 1931
Eleanor, Jan. 22, 1931
Elizabeth T., w. of Dr. William Gwathmey, Oct. 30, 1879
Emilie B., d. of R. T. and Leonora S. Gwathmey, Sept. 4, 1879
Eugenia K., d. of R. T. and L. S. Gwathmey, Oct. 29, 1857
Eugene Temple, s. of L. T. Gwathmey, May 20, 1886
Eva Baker (Mrs.), Feb. 6, 1908
Evelyn C., w. of Robert Temple Gwathmey, June 25, 1846
Hardinia Morris, Oct. 5, 1905
James Taylor, s. of R. Gwathmey, Aug. 12, 1852
Jeannette Garnett Ryland, w. of Joseph H. Gwathmey, mother of Dr. William Gwathmey, Aug. 26, Oct. 21, 1915
John Hill, Apr. 5, 1839
Joseph H., Mar. 28, 1918
Leonora S., w. of R. T. Gwathmey, Mar. 27, 1862
Lewis Temple, Sept. 15, 1881
Lucy Taylor, w. of Judge O. O. Gwathmey, Apr. 15, 1926
Maria W., Nov. 5, 1857
Mary, Nov. 11, 1836
Mary A., w. of George N. Gwathmey, d. of John L. Ligon, June 26, 1879
Mary Atwood, d. of Dr. William Gwathmey, Mar. 26, 1868
Mary Fanny, d. of Dr. William Gwathmey, Mar. 2, 1832
Mary Garlick (Mrs.), Oct. 24, 1867
R. R., Oct. 9 and 30, 1919

OBITUARY NOTICES IN THE RELIGIOUS HERALD WITH DATES OF PUBLICATION

Richard, s. of Richard Gwathmey, Sept. 23, 1852
Richard, Jan. 4, July 26, 1866
Sarah T. (Mrs.), May 8, 1835
Susan Wood, w. of L. T. Gwathmey, d. of Benjamin Carlton, Apr. 16, 1874
T. Hinton, July 25, 1867
W. H. (Dr.), May 6, June 10, July 15, 1886
W. W., Nov. 24, 1898
William, Apr. 1 and 8, May 13, 1858
William (Dr.), Dec. 2, 1875
Willie Ryland, w. of Alfred B. Gwathmey, d. of William Semple Ryland, Dec. 26, 1901

GWIN

Crawford David, s. of Rev. D. W. and Jennie C. Gwin, July 15, 1897
D. W. (Rev.), Aug. 21, 1884
Frances J. T., w. of David S. Gwin, Jan. 18, 1872
George B., s. of D. S. and Frances J. T. Gwin, Sept. 9 and 30, 1858
Howell B. (Dr.), Oct. 14, 1926
J. Alexander, s. of D. and F. T. Gwin, June 3, 1841
W. W. (Rev.), June 3 and 17, July 29, 1875

GWINN

E. J., July 14, 1887

GWYN

Frances B., w. of Hugh B. Gwyn, Feb. 25, 1858

H

HABEL
Pilcher, s. of Rev. Samuel T. and Mary Louise Habel, Feb. 7, 1918

HACKETT
Agnes, d. of Capt. Pleasant Hackett, July 4, 1828
Horatia B. (Dr.), Nov. 18, 1875
Mary P., w. of Dr. William R. Hackett, Oct. 14, 1847
Sarah Jane, Apr. 13, 1838
Susan (Mrs.), d. of William Waldrop, Jan. 13, 1887

HACKLEY
Marion Alice, w. of W. E. Hackley, Aug. 21, 1924

HACKNEY
John Robert, Apr. 30, 1840

HADEN
Mollie Gray (Mrs.), Mar. 2, 1899
Pamelia A. (Mrs.), Oct. 22, 1891
Robert B., Nov. 17, 1870

HAGAN
Charles H., July 5, 1934
Charles H. (Mrs.), Nov. 19, 1936
Eugene Hardaway, s. of R. E. and Lucy P. Hagan, Dec. 4, 1879
Mary L. (Mrs.), Oct. 29, 1936

HAGERMEYER
Alice J. (Mrs.), d. of A. W. and R. C. Jones, Jan. 31, 1884

HAIGHT
Willard R. (Rev.), Apr. 8 and 29, 1926

HAILE
Matilda Roland Wright, w. of John Haile, June 20, 1907
1907
Robert, Sept. 10, 1885
Mary C., w. of R. L. Haile, Sept. 14, 1882
Willoughby Newton, Oct. 18, 1883

HAILEY
B. T., s. of J. E. and M. H. Hailey, Feb. 9, 1893
Elizabeth (Mrs.), Sept. 12, 1889

HAINES
E. G. (Col.), Dec. 23, 1858

HAIR
Peter (Maj.), Oct. 26, 1882

HAIRSTON
Samuel, s. of Samuel and Agnes Hairston, Sept. 25, 1845

HAISLIP
Basil Vivian, Aug. 8, 1918
Catherine D. (Mrs.), July 27, 1871
George W., June 9, 1881
Lee Elsom (Mrs.), Jan. 22 and 29, Feb. 19, 1931

HALCROFT
Mary Jane, Feb. 5, 1852

HALDANE
Robert, Mar. 2, 1843

HALE
Joel Ezra, s. of Joel and Lizzie Hale, Feb. 2, 1888
Joel M., Sept. 22, 1898
Lemuel Bryan, s. of Joel and Lizzie H. Hale, June 30, 1898
Orleana B., w. of F. O. Hale, May 14, 1874

HALES
John H., Nov. 23, 1838

HALEY
Callie Goode, w. of Floyd Haley, d. of S. D. Goode, May 5, 1898
Douglas, s. of Rev. James T. Haley, June 25, 1904
Fanny, w. of Joseph Haley, March 21, 1895

-144-

OBITUARY NOTICES IN THE RELIGIOUS HERALD WITH DATES OF PUBLICATION

J. T., Feb. 6, 1930
Joseph C., Mar. 1, 1877
Julia Bet, w. of W. P. Haley, June 2 and 16, 1921
L. J. (Rev.), Feb. 22, 1917
Lewis, July 16, 1846
Sarah E. (Mrs.), Dec. 20, 1877
Sarah W., w. of J. C. Haley, Mar. 1, 1877
T. A. (Mrs.), w. of Dr. T. H. Haley, Feb. 5, 1914
W. W. (Mrs.), Mar. 8, 1923

HALL
A. C., May 14, 1903
Addison (Rev.), Apr. 13 and 20, 1871
Addison Taylor, June 30, 1910
Ambrose, July 14, 1870
Ann Judson, w. of William Hall and d. of Col. Robert Alexander, June 25, 1863
Annie E., d. of T. D. and M. A. Hall, Dec. 5, 1878
Annie G., d. of Maj. and Julia Hall, Mar. 10 and 17, 1870
Annie Kate, d. of W. G. and Mary Ida Hall, Mar. 1, 1877
Archie, child of Maj. and Julia Hall, Mar. 17, 1870
C. D., May 10, 1900
Catherine C., w. of Rev. Addison Hall, Oct. 18, 1849
Charles, Feb. 16, 1893
Clarence, s. of Rev. Addison and L. N. Hall, Nov. 26, 1863
Columbia H., w. of Shelton H. Hall, d. of Elder George Northam, Aug. 21, 1856
Daniel, May 13, 1875
Dinah, Feb. 28, 1867
E. M. (Mrs.), Nov. 16, 1893
Edward D., Aug. 23, 1860

F. H. (Rev.), s. of Addison Hall, June 29, 1893
Eli M., July 12, 1911
Eliza A., w. of Rev. W. C. Hall, Apr. 21, May 19, 1881
Elizabeth (Mrs.), Feb. 13, 1851
Elspeth Bates, July 16, 1925
F. Hubert, s. of F. H. and M. D. Hall, Aug. 6, 1885
Fannie Elliot, d. of J. B. Hall, Aug. 2, 1877
Franklin, s. of Elder Addison and L. N. Hall, Nov. 26, 1863
G. A., May 6, 1920
George W., May 7, 1891
Henrietta, w. of R. M. Hall, Feb. 24, 1859
Henriotta L., d. of James and Hardenia O. Hall, Apr. 19, 1888
Henry Johnson, July 6, 1871
J. H. (Dr.), July 30, 1903
John, s. of Warner Hall, Nov. 10, 1842
John N. (Rev.), Dec. 14, 1905
Joseph M., s. of Rev. William C. and Ann Eliza Hall, Apr. 9, 1857
Lancelot, Nov. 6, 1873
Lucius Ferdinand, s. of Addison and Catherine C. Hall, Sept. 29, 1837
Lydia Bird (Mrs.), Nov. 15, 1928
Mamie, Oct. 16, 1924
Manlius, s. of Rev. Addison and L. N. Hall, Nov. 26, 1863
Martha A., w. of Edward D. Hall, Aug. 23, 1860
Mary, w. of Henley Hall, Nov. 22, 1849
Mary, w. of Alexander Hall, Apr. 29, 1915

OBITUARY NOTICES IN THE RELIGIOUS HERALD WITH DATES OF PUBLICATION

Mary Ann, w. of
  William B. Hall,
  June 15, 1843
Mary K., w. of Dr. Julius
  T. Hall, Oct. 10, 1912
Mary L., Mar. 7, 1929
Mary Lizzie, d. of W.
  G. and Mary Ida Hall,
  Mar. 1, 1877
Mary P., w. of Rev. T.
  A. Hall, d. of Robert
  Allison, May 27, 1886
R. L. (Mrs.), Sept. 18,
  1884
Richard M. (Elder), Nov.
  1, 1860
Robert (Rev.), May 6, 1831
Roberta Alexander, d. of
  William and Ann J. Hall,
  Aug. 22, 1861
Sarah, May 11, 1843
Sarah, w. of Robert
  Marshall Hall, Apr.
  6, 1899
Sarah A., d. of Isaac and
  Matilda Hall, May 4, 1854
Selina Melvina, w. of C.
  Frank Hall, Mar. 26, 1885
Sibbie Walker, Feb. 24,
  1921
Silas B., May 11, 1843
Spence, June 8, 1871
Susan, w. of Col.
  Addison Hall, Jan. 13,
  1832
Susie E., Apr. 5, 1934
T. A. (Mrs.), w. of Rev.
  T. A. Hall, May 27, 1886
T. A., Mar. 14, 1929
Thomas D., June 4, 1903
Thomas H., June 25, 1896
Thomas H., Oct. 4, 1923
Timothy A. (Mrs.), w. of
  Rev. Timothy A. Hall,
  Feb. 7, 1929
W. C. (Rev.), Dec. 8, 1892
W. R., Apr. 15, 1937
William (Mrs.), Apr. 26,
  1928
William B., June 25, 1868
William H., Feb. 19, 1880
Willie Edward Lee, s. of
  Jerome B. and Fannie E.
  Hall, Aug. 3, 1871
Zadoc J., June 9, 1904
HALLER
  Louisa, Mar. 22, 1849
HALLET
  Lucy A., w. of Edward M.
    Hallet and d. of Capt.
    William Dixon, Jan. 13,
    1859
  Sarah, Sept. 22, 1898
HALLEY
  Ann M., w. of Dr. S. H.
    Halley, Apr. 25, 1878
  Boyce Gibson, s. of James W.
    and Mary A. Halley,
    June 10, 1875
  Henry S., Dec. 21, 1838
HALLIBURTON
  Martha R., w. of Thomas
    Halliburton, Mar. 14,
    1834
HALSEY
  Mary, w. of William A.
    Halsey, Mar. 25, 1858
  William A., Mar. 2, 1832
HALSTEAD
  Deborah A., w. of K. W.
    Halstead, June 28, 1888
HAM
  Trannie A., w. of M. H.
    Ham, May 5, 1887
HAMBERLIN
  L. R., May 1, 1902
HAMBLETON
  Nancy M. (Mrs.), Apr. 25,
    1901
  Virginia A., w. of J.
    P. Hambleton, Jan. 9,
    1919
HAMBLIN
  John, Apr. 1, 1836
HAMBRICK
  Andrew L., Apr. 28, 1887
HAMILTON
  A. L. (Capt.), May 28,
    1936
  B. F., Sept. 7, 1933

OBITUARY NOTICES IN THE RELIGIOUS HERALD WITH DATES OF PUBLICATION

Benjamin F. (Mrs.), June 5, 1924
John S., Mar. 24, 1898
Kate Tupper, Nov. 20, 1884
Mary W., w. of B. F. Hamilton, Apr. 30, 1925
W. P., father of Dr. W. W. Hamilton, July 29, Aug. 4, 1910

HAMLET
Bettie, d. of James and Sarah H. Hamlet, May 15, 1862
James, Sr., Feb. 12, 1836
James, Mar. 17, 1892
James William, s. of James and S. H. Hamlet, May 15, 1862
James Marshall, s. of James Hamlet, Sept. 24, 1863
Mary E. (Mrs.), d. of John W. Marshall, June 23, 1904
Nancy P., w. of Capt. James Hamlet, Aug. 3, 1848
R. A., Jan. 24, 1901
Rose Lilly, Dec. 3, 1914
Sarah, w. of Thomas Hamlet, Sept. 13, 1860
Sarah Ann, d. of Alexander Roberts, Feb. 23, 1854
Sarah H., w. of James Hamlet, Jan. 10, 1861
Sarah O., w. of Armistead Hamlet, July 23, 1863
Thomas, Feb. 3, 1870

HAMLIN
Cattie, w. of L. J. Hamlin, d. of John G. Powell, Feb. 2, 1888
Emily, w. of William Hamlin, d. of R. B. Jones, Oct. 18, 1888
John William, s. of L. J. Hamlin, Feb. 18, 1886

HAMM
Cornelia L., d. of J. C. Hamm, Aug. 23, 1883

HAMMACK
Mariah E. (Mrs.), Jan. 11, 1906

HAMMER
Jane, June 26, 1862

HAMMOND
R. H. (Capt.), Dec. 22, 1910

HAMNE
Susan G., w. of J. B. Hamne, Feb. 13, 1908

HAMNER
Charlie Russel, s. of Dr. William and Jane M. Hamner, July 26, 1860
Isabella, w. of James Hamner, Nov. 18, 1875
J. C. (Rev.), May 6, Aug. 5, 1875
James, s. of Nicholas and Mary Hamner, Aug. 25, 1910
Mattie Shepherd, w. of Howard Hamner, July 14, 1887
Nannie, d. of Robert Hamner, Mar. 24, 1870
Nathaneal Garland, June 23, 1904
Salley B., Oct. 11, 1917
Sallie A., w. of Charles W. Hamner, May 24, 1855
Sallie Allen, d. of Dr. W. W. and Jane M. Hamner, Apr. 23, 1863
Sarah A. F., w. of Edward D. Hamner, Sept. 6, 1855
Virginia, d. of John T. Hamner, Sept. 6, 1923
W. J., July 5, 1883
Wyatt W. (Dr.), Oct. 21, 1869

HAMPTON
Henry (Col.), Jan. 24, 1878
Margaret Steele, w. of S. W. Hampton, d. of John A. and Catherine Steele, Feb. 11, 1892
Susan F., Jan. 16, 1873

HAMRICK
J. M. (Rev.), July 11, 1929

HANCOCK
Annanias, Feb. 24, 1837
Arietta, w. of H. Horace

OBITUARY NOTICES IN THE RELIGIOUS HERALD WITH DATES OF PUBLICATION

Hancock, July 26, 1860
Beverly Augusta (Judge), Jan. 28, Apr. 14, 1904
Beverly C. (Elder), Oct. 4, 1849
Charles W., Mar. 15, 1928
Daniel Beasley, Feb. 14, 1878
Elizabeth, w. of Rev. Francis Hancock, June 21, 1860
Ella F. B., d. of Mrs. Mary F. Hancock, Dec. 10, 1863
Emma, w. of C. W. Hancock, June 16, 1921
Frank A., d. of A. E. and O. E. Hancock, Aug. 15, 1872
Hannah Walthall, w. of Capt. Higgison Hancock, Oct. 14, 1880
Henry Albert, Aug. 11, 1870
James (Dr.), Dec. 23, 1869
Jefferson (Dr.), July 23, 1857
Keziah, w. of Ananias Hancock, Sept. 9, 1836
Madison H., July 12, 1855
Marie E., w. of Matthew W. Hancock, Oct. 2, 1862
Martha L., Feb. 14, 1861
Martin, Oct. 19, 1838
Mary A., w. of Dr. Jefferson Hancock, Aug. 12, 1852
Mary D., w. of Col. Woodson W. Hancock, Oct. 22, 1846
Mary F., w. of Col. W. W. Hancock, Dec. 20, 1894
Maud G., d. of F. G. and Bettie Hancock, July 8, 1858
Melville Cardoza, child of Mrs. Bettie Hancock, Mar. 1, 1866
Orson Victor, s. of Col. W. W. Hancock, Apr. 2, 1863
Samuel (Col.), Oct. 23, 1856
Samuel A., Nov. 10, 1864
Sarah Catharine, Feb. 14, 1895
Tommy, s. of Daniel B. and and Molly E. Hancock, July 28, 1859
Walter Martin, Oct. 10, 1935
Willard M., Jan. 2, 1936
Willie, child of Daniel B. and Molly E. Hancock, July 28, 1859

HANCOX
Joseph N. (Mrs.), w. of Capt. Joseph N. Hancox, Dec. 24, 1891
Joseph N., Nov. 12, 1896

HANDY
Henry J. (Rev.), Apr. 4, 1907
Marianna, w. of Rev. H. J. Handy, d. of Paymaster Speiden, U. S. Navy, Oct. 5, 1876
Marianna, d. of Rev. H. J. Handy, Aug. 18, 1881

HANES
Thomas C., s. of Garland Hanes, July 3, 1856

HANEY
Wilson, s. of John W. and Hattie E. Haney, Nov. 15, 1877

HANGER
John Newton (Mrs.), Apr. 10, 1919
Lannie Broadus (Mrs.), Sept. 18, 1919*

HANKINS
Daniel, May 20, 1847
Ezra, May 19, 1859
George A., s. of Ezra and Elizabeth Hankins, Aug. 11, 1910
J. (Capt.), Oct. 5, 1854
Joseph Henry, Sept. 2, Oct. 7, 1915

* Possible inaccuracy in name, or spelling, but given as printed

OBITUARY NOTICES IN THE RELIGIOUS HERALD WITH DATES OF PUBLICATION

Mildred J., w. of Rev.
  William Hankins, May 30,
  1895
Thomas L., s. of Daniel
  Hankins, Sept. 14, 1848
HANKS
  Willie A., w. of G. W.
    Hanks, Sept. 8, 1892
HANNAH
  Thomas, Oct. 17, 1918
HANSFORD
  Elizabeth (Mrs.), June 3,
    1836
HARCAM
  William P. (Col.), Mar.
    31, 1853
HARCUM
  W. T., Dec. 1, 1938
HARDAWAY
  John S. (Rev.), June 25,
    July 9, 1925
  Nannie Winston, d. of
    John S. and Sally Steger
    Hardaway, May 15, 1890
  Robert Horace, s. of
    John S. and Anna H.
    Hardaway, June 9, 1898
  Sally Gaines, May 19, 1932
HARDBARGER
  C. W., Feb. 28, 1924
HARDCASTLE
  Aaron Bascom (Col.), Mar.
    18, 1915
  E. L. (Rev.), s. of Col.
    A. B. Hardcastle, Apr.
    9, Mar. 19, 1936
  Sarah E., w. of Rev. E.
    L. Hardcastle, Aug.
    25, Sept. 1, 8, and 15,
    Nov. 10, 1932
HARDGROVE
  Benjamin Franklin, s. of
    Thomas and Mary W. Hard-
    grove, Jan. 19, 1843
  E. M., w. of Samuel Hard-
    grove, Mar. 11, 1847
  Samuel, Nov. 6, 1862
  Thomas, Mar. 22, 1866
HARDIE
  Sophia, w. of William
    Hardie, Mar. 6, 1829
  Virginia, Feb. 10, 1859
HARDIN
  Annie Lizzie, Nov. 23, 1876
  Charles W. (Dr.), Feb. 9,
    1899
  James, Sept. 5, 1872
HARDING
  Cyrus Blackwell, s. of Cyrus
    and Laura E. Harding,
    Dec. 31, 1863
  Dora (Mrs.), Sept. 28, 1933
  James W., s. of James H.
    and Emily S. Harding,
    May 16, 1872
  Laura E. (Mrs.), Jan. 4, 1877
  Nannie Blackwell, d. of Capt.
    Cyrus and Laura E. Harding,
    Dec. 1, 1864
HARDMAN
  Ann Jane (Mrs.), Apr. 4, 1861
HARDWICK
  Andrew Fuller, s. of Dr.
    J. B. Hardwick, Apr. 2
    and 9, 1885
  Leola, d. of Rev. J. B.
    and M. J. Hardwick, Aug.
    25, 1864
HARDY
  A. F. (Mrs.), July 3, 1902
  Allen F. (Rev.), July 21,
    1892
  Ann N., w. of William T.
    Hardy, d. of John G.
    and Margaret Thompson,
    June 2, 1904
  Drury A., s. of George W.
    and Mary A. Hardy, July
    16, 1857
  Eleanor Frances, d. of Rev.
    F. L. Hardy, Sept. 16,
    1909
  Frank L. (Dr.), Oct. 26,
    Nov. 9, 1933
  Hannah (Mrs.), Dec. 18,
    1829
  John, Sr., Dec. 6, 1888
  Kate M. (Mrs.), d. of
    Samuel T. Miller, Mar.
    12, 1936

OBITUARY NOTICES IN THE RELIGIOUS HERALD WITH DATES OF PUBLICATION

Louisa Anne, Mar. 14, 1907
Lulu E. H., w. of Capt.
  L. T. Hardy, d. of Z. H.
  McGruder, Mar. 10, 1870
Mary, w. of R. C. Hardy,
  May 27, Sept. 2, 1852
Mary A., w. of George W.
  Hardy, Jan. 12, 1865
Mary Sue, d. of William and
  Mary Hardy, July 18, 1861
R. Henry, s. of William and
  Mary Hardy, July 18, 1861
Sarah W. (Mrs.), Oct. 15,
  1891
Vincent I., Feb. 9, 1838
William Leslie, s. of Leslie
  T. and Lula E. Hardy,
  Sept. 3, 1857
HARGRAVE
  Garland, Mar. 16, 1876
  J. Hunt (Mrs.), Oct. 20,
    1932
  J. Hunt, Apr. 11 and 18,
    1935
  Jesse H., Sept. 22, Nov.
    17, 1921
  Lucy W., w. of Garland
    Hargrave, d. of David
    Bibb, Jan. 3, 1856
  Robert L., Apr. 18, 1889
  Ruth, July 31, 1862
  Sallie Tate, Aug. 18,
    Oct. 6, 1932
HARGREAVES
  Jack, Nov. 30, 1911
HARGROVE
  child of James Hargrove,
    Apr. 18, 1867
  Mary W., w. of Maj. John
    D. Hargrove, Nov. 25,
    1875
  Susan (Mrs.), Oct. 1,
    1874
HARLEY
  Mary G. (Mrs.), Feb. 23,
    Mar. 2, 1882
HARLOW*
  Addie, d. of Richard and
    Fannie Harlow, Dec. 22,
    1887

John Hervey, s. of John M.
  and Julia Ann Harlow,
  Jan. 4, 1855
Margaret, w. of John M.
  Harlow, Mar. 4, 1847
HARLOWE*
  John M. (Rev.), Mar. 25,
    1915
  Julia A., w. of Rev. John
    M. Harlowe, Mar. 18, 1886
  Melissa Adelaide, d. of
    John M. and Julia Ann
    Harlowe, Dec. 6, 1860
HARMON
  Edward P., s. of J. R.
    Harmon, Apr. 4, 1861
  Josie Belle (Mrs.), Nov.
    20, 1924
  Lawrence Eugene, s. of
    Benjamin Franklin and
    Mollie Euphemia Harmon,
    Apr. 25, 1878
  Mary (Mrs.), Apr. 3, 1873
HARP
  W. I., Dec. 17, 1925
HARPER
  George W., Apr. 17, 1924
  Martha, Dec. 23, 1869
  Mary A. M., May 4, 1854
  N. M., June 12, 1879
  Will W., s. of Byrd S.
    and M. A. Harper, Nov.
    29, 1900
  William H. (Col.), Dec.
    16, 1875
HARRALL
  David K., June 22, 1922
HARRELL
  Edward A., s. of John W.
    and Media Harrell, Aug.
    11, 1887
  Eugenia Wortley, Feb. 14,
    1924
  Mary Gravat, July 14, 1927*
  Virginia, Mar. 8, 1923
HARRIEL
  Richard (Dr.), Dec. 1 and 8,
    1870
HARRINGTON
  Bettie E., w. of George W.

* Possible inaccuracy in name, or spelling, but given as printed

OBITUARY NOTICES IN THE RELIGIOUS HERALD WITH DATES OF PUBLICATION

Harrington, Aug. 18, 1859
John, Sept. 25, 1862
Mary A., Mar. 21, 1878
Willie Henry, s. of John and Mary Harrington, Feb. 27, 1862

HARRIS
Abraham (Dr.), Jan. 29, 1891
Alexander (Dr.), June 27, July 11, 1889
Andrew J., Dec. 31, 1863
Ann Virginia, Apr. 3, 1852
Benjamin, s. of Mrs. Jane Harris, June 9, 1859
Bettie Young (Mrs.), Feb. 13, 1919
C. C. (Mrs.), July 3, 1890
C. V. (Mrs.), d. of Rev. Jordan Martin, Mar. 18, 1897
Carolina C. (Mrs.), Oct. 11, 1888
Carrie, d. of Robert and Ellen Harris, Mar. 2, 1876
Carter J., Aug. 9, 1894
Clement F., Aug. 15, 1867
Diana (Mrs.), Dec. 13, 1849
Effie Park, w. of Dr. W. A. Harris, Feb. 17, 1898
Eldonia J., w. of J. S. Harris, d. of German Gilliam, May 19, 1881
Eleanor Mary Lloyd, w. of Robert Poindexter Harris, Nov. 23, 1916
Elizabeth, w. of William B. Harris, Oct. 14, 1847
Elizabeth (Mrs.), July 26, 1866
Ella Watson, June 24, 1920
Emma Bibb (Mrs.), Aug. 1, 1912
Eusebia Temple, d. of John T. and Caroline C. Harris, June 21, 1849

F. C., w. of J. W. Harris, June 11, 1828
F. F., Sept. 25, Dec. 25, 1924
Faitha, Apr. 18, 1861
Fannie Nelson, d. of Rev. Samuel and Mary A. Harris, Oct. 27, 1870
Flora W. (Mrs.), Nov. 23, 1838
Frances, w. of Jeremiah C. Harris, Apr. 26, 1855
Frances A., w. of Robert Harris, Mar. 1, 1860
Frances O. (Mrs.), Apr. 7, 1853
Frank, s. of Rev. W. F. Harris, Aug. 6, 1891
George W. (Rev.), Dec. 22, 1870
George Washington, May 30, 1929
Henry, Sept. 12, 1872
Henry Herbert (Dr.), Feb. 11, 1897
Henry Herbert, Sept. 12, 1935
Henry Judson, June 7, 1934
Hugh G., s. of H. H. and Emma J. Harris, Aug. 3, 1871
Ida E., May 15, 1890
J. F. (Rev.), Mar. 16, 1899
J. Lysander, Dec. 17, 1863
J. M., Nov. 20, 1919; Feb. 19, 1920
J. R. (Mrs.), Dec. 17, 1936
J. W., July 11, 1828
Jacintha, w. of James M. Harris, d. of Capt. M. Roles, Jan. 10, 1861
James Madison, Sept. 30, 1869
James Montague, s. of Clifton and Bettie H. Harris, Mar. 29, 1894
James O., July 30, 1891
Janie Ligon, d. of William H. Harris, Apr. 2, 1908
John (Capt.), Dec. 30, 1831
John G., Oct. 23, 1873
John Henry (Rev.), Feb. 4,

OBITUARY NOTICES IN THE RELIGIOUS HERALD WITH DATES OF PUBLICATION

1915
John L., s. of Samuel and Mary A. Harris, Mar. 13, 1851
John P., June 27, 1861
John R., May 12, 1859
John T., Dec. 16, 1886
John W. (Rev.), June 17, 1897
John William, July 20, Aug. 12, Sept. 30, 1897
Joseph Q., s. of Rev. William Harris, Oct. 15, 1863
Lillie L., w. of Thomas H. Harris, Mar. 15, 1888
Louisa, d. of Robert I. and Frances Harris, Mar. 14, 1861
Lucy M. (Mrs.), d. of Dr. Robert Berkeley, gr.d. of Councillor Carter, Oct. 1, 1891
Luella, d. of George W. and Ann M. Harris, Aug. 26, 1858
M. H., w. of Dr. William Harris, May 5, 1870
M. J. PUGH, w. of B. D. Harris, Aug. 26, 1880
Mackenzie Beverly, s. of Charles Harris, Aug. 23, 1883
Martha Ann, d. of George W. Harris, Nov. 27, 1862
Mary, w. of John Harris, mother of Rev. William Harris, Apr. 26, 1833
Mary, w. of John G. Harris, July 28, 1853
Mary, Sept. 9, 1858
Mary, d. of Mrs. Jane Harris, June 9, 1859
Mary E., Oct. 1, 1874
Mary F., w. of William E. Harris, Apr. 19, 1849
Mary Hart, w. of Henry J. Harris, Mar. 7, 1907
Mary Jane (Mrs.), d. of Nathan Thomas, May 21,

1863
Mary Payne (Mrs.), Jan. 22, 1920
Mary Pollard, d. of Rev. Samuel Harris, Feb. 12, 1914
Matthew M., Feb. 4, 1858
Mildred Ann, s. of William H. and Susan Jane Harris, July 26, 1860
Milton, s. of John T. and Caroline C. Harris, Sept. 5, 1844
Mollie P., May 19, 1859
Mollie P., Feb. 19, 1914
Nannie, Dec. 23, 1920
Nannie J., d. of R. W. and Mary E. Harris, Apr. 27, 1893
Newett, Apr. 7, 1881*
Newit, Jan. 13, 1859*
Octavia, d. of Mrs. Frances H. Harris, Dec. 25, 1845
R. F., Dec. 11, 1930
Rebecca (Mrs.), May 23, 1844
Richard Henry, s. of W. B. Harris, Sept. 23, 1852
Robert, Nov. 26, 1840
Robert Nelson, Sept. 2, 1926
Robert Ryland, s. of Elder Samuel Harris, Nov. 9, 1843
Robert W., Oct. 26, 1899
Sallie, d. of H. H. and E. J. Harris, Aug. 16, 1877
Sally Hundley, w. of Alexander Mason Harris, d. of George A. and Maria Kesie Hundley, Dec. 7, 1933
Samuel (Rev.), s. of William and Mary Pollard Harris, Apr. 23, June 11 and 18, 1891
Samuel (Mrs.), w. of Rev. Samuel Harris, Apr. 23,

* Possible inaccuracy in name, or spelling, but given as printed

OBITUARY NOTICES IN THE RELIGIOUS HERALD WITH DATES OF PUBLICATION

June 11, 1891
Samuel J., Sept. 28, 1922
Samuel Tyree, s. of Robert
  P. Harris, Aug. 20, 1874
Sarah, w. of Henry Harris,
  Mar. 24, 1870
Sarah, w. of William Harris,
  Oct. 28, 1875
Sarah A., Nov. 18, 1841
Sarah C. (Mrs.), June 24,
  1847
Stephen B., s. of Rev.
  William Harris, June 4,
  1863
Susan, Sept. 9, 1831
Thomas, Dec. 1, 1864
Thomas D., May 2, 1834
Thomas T. (Rev.), Sept.
  20, 1839
Tyree, May 6, 1836
Uriah, Aug. 19, 1858
Victoria M., w. of Abner
  Harris, Jan. 22, 1920
Virginia, d. of Mrs. Jane
  Harris, June 9, 1859
W. S., Oct. 31, 1929
William (Elder), Nov. 16,
  1865; Mar. 15, Sept. 6,
  and Oct. 18, 1866
William Alexander, s. of
  Elder Samuel and Mary
  A. Harris, July 17,
  1845
William Bryce, July 3, 1873
William F., Nov. 17, 1898
William L., June 10, 1847
HARRISON
Adam S., May 16, 1929
Ann, w. of Smith Harrison,
  d. of Wilson Turbiville,
  Oct. 4, 1860
Ann, Dec. 10, 1874
Anna Carrington, w. of Rev.
  J. Hartwell Harrison, d.
  of Isaac H. Carrington,
  Aug. 29, 1918
Anna V., d. of Thomas A.
  Harrison, June 3, 1880
Augusta, w. of S. A.
  Harrison, Jan. 31, 1924

Bewley Holmes, d. of G. A.
  and S. C. Harrison, Jan.
  19, 1888
Caroline Scott, w. of former
  President Harrison,
  Nov. 3, 1892
Charles A., Nov. 18, Dec.
  9, 1847
Charles Carter, s. of
  Gessner Harrison, Mar.
  2, 1882
Charles T., s. of Rev.
  J. R. Harrison, Dec. 8,
  1898
Edmond, Mar. 23 and 30,
  1916
Eliza Catharine, w. of
  Henry P. Harrison, Jan.
  16, 1851
Ella Green (Mrs.), Mar.
  19, 1914
Gessner (Dr.), Nov. 26,
  1874
Isaac Curts, s. of William
  H. and Annie M. Harrison,
  Dec. 4, 1884*
J. B. (Rev.), Mar. 6, 1890
J. R., June 27, 1901
James, Mar. 20, 1829
James, s. of William S.
  and Lucinie Harrison,
  Sept. 9, 1841
James, Jan. 13, 1887
Jaqueline (Mrs.), Oct. 13,
  1898
John H. (Elder), Jan. 9,
  1851
John R., Oct. 16, 1862
Johnnie Willie, s. of Rev.
  J. R. and Sarah E.
  Harrison, June 12, 1879
Lucie Wyche, d. of Joseph
  and Flora W. Harrison,
  July 30, 1885
Lucy A., w. of William
  H. Harrison, Jan. 12,
  1882
M. L., Feb. 1 and 8, 1934
M. T. (Dr.), Oct. 7, 1858
Martha (Mrs.), May 28, 1830

* Possible inaccuracy in name, or spelling, but given as printed

OBITUARY NOTICES IN THE RELIGIOUS HERALD WITH DATES OF PUBLICATION

Mary (Mrs.), Oct. 9, 1856
Mary (Mrs.), Dec. 2, 1869
Mary B., June 7, 1855
Mary C., d. of Brackston Harrison, May 25, 1848 *
Oceanna, d. of Mrs. Camilla A. M. Harrison, Oct. 2, 1851
R. L., Jan. 18, Feb. 1, 1917
Randolph (Col.), June 25, 1894
S. A., June 26, 1924
Sarah E., w. of Rev. J. R. Harrison, Oct. 2, 1890
Sophia, w. of Col. Richard Harrison, July 25, 1828
William H., Feb. 5, 1857
William H., Dec. 29, 1881
William H., Jan. 12 and 19, 1882

HARROLD
Lawrence M., June 24, 1858
Thomasia C., w. of Lawrence M. Harrold, Dec. 19, 1878

HARROW
J. W. (Dr.), June 25, 1868

HART
Ann E., w. of F. Hart, May 16, 1850
Carolyn, d. of Rev. J. L. Hart, Feb. 8, 1917
Coleman, s. of John and Sallie L. Hart, May 26, 1887
Eliza J., d. of Rev. John Spotts, May 1, 1879
Elizabeth Georgianna, d. of Mrs. Margaret A. R. Hart, Apr. 14, 1853
Emmet Wilson, Oct. 25, 1923; Apr. 3, 1924
J. W., Aug. 2, 1888
J. W. (Rev.), Aug. 20, Sept. 3, 1914
James, July 12, 1855
James D., June 11, 1931
James R., May 9, 1872
Jane, d. of John Hart, Aug. 22, 1850

Jennie, d. of Rev. J. W. and C. B. Hart, Mar. 31, 1881
Jesse B., Aug. 10, 1876
John, Dec. 6, 1855
John, July 25, 1895
Joseph, Nov. 1, 1860
Lewis C., Sept. 28, 1882
Lizzie, d. of John and Sallie L. Hart, July 28, 1859
Lottie, Feb. 13, 1919
Malcolm, s. of John and Sallie L. Hart, Aug. 22, 1872
Malcolm (Capt.), Sept. 23, 1880
Martha Jane, d. of Francis B. Hart, Mar. 3, 1853
Mary Ann, w. of T. B. Hart, Nov. 19, 1868
Mary Columbia, w. of Rev. Joseph W. Hart, June 17, 1883
Robert M., Sept. 21, 1922
Sarah E. (Mrs.), Mar. 20, 1851
Sarah Eubank, w. of B. F. Hart, Mar. 11, 1920
Sudie Terrill, w. of Rev. Joseph W. Hart, d. of Robert and Elizabeth Terrill, Jan. 10, 1901
Thomas B., Nov. 28, 1867
Thomas W. (Rev.), Nov. 4, 1926
W. T., Jan. 27, 1898
Walker D., Apr. 20, 1843
William (Mrs.), Nov. 8, 1894

HARTBARGER*
Hiram Jefferson, Dec. 11, 1924

HARTBERGER*
Hiram Jefferson, Dec. 25, 1924

HARTE
J. D. (Rev.), Nov. 16 and 30, 1933
J. D. (Mrs.), Dec. 19, 1935

HARTLEY
Lou Creath (Mrs.), d. of Rev. Thomas B. Creath, Oct. 18, Nov. 1, 1923
R. B., Nov. 5, 1914

* Possible inaccuracy in name, or spelling, but given as printed

OBITUARY NOTICES IN THE RELIGIOUS HERALD WITH DATES OF PUBLICATION

HARTMAN
B. P., Nov. 3, 1910
Willie A., s. of Dr.
John H. and Millie
Hill Hartman, July
24, 1873
HARTSHORN
J. C., July 25, 1889
HARTSOCK
Ida, Aug. 28, 1915
George, Oct. 13, 1859
HARTWELL
(Mrs.), Sept. 1, 1870
Charlie, Mar. 15, 1928
J. B. (Dr.), Jan. 11, 1912
Virginia T., w. of Charles Hartwell, May 18, 1848
HARVEY
Addie Bruce, d. of E. C. and M. J. Harvey, Sept. 8, 1864
Albert G., May 21, 1863
Ann Bruce, d. of E. C. Harvey, Sept. 22, 1864
Ann W., w. of Col. Joseph F. Harvey, Feb. 20, 1851
Booker, Aug. 27, 1891
Drusilla, w. of Isham Harvey, May 31, 1860
Elizabeth, w. of Col. John Harvey, Mar. 30, 1838
Frankie H., w. of Thomas Harvey, Nov. 26, 1891
Geneva Jackson (Mrs.), Nov. 8, 1934
John (Col.), May 6, 1858
John William, s. of Hezekiah H. Harvey, May 27, 1909
Lucinda W., d. of Thomas Harvey, May 17, 1883
M. A., Dec. 7, 1871
Mary, w. of Nathan Harvey, Feb. 25, 1831
Mollie Comer, w. of Edward P. Harvey, d. of J. M. Comer, Oct. 14, 1937

Nathan Thomas, s. of E. C. and M. J. Harvey, Mar. 10, 1864
Sallie E., w. of S. W. Harvey, d. of Col. John Foster, Feb. 3, 1910
Samuel H., s. of Col. John Harvey, Feb. 20, 1862
Sarah C., d. of Jesse Harvey, July 27, 1854
Thomas, Mar. 20, 1873
Thomas, Nov. 26, 1891
Virginia A. (Mrs.), June 25, 1863
William W., Mar. 10, 1864
William Watkins (Lt.), s. of Jesse Harvey, Jan. 8, 1863
HARWOOD
Abel (Rev.), Apr. 21, 1837
Alice Newton Drinkard, w. of John William Harwood, Oct. 5, 1933; Feb. 15, 1934
Bessie Newton, d. of John William and Alice Newton Harwood, Nov. 27, 1884
Columbia A., w. of Thomas M. Harwood, d. of Allen and Sarah Lee Davis, June 13, 1901
Ellen, w. of John William Harwood, Dec. 19, 1878
Frances (Mrs.), Apr. 17, 1835
Frances N., w. of Joseph L. Harwood, Apr. 11, 1861
John, Mar. 3, 1837
John B. (Lt.), Jan. 5, 1865
John S. (Col.), Oct. 2, 1913
John S. (Mrs.), Sept. 23, 1926
John W., Apr. 22, 1909
Joseph U., Nov. 14, 1918
Josephine B. Bell, d. of James A. and Georgella B. Harwood, July 4, 1850
Judith (Mrs.), Sept. 24, 1830
Lizzie, d. of John William

OBITUARY NOTICES IN THE RELIGIOUS HERALD WITH DATES OF PUBLICATION

and Ellen Harwood, Dec. 19, 1878
Maria Susan, Sept. 27, 1860
Martha (Mrs.), Aug. 28, 1862
Martha M., Sept. 30, 1847
Martha S., Dec. 21, 1876
Mary, w. of Richard Henry Harwood, Aug. 22, 1872
Mary E., May 1, 1884
Philip B., July 5, 1855
Priscilla, Aug. 15, 1861; Feb. 20, 1862
Richard Henry, Jr., s. of Richard H. Harwood, Apr. 23, 1840
Richard Henry, Aug. 22, 1872
Virginia, w. of William Harwood, June 5, 1902
William Franklin, Aug. 31, Oct. 5, 1893
William Henry, Aug. 18, 1881

HASH
  A. G. (Rev.), Mar. 14, 1912

HASKER
  A. A. (Mrs.), Apr. 8, 1926

HASKINS
  Bertie, w. of E. L. Haskins, Dec. 19, 1889
  Edward (Capt.), May 12, 1837
  Edward (Capt.), July 19, 1855
  Eliza, w. of Robert Haskins, Jan. 16, 1845
  James Addison, s. of Capt. Edward Haskins, July 13, 1854
  Martha M., July 19, 1855
  Prudence H., w. of Creed T. Haskins, Dec. 8, 1859
  Sallie Pattie, d. of Capt. E. L. Haskins, Jan. 15, 1885
  T. J. (Mrs.), Apr. 20, 1905
  Virginia, d. of Capt. Edward and Martha Haskins, Oct. 14, 1852

HASLOP
  Eleanor Long, w. of Horace M. Haslop, Aug. 31, 1854

HATCHER
  (Dr.), Aug. 29, 1912
  A. E. (Mrs.), Feb. 5, 1857
  Amanda, w. of C. W. Hatcher, May 29, 1913
  C., Feb. 18, 1864
  Dora, d. of Thomas Hatcher, Jan. 2, 1868
  Elsie Davis, d. of Rev. William E. Hatcher, July 19, 1883
  Eugene P. (Mrs.), Oct. 5, 1922
  Fanny, w. of Julius Hatcher, Jan. 8, 1857
  Florentine M., w. of Caleb H. Hatcher, Feb. 17, 1876
  Frances B., w. of Julius H. Hatcher, Jan. 15, 1857
  Frances O. L., d. of Hardaway Hatcher, Apr. 9, 1840
  H. E. (Rev.), Sept. 15, 1892
  Harvey (Dr.), Jan. 19, Feb. 2 and 23, 1905
  J. L., s. of Jerry G. Hatcher, Jan. 18, 1872
  James Henry, s. of J. G. and A. W. Hatcher, Dec. 29, 1864
  Jeremiah G., Feb. 11, 1892
  Judson L., s. of Jerry G. Hatcher, Jan. 18, 1872
  Julius, Jan. 2, 1868
  Julius W., Dec. 14, 1876
  Lemuel G. (Elder), Sept. 5, 1844
  Lucy R., w. of Daniel Hatcher, May 10, 1849
  Martha, w. of Maj. John Hatcher, Sept. 26, 1895
  Martin Luther, Oct. 8, 1914
  Mary Lelia, d. of Rev. Harvey and Pattie Hatcher, July 27, 1871
  Nancy, w. of Rev. William Hatcher, Feb. 28, 1884
  Samuel, Nov. 30, 1854
  Susan G. (Mrs.), Oct. 4, 1855

OBITUARY NOTICES IN THE RELIGIOUS HERALD WITH DATES OF PUBLICATION

HATCHETT
  Maria H., d. of Elder
    William Hatchett, Oct.
    6, 1853
  Mary E., w. of William T.
    Hatchett, Jan. 20, 1887
  Sarah Albina, w. of Americus
    Hatchett, Oct. 13, 1892
  Sarah C., w. of A. Hatchett,
    d. of Thomas B. Collier,
    Oct. 22, 1857
  Thomas M., s. of Elder
    William Hatchett, Oct. 20,
    1853
  William (Rev.), Oct. 5, 1854

HATHAWAY
  Charles G., June 20, 1929
  Elizabeth, d. of Charles G.
    and Blanche Hathaway, Dec.
    30, 1886
  Harriet E., w. of H. S.
    Hathaway, d. of Col. Ralph
    Edmonds, Apr. 8, 1858
  Henry S., Oct. 20, 1892
  John R., Dec. 13, 1894
  L., July 18, 1844
  Lillie Augusta, d. of Henry
    S. Hathaway, May 27, 1869
  Lucellus O., Apr. 22, 1920
  Mary Ann, w. of James H.
    Hathaway, Nov. 23, 1854
  Sarah T., w. of James H.
    Hathaway, July 1, 1841

HATHWAY
  L. O. (Mrs.), Dec. 14, 1933

HATTON
  Catherine, w. of Thomas
    Hatton, June 10, 1858

HAWES
  Charlotte, June 12, 1873
  Mary A. (Mrs.), d. of Gen. B.
    W. Pryor, Nov. 24, 1870

HAWKINS
  Ann, w. of Laban D. Hawkins, Oct. 29, 1846
  Catharine (Mrs.), Nov. 10, 1842
  Charles A., s. of Edward P.
    and M. J. Hawkins,
    July 5, 1855

Edward Pinkard, June 29, Aug.
    3, 1916
Ella Talcott, d. of Lee M.
    Hawkins, Jan. 3, 1867
Emma, d. of Rev. E. P.
    Hawkins, June 22, 1876
Harvey, July 23, 1908
Hennie, w. of M. V. Hawkins,
    Dec. 5, 1889
Huldah Herndon (Mrs.), Aug.
    3, 1916
James A., Jan. 25, 1900
Little, July 17, 1884
Lucy, Feb 25, 1897
Lucy W., w. of James P.
    Hawkins, Aug. 16, 1866
Martha. w. of Allen W.
    Hawkins, d. of Spencer
    Pinkard, July 13, 1838
Martha J., w. of Rev. E.
    P. Hawkins, July 7, 1881
Martha R. (Mrs.), Feb. 13,
    1879
Mary, Sept. 25, 1829
Mary, w. of Capt. Thomas
    Hawkins, May 28, 1840
Matilda, w. of Thomas R.
    Hawkins, Aug. 19, 1836
Mildred H., w. of S. S.
    Hawkins, Oct. 5, 1876
P. F. (Mrs.), June 4, 1903
Russell (Dr.), Feb. 11,
    1897
Sallie J., d. of Rev. E. P.
    and Mary J. Hawkins, Dec.
    14, 1871
Sarah A., d. of James and
    Adeline Hawkins, Aug. 1,
    1834
Thomas (Capt.), Apr. 30, 1840
Thomas (Rev.), June 18, 1885
William G., Nov. 11, 1847
William S. (Elder), Aug. 30,
    Oct. 4, 1883

HAWLEY
  Mary P., w. of George W.
    Hawley, Apr. 24, 1856
  Thomas, May 26, 1853

HAWTHORN
  D. S., Apr. 24, 1884

OBITUARY NOTICES IN THE RELIGIOUS HERALD WITH DATES OF PUBLICATION

Eliza J., w. of L. R. Hawthorn, June 2, 1881
HAWTHORNE
  Charlotte Tupper, d. of Hartwell K. and Lottie Tupper Hawthorne, Oct. 22, 1896
  Emma, d. of Hartwell K. and Lottie Tupper Hawthorne, July 24, 1890
  Hugh C., June 23, 1881
  J. B. (Rev.), Mar. 10, 1910
  Martha, w. of Rev. K. Hawthorne, Oct. 24, 1872
  W. J., Aug. 4, 1887
HAY
  George, son-in-law of James Monroe, Oct. 1, 1830
  Joseph (Rev.), Jan. 15, 1874
  Nannie, w. of Rev. Joseph Hay, Aug. 26, 1858
  William, Jr., Jan. 23, 1835
HAYDON
  Jesse, Sept. 3, 1846
  T. J. (Mrs.), Dec. 17, 1925
HAYES
  Ann E., w. of Henry Hayes, Oct. 14, 1869
  C. H., Feb. 19, 1857
  Dollie B., w. of Thomas W. Hayes, Feb. 4, 1869
  Lillie N., May 31, 1928
  Lucy A. (Mrs.), Mar. 30, 1893
  Mary E., w. of Capt. O. J. Hayes, Oct. 9, 1879
  Rutherford B., Jan. 9, 1902
  Susan Alexander Bruce, w. of Nicholas E. Hayes, May 7, 1914
  W. L. (Rev.), June 27, 1918
  William Judson, s. of William and Fannie Hayes, Mar. 4, 1880
HAYMES
  William (Capt.), July 4, 1912
HAYNE
  Robert Y. (Gen.), Oct. 18, 1839
HAYNES
  Alice Brooks, w. of Robert R. Haynes, June 17, 1909
  Andrew L., Sept. 9, 1915
  Ann R., w. of J. W. Haynes, Oct. 12, 1876
  Austin B., Sept. 22, 1887
  Catharine, w. of Austin B. Haynes, d. of Richard Street, Aug. 2, 1900
  Celia, w. of William T. Haynes, Mar. 14, 1901*
  Emily S. (Mrs.), June 3, 1926
  Fanny W., Feb. 11, 1926
  Frances, d. of Maj. William H. Haynes, July 10, 1884
  Francis Marion, s. of William and Emily F. Haynes, July 7, 1842
  George L., Dec. 28, 1922
  James Anthony (Rev.), Apr. 8, 1880
  Jennie L. (Mrs.), Dec. 7, 1882
  John R., Oct. 13, 1870
  Lucy Mason, d. of J. A. and M. C. Haynes, Aug. 24, 1854
  Martha, w. of Capt. Thomas Haynes, Nov. 25, 1831
  Mary Brown, d. of William T. and Cecilia Haynes, Dec. 10, 1868*
  Mary Camm, w. of Rev. James A. Haynes, Feb. 7, 1895
  Mattie, d. of A. B. and Catharine Haynes, July 1, 1875
  Rosannah, July 30, 1885
  Sarah B. (Mrs.), Dec. 13, 1877
  Susan, w. of John R. Haynes, Aug. 9, 1839
  Susan Ann, w. of John R. Haynes, Apr. 12, 1882
  Thomas (Capt.), July 26, 1860; Nov. 29, 1877; Sept. 17, 1885
  W. S. (Mrs.), June 25, 1903
  W. T. (Capt.), May 22, 1919

* Possible inaccuracy in name, or spelling, but given as printed

OBITUARY NOTICES IN THE RELIGIOUS HERALD WITH DATES OF PUBLICATION

William Cornelius, s. of John R. and Susanna Bagby Haynes, Sept. 22, 1898
HAYNIE
  E. E. (Mrs.), Feb. 25, 1904
  Eliza J., d. of William H. and Nancy B. Haynie, Mar. 14, 1872
  Julia Tankard, d. of Cyrus L. and Nannie B. Haynie, Oct. 11, 1888
  Martha F., w. of Dr. Thomas Haynie, d. of Rev. John G. Mills, May 7, 1868
  Nannie C., d. of William H. and Nancy B. Haynie, Mar. 14, 1872
  William H., Oct. 9, 1879
HAYNSWORTH
  Mary, d. of William F. B. and Mary C. Haynsworth, Feb. 11, 1875
HAYS
  Henry Huston, s. of James M. Hays, Apr. 29, 1920
  Mary, w. of William H. Hays, Mar. 31, 1887
  Susan, w. of James T. Hays, June 25, 1854
  Thomas, Mar. 17, 1864
HAYTHE
  Ella (Mrs.), Aug. 17, 1922
  Mattie E., w. of M. B. Haythe, d. of George A. and Mary S. Haynes, Jan. 19, 1888
HAYWOOD
  Julian, s. of Coleman and Macon Haywood, Nov. 24, 1887
HAZELGROVE
  Henry H., July 23, 1863
  Marcellus Harrison, May 6, 1926
  Olivia Timberlake (Mrs.), July 1, 1915
  Percy Macon, Nov. 21, 1935
HAZELWOOD
  William H. (Lt.), Oct. 2, 1862
HAZLEGROVE

  Edna M., June 28, 1894
  Richard L., July 19, 1888
HEAD
  Eliza, w. of William S. Head Sept. 5, 1872
  Fanny, w. of Milton Head, d. of John Huckstep, Nov. 26, 1868
  Joyce M., w. of Emanuel Head, Aug. 14, 1829
  M. W., Dec. 5, 1878
  Mary A., d. of Henry and Mary A. Head, Feb. 28, 1884
  Mary L., w. of John R. Head, d. of David R. Jones, Feb. 19, 1836
  O. V., Jan. 24, 1924
HEADEN
  Eva, d. of J. F. Headen, Dec. 18, 1902
  John F., Oct. 14, 1926
  Maria, d. of John Headen, June 27, 1828
HEADLEY
  A. J., Mar. 4, 1926
  Albert, Feb. 10, 1921
  Cromwell Christopher, s. of Septimus and Ann Headley, Jan. 3, 1878
  William W., Oct. 20, 1859
  Willie C., Nov. 26, 1936
HEALEY
  Maria, w. of Walter Healey, Mar. 10, 1870
  Mary Ann, w. of Elder Nathan Healey, May 1, 1856
HEALY
  Amy E., Apr. 7, 1927
  Annie Elizabeth, w. of J. L. Healy, July 5, 1917
  Betty T. C. (Mrs.), July 31, 1845
  Elizabeth A., w. of S. L. S. Healy, July 14, 1887
  Elizabeth O., w. of Edmund Healy, Mar. 9, 1838
  Enos, June 21, 1866
  George T. R., Feb. 25, 1841
  James E. (Dr.), Aug. 8, 1867

OBITUARY NOTICES IN THE RELIGIOUS HERALD WITH DATES OF PUBLICATION

Roberta Fauntleroy, d. of
  Robert and Georgia Lorimer
  Healy, Feb. 21, 1878
S. L. S., Oct. 24, Dec. 19,
  1895
S. Lacy, May 28, 1925
Thomas Sinclair, s. of
  Granville S. and Mary A.
  Healy, May 20, 1886
W. H., July 14, 1904
Walter, Jan. 28, 1858
HEARRING
  G. L., Oct. 26, 1875
HEATH
  Josiah, Jan. 1, 1852
  Ophelia Durham (Mrs.),
    July 10, 1919
  Parks, Apr. 4, 1878
  Sarah A., w. of Lewis D.
    Heath, June 18, 1857
  Sophia, w. of Parks Heath,
    Apr. 4, 1878
  Virginia R., w. of Leo Heath,
    May 16, 1872
HEBERT
  Francis M., s. of Francis
    C. and Mary E. Hebert,
    Jan. 10, 1856
HECK
  Fannie E. S., Sept. 2, 1915
  J. M. (Col.), Feb. 15, 1894
HEDLEY
  William Edward B. (Rev.),
    Dec. 7, 1933; Jan. 11,
    1934
  Winifred, d. of Rev. William Hedley, June 26, 1902
HEFFLING
  Lizzie Maude, d. of Cornelius
    D. and Mary Heffling, Oct.
    31, 1872
HEFLIN
  Hosea, May 23, 1878
  Wilbur E., s. of S. J. and
    M. E. Heflin, July 3, 1890
HEIDWOHL
  James Mason, Dec. 19, 1907
HELM
  Carter C., s. of William T.
    Helm, Dec. 25, 1856

  Martha, w. of William B.
    Helm, Jan. 19, 1865
  Mary P. (Mrs.), Dec. 23, 1847
  Meredith, Jr., Dec. 31, 1846
  Sally Page, Nov. 19, Dec. 10,
    1885
  William B., s. of William T.
    Helm, Feb. 21, 1889
  William P., Sept. 6, 1860
HELVESTINE
  C. A., Mar. 27, 1930
HENDERSON
  Ellen, w. of Stephen Henderson,
    July 31, 1845
  Frances S., w. of James Henderson, Feb. 18, 1831
  Giles K., s. of Giles G. and
    Celinda M. H. Henderson,
    Apr. 5, 1860
  Harriet Jane, w. of James Henderson, Feb. 15, 1828
  Helen Timmons, w. of R. A.
    Henderson, Aug. 13, 1925
  John C., Dec. 21, 1838
  Martha, w. of Stephen Henderson, Nov. 19, 1857
  Mary Elizabeth, w. of Dr. A.
    J. Henderson, Nov. 26, 1891
  Mary Emma, d. of Dr. Andrew
    J. and M. E. Henderson, Oct.
    26, Dec. 7, 1882
  R. A. (Mrs.), Oct. 8, 1925
  Samuel (Rev.), Mar. 6, 1890
  Whitfield W., s. of James T.
    and Fannie Henderson, July
    5, 1883
HENDREN
  Henrietta (Mrs.), Mar. 30,
    1899
  Jeremiah (Rev.), Jan. 23,
    1868
  Lois, d. of Jeremiah and
    Sarah Hendren, Feb. 28, 1856
  Michael, July 6, 1871
  Sarah, w. of Rev. Jeremiah
    Hendren, June 23, 1859
HENDRICK
  Ann (Mrs.), July 26, 1839
  Arianna, w. of William J.
    Hendrick, Jan. 3, 1878

OBITUARY NOTICES IN THE RELIGIOUS HERALD WITH DATES OF PUBLICATION

Barbara, d. of Joseph C.
  Hendrick, June 29, 1832
Eliza A., w. of William
  J. Hendrick, Oct. 17,
  1850
Ellen D. (Mrs.), d. of George
  Crissaney Taylor, July 8,
  1880
Joseph C., Jan. 25, 1877
Mary Ann, June 29, 1832
Mary Ellen, d. of William
  Hendrick, Feb. 20, 1873
Mary T., w. of Joseph C.
  Hendrick, Dec. 16, 1852
Peter, June 29, 1832
William, Apr. 29, 1875
HENDRICKSON
  C. R. (Rev.), Nov. 10, 1881
  Ellen F., w. of Rev. C. R.
    Hendrickson, d. of
    Amaryllis Dwight, July 13,
    1854
  G. Crawford, Oct. 28, 1875
  Rebecca (Mrs.), Feb. 14,
    1861
HENEREY
  William S., Oct. 19, 1871
HENING
  Agatha (Mrs.), Apr. 18, 1828
  Charles Kennon, s. of Dr.
    William H. and Olivia H.
    Hening, Mar. 22, 1900*
  Eliza P. (Mrs.), July 17,
    1879*
  George Edward, Sept. 26, 1912
  Margaret J., w. of James B.
    Hening, Sept. 16, 1875
  Mary Elizabeth, w. of Oscar
    Hening, d. of William S.
    Walton, July 2 and 16,
    1903
  Wane, Mar. 23, 1916
  William Walter, Apr. 11,
    1828
HENLEY
  Bertha May, d. of M. B. and
    A. V. Henley, Aug. 2, 1877
  Charlotte R. (Mrs.), May 22,
    1879
  Elizabeth, w. of Leonard
    Henley, Feb. 6, 1845
  Elizabeth, w. of Capt.
    Hezekiah Henley, Dec. 20,
    1849
  Ella Jane, w. of Maj. John
    A. Henley, Apr. 5, 1883
  Hezekiah (Capt.), Feb. 1, 1839
  John, Mar. 20, 1835
  Leonard, Feb. 11, 1831
  Louisa F., w. of Elder R. Y.
    Henley, d. of Sublet Mc-
    Gruder, July 30, 1863
  Millie T., d. of Richardson
    Henley, July 9, 1863
  Richardson, Sept. 14, 1843
  Richardson, Dec. 25, 1890
  Robert (Capt.), Oct. 17, 1828
  William (Maj.), Feb. 16, 1838
HENNING
  Eliza P., Dec. 11, 1862*
  Julia, w. of Dr. William H.
    Henning, d. of Theodore N.
    Davis, May 12, 1859*
  Virginia A., Dec. 11, 1862
HENRY
  Elizabeth R. J., w. of
    Thomas S. Henry, d. of
    C. W. and S. S. Roach,
    Mar. 30, 1843
  Ludwell B., s. of Dr. W.
    D. and Lucy B. Henry,
    Mar. 20, 1879
  Martha, w. of John Henry,
    Feb. 1, 1844
  Mary (Mrs.), Jan. 15, 1846
  Sarah, w. of Fountain F.
    Henry, Jan. 13, 1837
  Susan, w. of Joel Henry,
    Jan. 5, 1843
HENSHAW
  Charles T., s. of Mrs. A.
    S. Henshaw, Sept. 6, 1849
  Edmund (Maj.), June 24, 1841
  Fanny Helen, June 16, 1881
  Fred, Aug. 26, 1915
  Venetia (Mrs.), Aug. 12, 1915
HENSLEY
  Birchie Maynard, d. of James
    O. and M. F. Hensley, Feb.
    21, 1878

* Possible inaccuracy in name, or spelling, but given as printed

OBITUARY NOTICES IN THE RELIGIOUS HERALD WITH DATES OF PUBLICATION

HENSON
  (Dr.), May 7, 1914
  B. A. (Col.), Mar. 9, 1882
  David B., s. of Clifton
    R. Henson, Aug. 27, 1840
  Hudson L., Dec. 29, 1864
  J. W. (Rev.), Dec. 18, 1873
  J. Waller (Rev.), Mar. 19,
    1874
  Mary P., w. of Benjamin
    Henson, Apr. 8, 1858
  Mattie E., d. of Benjamin
    Henson, Mar. 11, 1869
  Nellie, d. of Walter J. and
    Cornelia A. Henson, Oct.
    17, 1889
  Samuel B., Mar. 10, 1898
  Willie S., child of
    Benjamin and Lucy Henson,
    Mar. 11, 1869
HEPBURN
  David (Rev.), Apr. 23 and
    30, 1931
HEPLER
  Margaret M., Dec. 9, 1875
HERBERT
  Elizabeth C., Jan. 10, 1856
  Elizabeth S., w. of Francis
    C. Herbert, Aug. 6, 1840
  Mary E., w. of Francis C.
    Herbert, Jan. 10, 1856
  Thomas B., Jan. 10, 1856
HEREFORD
  Josiah W. (Capt.), Feb. 12,
    1891
  Mary, w. of William P.
    Hereford, Sept. 7, 1838
HERING
  W., Mar. 18, 1880
HERNDON
  A. W., s. of Thaddeus
    Herndon, July 14, 1910
  Alexander, s. of Dr. Z.
    B. and M. G. Herndon,
    Mar. 23, 1871
  Alexander, Sept. 21, 1876
  Alice, w. of Elder John C.
    Herndon, Sept. 21, 1838
  Amanda L. (Mrs.), Nov. 22,
    1923
  Ann, w. of Elder Thaddeus
    Herndon, Dec. 12, 1839
  Ann Hasseltine, d. of Elder
    T. D. Herndon, Oct. 20,
    1837
  Anne, w. of Alexander Herndon,
    d. of Elder John A. Billing-
    sley, Aug. 1, 1878
  Betsey, w. of Thomas D. Hern-
    don, d. of J. A. Billingsley,
    Mar. 15, 1883
  C. D., Mar. 9, 1882
  Charles Traverse (Rev.), Jan.
    9, Feb. 20, 1936
  Elizabeth June, w. of Rev.
    Richard N. Herndon, Nov.
    3, 1898
  Emily J., w. of James C. Hern-
    don, Feb. 16, 1871
  Fannie Gregory, w. of Dr.
    Thomas Herndon, Jan. 2, 1873
  George Latham, s. of Elder
    Thaddeus Herndon, June 29,
    1848
  George W., s. of Elder John C.
    Herndon, Dec. 3, 1840
  Henry T., Jan. 24, 1834
  Jacob W. (Elder), Aug. 17,
    1848
  James, May 28, 1857
  John C. (Elder), Jan. 20, 1848
  John G., Apr. 5, 1928
  John Joseph, s. of Alexander
    Herndon, Apr. 11, 1895
  Joseph, Feb. 17, 1832
  Julian, Nov. 19, 1863
  Louisa Hule Love, w. of Rev.
    Traverse D. Herndon, d. of
    Col. George and Mary Love,
    Jan. 30, Feb. 6, 1890
  Lucy, w. of Joseph Herndon,
    June 18, 1840
  Lucy Ann (Mrs.), d. of Capt.
    Thomas Thornton, Apr. 26,
    1860
  M. A., w. of Rev. Thaddeus
    Herndon, Aug. 16, 1888
  Mahala, w. of Robert W. Hern-
    don, Dec. 11, 1924
  Margaret G., w. of Elder

OBITUARY NOTICES IN THE RELIGIOUS HERALD WITH DATES OF PUBLICATION

Richard N. Herndon, Feb. 3, 1842
Maria Ann, w. of Archibald Herndon, June 4, 1857
Maria G., w. of Dr. Z. B. Herndon, Nov. 17, 1881
Mary Ann, d. of Joseph Herndon, Jan. 9, 1840
Mary Elizabeth (Mrs.), Feb. 7, 1895
Mildred (Mrs.), Sept. 10, 1903
Nannie, d. of Alexander Herndon, Jan. 4, 1872
Richard N. (Rev.), s. of Rev. J. C. Herndon, Nov. 15, 1866
Susan Elizabeth, d. of Mrs. Matilda Crawford, Mar. 4, 1852
T. D., Feb. 3, 1853
T. D. (Elder), Sept. 28, 1854
Thomas (Dr.), Nov. 6, 1873
Traverse D. (Elder), Oct. 5, 1854
Virginia L., d. of Alexander Herndon, Nov. 30, 1893
Virginia P., d. of Thomas M. Herndon, Sept. 6, 1833
William A. (Dr.), Sept. 14, 1871
William Albert, Aug. 8, 1828
William Gregory, Nov. 17, 1881
William I., s. of Elder John C. Herndon, Dec. 3, 1840

HERON
James, Sept. 11, 1829

HERRICK
Margaret (Mrs.), Sept. 29, 1881

HERRIN
child of B. W. and M. J. Herrin, Oct. 1, 1868
Burgess W., Mar. 10, 1881
Otelia M., w. of R. M. Herrin, d. of Merritt Joyner, Nov. 1, 1906

HERRING
Albert L., s. of Wilson Herring, Nov. 11, 1841
Curtis O., June 28, 1923
Frank Hunter, Oct. 18, 1928
George Edward, Oct. 3, 1912
Lavinia Lewis, d. of George J. and Mary P. Herring, July 31, 1856
Maria Louise, w. of George Edward Herring, Feb. 17, 1916
Mollie P., Feb. 21, 1889
Oscar, Aug. 11, 1887
Richard G., s. of Oscar and Mary E. Herring, May 3, 1888

HERVEY
J., Sept. 26, 1834

HESKETT
Maggie A. (Mrs.), Dec. 31, 1903

HESTER
Benton R., Mar. 24, 1921; Mar. 30, 1922; Mar. 22, 1923; Apr. 3, 1924

HETFIELD
E. H., w. of Capt. John C. Hetfield, Apr. 30, 1885

HEWETT
Griffin, Feb. 20, 1908

HEWITT
James, Oct. 15, 1868
Mary E. (Mrs.), Dec. 25, 1924

HEWLETT
Charles N. (Capt.), Aug. 15, 1878
Frances H., w. of Thomas B. Hewlett, Mar. 7, 1850
Mary Frances, d. of C. A. Hewlett, Aug. 2, 1855
Matilda, d. of C. A. Hewlett, Oct. 14, 1858
W. C., child of A. D. and Margaret Hewlett, May 27, 1858

HEYWOOD
Ann B., w. of Robert Heywood, Sept. 18, 1879
B. F., Aug. 23, 1900

OBITUARY NOTICES IN THE RELIGIOUS HERALD WITH DATES OF PUBLICATION

Caroline Sims, w. of Thomas
R. Heywood, d. of Mickle-
borough Young, Sept. 23 and
30, 1886
Kate (Mrs.), Feb. 24, 1916
R. S., Apr. 24, 1873
Richard Coleman, Oct. 19,
1893
HICKERSON
Florence B. (Mrs.), Feb. 10,
1921
HICKMAN
Agnes (Mrs.), May 18, 1848
Angelia, w. of Charles W.
Hickman, Apr. 15, 1886
H. H., Mar. 3, 1904
William (Elder), Sept. 23,
1869
HICKS
Ann E., w. of Meshack
Hicks, Oct. 1, 1874
E. P., Dec. 4, 1913
Elvira D. (Mrs.), Nov. 28,
1907
Frederick, May 16, 1850
Hugh (Mrs.), Dec. 29, 1853
J. Emerson (Dr.), July 14,
1932
John Franklin (Dr.), May
13, 1920
Lee M., June 24, 1920
Marcus Daniel, s. of Rev.
R. F. Hicks, July 27,
Aug. 3 and 10, 1922
Mary McCormick, w. of Dr.
J. F. Hicks, July 19, 1928
Nancy S. (Mrs.), Nov. 18, 1841
Sarah A. (Mrs.), Nov. 13, 1884
Tabitha (Mrs.), Apr. 16, 1857
William D., Feb. 1, 1872
Willie, child of Capt. W. D.
Hicks, July 21, 1870
HICKSON
Allen, s. of R. L. Hickson,
Aug. 27, 1891
George, Nov. 19, 1830
Samuel M., s. of R. L.
Hickson, Aug. 27, 1891
William, Sept. 3, 1830
HIDEN

Cordelia (Mrs.), Oct. 3 and
17, 1889
Henry, Aug. 23, 1866
James (Rev.), Oct. 24 and
31, 1918
Joseph, Apr. 29, 1869
Mary, w. of Henry Hiden,
June 22, 1882
Susette Rogers, d. of Rev.
Joseph H. and Nelly B.
Hiden, Nov. 23, 1893
HIETT
Elizabeth C., w. of H.
Hiett, July 10, 1845
HIGGASON
E. T. (Rev.), May 24, 1917
HIGGINBOTHAM
Chester J., July 17, 1924
Edwin, Dec. 25, 1862
Florence, Dec. 17, 1903
William F., Apr. 11, 1889
HIGH
Judith B. (Mrs.), Sept. 10,
1857
HIGHT
Elizabeth, May 13, 1869
HILL
(Rev. Father, Vicar General
of the Bishop of Ohio),
Mar. 5, 1830
A. G. (Mrs.), June 16, 1938
Agnes R., d. of Baylor Hill,
May 7, 1846
Albert H., May 18, 1933
Ann McChesney, w. of Col. F.
H. Hill, Jan. 29, 1891
Baylor, Oct. 17, 1850
Betsy, Dec. 7, 1882
Bettie Garlick, Jan. 16,
Feb. 13, 1908
Booton J. (Maj.), Dec. 4,
1913*
C. B., May 16, 1889
Catharine, w. of Capt.
Robert B. Hill, May 12,
1842
Charles B., July 1, 1858
Davis, Oct. 27, 1842
E. B. (Maj.), Feb. 27, 1890
Edgar Tutt, s. of James Polk

* Possible inaccuracy in name, or spelling, but given as printed

OBITUARY NOTICES IN THE RELIGIOUS HERALD WITH DATES OF PUBLICATION

and M. Ella Hill, Sept. 25, 1879
Edward, Mar. 17, 1870
Edward B. (Maj.), Apr. 10, 1890
Edward B. R., s. of Russell Hill, June 23, 1837
Edwin Scott, s. of Edwin F. and Lucy T. S. Hill, May 10, 1849
Elizabeth, w. of John A. Hill, July 27, 1854
Elizabeth, June 30, 1859
Elizabeth G., w. of Thomas Hill, Aug. 3, 1848
Elizabeth T., w. of Edward Hill, June 2, 1859
Emily Brooke, w. of Nathaniel B. Hill, Aug. 22, 1834
Evelyn, June 15, 1905
Fannie Garlick, w. of Robert Pollard Hill, d. of Edward Garlick, Apr. 19, 1900
Fanny C., d. of Edward and Elizabeth T. Hill, Nov. 15, 1855
Frances, w. of Robert Hill, Aug. 31, 1838
Frances A., d. of Thomas Hill, Jr., Jan. 11, 1849
Frances Anne, w. of John P. Hill, Dec. 30, 1852
Frances Everline, w. of Col. Henry Hill, Mar. 12 and 19, 1868
George, Oct. 11, 1855
George Harvey, s. of Albert Hill, Aug. 12, 1847
Harriet N., w. of Capt. James C. Hill, June 25, 1863
Henry (Col.), Sept. 27, 1866
Humphrey, May 15, 1851
J. D. W., June 12, 1873
Jane S., w. of Henry Hill, Feb. 24, 1848
John, July 7, 1837
John, s. of Edward and

Elizabeth Tucker Hill, Mar. 25, Apr. 1, 1909
John Booten (Maj.), s. of Dr. William S. and Judith F. Hill, June 25, 1914*
John S., s. of Elder William Hill, Aug. 8, 1844
Johnnie, s. of Capt. James C. and Harriet Hill, Feb. 19, 1863
Joshua Fry, s. of Edward F. and Lucy T. S. Hill, May 10, 1849
Judith, w. of Capt. Robert Hill, Mar. 27, 1845
Julia Henry, d. of Rev. W. A. and J. F. Hill, Feb. 28, Apr. 4, 1889
Lucian, s. of Robert and Fanny T. Hill, Jan. 12, 1871
Lydia H. (Mrs.), Jan. 22, Feb. 5, 1874
Margaret L., w. of Capt. E. Y. Hill, d. of Rev. Edward Baptist, Aug. 20, 1863
Maria Louisa, w. of Rev. Stephen Hill, Oct. 17, 1834
Martha (Mrs.), Dec. 19, 1839
Martha Sneed, d. of A. Govan and Bettie V. Hill, June 16, 1887
Mary, w. of William H. Hill, and d. of Edmond and Mary Nelson, May 29, 1856
Mary Douglas, w. of William P. Hill, d. of John D. McGill, Nov. 21, 1878
Mary Emory (Mrs.), Oct. 31, 1929
Mary J. (Mrs.), Feb. 12, 1874
Mary L., Jan. 17, 1867
Mary Wythe, w. of Baylor Hill, Oct. 5, 1838
Matilda, w. of Henry Hill, Aug. 15, 1889
Nathanael Boush, Mar. 17, 1892

* Possible inaccuracy in name, or spelling, but given as printed

OBITUARY NOTICES IN THE RELIGIOUS HERALD WITH DATES OF PUBLICATION

Owen B. (Dr.), Aug. 7, 1862
Perkins, Apr. 5, 1839
R. F. (Mrs.), Apr. 22, 1926
Richard C., Mar. 16, 1865
Robert B. (Capt.), July 18, 1834
Robert J., s. of William H. Hill, June 7, 1860
Robert R., Sept. 30, 1841
Sallie Adams, w. of R. C. Hill, Jan. 1, 1931
Samuel D., July 29, 1852
Sarah Jane, w. of Henry Hill, Nov. 22, 1849
Sarah W., Sept. 9, 1836
Sue Walker, Oct. 1, 1885
W. W., Mar. 5, 1931
William M., Jan. 10, 1918
William Powell, s. of Rev. W. A. Hill, May 30, 1929

HILLIARD
Alexander, Dec. 2, 1851
James, July 16, 1874
John L., s. of R. D. Hilliard, May 24, 1906
Mary Ann (Mrs.), Aug. 29, 1850
Mary L., w. of William F. Hilliard, Apr. 7, 1859
Meredith, Aug. 22, 1844
Richard Daniel, May 6, 1915
William James, Jan. 21, 1904

HILLYARD
Betty Parker, Jan. 31, 1878
Frances Ann, July 29, 1852
Henry, June 16, 1842
Joseph, Feb. 10, 1853
Mary, w. of Elder John W. Hillyard, Jan. 19, 1843
Mary Eliza, w. of Joseph Hillyard, May 1, 1879

HILYARD*
Robert Baylor, s. of Mary E. Hilyard, Nov. 9, 1843

HINDMAN
Samuel B., Jan. 27, 1887

HINE
James, Feb. 13, 1868

HINES
George F., July 14, 1887
Mansfield, Oct. 23, 1862
Martha E., w. of John H. Hines, Aug. 30, 1894
Nancy (Mrs.), Oct. 26, 1922
Nelson S., Feb. 8, 1844
Orris Q., Dec. 11, 1873
W. S., Jan. 10, 1901

HINTON
J. H. (Rev.), Jan. 22, 1874
James S., s. of Elder I. T. Hinton, Aug. 22, 1834

HISCOX
E. T. (Dr.), Jan. 2, 1902

HITCHCOCK
Josiah C., May 6, 1831
Ruth, d. of John and Eleanor Hitchcock, Aug. 11, 1887

HITE
Catherine E., w. of Capt. J. F. Hite, d. of Peter Lucas, Sept. 8, 1870
Reuben Stanley, Jan. 11, 1934

HITER
H. D., s. of William Y. Hiter, gr.s. of Rev. W. Y. Hiter, Aug. 31, 1911
Henry, s. of Peter M. and Mattie L. Hiter, Mar. 17, 1898
Henry Harris, s. of Hugh and Susan Hiter, Feb. 3, 1853
Hugh G., Jr., s. of Hugh G., Sr., and Susan H. Hiter, Jan. 12, 1865
Lucy M., w. of James Hiter, Jan. 13, 1848
Sarah M., w. of W. Y. Hiter, Feb. 24, 1887
W. Y., s. of Rev. W. Y. Hiter, Feb. 24, 1887
W. Y., Sr., gr.s. of Rev. Hiter, Mar. 30, 1911
William Y. (Elder), Oct. 12, 1848

HITT

* Possible inaccuracy in name, or spelling, but given as printed

OBITUARY NOTICES IN THE RELIGIOUS HERALD WITH DATES OF PUBLICATION

Fannie, w. of M. L.
Hitt, d. of Thomas H.
Johnson, Aug. 26, 1886
Wesley Worth, s. of Charles
Hitt, Apr. 2, 1874

HIX
M. F., June 26, 1902
Sally (Mrs.), Dec. 19, 1850
Thomas W. (Dr.), July 10, 1884

HOBBS
Annie, d. of Capt. Alexander R. Hobbs, Mar. 16, 1905
C. Kelly (Mrs.), Apr. 7, 1932
Caleb Daniel, s. of Daniel and Elizabeth Nixon Hobbs, Mar. 6, 1919
Charles Kelly (Rev.), June 27, July 25, 1935
Martha, d. of John Hobbs, Aug. 5, 1858

HOBDAY
George J., Jan. 3, 1929
Mollie, w. of Rev. George J. Hobday, Mar. 10, 1932

HOBGOOD
Carrie Lee (Mrs.), Nov. 17, 1938
F. P., Feb. 28, 1924
Joseph F., Feb. 15, 1906

HOBSON
Ann Eliza, Nov. 29, 1877
Ann Elizabeth, d. of Julius A. and Mary A. Hobson, Nov. 24, 1853
Bettie, w. of James W. Hobson, Sept. 25, 1919
Edward, s. of Benjamin N. Hobson, June 20, 1872
Elizabeth W. (Mrs.), Jan. 27, 1876
Julius A., Oct. 20, 1870
Samuel, Oct. 14, 1852

HOCKADAY
John, Mar. 22, 1849

HOCKETT
Mary Alice, w. of John Cornelius Hockett, May 23, 1929

HODGES
Bettie S. (Mrs.), Apr. 20, 1876
Jesse, June 23, 1842
Martha (Mrs.), Dec. 12, 1839
Mary L., d. of Gen. John Hodges, May 1, 1845
S. C., June 8, 1922
Sallie B., w. of J. W. Hodges, Mar. 6, 1902
Sarah Richardson, w. of John T. Hodges, Mar. 12, 1936
Thomas, Nov. 3, 1842
Wilson H., s. of W. S. and K. Hodges, Aug. 31, 1871

HODNETT
Mary F. (Mrs.), Aug. 10, 1905

HOFFMAN
Sarah B. (Mrs.), June 29, 1876
William, Feb. 9, 1899

HOGAN
Frances (Mrs.), Oct. 6, 1904

HOGE
B. Lacy (Rev.), Sept. 25, 1924
Cassie E., w. of P. B. Hoge, May 8, 1862
Mary L., w. of John H. Hoge, Jan. 23, 1896
P. C. (Rev.), July 27, Aug. 24, 1876; Apr. 5, 1877
Sarah, w. of Elder Peter C. Hoge, Oct. 10, 1872

HOGG
Charles J., Feb. 19, 1914
Cornelia (Mrs.), July 27, 1916
J., w. of Thomas Hogg, Apr. 23, 1857
Joseph T., Feb. 19, 1914
Lucy (Mrs.), Aug. 21, 1924
Maud A., d. of W. H. and A. F. Hogg, Sept. 13, 1883

OBITUARY NOTICES IN THE RELIGIOUS HERALD WITH DATES OF PUBLICATION

HOGGE
  Cora Lee, Apr. 9, 1895
  Hinton, s. of S. Scott and
    Celestia, Oct. 4, 1883
  S. S., Feb. 13, 1919
HOGUE
  William M., Feb. 8, 1866
HOLCOMB
  Bettie (Mrs.), Oct. 6, 1859
HOLCOMBE
  Hosea (Rev.), Sept. 30, 1841
  J. P., Sept. 4, 1873
HOLCROFT
  John T., Sept. 16, 1852
HOLDCROFT
  F. S., Feb. 24, 1898
  James, Jan. 10, Sept. 26,
    1889
  Rebecca Judkins, w. of J.
    E. Holdcroft, July 26,
    1906
HOLDEN
  W. H., Aug. 26, 1858
HOLIDAY
  John Reed, s. of William J.
    and Lucy R. Holiday, Aug.
    30, 1860
HOLLADAY
  Agnes, May 4, 1848
  Elizabeth Jane, Jan. 18, 1934
  Frances A., Aug. 1, 1878
  Huldah F., w. of Waller
    Holladay, Nov. 12, 1863
  J. P. (Mrs.), Aug. 2, 1923
  James P., May 10, 1917
  Lewis L., July 30, 1891
  Mary E. (Mrs.), mother of
    Dr. J. W. Garnett, d. of
    Elder L. Willis, Oct. 28,
    1886
  Elizabeth W. (Mrs.), d. of
    John P. Kelley, Nov. 17,
    1853
HOLLAND
  Alpha Harman, s. of John E.
    and S. Holland, Aug. 6,
    1846
  Asa (Capt.), Oct. 30, 1879
  Cephas, s. of H. R. and
    Pattie J. Holland, Apr.
    4, 1878
  Christopher Grant, Aug. 27,
    1896
  Georgie Morris (Mrs.), Jan.
    20, 1927
  Henry M., Dec. 14, 1871
  Joe, Feb. 5, 1891
  John, Dec. 23, 1852
  John C. (Capt.), Mar. 7,
    1881
  John Oscar, s. of J. P.
    Holland, Oct. 12, 1876
  John W., Aug. 13, 1857
  John W., Dec. 22, 1932
  K. G., July 14, 1887
  Mary Thomas Bell, w. of
    Alvin Holland, d. of
    Charles C. Bell, Feb.
    6, 1919
  Nancy B., w. of K. G.
    Holland, May 21, 1863
  Nancy W., d. of Richard
    and Lucy Holland, Feb.
    2, 1838
  Robert E., s. of John C.
    and Sarah E. Holland,
    Feb. 20, 1879
  Robert Madison, s. of John
    P. and S. Emma Holland,
    July 24, 1873
  Robert Watson, s. of John
    W. and Amanda W. Holland,
    Aug. 29, 1889
  Sarah C., Apr. 12, 1923
  Sarah E., Sept. 25, 1902
  Thomas J., s. of Robert S.
    and Lucy H. Holland,
    Aug. 3, 1871
  William W. (Dr.), Mar. 22,
    1849
  Williamson P. (Dr.), Jan.
    26, 1854
HOLLEMAN
  Annie C., d. of A. S.
    Holleman, Dec. 18, 1884
  Mary H., w. of Arthur
    Holleman, Feb. 16, 1843
  Nancy, w. of J. Holleman
    July 25, 1844
HOLLIDAY

OBITUARY NOTICES IN THE RELIGIOUS HERALD WITH DATES OF PUBLICATION

Arabella, Dec. 21, 1854
G. M., Apr. 14, 1898
Mary, w. of Capt. William
  Holliday, July 2, 1846
HOLLINS
  Hardenia, w. of William
    C. Hollins, Jan. 3, 1856*
  John, Apr. 21, 1859
  Mary E., d. of William C.
    and Hardena Hollins,
    Dec. 1, 1853*
  Robert E., s. of W. C. and H.
    A. Hollins, Feb. 24, 1853
  W. C., Apr. 29, 1858
  William G., May 20, 1858
HOLLOWAY
  A. C., Feb. 20 and 27, 1873
  Elizabeth B. (Mrs.), Mar.
    14, 1867
  Frances E., d. of Silas
    and Ann H. Holloway, Dec.
    25, 1856
  James G., Sept. 2, 1886
  Silas, Feb. 16, 1860
  William, Oct. 21, 1886
HOLMAN
  Elizabeth, w. of Joseph
    Holman, Apr. 19, 1839
  Joseph, Aug. 24, 1848
  Lucy Noel, w. of James
    Henry Holman, May 2,
    1929
  Pattie E., w. of T. Holman,
    d. of John C. and Bettie
    Amos, Mar. 28,
    1889
HOLMES
  Annie M., w. of George
    C. Holmes, June 17,
    1920
  B. W., July 28, 1904
  Carrie H., w. of Rev. J. E.
    L. Holmes, d. of Dr.
    S. H. and Bettie F. Hud-
    nall, Feb. 22, 1883
  Deanie, child of William G.
    and C. V. Holmes, July 30,
    1874
  George C., Dec. 20, 1906
  J. L. (Dr.), Apr. 26,
    1894
  Jane (Mrs.), Apr. 4, 1878
  Julius C. (Mrs.), Aug. 23,
    1906
  Lizzie D., d. of W. G. and
    C. V. Holmes, Apr. 27,
    1899
  Sarah Ann, w. of S. H. Holmes,
    Nov. 23, 1854
  William H., Oct. 28, 1847
  William M. (Mrs.), Dec. 1,
    1938
HOLT
  Amelia Joseph, w. of Jacob
    Holt, d. of Capt. Vincent
    Phillips, Oct. 3, 1895
  Ann (Mrs.), July 20, 1871
  Clarissa C., w. of William
    L. Holt, Oct. 6, 1870
  Daniel, Mar. 16, 1871
  E. V. (Capt.) May 24, 1888
  Elizabeth, w. of Giles
    Holt, July 1, 1880
  George (Capt.), Mar. 23,
    1843
  George Herbert, s. of William
    L. and Clarissa C. Holt,
    Apr. 17, 1856
  Henry, s. of Giles Holt,
    Feb. 15, 1855
  Jacob W., Oct. 28, 1880
  R. B., Feb. 17, 1921
  Rebecca, w. of Thomas Holt,
    Oct. 17, 1850
  Robert, s. of A. J. and Emma
    Holt, Jan. 17, 1878
  Thomas H., July 10, 1884
HOLTZMAN
  Aylett T., Sept. 3, 1925
  Hannah L., w. of John
    A. Holtzman, Jan. 31,
    Feb. 14, 1907
  John A., Sept. 23, 1915
  Louisa, w. of Thomas Holtz-
    man, May 27, 1841
  Thomas (Rev.), Feb. 20,
    1879
  William F., Oct. 17, 1907

* Possible inaccuracy in name, or spelling, but given as printed

OBITUARY NOTICES IN THE RELIGIOUS HERALD WITH DATES OF PUBLICATION

HOMES
    Benjamin J., Sept. 20, 1866
    Mollie J., d. of Benjamin J. Homes, Sept. 20, 1866

HONE
    Emeline BOURNE (Mrs.), Mar. 24, 1910

HOOD
    Elizabeth Prince, w. of Samuel C. Hood, Aug. 6, 1908
    Emmett Randolph, Sept. 5, 1935
    Joel Prince, June 10, 1915
    S. C., Oct. 1, 1896
    Thomas, Apr. 18, 1828

HOOKER
    Esther Cheatham, w. of Dr. Raymond C. Hooker, July 2, 1936
    Virginia (Mrs.), Apr. 12, 1888

HOOPER
    Eliza L. (Mrs.), Feb. 18, 1892
    George J., Sr., Apr. 12, 1900
    George J., Jan. 16, 1936
    George L., s. of Benjamin Hooper, Aug. 12, 1858
    Judith (Mrs.), Feb. 17, 1859
    Mary Hix (Mrs.), Sept. 23, 1926
    Nancy, Feb. 1, 1849
    Susan (Mrs.), June 1, 1858
    William, Sept. 22, 1864
    William (Rev.), Aug. 31, 1876

HOOVER
    Nellie Chambers, w. of Milton J. Hoover, Aug. 16, 1906

HOPE
    Elizabeth, w. of Benjamin B. Hope, June 19, 1829
    Fannie (Mrs.), Oct. 12, 1843
    John, July 20, 1838
    John (Capt.), Dec. 21, 1843
    Lucy B. (Mrs.), Feb. 3, 1876
    Mary, w. of Capt. John Hope, Aug. 11, 1837
    Mary (Mrs.), Sept. 3, 1846
    Mary, d. of David M. and Sarah J. Hope, June 25, 1854
    Russell, child of Rev. H. M. Hope, Sept. 27, 1894
    Sallie L. w. of James W. Hope, Apr. 26, 1877
    Sarah, w. of Giles Hope, Sr., Mar. 2, 1843
    William, Aug. 11, 1837

HOPKINS
    Armstead S., May 28, 1830
    Bettie J., w. of John N. Hopkins, Apr. 19, 1866
    C. R., Mar. 12, 1868
    Carrie Knight (Mrs.), d. of John W. and Sarah Knight, Apr. 15, 1920
    David McCaw, s. of LeRoy and Mary Hopkins, July 4, 1850
    Edith Matilda Jenkins, w. of R. F. Hopkins, Feb. 18, 1909
    Erasmus, Sept. 21, 1876
    Frances G., w. of Price Hopkins, Mar. 8, 1860
    Hattie, d. of Thomas J. and Amanda E. Hopkins, Sept. 22, 1859
    Horace, s. of George H. and Elizabeth Hopkins, Dec. 10, 1857
    J. Hayward, Oct. 2, 1884
    John A. (Rev.), Sept. 16, 1880
    John J., Aug. 17, 1899
    Lottie W., June 13, 1889
    Maria M., w. of John C. Hopkins, July 13, 1843
    Martha Jones, w. of W. F. Hopkins, July 4, 1901

OBITUARY NOTICES IN THE RELIGIOUS HERALD WITH DATES OF PUBLICATION

Mary, w. of Col. John
  Hopkins, Mar. 29, 1839
Mary E., d. of C. A.
  Hopkins, Aug. 15, 1872
Norella Thomas (Mrs.), d.
  of Henry A. Thomas, June
  27, 1929
R. F. (Mrs.), w. of R. F.
  Hopkins, Feb. 4, 1909
Robert E., Nov. 8, 1849
Rowland, July 21, 1859
Sarah R., w. of Elder John
  Hopkins, Aug. 4, 1853
William C., s. of Rev.
  John Hopkins, Aug. 29,
  1867
William F., June 23, 1921
HORDE
  Deliah E. (Mrs.), Oct. 4,
  1855
HORN
  Miles, Mar. 15, 1855
  Robert E., May 1, 1856
HORNE
  Daisy E., May 9, 1889
  George E., s. of Robert
  Horne, May 21, 1840
  India C. (Mrs.), Jan. 16,
  1879
  Mary Ann, w. of Robert R.
  Horne, Mar. 22, 1855
  Ralph, Oct. 9, 1829
HORNER
  A. O., w. of Rev. L. D.
  Horner, Dec. 23, 1875
  Eulalia J., July 7, 1870
  Levi D. (Mrs.), w. of Elder
  Levi D. Horner, Dec. 19,
  1839
  Martha Ann, w. of Elder
  Levi D. Horner, May 18,
  1854
HORNOR
  James Yard, Jan. 16, 1873
HORNSEY
  C., Jan. 29, 1885
HORR
  George E. (Rev.), Feb. 11,
  1897
HORTON

Frances, w. of T. S.
  Horton, Dec. 20, 1860
J. W. (Rev.), June 8, 1922
HOSKINS
  George S., s. of Capt.
  George Hoskins, Oct. 19,
  1843
HOSSLEY
  William H. (Mrs.), Feb.
  12, 1931
  William Henry, May 24, 1928
HOSTRANDER
  D. E., Feb. 1, 1912
HOTCHKISS
  J. (Maj.), Jan. 26, 1899
  N. H. (Maj.), Apr. 30,
  1891
HOUCHENS
  William, June 30, 1859
HOUCHINS
  Celestia, d. of Joseph A.
  and America S. Houchins,
  Mar. 28, 1861
  Susan W., w. of James
  Houchins, Dec. 6, 1860
HOUGH
  Isabella, w. of Thomas Hough,
  Jan. 25, 1849
HOUSE
  S. H., Oct. 17, 1844
HOUSTON
  Calvin N., Dec. 7, 1922
  Elizabeth, w. of Page Houston,
  Dec. 13, 1900
  J. R. P., Sept. 8, 1892
  Jane, Apr. 3, 1862
  Margaret M., w. of Gen.
  Sam Houston, Jan. 2, 1868
  Mary (Mrs.), June 23, 1842
HOVEY
  Alvah (Dr.), Oct. 1, 1903
HOWARD
  Carrie O., w. of George M.
  Howard, d. of John T. and
  Caroline C. Harris, Oct.
  21, 1897
  Claudia Alma, d. of R. J.
  and Mary J. Howard, May
  19, 1881
  E. C., Aug. 11, 1864

OBITUARY NOTICES IN THE RELIGIOUS HERALD WITH DATES OF PUBLICATION

Elizabeth, w. of Thomas Howard, Mar. 27, 1856
Francis Mallory, Feb. 6, 1873
John, Mar. 16, 1899
John James, Dec. 14, 1854
Joseph, Feb. 28, Mar. 7, 1861
Mary Ann, w. of Joseph C. Howard, Dec. 12, 1844
Susan S. (Mrs.), Dec. 28, 1854
Susanna (Mrs.), Oct. 19, 1838
Thomas (Rev.), Apr. 28, 1932

HOWARTH
John H. (Capt.), Sept. 10, 1887

HOWELL
Asemath (Mrs.), Feb. 26, 1931
C. D. B., Aug. 7, 1856
Charles Trabue, s. of Elder R. B. C. Howell, Aug. 16, 1839
E. J. (Mrs.), Mar. 11, 1926
Isaac E., Mar. 20, 1930
Isabel Elliott, w. of Morton B. Howell, May 7, 1868
Josephus, Oct. 1, 1891
Paul, May 23, 1828
R. B. C. (Rev.), Apr. 16, May 7, 1868
Robert Bruce, Apr. 7, 1921

HOWERTON
Elizabeth (Mrs.), Apr. 22, 1836
Ellie H., May 25, 1899
Kate M., w. of Richard T. Howerton, d. of Henry R. and Mary Bishamer, Apr. 14, 1870.
Kate Powell, d. of William T. Howerton, Feb. 1, 1872
Mary F. (Mrs.), Nov. 15, 1888
Minnie Grey, Feb. 1, 1872
Robert G., May 25, 1854
Robert G., Jr., s. of Robert G. Howerton, Feb. 1, 1872
S. D., w. of Thomas J. Howerton, Feb. 8, 1855
Sarah A., w. of R. G. Howerton, Feb. 1, 1872
Sarah A. (Mrs.), July 27, 1876
Thomas J., July 4, 1878
Virginia, w. of William T. Howerton, Feb. 1, 1872
William J., Jr., Feb. 15, 1900
Willie, child of William T. Howerton, Feb. 1, 1872

HOWL
Emma J., w. of James D. Howl, Mar. 12, 1868

HOWLE
Elizabeth, w. of Thomas R. Howle, Oct. 3, 1872
Mary E., w. of Thomas R. Howle, d. of Henry C. and Eliza Carter Binford, Apr. 8, 1920
Patsy, May 1, 1862
William M., May 25, 1843
William Spencer, s. of John W. and Amanda D. Howle, Aug. 25, 1853

HOWLETT
Elizabeth (Mrs.), Aug. 20, 1840
Martha E. (Mrs.), Nov. 4, 1880
William, Dec. 5, 1828

HOWLEY
Robert Henderson, s. of James H. and Catherine J. Howley, Feb. 16, 1865

HOYT
James A., June 23, 1904
John J., Mar. 12, 1891
Joseph B., Jan. 10, 1889

HUBBARD
Ann Maria, w. of Dr. Hiram C. Hubbard, Sept. 16, 1852

OBITUARY NOTICES IN THE RELIGIOUS HERALD WITH DATES OF PUBLICATION

Charles B., Mar. 13, 1884
Cornelius, Aug. 9, 1866
Edgar Overton, May 25, 1916
Joel (Rev.), Nov. 4, 1880
Joshua S., Jan. 25, Mar. 8, 1883
Maude, d. of E. O. Hubbard, Feb. 2, 1899
R. C. (Rev.), Sept. 12, 1918
Rawley, s. of Rawley and Emma Hubbard, July 19, 1888
Rawley Thompson, Aug. 17, 1916; Feb. 8, 1917
Robert R., Apr. 21, 1864
Robert S., Feb. 28, 1889
Samuel, Nov. 7, 1828
Susan D., w. of Jesse Hubbard, Dec. 10, 1891
William, Nov. 7, 1828
HUCKSTEP
George Holman, Apr. 25, 1935
Mildred Anne (Mrs.), Apr. 19, 1894
Willie (Rev.), Mar. 7, 1867
HUDDLESTON
Steven, July 8, 1841
HUDGENS
Benjamin, Nov. 13, 1879*
Dennis Ashby, s. of Alfred S. and Marie A. Hudgens, June 29, 1876*
Mary Josephine, w. of Thomas E. Hudgens, Oct. 28, 1909
HUDGINS
Albert G. (Dr.), Mar. 10, 1853
Ann (Mrs.), Dec. 21, 1843
Benjamin Franklin, Apr. 5, 1839*
Bettie M., d. of Mrs. Louisa Hudgins, June 18, 1857
Eliza B., May 28, June 4, 1908
Elizabeth, w. of Anthony Hudgins, May 10, 1839
Elizabeth G., w. of Thomas Hudgins, Nov. 15, 1833
Elizabeth V. (Mrs.), Feb. 25, 1841

Henry Preston, s. of H. H. and S. E. Hudgins, Sept. 28, 1899
James Campbell, s. of Dr. A. G. and R. V. Hudgins, Mar. 22, 1855
John, Jan. 6, 1859
Louisa A., w. of Henry V. Hudgins, Apr. 13, 1876
Louisa F., d. of Mrs. Louisa Hudgins, June 18, 1857
Marie A., w. of Benjamin Hudgins, Jan. 8, 1885*
Mary, w. of John L. Hudgins, Feb. 22, 1844
Mary Braxton (Mrs.), Nov. 2, 1905
Mattie Lee, d. of Dr. A. G. Hudgins, May 14, 1868
Milton F., Dec. 21, 1893
Nannie Jane, w. of Thomas W. Hudgins, June 16, 1853
Preston Marion, Dec. 29, 1898
Rebecca V., w. of Dr. Albert Hudgins, d. of Col. Thomas Hudgins, Sept. 20, 1860
Robert, June 7, 1860
Robert H., Dec. 23, 1915
Sarah B., w. of Andrew G. Hudgins, June 3, 1858
Thomas (Col.), Dec. 11, 1862
Thomas S., Mar. 2, 1865
HUDNALL
Agnes, w. of Lawson Hudnall, Nov. 27, 1851
Bettie F. (Mrs.), Jan. 12, 1911
Chloe E., w. of James H. Hudnall, Mar. 7, 1867
Ezekiel Wayles, Sept. 28, 1854
Henry (Mrs.), w. of Capt. Henry Hudnall, July 12, 1888
Richard H. (Dr.), June 29, July 20, 1916
S. H. (Dr.), Jan. 9, 1902
HUDSON
d. of H. Calvin Hudson, Dec.

* Possible inaccuracy in name, or spelling, but given as printed

OBITUARY NOTICES IN THE RELIGIOUS HERALD WITH DATES OF PUBLICATION

25, 1884
Abbott M., May 21, 1857
Abner, June 10, 1869
Addison P., Apr. 21, 1892
C. F., Aug. 20, 1936
Charles B. (Capt.), Jan. 6, 1876
Clara P., d. of James G. and M. C. Hudson, Aug. 28, 1856
Eliza, w. of Addison P. Hudson, Dec. 1, 1892
Eliza Murphy (Mrs.), Feb. 10, 1916
Ellen Palmer (Mrs.), Sept. 26, 1907
Elliott Woodville, s. of John D. Hudson, May 10, 1877
Franklin, Oct. 23, 1879
Georgianna H. (Mrs.), June 22, 1882
Grief C., s. of David P. and Mary P. Hudson, Aug. 11, 1864
James G., June 6, 1844
James G., Dec. 31, 1863
John Bustard, Mar. 19, 1931
John G., s. of William and Lavinia Hudson, Apr. 16, 1863
Julius C., Aug. 26, 1937
Lavinia C., Dec. 31, 1885
Martha, d. of A. G. and Sarah Hudson, Feb. 7, 1850
Mary (Mrs.), Aug. 5, Sept. 23, 1852
Mollie E., Dec. 23, 1875
Nellie, d. of R. O. and A. E. Hudson, Jan. 11, 1894
O. S., June 4, 1936
Sally, d. of Mrs. Mary Hudson, July 31, 1845
Sarah Elizabeth, w. of John W. Hudson, June 9, 1859
Sarah Frances (Mrs.), Mar. 5, 1931
Susan Penelope, d. of Robert Hudson, Dec. 21, 1854
William (Mrs.), Apr. 22, 1886
William Royal, s. of Julius C. and Jennie Hudson, May 16, 1895

HUFF
Bettie Jurey, w. of Rev. Samuel P. Huff, Mar. 7, 1912
D., s. of Col. Daniel Huff, July 30, 1874
D. (Col.), Oct. 12, 1882
Henry Clay, s. of John S. and Emily B. Huff, Jan. 22, 1863
Preston Brooks, Dec. 22, 1887
S. P. (Rev.), Jan. 16, 1896
Sallie A. (Mrs.), Mar. 6, 1902

HUFFMAN
Edward V., Nov. 14, 1935
Giles C., Sept. 6, 1888
Lucy B. (Mrs.), Dec. 24, 1936
Patrick Henry, May 18, 1893

HUGGINS
Samuel J. (Rev.), Nov. 30, 1838

HUGGINS
Ida J. (Mrs.), d. of W. H. Huggins, Dec. 23, 1880

HUGHART
Virginia S., w. of Rev. O. W. Hughart, July 25, 1872
William H. (Dr.), Nov. 19, 1868

HUGHES
Annie DeCormas, d. of Thomas W. Hughes, Feb. 18, 1892
Edward M., s. of Richard A. and Dahlia Z. Hughes, May 29, 1879
Ellen M. (Mrs.), Jan. 31, 1924
Fannie B., d. of George P. Hughes, July 25, 1901
Fanny T., Jan. 26, 1854
Jacob Thomas, s. of George S.

OBITUARY NOTICES IN THE RELIGIOUS HERALD WITH DATES OF PUBLICATION

Hughes, Nov. 15, 1888
Jesse R., Feb. 12, 1880
John E., July 12, 1877
John H., Feb. 22, 1894
John J., July 19, 1839
Joseph A., s. of John C. and Lucy Ann Hughes, Nov. 13, 1884
Maggie, w. of J. A. Hughes, Dec. 22, 1921
Martha (Mrs.), Oct. 25, 1860
Martha P., w. of P. A. Hughes, Sept. 11, 1856
Mary M., w. of Charles S. Hughes, Jan. 21, 1858
Nancy J., w. of A. Hughes, Sept. 10, 1846
Sallie (Mrs.), Dec. 14, 1905
Susan (Mrs.), June 26, 1913
Virgie Belle, d. of Ben and Susan Hughes, Sept. 15, 1881
Virgie Thomas, w. of George S. Hughes, d. of Jacob and Fannie Thomas, Dec. 20, 1888
W. S., Sept. 27, 1888
William B., Mar. 16, 1843

HUGHLETT
Amarose B., July 12, 1855

HUGHS
Elizabeth, Feb. 3, 1832

HUGHSON
Lattie Randolph, w. of Dr. John S. Hughson, d. of Shirley C. Turner, Feb. 3, 1876
N. C., July 12, 1934

HULCE
Robert Emmett, s. of Samuel T. and Elizabeth Hulce, Dec. 7, 1854
Samuel T., July 24, 1873

HULETT
Willie C., s. of A. D. Hulett, June 10, 1858

HULFISH
S. M. (Mrs.), June 8, 1922

HULL
Brodie S., s. of John and Martha Hull, Nov. 9, 1838*
Elizabeth G., w. of Brodil S. Hull, July 3, 1835*
Hallie Winston, d. of John M. and Anna M. Hull, Apr. 17, 1873
Hannah, d. of Mrs. Mary Hull, Sept. 6, 1833
John G., Sept. 23, 1841
John Moncure, s. of Paul Hull, Oct. 2, 1862
Martha (Mrs.), Sept. 20, 1839
Mary, w. of Thomas Hull, Mar. 6, 1845
Paul, Feb. 11, 1892
Richard Gascoigne, s. of Paul Hull, June 9 and 16, 1870
Sallie Moncure, Feb. 11, 1892
Samuel S., s. of John and Martha Hull, Nov. 9, 1838
William E., Feb. 27, 1936

HULVEY
D. O., May 10, 1934
Raymond C., Aug. 9, 1917

HUME
Elizabeth (Mrs.), May 1, 1851
Elizabeth H., d. of Rev. Thomas Hume, Nov. 21, 1844
Jeter, s. of Elder Thomas Hume, Aug. 22, 1850
Lizzie Braxton, w. of Rev. Thomas Hume, July 8, Aug. 5, 1869
Lizzie Braxton, d. of Rev. Thomas and Lizzie B. Hume, Aug. 26, 1869
Mary Ann, w. of Rev. Thomas Hume, Apr. 17, 1862
Thomas (Rev.), Mar. 18, Apr. 1, 22, and 29, 1875
Thomas (Rev.), Aug. 8 and 22, 1912
Willie, s. of Rev. Thomas Hume, Aug. 3, 1854

HUMPHRAS
Nahari, Apr. 17, 1856

HUMPHREY

* Possible inaccuracy in name, or spelling, but given as printed

OBITUARY NOTICES IN THE RELIGIOUS HERALD WITH DATES OF PUBLICATION

Eliza Ann, w. of Minor T. Humphrey, Sept. 22, 1859
Frances Ruth A., w. of George Humphrey, Nov. 28, 1867

HUMPHREYS
Elizabeth, w. of Ezekiel Humphreys, Sept. 23, 1836
Isabella C., Aug. 12, 1847
J. T. (Dr.), Dec. 6, 1888
Susan J. (Mrs.), Sept. 6, 1849
William, June 5, 1873

HUMPHRIES
Alexander Hamilton, s. of J. R. P. Humphries, May 6, 1915
C. L., May 23, 1895
James T. (Lt.), Jan. 26, 1865
John, Sr., Apr. 13, 1838

HUNDLEY
Eliza Booth, w. of Capt. Larkin Hundley, Apr. 7, 1853
Elizabeth, w. of Josiah Hundley, Aug. 11, 1837
Elizabeth (Mrs.), Sept. 16, 1847
Frank, s. of William T. and Nannie L. Hundley, June 19, 1879
Harriet Russell (Mrs.), May 1 and 15, 1913
John W. (Rev.), Jan. 30, 1890
John W. (Rev.), Mar. 28, 1912
John Walker, Oct. 29, Dec. 17, 1914; Jan. 28, 1915
Kelsic Coleman, Oct. 6, 1938
Martha M., w. of Richard A. Hundley, Mar. 7, 1867
Mary Hamilton, Apr. 2, 1931
Maude, d. of Rev. William T. and Nannie L. Hundley, June 22, 1882
R. B., May 24, 1917
R. H., Apr. 28, 1898
Sarah B. (Mrs.), Nov. 4, 1880
Sydney, s. of Rev. J. Hervey and Sophronia Hundley, Dec. 19, 1867
Willie W., child of Robert B. and H. B. Hundley, Aug. 29, 1861

HUNLEY
Ida B. (Mrs.), d. of Philip Gibson, Sept. 22, 1898
Margaret A. T., w. of Thomas M. Hunley, Oct. 13, 1842

HUNNICUTT
John W., Nov. 29, 1877
Martha Ann, d. of J. W. Hunnicutt, Mar. 25, 1847
Rosa, d. of John W. Hunnicutt, Feb. 16, 1860

HUNT
Catherine (Mrs.), Jan. 6, 1832
Elijah, Feb. 6, 1902
John, Sept. 27, 1839
John (Capt.), July 15, 1841
John D., June 30, 1859
Lucinda L., w. of John Hunt, Jan. 27, 1842
M. A. (Mrs.), Dec. 5, 1878
Mahala (Mrs.), Mar. 5, 1830
Susan E., w. of J. D. Hunt, July 8, 1858

HUNTER
Alice Swain (Mrs.), Dec. 8, 1898
Andrew, Nov. 29, 1888
John Robert, s. of William H. and Ann M. Hunter, Dec. 30, 1852
Maria Lewis, d. of William H. and Ann M. Hunter, Dec. 30, 1852

HUNTINGTON
A. J., w. of Dr. A. J. Huntington, Oct. 3, 1889
A. J. (Dr.), July 23, 1903
Adoniram Judson, Feb. 25, 1904

OBITUARY NOTICES IN THE RELIGIOUS HERALD WITH DATES OF PUBLICATION

HUNTON
 William, July 27, 1838
 William A., Feb. 19, 1863
HURST
 William (Capt.), Dec. 3,
  1857
HURT
 Adolphus C., s. of James B.
  and Eliza A. B. Hurt,
  July 28, 1837
 Alice Bell, d. of P. H. Hurt,
  Aug. 22, 1861
 Alvin Judson (Dr.), Sept. 3,
  1936
 Ashley D., s. of Ashley D.
  and Mary Hurt, Apr. 11,
  1861
 Caroline C. (Mrs.), June 20,
  1872
 Elizabeth D., d. of Elder R.
  S. Hurt, Feb. 12, 1852
 George S., Sept. 14, 1905
 George W. (Rev.), Mar. 3
  and 31, 1932; Mar. 30,
  1933
 H. H. (Gen.), Aug. 9, 1888
 Jennie Johnson (Mrs.),
  July 18, 1929
 Lavinia, w. of Elder Robert
  S. Hurt, Oct. 14, 1858
 Louisa, w. of Dr. Hurt,
  Aug. 28, 1856
 Maria L., w. of Col.
  William Hurt, Mar. 15,
  1888
 Mary M. (Mrs.), Aug. 23,
  1888
 Mathew M., s. of Milton R.
  and Bettie Hurt, Dec. 10,
  1857
 Nancy Ann, w. of P. H. Hurt,
  d. of Joseph Duckwiler,
  Apr. 11, 1861
 S. C., Apr. 14, 1898
 Sallie E., d. of Ira Hurt,
  Nov. 21, 1872
 Sallie Yates, Jan. 27,
  Mar, 25, 1916
 Thomas, Aug. 18, 1870
 Werter W., s. of George S.
  Hurt, Sept. 13, 1883
 William E. (Rev.), Nov. 13,
  1930
 William P., s. of William
  Hurt, Aug. 7, 1856
HUTCHERSON
 Nannie (Mrs.), June 2,
  1921
HUTCHESON
 Mary C. (Mrs.), Mar. 21,
  1861
 Serena, w. of A. B. Hutche-
  son, May 12, 1898
HUTCHINGS
 child of Willie Hutchings,
  July 6, 1893
 Elizabeth Parmly, w. of
  William D. Hutchings,
  Sept. 2, 1880
 Fannie, w. of Willis Hutch-
  ings, June 15, 1893
HUTCHINSON
 Elizabeth, Dec. 24, 1857
 Helen (Mrs.), Oct. 13,
  1887
 Jefferson Davis, s. of
  W. W. and M. E. Hutchin-
  son, Dec. 18, 1862
 Jeter Overton, Aug. 28, 1930
 Lucien M., s. of Warner W.
  Hutchinson, Nov. 17, 1904
 Mary E., w. of Warner W.
  Hutchinson, Aug. 20,
  1891
 Virgil, Mar. 18, 1875
 Warner W., Sept. 17, 1891
HUTCHISON
 Annie Lou, d. of Westwood
  and Susan Hutchison,
  Oct. 28, 1875
 B. O., Nov. 26, 1925
 Elizabeth, w. of John Hutchi-
  son, d. of Richard L. and
  Nancy H. Rogers, June 11,
  1903
 G. A., July 17, 1924
 Ida Lee, d. of J. O. Hutchi-
  son, June 13, 1929
 Jane (Mrs.), Nov. 21, 1850
 Westwood (Rev.), Sept. 21, 1933

OBITUARY NOTICES IN THE RELIGIOUS HERALD WITH DATES OF PUBLICATION

Westwood (Mrs.), Jan. 10, 1935
HUTSON
 Araminta H., w. of James Hutson, d. of W. G. Goode, May 13, 1869
 J. E. (Rev.), Feb. 18 and 25, Mar. 18, 1915
 Margaret (Mrs.), d. of John T. Bidgood, June 13, 1907
HUTTSON
 Patsy, w. of Capt. Huttson, Aug. 11, 1853
HYDE
 Anna J., w. of Rev. G. W. Hyde, d. of Bennett C. and Margaret H. Clark, Aug. 8, 1878
 Richard S., Dec. 14, 1871
 Robert (Capt.), Dec. 18, 1835
 Sallie Garnett, w. of J. B. Hyde, Aug. 8, 1878
 William S., June 5, 1862

I J

I'ANSON
  Betty Lee, w. of Dr. Henry
    I'Anson, May 4, 1876
INGE
  D. P., Aug. 10, 1911
INGRAHAM
  Cyrus D., May 1, 1862
INGRAM
  I. H. (Mrs.), June 26, 1919
  Orson, Aug. 11, 1853
IRBY
  Mattie, Apr. 30, 1936
  William Rufus (Capt.), June 26, 1879
IRVIN
  Crawford, Nov. 6, 1829*
IRVINE
  A. M. (Miss), June 24, 1858
  Sarah, w. of Crawford Irvine, Apr. 3, 1829*
IRVING
  Lena Rosa (Mrs.), Dec. 19, 1918
IRWIN
  C. M. (Mrs.), w. of Rev. C. M. Irwin, Feb. 11, 1886
  Susan B., w. of Dr. W. B. Irwin, May 17, 1860
ISAACS
  Richard M., Aug. 13, 1874
ISBELL
  A. L., Oct. 8, 1903
  Abner Clopton (Dr.), Nov. 8, 1855
  Adronicus Parkinson, child of Francis T. and Tabitha W. Isbell, Mar. 26, 1846
  Henry E., s. of George Isbell, Oct. 24, 1844
  Patrick, May 2, 1901
  Patrick J., June 6, 1878
IVES
  Hilda Beryl, d. of Amos L. Ives, Sept. 14, 1899
  Ida, d. of William Leslie and Nancy Frances Ives Dec. 4, 1879
  J. H., Jan. 2, 1908
IVEY
  Edward T., Jan. 9, 1913
IVY
  P. H., Nov. 2, 1899
  William Farrow, May 7, 1891

JACKSON
  Charles Thomas, Jan. 2, 1930
  Charles William, s. of J. H. and M. D. Jackson, June 15, 1848
  Crawford, Apr. 23, 1874
  Daniel, May 2, 1872
  Eugene B. (Mrs.), May 5, June 2, 1932
  Frank Floor, s. of J. Tyler and Emma H. Jackson, Aug. 15, 1878
  Franklin D., July 9, 1863
  George M. Dallas, s. of J. B. and Martha A. Jackson, July 16, 1846
  Howard Aubray, s. of J. Tyler and Emma H. Jackson, Oct. 3, 1872
  J. B. (Rev.), Dec. 25, 1919
  James B., Feb. 5, 1891
  John R., Jan. 1, 1880
  Josephine W., d. of Dr. Robert S. and Ann C. Jackson, Aug. 23, 1860
  Laura F. (Mrs.), May 28, 1903
  Lou A., Nov. 4, Dec. 16, 1920
  Margery, Oct. 22, 1846
  Maria, w. of Thomas A. Jackson, June 16, 1881
  Martha, w. of Frederick Jackson, Feb. 13, 1851
  Moat A., June 2, 1927
  Mollie Huntington, d. of Howard C. and Naomi F.

---

* Possible inaccuracy in name, or spelling, but given as printed

OBITUARY NOTICES IN THE RELIGIOUS HERALD WITH DATES OF PUBLICATION

Jackson, Oct. 9, 1862
Nancy A., w. of Franklin D.
  Jackson, July 9, 1863
Narcissa C., w. of Rev.
  Matthew W. Jackson, d. of
  Richard and Amey Pente-
  cost, Aug. 20, 1874
Penelope, w. of W. A. Jack-
  son, d. of George W. and
  Elizabeth Pendleton, Nov.
  29, 1906
Permelia Ann, w. of James
  Jackson, June 28, 1839
Phebe H., d. of Daniel and
  Mary Jackson, Dec. 19,
  1895
R. S. (Rev.), Sept. 24, 1874;
  Jan. 14, 1875
Virginia A., d. of John B.
  and Elizabeth Jackson,
  Jan. 16, 1873
W. A., Jan. 12, 1905
W. J., Mar. 29, 1934
W. S. (Rev.), July 4, 1918
William A., Feb. 2, 1888

JACOB
  B. A., Jan. 21, 1937
  Caleb, Oct. 6, 1904
  Caleb Lee, s. of Caleb and
    J. L. Jacob, Feb. 1, 1866
  Ella Virginia, w. of Capt.
    B. A. Jacob, Sept. 23,
    1915
  John, Aug. 11, 1864
  Mary Ann Eliza, w. of Joseph
    C. Jacob, Nov. 27, 1851
  Walter Ellis, Feb. 27, 1879
JACOBBS*
  Allen, Dec. 9, 1875
JACOBS
  Benjamin Aylwin, May 28,
    1846
  Ida, d. of R. T. and J. V.
    Jacobs, Apr. 13, 1876
  J. B., May 26, 1887
  John Frances, June 16, 1921
  John W., June 16, 1881
  Martha W. (Mrs.), Aug. 17,
    1933
  Missouri M., w. of Dr. William

  Jacobs, Dec. 2, 1875
  R. P., Mar. 21, 1889
  Rebecca, w. of James B.
    Jacobs, Dec. 15, 1859
  Robert H., Sr., May 14, 1931
  Sarah Ann, Aug. 6,
    1840
JACQUES
  B. R. Q., Nov. 6, 1879
JAMAR
  Annie Roberts (Mrs.), Oct.
    17, 1929
JAMES
  B. C. (Rev.), Nov. 8, Dec.
    20, 1906
  Benjamin Hiter, Mar. 2,
    1899
  Bettie C., w. of James B.
    James, Mar. 28, 1872
  Carrie, Oct. 6, 1921
  Carrie A. (Mrs.), June 23,
    1921
  Charles F. (Dr.), Dec. 18
    and 25, 1902
  David Ryland, Sr., Sept. 18,
    1924
  Eliza M., w. of Thomas L. P.
    James, Oct. 5, 1843
  Fannie, Mar. 20, 1930
  Fleet H. (Rev.), May 8,
    1919
  H. A., Nov. 24, 1887
  J. Sexton (Dr.), July 20,
    1848
  J. Sexton (Mrs.), w. of
    Dr. J. Sexton James,
    July 20, 1848
  James B., Aug. 31, 1876
  James L. (Dr.), Sept. 14
    and 28, 1876
  John, June 9, 1921
  Joseph T., Jan. 19 and 26,
    1905
  Margaret, d. of Dr. W. C.
    James, Nov. 26, 1931
  Mary (Mrs.), Jan. 22, 1885
  Mary Estelle, d. of R. D.
    James, Sept. 7, 1905
  Mason, June 17, 1897
  Matson, Dec. 13, 1877

* Possible inaccuracy in name, or spelling, but given as printed

OBITUARY NOTICES IN THE RELIGIOUS HERALD WITH DATES OF PUBLICATION

Nancie (Mrs.), Oct. 23, 1902
Orma Whitson, Feb. 23, 1933
Patience, Aug. 2, 1900
Richard D. (Mrs.), July 15, 1915
Robert (Mrs.), Jan. 3, 1895
Sarah E., d. of Dr. A. James, May 3, 1860
Susan, w. of Wright James d. of John M. Young, Oct. 11, 1860
W. A. (Mrs.), Feb. 2, 1893
W. B., Dec. 20, 1906
Wiley, Aug. 16, 1855
William Matson, May 12, 1932
Willie, child of Dr. M. L. and Julia James, Mar. 23, 1871
Willie H., Sept. 29, 1921
Winifred, w. of Robert James Nov. 19, 1885

JAMESON
S. Y. (Dr.), Mar. 24, 1921

JAMIESON
Elizabeth, Sept. 27, 1839

JARGARONA
Mary Eubank (Mrs.), Feb. 4, 1926

JARMAN
Thomas B., Jan. 31, 1929

JARRAD
Joseph (Mrs.), Mar. 3, 1842

JARRATT
Elizabeth M., w. of Jesse Jarratt, Oct. 28, 1886
J. N., May 21, 1931
Jesse, May 25, 1893
Mary, w. of N. Jarratt, Aug. 28, 1856
Nicholas, Apr. 1, 1852
Sallie, May 6, 1926
William N., Sr., Apr. 21, 1881

JARRETT
Martha E., w. of A. L. Jarrett, d. of David Philpott, Jan. 22, 1857

JARVIS
Lucinda (Mrs.), July 17, 1919

Maggie L., d. of H. S. and M. E. Jarvis, May 22, 1884
Mattie, w. of Henry S. Jarvis, July 8, 1920

JEFFERSON
Elizabeth J., w. of George Jefferson, Sept. 6, 1833
George C., Apr. 23, 1931
Jennie E., w. of Lt. E. E. Jefferson, d. of Col. A. Fitzpatrick, Feb. 22, 1866
John P., Mar. 15, 1860
Lewis, Apr. 8, 1858
Mary, w. of Elder E. Jefferson, May 21, 1863
Sallie, d. of Elder E. G. Jefferson, Aug. 22, 1861

JEFFRESS
A. G., Oct. 5, 1893
Anna Meredith (Mrs.), Feb. 17, 1927
Charley Richard, s. of S. E. F. and A. F. Jeffress, Feb. 23, 1865
Charlie, Sept. 8, 1864
Edward (Mrs.), w. of Col. Edward T. Jeffress, Mar. 18, 1858
Edward T. (Col.), May 1, 1873
Edwin T., s. of J. M. Jeffress, Feb. 9, 1838
Elizabeth Ann, w. of Col. William Jeffress, July 3, 1851
Ella B., w. of Albert G. Jeffress, June 28, 1888
Emma, d. of Col. William C. and Margaret B. Jeffress, Oct. 3, 1861
Fleming James (Capt.), Aug. 11, 1859
Hilary Thomas, June 6, 1895
James H., July 2, 1874
Jennings M. (Capt.), May 6, 1852

OBITUARY NOTICES IN THE RELIGIOUS HERALD WITH DATES OF PUBLICATION

Jethro Alexander, s. of L. C. Jeffress, July 31, 1845
Margaret B., w. of Capt. William C. Jeffress, Oct. 1, 1863
Mary C. (Mrs.), Apr. 5, 1855
Nancy B., w. of James H. Jeffress, Aug. 19, 1869
Sally Betts (Mrs.), Nov. 15, 1849
Sallie T., w. of Col. W. C. Jeffress, Oct. 22, 1885
Sarah E. F., w. of Albert G. Jeffress, Jan. 3, 1867
Susan D., w. of Capt. Jennings M. Jeffress, Mar. 5, 1840*
William C. (Mrs.), w. of Col. Jeffress, Nov. 5, 1885

JEFFRIES
Ann J., May 6, 1852
Ann Elizabeth, d. of Orville and Mary Jeffries, July 5, 1839
Anne C., w. of Richard Jeffries, Apr. 26, 1855
Bettie Diggs (Mrs.), July 17, 1930
Edwin T., s. of Jennings and Susan Jeffries, Apr. 13, 1838*
Elizabeth, w. of Enoch Jeffries, Apr. 13, 1893
Elizabeth R., w. of William S. Jeffries, Nov. 9, Dec. 14, 1848
Enoch, Aug. 17, 1876
James E., Oct. 30, 1856
James L., s. of Lewis and Martha A. Jeffries, Nov. 4, 1841
James P., s. of James P. Jeffries, June 19, 1890
Lewis, Aug. 16, 1866
Louise Howard, d. of Joseph A. and Camilla H. Jeffries, Aug. 11, 1881
M. M. (Mrs.), May 12, 1910
Maria, w. of Thomas H. Jeffries, Nov. 27, 1851
Martha, w. of Lewis Jeffries, May 1, 1845
Martha S., d. of Lewis and Martha A. Jeffries, Nov. 4, 1841
Mary, w. of O. Jeffries, Sept. 27, 1860
Mary J., w. of Ambrose Jeffries, Oct. 24, 1889
N. Janey, w. of Melville Jeffries, d. of Capt. A. F. and Fannie S. Bagby, Jan. 29, 1891
Richard (Capt.), June 7, 1849
Rosa, w. of John Jeffries, Dec. 5, 1867
Susan, w. of Ambrose Jeffries, Feb. 3, 1837
William G. (Dr.), May 25, 1899
William Jennings, Jan. 14, 1926
William S., Sept. 15, 1859

JEFFRY
Ann (Mrs.), July 16, 1840

JENKINS
A. B., Sept. 8, 1921
A. D. (Mrs.), Apr. 23, 1908
A. R. (Mrs.), Jan. 2, 1902
Ann T., w. of William Jenkins, Jr., Jan. 15, 1852
Charlie Vernon, s. of A. M. Jenkins, May 20, 1890
Eliza, Jan. 10, 1907
J. P. (Mrs.), Feb. 21, 1918
J. W., Sr., Apr. 15, 1920
John D. (Col.), June 14, 1888
Joseph (Elder), Aug. 25, Sept. 22, 1853
Joseph Philip, Aug. 31, 1933
Luther H., Mar. 7 and 14, 1935

* Possible inaccuracy in name, or spelling, but given as printed

OBITUARY NOTICES IN THE RELIGIOUS HERALD WITH DATES OF PUBLICATION

Maria B., w. of Col. John D.
Jenkins, d. of Capt. Willis
Sanderson, July 5, 1850
Martha (Mrs.), June 26, 1856
Melzer A. (Sgt.), s. of John
B. and Margaret A. Jenkins,
July 30, 1863
Nancy (Mrs.), May 19, 1853
Orra Lee, w. of W. S. Jenkins,
Oct. 20, 1921
Robert Lee, June 1, 1911
William (Capt.), Sept. 20,
1866
William G., Mar. 17, 1892

JENKS
Augustus A., s. of A. A.
Jenks, Jan. 20, 1859
Laura K., w. of Dr. O. B.
Jenks, d. of Dr. W. H.
Twyman, Dec. 16, 1875
O. B. (Dr.), July 6, 1876

JENNETT
Elizabeth J. (Mrs.), July
12, 1860

JENNETTE
John A., Dec. 19, 1907

JENNINGS
Alfred Carola, Nov. 2, 1893
Ann, Feb. 17, 1859
Anna Deaner, w. of W. E.
Jennings, Mar. 2, 1922
Annie Baldwin, d. of J. T.
Jennings, Feb. 9, 1899
B., July 28, 1892
Catharine (Mrs.), Sept. 21,
1843
E. N.(Mrs.), May 7, 1858
Edward R., Jan. 9, 1835
Eliza A. (Mrs.), Apr. 15, 1885
Griffin S., Apr. 7, 1881
Irena Ann (Mrs.), Dec. 22,
1881
James P., June 11, 1903
Jimmie Hamlet, s. of James
and Nannie J. Jennings
Aug. 31, 1876
John H., Jan. 23, 1845
John W., May 20, 1886
Judith E., w. of Dr. Alvin
Jennings, Feb. 8, 1855

Larkin D., Oct. 19, 1838
Lelia M., July 24, 1902
Lilly Booker, w. of R. F.
Jennings, Sept. 3, 1891
Lucy A., w. of James W.
Jennings, June 21, 1866
Lucy J., d. of John W.
Jennings, Oct. 30, 1856
M. A., w. of George D.
Jennings, Mar. 11, 1926
Martha (Mrs.), Apr. 27,
1838
Martha, Jan. 30, 1840
Martha F., d. of Joseph S.
and Sarah Jennings, May
17, 1850
Martha Glass (Mrs.), July
26, 1923
Martha T., w. of Anderson
M. Jennings, Apr. 6, 1843
Mary B., Apr. 29, 1841
Mary C. (Mrs.), Nov. 21,
1901
Mattie (Mrs.), Nov. 11,
1937
Mollie, Feb. 19, 1857
Nannie, w. of H. B. Jennings,
Oct. 4, 1917
Rosalie Ianthe, d. of James
H. and Nannie J. Jennings,
Oct. 3, 1872
Rosalie L. (Mrs.), July 23,
1868
Thomas, Dec. 17, 1840
Thomas C., Nov. 1, 1860
Thomas M., s. of Anderson M.
Jennings, Sept. 24, 1863
William T., s. of James P.
Jennings, Sept. 24, 1863

JERDONE
Lillie E., w. of John Jerdone,
Sept. 23, 1886

JERKINS
Susan C., w. of A. T. Jerkins
June 15, 1911

JERREL
V. M. (Dr.), Jan. 20, 1859

JERRELL
T. C., Apr. 22, 1858

JERRELLE

OBITUARY NOTICES IN THE RELIGIOUS HERALD WITH DATES OF PUBLICATION

Ann, w. of Pembleton Jer-
   relle, Apr. 29, 1841
JESPER
   H. (Mrs.), Mar. 8, 1855
JESSE
   Jane E., w. of William T.
      Jesse, Feb. 20, 1829
   M. D., w. of R. Jesse,
      Apr. 2, 1857
   Mary D., w. of William T.
      Jesse, d. of Rev. Richard
      Claybrook, Jan. 12, 1882
   Mary E. (Mrs.), Dec. 12, 1834
JESSEE
   James, Sept. 15, 1887
   James P., Sept. 12, 1861
   Liza (Mrs.), July 20, 1922
   Stanford L., May 29, 1862
JESSY
   Bettie Price, d. of William
      P. and Emily T. Jessy,
      Nov. 24, 1859
JETER
   Asa V., s. of Sovereign
      Jeter, Oct. 16, 1845
   Charlotte, w. of Rev. J. B.
      Jeter, Aug. 22, 1861
   Elizabeth (Mrs.), Mar. 22, 1833
   Elizabeth W. (Mrs.), Aug. 1,
      1850
   Elliott, Mar. 30, 1876
   Gabriella G., w. of L. H.
      Jeter, June 11, 1857
   Jane E. (Mrs.), July 22,
      1836
   Jeremiah Bell (Rev.), Feb.
      26, 1880
   Jesse (Capt.), Apr. 10, 1862
   Lucy Ann, d. of William and
      Eliza Jeter, July 10, 1845
   Mary Catharine, w. of Rev.
      J. B. Jeter, d. of Henry
      and Araminta Williams,
      Sept. 29, Oct. 20, 1887
   Mary M., w. of William A.
      Jeter, Aug. 20, 1874
   Mattie D., w. of L. H. Jeter,
      Dec. 6, 1900
   Pleasant, Apr. 29, 1852
   Sarah A., w. of Elder J. B.
      Jeter, Nov. 4, 1847
   Susan, w. of Elder James
      Jeter, Mar. 28, 1834
   Susan, w. of Jesse Jeter,
      Sept. 11, 1873
JETT
   Bettie C., w. of Charles L.
      Jett, d. of Eldred and
      Mary A. Lee, Dec. 25, 1890
   John L., June 23, 1837
JEWETT
   Thomas, Mar. 6, 1851
JOHNS
   Edmund (Elder), Jan. 20,
      1837
   Elizabeth, Sept. 20, 1877
   Elizabeth C., w. of Joel
      Johns, d. of Branch Os-
      bourne, Sept. 6, 1855
   John (Rev.), Aug. 15, 1878
   Mary E., Sept. 5, 1844
   Mary E., w. of James S.
      Johns, Nov. 23, 1876
   Susannah, w. of Edmond Johns
      Apr. 18, June 13, 1844
   Thomas A., Sept. 5, 1844
JOHNSON
   A. Sidney, s. of William C.
      and M. L. Johnson, Oct.
      31, 1878
   Ada Roberta, d. of Benjamin
      and Ann E. Johnson, July 5,
      1860
   Alice (Mrs.), Aug. 26, 1926
   Alonzo W., June 29, 1876
   Amy (Mrs.), Apr. 22, 1869
   Andrew (Col.), Nov. 30, Dec.
      21, 1838
   Andrew, former President of the
      United States, Aug. 5 and 19,
      1875
   Andrew F., s. of Rev. Thomas
      N. Johnson, Apr. 3, 1890
   Ann, w. of Col. Valentine
      Johnson, Sept. 16, 1847
   Ann, w. of Rev. Anderson
      Johnson, Mar. 22, 1849
   Anna (Mrs.), Nov. 29, 1849
   Anne D., w. of John Johnson,
      Feb. 11, 1847

OBITUARY NOTICES IN THE RELIGIOUS HERALD WITH DATES OF PUBLICATION

Annie May, d. of Alonzo W. and Anna C. Johnson, May 31, 1888
Aquila, Sept. 9, 1852
Bailey S., July 16, 1830
Belfield Cave, Feb. 19, 1885
Benjamin, June 25, 1857
Bettie, Mar. 16, 1922
Bettie A., Oct. 2, 1862
Burrows, s. of F. D. Johnson, Apr. 19, 1917
Caroline W., w. of D. H. Johnson, Apr. 3, 1919
Catharine L., w. of Elder T. N. Johnson, Sept. 30, 1841
Catherine, May 22, 1862
Charlie, s. of Thomas Johnson, Sept. 27, 1894
Christianne, Mar. 9, 1905
D. Newton, s. of John Johnson, Dec. 4, 1862
David Dye, s. of William Johnson, June 18, 1914
Edward R., Nov. 6, 1884
Edwin, Oct. 31, 1850
Elias H. (Dr.), Mar. 22, 1906
Elijah, Mar. 27, 1862
Eliza, w. of William Johnson, Apr. 28, 1853
Eliza A. (Mrs.), Feb. 19, 1885
Elizabeth (Mrs.), Nov. 4, 1869
Elizabeth, w. of William Johnson, d. of Daniel and Theresa Dye, Oct. 20, 1870
Elizabeth, w. of Samuel B. Johnson, Sept. 7, 1871
Ella Moseley, d. of T. N. and Mary E. Johnson, Sept. 18, 1845
Ella W., Sept. 26, 1935
Emma Jane, Dec. 20, 1877
Enoch Dye, s. of William Johnson, Apr. 22, 1915
Eva Ivey, d. of Joseph H. and Mary A. Johnson, Nov. 30, 1871

Eveline Eudora, d. of William D. Johnson, Nov. 29, 1849
Fanny, w. of Jonathan Johnson, June 25, 1863
Frances T., w. of Mosby Johnson, Jan. 14, 1847
Frank C., Dec. 4, 1890
Frank Wheatley, s. of B. F. and Blanche Wynne Johnson, Feb. 8, 1900
George, Dec. 20, 1877
George H., s. of Thomas Johnson, Apr. 30, 1863
George H., Aug. 13, 1926
George W., May 1, 1862
Helen, Dec. 22, 1910
Herman, s. of W. A. Johnson, Feb. 4, 1915
Hudson, Aug. 9, 1833
J. A., Jan. 17, 1918
J. E. (Mrs.), Mar. 25, 1937
J. R., Apr. 20, 1916
Jacob Allen, s. of Jesse B. and Mary C. Johnson, Mar. 7, 1918
James B., Apr. 14, 1881
James E., s. of M. S. and W. R. Johnson, Apr. 17, 1884
James J., Mar. 6, 1862
Jane (Mrs.), June 12, 1851
Jason L., Feb. 16, 1928
Jeremiah Dale, Mar. 1, 1877
John, May 20, 1847
John I., July 25, 1828
John L. (Rev.), Mar. 11 and 18, 1915
John Lipscomb (Mrs.), d. of Thomas Dallam Toy, May 22, 1930
John N. (Rev.), Oct. 17, 1850
John S., June 29, 1832
John S. W., Mar. 6, 1862
John T., Apr. 15, 1920
Joseph, s. of William and Mary Johnson, Mar. 10, 1842
Joseph, Jr., Oct. 8, 1857
Josiah, July 18, 1872
Julia Mason (Mrs.), July 1,

OBITUARY NOTICES IN THE RELIGIOUS HERALD WITH DATES OF PUBLICATION

1897
Julius P., Feb. 26, 1852
Keziah J., s. of James Johnson, Jan. 27, 1859
Laura Buck, w. of George Henry Johnson, Jan. 28, 1932
Lavinia, w. of W. L. Johnson, Dec. 4, 1890
Livingston (Dr.), Feb. 12, 1931
Louisa A., w. of Robert Johnson, July 23, 1863
Lucie Barbour, d. of Benjamin V. and Amanda M. Johnson, June 27, 1850
Lucy, w. of Benjamin Johnson, Apr. 26, 1849
Lucy Ann, Feb. 28, 1889
Lucy Ann Margaret, d. of John Johnson, Aug. 18, 1837
Lucy Ida, d. of T. L. and M. L. Johnson, July 30, 1885
M. A. (Miss), June 27, 1895
M. C. (Miss), Mar. 16, 1905
M. L. (Mrs.), July 26, 1928
Mabel, May 11, 1893
Maria Lou (Mrs.), Apr. 5, 1866
Marietta, d. of William and Mary Johnson, Apr. 14, 1842
Marshall, Apr. 22, 1852
Martha, w. of John Johnson, d. of Rev. Robert Lilly, Feb. 10, 1881
Martha Ella, Dec. 20, 1877
Mary, w. of Elder Anderson Johnson, Jan. 6, 1842
Mary, w. of Obediah Johnson, Feb. 20, 1845
Mary, w. of Elder T. N. Johnson, June 5, 1873
Mary A. E., w. of James Johnson, June 5, 1873
Mary E., w. of William C. Johnson, Mar. 10, 1870
Mary Elizabeth, w. of Elder T. N. Johnson, July 12, 1849
Mary M. (Mrs.), Dec. 9, 1915
Mary Nelson, d. of Lawrence T. and Eliza Johnson, Aug. 2, 1860
Mary P., w. of John Johnson, June 20, 1844
Mildred L. (Mrs.), May 21, 1863
Nancy, d. of Thomas Johnson, Sr., Mar. 23, 1838
Nancy J., Apr. 10, 1879
Nancy T., w. of John Johnson June 29, 1838
Nancy T., w. of George Johnson, Nov. 10, 1853
Nathanael D., Dec. 8, 1881
Nellie, d. of R. N. Johnson, Sept. 26, 1878
Otelia P., w. of George Dallas Johnson, Dec. 25, 1890
Peter, Oct. 26, 1838
Polly T., w. of John Johnson, July 4, 1844
R. M. (Dr.), Oct. 28, 1915
Rachel Elizabeth (Mrs.) Feb. 2, 1888
Reuben W., s. of John S. W. Johnson, Dec. 24, 1857
Robert, s. of Thomas Johnson, Sept. 27, 1894
Robert H., Feb. 17, 1898
Robert Henry, s. of Samuel B. and Elizabeth Johnson, Dec. 29, 1853
Robert M., Aug. 27, 1874
Robert N., Jan. 30, Mar. 27, 1913
Robert W., Sept. 11, 1890
Sallie F., d. of George and Caroline Johnson, Sept. 1, 1859
Samuel, Aug. 3, 1876
Sarah, June 2, 1853
Sarah, w. of Marshall Johnson Feb. 10, 1870
Sarah, Mar. 8, 1923
Sarah C., w. of James B. Johnson, Apr. 8, 1897
Sarah F., June 7, 1917
Sarah P. (Mrs.), Oct. 27, 1910

OBITUARY NOTICES IN THE RELIGIOUS HERALD WITH DATES OF PUBLICATION

Silas J. (Dr.), Feb. 4, Mar. 10, 1904
Stephen, May 24, 1855
Susanna V., Apr. 10, 1879
Susie Wood, Mar. 29, 1928
T. B., Nov. 7, 1901
Thomas, Jan. 8, 1863
Thomas N., Apr. 16, 1896
Thomas Nathaniel (Rev.), Sept. 20, Oct. 11, 1894
Thomas P., Oct. 25, 1900
Valentine (Col.), Sept. 7, 1848
W. C., s. of John and Anna Chewning Johnson, Mar. 3, 1910
W. I., Mar. 7, 1912
William, s. of William and Mary Johnson, July 28, 1842
William, Mar. 23, Apr. 27, 1871
William B. (Rev.), Jan. 3, 1867
William D., Nov. 19, 1868
William F., May 30, 1929
William I., s. of Mrs. Bessie A. Johnson, June 26, 1919
William M., s. of A. J. and S. J. Johnson, Mar. 17, 1859
William R., s. of Henry T. and Martha M. Johnson, Oct. 31, 1867
William S., Feb. 10, 1887
Willie, s. of Thomas Johnson, Sept. 27, 1894
Willie J., Nov. 17, 1892

JOHNSTON
Alice Boyd, w. of Walter N. Johnston, d. of William W. Boyd, June 24, 1875
Bettie Alexander, w. of Maj. John W. Johnston, d. of Samuel and Mary Alexander, May 23, 1889
Charles A. (Mrs.), Aug. 11, 1932
David E. (Judge), Sept. 20, 1917
Elizabeth O., w. of Elder John Nash Johnston, Apr. 11, 1878
Helen, w. of Rev. P. B. Johnston, Apr. 23, May 7, 1874
James, June 23, 1842
John W., s. of Samuel B. and Elizabeth Johnston, Aug. 10, 1854
John Nash (Elder), Aug. 1, 1850
Malinda Michie, w. of William Joseph Johnston, Mar. 28, 1929
Marianna, d. of Elder John Nash and Eliza O. Johnston, Apr. 11, 1901
Peter B. (Rev.), Jan. 13, 1887
Sallie Strange, w. of Dr. A. Nash Johnston, d. of Maj. James M. and Harriet G. Strange, Nov. 29, 1888
Walter N., Dec. 9, 1886
William Preston (Col.), s. of Gen. Albert Sidney Johnston, July 20, 1899

JOINER
Jeanette, July 23, 1903
Oney D., w. of Peter G. Joiner, Feb. 25, 1864
William (Rev.), s. of William Joiner, May 5, 1864

JOLLY
Asa (Judge), June 15, 1871
James Gary, s. of Rev. W. T. Jolly, June 24, 1897
W. T. (Rev.), Mar. 24, 1898

JONES
A. Judson, Dec. 2, 1875
Ada, d. of J. L. Jones, June 15, 1876
Adolphus, Jan. 27, 1881
Alberter C., s. of Philip C. and Permelia Jones, Apr. 14, 1870
Alexander Marion (Mrs.), Oct. 12, 1922
Almeda E. B., Oct. 9, 1873
Amy Parsons, d. of Rev. J. J. Parsons, Oct. 22, 1914
Ann E., w. of J. R. Jones, Apr. 17, 1913

OBITUARY NOTICES IN THE RELIGIOUS HERALD WITH DATES OF PUBLICATION

Ann Timson, w. of Rev. Scervant Jones, June 21, 1849
Ann Keeling (Mrs.), Oct. 24, 1928
Anne, w. of Dr. Carter Helm Jones, d. of Dr. J. W. McCown, Feb. 1, 1906
Annie, d. of James B. Jones, Sept. 10, 1857
Annie Bell, June 25, July 9, 1885
Austin W., Oct. 16, 1890
Benjamin A., Feb. 6, 1873
Benjamin Frederick, July 11, 1889
Benjamin S., Apr. 7, 1870
Bettie C., w. of Robert J. Jones, d. of J. B. Wood, Aug. 28, 1873
Bettie Lewis, d. of William and Bettie Jones, June 21, 1883
Betty Hill, w. of Robert Brooke Jones, June 12, 1873
Beverley, May 19, 1887
Byrd Dunn, w. of Frank E. Jones, Apr. 12, 1928
Carrie B., d. of J. J. Jones, Feb. 2, 1899
Catharine, Feb. 25, 1841
Catherine E. (Mrs.), Sept. 7, 1905
Charles, s. of T. W. Jones, Aug. 20, 1863
Charles E., Feb. 12, June 18, 1925
Charles L., Jan. 9, 1896
Charles M., s. of Silas B. Jones, Mar. 27, 1856
Charles S., Feb. 21, 1850
Charles W., Aug. 4, 1842
Charles W., Feb. 7, 1878
Claggett B. (Judge), Mar. 26, 1931
David R., Oct. 21, 1852
Doras H., Jan. 31, Feb. 14, 1924
E. D. (Dr.), July 15, 1841
Edna, Sept. 22, 1921

Edward, s. of William I. Jones, Jan. 4, 1877
Edward T., Dec. 2, 1920
Edwina Chandler (Mrs.), Nov. 11, 1937
Eleanor, Nov. 17, 1859
Eli M., July 29, 1880
Eliza G., w. of T. C. Jones, Sept. 7, 1871
Eliza Miller, w. of James Brereton Jones, Apr. 13, 1899
Elizabeth, w. of Willis Jones, Apr. 20, 1832
Elizabeth, w. of Albert Jones, Apr. 28, 1837
Elizabeth (Mrs.), Apr. 29, 1852
Elizabeth, w. of Jesse W. Jones, Aug. 16, 1855
Elizabeth, w. of Col. John Jones, June 27, 1867
Elizabeth, w. of R. B. Jones, Jan. 3, 1878
Elizabeth Harriet, d. of Philip C. and Permelia Jane Jones, Jan. 8, 1863
Elizabeth S., w. of Charles W. Jones, Dec. 9, 1858
Elizabeth W., w. of Rev. John W. Jones, Feb. 2, 1899
Elizabeth Walden, w. of John B. Jones, July 18, 1878
Emily B. MINOR (Mrs.), Feb. 28, 1889
Emma Ann, d. of Philip C. and Permelia Jones, Jan. 8, 1863
Emma Price, d. of N. B. and Amanda M. Jones, Oct. 23, 1884
Evan, s. of Mattie Hood Jones, Sept. 16, 1897
F. H. (Rev.), Dec. 28, 1911
F. W. (Col.), Feb. 13, 1890
Fannie, Jan. 27, 1898
Fanny W., w. of John R. Jones, d. of Elder George C. Richards, June 16, 1859
Frances, d. of Dr. E. Pendleton

OBITUARY NOTICES IN THE RELIGIOUS HERALD WITH DATES OF PUBLICATION

Jones, July 15, 1957
Francis T. (Mrs.), Jan. 21, 1864
George, Nov. 8, 1883
George R., May 7, 1908
George S., s. of William J. and Sarah Jones, Aug. 17, 1854
George W., Mar. 17, 1910
George W. (Mrs.), Mar. 3, 1921
Gordon Emma, Jan. 7, 1926
Granderson, Apr. 16, 1857
H. C. (Mrs.), Apr. 16, 1903
Harrison, Sept. 4, 1829
Harrison B., Sept. 11, 1856
Harrison B., Sept. 9, 1897
Helen Lee, w. of Charles E. Jones, d. of George J. and Lucy M. Sumner, May 15, 1890
Henry, m. Alice Holleman, Feb. 11, 1904
Howard Lee (Dr.), Sept. 30, 1915
Ida, w. of M. S. Jones, July 25, 1907
J. E. (Rev.), Apr. 18, June 27, 1912
J. H. C. (Judge), Sept. 17, Nov. 26, 1885
J. Harrison (Mrs.), Jan. 13, 1921
J. R., Nov. 24, Dec. 8, 1881
J. W., May 9, 1907
J. W., Apr. 19, 1923
J. Washington, Sept. 30, 1875
James (Capt.), May 7, 1840
James B., Dec. 24, 1840
James B., June 25, 1868
James E. (Rev.), Apr. 18, 1912
James G., Nov. 20, 1873
James L., s. of Col. F. W. Jones, Aug. 28, 1884
James Norvell, s. of Samuel T. and Lavinia M. Jones, June 27, 1844
James S., Dec. 24, 1846
James Saunders (Rev.), Jan. 9, Feb. 27, 1930
James Smith, June 28, 1894
Jane (Mrs.), Oct. 27, 1837
Joel Patrick, s. of Albert S. and Frances Jones, Oct. 6, 1859
John, Sept. 7, 1838
John (Mrs.), July 21, 1842
John (Col.), July 2, 1868
John A., Mar. 6, 1862
John R., Mar. 25, 1858
John Taliaferro (Dr.), Dec. 24, 1903
John W., Mar. 14, 1872
John W. (Rev.), Aug. 21, 1873
John W., Aug. 13, 1874
John William, s. of Rev. M. Ashby and May Turner Jones, Aug. 6, 1896
John William (Dr.), Mar. 25, 1909
Joseph H. (Rev.), Jan. 11 and 18, Feb. 1, 1872
Joseph Samuel, s. of L. W. and M. J. Jones, Feb. 3, 1876
Joseph Witt, s. of Paul T. Jones, Mar. 5, 1885
Judith Page, w. of Dr. J. William Jones, Jan. 22, 1925
L. Byrdie, w. of T. T. Jones, d. of John Coleman, Jan. 1, 1885
L. W., Apr. 21, 1870
Landy, Dec. 28, 1843
Lavinia V., d. of William A. Jones, Dec. 23, 1852
Letitia B., Aug. 23, 1877
Levinia M., w. of Samuel T. Jones, July 24, 1851
Lucetta M., w. of A. J. Jones, d. of William Hancock, Apr. 12, 1877
Lucian Ryland, d. of Silas B. Jones, Aug. 12, 1847
Lucy B., w. of Rowland Jones, June 10, 1858
Lucy B. (Mrs.), sister of Ann L. Semple, Dec. 13, 1900
M. V., w. of Capt. S. Jones,

OBITUARY NOTICES IN THE RELIGIOUS HERALD WITH DATES OF PUBLICATION

Oct. 7, 1858
Margaret (Mrs.), Feb. 21, 1924
Martha (Mrs.), Oct. 24, 1828
Martha, w. of Christopher Jones, Nov. 27, 1851
Martha (Mrs.), Dec. 23, 1926
Martha A., w. of Dr. J. L. Jones, Mar. 7, 1889
Martha B. (Mrs.), Sept. 24, 1896
Martha J., d. of Elijah Jones, Oct. 13, 1853
Martha J. (Mrs.), d. of Charles Massie, May 23, 1901
Martha Jane (Mrs.), Feb. 26, 1920
Martha M., w. of William H. Jones, Apr. 8, 1836
Martha M. (Mrs.), June 16, 1904
Martha R., w. of John W. Jones, Dec. 23 and 30, 1847
Martha Ridley, July 22, Sept. 9, 1920
Mary, Dec. 25, 1879
Mary (Mrs.), July 14, 1938
Mary A. (Mrs.), Apr. 3, 1890
Mary A. Perry, w. of M. M. Jones, Apr. 3, 1875
Mary Ann S. (Mrs.), July 13, 1848
Mary H., w. of Thomas M. Jones, Jan. 21, 1847
Mary L., w. of William P. Jones, Apr. 26, 1888
Mary R., w. of Thomas M. Jones, Jan. 6, 1842
Mary W., d. of Rev. Reuben and Lanetta C. Jones, May 4, 1854
Maryus, Apr. 5, 1923
Matilda, w. of Thomas Jones, May 10, 1849
Mattie Hood (Mrs.), Apr. 21 and 28, 1898
Melinda V. (Mrs.), Aug. 2, 1917
Michael R., Mar. 25, 1847

Mollie, w. of William L. Jones, May 17, 1883
Myra Irene, d. of John and Maggie Jones, July 27, 1893
N. B., Apr. 3, 1890
N. S., Feb. 20, 1879
Nanna M. (Mrs.), Mar. 30, 1933
Nannie Kate (Mrs.), Mar. 19, 1931
Nannie Sue, d. of N. B. Jones, Mar. 14, 1872
Naomi, d. of Calvin and Sally Jones, Jan. 22, 1846
P. E., May 7, 1863
Parthenia A., w. of Thomas R. Jones, Jan. 25, 1844
Paul T., Mar. 21, 1907
Peter, Mar. 20, 1829
Peter Ridley, Feb. 13, 1879
Philip B., Sr., Mar. 9, 1882
R., Oct. 18, 1855
R. B. (Rev.), Feb. 13, 1868
R. Baxter, Sept. 26, 1889
R. T. (Capt.), Oct. 14, 1852
Rebecca J., w. of William A. Jones, July 8, 1858
Reuben (Rev.), Dec. 17 and 31, 1885
Reubenneta C., d. of Rev. R. Jones, Nov. 14, 1867
Robert, Oct. 3, 1844
Robert, Mar. 28, 1901
Robert Blackwell, Jan. 29, 1863
Robert Brooke, Nov. 10, 1864
Robert Brooke, s. of Dr. J. T. Jones, Sept. 16, 1875
Robert Brooke, s. of Rev. J. William and Page Helm Jones, July 10, 1879
Robert S., Apr. 7, 1859
Robert T., Apr. 7, 1881
Roberterie Cary, d. of William E. and Martha Jones, Sept. 8, 1853
Rosa, d. of C. G. and Rosa E. Jones, Mar. 16, 1893
Rosa Ann, w. of John Jones, Dec. 30, 1880
S., Sept. 5, 1844

OBITUARY NOTICES IN THE RELIGIOUS HERALD WITH DATES OF PUBLICATION

Sallie, w. of George Jones, July 20, 1876
Sallie, Dec. 25, 1890
Sallie A., d. of Mrs. William A. Jones, June 28, 1860
Sallie B., d. of Capt. David N. and Lavinia Jones, Oct. 15, 1857*
Sallie T., May 2, 1929
Samuel, June 17, 1886
Samuel Edward (Mrs.), Feb. 21, 1935
Samuel Porter, Oct. 18, 1906
Samuel T., s. of Samuel T. and Levinia M. Jones, Aug. 4, 1842*
Sarah (Mrs.), Jan. 13, 1837
Sarah (Mrs.), Aug. 2, 1849
Sarah, w. of Elder Jesse Jones, May 20, 1852
Sarah (Mrs.), Mar. 14, 1861
Sarah DeVany (Mrs.), May 26, 1932
Sarah J. (Mrs.), Feb. 21, 1878
Spencer (Col.), May 6, 1915
Susan, w. of Capt. John Jones, Oct. 11, Nov. 8, 1849
Susan J. (Sister), May 5, 1864
Susunnah G., d. of David R. Jones, Jan. 14, 1831
T. G. (Mrs.), w. of Dr. T. G. Jones, d. of Richard and Jane Reins, Oct. 31, Nov. 21, 1867
T. L., Jan. 6, 1876
Temperance H., w. of Capt. David N. Jones, Dec. 11, 1835
Thomas, Sept. 28, 1838
Thomas, May 15, 1856
Thomas L., Apr. 24, 1862
Thomas Magoon, s. of Samuel T. and Levinia M. Jones, May 20, 1847*
Thomas N., s. of Laney Jones, June 13, 1844
Thomas Neverson, Jan. 22, 1920
Thomas S., Oct. 11, 1860
Thomas W. (Maj.), Apr. 17, 1862
Thomas W., Dec. 22, 1892
Tiberius Gracchus (Rev.), s. of Wood Jones, July 4, 1895
Virginia J., w. of William S. Jones, Mar. 21, 1901
W. L., July 23, 1857
W. Stanfield, Aug. 13, 1903
W. T. (Rev.), Sept. 14, 1899
Walker (Dr.), Dec. 3, 1891
Walter T., s. of Thomas Jones, May 13, 1875
William, May 16, 1861
William A., Nov. 8, 1855
William A. W. (Mrs.), Mar. 16, 1871
William Alfred (Dr.), Sept. 13, 1917
William Catesby, s. of Maryus Jones, Feb. 4, 1904
William E., Dec. 3, 1885
William I., June 3, 1880
William Parker, June 6, 1828
William R., Mar. 13, 1879
William T., Apr. 3, 1856
William Wiggenton, Apr. 3, 1835
Willianna Elizabeth, d. of Samuel T. and Levinia M. Jones, June 3, 1841*
Willie H., Nov. 18, 1920
Willis Armistead, s. of Benjamin S. and Rebecca Ann Jones, Dec. 24, 1896

JORDAN

Ann B. (Mrs.), Apr. 5, 1839
Byrd A., Dec. 3, 1863
E. V., June 26, 1913
Eastham, Sept. 11, 1890
Elijah, Apr. 1, 1886
Ellen (Mrs.), Dec. 2, 1831
G. H., Apr. 4, 1889
George Wilson, s. of Dr. George H. and S. Lizzie Jordan, Oct. 6, 1881
James Robert, s. of Dr. George H. Jordan, Mar. 22, 1923

* Possible inaccuracy in name, or spelling, but given as printed

OBITUARY NOTICES IN THE RELIGIOUS HERALD WITH DATES OF PUBLICATION

Jennie Lou, d. of J. L. and Lucy E. Jordan, Mar. 28, 1882
John Lawrence, Jan. 15, 1925
John M., June 27, 1861
Judith, w. of William Jordan, Sept. 20, 1849
Judith Alice, d. of William and Mary F. Jordan, Oct. 29, 1863*
Martha (Mrs.), Feb. 5, 1863
Mary Alice, d. of William and Mary F. Jordan, Apr. 14, 1859*
Rebecca (Mrs.), June 19, 1851
Robert E., Jan. 10, 1895
Samuel H., Dec. 7, 1871
Sarah (Mrs.), Dec. 20, 1855
Selah F., June 30, 1842
Susan G., w. of John M. Jordan, Jan. 18, 1872
Thomas, Aug. 1, 1844
Virginia A., w. of John M. Jordan, Sept. 10, 1846
William Hill, Oct. 25, 1883
William M., Nov. 25, 1841
Willie A., s. of W. H. and M. F. Jordan, Nov. 5, 1863
Willie Byrd, s. of William and Mary F. Jordan, Dec. 22, 1870*

JORDON*
George Edgar, s. of William and Mary F. Jordon, Apr. 13, 1882
George Edward, s. of William and Mary F. Jordon, Apr. 6, 1882

JOSEPH
Mary W. M., w. of Robert Joseph, Aug. 24, 1848
Thomas Pemberton, s. of T. W. and M. M. Joseph, Nov. 10, 1892

JOYCE
Charles F., s. of Charles and Atha Joyce, July 19, 1858
Edwin C., July 18, 1912

Nancy, w. of Andrew Joyce, Feb. 26, 1852

JOYNER
Madaline Baird, d. of C. F. Joyner, Aug. 15, 1901
Martha James, w. of Baker Joyner, June 12, 1879
Roland Lee, Aug. 31, 1882

JOYNES
Leah Jane, w. of Capt. William F. Joynes, June 10, 1915

JUDAH
Bareech H., Oct. 1, 1830

JUDE
John Croxton, s. of Leander M. and Sarah Jude, Aug. 3, 1848
Rhoda, w. of John H. Jude, Sept. 26, 1850

JUDKINS
Sarah D., w. of William H. Judkins, July 26, 1860

JUDSON
Abigail, w. of Rev. Adoniram Judson, Mar. 9, 1843
C. H. (Mrs.), w. of Dr. C. H. Judson, May 28, 1903
Edward (Dr.), Oct. 29, 1914
Sarah Boardman, w. of Adoniram Judson, Mar. 5, 1846

JUREY
Anne, w. of Rees Jurey, d. of Col. John S. Slaughter, June 13, 1867
F. A., Mar. 9, 1899
Margaret M., Mar. 9, 1899

JUSTICE
Mattie (Mrs.), Apr. 3, 1930
Quincy E., Feb. 24, 1927

JUSTIS
Bettie Watkins (Mrs.), May 22, 1924
Henson P., Aug. 28, 1913
R. A., Feb. 9, 1911
Sarah (Mrs.), Feb. 22, 1872
W. W. (Mrs.), Sept. 21, 1893

* Possible inaccuracy in name, or spelling, but given as printed

-K-

KABLER
 Elizabeth Hester, w. of
  William S. Kabler, Jan.
  21, 1904
KAHL
 Maggie, Feb. 9, 1905
KANE
 Thomas M., Aug. 6, 1846
KARNES
 Malinda P., w. of W. H.
  Karnes, May 23, 1861
KAY
 Ada Gravatt (Mrs.), Mar. 1,
  1928
 Albert, Jan. 1, 1863
 Calendonia, d. of Edmond T.
  and Carrie Kay, June 1, 1882
 Challonia, w. of James H. Kay,
  Aug. 14, 1913
 Ellen, July 7, 1870
 Fanny G. (Mrs.), May 6, 1880
 Jimmie Trice, s. of Robert A.
  and Urania G. Kay, Jan. 2,
  1873
 John, Apr. 2, 1885
 Mildred A. (Mrs.), d. of
  Philip Green, Mar. 31, 1853
 Sarah A. H. (Mrs.), June 7,
  1900
 W. W., Jan. 24, 1884
KEAN
 Catherine S., w. of James L.
  Kean, Sept. 12, 1872
 Richard M. G., s. of James L.
  and Catherine S. Kean,
  Sept. 24, 1863
KEARFOTT
 C. P. (Mrs.), Oct. 11, 1928
 Clarence P. (Dr.), Nov. 11,
  1920
 J. Baker, father of Drs.
  Clarence and Joseph
  Kearfott, Jan. 4, 1900
 John P., July 21, 1881
KEATON
 Elizabeth (Mrs.), Dec. 3, 1840
KEEBLE
 H. H., June 11, 1874
KEEFE
 Viola (Mrs.), July 17, 1924
KEELING
 Elizabeth C. (Mrs.), d. of
  William and Elizabeth
  Braithwaite, Aug. 12, 1915
 Henry (Rev.), Nov. 24, Dec.
  15, 1870
 Robert Fulton, July 1, 1926
 Robert Henry (Capt.), Oct.
  16, 1862
KEEN
 Amanda, w. of John Keen, d.
  of William F. Broaddus,
  Apr. 12, 1860*
KEENE
 Sarah F., d. of John Keene
  Oct. 29, 1846*
KEESE
 Levi (Dr.), Apr. 15, 1880
KEESEE
 Frances, w. of George Keesee,
  Apr. 2, 1840
 Jesse F., Nov. 24, 1881
 Lucy Frances, d. of Thomas
  Keesee, Oct. 27, 1842
KEETON
 Susan K., d. of Mrs. Lucy
  Keeton, Apr. 10, 1862
 Warner C., Aug. 27, 1857
KEFAUVER
 Jacob, Feb. 18, 1864
KEIT
 Thomas G., s. of William
  B. Keit, May 14, 1857
KELLER
 Elizabeth R. (Mrs.), d. of
  J. H. and Elizabeth R.
  McLeod, Jan. 22, 1914
KELLEY
 Elizabeth A. L., w. of Col.
  Hugh H. Kelley, Sept. 23,
  1858
 John G., Nov. 15, 1866
 Lottie Booker (Mrs.), June
  2, 1927

* Possible inaccuracy in name, or spelling, but given as printed

OBITUARY NOTICES IN THE RELIGIOUS HERALD WITH DATES OF PUBLICATION

William Samuel, s. of John
  A. and Maria E. Kelley,
  Mar. 28, 1861
KELLO
  Lula B., d. of Dr. S. B. and
    Virginia E. Kello, Sept. 15,
    1904
  Samuel B. (Dr.), Aug. 23, 1888
  Virginia E., w. of Dr. Samuel
    B. Kello, July 23, 1903
KELLUM
  George W., Mar. 1, 1920
KELLY
  C. C. (Mrs.), Aug. 8, 1929
  Hattie (Mrs.), Dec. 22, 1887
  James M., s. of Granville J.
    and Harriet Kelly, Jan. 7,
    1858
  John P., June 29, 1871
  Lucinda, June 8, 1854
  Margaret J., d. of Granville
    and Harriet Kelly, Jan. 7,
    1858
  Martha J., d. of Hugh H.
    Kelly, Oct. 2, 1845
  Mary F., Mar. 30, 1882
  Mary J., d. of Granville and
    Harriet Kelly, Jan. 7, 1858
  William, Jan. 25, Mar. 14,
    Sept. 12, 1872
KELSEY
  Burton, Dec. 21, 1832
  Elizabeth A. (Mrs.), Dec.
    3, 1925
KEMP
  Matthew S., Aug. 8, 1828
  Oswald S., May 31, 1866
  Parke Christian, w. of
    Oswald S. Kemp, Dec.
    28, 1899
KEMPER
  Eliza J., Mar. 11, 1858
  Ellen Virginia, June 1, 1876
  John S., June 16, 1887
  Juliet Frances (Mrs.), Jan.
    20, 1916
  Laura F., w. of Rev. J. F.
    Kemper, Nov. 11, 1909
  Lavinia, Mar. 25, 1915
KENDALL

Lizzie, d. of F. M. and Isa
  B. Kendall, Aug. 5, 1880
  Virginia, Jan. 30, 1879
  William Washington, Apr.
    17, 1884
KENDRICK
  Albert A., Nov. 26, 1885
  Christopher, Jan. 27, 1848
  Mary Frances Emma, d. of
    William and Ellen Kendrick,
    July 30, 1846
  Nathaniel (Dr.), Sept. 28,
    1848
  William L., Dec. 4, 1851
KENNAN
  Catherine L. (Mrs.), Dec. 8,
    1859
KENNARD
  David (Dr.), July 7, 1842
  George S. (Rev.), Nov.
    26, 1936
KENNEDY
  Arline, d. of D. S. and
    Estelle Kennedy, Nov. 26,
    1891
  D. B. (Mrs.), Apr. 8, 1926
  Frances H., w. of Dr. Thomas
    H. Kennedy, Oct. 23, 1851
  G. E., Mar. 24, 1910
  Maria W. (Mrs.), Feb. 1, 1934
KENNER
  R. P., May 24, 1883
KENT
  Annie Lee, d. of G. H. and
    Florence M. Kent, Nov. 25,
    1897
  Claude M., Feb. 9, 1888
  Elizabeth, w. of John Kent,
    May 27, 1852
  Gideon S., s. of John Kent,
    Feb. 23, 1865
  Henry T., June 28, 1849
  Henry T., s. of John T. and
    Mary C. Kent, Oct. 8, 1857
  Horatio T., June 28, 1849
  James M., Jr., Sept. 13, 1883
  James M., Sr. (Rev.), July
    25, 1889
  John S., June 20, 1856
  John S., Feb. 5, 1885

OBITUARY NOTICES IN THE RELIGIOUS HERALD WITH DATES OF PUBLICATION

Joseph E., s. of Rev. James M. Kent, Sept. 11, 1862
Judith, w. of William C. Kent, Jan. 4, 1839
Kate J., d. of John T. and Mary C. Kent, Oct. 8, 1857
L. Fannie WHALEY, w. of Oscar R. Kent, Nov. 17, 1904
Lucy Ann Elizabeth, d. of Mary Kent, June 17, 1836
Lucy Susan, d. of Robert Kent, Jr., Apr. 12, 1833
M. E. (Mrs.), Mar. 6, 1902
M. Flornie, d. of Mrs. M. C. Kent, May 21, 1885
Martha D., w. of R. A. Kent, July 19, 1900
Mary A., w. of Rev. John Kent, July 17, 1879
Mason L., Oct. 30, 1851
Mattie, May 29, 1924
Mildred Ann, d. of Robert Kent Jr., Jan. 11, 1839
Minor Harmon, s. of Robert Kent, Sept. 28, 1838
O. R., Sept. 8 and 15, 1921
Rebecca (Mrs.), Feb. 13, 1879
Robert, Dec. 10, 1840
Robert, Feb. 11, 1863
Robert A., Mar. 29, 1877
Robert C., Apr. 12, 1900
Samuel H., s. of R. A. and Martha D. Kent, Dec. 24, 1846
Sarah Ann (Mrs.), May 9, 1828
Sarah Jane, Feb. 20, 1898
Sarah S., w. of Robert A. Kent, d. of Elder Robert Lilly, July 21, 1837
Sarah T., w. of William Kent, Feb. 19, 1863
Spottswood P., Dec. 21, 1838
William C., Oct. 5, 1871
William James, s. of John S. and Ann E. Kent, June 26, 1856
William Joseph, s. of Robert A. Kent, Feb. 14, 1834

William Semple (Rev.), Apr. 11, 1901
KEISER
Henrietta E. (Mrs.), d. of Charles S. and Henrietta E. Petty, July 18, 1907
KERFOOT
Daniel S., s. of William C. Kerfoot, Dec. 21, 1865
Daniel S., Sept. 18, 1884
Eliza Ann, w. of William C. Kerfoot, July 9, 1868
Ella, d. of Daniel Kerfoot, July 13, 1916
F. J. (Dr.), Oct. 4, 1888
Frank W. (Rev.), Sept. 5 and 19, 1918
George L., Sept. 27, 1855
H. D. (Dr.), Apr. 23, 1903
Harriet E., w. of Dr. F. J. Kerfoot, Sept. 11, 1851
John, Dec. 30, 1841
Judson George, Feb. 27, 1908
Lucy J., w. of George L. Kerfoot, May 5, 1881
Marion, d. of William T. and Ella C. Kerfoot, Dec. 24, 1896
Olivia Duncan, w. of James F. Kerfoot, June 28, 1906
Warren Slaughter, s. of Dr. F. J. Kerfoot, Oct. 4, 1888
William C., July 1 and 8, 1880
William F., Feb. 20, 1890
William Turner, June 25, 1936
KERR
Ann Eliza, w. of John Kerr, Oct. 28, Dec. 30, 1915
Elizabeth, w. of Elder John Kerr, Nov. 28, 1834
Grace A., July 24, 1919
Grace Adelaide, d. of Judge John and Ann Eliza Kerr, Jan. 15, 1920
H. W. (Mrs.), Sept. 7, 1933
John (Rev.), Sept. 29, 1870
Laura, Sept. 27, 1923
M. C., Aug. 24, 1876
KERSEY

OBITUARY NOTICES IN THE RELIGIOUS HERALD WITH DATES OF PUBLICATION

Ballard S., Sept. 30, 1880
Emma Cornelia, w. of Philip W.
 Kersey, June 13, 1929
P. W., Jan. 26, 1904
KESLER
 Samuel, Jan. 8, 1857
KESTER
 J. Marcus (Dr.), Apr. 9, 1936
KESTERSON
 Kitty, w. of James Kesterson,
  Apr. 26, 1833
KEWIN
 Eloisa, w. of John P. Kewin,
  Feb. 28, 1834
KEY
 (Mrs.), Aug. 2, 1833
 Anna, w. of Martin Key,
  Sept. 10, 1863
 George W., June 5, 1873
 Martin, Oct. 21, 1847
 Martin A., Aug. 30, 1849
 Robert D., June 24, 1841
 William J., Mar. 8, 1883
KEYES
 Elizabeth (Mrs.), Apr. 22,
  1869
KEYS
 Sarah (Mrs.), Dec. 1, 1932
KEYSER
 Annie Miller (Mrs.), Jan. 23,
  1936
 Loula Rixey (Mrs.), Mar. 5,
  1931
KIDD
 Alvis Mayhew, d. of Joel C.
  and Ann Willis Kidd, Sept.
  20, 1900
 Ann, w. of Thomas Kidd, Aug.
  24, 1838
 Ann, w. of John Kidd, July
  22, 1847
 Benjamin F. (Dr.), June 1,
  1905
 Cynthia C. (Mrs.), Apr. 25,
  1861
 Elsie Etta, d. of John Kidd,
  July 16, 1896
 John Jr., Oct. 7, 1836
 John, June 28, 1839
 Lucy (Mrs.), Oct. 1, 1868

Maria Louisa, Apr. 28, 1853
Mozell Broaddus, June 14,
 1923
Nicholas, s. of Joseph Kidd,
 July 29, 1858
Pocahontas, d. of Joseph Kidd,
 July 29, 1858
Thomas B., June 6, 1878
W. H. (Mrs.), Jan. 3, 1895
William B., Jan. 13, 1876
William J., Apr. 24, 1902
KILBY
 Ann P., d. of Henry and Susan
  B. Kilby, Sept. 22, 1864
 Aurelia P. (Mrs.), Mar. 3,
  1938
 Turpin (Capt.), Jan. 11, 1833
KILGORE
 Charles F., Apr. 20, 1922
 Rhoda Elizabeth, w. of Rev.
  G. W. Kilgore, July 2,
  1896
KILGRO
 Margaret A. (Mrs.), July 3,
  1924
KILLMON
 T. O., Apr. 26, 1934
KIMBALL
 Louisa Virginia, d. of Rev.
  J. A. and Lucy Hiter Kimball,
  Oct. 20, 1881
KIMBROUGH
 Edward W., Dec. 4, 1856
 John, May 25, 1843
 Munroe, s. of E. W. Kimbrough,
  July 22, 1852
 Sarah, w. of Richard H. Kimbrough,
  d. of Gen. Thomas M.
  White, Sept. 14, 1876
KINCAID
 Sabina, w. of Thomas M. Kincaid,
  Aug. 26, 1869
KINCANON
 M. E., w. of Dr. J. T. Kincanon,
  Feb. 1, 1883
KINCANNON
 Charles Thomas (Rev.), Mar. 11,
  1920
 J. T. (Rev.), s. of Francis and
  Martha Kincannon, Dec. 18, 1924

OBITUARY NOTICES IN THE RELIGIOUS HERALD WITH DATES OF PUBLICATION

KINCHELOE
    Robbie, s. of R. E. and Alice Kincheloe, Oct. 30, 1873
KINDRED
    Sidney, d. of E. T. and M. T. Kindred, Dec. 22, 1870
KING
    Ann E., w. of Samuel R. King, Oct. 15, 1857
    Charles, Jan. 11, 1866
    Eleanor (Mrs.), Jan. 31, 1929
    Elfleda A., d. of J. J. King, Feb. 17, 1876
    Elizabeth (Mrs.), Feb. 2, 1838
    Emma Cary, d. of Eliza F. King, June 2, 1859
    George W., Sept. 27, 1900
    Henry, Dec. 1, 1870
    Henry C. (Capt.), Dec. 19, 1929
    James J., July 31, 1862
    Lucy W. H., w. of Charles King, June 3 and 24, 1869
    Luther Addison, Aug. 10, 1916
    Mary (Mrs.), Sept. 22, 1864
    Mary Ann, w. of Rev. Thomas King, May 9, 1878
    Mary E., d. of William and Maria J. King, July 29, 1858
    Mary Elizabeth, Mar. 12, 1908
    Mollie K., w. of William I. King, d. of Capt. James P. and Arrena H. Wooddy, May 13, 1897
    Nancy, w. of Charles King, Aug. 3, 1843
    Nannie, w. of Marcellus King, Dec. 22, 1921
    Sarah Ann Margaret, w. of Rev. Thomas King, Dec. 18, 1851
    Susan E., w. of Capt. John J. King, Dec. 8, 1910
    Theodosia L., w. of Charles E. King, d. of Minerva A. Lemon, Apr. 22, 1880
    Thomas (Rev.), Mar. 1, 1883
    William J., Jan. 16, 1913
    William N., s. of John D. and Keturah King, Dec. 18, 1845
KINGERY
    Joel R., Jan. 9, 1919
KINGSLEY
    Chester W. (Mr. and Mrs.), Jan. 14, 1904
KINNAIRD
    George T. (Elder), Mar. 14, 1867
KINNEAR
    George F., Oct. 11, 1923
    Olive Almond (Mrs.), Feb. 24, 1927
KINNIER
    Ann Elizabeth, w. of Andrew Kinnier, Aug. 21, 1851
KINSOLVING
    Lavina, d. of James and Margaret Kinsolving, June 15, 1852
KINZER
    George L. M., Feb. 13, 1868
KIRBY
    Emory T., Feb. 10, 1916
    Susan, Oct. 29, 1857
KIRK
    Bernard Semple, s. of Rev. James O. and Carrie F. Kirk, July 19, 1877
    Carrie V. FLEET, w. of Rev. J. O. Kirk, May 14, 1896
    Elizabeth, Feb. 20, 1829
    Elizabeth M., w. of Elder William H. Kirk, Aug. 11, 1853
    Fannie, w. of Charles R. Kirk, Sept. 9, 1880
    Lucy Burnley, d. of Rev. James O. Kirk, Apr. 21, 1904
    Nella Sadler (Mrs.), Feb. 24, 1916
    W. Fleet, Dec. 6, 1934
    William H. (Dr.), Mar. 27, 1884
    William M. (Dr.), Sept. 5, 1918; Apr. 3, 1919
KIRKHAM
    Lucy Josephine, w. of John Braxton Kirkham, May 3, 1888
KIRTLEY
    Martha A., May 30, 1867
KITCHEN
    India B., Aug. 17, 1922

OBITUARY NOTICES IN THE RELIGIOUS HERALD WITH DATES OF PUBLICATION

Mollie K., d. of Dixon W. and Mary E. Kitchen, Oct. 3, 1872
Polly (Mrs.), Aug. 23, 1888

KNAPP
Julia Meade, d. of Fred W. Knapp, Jan. 19, 1838
Mamie Lewis, d. of Rev. T. J. and N. Knapp, Sept. 24, 1868

KNAUFF
John C., July 15, 1869
Susan, w. of John C. Kanuff, Oct. 17, 1867

KNIBB
Francis Rebecca, w. of J. B. Knibb, Dec. 7, 1911*
John B., m. Frances R. Bowles, Oct. 11, 1906

KNIGHT
A. B. (Rev.), Apr. 20, 1899
Horace N., May 16, 1907
Joseph (Rev.), Apr. 8, 1841
Margaret (Mrs.), May 9, 1828
Matthews W., s. of Sherwood W. and Martha Ann Knight, Jan. 26, 1865
Sherwood, Sept. 3, 1874

KNIGHTON
Ella, May 9, 1878

KNOTE
Woodson C., s. of William and Susan F. Knote, Aug. 14, 1851

KNOTT
J. B., Sept. 9, 1915

KNOWLES
James Davis (Rev.), June 15, 1838

KOGER
Catherine M., July 27, 1922

KUHN
Henry H., Sept. 11, 1829
John, June 5, 1835
Pocahontas F., w. of A. J. Kuhn, d. of Elijah Brummell, Sept. 18 and 25, 1856

KUMAN
George, July 1, 1836

L

LaBOYTEAUX
  M. D. (Mrs.), Mar. 11, 1926
LACKEY
  Willie, w. of George W. Lackey, d. of Paul Burruss, Sept. 30, 1880
LACKS
  Lawrence Daniel, Mar. 25, 1926
  Ruby Snedker (Mrs.), Sept. 2, 1926
LACY
  Allen, Aug. 8, 1895
  Alonzo L., Apr. 3, 1924
  Bettie B., d. of Rev. J. H. Lacy, Aug. 26, 1875
  Elizabeth, w. of Allen R. Lacy, Aug. 25, 1870
  Elizabeth H., Nov. 16, 1871
  J. H. (Rev.), May 19, 1881
  John L. (Rev.), June 27, 1872
  M. Jennie, w. of Rev. J. H. Lacy, Dec. 23, 1869
  Maria S., d. of Thomas A. and Anna E. Lacy, Aug. 23, 1855
  Martha A., w. of Col. Theophilus A. Lacy, Mar. 28, 1844
  Mary Allen Hardy, w. of Rev. John H. Lacy, Dec. 15, 1910
  Mary Ann, w. of Archibald C. Lacy, d. of Mrs. Mary E. Johnson, Feb. 19, 1880
  Mary E. M., w. of John R. Lacy, Sept. 21, 1854
  Moranda, w. of Allen Lacy, Sept. 21, 1893
  Nora F., w. of William J. Lacy, July 4, 1878
  O. C., w. of Rev. J. H. Lacy, d. of Elder J. G. Barkley, May 17, 1866
  Robert D. (Maj.), Aug. 17, 1843
  Samuel M., Oct. 18, 1855
  Theophilus A., July 10, 1884
LADD
  Mary (Mrs.), Dec. 21, 1843
  Thomas, June 20, 1834
LAFOE
  Jane F. (Mrs.), Oct. 18, 1877
LAIR
  Margaret (Mrs.), Oct. 23, 1879
LAKE
  Beverly Hunt, s. of Rev. I. B. Lake, Sept. 26, 1867
  Isaac Beverly (Rev.), s. of Ludwell and Agnes Martin Lake, Sept. 14, 1922
  James L. (Mrs.), Nov. 1, 1906
  Rosa JONES, w. of George B. Lake, July 18, 1907
LAMAN
  Charlotte (Mrs.), Feb. 1, 1877
LAMB
  B. F., Apr. 28, 1938
  Emma J. (Mrs.), Feb. 17, 1881
  M. A., w. of Rev. J. M. Lamb, Mar. 28, 1878
LAMBERT
  Archer, Aug. 22, 1861
  Thomas J., July 24, 1873
LAMBKIN
  J. M., father of James Lambkin, Jan. 18, 1894
LANCASTER
  A. (Sister), Feb. 8, 1812
  Belle Alderson, w. of C. C. Lancaster, Oct. 6, 1881
  D. G. (Rev.), Mar. 17, 1927
  Mary (Mrs.), Aug. 10, 1922
  Nathaniel Edwards, s. of John L. and Mary Jane Lancaster, Sept. 12, 1872
  Owen C. (Mr. and Mrs.), Mar.

OBITUARY NOTICES IN THE RELIGIOUS HERALD WITH DATES OF PUBLICATION

19, 1914
Warren Overstreet, s. of S. C. and C. A. Lancaster, Sept. 16, 1880

LAND
Ann E., w. of Elder Robert H. Land, Sept. 4, 1851
Annie, d. of Rev. R. H. Land, Mar. 27, 1873
Charles Urquhart, s. of Maj. A. L. and Mary Lou Land, Nov. 18, 1869
Eliza Hill, d. of Maj. A. L. L. and Mary L. Land, Sept. 19, 1867
Esther (Mrs.), Dec. 25, 1873
H. C., Nov. 15, 1877
John B., s. of George R. Land, Dec. 28, 1899
Judson Rochelle, s. of Rev. R. H. Land, May 14, 1908
Mary, d. of George R. and Dora Land, July 5, 1894
Mary D., w. of John Land, Jan. 16, 1845
Mary F. (Mrs.), Feb. 23, 1899
Nathaniel D. (Capt.), Jan. 23, 1840
R. H. (Rev.), Aug. 4 and 25, 1881
Richard, Sr., Oct. 20, 1859
Theodosia, w. of John Land, Jan. 31, 1889
William R., Oct. 7, 1852

LANDCRAFT
Sarah B., w. of Nathaniel Landcraft, June 8, 1843

LANDRAM
Edmonia J., w. of L. W. Landram, July 1, 1909
Eliza, w. of Walker Landram, May 2, 1901

LANDRUM
Annie Camilla, Apr. 4, 1907
Edward, s. of W. H. L. and S. R. Landrum, Aug. 8, 1889
Eliza Warren (Mrs.), mother of Dr. W. W. Landrum, Dec. 15, 1898
Ida Dunster, w. of William Warren Landrum, Mar. 26, 1885
John G., Jan. 26, 1882
Sylvanus (Rev.), Nov. 25, 1886
Thomas (Dr.), July 23, 1863
W. W. (Dr.), Feb. 4, 1926

LANE
A. Carter, Jan. 18, 1912
Calvin B., June 11, 1874
Fanny, w. of John Lane, Aug. 31, 1854
Jane (Mrs.), d. of Charles Smith, June 24, 1869
Joel, s. of John D. and Cherry Lane, Jan. 11, 1844
John B. (Mrs.), Feb. 7 and 28, 1935
John D., June 12, 1873
Lizzie Jordan, d. of L. Winder and Lizzie L. Lane, Sept. 4, 1890
Louisa T., w. of James Lane, Nov. 1, 1855
Nancy C. (Mrs.), May 10, 1877
P. H., June 17, 1875
William N., Apr. 29, 1875

LANFORD
J. W., Apr. 16, 1914
Mary Archer, w. of J. W. Lanford, Nov. 24, 1927

LANG
Sarah (Mrs.), Oct. 3, 1828

LANGHORNE
Elizabeth Omohundro, Feb. 25, 1915

LANGSTON
Thomas W. (Rev.), June 18, 1885

LANHAM
Eliza, Feb. 20, 1890

LANKFORD
Lucille, d. of Dr. L. B. Lankford, Dec. 24, 1885
Lucille, d. of Dr. L. and Mary B. Lankford, July 14, 1887
Martha A., w. of Menalcus

OBITUARY NOTICES IN THE RELIGIOUS HERALD WITH DATES OF PUBLICATION

Lankford, Jan. 14, 1897
Menalcus, June 22, 1905
Miriam, w. of Jesse Lankford, July 28, 1870
William, s. of Jesse Lankford, July 28, 1870
William E. (Rev.), Dec. 14 and 21, 1922

LANSDELL
Ann, w. of Thomas H. Lansdell, d. of Royston Betts, Jr., Nov. 4, 1831
George W., s. of Henry T. and Mary B. Lansdell, July 18, 1861
R. Addison (Dr.), Feb. 11 and 25, 1937

LAPRADE
Andrew (Dr.), Aug. 25, 1859

LaROQUE
George Paul (Dr.), May 31, 1934

LARRY
Maria Abigail, d. of James and Martha Jane Larry, Mar. 26, 1857

LARUE
Fanny (Mrs.), Mar. 18, 1847

LASH
Lucy J., w. of William A. Lash, d. of Robert and Lucy A. Pollard, Nov. 10, 1892

LASSITER
Alice, w. of John T. Lassiter, d. of William Low, Mar. 31, 1881

LASTLEY
Mollie Washington, d. of Erasmus H. and Lucy M. Lastley, May 31, 1860

LATANE
Thomas N. (Dr.), Aug. 23, 1906
William, Dec. 25, 1884; Jan. 29, 1885

LATHAM
Fayette M., s. of F. M. and Bettie W. Latham, Aug. 17, 1893
George H., June 30, 1910
George W. (Rev.), Feb. 11, 1847
Kitty Mauzy, w. of John F. Latham, Feb. 14, 1884
Lucy, Jan. 7, 1869
Mildred L., Feb. 4, 1858
P. (Miss), July 15, 1880
S., d. of Rev. G. W. Latham, July 20, 1854
Sallie, Apr. 9, 1891

LATIMER
Atla Vick, Sept. 15, 1892
Ella B., d. of J. R. Latimer, June 28, 1883
Frances Ann (Mrs.), May 8, 1890
Mary Ann (Mrs.), Mar. 1, 1928

LAUGHLIN
Elizabeth, d. of James Laughlin, Apr. 15, 1841
Sarah (Mrs.), Nov. 12, 1840
Susan M. (Mrs.), Oct. 14, 1847

LAUGHTON
Catharine, w. of John E. Laughton, Mar. 16, 1838
Sarah A., w. of John E. Laughton, Oct. 23, 1856

LAURINE
Rosa, d. of James M. Laurine, Jr., Mar. 8, 1833

LAVENDER
Giles O., Nov. 12, 1863

LAVINDER
Lola (Mrs.), Apr. 3, 1924

LAW
Emma J., Apr. 7, 1921
Martha Susan, July 10, 1924

LAWLESS
Emma Barker, w. of Dr. J. L. Lawless, Apr. 12, 1923
John Lee, Dec. 20, 1928
John Leland, Feb. 14, 1929

LAWMAN
Nancy (Mrs.), Apr. 3, 1890

LAWRASON
W. W., Feb. 3, 1870

OBITUARY NOTICES IN THE RELIGIOUS HERALD WITH DATES OF PUBLICATION

LAWRENCE
  Ann R., w. of John T. Lawrence, d. of Col. D. Allen, Jan. 16, 1873
  Clarence William, s. of James T. and Della Lawrence, June 20, 1912
  J. Lee, Oct. 27, 1892
  Joshua (Elder), Mar. 2, 1843
  Julia Harry, d. of Mrs. Ella Lawrence, Oct. 20, 1892
  Ludlow, Oct. 4, 1883
  Mary Frances (Mrs.), Oct. 9, 1930

LAWS
  Ann, w. of Newton Laws, Feb. 14, 1861
  Edward Dulin, Jan. 2, 1919
  Georgia Kerfoot (Mrs.), Feb. 23, 1922
  Joel Newton, Feb. 17, 1910
  Joel Newton (Mrs.), d. of William G. Kerfoot, Feb. 2, 1922
  John, Dec. 26, 1839
  Laura J. (Mrs.), July 20, 1916
  Mable, d. of George and J. N. Laws, Feb. 10, 1881
  Mahala J., w. of Z. C. Laws, Mar. 21, 1844
  Sarah, w. of Elder William Laws, Nov. 28, 1839

LAWSON
  Cora Chambers, w. of Rev. W. H. Lawson, Jan. 28, 1937
  Flora Eleonor, d. of J. R. and L. V. Lawson, May 14, 1891
  Ida Elizabeth, Oct. 13, 1870
  J. R. (Mrs.), Sept. 30, 1909
  John R., June 1, 1905
  W. H., Mar. 4, 1926

LAWTON
  Alexander J. (Col.), May 25, 1876
  T. O. (Mrs.), mother of Rev. W. W. Lawton, Apr. 2, 1903

LAYMAN
  Helen, d. of C. E. Layman, Feb. 1, 1906

LAYNE
  Ariadne (Mrs.), Apr. 13, 1848
  Benjamin Paty, s. of R. F. and W. A. Layne, June 28, 1888
  Ellen S., w. of John T. Layne, Dec. 28, 1905
  George F., Feb. 14, 1884
  J. W., Nov. 19, 1931
  L., Jan. 6, 1859
  Mary, July 14, 1859
  Mary E., w. of Alexander S. Layne, d. of William A. Lightfoot, Aug. 30, 1855
  Mary V., w. of George F. Layne, d. of Thomas Boatwright, June 7, 1917
  Robert J., Aug. 12, 1920
  Rosa Lee, d. of W. L. and M. A. Layne, Nov. 26, 1885
  Sallie Alice, d. of N. B. and S. A. Layne, Oct. 16, 1862
  Sarah Lewis, d. of John R. Layne, Apr. 3, 1862
  Tebitha, w. of Lycurgus Layne, Feb. 20, 1851*
  William G. M., s. of G. C. and Elizabeth Layne, May 1, 1845

LEA
  Carrie, d. of John G. and Nannie R. Lea, Sept. 5, 1878
  Fannie E. B., w. of S. S. Lea, Oct. 28, 1886
  Nannie R., w. of John G. Lea, d. of William F. Thomas, May 31, 1883
  Rachel (Mrs.), mother of Mrs. Jane Poor, June 8, 1843
  Tommie, s. of T. L. and Sallie K. Lea, Jan. 7, 1886

LEACH
  Alutus, Dec. 3, 1925

LEACHMAN
  d. of Rev. J. D. Leachman, Apr. 22, 1875
  Mary (Mrs.), mother of Rev. Jeremiah Dale, May 14, 1874
  Tabitha E., d. of Elder J. D. Leachman, Apr. 8, 1875
  Thomas D., s. of Elder J. D. and Emeline Leachman, June

* Possible inaccuracy in name, or spelling, but given as printed

OBITUARY NOTICES IN THE RELIGIOUS HERALD WITH DATES OF PUBLICATION

3, 1875
LEAKE
  Elizabeth F., w. of Robert
    S. Leake, d. of James R.
    True, Jan. 27, 1876
  John H. W., s. of Peter J.
    and Elizabeth Leake, May
    3, 1866
  O. P., Nov. 17, 1932
  Samuel (Col.), Jan. 31, 1856
  W. S. (Mrs.), July 25, Aug.
    1 and 8, 1912
  W. S. (Rev.), Feb. 24, Mar.
    17, 1938
LEAR
  J. J., Oct. 25, 1906
LEASTER
  Ann Eliza (Mrs.), Nov. 25,
    1875
LEATH
  Walter, Mar. 19, 1885
LEATHERS
  Jonathan, May 26, 1887
LEBER
  Mary W. Forman, d. of Will-
    iam Gorman and Caroline V.
    Leber, Apr. 29, 1880
LEE
  Aaron B., Aug. 6, 1863
  Andrew J., Dec. 1, 1892
  Annie Brinson, Sept. 30, 1926
  B. W. (Mrs.), d. of Mrs. R. C.
    Parker, Jan. 29, 1891
  Betsy B., d. of Arthur Lee,
    Dec. 31, 1846
  Blair H., s. of E. P. B. and
    S. L. Lee, Dec. 26, 1850
  C. T., w. of E. C. C. Lee,
    Feb. 25, 1886
  Caroline, w. of George H.
    Lee, Dec. 7, 1854
  Caroline (Mrs.), July 25,
    1901
  Charles, Jan. 20, 1832
  Cordelia, Aug. 19, 1869
  E. (Mrs.), Oct. 7, 1858
  Edaline J., w. of Elder J. B.
    Lee, Oct. 9, 1862
  Elizabeth, w. of Elder John S.
    Lee, Mar. 26, 1868

  Elsie Densmore, Apr. 3, 1919
  Fanny P., w. of Littleton
    Lee, Dec. 13, 1900
  Gustavus B., Aug. 11, 1887
  Hardenia B., w. of Edward P.
    Lee, Jan. 15, 1852
  Hubert Brightwell, Sept. 21,
    1893
  J. S. (Elder), Jan. 21, 1858
  J. W. (Mrs.), Nov. 8, 1928
  James, Oct. 9, 1845
  John (Elder), Feb. 27, 1840
  John H., May 31, 1888
  John Harrison, June 16, 1870
  John S. (Rev.), Dec. 17, 1857
  Leroy M., Jan. 17, 1918
  Louisa C., w. of James Lee,
    Sept. 30, 1841
  Lucy, w. of Erastus L. Lee,
    Jan. 22, 1885
  Mabel Livingston, Oct. 30,
    1902
  Margaret (Mrs.), July 31,
    1884
  Mary A., w. of O. W. Lee,
    Jan. 15, 1852
  Mary B., d. of Elder J. B.
    Lee, Oct. 9, 1862
  Mary Jane, w. of Elder R. N.
    Lee, Oct. 29, 1863
  Missouri, Apr. 19, 1923
  Peachy Brown, d. of Rev. R. N.
    and Margaret E. Lee, May
    18, 1871
  R. E. (Gen.), Oct. 20 and 27,
    1870
  R. N. (Rev.), Sept. 23, 1875
  Richard Henry, Aug. 5, 1926
  Samuel E., Dec. 17, 1863
  Sarah (Mrs.), Dec. 13, 1883
  Susie R., w. of James W. Lee,
    d. of Rev. Newton Short,
    June 26, 1879
  Tabitha, w. of Richard Lee,
    July 11, 1828
  William F. (Rev.), May 26,
    1837
LEFEVER
  John, May 9, 1872
LEFOE

OBITUARY NOTICES IN THE RELIGIOUS HERALD WITH DATES OF PUBLICATION

Bettie, w. of Frank Lefoe, Dec. 14, 1905
Willie, s. of J. F. Lefoe, Oct. 13, 1881
LEFTWICH
  Ann (Mrs.), Oct. 21, 1841
  Ann B. BILBRO, w. of Rev. James Leftwich, Nov. 20, 1884; May 28, 1885*
  Caroline, w. of Rev. George Whitfield Leftwich, June 8, 1882
  Carrie S., d. of Rev. George W. Leftwich, July 19, 1866
  Ella L., d. of Rev. James and Anne Bilbre Leftwich, Oct. 13, 1921*
  Fanny, w. of Thomas Leftwich, Mar. 21, 1867
  George M., Nov. 6, 1862; Feb. 12, 1863
  George Whitefield (Rev.), s. of Rev. William Leftwich, Mar. 5, June 18, 1868
  James, Nov. 16, 1854
  James, May 18, 1882
  James W., s. of Col. William W. Leftwich, July 21, 1870
  John Marshall, s. of William and Sarah Leftwich, Sept. 15, 1837
  John W. (Dr.), s. of Rev. James Leftwich, Feb. 20, Mar. 12, 1868
  Martha Jane Smith, d. of Elder George W. and Caroline M. Leftwich, Sept. 25, 1845
  Mary, w. of Elder William Leftwich, Oct. 5, 1838
  Mildred Ann, d. of Thomas and Frances Leftwich, Apr. 8, 1847
  Mildred B., d. of Rev. James Leftwich, Apr. 8, 1858
  Sallie Ann, w. of Maj. William Leftwich, Aug. 1, 1850
  Sarah C., w. of Maj. William Leftwich, Feb. 6, 1845
  Serana C., w. of William M. Leftwich, Jan. 6, 1848

  William (Rev.), July 13, 1848
LeGRAND
  A. A., Apr. 10, May 2, 1879
  Caroline M., w. of A. A. LeGrand, d. of Maj. Benjamin Hunter, Aug. 6, 1857
  Rebecca, w. of S. C. LeGrand, Mar. 24, 1881
  Samuel C., Sept. 3, 1857
  Samuel Thomas, Jan. 6, 1927
  Sarah Ann (Mrs.), Apr. 24, 1924
  Thomas A. (Rev.), Mar. 9, 1848
  Thomas S., Feb. 4, 1869
LEIGH
  Benjamin Watkins, Feb. 8, 1849
  Henry, Dec. 3, 1885
  Mary Jane Tabitha (Mrs.), d. of John G. and Lucy Adams, July 13, 1843
LEIPFERT
  Rosa, Aug. 27, 1936
LEITCH
  John Francis, Oct. 2, 1890
  Lucy B., w. of Dr. George H. Leitch, Apr. 1, 1858
LELAND
  Aaron (Elder), Sept. 21, 1832
  John (Rev.), Mar. 4, 1841
LEMON
  Ellwra S., Dec. 18, 1913*
LENZ
  F. C. (Mrs.), Jr., Oct. 6, 1938
LESLIE
  Jonathan, Mar. 18, 1858
  Jonathan D., s. of C. H. Leslie, Mar. 27, 1856
  Samuel D. (Capt.), Nov. 6, 1902
LESTER
  Benjamin, Apr. 25, 1878
  Bryan W., Sept. 29, 1838
  E. S. (Dr.), Jan. 28, 1937
  Elizabeth, w. of Bryan W. Lester, Sept. 28, 1838
  Fannie Ann ATKINSON, w. of John Benjamin Lester, Aug. 13, 1885
  James Edward, Dec. 22, 1927

* Possible inaccuracy in name, or spelling, but given as printed

OBITUARY NOTICES IN THE RELIGIOUS HERALD WITH DATES OF PUBLICATION

Lucy R., w. of Benjamin F. Lester, Oct. 15, 1874
Mabel Clare, d. of Lee B. and Lillie M. Lester, July 1, 1886
Margaret Ruth, d. of Mills H. and Mollie L. Lester, May 31, 1906
Mary, w. of James M. Lester, Oct. 15, 1868
William, May 16, 1861
William, Jan. 26, 1865
William E., Sept. 4, 1930

LETT
Bessie Imogene, d. of S. G. Lett, Apr. 2, 1885
Mary A., w. of Hardiway Lett, Jan. 10, 1856
P. E. (Dr.), July 27, 1876

LETTS
Elizabeth, Apr. 22, 1847

LEVI
Mary Ann, d. of William H. Levi, Feb. 12, 1857
Thomas Braxton, Sept. 1, 1921

LEVY
Mary S. (Mrs.), Jan. 10, 17, and 24, 1895

LEWIS
Alice L. (Mrs.), Nov. 23, 1876
Amanda C., d. of William S. and Fannie Lewis, Feb. 23, 1860
Annie Elizabeth, Apr. 14, 1932
Cadwallader (Rev.), May 4, 1882
Catherine Price (Mrs.), Nov. 6, 1873
Charles A. L., Sept. 4, 1845
Daniel V., Dec. 27, 1860
E. W., June 21, 1855
Elizabeth J., w. of William Lewis, Apr. 2, 1858
Elizabeth Jane, w. of William B. Lewis, Dec. 11, 1862
Eva Alderson, d. of Ross and Lucy Alderson Lewis, July 23, 1891*
Fannie Jeffries, d. of W.
Wallis and Mary E. Lewis, Aug. 30, 1883
Felicia (Mrs.), May 19, 1921
Francis W., July 25, 1867
J. E., Jan. 26, 1922
J. L. (Rev.), Apr. 12, 1877
J. Matthew, Aug. 18, 1927
J. T., Dec. 12, 1929.
J. W., Feb. 28, 1901
Jacob, Oct. 29, 1840
John (Capt.), July 26, 1866
John C., s. of Tarlton P. and Mary S. Lewis, Aug. 11, 1864
John Henry, Dec. 11, 1851
John R. C. (Col.), Dec. 22, 1898
John T., Aug. 13, 1885
Joseph, Mar. 17, 1864
Lorine H. SHADRACH, w. of J. W. Lewis, July 28, Oct. 27, Nov. 10, 1892
Lucie Alderson, w. of E. R. Lewis, Feb. 4, 1886*
Lucinda, w. of William Lewis, Nov. 4, 1858
Lucy S., d. of Dr. J. S. and Octavia Lewis, Feb. 25, 1858
Luke, Nov. 11, 1852
M. L. A., w. of Dr. Z. Lewis, Sept. 2, 1869
Margaret (Mrs.), Mar. 9, 1922
Martha (Mrs.), June 11, 1840
Martha J., w. of Alfred B. Lewis, d. of James Clovin, Mar. 29, 1855
Mary Collier, Feb. 2, 1888
Mary E., w. of W. Wallis Lewis, Mar. 13, 1884
Mary Elizabeth, June 3, 1920
Mary Lee, d. of William and Mary Lewis, Nov. 6, 1879
Mary W., w. of Charles A. L. Lewis, Dec. 23, 1858
Pamela P., d. of R. Lewis, July 20, 1832
Paul, s. of William and Mary Lewis, Nov. 6, 1879
R. E., May 7, 1914
Richard Enlaw, Oct. 23, 1919

* Possible inaccuracy in name, or spelling, but given as printed

OBITUARY NOTICES IN THE RELIGIOUS HERALD WITH DATES OF PUBLICATION

Robert (Mayor), Jan. 23, 1829
S. A., Nov. 3, 1887
S. B. (Mrs.), Sept. 28, 1882
S. Roe (Miss), July 19, 1928
Sarah C., d. of Rev. Robert and S. Lewis, July 5, 1860
Sellia O., d. of Dr. J. S. and Octavia Lewis, Feb. 25, 1858
Sophia, w. of Lawrence B. Lewis, Apr. 6, 1848
Susan Ann, w. of Rev. Robert Lewis, Apr. 3, 1862
Thomas M., June 11, 1863
Thomas W. (Rev.), June 8, 1905
W. T., Apr. 20, 1905
William, Mar. 9, 1832
William B. (Dr.), May 10, 1866
William I. (Col.), Nov. 14, 1828
Zachary (Dr.), July 7, 1859

LIBBY
Sylvia, Mar. 14, 1895

LIDE
D. R., Oct. 22, 1874
Dora, w. of Rev. R. W. Lide, Jan. 30, 1879
Elizabeth D., w. of T. P. Lide, Sept. 26, 1878
Leslie Bacot, s. of Rev. R. W. and Dora Lide, Jan. 30, 1879
Thomas P., Aug. 10, 1882

LIENTZ
Ann E., w. of M. P. Lientz, d. of Hugh and Mary Rogers, Dec. 9, 1886

LIFSEY
John, Nov. 4, 1836
Laura (Mrs.), Mar. 12, 1868
Sallie (Mrs.), Apr. 9, 1857
William J., June 1, 1854

LIGGON
Jane M. (Mrs.), July 28, 1904
W. R. (Mrs.), Oct. 17, 1889

LIGHT
E. P., June 17, 1858
Jemima H., w. of John Light, Sr., Oct. 21, 1858

LIGHTFOOT
Edward V., s. of John T. and Lucie E. Lightfoot, Oct. 31, 1918
Elizabeth, w. of Edward Lightfoot, July 6, 1838
J. T., July 9, 1914
John, July 31, 1856
John (Capt.), Oct. 21, 1880
Julia Ann, gr.d. of Robert T. Daniel, May 31, 1833
K. A. (Mrs.), Aug. 4, 1881
Lizzie W., June 26, 1919
Nannie Valentine, w. of Capt. John Lightfoot, July 10 and 17, 1884
William, s. of Armistead N. Lightfoot, Feb. 3, 1853

LIGION
Lewis L., Dec. 17, 1857

LIGON
Ann, d. of Joseph S. Ligon, Sept. 10, 1857
G. William, Apr. 18, 1889
John, Apr. 18, 1861
John L., Dec. 19, 1867
Julia A., w. of William D. Ligon, May 27, 1926
Louisa C., w. of Henry A. Ligon, June 22, 1838
Minerva C., w. of Smith Ligon, d. of Hiram R. Stephens, Mar. 3, 1904
Nancy, w. of John Ligon, Sept. 25, 1873
Robert Wilber, s. of Smith W. and Minerva C. Ligon, Sept. 30, 1880
Thomas, Aug. 19, 1841
Warren B. B., Apr. 9, 1874
William C. (Rev.), May 16, 1878

LILES
Ellen Lee MOORE, w. of W. P. Liles, Aug. 24, 1922

LILLARD
Benjamin (Capt.), Feb. 20, 1868

LILLEY

OBITUARY NOTICES IN THE RELIGIOUS HERALD WITH DATES OF PUBLICATION

Nathaniel, May 31, 1860
LILLY
    Armigor, child of Samuel Lilly, June 3, 1836
    Dicy, w. of Elder Robert Lilly, Sept. 5 and 19, 1844
    Garland, s. of Elder Robert Lilly, Sept. 20, 1860
    John Leland, s. of Elder Robert Lilly, Apr. 23, 1830
    Mary, d. of Samuel Lilly, Nov. 21, 1844
    Pamelia, w. of Garland Lilly, Nov. 5, 1830
    Robert (Elder), Dec. 18, 1856
LINCOLN
    Ensign (Rev.), Dec. 14, 1832
    Hetty G., w. of Heman Lincoln, d. of John Holme, Feb. 21, 1867
LINDGREN
    Ora Barcroft (Mrs.), July 23, 1925
LINDSAY
    E. C. (Mrs.), Aug. 25, 1859
    Elizabeth (Mrs.), Aug. 11, 1837
    Elizabeth, w. of William Lindsay, June 25, 1857
    Ellen J., d. of Mrs. E. C. Lindsay, Nov. 1, 1855
    Jane, w. of Rev. John Lindsay, Mar. 26, 1830
    Martha Eliza, d. of William C. and Ellen C. Lindsay, Mar. 5, 1840
    Matilda A., d. of M. E. and G. R. Lindsay, May 22, 1873
    Robert, Jan. 12, 1843
    Rosalie Winder, w. of G. R. Lindsay, d. of L. Y. Winder, May 31, Sept. 20, 1888
    S. E., w. of G. R. Lindsay, Feb. 6, 1873
    Sallie A. V., w. of Rev. W. T. Lindsay, July 6, 1871
    William, Dec. 6, 1855
    William C., July 24, 1851
    William T. (Rev.), June 8, 1882
    William Winder, s. of George R. Lindsay, July 20, 1882
LINDSEY
    Ann M. (Mrs.), Oct. 6, 1853
    Elizabeth C., w. of Capt. James H. Lindsey, Mar. 3, 1859
    Martha Ann, w. of Bishop William T. Lindsey, Sept. 6, 1849
    William, July 30, 1863
    William S., July 16, 1863
    William T. (Rev.), Jan. 12, 1882
LIPFORD
    William A., Mar. 6, 1862
LIPSCOMB
    Charles R., Feb. 10, 1881
    Charles Wily, Oct. 11, 1923
    David, June 20, 1850
    Ella Judson, w. of Bernard F. Lipscomb, d. of Lewis McLaurine, July 10, 1873
    Frances, w. of Joseph Lipscomb, Apr. 10, 1829
    Frances Todd, w. of W. C. Lipscomb, d. of William Barton, Apr. 5, 1883
    George Wiley, Dec. 29, 1887
    James R., Jan. 12, 1865
    Jane Lambert, d. of William C. and Frances T. Lipscomb, Mar. 17, 1853
    Lavina J., July 25, 1834
    Louisa (Mrs.), Feb. 21, 1889
    Lucy P. B. (Mrs.), Mar. 16, May 4, 1876
    Martha, w. of David Lipscomb, Mar. 3, 1842
    P. Emmett, Feb. 10, 1910
    Sallie Bland, d. of Hudson Lipscomb, May 19, 1881
    Sterling (Capt.), Feb. 13, 1868
    William J., Apr. 18, 1878
    William T. (Capt.), Mar. 3, 1853
LIPSCOMBE
    Robert Samuel, June 15, 1916
    William Y. (Dr.), Jan. 14, 1864

OBITUARY NOTICES IN THE RELIGIOUS HERALD WITH DATES OF PUBLICATION

LITCHFIELD
  Sarah J., d. of David
  C. Litchfield, Apr. 20,
  1876
LITCHFIELDS
  Sarah Jane, Apr. 13, 1876
LITCHFORD
  Evies (Mrs.), May 30, 1918
LITTLE
  Charlotte H., Aug. 6, 1857
  Ella A. R., d. of James H.
  and Catharine P. Little,
  Aug. 25, 1853
  Evelyn L. (Mrs.), Apr. 13,
  1911
  John T., Sept. 2, 1875
  Joseph L., June 19, 1930
  Vincent, Feb. 9, 1854
  Virginia Kathleen, d. of J.
  Frank and Virginia Bickers
  Little, July 30, 1896
LITTLETON
  Helen Smith, d. of Thomas J.
  and Nellie Smith Littleton,
  Feb. 7, 1918
LITTRELL
  Thomas Edward, May 24, 1934
LIVELY
  Aramitta E., d. of Mrs. M.
  E. Bowles, July 17, 1879
  Jane, w. of James Lively,
  Mar. 15, 1833
  Mary Ann (Mrs.), Dec. 18,
  1884
LIVERMON
  George W., Sept. 7, Aug. 31,
  1922
  J. L. (Mrs.), Mar. 5, 1936
LIVERMORE
  Charles Frederick, s. of Rev.
  Silas and Eliza M. Liver-
  more, Sept. 20, 1860
  Eliza M., w. of Rev. Silas
  Livermore, Sept. 20, 1860
LIVINGSTON
  Douglass, s. of James Living-
  ston, Aug. 15, 1850
  James, July 2, 1874
  Sallie Watkins, w. of Dr. A.
  B. Livingston, Oct. 21, 1897*

LIVINGSTONE*
  A. B. (Dr.), May 20, 1920
  James Patterson, s. of
  Dr. A. B. and Sallie
  Livingstone, June 25, 1891
LLOYD
  Andrew, June 20, 1872
  Hugh Walton, s. of Rev. J.
  R. and M. D. Lloyd, Aug.
  27, 1891
  J. L. (Mrs.), d. of Etheldred
  Henderson, Dec. 2, 1875
  Joseph R. (Rev.), Feb. 13,
  1902
  Marcellus Bitting, s. of J.
  R. and M. D. Lloyd, Dec.
  22, 1881
  Mary Jeter, d. of Rev. J.
  R. and M. D. Lloyd, Dec.
  25, 1890
  Matilda, w. of Moses B. Lloyd,
  Jan. 10, 1856
  Moses B., July 16, 1868
  Ward Harrison, s. of J. R.
  and M. D. Lloyd, Jan. 17,
  1878
LOAFMAN
  William, Aug. 17, 1882
LOCKE
  Elizabeth H., w. of Addison
  Locke, Sept. 16, 1836
  Polly, Feb. 17, 1837
LOCKER
  Myrtle Park, d. of J. M. and
  S. A. Locker, Apr. 17, 1884
LOCKETT
  Basil Lee (Dr.), Nov. 16, 1933
  Charles, Jan. 19, 1838
  Charles, Sept. 2, 1847
  Edmond, (Capt.), Aug. 1, 1834
  Edward Frances, w. of Capt.
  E. F. Lockett, Dec. 2, 1926
  J. S., Feb. 6, 1896
  John, Feb. 1, 1844
  Mary Clay, w. of Stephen C.
  Lockett, May 16, 1834
  Robert Eugene, s. of E.
  F. Lockett, Apr. 20,
  1905
  William O., Apr. 27, 1871

* Possible inaccuracy in name, or spelling, but given as printed

OBITUARY NOTICES IN THE RELIGIOUS HERALD WITH DATES OF PUBLICATION

LOCKHEART
 E. G. (Mrs.), Apr. 26, 1877
LOCKNANE
 Martha F., d. of Miles B.
  Locknane, May 22, 1845
LODGE
 Lelia E., w. of Lee Davis
  Lodge, d. of Rev. S. R.
  White, May 9, 1895
 Llewellyn Warfield, s. of
  Rev. J. L. and Alice V.
  Lodge, July 27, 1876
LOFTIS
 William A., Sr., Mar. 2, 1899
LOGAN
 Emily G., w. of John S.
  Logan, Jan. 7, 1847
 Frances M., Aug. 3, 1854
 Nancy W. (Mrs.), May 11,
  1871
LOHR
 Sallie, w. of E. C. Lohr,
  May 29, 1919
LONG
 A. L. (Gen.), May 7, 1891
 Amelia H., w. of James
  Long, May 22, 1862
 Amy (Mrs.), Feb. 8, 1849
 Armistead Ragland, Feb. 1,
  1934
 Cora Lee (Mrs.), Jan. 23,
  1930
 Ernest Mayo, Oct. 7, Dec. 9,
  1937
 Fanny, July 12, 1855
 George, June 3, 1880
 James F., Jr., Nov. 30, 1854
 John C. (Dr.), Aug. 9, 1894
 John T. (Mrs.), Apr. 30, 1931
 John W., Aug. 26, 1841
 Joseph R., Mar. 24, 1932
 Lizzie Dabney, d. of James
  Long, May 22, 1862
 Mary Ann, w. of M. Long,
  June 26, 1851
 Mary C., Sept. 21, 1899
 Oppie Day, d. of James Long,
  May 22, 1862
 Vernon Richards, s. of John
  G. Long, June 14, 1877

LONGAN
 Martha, w. of William Longan,
  Apr. 3, 1856
LONGANACRE
 James (Rev.), Nov. 7, 1850
LOOK
 N. L. (Mrs.), Aug. 21, Oct.
  30, 1902
LOPUS
 Joseph, Nov. 17, 1842
LOUTHAM*
 E. M. (Mrs.), w. of Rev. E. M.
  Louthan, d. of Rev. N.
  Richards, July 31, 1924
LOUTHAN
 C. M. (Mrs.), May 26, 1932
 Ella B. (Mrs.), d. of Capt.
  Charles Brown, Apr. 16, 1885
 Ellen Francis, w. of John K.
  Louthan, Feb. 5, 1920
 Lydia (Mrs.), Nov. 15, 1866
 Lydia Annie, d. of Carter M.
  and Ella M. Louthan, Feb.
  4, 1869
 William P., Sept. 5, 1861
LOVE
 A. (Dr.), Apr. 18, 1850
 Charles, June 27, 1844
 George (Elder), Oct. 6, 1853
 James F. (Rev.), May 10, 17,
  and 24, June 28, 1928
 James F. (Mrs.), w. of Dr. J.
  F. Love, Oct. 18, 1928
 Mary Smith, w. of Elder George
  Love, Jan. 22, 1863
 Olonza Robert (Rev.), Dec.
  24, 1925
 Patsy, Nov. 6, 1873
LOVELACE
 Jennie, w. of J. H. Lovelace,
  Oct. 8, 1925
 Martha A., w. of James S.
  Lovelace, Aug. 2, 1855
LOVELL
 Ellen, w. of Robert Lovell,
  June 7, 1883
 Jane, w. of William Lovell,
  Feb. 5, 1903
 Robert T., Jan. 13, 1881
 William, Feb. 4, 1892

* Possible inaccuracy in name, or spelling, but given as printed

OBITUARY NOTICES IN THE RELIGIOUS HERALD WITH DATES OF PUBLICATION

LOVING
  Betsy (Mrs.), Apr. 3, 1856
  Charles T. (Dr.), s. of James
    L. and Elizabeth L. Loving,
    Nov. 28, 1895
  Eliza Mildred, mother of Revs.
    A. G., O. D., and W. B.
    Loving, Jan. 13, 1910
  Elizabeth, w. of James L.
    Loving, June 18, 1863
  Emma, d. of James L. Loving,
    Sept. 14, 1876
  Fannie L., w. of Edward B.
    Loving, d. of Daniel and
    Margaret Goode, May 7,
    1908
  George, Aug. 29, 1834
  Haden, Nov. 23, 1893
  James L., Nov. 16 and 23,
    1899
  John D., Mar. 6, 1856
  Joseph B., July 10, 1924
  Lula Shadrach (Mrs.), Oct.
    26, 1920
  Mary, w. of Thomas Loving,
    May 30, 1872
  Mary Walton, d. of Richard
    E. and Sallie A. Loving,
    Oct. 31, Nov. 21, 1901
  Oscar Deane (Rev.), Aug. 7,
    1924
  Richard, May 26, 1842
  Robert Semple, May 21,
    1885
  Russell T., s. of Edwin B.
    and Alice Loving, Jan. 26,
    1882
  Sallie A. (Mrs.), Oct. 12,
    Dec. 21, 1916
  Sallie Nelson (Mrs.), Oct.
    15, 1936
  T. G., gr.s. of Rev. G. C.
    Travillian, Apr. 9, 1857
  Thomas H., Feb. 10, 1859
  Thomas R., May 12, 1927
  William D., Mar. 12, 1891
  William Ely, s. of Joseph
    B. and Lula L. Loving,
    Apr. 14, 1904
LOWE
  Ida J., d. of A. J. and Diana
    E. Lowe, Aug. 5, 1858
LOWMAN
  Elizabeth S. (Mrs.), d. of Rev.
    William Harris, Mar. 31,
    1904
  Lizzie, d. of Abel and Eliza-
    beth S. Lowman, Mar. 12,
    1863
LOWNES
  Alonzo, s. of Birkett Lownes,
    Mar. 15, 1860
  Eliza G. (Mrs.), Apr. 26,
    1877
LOWRY
  Ann Eliza, d. of Nelson E.
    and Catherine T. Lowry,
    Oct. 8, 1846
  Cary Judson, s. of James V.
    Lowry, May 3, 1855
  Catharine E., w. of James
    Lowry, d. of G. Hargrave,
    Dec. 7, 1854
  Edward, Jr., Feb. 16, 1843
  Henry W., s. of Wilson and
    Mary Lowry, July 29, 1858
  Jemima H., w. of Henry S.
    Lowry, May 27, 1852
  Jemima H., d. of Henry S.
    Lowry, Mar. 9, 1854
  M. P. (Gen.), Mar. 5 and 12,
    1885
  Mary (Mrs.), Feb. 8, 1855
  Mary P., w. of Albert A.
    Lowry, May 19, 1881
  Nannie, d. of R. W. Lowry,
    Sept. 27, 1866
  Nelson E., May 16, 1878
LOYD
  E. G., s. of J. R. Loyd,
    July 23, 1903
  James T., s. of James M.
    Loyd, Mar. 17, 1859
  Martha J., w. of James Loyd,
    Mar. 17, 1859
  Myrtilda Hoge, d. of J. R.
    and M. D. Loyd, Jan. 28,
    1875
LUCADO
  Amine, w. of Leonard F. Lucado,

OBITUARY NOTICES IN THE RELIGIOUS HERALD WITH DATES OF PUBLICATION

June 30, 1859
Mary Fannie, d. of L. A.
and Eliza Lucado, Aug.
17, 1871
LUCAS
  Price, Aug. 20, 1874
  Virginia M., w. of Price
  Lucas, Aug. 20, 1874
  Zachariah, May 16, 1828
LUCK
  Beulah Virginia, w. of Rev.
  Norman Luck, Mar. 17 and
  31, 1938
  Catherine, w. of Clinton B.
  Luck, Sept. 3, 1863
  Eleanore, w. of Robert S.
  Luck, Jan. 18, 1866
  Elizabeth, w. of Samuel P.
  Luck, Dec. 20, 1849
  Elizabeth, w. of Napoleon P.
  Luck, Sept. 9, 1852
  Elvira, w. of William R.
  Luck, Mar. 17, 1892
  George P. (Rev.), Oct. 22,
  Nov. 26, 1891
  George S. (Dr.), Apr. 13,
  1911
  James F., s. of W. F. Luck,
  Jan. 31, 1884
  James Paschal (Rev.), s. of
  Rev. George and Nancy
  Buford Luck, Dec. 11, 1913;
  Feb. 5, 1914
  Joel T., Nov. 16, 1876
  John, Apr. 22, 1858
  John K., Sept. 13, Oct. 18,
  1860
  Julian M. (Mrs.), w. of Rev.
  J. M. Luck, Mar. 8 and 22,
  1917
  Julian M. (Rev.), Jan. 16,
  1930
  Loula, w. of Willie Luck,
  June 26, 1924
  Lucy N. (Mrs.), June 16,
  1859
  Maria Louisa, d. of Samuel
  P. Luck, Aug. 30, 1849
  Martha J., w. of B. J. D.
  Luck, Nov. 18, 1858
  Mary A., Nov. 20, 1902
  Mary Bell, d. of Rev. J. M.
  and O. F. Luck, Sept. 6,
  1877
  Mary Marshall, d. of John M.
  and Mary A. Luck, Sept. 5,
  1867
  Mildred J., d. of R. S. Luck,
  May 1, 1873
  Nannie, w. of Rev. G. P. Luck,
  mother of Rev. J. M. Luck,
  Sept. 2, 1886
  Nettie Lee, d. of William K.
  and Elvira Luck, Apr. 24,
  1873
  Robert Moorman, s. of Dr.
  George S. Luck, Feb. 3, 1881
  Samuel, Feb. 2, 1828
  W. K., May 7, 1891
LUCKADO
  Edward White, s. of Berry
  Luckado, June 11, 1863
  Isaac (Elder), Oct. 15, 1874
LUCKETT
  Francis W., Apr. 1, 1869
  James Thornton, s. of James
  T. and Lucie J. Luckett,
  May 25, 1876
LUCY
  M. E. (Mrs.), June 6, 1907
  Samuel K. (Maj.), Feb. 15,
  1877
LUKE
  Euphrates R., child of J. M.
  C. and Catherine H. Luke,
  Aug. 26, 1858
  J. M. C. (Rev.), Feb. 22, 1877
LULL
  Frances V. A. (Mrs.), d. of
  Pleasant Tucker, Mar. 19,
  1885
LUMPKIN
  Achilles, May 26, 1859
  Amanda (Mrs.), Mar. 25, 1880
  Ann, w. of Capt. John Lumpkin,
  Feb. 27, 1835
  George Thomas (Rev.), Feb.
  22, 1934
  Mary T., d. of Rev. Thomas W.
  Lumpkin, Aug. 11, 1853

OBITUARY NOTICES IN THE RELIGIOUS HERALD WITH DATES OF PUBLICATION

Priscilla, w. of Richardson
    Lumpkin, Apr. 7, 1842
Richardson, July 16, 1863
Susan F. (Mrs.), Mar. 7, 1861
LUMPKINS
    Sallie W., d. of W. L. and E.
    F. Lumpkins, Feb. 28, 1889
LUMSDEN
    Mary L., w. of William D.
    Lumsden, Apr. 24, 1851
    Vernon Oakley, May 26, 1927
LUMSDON
    Mary H., d. of George Lumsdon, July 29, 1841
LUNCEFORD
    Harriet Griffith, w. of C.
    Lunceford, Dec. 24, 1914
LUNDQUIST
    C. R., Sept. 8, 1927
LUNDY
    P. H., Sept. 11, 1873
    Rebecca J., w. of Dr. E.
    Lundy, May 22, 1879
    Roger B., s. of Dr. E. W.
    Lundy, Oct. 2, 1873
    Rosa A., w. of William T.
    Lundy, Sept. 17, 1868
    William T. (Col.), June 3, 1869
LUNSFORD
    Edwin (Dr.), Oct. 11, 1877
    Elizabeth, w. of Thomas
    Lunsford, Dec. 11, 1862
    Jane E., w. of Louis Lunsford, Oct. 4, 1883
    Sally, w. of Dr. E. Lunsford, Sept. 5, 1861
    Thomas, Mar. 5, 1863
    William (Dr.), June 9, 1927
LUPTON
    Josephine (Mrs.), Mar. 23, 1882
LUSHBAUGH
    Nettie (Mrs.), Oct. 8, 1925
    Rose (Mrs.), Dec. 28, 1922
LUTTRELL
    John P., May 22, 1851
    Mary Ritchie (Mrs.), May 20, 1909
LYELL

Fannie L. (Mrs.), d. of
    R. L. Pitts, Oct. 12, 1854
LYLE
    G. W. (Dr.), Mar. 29, 1928
LYMAN
    Fannie Ella, w. of William L.
    Lyman, d. of Werner Eubank, Oct. 1, 1885
    Henry A., Jan. 30, 1902
    Nannie W. (Mrs.), d. of
    George I. and Mary P. Herring, July 27, 1882
LYNCH
    J. C., July 31, 1902
    John, July 7, 1842
    Jordan M., Mar. 22, 1849
    Mary, w. of John Lynch,
    Aug. 14, 1829
    Mary (Sister), May 25, 1899
    Samuel, Apr. 24, 1919
    Willoughby, Sept. 2, 1875
LYND
    S. W. (Dr.), July 6, 1876
LYNE
    Alpheus Garnett, s. of
    Thomas Lyne, Jan. 22, 1885
    Cassie Oliver (Mrs.), Apr. 5, 1934
    Lucy F., Feb. 10, 1887
    Robert Baylor (Dr.), Oct. 25, 1866
LYNN
    A. T. (Rev.), Sept. 25, 1924
    B. W. (Maj.), Oct. 4, Nov. 29, 1917
    G. S., s. of Maj. B. W. Lynn,
    Sept. 15, 1898
    James Shirley (Rev.), Dec. 24, 1914; Jan. 21, 1915
    Jennie H., w. of H. Clay Lynn,
    June 23, 1892
    Myrtle, d. of Maj. B. W.
    Lynn, Sept. 15, 1898
    Robert Ellwood, s. of A. J. and
    Nannie Lynn, Mar. 17, 1881
LYON
    Amoret, w. of Allen M. Lyon,
    Sept. 5, 1861
    P., w. of J. Lyon, Jr., Apr. 25, 1844

·M·

MABRY
  Marie Elizabeth, w. of Dr. J. H. Mabry, d. of W. L. Boatwright, Sept. 13, 1917
McADAMS
  I. J. (Mrs.), July 17, 1913
McALEXANDER
  Alexander (Capt.), Feb. 25, 1841
McALISTER
  Polly, June 5, 1884
McALLISTER
  James, Sept. 12, 1828
  James, Mar. 4, 1880
  Pattie L., w. of Dr. W. T. McAllister, May 2, 1872
  Phebe (Mrs.), Feb. 9, 1882
McARDLE
  Jane E., w. of H. A. McArdle, d. of William B. Smith, May 26, 1870
MacARTHUR
  (Dr.), Mar. 1, 1923
McBRIDE
  Robert, s. of Dr. Hugh Malcolm and Anne Wording McBride, Sept. 30, 1909
McCABE
  Rosa Newman (Mrs.), June 14, 1923
  W. O. (Dr.), Mar. 12, 1936
McCADDER
  Fannie, July 14, 1853
McCAIN
  William (Rev.), Jan. 19, 1871
McCALLEY
  M. Ella, Mar. 13, 1879
McCALLY
  Elizabeth Ann (Mrs.), Aug. 8, 1878
McCANTS
  F. C., Feb. 27, 1879
McCARGO
  Elizabeth, w. of Littlejohn, McCargo, Jan. 18, 1855
  Virginia, d. of William McCargo, Dec. 27, 1849
McCARTER
  Jessa (Mrs.), Aug. 19, 1920
McCARTIN
  Carlton, Apr. 23, 1936
  John H., Feb. 10, 1859
McCARTY
  Alice C., d. of William McCarty, June 9, 1857
  Olivia, w. of Madison McCarty, Nov. 8, 1860
McCAUL
  Lucy M., Mar. 22, 1860
McCAULEY
  Sarah E., d. of James McCauley, Mar. 2, 1865
McCLANAHAN
  Augustine, Sr., Oct. 12, 1876
McCLANNAHAN
  Gertrude, d. of Dr. R. S. and Alice McClannahan, June 8, 1882
  Lucy (Mrs.), Mar. 3, 1853
M'CLANNEN
  William, Mar. 20, 1862
McCLENNEY
  Sarah, Sept. 9, 1836
McCLENNY
  Martha, w. of William D. McClenny, Apr. 24, 1873
  Mary (Mrs.), July 7, 1859
  Mary E., Apr. 9, 1857
  Nancy, Apr. 11, 1889
McCLUER
  Elizabeth, d. of R. S. and Bettie B. McCluer, Aug. 22, 1889
McCLUN
  John R., s. of William W. and Cynthia McClun, Aug. 6, 1857
McCLUNG
  Abigal Ann, d. of John McClung, Feb. 14, 1861
  Harry Lipscomb, s. of John H.

OBITUARY NOTICES IN THE RELIGIOUS HERALD WITH DATES OF PUBLICATION

and Bettie McClung,
Sept. 25, 1873
Lusina Virginia, w. of W. T.
McClung, Sept. 5, 1935
Minerva Margaret, d. of John
McClung, Feb. 14, 1861
Monte, s. of J. H. and Bettie
McClung, Aug. 14, 1873
Virginia Catherine, d. of
John McClung, Feb. 14,
1861
W. C. (Dr.), Dec. 16, 1937
William Stanton, Nov. 15,
1888

McCOLLOM
Elizabeth J. (Mrs.), Feb. 28,
1878

McCOMB
Nannie, w. of Gen. William
McComb, Aug. 15, 1895

MACCOMMACK
Pleasant, Aug. 15, 1851

McCONIHEAY
Hannah, w. of Samuel
McConiheay, Feb. 21, 1856

McCONNELL
F. C. (Dr.), Jan. 17, 1929

McCORD
L. T. (Mrs.), Mar. 29, 1923

McCORMICK
Hugh P., Oct. 24, 1920
Robert Burns, June 27, 1901

McCOUCHIE
James (Mrs.), Aug. 6, 1914

McCOWN
John Westley (Dr.), Jan. 13
and 20, Feb, 10, 1910
Permelia, w. of Joseph
McCown, d. of Reuben
Hughes, Nov. 5, 1885;
May 27, 1886

McCOY
Isaac (Elder), July 9, 1846
Mary Virginia, Sept. 4, 1913
Sadie, Mar. 24, 1921
William, July 3, 1851
William Kenneth (Sgt.),
June 25, 1863

McCRAW
A. C. (Lt.), May 21, 1863

Bettie Gilliam, w. of William Emmett McCraw, Nov. 2
and 16, 1922
Ellen Blair, d. of John A.
and Lucie A. McCraw, Aug. 4,
1864
Emma D., w. of W. D. McCraw,
d. of Thomas Clark, Apr. 27,
1854
John A. (Col.), Aug. 16, 1894
Josephene Lavinia, d. of F.
D. McCraw, Feb. 11, 1869*
Lucie A. SYDNOR, w. of Col.
John A. McCraw, d. of Beverly and Ann Spotswood
Sydnor, Apr. 26, May 29,
1917
Richard Miller, Feb. 20, 1862
Sallie Harrison, d. of F. D.
McCraw, Sept. 30, 1869
William Emmett, June 3, 1920

McCULLOCK
Annie, d. of Adam G. and
Beatrice McCullock, July 24,
1873

McCUNE
Susan, w. of Robert McCune,
Sept. 9, 1841

McCURDY
W. D. (Mrs.), Feb. 4,
1909

McCUTCHEN
Abigail D., w. of Robert
McCutchen, July 23, 1868

McCUTCHEON
Charles, Apr. 24, 1862
John E., Mar. 7, 1844
Lucy Ann (Mrs.), d. of Philip
Thurmond, May 22, 1890
Prudence, w. of Charles McCutcheon, Aug. 21, 1856

McDANIEL
Delia, w. of R. E. McDaniel,
Sept. 4, 1851
George W. (Dr.), Aug. 25,
Sept. 28, 1927
Mary T., w. of Rev. James
McDaniel, Aug. 5, 1869
Robert W., s. of R. E. McDaniel, Jan. 22, 1857

* Possible inaccuracy in name, or spelling, but given as printed

OBITUARY NOTICES IN THE RELIGIOUS HERALD WITH DATES OF PUBLICATION

McDANNALD
　Samuel Merle, s. of W. H.
　and S. B. McDannald,
　Nov. 6, 1873
McDEARMAN
　Elmina A. (Mrs.), Sept. 30,
　1841
McDEARMON
　Thelma Demetris, Dec. 17,
　1903
McDERMED
　Daniel, Oct. 27, 1853
McDONALD
　John Alexander, s. of Rev.
　William R. McDonald,
　Sept. 5, and 12, 1867
　Mary G., w. of James Mc-
　Donald, Sr., Feb. 16,
　1854
　Sarah Elizabeth (Mrs.),
　Nov. 20, 1924
　Thomas D., Nov. 18, 1841
　W. R. (Rev.), Aug. 5 and
　26, Sept. 9, 1869
McDOUGAL
　Mabel Floyd, Nov. 5, 1896
McDOWALL
　John Robert (Rev.), Dec.
　30, 1836
McDOWELL
　A. (Rev.), June 9 and
　23, 1891
　E. A. (Rev.), Jan. 20,
　1938
　George Clifford, s. of J.
　W. and Z. A. McDowell,
　Oct. 1, 1874
　James, Mar. 3, 1881
　James S., Oct. 26, 1916
　Joseph P., Sr., Sept. 13,
　Oct. 25, 1928
　Otis L., Mar. 25, 1937
McELEREE
　Martha A., Nov. 6, 1884
McELLROY
　William C. (Rev.), June 9,
　1837
McELORY
　Edward C., s. of Ellis S.
　and Caroline M. McElory,
　Dec. 2, 1858
McFADDEN
　Mary Witt, d. of Jackson
　McFadden, Mar. 14, 1872
McFADEN
　Frank T. (Dr.), Aug. 10,
　1933
McFARLAND
　Frances (Mrs.), June 11,
　1936
MACFEE
　W. V. (Rev.), May 16, 1889
McGEE
　John E., Feb. 15, 1923
　Joseph, Sept. 3, 1830
　Sallie M. (Mrs.), d. of Rev.
　E. G. Shipp, Feb. 1, 1883
McGEHEE
　David B. (Elder), June 17,
　1847
　Eliza A., d. of Elder D. B.
　McGehee, Oct. 31, 1850
　Elizabeth, w. of Elder D. B.
　McGehee, Oct. 31, 1850
　Elizabeth Sarah, d. of John
　McGehee, Sept. 22, 1837
　Garrett C. (Col.), Oct. 3,
　1878
　Jacob Owen, May 5, 1932
　James W., s. of Thomas B.
　and Lucy A. McGehee,
　Aug. 6, 1846
　John, Aug. 5, 1875
　John B., Sept. 22, 1870
　John F., s. of Thomas B. and
　Lucy A. McGehee, Aug. 6,
　1846
　Judith A. (Mrs.), Jan. 19,
　1865
　Martha, w. of Francis Mc-
　Gehee, June 18, 1846
　Mary, w. of John McGehee,
　Nov. 5, 1846
　Nelson Booker, s. of John
　McGehee, Feb. 11, 1864
　Sarah E., w. of David B.
　McGehee, Oct. 23, 1902
　Sarah Elizabeth, w. of
　George D. McGehee, Feb. 1,
　1830

OBITUARY NOTICES IN THE RELIGIOUS HERALD WITH DATES OF PUBLICATION

W. C. (Mrs.), June 27, 1889
McGEORGE
  Evelyn B., w. of John F.
    McGeorge, Nov. 24, 1853
  J. L., Jan. 28, 1869
  Lawrence, Mar. 5, 1863
  Reuben, Apr. 20, 1871
  Sarah A. (Mrs.), May 20, 1875
M'GHEE*
  Elmira Houston, w. of Foster M'Ghee, May 25, 1899
McGHEE
  James L., s. of John and Lavinia McGhee, Oct. 22, 1863
  Lavinia E., w. of John McGhee, d. of Benjamin Falls, Oct. 22, 1863
  Mary Bettie, d. of Foster McGhee, July 23, 1891*
  Z. B., s. of I. Foster and Elmira McGhee, Oct. 31, 1889*
McGILL
  Ann, w. of John D. McGill, Jan. 26, 1843
  Cordelia A., w. of Robert T. McGill, Nov. 12, 1874
  John D., Feb. 7, 1856
  Louisa (Mrs.), d. of Joseph Schoolfield, Aug. 24, 1893
  Mattie Douglas, d. of Robert T. McGill, Sept. 6, 1866
McGILVRAY
  William B. (Rev.), Dec. 3, 1891
McGLAMRE
  John, s. of Elder John McGlamre, Aug. 21, 1851
McGLOTHLIN
  J. T. (Dr.), June 14, 1934
  W. J. (Mrs.), w. of Dr. McGlothlin, May 25, 1933
McGRUDER
  Elizabeth, w. of Capt. William McGruder, Sept. 12, 1872

Hardaway, June 2, 1859
  Louisa T., w. of Z. McGruder, Nov. 5, 1874
  Mary, w. of Zebedee McGruder, Sept. 30, 1858
  Susan E., w. of H. McGruder, d. of Milton P. and Elizabeth Atkinson, July 26, 1855
  William G. (Dr.), s. of William McGruder, Feb. 13, 1851
  Zephaniah, Sept. 19, 1844
McGUFFEY
  William H. (Dr.), May 15 and 22, 1873
McGUIRE
  Hunter, Sept. 27, 1900
  John P., May 3, 1906
MACHLIN
  John, Aug. 13, 1857
McILWAINE
  Lucy A. (Mrs.), mother of Senator William B. McIlwaine, sister of Gen. Roger Pryor, Mar. 28, 1901
McINNIS
  Elizabeth C., w. of M. McInnis, d. of Robert Hill, Dec. 24, 1857
McINTOSH
  John (Dr.), Feb. 20, 1879
  Mary (Mrs.), Dec. 25, 1835
McIVER
  d. of George W. McIver, June 17, 1886
  Hannah M., w. of P. K. McIver, Dec. 5, 1867
  John K. (Dr.), Dec. 3, 1846
  Lucy Quisenbery, w. of J. McIver, Apr. 15, 1926
  Martha E., w. of Rev. D. R. W. McIver, Jan. 25, 1883
MACKAN
  Thomas E., s. of Dr. H. M. Mackan, Sept. 21, Nov. 16, 1876
McKANN
  Anne (Mrs.), July 15, 1926
McKEE
  Dallas, s. of M. S. McKee,

* Possible inaccuracy in name, or spelling, but given as printed

OBITUARY NOTICES IN THE RELIGIOUS HERALD WITH DATES OF PUBLICATION

Nov. 21, 1918
Susanna M., w. of Robert
L. McKee, Nov. 19, 1846
McKENNEY
  Evie Elizabeth, Nov. 8,
  1923
McKENNY
  Betsy, Apr. 19, 1855
  Clarence, Jan. 24, 1924
  Julia Lee, July 18, 1889
McKENZIE
  Benedict M., s. of Benedict
  and Martha McKenzie,
  Dec. 3, 1840
  Martha, w. of B. McKenzie,
  Jan. 29, 1846
  William, June 12, 1829
  William C., s. of James M.
  and Sciana F. McKenzie,
  Oct. 1, 1846
MACKIE
  Ann E. (Mrs.), Sept. 27,
  1877
McKIM
  Bettie A. (Mrs.), Jan. 27,
  1938
  Caroline S., w. of William A. McKim, Mar. 4,
  1858
  Carrie F., Mar. 9, 1882
  Elizabeth, w. of William
  McKim, Jan. 29, 1830
  Elizabeth, w. of Robert
  McKim, Oct. 18, 1855
  Joseph, Sept. 9, 1836
McKINLEY
  William (Mrs.), w. of former
  President McKinley,
  June 6, 1907
McKINNEY
  Eliza D., d. of Peter J.
  McKinney, Jan. 29, 1874
  G. H., Oct. 29, 1874
  J. S., Feb. 20, 1936
  Lucy Coleman (Mrs.),
  Sept. 14, 1933
  Martha G. (Mrs.), Nov. 25,
  1875
  Sallie, w. of Peter J.
  McKinney, Jan. 29, 1874

Sallie I., Dec. 22, 1881
T. A. (Mrs.), Dec. 16,
1926
McKISSICK
  E. P., Oct. 2, 1902
McLAREN
  Alexander (Rev.), May 19,
  and 26, 1910
  David, Aug. 29, 1850
McLAUGHLIN
  J. T. (Rev.), Oct. 30, 1902
  Nena D., d. of Rev. James
  T. and Ann M. McLaughlin,
  June 21, 1923
  Thomas, Aug. 31, 1838
McLAURIN*
  Lewis, Mar. 2, 1865
  Mary E., d. of Lewis and
  Rebecca McLaurin, Mar. 2,
  1865
  Rebecca, d. of Lewis and
  Rebecca McLaurin, Mar. 2,
  1865
  Rebecca F., May 12, 1864
McLAURINE*
  Henry, Sept. 14, 1876
  Lewis, Mar. 15, 1883
  Marie Louise, d. of George
  W. McLaurine, Jan. 14,
  1909
  Milton, s. of Lewis and
  Rebecca McLaurine, Apr. 9,
  and 30, 1914
  Milton (Mrs.), Jan. 16,
  1930
  R. Lewis, s. of Lewis and
  Rebecca McLaurine, Nov. 5,
  1863
  Rebecca, w. of Lewis McLaurine, Aug. 3, 1871
MACLENNAN
  Lucy Ann Frances, w. of Rev.
  James Maclennan, d. of
  Capt. J. and Susanna
  Beazley, Apr. 20, 1848
McLEOD
  Belinda (Mrs.), May 6,
  1858
  Cazneau, Jan. 3, 1901
  William J., s. of William

* Possible inaccuracy in name, or spelling, but given as printed

OBITUARY NOTICES IN THE RELIGIOUS HERALD WITH DATES OF PUBLICATION

McLeod, June 8, 1836
MACLIN
  Henry Austin, s. of John Henry and Sarah Hill Maclin, May 18, 1893
  Thomas, May 31, 1866*
McMANAWAY
  Graham V., s. of Rev. A. G. McManaway, July 23, 1914
  James M. (Rev.), Apr. 27, 1922
  John Eugene (Rev.), Mar. 27, Apr. 10, 1930
  Maria Josephine, w. of Rev. Alexander G. McManaway, Mar. 3, 1927
  Mary Morgan, w. of Dr. James M. McManaway, Oct. 20, 1938
McMENAMIN
  Lelia (Mrs.), Mar. 26, 1896
McMICHAEL
  J. C., Oct. 31, 1895
McMICKING
  Mary, Nov. 8, 1934
McMILLAN
  W. R. (Rev.), Feb. 12, 1920
McMULLAN
  Blannie, d. of Edward B. and Fannie D. McMullan, Aug. 3, 1876
McMULLEN
  Peachy, w. of John Mc-mullen, gr.d. of Adam Banks, Aug. 20, 1874
McNEALE
  Isabella (Mrs.), June 4, 1857
McNEILL
  John (Dr.), Mar. 4, 1937
McNENY
  Alice, w. of Thomas Mc-Neny, d. of Edwin Price Thompson, Nov. 22 and 29, 1923
  Thomas, Feb. 8, 1923
MacNIEL
  John S., Apr. 6, 1933
McPHERSON
  Rebecca H., w. of Capt. J. S. McPherson, Jan. 7, 1892
  Samuel (Rev.), Sept. 5, 1828
McQUEEN
  Archibald (Elder), Aug. 27, 1840
  David (Dr.), Mar. 22, 1855
  Margaret, May 6, 1862
McQUIE
  Mary J., w. of Elder Walter McQuie, d. of Jesse Baskett, Apr. 8, 1858
McRAE
  Charles F., June 18, 1885
  Emily S. Turpin, w. of John H. McRae, Sept. 13, 1906
McREYNOLDS
  Noah C., Feb. 12, 1914
McTYRE
  James R., June 9, 1881
  James Wilds, s. of James R. and Martha J. McTyre, Aug. 9, 1855
  Martha J., w. of J. R. McTyre, d. of Elder Jordan Martin, Nov. 10, 1864
McVEIGH
  E. (Mrs.), Sept. 19, 1872
  Harvey, May 17, 1923
  Harvey (Mrs.), May 14, 1925
  Jesse, Oct. 30, 1856
  Rosanna, d. of Eli McVeigh, Oct. 5, 1843
McWHIRT
  Mary A., d. of Franklin McWhirt, Apr. 9, 1903

* Possible inaccuracy in name, or spelling, but given as printed

OBITUARY NOTICES IN THE RELIGIOUS HERALD WITH DATES OF PUBLICATION

MADDOX
    Elizabeth S., w. of Elder William H. Maddox, Mar. 24, 1842
    Jane, w. of William Maddox, Dec. 10, 1857
    John (Mrs.), Sept. 25, 1930
    Judith J., w. of William H. Maddox, Aug. 30, 1839
    Lucy F., w. of Robert Maddox, Sept. 25, 1851
    Martha Claiborn, w. of Elder William H. Maddox, Oct. 3, 1844
    Samuel, father of Mrs. J. A. Flannagan, July 18, 1912
    Sarah (Mrs.), Mar. 4, 1909
    William J., Apr. 19, 1855

MADDUX
    George B., s. of E. B. Maddux, Dec. 10, 1885
    J. W., July 30, 1914
    Thomas Samuel, Nov. 13, 1913

MADISON
    Eleanor (Mrs.), mother of former President Madison, Feb. 20, 1829
    Emma Louise, w. of M. O. Madison, d. of William H. Ryals, Mar. 3, 1921
    Eugene Franklin, s. of William Lewis and Martha A. Madison, Feb. 15, Mar. 14, 1872
    Henry, Dec. 12, 1839
    Ida, Dec. 22, 1881
    Lucy Ann (Mrs.), June 16, 1859
    Lucy M., w. of Dr. James A. Madison, Aug. 12 and 26, 1886
    Robert L., s. of Gen. Madison, nephew of former President Madison, Mar. 7, 1828
    William L. (Capt.), July 7, 1859

MAGEE
    Julia W. (Mrs.), d. of B. M. Robertson, Feb. 23, Mar. 2, 1882

MAGOON
    W. of Rev. Magoon, Feb. 20, 1879
    Josiah (Elder), May 13, 1841

MAHON
    Emily, w. of Carter Mahon, Mar. 28, 1872
    John Newton, July 23, 1868
    Lizzie Butler, w. of Joseph C. Mahon, d. of Col. I. O. and Nannie Butler, Mar. 2, 1905
    Mollie W., Apr. 2, 1874
    Phebe, w. of Thomas Mahon, Nov. 6, 1856
    Silas, Jan. 25, 1872
    William Luther, Sept. 5, 1868

MAIDEN
    James Franklin (Elder), Dec. 17, 1903

MAJER
    John H., June 16, 1859

MAJOR
    Carrington, s. of S. A. Major, Jr., July 27, 1899
    Catherine K., w. of Spotswood Major, Oct. 8, 1863
    Cleopatra, w. of Harwood Major, Mar. 13, 1884
    Cleopatra (Mrs.), Jan. 25, 1900
    George W. (Mrs.), Oct. 29, 1840
    H. (Mrs.), Mar. 20, 1884
    Howard A., Oct. 8, 1863

OBITUARY NOTICES IN THE RELIGIOUS HERALD WITH DATES OF PUBLICATION

John C., Mar. 11, 1886
MAKEPIECE
  Martha Ann, w. of A. S.
    Makepiece. May 29,
    1851
MALCOM
  Howard (Rev.), Apr. 3,
    1879
  Lydia M., w. of Rev.
    Howard Malcom, Feb. 15,
    1833
MALLONEE
  father of John K. Mal-
    lonee, Sept. 9, 1880
  Charles W., s. of Leonard
    Mallonee, Mar. 19,
    1874
  Thomazine, w. of Will-
    iam Mallonee, Mar. 13,
    1879
MALLORY
  Ann Curtis, w. of Bickerton
    Winston Mallory, Aug. 27,
    1891
  B. W., July 26, 1849
  Elizabeth, w. of Edward
    T. Mallory, Sept. 14,
    1848
  Emma Alice (Mrs.), Apr. 21,
    1921
  Estelle, d. of B. W. and
    Ann C. Mallory, Apr. 1,
    1841
  Forrest, Nov. 7, 1929
  Frances L., w. of Charles
    K. Mallory, July 3,
    1845
  James, s. of Uriel
    Mallory, Nov. 29,
    1877
  Lucie Anna, d. of G. W.
    and Henrietta K.
    Mallory, Oct. 22,
    1857
  Margaret M., w. of
    Jesse H. Mallory, d.
    of Joel and Susan
    Thomas, Jan. 23 and 30,
    1873
  Mary, w. of William
    Mallory, Aug. 21,
    1851
  Mary Frances (Mrs.), May 14,
    1891
  Mary HUNT, w. of Charles E.
    Mallory, d. of Dr. Ander-
    son Hunt, Sept. 27,
    1894
  Pamelia H. (Mrs.), Oct. 6,
    1859
  Richard, Apr. 13, 1843
  Sammie C., Sept. 1,
    1892
  Susan, July 27, 1848
  Uriel, Sept. 10, 1840
  William, Feb. 22, 1855
  William (Col.), Sept. 20,
    1866
MALONE
  Anderson, Aug. 9, 1860
  H. O. (Mrs.), Apr. 14,
    1932
  James, Jr., Mar. 15,
    1855
  Lou, w. of Robert Malone,
    July 21, 1892
  Mary (Mrs.), Apr. 27,
    1848
MANDLEBAUM
  Annie (Mrs.), Dec. 31,
    1891
MANGHUM
  Lucy Arvine, d. of N.
    R. and Lucy Manghum,
    July 27, 1871
MANGRAM
  Joel, Jan. 22, 1863
MANIPLY
  N. N., Mar. 17, 1892
MANLY
  Alice, d. of Rev. B. and
    C. E. Manly, Jr., Aug.
    16, 1866
  B., Sr. (Dr.), July 11,
    1872
  Basil R., s. of Dr. B.
    Manly, Sept. 30,
    1880
  Mary, d. of Rev. Charles
    Manly, Apr. 7 and 17

OBITUARY NOTICES IN THE RELIGIOUS HERALD WITH DATES OF PUBLICATION

1910
Mary Lane, d. of Rev. B. Manly, Sept. 16, 1880
Rosa, d. of Dr. Basil and Hattie S. Manly, Feb. 12, 1880
Sarah M., w. of Rev. Basil Manly, Sr., Sept. 20, 1894

MANN
Annie C., d. of James J. and M. Estelle Mann, Dec. 16, 1886
Bettie W., w. of H. K. Mann, d. of J. H. and Judith Shelton, Dec. 19, 1895; Jan. 2, 1896
Caroline (Mrs.), Sept. 27, 1900
E. Jamie, child of James J. and M. Estelle Mann, Dec. 16, 1886
E. W., Aug. 26, 1858
Elizabeth Ann (Mrs.), May 8, 1835
Frances (Mrs.), Apr. 19, 1855
Henley, June 12, 1879
J. P. (Mrs.), Sept. 18, 1890
James H., Jan. 28, 1831
James J., Mar. 8, 1917
John Robert (Lt.), Aug. 7, 1862
Lawrence, Jan. 31, 1895
Levi, Apr. 27, 1854
Meekey S., w. of Richard H. Mann, July 2, 1857
Philip G., s. of William Mann, Aug. 20, 1830
Susan D., Aug. 17, 1882
Susannah H. (Mrs.), Sept. 16, 1831
William, Apr. 1, 1852

MANNION
Charles (Mrs.), Dec. 19, 1929

MANSER
Miles, m. Catharine Morris, Jan. 29, 1874

MANSFIELD
E., Mar. 24, 1910
John W. (Capt.), Mar. 15, 1860
Mary, w. of John Mansfield, d. of Rev. Christian Street, July 20, 1871
Robert G., Aug. 27, 1863
Susan, w. of Elder William A. Mansfield, Jan. 2, 1845
Thomas Parker, s. of Edward and Lizzie Mansfield, Sept. 4, 1856
William D., Aug. 16, 1860

MANTIPLY
Susan, w. of Capt. Winston Mantiply, Apr. 15, 1858
William, Apr. 21, 1864

MANTLO
Emma Gertrude, d. of John G. and India Mantlo, Mar. 9, 1865

MAPLES
S. P., w. of S. Maples, d. of Henry and Sallie Townsend, Mar. 19, 1857

MAPP
Elizabeth N., w. of Victor A. Mapp, d. of Thomas G. and Elizabeth N. Scott, Oct. 16, 1873

MARABLE
Ann, w. of W. H. Marable, d. of Rev. James T. Gwaltney, Jan. 29, 1874
Elizabeth, w. of William H. Marable, Dec. 4, 1879
Jennie A., w. of Rev. B. F. Marable, June 18, 1857
Sallie (Mrs.), Mar. 3, 1859
Thomas E., Mar. 31, 1921
William H., Sr., Oct. 26, Nov. 9, 1854

MARBLE
Susan W., w. of Benjamin Marble, Oct. 15, 1840

MARCH
Peter S., Mar. 9, 1899
Seth, Mar. 31, 1870
Virginia J., w. of Seth March, Jan. 24, 1878

MARCHANT

OBITUARY NOTICES IN THE RELIGIOUS HERALD WITH DATES OF PUBLICATION

A., Mar. 12 and 19, 1857
James B., Oct. 1, 1874
James D., Aug. 13, 1874
John, Nov. 11, 1841
Leonora T., Apr. 2, 1925
Lucy (Mrs.), Dec. 22, 1859
Mary E., w. of J. W. Marchant, July 2, 1896
Stanley F., June 17, 1897
Susan J., Mar. 29, 1923
MARCHELL
   Lucy Johnson, w. of F. O. R. Marchell, June 25, 1885
MARDERS
   Eliza, w. of Rev. L. Marders, June 28, 1849
   Sarah F., w. of Elder Lovell Marders, Mar. 31, 1837
MARGRAVE
   Margaret, w. of Elder William G. Margrave, Apr. 2, 1863
   Mary (Mrs.), Jan. 11, 1833
   William G. (Elder), Mar. 21, 1867
MARINER
   Julia A. S., d. of Mrs. Ann Mariner, Aug. 15, 1844
   Richard A., Apr. 5, 1888
   W. (Maj.), Feb. 24, 1927
MARKHAM
   Barnard H., s. of E. L. and C. C. Markham, Aug. 17, 1871
   Julia F., w. of Vincent D. Markham, Aug. 28, 1856
   Samuel P., May 1, 1862
   Willie V. (Mrs.), Jan. 3, 1929
MARKS
   John Gwathmey, s. of John R. and Mary L. Marks, Dec. 7, 1876
   L. Lilburne (Mrs.), Feb. 9, 1911
   Lansdelle, s. of William E. and H. W. Marks, Feb. 5, 1863
   W. D., May 1, 1924
MARKWOOD

   Milton H., Aug. 1, 1895
MARQUIS
   Sarah (Mrs.), Dec. 23, 1831
MARRINET
   Louisa M., w. of William T. Marrinet, Feb. 6, 1873
MARSH
   Cyrus, Mar. 6, 1919
   Ella, w. of Dr. H. W. Marsh, d. of Rev. A. J. Hires, Sept. 19, 1878
   Mary Lou (Mrs.), Apr. 12, 1934
   W. J., Oct. 15, 1925
MARSHALL
   Andrew Broaddus, Feb. 5, 1931
   Bettie Lumpkin, d. of Thomas and Lucy Marshall, Sept. 27, 1855
   Clara M., w. of Thomas E. Marshall, d. of Capt. Joseph F. Price, Feb. 11, 1858
   Coleman, Oct. 29, 1874
   Elizabeth L., w. of Capt. Thomas Marshall, Oct. 7, 1841
   Fannie (Mrs.), June 28, 1934
   Frances, w. of Thomas Marshall, Aug. 2, 1849
   Francis, June 3, 1858
   George W., May 23, 1872; Dec. 10, 1874
   Howard, Mar. 28, 1895
   J. E. (Mrs.), Mar. 19, 1931
   John W., Apr. 12, 1839
   Josiah, Mar. 6, 1845
   Judith P., w. of George W. Marshall, Sept. 6, 1849
   Lucy, w. of Thomas Marshall, Dec. 13, 1877
   Minerva, Mar. 26, 1830
   Philip, Oct. 7, 1880
   R. Thomas, June 18, 1863
   Richard A. (Maj.), Oct. 27, 1887
   Richard S., July 5, 1860
   Robert A. (Mrs.), Nov. 30, 1933

OBITUARY NOTICES IN THE RELIGIOUS HERALD WITH DATES OF PUBLICATION

Robert Semple, s. of George Marshall, Mar. 8, 1855
Susan T., w. of Presley B. Marshall, Feb. 18, 1864
Theresa, w. of George Marshall, June 15, 1871
Thomas (Capt.), Feb. 16, 1838
Thomas, Oct. 14, 1880
William A., Feb. 13, 1918
William Thomas, s. of Thomas and Lucy Marshall, Oct. 26, 1854

MARSTON
Addie Tribble, May 16, 1929
John W., Jan. 9, 1919
Johnnie, s. of John W. and Addie Marston, Dec. 30, 1880
Lillian R. (Mrs.), Feb. 7, 1935
O. D. (Mrs.), Feb. 26, 1914
O. D., Apr. 26, 1928
T. Beal, Aug. 10, 1933

MARTIN
A. B. (Mrs.), Feb. 9, 1933
A. E., w. of Francis Martin, Aug. 25, 1881
Ada Augusta, d. of J. H. and E. J. Martin, July 31, 1856
Adam, Apr. 30, 1914
Alfred Broadus, Aug. 12, 1926*
Ann, Oct. 6, 1837
Ann Edwards, w. of Dr. William Martin, Mar. 24, 1881
Annie Cora, May 22, 1902
Annie L., d. of William B. and E. F. Martin, June 25, 1891
Arthur Lewis (Dr.), Mar. 29, 1928
Bessie, Apr. 10, 1879
Bettie, Apr. 4, 1861
Bettie Elizabeth, d. of Joseph F. Martin, July 21, 1898
Brown Reid (Mrs.), Mar. 24, 1927
C. A. (Mrs.), d. of Mrs. Mary A. Thomas, Feb. 15, 1906

Caroline L., w. of A. T. Martin, Oct. 15, 1874
Catharine, w. of John Martin, Jan. 15, 1852
Charles Anderson, Jr., Mar. 18, 1920
Charlotte (Mrs.), Jan. 29, 1863
Cornelias, w. of John G. Martin, Mar. 5, 1885
Eliza A. (Mrs.), Mar. 24, 1859
Elizabeth, w. of Capt. Henry C. Martin, May 3, 1860
Elizabeth A., w. of William A. Martin, July 14, 1859
Ellen (Mrs.), May 11, 1882
Emeline Johnston (Mrs.), Jan. 31, 1929
Emily D., w. of Dr. Charles F. Martin, Sept. 20, 1894
Emma J., Mar. 25, 1875
Eugene, Mar. 12, 1896
Fannie A. (Mrs.), Oct. 2, 1873
Fannie J., w. of J. W. Martin, Nov. 16, 1876
Fanny, Oct. 8, 1885
Frank, Sept. 15, 1892
Furman H. (Dr.), Feb. 13, 1936
Grace, Jan. 12, 1922
Hattie L., May 6, 1920
J. J., Dec. 26, 1901
J. L., Nov. 20, 1919
J. W. (Rev.), July 6, 1911
J. W., July 17, 1919
James F. (Mrs.), Jan. 4, 1912
James F., May 22, 1919
James M., Jan. 16, 1873
James S., June 25, 1868
Jerry W., Jan. 21, 1892
John, Apr. 10, 1829
John H., Mar. 12, 1903
John Richie, s. of Chesley Martin, Aug. 17, 1848
John W. (Rev.), Aug. 17, 1911
John Younger, s. of Thomas

* Possible inaccuracy in name, or spelling, but given as printed

OBITUARY NOTICES IN THE RELIGIOUS HERALD WITH DATES OF PUBLICATION

C. Martin, Dec. 15, 1910
Johnnie, s. of J. L. Martin, June 25, 1896
Jordan (Elder), Jan. 4, Feb. 1, 1849
Joseph (Col.), Nov. 24, 1859
Laura, w. of William F. Martin, Nov. 13, 1873
Leonard, Nov. 24, 1842
Lizzie, w. of William A. Martin, Sept. 24, 1868
Lucie Mildred, d. of Garret and Sallie F. Martin, Feb. 5, 1863
Lucy Catherine, w. of Marcellus D. Martin, d. of John M. and Virginia A. Jordan, July 20, 1882
M. W., Aug. 23, 1888
Martha, w. of William Martin, Apr. 1, 1841
Martha J., w. of Elder Jordan Martin, Mar. 23, 1848
Mary F., w. of William M. Martin, June 13, 1867
Mattie, June 21, 1928
Morris B., s. of Thomas and Mary Martin, June 28, 1888
Moses E., Mar. 2, 1854
Nancy (Mrs.), Mar. 24, 1853
Neville, w. of Dr. B. H. Martin, d. of J. B. Watkins, Apr. 7, May 5, 1927
Nora Lea, d. of J. W. and F. J. Martin, Aug. 25, 1870
O. J., w. of W. E. Martin, d. of Col. Lawson Burfoot, Sept. 3, 1896
Olivia Ann, d. of William M. and Mellie S. Martin, Mar. 30, 1871
Ollie, July 17, 1924
Rebecca Lewis, w. of John Younger Martin, Dec. 23, 1909
Rebecca M., w. of Dr. Chesley Martin, Feb. 9, 1888
Royal, Aug. 23, 1855
Sallie (Mrs.), Jan. 25, 1872
Sallie (Mrs.), Apr. 3, 1924

Sallie A., d. of W. M. Martin, June 16, 1904
Theodosia F., w. of J. L. Martin, Aug. 21, 1924
Thomas B., Jan. 26, 1854
Thomas J. (Col.), Sept. 11, 1862
Thorburn Clarke, s. of Melvin A. and Alberta G. Martin, Sept. 23, 1875
Virginia Ida, May 21, 1891
W. H. (Mrs.), May 20, 1897
W. M. (Mrs.), May 12, 1887
William, Aug. 17, 1838
William (Rev.), Apr. 21, 1887
William A. (Capt.), s. of Mrs. E. A. Martin, May 28, 1857
William B., May 12, 1927
Williette Gertrude, d. of William and Harriette Martin, Feb. 17, 1859
Williette H., d. of William B. Martin, Jan. 2, 1851
Younger, Jan. 31, 1861
MASON
Allen S., Dec. 31, 1903
Camillus A., Dec. 25, 1862
Drusilla W. (Mrs.), Apr. 14, 1859
Edwin, Oct. 28, 1886
Elizabeth, w. of Elder V. M. Mason, Dec. 30, 1841
Elizabeth (Mrs.), Aug. 28, 1856
Elizabeth V., d. of Elder V. M. Mason, Oct. 22, 1840
Emily Ann, w. of Dr. William H. Mason, Aug. 10, 1843
Fanny, Oct. 8, 1857
Francis M., s. of Maj. W. M. Mason, Dec. 25, 1862
Francis Terry (Mrs.), Dec. 22, 1927
Frederick Davidson, Mar. 29, 1934
George, Apr. 15, 1841
George W., s. of Lewis G. and Catherine J. Mason, Apr. 16, 1863
Gilbert, s. of Rev. Gilbert

OBITUARY NOTICES IN THE RELIGIOUS HERALD WITH DATES OF PUBLICATION

Mason, Dec. 18, 1862
Gilbert (Rev.), Mar. 27, 1873
Guy French, s. of W. B. Mason, Dec. 22, 1898
Henrietta S., Feb. 9, 1865
J. S. (Mrs.), w. of Elder J. S. Mason, Jan. 12, 1860
James H. (Mrs.), July 17, 1930
James Jordan, Nov. 2, 1923
John, Aug. 27, 1857
John S. (Rev.), Dec. 15, 1892
John Y., Mar. 15, 1928
L. S. (Mrs.), Aug. 27, 1908
Lucy Roy, Dec. 22, 1870
Lydia, w. of Samuel Mason, Jan. 18, 1844
Margaret, w. of Capt. Claiborne R. Mason, May 29, 1890
Margaret Ellen, d. of Col. Miles F. Mason, Apr. 28, 1859
Mary I., w. of William B. Mason, d. of Capt. Guy D. and A. D. French, Mar. 31, 1887
Mary J., w. of Edward Mason, Jan. 15, 1891
Mary Jane, d. of Christopher and Ruth Mason, June 23, 1859
Mattie J. (Sister), Sept. 20, 1894
N. J., Feb. 13, 1896
Nellie, d. of Eben E. and Elizabeth T. Mason, Apr. 20, 1871
Oswald (Mrs.), Mar. 12, 1936
Otis T.(Mrs.), July 12, 1900
Pattie L. (Mrs.), Mar. 16, 1905
Polly T., Sept. 7, 1838
Rachel Lincoln, May 16, 1889
Sallie E., w. of W. M. Mason, Mar. 26, 1874
Samuel Griffin (Rev.), Feb. 13, Mar. 6, Apr. 24, May 1, 1890
Sarah, w. of Samuel Mason, Dec. 26, 1839
Sarah, w. of Jonathan Mason, May 6, 1926
Sue Tyler, w. of Rev. J. G. Mason, Mar. 11, 1875
Susan M., w. of Sanders Mason, Feb. 20, 1879
T. P. (Rev.), May 27, 1915
Thomas Pettus, s. of N. J. and P. L. Mason, Nov. 10, 1892
Warner M. (Maj.), Apr. 16, 1885
William, s. of Rev. V. M. Mason, Dec. 25, 1835
William B., s. of Rev. John S. Mason, Apr. 30, 1863
William Henry (Dr.), Aug. 30, 1840
Willia A., s. of Elder S. G. and S. F. Mason, Jan. 29, 1857

MASSENBURG
Carrie Rea (Mrs.), Feb. 24, 1938

MASSEY
Benjamin, Mar. 7, 1872
Edward, s. of Rev. J. E. and M. A. Massey, Feb. 2, 1854
Elizabeth, w. of Benjamin Massey, Aug. 2, 1855
George Henry, s. of Rev. Joseph T. Massey, Oct. 28, 1847
Joseph T. (Rev.), brother of John E. Massey, Feb. 26, 1891
Katie E., d. of Rev. J. T. Massey, Aug. 25, 1870
Louisa Love, d. of Rev. J. T. Massey, Sept. 23, 1869
Lucy Mary, w. of E. W. Massey, d. of Robert and Susan Hart, Apr. 21, 1881
Margaret Ann, w. of Lieutenant Governor John E. Massey, d. of John and Elizabeth Kable, Aug. 8, 1889

OBITUARY NOTICES IN THE RELIGIOUS HERALD WITH DATES OF PUBLICATION

S., w. of Thomas D. Massey,
  Feb. 1, 1855
Thomas P., Oct. 17, 1861
Walter W., m. Mary H. Edge,
  s. of John E. Messey,
  Feb. 11, 1904
MASSIE
  Bettie A. (Mrs.), May 19,
    1881
  Catharine, w. of James Massie,
    June 16, 1853
  Charles, Apr. 10, 1879
  Hardin (Dr.), Nov. 2, 1848
  James S., June 2, 1892
  Mary H. (Mrs.), Dec. 14, 1848
  Nannie Rodes, d. of Nathaniel
    Massie, Oct. 16, 1856
  Paulus Powell (Rev.), Apr. 23,
    1936
  Rodes, May 29, 1902
  S. P. (Mrs.), w. of Rev. S. P.
    Massie, Feb. 25, 1909
  Walter P, (Mrs.), d. of Dr.
    James M. Taliferro, May 21,
    1925
  Walter Price, May 8, 1930
  William Henry, June 2, 1892
MASTERS
  A. W. (Capt.), Feb. 26, 1891
MATHEWS
  Alexina Gertrude, d. of
    George A. Mathews, Aug.
    21, 1862
  C. J., Mar. 1, 1900
  Eliza A. (Mrs.), d. of Robert
    Stringfellow, Jan. 27, 1876
  Frank (Mrs.), Aug. 7, 1919
  S. F., July 15, 1858
  William L., s. of James B.
    Mathews, Apr. 16, 1863
  William Thomas, June 9, 1927
MATHIAS
  Margarette A., Apr. 15, 1886
MATTHEWS
  Baldwin S., Jan. 27, 1832
  Devilla, d. of J. B. and
    E. J. Matthews, Apr. 15,
    1869
  Eliza J., Feb. 4, 1892
  Elizabeth, d. of Anderson
    Matthews, Apr. 12, 1833
  Elizabeth, May 13, 1847
  Elizabeth, w. of Thomas
    Matthews, Nov. 4, 1847
  Emily Jane, d. of Andrew
    Matthews, Apr. 12, 1833
  Hattie D., d. of Daniel and
    Emily Matthews, Sept. 18,
    1862
  J. C., Nov. 23, 1933
  James N., July 15, 1926
  John, Oct. 13, 1853
  John J., s. of William
    Matthews, Sept. 25, 1851
  Lucy Littleberry, d. of John
    and Lucy B. D. Matthews,
    Oct. 25, 1839
  Margaret A., w. of Capt. David
    Matthews, Nov. 15, 1855
  Mary, d. of John Matthews,
    Sept. 1, 1842
  Mollie, d. of J. B. and E. J.
    Matthews, Apr. 15, 1869
  Nancy, d. of Andrew Matthews,
    Apr. 12, 1833
  Nancy (Mrs.), Oct. 12, 1876
  Philip (Elder), Sept. 6, 1839
  Rebecca (Mrs.), Mar. 26, 1830
  Rebecca Jane, Jan. 26, 1854
  Richard L. (Rev.), June 27,
    Oct. 17, 1935
  S. H., Apr. 23, 1857
  Sophia W., w. of Albert
    Matthews, Jan. 22, 1857
  Thomas P., Jan. 19, 1905
  W. P. (Dr.), s. of Dr. T. P.
    Matthews, Aug. 1, 1918
  William, Nov. 24, 1859
  William D., July 12, 1855
  William H. (Rev.), Nov. 24,
    1898
  William Thomas, s. of Andrew
    Matthews, Apr. 12, 1833
  Willie Marshall, s. of Dr.
    Thomas P. and Bettie B.
    Matthews, Feb. 27, 1862
MATTHIAS
  Joshua, Mar. 3, 1881
MATTOX
  Gladys May, Mar. 31, 1927

OBITUARY NOTICES IN THE RELIGIOUS HERALD WITH DATES OF PUBLICATION

MAULDIN
  B. O., Oct. 29, 1874
MAUPIN
  Addison, Apr. 18, 1872
  Catharine P., w. of Chapman W. Maupin, Oct. 11, 1855
  Eliza Ann, w. of Lilburn Maupin, July 14, 1837
  Eliza Jane, d. of Ira and Virginia Maupin, Sept. 18, 1862
  Lucy Taylor, w. of Addison Maupin, Sr., Aug. 16, 1894
  Mary S., w. of C. F. Maupin, Feb. 5, 1885
  William A. (Dr.), June 22, 1848
MAURING
  Henry (Elder), Apr. 27, 1838
MAURY
  Anne Herndon, w. of Commodore Matthew F. Maury, Feb. 21, 1901
  Sarah Ann, w. of Robert H. Maury, d. of Richard C. Wortham, Oct. 8, 1846
MAWYER
  Ada I. (Mrs.), Jan. 5, 1928
  Elizabeth M., w. of Hardin M. Mawyer, Apr. 20, 1899
MAXCY
  Bettie, d. of Sally M. Maxcy, Aug. 21, 1851
  Sally M. (Mrs.), Aug. 21, 1851
MAXEY
  A. T., Mar. 12, 1931
  Abner W. (Capt.), June 29, 1876*
  Abram B., Nov. 27, 1862
  Agnes, July 30, 1846
  Albert J., Jan. 24, 1884
  Alice Spencer, w. of Frank Maxey, July 27, 1916
  E. L., s. of Artaxerxes Maxey, Aug. 28, 1862
  Elizabeth, w. of Obediah Maxey, Oct. 8, 1840
  F. N., Jan. 14 and 21, 1904
  G. W., Jan. 22, 1891

  Harriet V., w. of Maj. Robert Maxey, Jan. 16, 1873
  J. C. (Mrs.), Dec. 5, 1901
  Maggie, Jan. 4, 1872
  Queen Victoria (Mrs.), Mar. 1, 1923
  R. W., Jan. 11, 1934
MAXWELL
  Elizabeth Harrison, w. of Capt John Maxwell, Oct. 24, 1872
  Sallie (Mrs.), Dec. 6, 1883
  Thomas Owen, s. of William W. and Lily Garrett Maxwell, Apr. 9, 1903
MAXY
  Mary A., w. of Capt. Abner Maxy, gr.d. of Rev. John Williams, Apr. 7, 1870*
MAY
  Anna A., Dec. 7, 1882
  Irving N. (Dr.), s. of Rev. I. N. and Jane Dickinson May, Sept. 25, 1902
  J. F. (Mrs.), May 17, 1917
  Lucy A., Nov. 1, 1860
  Philip Pendleton (Dr.), May 30, 1918
  Susie, d. of Dr. J. F. May, July 9, 1896
  Susie Johnson (Mrs.), May 10, 1917
MAYES
  Charles Henry, June 27, 1929
  Joseph G., Mar. 25, 1886
  Lucy A. (Mrs.), Feb. 7, 1895
  M. A. (Miss), Oct. 14, 1875
  Mary Ann Semantha, Feb. 7, 1856
  Susan (Mrs.), Sept. 13, 1928
  William J., s. of Joseph Mayes Mar. 30, 1843
MAYNARD
  Nathan (Mrs.), Dec. 20, 1934; Jan. 3, 1935
MAYNOR
  Peyton, June 4, 1863
MAYO
  Agnes P., Mar. 11, 1831
  Ann Maria, w. of Charles A.

* Possible inaccuracy in name, or spelling, but given as printed

OBITUARY NOTICES IN THE RELIGIOUS HERALD WITH DATES OF PUBLICATION

Mayo, d. of Thomas Howard,
  Apr. 30, 1863
Catharine, w. of Capt. William Mayo, Dec. 28, 1843
James S. (Mrs.), May 9,
  1912
Joseph, Nov. 21, 1828
Joseph Albert (Dr.), Aug. 30,
  1877
Kate Fitzhugh (Mrs.),
  Oct. 15, 1936
M. E. (Miss), Nov. 28,
  1907
M. Ella, Nov. 6, 1862
M. T. (Mrs.), May 15,
  1919
Martha S., w. of Dr.
  Joseph A. Mayo, Mar. 21,
  1850
Niel Campbell, s. of Col.
  R. M. Mayo, Dec. 13,
  1877
Robert Murphy, s. of Col.
  R. M. Mayo, Dec. 13,
  1877
MAYS
  Lillie, d. of William P.
    and Dora A. Mays,
    Jan. 22, 1863
  S. R., w. of Rev. J. F. B.
    Mays, June 12, 1873
MAYSE
  Sarah, w. of C. P. Mayse,
    Feb. 23, 1854
MAYTON
  Olivia S., w. of George R.
    Mayton, Feb. 20, 1879
MAYZE
  Thomas, June 25, 1857
MEADE
  w. of Rev. Meade, d. of
    Rev. Pike Powers,
    June 4, 1891
  Bettie, Mar. 22, 1906
  Charlotte Randolph,
    Dec. 30, 1915
  Mary Overton, w. of William
    E. Meade, Dec. 21, 1865
  N. B. (Judge), June 7, 1888
  W. E., s. of William Everard
    and Mary Stegar Meade,
    Feb. 11, 1915
MEADER
  Drucilla, w. of John
    Meader, Jan. 11, 1844
MEADOR
  Ann C., w. of C. C. Meador,
    d. of W. C. Shields,
    Mar. 8, 1900
  C. C. (Rev.), Apr. 14, 1898
  C. C. (Rev.), Nov. 17 and
    24, 1904
  Clara P., w. of E. R.
    Meador, d. of Rev. R.
    Pack, Sept. 21, 1876
  Dollie (Mrs.), May 13,
    1926
  John, July 23, 1863
  Leslie L., s. of Fannie A.
    and Amos W. Meador,
    Dec. 18, 1884
  R. James, Sept. 14, 1911
  R. L. (Mrs.), May 15,
    1919
  Rachel Elizabeth (Mrs.),
    Dec. 23, 1926
  Russell Earl, Apr. 10,
    1919
  Thomas Rucker, s. of Sylvester and Dora Meador,
    Dec. 28, 1911
MEADORS
  Mary A. E., w. of Rev.
    Joel Meadors, Nov. 11,
    1897
MEANLY
  Ann Maria (Mrs.), Mar. 2,
    1882
  Sarah Meredith, w. of William A. Meanly, Oct. 13,
    1887
MEARS
  John Henry, Jan. 13, 1916
  Mary Ann (Mrs.), Feb. 18,
    1886
MEDLEY
  Dandridge F., s. of James
    B. Medley, Oct. 24,
    1850
MEEKS

OBITUARY NOTICES IN THE RELIGIOUS HERALD WITH DATES OF PUBLICATION

Albert L., Feb. 20, 1879
Anna Ragland, d. of Albert
   L. and Hyacinth Meeks,
   July 17, 1862
MEENLEY
   Archibald Harrison, s.
      of John F. and Catherine
      W. Meenley, Mar. 28,
      1844
   Mary Ann, Jan. 18, 1839
   Napoleon C., s. of Samuel
      and Julia Ann Meenley,
      Sept. 1, 1837
MEGGINSON
   Ella, d. of Dr. B. C.
      Megginson, May 14, 1863
   Joseph A., s. of Dr. B.
      C. Megginson, Mar. 12,
      1863
MELONE
   William, Aug. 11, 1892
MELTON
   Elizabeth, Dec. 10, 1874
   Helen Hites, w. of J. W.
      Melton, gr.d. of Rev.
      William Y. Hites,
      Aug. 7, 1913
   John T. (Dr.), Mar. 31,
      1881
   John W., Dec. 10, 1877
   Laura Nelson, w. of Dr.
      Sparks W. Melton,
      Jan. 24 and 31, 1918
MELVILLE
   Henry (Rev.), Mar. 9,
      1871
MELVIN
   Margaret, w. of Josiah
      Melvin, Apr. 7, 1837
MERCER
   I. M. (Mrs.), Apr. 14,
      1892
   Sylvia, w. of Carver
      Mercer, Aug. 3, 1848
   Virginia, Aug. 8, 1850
MEREDITH
   Ann E. (Mrs.), Dec. 4,
      1835
   Ann S., w. of Maj. John
      Meredith, Feb. 20, 1835
   Emily Virginia, d. of
      Thomas E. Meredith,
      Aug. 7, 1873
   Josephine, Aug. 21, 1851
   Mittie Marion, d. of J.
      D. and Mittie R. Lewis
      Meredith, May 20,
      1858
   Samuel, Dec. 10, 1874
   Thomas, Nov. 9, 1843
   Thomas William, Aug. 9,
      1866
MERIWETHER
   W. D. (Mrs.), Jan. 30,
      1879
MERRETT
   Julia Ann, w. of E. D.
      Merrett, Feb. 9, 1854*
MERRILL
   E. A. (Mrs.), Apr. 20,
      1922
MERRIMAN
   Elizabeth E., w. of S.
      Merriman, Apr. 24,
      1862
MERRITT
   Catharine Eulalie, w. of
      R. D. Merritt, d. of
      Thomas G. Moorefield,
      Apr. 4, 1929
   Dellah Hazeltine, June 2,
      1921
   Mary C., d. of Elijah D.
      and Julia Merritt,
      May 8, 1851*
MERRIWETHER
   V. N., w. of Judge Merri-
      wether, d. of Mrs. Mary
      A. R. Shackelton, Jan. 28,
      1858
MERRY
   Bertha E., d. of O. F.
      and Rhoda E. Merry,
      Jan. 30, 1890
MERRYMAN
   C. G. (Rev.), July 12,
      1894
   Fanny B., w. of B. Merryman,
      Sept. 28, 1871
   Margaret (Mrs.), May 5,

* Possible inaccuracy in name, or spelling, but given as printed

OBITUARY NOTICES IN THE RELIGIOUS HERALD WITH DATES OF PUBLICATION

1853
MESMER
    Thomas J., Oct. 10, 1935
MESSER
    Asa (Rev.), Nov. 4, 1836
METCALF
    Ned, s. of Charlie and Alice Metcalf, Feb. 5, 1880
MEWBERN
    William, Mar. 13, 1829
MEYER
    F. B. (Rev.), Apr. 18, 1929
    Martha Louis, Jan. 8, 1863
MEYERS
    John O., Oct. 12, 1922
    William W., Apr. 23, 1885
MIARS
    Moses, Oct. 13, 1859
MICHAEL
    Charles Clinton, Nov. 29, 1923
MICHAELS
    Albert, Mar. 17, 1887
    Cordelia Clopton (Mrs.), Oct. 20, 1870
    M. V. (Mrs.), Nov. 21, 1918
    Thomas S. (Dr.), s. of A. Michaels, Feb. 25, 1886
MICHAUX
    Jacob (Maj.), Apr. 22, 1847
    Martha (Mrs.), Apr. 27, 1882
    Tscharnar, Apr. 27, 1882
MICHIE
    J. W. (Mrs.), June 29, 1933
    William (Capt.), Oct. 23, 1851
MICOU
    Ann O. L., d. of James Roy Micou, Jan. 16, 1840
    B. M., w. of Albert Micou, Jan. 2, 1845
    Ellen R., Mar. 23, 1871
    James Ray, Apr. 20, May 4, 1843
    John (Elder), Nov. 3, 1870
    Louisa, June 5, 1845
    Maria J. (Mrs.), Mar. 14, 1878
    Virginia Tayloe, May 1, 1851
    William A., s. of Elder John Micou, Jan. 26, 1871
    William D., s. of W. F. Micou, July 19, 1877
    William F., July 30, 1830
MIDDLETON
    Elizabeth A., Oct. 2, 1829
MILAM
    George P., Sept. 2, 1909
MILBOURNE
    L. R. (Rev.), Mar. 8, 1906
    Lizzie J., w. of Rev. L. R. Milbourne, Oct. 26, 1882
MILES
    Elizabeth, w. of John Miles, Nov. 3, 1853
    H. T. (Mrs.), Feb. 28, 1924
    Harriet C., w. of J. J. Miles, Sept. 12, 1872
    Hattie J., Apr. 6, 1876
    John Andrew, s. of A. Rutlege Miles, Jan. 6, 1876
    Lacy (Mrs.), Oct. 24, 1918
    William B., Apr. 19, July 5, 1866
MILLAM
    Benjamin R., May 8, 1845
MILLAN
    Mary Cooper, d. of Walker R. and Columbia Cooper Millan, July 13, 1933
MILLER
    Alexander (Rev.), May 24, 1923
    Alfred H., June 16, 1892
    Alfred Leslie, s. of Alfred H. and Rebecca F. Miller, July 20, 1871
    Alice S., d. of B. F. and Sarah E. Miller, Mar. 16,

OBITUARY NOTICES IN THE RELIGIOUS HERALD WITH DATES OF PUBLICATION

1916
Ann C., w. of Middleton Miller, May 15, 1845
Ann S. (Mrs.), Oct. 11, 1877
Archie S., Nov. 24, 1898
B. F., July 6, 1882
Bernice James (Mrs.), Oct. 6, 1938
Bertha, d. of Henry Adolph Miller, Aug. 23, 1888
David P., s. of Samuel T. Miller, Dec. 28, 1854
David P., May 20, 1880
Edward B., Feb. 3, 1853
Edward T., Dec. 7, 1876
Elizabeth, d. of John and Margaret Miller, Nov. 21, 1828
Elizabeth (Mrs.), Oct. 27, 1859
Fannie, Sept. 13, 1860
Fannie F., May 12, 1927
J. H. (Rev.), May 14, 1863
J. N. (Mrs.), Mar. 25, 1915
James, Mar. 13, 1884
James Cabell, s. of Alfred H. and Rebecca F. Miller, Nov. 26, 1868
Joanna, w. of Capt. William H. Miller, Mar. 29, 1839
John Dabney, Feb. 5, 1891
John Henry, Sept. 12, 1935
John T., s. of William H. and Ann E. Miller, Oct. 1, 1857
L. O., May 3, 1917
Laura Cabell, d. of William A. and Margaret A. Miller, Sept. 13, 1860
Lily N., d. of G. W. and M. T. Miller, Jan. 10, 1884
Louisa E., Oct. 8, 1885
Margaret Ann, w. of William A. Miller, Mar. 3 and 31, 1881
Martha J., w. of C. Miller, Sept. 25, 1879

Mary, d. of John and Margaret Miller, Nov. 21, 1828
Mary (Mrs.), Feb. 3, 1870
Mary B. (Mrs.), Jan. 11, 1883
Mary Hunt, w. of Thomas O. Miller, June 21, 1888
Mary Maffit, d. of Samuel T. Miller, Dec. 28, 1854
Mattie J., July 28, 1881
Rebecca J., w. of John B. Miller, d. of Cornelius Smith, Mar. 18, 1886
Robert R., Feb. 9, 1843
Samuel T., May 5, 1870
Sarah E., w. of B. F. Miller, Apr. 27, 1911
Sarah Elizabeth JOHNSON, w. of Daniel Miller, Aug. 2, 1888
Sarah P. (Mrs.), Sept. 12, 1850
T. A., May 29, 1924
Thomas, Nov. 13, 1845
Thomas Porter, May 11, 1893
William A., Jan. 3, 1924

MILLIKEN
Leonard Hugh (Rev.), s. of William and Mary Milliken, Mar. 13, 1884

MILLINGTON
Henry W. O. (Dr.), Mar. 24, 1938

MILLNER
Alice L. (Mrs.), Apr. 24, 1884

MILLS
Amanda, w. of R. S. Mills, d. of Bird L. Ferrill, May 14, 1868
Ann Eliza, d. of Nathaniel Mills, Apr. 1, 1836
Ann Eliza, w. of William H. Mills, d. of Capt. John Simpson, Nov. 18, 1841
Catharine (Mrs.), Jan. 25, 1877
Catharine V., d. of Nathaniel Mills, Nov. 21, 1844
Charles H., s. of Nathaniel Mills, Nov. 21, 1844

OBITUARY NOTICES IN THE RELIGIOUS HERALD WITH DATES OF PUBLICATION

George W., Sept. 1, 1859
Harriet C., w. of J. J. Mills, d. of John Pulliam, Oct. 3, 1872
John G. (Elder), Jan. 5, Feb. 23, Sept. 13, 1860
John H., Dec. 29, 1898
M. A., w. of N. H. Mills, Feb. 22, 1923
Minnie R. (Mrs.), Dec. 9, 1897
N., Apr. 7, 1859
Norman L., June 9, 1932
R. G., June 25, 1854
Robert Garland, s. of Mrs. Susanna D. Mills, Sept. 29, 1859
Robert S., s. of Rev. John G. Mills, Mar. 22, 1866
S. D. (Mrs.), Nov. 24, 1887

MILLY
William, Mar. 7, 1828

MILMAN
Henry Hart (Rev.), s. of Sir Francis Milman, Oct. 1, 1868

MILNER
William H. (Lt.), s. of Capt. John and Rebecca T. Milner, June 11, 1863

MILNOR
James (Rev.), May 8, 1845

MIMMS
Susan K. Dudley, w. of George W. Mimms, Sr., Dec. 7, 1882

MIMS
James S., s. of Samuel Mims, Aug. 6, 1868

MINNICK
Mattie, Dec. 28, 1922

MINOR
Albenia Brand, w. of C. C. Minor, d. of Capt. W. W. Brand, Aug. 10, 1916
Ann (Mrs.), Sept. 26, 1844
C., June 17, 1858
Diana, w. of Richard Minor, Mar. 15, 1833
E. C., Feb. 14, 1901
Elizabeth, w. of Capt. Vivian Minor, Apr. 16, 1846
Ella, Feb. 28, 1918
George A., Feb. 4, 1904
Henry Laurens, Sept. 21, 1832
Henry Wallace, s. of John M. and Sarah J. Minor, Nov. 10, 1853
John B., Aug. 1, 1895
John Thomas, s. of John W. and Frances A. Minor, Feb. 28, 1861
Lancelot B., s. of Gen. Minor, Oct. 12, 1843
Laura A., Sept. 8, 1921
Lucian, Aug. 12, 1858
Lucy (Mrs.), May 5, 1861
Lucy M., w. of William S. Minor, July 31, 1890
Martha R., w. of Elder Raymond Minor, June 4, 1846
Mary (Mrs.), June 21, 1850
Maud (Mrs.), d. of Lewis M. and Mary Ambler Coleman, Oct. 16, 1879
Sarah Jane, w. of John W. Minor, d. of Rev. Henry Mouring, Sept. 6, 1888
Thomas, Feb. 23, 1838
William, Apr. 10, 1829
William M., June 11, 1857
William S., July 10, 1884

MINSEN
John C., Oct. 30, 1862

MINSON
Elizabeth, w. of Edward Minson, Mar. 29, 1877

MINSTER
Jane D., Aug. 1, 1844

MINTER
Caroline E., w. of William J. Minter, Feb. 13, July 4, Aug. 15, 1861

OBITUARY NOTICES IN THE RELIGIOUS HERALD WITH DATES OF PUBLICATION

Jane (Mrs.), May 29, 1845
Jesse L., s. of Jesse
  Minter, Mar. 10, 1864
Ruth Pendleton, w. of Miles
  W. Minter, July 19,
  1888
MINTON
  Claud B. (Mrs.), Apr. 3,
    1919
  Claudius T., June 11, 1931
  Eliza W., w. of Dr. William
    Minton, Aug. 20, 1840
MIRICK
  S. H. (Rev.), Nov. 15,
    1883
MISKELL
  Ann Hasseltine, d. of
    William and Lucy Miskell
    Nov. 21, 1839
  George H., Oct. 6, 1853
MITCHELL
  A. R., July 21, 1904
  Ada Blake (Mrs.), June
    3, 1926
  Archelaus, Jr., Aug. 31,
    1838
  Bettie I., d. of O. T.
    Mitchell, Nov. 6, 1862
  Burden, Mar. 10, 1921
  Carter A., Aug. 2, 1855
  Charles M., Aug. 16, 1839
  Eliza H., Dec. 25, 1835
  Elizabeth O., w. of O. T.
    Mitchell, Sept. 4, 1856
  Fannie Carter (Mrs.), July
    12, 1906
  Hanora Jane, d. of C. C.
    and Margaret Mitchell,
    May 13, 1847
  J. D. (Mrs.), July 13, 1882
  J. R. (Mrs.), Sept. 25, 1902
  J. W. (Dr.), Nov. 23, Dec. 7,
    1933
  James W. (Mrs.), May 4, 1871
  John D., Aug. 19, 1858
  Lizzie May, d. of William
    A. and Fannie Mitchell,
    Mar. 27, 1873
  Lutie T., w. of William
    Tell Mitchell, Apr. 7, 1921

  M. E., w. of William E.
    Mitchell, July 14,
    1921
  Maggie Herndon, w. of R.
    Fairfax Mitchell, d. of
    Rev. Richard N. Herndon,
    Nov. 29, 1894
  Maggie Meador, w. of B. L.
    Mitchell, Apr. 5, 1906
  Mary E. (Mrs.), Mar. 3,
    1859
  Mary Virginia, w. of Rev.
    William W. Mitchell,
    Jan. 26, 1854
  Nancy E., Nov. 10, 1881
  O. T., Mar. 27, 1879
  Perry (Mrs.), w. of Rev.
    Perry Mitchell, Mar. 14,
    1918
  Richard Dennett, Dec. 27,
    1883
  Robert Bladen, Dec. 15,
    1842
  Virginia M., d. of O. T.
    and Elizabeth O. Mitchell,
    June 13, 1844
  W. B., Dec. 15, 1892
MITTER
  Augusta Rhoda, w. of Ferdi-
    nand Mitter, Dec. 9,
    1880
MOBLEY
  Nannie T., d. of Dr. Isaiah
    Mobley, Apr. 4, 1867
MODENA
  James William, s. of Benjamin
    J. and Bettie F. Modena,
    July 24, 1890
MOFFETT
  Anderson (Elder), Aug. 7,
    1873
  J. R. (Rev.), Dec. 1, 1892
  Lucinda M., w. of Horatio
    G. Moffett, Sept. 3, 1863
  Sarah C. (Mrs.), d. of Col.
    Thomas Pugh, June 2, 1859
  William D. (Capt.), July
    15, 1869
  William Walter (Mrs.), Aug.
    29, 1935

OBITUARY NOTICES IN THE RELIGIOUS HERALD WITH DATES OF PUBLICATION

MOFFITT
  John, Feb. 20, 1868
  Walter F., s. of Horatio
    G. Moffitt, Jan. 12,
    1865
MOFFITTE
  Mollie, d. of Horatio G.
    and Lucinda Moffitte,
    Mar. 5, 1863
MOHORN
  Mary E., d. of Thomas
    Mohorn, Nov. 23,
    1854
MONCURE
  Eustace (Mrs.), Oct. 18,
    1923
  Eustace Conway (Judge),
    July 21, 1921
  Fannie Irby (Mrs.), Aug.
    16, 1923
  Frances Daniel, w. of
    John Moncure, Sept. 28,
    1871
  Frances Daniel, d. of Rev.
    W. R. D. Moncure, Mar.
    3, 1910
  Harriet Eustace, d. of W.
    R. D. and M. C. Moncure,
    Jan. 27, 1887
  John (Rev.), Apr. 10,
    1930
  Ruby Richerson (Mrs.),
    May 12 and 19, 1898
  Sallie Hull, Jan. 3, 1929
  W. R. D. (Rev.), Nov. 8,
    1900; Dec. 25, 1905
  William A., Mar. 27, 1862
  William R., Apr. 25, 1883
MONDS
  George William Cecil, s.
    of Rev. R. S. Monds, Oct.
    17, 1918
MONROE
  Ida Tate (Mrs.), Apr. 18,
    1889
  James, former President,
    July 15, 1831
  Lucy, w. of former
    President Monroe,
    Oct. 1, 1830

MONTAGUE
  Andrew P. (Dr.), Dec. 13,
    1928
  Anna Lee, d. of Peter H.
    Montague, Feb. 1, 1866
  Catharine (Mrs.), Feb. 1,
    1844
  Cordelia Gay, w. of Robert
    L. Montague, d. of James
    C. Eubank, Feb. 12, 1885
  Elizabeth, Mar. 6, 1856
  Fannie, d. of R. C. Montague,
    Oct. 6, 1881
  Frank H., Aug. 17, 1905
  Henry B., Apr. 26, 1855
  Howard W. (Rev.), June
    22, July 6, 1876
  J. J. (Mrs.), Jan. 5, 1905
  Jane, w. of Lewis L. Montague,
    Aug. 30, 1860
  Jessie Carrington, d. of
    Dr. L. B. and Rosa Montague,
    Aug. 15, 1872
  John C. (Elder), Mar. 6,
    1851
  John E. (Rev.), May 26, 1887
  Judith, w. of William Montague,
    Dec. 1, 1853
  Lewis B., Aug. 20, 1868
  Lewis Latane, Oct. 23, 1873
  Mary, w. of William W.
    Montague, Sept. 5, 1834
  Mary A. B., w. of Capt.
    Thomas B. Montague, d.
    of Joseph Pollard, Dec.
    30, 1886
  Mary F., Apr. 4, 1878
  Mary Winston, d. of Hill
    Montague, July 27, 1899
  May Christian, w. of
    Andrew P. Montague,
    May 24, 1906
  Mildred Columbia (Mrs.), Feb.
    8, Dec. 19, 1901
  Nannie Steger, d. of Hill
    and Mary Winston Montague,
    July 27, 1899
  Philip (Elder), Mar. 18
    and 25, 1852
  Philip H. L., s. of Elder

OBITUARY NOTICES IN THE RELIGIOUS HERALD WITH DATES OF PUBLICATION

Philip Montague, Jan. 31, 1861
Philip T. (Elder), Aug. 13, 1846
Robert L. (Judge), Mar. 11, Apr. 22, 1880
Robert Lynch, Mar. 17, Jan. 28, 1932
Rosa Young, w. of Dr. L. B. Montague, d. of John W. and Mary A. Young, Apr. 3, 1890
Susan M. (Mrs.), Feb. 13, 1908
Susan M., w. of John N. Montague, Nov. 11, 1909

MONTEIRO
Edward H., July 26, 1866

MONTGOMERY
Aileen, d. of John T. and Eliza D. Montgomery, Aug. 31, 1876
Andrew I., s. of Andrew Montgomery, Dec. 26, 1834
Elizabeth W., w. of James Montgomery, Aug. 27, 1840
Elizabeth, d. of Robert H., Montgomery, Oct. 10, 1844
Frances L., Jan. 27, 1842
R. H., May 8, 1851
Sarah (Mrs.), Sept. 25, 1829
Thomas, May 16, 1828
William H., s. of Mrs. Lucy T. Montgomery, July 18, 1872

MOODY
Alonzo Dew (Mrs.), Oct. 6 and 20, 1921
Amey, w. of James Moody, Apr. 15, 1858
Ann P., w. of William M. Moody, Oct. 6, 1857
Jamison, Oct. 27, 1842
Phebe (Mrs.), Aug. 15, 1867
Polly (Mrs.), Dec. 14, 1843
Samuel J., s. of J. W. and Anna Moody, Apr. 6, 1882
Sarah Rebecca (Mrs.), Feb. 8, 1923
T. N. (Rev.), Jan. 3, 24, and 31, 1935
William, May 31, 1849
Willie, Apr. 26, 1883

MOOKLAR
Mary Sue, d. of Atwell T. and Fanny E. Mooklar, July 4, 1867

MOOMAW
J. Lucian, Apr. 2 and 16, 1914
Ruth Tillman, w. of O. D. Moomaw, July 13, 1933

MOON
Anna Maria, w. of Edward Moon, Aug. 25, 1870
Edward H., Feb. 17, 1853
Elizabeth (Mrs.), Dec. 10, 1891
Gilmer, s. of John S. Moon, Feb. 5, 1852
John D., Mar. 5, 1863
Lilly A., w. of Daniel P. Moon, Jan. 21, 1864
Lottie, Feb. 13, Apr. 3, 1913
Mary W., d. of Richard Moon, June 16, 1853
Nancy (Mrs.), Jan. 17, 1861
Olga, s. of J. N. and Alice Moon, Aug. 20, 1891

MOORE
Aceneth, w. of Rev. L. W. Moore, d. of Gen. Hunt, Feb. 25, 1886
Alese, d. of W. J. Moore, Dec. 1, 1927
Beulah (Mrs.), Jan. 30, 1919
David, Oct. 16, 1845
Eddie W., Mar. 10, 1881
Elizabeth (Mrs.), Jan. 16, 1868
Elizabeth Johnson, w. of Rev. William Moore, May 6, 1852
Ella Florence, d. of John A. and Emma Moore, Apr. 11, 1878
Elviro Jennings, d. of J.

OBITUARY NOTICES IN THE RELIGIOUS HERALD WITH DATES OF PUBLICATION

B. and C. M. Moore, Sept. 20, 1888
Emma Cobbs, w. of A. A. Moore, Sept. 17, 1903
Frances, w. of Robert Moore, Aug. 14, 1862
Frances B., May 23, 1844
Frank, s. of Dr. J. B. and V. A. Moore, Dec. 22, 1881
Frederick, May 6, 1847
Frederick W., Oct. 15 and 22, 1931
Geneva H. (Mrs.), Feb. 26, 1903
George L., s. of James Moore, Oct. 25, 1860
George Thomas, s. of William H. and M. L. Moore, June 19, 1890
Gertrude, d. of Dr. J. B. and Victoria A. Moore, Sept. 24, 1885
Harriet L., w. of John B. Moore, Sept. 14, 1876
Herbert Sydnor, s. of Dr. John W. and Sallie McLaughlin Moore, Dec. 27, 1877
J. W. (Mrs.), w. of Dr. J. W. Moore, d. of Rev. James T. and Ann Miller McLaughlin, Sept. 12, 1878
James, Feb. 9, 1882
Jennie, w. of John A. Moore, d. of C. W. Williamson, Sept. 21, 1871
Jennie, w. of C. W. Moore, Dec. 25, 1890
Jessie Hartwell, May 6, 1915
John Calvin, s. of Rev. Henry Moore, Mar. 21, June 6, 1929
John W. (Dr.), Dec. 27, 1877
John W. (Capt.), Jan. 29, 1891
John W., s. of Amos Moore, Jan. 30, 1913
Judith F., w. of Temple C. Moore, Mar. 1, 1839
Laura Fant, d. of James and Maria Moore, Mar. 20, 1862
Laura Virginia, Mar. 15, 1934
Lucie Eliza, w. of Dr. John W. Moore, Aug. 26, 1875
Martha A., w. of A. A. Moore, June 16, 1892
Martha Julia, d. of William Moore, Apr. 13, 1838
Mary, w. of James E. Moore, Dec. 25, 1890
Mary Frances, w. of E. E. Moore, Sept. 6, 1894
Mary M., w. of E. C. Moore, Oct. 12, 1843
Mary W., w. of Rev. William Moore, May 4, 1876
Neva, w. of Goodwin Moore, June 30, 1921
Octavia, w. of Elder L. W. Moore, Aug. 11, 1864
Rebecca (Mrs.), Feb. 25, 1841
Reuben (Capt.), Aug. 9, 1839
Richard H., Sept. 30, 1841
Rosalie R., Sept. 2, 1926
Sallie E., w. of Samuel Moore, Nov. 29, 1860
Sallie Elizabeth (Mrs.), May 23, 1935
Sarah, w. of Malachi Moore, July 3, 1835
Sarah Ann, w. of David Moore, Dec. 23, 1852
Sarah F., w. of Dr. J. E. Moore, Sept. 20, 1906
T. V. (Rev.), Aug. 24, 1871
Virgie, w. of E. B. Moore, Nov. 28, 1929
W. H., Sept. 8, 1910
W. W. (Dr.), June 17, 1926
Walter J., Mar. 24, 1904
William E. (Capt.), Apr. 14, 1837
William Jefferson, Dec. 3, 1931
William R., Mar. 12, 1925

MOORFIELD
Rebecca, July 27, 1854
Theodore, May 18, 1922

MOORMAN
Dora Olivia, Sept. 14, 1882

MORAN

OBITUARY NOTICES IN THE RELIGIOUS HERALD WITH DATES OF PUBLICATION

Emma Roberta Fox (Mrs.), Feb. 25, 1915
MORANDEAU
 Marie Antoinette (Mrs.), Aug. 29, 1828
MORCOCK
 William A., s. of Rev. William James and Julia F. Morcock, Feb. 1, 1872
 William J. (Rev.), July 31, Aug. 21, 1872
MORE
 David (Mrs.), w. of Rev. David More, May 8, 1884
MOREHEAD
 James W., Dec. 3, 1903
MOREN
 Mary E. (Mrs.), Mar. 6, 1930
 Maude Garnett, d. of J. F. and Bessie Moren, Jan. 25, 1923
MOREY
 Robert, July 19, 1923
MORFIT
 Harry, s. of Maj. Mason Morfit, Dec. 14, 1876
 Richard Gregory, s. of Mason and Lizzie Morfit, Aug. 5, 1873
MORGAN
 Adela Rutherford Coulter (Mrs), Aug. 5, 1926
 Alma Clay, Feb. 4, 1937
 B. W. (Mrs.), mother of Rev. John W. Morgan, Oct. 11, 1906
 Daniel S. (Dr.), Feb. 18, 1864
 Enoch, Aug. 6, Sept. 24, 1914
 J. W. (Mrs.), Aug. 12, 1926
 John Gilbert, s. of E. L. and Grace Morgan, Nov. 20, 1902
 L. J. (Mrs.), Jan. 22, 1914
 Meredith, Mar. 13, 1829
 Mollie A. (Mrs.), d. of Thomas B. Campbell, May 16, 1861

Rebecca, Mar. 15, 1855
Rosa Wingo (Mrs.), June 14, 1923
MORRIS
 Alexander M., Mar. 19, 1874
 Annie Tompkins, d. of B. M. and Bettie B. Morris, Apr. 9, 1863
 Bessie, d. of J. R. Morris, Jan. 28, 1886
 Bettie A., d. of Robert W. and Sallie Morris, Jan. 29, 1863
 C. M. (Mrs.), Jan. 13, 1927
 Caroline E., w. of Adolphus Morris, Feb. 19, 1857
 Carrie L., Aug. 28, 1884
 Charles, Sept. 22, 1842
 Charles M., Feb. 6, 1936
 Dabney (Capt.), July 5, 1833
 Edlow, Jan. 16, 1873
 Elizabeth, Nov. 26, 1885
 Fielding W. (Rev.), Mar. 31, 1881
 George W., July 10, 1862
 Georgia Lillie, w. of Rev. E. Bassett Morris, Aug. 15, 1895
 Hattie V., d. of Robert W. and Sallie Morris, Jan. 29, 1863
 Henry N., Oct. 11, 1855
 Herbert L. (Mrs.), Mar. 22, 1906
 Hester Harman, d. of Elder Thomas S. and Mary Ann Morris, Feb. 9, 1843
 J. S., Sept. 20, 1906
 James, Sept. 15, 1853
 James, Aug. 25, 1864
 Jesse T., Jr., Feb. 16, 1928
 Jesse Thompson, Mar. 1 and 8, 1894
 John, May 19, 1881
 John B., s. of Robert W. and Sallie Morris, Jan. 29, 1863
 John G., Apr. 22, 1886
 John M., Dec. 31, 1846
 John Minor, s. of John M. and Eugenia H. Morris, Dec. 24, 1874

-237-

OBITUARY NOTICES IN THE RELIGIOUS HERALD WITH DATES OF PUBLICATION

Juliet Summers, d. of George H. and R. M. Morris, Apr. 18, July 25, 1878
Marion, Sept. 26, 1889
Martha, Sept. 22, 1887
Mary A., Mar. 16, 1854
Mary B., w. of Samuel F. Morris, Dec. 17, 1885
Mary E., w. of R. N. Morris, Mar. 28, 1901
Mary Jane, d. of Elder Thomas S. and Mary Jane Morris, Aug. 17, 1843
Mary Taylor, w. of Alexander M. Morris, June 21, 1866
Poindexter Paterson, s. of Robert W. and Sarah E. Morris, Oct. 3, 1850
R. M., July 30, 1885
Richard C., s. of Elder Thomas S. and Mary Ann Morris, Feb. 9, 1843
Robert (Elder), Mar. 8, 1855
Robert E., s. of J. O. and Sallie A. Morris, June 16, 1887
Robert W., Sept. 10, 1868
Sallie W., d. of Hazlewood Morris, Sept. 19, 1878
Sarah, w. of John Morris, May 3, 1833
Sarah, w. of James M. Morris, Jan. 18, 1855
Sarah Anne, w. of Jonathan O. Morris, July 21, 1859*
Sarah Elizabeth, d. of Jesse T. and Elizabeth F. Morris, Dec. 1, 1859
Susan E. (Mrs.), June 30, 1887
T. R. (Mrs.), July 22, Aug. 19, 1920
Teresa Tilman, d. of O. C. Morris, Dec. 30, 1831
Thomas, May 21, 1863
Thomas Rowson (Rev.). Dec. 20, 1923
Thomas S. (Elder), Apr. 14, May 5, 1859
Vivian Gray, s. of E. P. and M. Addie Morris, Apr. 17, 1884
W. K., Mar. 31, Apr. 7, 1881
William H., Sept. 3, 1896
William R., Oct. 16, 1890
William W., Aug. 21, 1850
Woodson B., s. of Robert W. and Sallie Morris, Jan. 29, 1863
MORRISETT
Lavinia (Mrs.), Dec. 12, 1889
Nannie E. (Mrs.), July 12, 1866
W. J., Nov. 11, 1909*
MORRISON
Amanda, w. of John Morrison, Aug. 25, 1842
Mary (Mrs.), Apr. 4, 1844
Mildred, d. of Dr. Robert Morrison, July 20, 1832
Mildred, w. of Dr. Morrison, Sept. 27, 1833
Robert (Dr.), Nov. 13, 1829
Samuel D. (Dr.), Feb. 14, 1901
William J., Sept. 25, 1862
MORRISS
Elizabeth B., w. of Charles R. Morriss, Dec. 24, 1857
James Y., s. of Charles R. Morriss, May 28, 1857
Jonathan Olds, Apr. 18, 1895*
Marion McDonald, s. of William Lewis and Anna Morriss, Jan. 24, 1918
Mary L., w. of Dr. B. P. Morriss, Dec. 28, 1916
Mary Preston, d. of Dr. B. P. Morriss, May 7, 1931
William L., Feb. 3, 1876
MORRISSETT
Lily May, d. of Lawson and Mollie Morrissett, Sept. 24, 1891
W. J., July 17, 1884*
Walter P., May 22, 1884
MORROW
John, Nov. 14, 1834
Joseph E., Dec. 7, 1865
MORTIMER
M. Bowles, s. of T. E. and

OBITUARY NOTICES IN THE RELIGIOUS HERALD WITH DATES OF PUBLICATION

Virgie B. Mortimer, Aug. 2, 1906

MORTON
Ann (Mrs.), Apr. 10, 1829
George W., July 11, 1867
I. (Mrs.), Mar. 3, 1892
Laura, w. of George W. Morton, July 3, 1884
Lottie, d. of George W. and Laura Morton, July 3, 1884
William Wallace, s. of Jeremiah and Charlotte Washington Morton, Feb. 9, 1933

MOSBY
Arthur, Aug. 4, 1837
Benjamin, Mar. 8, 1849
Edward, Jan. 11, 1855
Eliza H. (Mrs.), Jan. 14, 1858
Jane P. (Mrs.), d. of Capt. Philip Woodson, June 12, 1835
Langston, Mar. 12, 1863
Lucy, w. of L. Mosby, Dec. 9, 1858
Lucy Ann, d. of Dr. Joseph Mosby, Dec. 3, 1840
Lucy Ann, w. of W. T. Mosby, d. of Garland Mallory, Nov. 24, 1853
Martha A., w. of Benjamin Mosby, Sept. 16, 1847
Mary Jane, d. of Dr. Joseph Mosby, Dec. 3, 1840
Overton A., Sept. 9, 1852
Robert, s. of Gen. Littlebury Mosby, Apr. 5, 1839
Samuel D., Nov. 11, 1841
William T., Aug. 7, 1873

MOSELEY
Anna B. (Mrs.), Feb. 26, 1914
E. J. (Mrs.), Mar. 3, 1910
Edward A., June 14, 1900
Edward H., Oct. 3, 1867
Eliza H., w. of Robert Moseley, June 21, 1860
Elizabeth F., w. of Alfred Moseley, Mar. 22, 1855
Emily, May 23, 1861
Hillary (Capt.), Oct. 30, 1835*
Hillery C., Aug. 4, 1870*
Isaac Alfred, Nov. 5, 1846
J. D. (Mrs.), Dec. 19, 1867
John M., s. of Dr. E. J. and Nannie Moseley, Mar. 20, 1873*
Lelia Davis, d. of John A. and Mary J. Moseley, July 24, 1845
Lelia J., w. of M. E. A. Moseley, d. of Benjamin A. Bailey, Jan. 21, 1886
Lewis Temple, s. of Dr. E. J. Moseley, Aug. 15, 1901*
M. J. (Mrs.), July 16, 1857
Mary Jane, w. of Josiah Moseley, Mar. 23, 1854
Matilda J., d. of L. and S. J. Moseley, Nov. 8, 1849
Octavia R., w. of Edward A. Moseley, Oct. 20, 1859
Rebecca A., w. of William R. Moseley, Mar. 29, 1861
Robert A., May 29, 1902
Sarah (Mrs.), Apr. 16, 1846
Susan A. (Mrs.), Sept. 24, 1914
William, June 1, 1838
William, May 23, 1861
William A., s. of W. G. and M. Moseley, Feb. 20, 1873
Willie G., child of R. E. Moseley, Feb. 21, 1867
Willie J., Sept. 8, 1864

MOSELY
Edward Julian (Dr.), May 1, 1924*
Robert E., May 1, 1884
Temple, s. of Dr. E. J. Mosely, July 4, 1901*
William O., Jr. (Dr.), Aug. 28, 1879

MOSES
Annie Leonora, d. of Robert Moses, Apr. 1, 1886
C. Reed, Aug. 7, 1902
Charles A. (Rev.), June 5, 1924

* Possible inaccuracy in name, or spelling, but given as printed

OBITUARY NOTICES IN THE RELIGIOUS HERALD WITH DATES OF PUBLICATION

Kate S. (Mrs.), d. of Capt. Jeremiah W. and Kathleen Spiller Boxley Graves, Dec. 24, 1914
N. A. (Dr.), Mar. 12, 1891
R. A. (Mrs.), w. of Robert A. Moses, Apr. 25, 1918
W. W., Jr. (Mrs.), Mar. 8, 1923

MOSHENECK
Beulah Clements (Mrs.), July 15, 1937

MOSLEY
Lucy, w. of Green Mosley, Apr. 1, 1841
Nannie J., w. of W. H. Mosley, July 19, 1888

MOSLY
Mary (Mrs.), Jan. 22, 1836

MOSS
C. R. (Rev.), July 24, 1902
Catherine, w. of William Moss, May 31, 1894
Ella Gertrude, Aug. 28, 1884
Frances, d. of A. H. Moss, gr.d. of Rev. J. M. Perry, Feb. 3, 1910
G. W., Aug. 31, 1876
J. Calvin, June 10, 1937
Nellie C., Mar. 19, 1925
Richard Toler, May 22, 1924
Rosa, Oct. 14 and 28, 1909
Sarah, w. of Joshua Moss, Jan. 14, 1841
Townsend McVeigh, s. of William V. and Blanche Moss, May 30, 1872
Tyree Garland, gr. child of Mrs. P. E. Burton, Oct. 19, 1871

MOTHERSHEAD
Carra, child of J. K. and M. L. Mothershead, gr. child of P. F. Archer, Jan. 27, 1876
John D., s. of Samuel D. and Mary F. Mothershead, May 24, 1860
Martha L. (Mrs.), d. of Peter F. and Caroline E. Archer, Jan. 18, 1877

MOTLEY
Adalaide B. (Mrs.), July 24, 1873
Alice, Sept. 15, 1921
Allie Lewis, Dec. 4, 1924
Ann (Mrs.), Feb. 14, 1850
Annie Alston, w. of Rev. R. L. Motley, May 13, 1920
Bettie Floyd, w. of George C. Motley, d. of Capt. James M. Williams, Mar. 22 and 29, 1877
Charles H., Dec. 2, 1920
Edmund S., Apr. 20, 1871
F. W., May 14, 1931
J. L. (Dr.), Feb. 1, 1894
J. Richard, Aug. 23, 1900
John G., Aug. 3, 1922
Laura Wirt, d. of Thomas and Lizzie Motley, June 18, 1896
Lucinda (Mrs.), Mar. 14, 1878
Lucy G., w. of Nathaniel Motley, July 19, 1849
Maria, w. of John L. Motley, July 9, 1908
Martha Adeline Gray, Nov. 4, 1880
Nathaniel, Mar. 21, 1867
Ora Lee, d. of Thomas Motley, Aug. 8, 1889
Pattie W., d. of John W. Motley, Oct. 22, 1868
Sue Mountcastle (Mrs.), Dec. 20, 1923; Jan. 3, 1924
Thomas Rabley, s. of Thomas Motley, Aug. 8, 1889

MOTTLEY
Mittie J., w. of J. H. Mottley, June 30, 1859

MOUNTCASTLE
Ann E., w. of John E. Mountcastle, Sept. 25, 1862
Richard Henry, s. of Richard

OBITUARY NOTICES IN THE RELIGIOUS HERALD WITH DATES OF PUBLICATION

T. and Melvina Mountcastle, Sept. 21, 1843
MOURING
  Henry Allen, s. of William T. and Susan T. Mouring, Nov. 10, 1833
  Lizzie, d. of William C. and Sue Mouring, Jan. 9, 1873
  Settie Morrow Davis, w. of T. R. Mouring, Dec. 29, 1904
MOXLEY
  Mary Jane, d. of John A. and Mary Moxley, Oct. 26, 1838
MUIRE
  Lucy B. (Mrs.), d. of A. Pointer, Feb. 25, 1864
MULLEN
  Edgar Young (Rev.), Nov. 29, Dec. 6 and 12, 1928
  George, Mar. 16, 1893
  John Henry, May 22, 1930
  Mary, w. of Charles Mullen, Mar. 11, 1858
MULLINS
  John W. (Lt.), Aug. 25, 1864
  S. G. (Mrs.), w. of Rev. S. G. Mullins, Jan. 28, 1915
MUMFORD
  W. J. (Mrs.), Nov. 22, 1923
MUNDAY
  Ann Elizabeth, w. of Burrus Munday, Feb. 15, 1872*
  Euphemia Marion, d. of Harrison and Elizabeth S. Munday, Sept. 24, 1840
  Harriet L., w. of Burruss Munday, Jr., May 14, 1857*
  Thomas W., Aug. 31, 1848
MUNDEN
  Eliva, w. of Noah Munden, Aug. 30, 1877
  James Paul, s. of John, Jr., and Louise W. Munden, Aug. 25, 1887
  John Harrison, May 19, 1892
  Mary F., w. of John H. Munden, Apr. 5, 1888
  Nathan M. (Rev.), Jan. 28, 1904
MUNDIE
  Fannie B., Mar. 1, 1906
MUNDIN
  Lydia A. (Mrs.), July 9, 1857
  Martha (Mrs.), Aug. 14, 1829
MUNDY
  A. (Capt.), Sept. 3, 1868
  Eliza B., w. of John D. Mundy, d. of H. H. Norris, May 24, 1888
  James A. (Mrs.), w. of Dr. James A. Mundy, d. of Rev. T. N. and Catherine Johnson, Aug. 7, 1913
  James Alexander (Rev.), June 23, July 7, 1910
MUNFORD
  Eliza A., w. of John D. Munford, May 8, 1851
  Robert (Dr.), Jan. 25, 1844
MUNGER
  Lewis (Rev.), May 29, 1879
MUNROE
  Margaret (Mrs.), Feb. 3, 1870
MUNSEY
  H. N., Mar. 20, 1902
MURCHIE
  John, Mar. 25, 1831
MURDEN
  Emily F., Aug. 12, 1897
  John (Mrs.), June 14, 1888
MURDOCH
  J. R. (Rev.), Feb. 1, 1906
  William M., Aug. 1, 1907
MURFEE
  Joseph Addison, Aug. 5, 1869
  Lydia, w. of Rev. Simon Murfee, Mar. 24, 1859
  Martha S., w. of J. T. Murfee, Apr. 30, 1857
  Ruth Robinson, d. of Edwin F. and Josephine E. Murfee, Feb. 7, 1856
MURFY
  Steven, Oct. 6, 1837
MURKLAND

* Possible inaccuracy in name, or spelling, but given as printed

OBITUARY NOTICES IN THE RELIGIOUS HERALD WITH DATES OF PUBLICATION

John McGregor, s. of S. R. Murkland, Aug. 23, 1888
MURPHY
  s. of Cornelius Murphy Oct. 16, 1845
  Cornelius, Oct. 16, 1845
  Letitia Walker (Mrs.), d. of William and Adaline Meredith, Jan. 19, 1882
MURRAY
  Alice Carr, d. of R. P. and Mary E. Murray, 1890
  Gordon P. (Mrs.), July 31, 1924
  James D., s. of R. P. Murray, Feb. 12, 1891
  Jane Thomas, w. of John Murray, Mar. 28, 1907
  John W. (Lt.), Sept. 10, 1863
  Junius F., s. of Reuben B. Murray, Jan. 29, 1852
  Olivia (Mrs.), May 21, 1846
  P. H. (Mrs.), w. of Rev. P. H. Murray, d. of William and Eliza Graves, Feb. 2, 1911
  Reuben, June 19, 1845
  Reuben B., Nov. 20, 1851
  Robert P., Oct. 3, 1889
  Susan Jane, Sept. 6, 1849
  Virginia H. (Mrs.), June 28, 1923
  William B., Sept. 1, 1859
  William J., Apr. 27, 1882
MURRELL
  Elizabeth A., d. of Robert and Rebecca Murrell, Aug. 12, 1858
  Emma Lou, w. of Jesse Murrell, Sept. 22, 1904
  Frances (Mrs.), Jan. 25, 1872
  John D., father of Dr. Thomas Murrell, Aug. 8, 1918
  Lillian Thomas, w. of Charles C. Murrell, d. of George Thomas, July 25, 1901
  Nancy, Nov. 1, 1855
  Rebecca J., d. of Robert Murrell, Aug. 12, 1858
MUSE
  Ann (Mrs.), May 18, 1882
  E. E. (Mrs.), Nov. 12, 1896
  J. J., Mar. 17, 1898
  James Archer, Feb. 17, 1921
  Mary W. (Mrs.), July 23, 1883
MUSGRAVE
  Carrie Lucille, d. of R. N. and Hattie S. Musgrave, Dec. 19, 1889
MUSSON
  J. A. (Rev.), Nov. 7, 1895
MUSTAIN
  Joel, May 13, 1875
  Martha (Mrs.), Dec. 10, 1891
MUSTOE
  A., Aug. 11, 1910
  Bettie Toney, w. of J. D. Mustoe, July 29, 1897
  J. D., Nov. 1, 1928
  Michael, Dec. 10, 1885
MYERS
  Amanda H., May 6, 1875
  Ardilsey, w. of Charles S. Myers, June 16, 1853
  David William R., Feb. 13, 1829
  Elizabeth (Mrs.), Jan. 16, 1829
  Frances Ann, d. of George and Lucy Ann Myers, Jan. 11, 1828
  Harry G., Oct. 31, 1935
  John Henry, s. of Chesley A. and Louisa R. Myers, Apr. 25, 1861
  John O. (Mrs.), May 7, 1914
  Lucy Ann HYDE (Mrs.), Aug. 27, 1874
  Sallie Lou, d. of John O. and Laura Myers, Nov. 7, 1901
  Samuel, Jr., Feb. 6, 1829
  Sarah J. (Mrs.), June 5, 1884
  William F., May 16, 1828
MYLNE
  William (Elder), May 5 and 12, 1864
MYRICK
  R. M. (Mrs.), June 20, 1878
  Walter, Apr. 27, 1871

N

NALLE
  Carrie Harris, w. of Dr. Orville Nalle, Oct. 28, 1909
  Elizabeth, w. of Martin Nalle, May 15, 1856
  John T., Dec. 19, 1912
  Martin, Feb. 29, 1844

NALLS
  Benjamin W., Feb. 4, 1909
  William M., Dec. 25, 1856

NANCE
  Julia Ann, d. of Z. Nance, Nov. 26, 1846
  Mary Toloula, w. of Capt. J. L. Nance, Oct. 5, 1893

NANNY
  Drury, Jan. 10, 1856

NASH
  David, Aug. 5, 1847
  Dewitt H., s. of James L. and Sarah A. Nash, Feb. 9, 1899
  Illinois (Mrs.), Jan. 27, 1921
  Joseph W., Sept. 24, 1846
  Myrtle O., d. of W. F. and M. J. Nash, Nov. 13, 1884
  Robert H., Mar. 8, 1849
  Sarah (Mrs.), Sept. 4, 1879
  Sarah A., w. of James L. Nash, May 3, 1883

NAYLOR
  Ella, w. of Rev. N. C. Naylor, Aug. 26, 1875

NEAL
  Dolly, w. of John M. Neal, Oct. 26, 1882
  Elizabeth E., Feb. 24, 1848
  Garnett, July 8, 1920
  Lucy, w. of Elder John Neal, June 9, 1842
  P. H., Jan. 11, 1883
  W. H. (Mrs.), June 3, 1915
  Willie Bernard, s. of W. A. and L. M. Neal, Apr. 24, 1884

  Zachariah (Elder), Jan. 17, 1850

NEALE
  C. C., Dec. 15, 1932
  Catharine (Mrs.), Oct. 18, 1894
  John (Elder), Feb. 25, 1847
  R. H. (Rev.), Oct. 2, 1879
  William, Apr. 10, 1829

NEATHRY
  Richard L., Oct. 8, 1863

NEAVES
  Hadrian A., Sept. 15, 1904*
  J. W., June 9, 1932
  Mary A., w. of Hadrian A. Neaves, d. of Dr. John M. Baugh, July 7, 1910*

NEEDHAM
  George C. (Rev.), Feb. 20, 1902
  William E. (Mrs.), w. of Rev. William E. Needham, Apr. 23 and 30, 1885

NEESE
  Mary Ann, w. of George Neese, June 19, 1835

NEISTER
  Catherine Elizabeth (Mrs.), Mar. 21, 1889
  Gillis, June 24, 1886
  Mattie Virginia, June 12, 1919

NELMES
  James Edward, July 26, 1906
  Margaret E. B., d. of M. C. and Martha E. H. Nelmes, Nov. 8, 1877

NELMS
  Ada G., w. of James E. Nelms, Mar. 3, 1881
  Byard, s. of Col. E. Nelms, Jan. 11, 1855
  C. F. (Mrs.), Oct. 4, 1888
  Catharine, w. of Edwin Nelms, Dec. 6, 1849

---

* Possible inaccuracy in name, or spelling, but given as printed

OBITUARY NOTICES IN THE RELIGIOUS HERALD WITH DATES OF PUBLICATION

E. (Col.), Feb. 7, 1867
Edward, s. of J. E. and
  V. C. Nelms, Aug. 30,
  1888
Edwin (Col.), Apr. 2, 1863
Elizabeth D., d. of Col.
  E. Nelms, Aug. 29, 1867
NELSON
  A. Ruggles, Dec. 17, 1914;
    Jan. 14, 1915
  Addie Bailey, d. of James
    R. and Martha A. Nelson,
    July 11, 1861
  Anderson H. (Mrs.), Apr. 29,
    1926
  Elizabeth, d. of Col.
    William Nelson, Apr. 1,
    1836
  Elizabeth, w. of J. Nelson,
    Aug. 11, 1853
  Elizabeth Ann, w. of Richard
    Lewis Nelson, Apr. 25, 1889
  Fanny (Mrs.), Dec. 27, 1877
  Frances A. (Mrs.), d. of
    Henry Lawrence, Sept. 19,
    1828
  James, Mar. 23, 1854
  John F., Sr., Dec. 30, 1909
  John James, s. of James R.
    and Martha Ann Nelson, Feb.
    1, 1855
  Juliette Luttrell (Mrs.),
    June 16, 1938
  Kinloch (Rev.), Nov. 1,
    1894
  Lewis Edward, s. of Richard L.
    and Elizabeth A. Nelson,
    Dec. 31, 1863
  Lucy, w. of Gen. Thomas Nelson,
    Oct. 1, 1830
  Martha O., Dec. 25, 1835
  Mary (Mrs.), Dec. 6, 1866
  Mary M. (Mrs.), Aug. 16,
    1839
  Mary Moncure (Mrs.), Aug. 23,
    1882
  Nyra Garner, w. of W. R. Nelsen,
    Jan. 11, 1923
  Peter C., Nov. 25, 1852
  Phebe C., w. of John L. Nelson,
    Feb. 3, 1832
  Rachel (Mrs.), Aug. 17,
    1843
  S. A. (Mrs.), July 14,
    1938
  Tabitha, w. of Thomas Nelson, Feb. 11, 1864
  Thomas, s. of Joseph Nelson,
    Feb. 12, 1857
  Thomas Hugh, s. of James
    Nelson, Sept. 2, 1836
  W. P., s. of James Nelson,
    Jan. 20, 1837
  W. R., Jan. 28, 1932
  William Carey, s. of John
    L. Nelson, Dec. 5, 1878
  William F. (Rev.), Apr.
    29, 1875
  Wilson Carey, Oct. 7, 1841
NESBIT
  E. M., Jan. 9 and 23, 1913*
NESBITT
  Francis Robertson, s. of E.
    M. and H. E. Nesbitt,
    Dec. 17, 1891*
NETTLES
  Genevieve, d. of Mollie E.
    and Rev. T. J. Nettles,
    Nov. 30, 1893
  Thomas Jefferson (Mrs.),
    June 2, 1921
NEVES
  Alice W., d. of Hadrian A.
    and Mary A. Neves, Nov.
    3, 1881*
NEVIL
  Mary (Mrs.), Apr. 9, 1863
NEVINS
  William (Rev.), Oct. 30,
    1835
NEW
  Ann Maria, d. of William D.
    and Elizabeth M. New, Feb.
    8, 1855
  George R., Nov. 17, 1837
  James Blakey, s. of L. B.
    and L. A. New, Jan. 5,
    1843
  John D., Feb. 2, 1905
  John Frank, s. of James F.

* Possible inaccuracy in name, or spelling, but given as printed

OBITUARY NOTICES IN THE RELIGIOUS HERALD WITH DATES OF PUBLICATION

and Margaret J. New, Nov. 15, 1855
Louisa M. (Mrs.), Sept. 14, 1876
Sarah Frances, d. of L. B. and L. A. New, Jan. 5, 1843
NEWBELL
R. A. (Dr.), July 20, 1876
NEWBILL
Ella, w. of Logan Newbill, Oct. 14, 1875
Fannie Taylor, Aug. 8, 1829
Hetty, w. of William Newbill, Oct. 3, 1844
J. H. (Mrs.), w. of Rev. J. H. Newbill, Jan. 29, 1914
John, Sept. 18, 1879
John Horace (Rev.), s. of John Armstead and Eliza Holland Newbill, Oct. 14, 1915
NEWBY
Elizabeth, w. of William P. Newby, Apr. 8, 1847
Robert C., Nov. 13, 1884; Jan. 29, 1885
NEWCOMB
Mabel Eubank, Mar. 31, 1938
NEWCOMER
Fannie R. (Mrs.), Apr. 22, 1886
NEWELL
Thornton, Dec. 22, 1842
NEWMAN
Eleanor Harris, July 12, 1928
G. R. J. (Mrs.), w. of G. R. J. Newman, May 12, 1921
George Reedy, s. of S. M. and M. Lee Newman, Mar. 18, 1875
Irvin (Lt.), May 12, 1921
John R., Dec. 15, 1892
Martha O., w. of Thomas Newman, Nov. 24, 1842
Pattie W. (Mrs.), Sept. 27, 1894
Reuben, Aug. 13, 1874
T. W. (Rev.), Dec. 24, 1903

NEWTON
James K. M., Dec. 21, 1899
John (Rev.), Sept. 19 and 26, 1828
John, Sept. 16, 1875
John B., June 3, 1897
John Milton, Sr., Mar. 14, 1935
Rebecca Susan, d. of John J. and Rebecca Newton, July 11, 1850
Sally (Mrs.), June 6, 1828
Thomas W., May 21, 1863
Virginius, June 2, 1904
NIBLETT
Eugene, s. of Williamson and Mollie J. Niblett, Nov. 4, 1880
NICELY
Hortense, d. of Archie Nicely, Dec. 9, 1909
NICHOLAS
Aria C. (Mrs.), Mar. 17, 1892
Frances, w. of Lewis Nicholas, Jan. 2, 1829
Henrietta Josephine, w. of I. M. Nicholas, Jan. 18, 1877
Henry L. (Rev.), Nov. 6 and 27, 1924
John Mason, s. of John H. and Mary M. Nicholas, Nov. 17, 1853
Lewis, Jan. 30, 1840
Mary M., w. of John H. Nicholas, June 16, 1881
Selina (Mrs.), May 11, 1922
Wilson Cary, s. of W. C. Nicholas, Aug. 29, 1828
NICHOLLS
George Bedloe, Dec. 22, 1938
Horace Dwight, s. of J. W. Nicholls, July 7, 1910
NICHOLS
Giles Young, Feb. 21, 1878
J. U., May 19, 1938
James H., Feb. 7, 1856
James R., June 8, 1882

OBITUARY NOTICES IN THE RELIGIOUS HERALD WITH DATES OF PUBLICATION

Lucy M., Apr. 1, 1858
Mary V., d. of G. R. and
  N. V. Nichols, July 5,
  1894
P. P. (Mrs.), Oct. 30, 1919
Willie L., s. of G. T.
  and J. L. Nichols, Mar. 5,
  1863
NICKOLS
  Alexander W., s. of Giles
    Y. and Jennie L. Nickols,
    July 14, 1859
NICKOLSON
  Ann, w. of Stith Nickolson,
    Nov. 5, 1857
NICOL
  C. E., w. of Judge C. E.
    Nicol, Jan. 23, 1902
  Charles Edgar, Nov. 6,
    1924
NOEL
  Albert Lowry, s. of Cornelius
    Noel, Aug. 25, 1864
  Alice, d. of Susan Noel,
    Oct. 23, 1856
  America E. (Mrs.), Oct. 12,
    1876
  Elizabeth F., w. of Edmond
    F. Noel, Feb. 7, 1867
  Ellen C., w. of J. R. Noel,
    d. of Mrs. Eliza P.
    Henning, Nov. 28, 1867
  G. C. (Mrs.), Feb. 7, 1935
  John, Sept. 15, 1853
  John E. (Capt.), May 11,
    1899
  Joseph, s. of Susan Noel,
    Oct. 23, 1856
  Lizzie F., w. of J. R. Noel,
    Jan. 8, 1863
  Lucinda H., Sept. 11, 1851
  Lucy L., Oct. 16, 1851
  Martha (Mrs.), Oct. 23, 1856
  Samuel F., s. of Mrs. Martha
    Noel, Oct. 23, 1856
  Silas M. (Elder), May 24,
    1839
NOELL
  Henry, July 22, 1847
  John C., Jan. 22, 1863

Lula Collins (Mrs.), Feb.
  14, 1935
Melvin B., s. of Marquis L.
  Noell, Oct. 15, 1863
Nancy (Mrs.), Apr. 22, 1875
Sarah A. (Mrs.), Dec. 14,
  1905
NOFFSINGER
  Hettie M., Apr. 16, 1908
  Margaret Elizabeth, d. of
    H. G. Noffsinger, Aug. 3,
    1935
NOFTSINGER
  Catherine M., w. of W. A.
    Noftsinger, June 18, 1914
  Emma, d. of William Noftsinger,
    Feb. 13, 1936
  William A., Feb. 27, 1913
NOISWORTHY
  Mahlon E., May 4, 1876
NOLAND
  Alice R., d. of Maj. George
    W. Noland, May 3, 1923
  George W. (Maj.), Aug. 3,
    1893
  Ruth H., w. of George W.
    Noland, d. of Stacy and
    Ruth Taylor, Dec. 8, 1904
  T. W. T., Apr. 30, 1925
NOLTING
  Linda J., d. of Harrison
    and Alberta Nolting, Apr. 2,
    1896
NORFLEET
  Bulah M., d. of M. L. Nor-
    fleet, Jan. 5, 1882
NORMAN
  Frances (Mrs.), Aug. 20,
    1868
NORMANT
  Charlotte, w. of Richard
    Normant, Oct. 10, 1850
NORMENT
  Catharine (Mrs.), May 3,
    1833
  Edgar M., s. of Richard H.
    Norment, July 24, 1851
  Emily (Mrs.), Dec. 9, 1836
  Mildred C., May 31, 1855
  Nola Bernice, d. of E. L.

OBITUARY NOTICES IN THE RELIGIOUS HERALD WITH DATES OF PUBLICATION

and Florence O. Norment, Sept. 1, 1892
Phillips Rennolds, May 3, 1906
Willie Mercer, d. of D. R. Norment, Aug. 16, 1883

NORRIS
Calvin Roah (Rev.), June 25, 1914
Elizabeth, w. of Rev. G. S. Norris, July 4, 1861
Eppa, Mar. 16, 1843
H. H., May 2, 1895
Henry H., s. of H. H. and L. A. Norris, May 21, 1863
James, Feb. 14, 1834
Johnson, s. of Henry H. and Lucy A. Norris, Aug. 12, 1858
Louisa Virginia, w. of Robert R. Norris, Apr. 12, 1917
Lucie, d. of Henry H. Norris, July 14, 1859
Lucy A. (Mrs.), d. of Belfield C. Johnson, Apr. 4, 1912
Mary H., d. of H. H. and L. A. Norris, May 14, 1863
Nellie Hunton, d. of E. T. Norris, Mar. 26, 1891
Nettie (Mrs.), Mar. 15, 1923
Rebecca, Oct. 25, 1906
Rufus D., Sept. 19, 1918

NORRISS
George (Elder), Feb. 1, 1844

NORTH
Charles P., Nov. 7, 1889
Elizabeth J., w. of Anthony A. North, Sept. 30, 1841
John, July 14, 1853
Mary Frances, d. of Anthony A. and Elizabeth J. North, Jan. 27, 1842
Nancy C., w. of Richard P. North, July 26, 1839
William P., Dec. 8, 1837

NORTHAM
Annie Watson, June 16, 1892
Deborah, d. of Elder George Northam, June 25, 1846
Elizabeth, w. of Elder George H. Northam, Sept. 25, 1856
George (Elder), Dec. 21, 1854
George (Rev.), s. of Maj. Northam, Feb. 21, 1856
George H., s. of Elder G. H. Northam, Oct. 30, 1856
Henry, Dec. 23, 1831
Nancy, w. of Rev. George Northam, Jan. 26, 1854
Susie, d. of Henry C. and Susan Northam, Jan. 18, 1872
Virginia B., d. of Elder George Northam, Feb. 24, 1853

NORTHCROSS
Rebecca (Mrs.), June 1, 1871

NORTHEN
Mary F., Feb. 6, 1902
Richard G., Dec. 12, 1839

NORTHERN
Alonzo, July 16, 1925
Mary Catherine, June 2, 1859
Richard L., s. of William S. Northern, Nov. 26, 1868

NORTON
Elizabeth D., w. of Jabez Norton, Feb. 21, 1878
George W., July 25, 1889
George W., Jr., Jan. 15, 1925
Nannie M. (Mrs.), Dec. 9, 1920

NORVELL
F. G. (Mrs.), June 25, 1874
Lola Thornhill, d. of Thomas B., Oct. 28, 1886
Woodson (Mrs.), Dec. 23, 1875

NORWOOD
Sarah (Mrs.), Aug. 11, 1859
William, June 22, 1922

NOTTINGHAM
Cora, Aug. 13, Sept. 3, 1925

OBITUARY NOTICES IN THE RELIGIOUS HERALD WITH DATES OF PUBLICATION

John E., Aug. 17 and 31, 1916
Lilly, d. of Mrs. V. G. Nottingham, Nov. 30, 1871
Malinda, w. of John E. Nottingham, Dec. 29, 1881
Malinda Rose Fisher, d. of John E. Nottingham, Jan. 18, 1883
Mary, w. of Thomas J. Nottingham, Aug. 19, 1886
Mary W. (Mrs.), Dec. 1, 1932
Pollie (Mrs.), Nov. 24, 1859
S. J. (Mrs.), Aug. 26, 1858
Thomas J., Sr., May 8, 1890; Sept. 24, 1891
Thomas W., Aug. 12, 1880
Virginia Face, w. of John A. Nottingham, Feb. 16, 1893

NOWLAN
David William (Rev.), Nov. 30, 1865

NOWLIN
Andrew J., Aug. 19, 1920
Belinda R. (Mrs.), Feb. 24, 1848
Beulah, d. of Casper W. and Loretta Nowlin, Mar. 13, 1873
Bryant (Capt.), May 24, 1860
Joseph Bryan, s. of Samuel and Frances P. Nowlin, May 29, 1856
Samuel, Feb. 12, 1863
Thomas A., s. of B. W. Nowlin, Jan. 15, 1852

NUCHOLS
Ella, July 27, 1922

NUCKOLLS
Amanda M., d. of Leyton Nuckolls, July 27, 1854
Caroline M., w. of Mordecai Nuckolls, July 13, 1848
Charles, Apr. 21, 1859
Edmond, Mar. 12, 1863
Edmond B., June 11, 1857
James D., Apr. 20, 1871
John N., Sept. 25, 1862
Leighton, May 2, 1872
Martha Ann (Mrs.), d. of James D. Nuckolls, Apr. 20, 1871
Martha S., w. of William Nuckolls, Oct. 3, 1861
Mordecai J., Aug. 31, 1848

NUCKOLS
Ann Olivia, d. of William H. Nuckols, Feb. 16, 1854
Annie, Jan. 23, 1868
B., July 15, 1858
Graham English, s. of Abner C. and Mattie C. Nuckols, Feb. 9, 1899
James, s. of Rev. Harding D. Nuckols, Mar. 28, 1907
Judith, w. of Lewis Nuckols, Dec. 14 and 28, 1848
Lewis, Nov. 11, 1847
Louisiana, w. of Nathaniel Nuckols, July 16, 1868
Martha J., w. of Andrew B. Nuckols, July 9, 1863
Mary Jane, d. of Henry R. and Lucy C. Nuckols, Mar. 5, 1863
Mary S. (Mrs.), June 21, 1877
Mathew W., Sept. 27, 1855
Mildred O. (Mrs.), Oct. 18, 1866
Nannie E. Talby, w. of David H. Nuckols, Feb. 15, 1912
Retter (Mrs.), Aug. 6, 1835
Ruth Gilbert, w. of Frank Nuckols, Nov. 17, 1938
Sarah Ann, Dec. 12, 1839
Sarah Francis, w. of Charles Nuchols, Feb. 15, 1900
W. M., Mar. 16, 1911

NUNN
Fanny A. (Mrs.), Mar. 24, 1870
John M. (Dr.), Dec. 24, 1846
Mary, w. of John Nunn, Dec. 9, 1858
William S., Oct. 29, 1863

NUNNALEY

OBITUARY NOTICES IN THE RELIGIOUS HERALD WITH DATES OF PUBLICATION

William T., Aug. 17, 1876
NUNNALLY
   John W., Dec. 25, 1862
   Julia, w. of Joseph Nunnally,
     June 5, 1851
   Washington, Mar. 1, 1839

NUNNELEE
   Martha, w. of Dr. Nunnelee,
     Nov. 14, 1872
NUTTALL
   James (Capt.), Oct. 18,
     1923

OAKHAM
  Nathan, July 4, 1872
  Thomas J., May 7, 1896
OAKLEY
  Newton Z., Aug. 20, 1925
OAKS
  Albert M., s. of Mortimer
    and Sarah A. Oaks, Aug.
    19, 1854
  Dora Ann Victoria, d. of
    Mortimer and Sarah A.
    Oaks, Aug. 19, 1858
  Mary Francis*, d. of
    Mortimer and Sarah A.
    Oaks, Aug. 19, 1858
O'BANNON
  Elizabeth Eggborn, w. of
    Walter O'Bannon, Dec.
    28, 1899
  Gay, Mar. 17, 1921
  Walter, Sept. 8, 1870
OBENCHAIN
  Anthony, June 11, 1857
  Mary Elizabeth, d. of Elder
    J. J. Obenchain, Mar. 1,
    1860
OBENSHAIN
  Lucy (Mrs.), Aug. 12, 1920
OBERRY
  Hubert (Mrs.), Mar. 17, 1921
O'BRIEN
  Nettie, w. of J. H. O'Brien,
    July 20, 1933
ODELL
  Euphenia A., w. of John C.
    Odell, d. of Maj. George
    W. Noland, Mar. 14, 1867
  Sarah Jane, d. of James
    Odell, Nov. 2 and 9, 1871
ODEN
  Bettie BURKE, w. of B. F.
    Oden, Jan. 29, 1914
  Garnett, Feb. 16, 1911
OESTERREICHEE
  Joseph Pilot, Oct. 31, 1872
O'FERRALL
  Charles F., former Governor
    of Virginia, Sept. 28, 1905
OGDEN
  A. T., Apr. 10, 1913
  Armstead H. (Rev.), Jan. 11,
    1883
  James M., Sept. 25, 1890
OGG
  N. F. (Mrs.), Oct. 26, 1882
OGILVIE
  Elizabeth A., w. of Rev.
    John Ogilvie, Aug. 10, 1882
  John, June 28, 1849
  Margaret Eliza, Oct. 14, 1920
  Matilda T., d. of Rev. John
    Ogilvie, Aug. 18, 1870
OLD
  A. P., Dec. 29, 1927
  Helen Cone, w. of Logan E.
    Old, d. of George W. Cone,
    Sept. 30, 1909
OLDHAM
  Mary Jane, w. of Thomas Old-
    ham, Dec. 6, 1849
  Thomas, Apr. 10, 1879
  William C., Nov. 4, 1869
OLIVER
  Ann A., w. of Isaac Oliver,
    Nov. 5, 1846
  B. F., Apr. 23, 1914
  Bettie Miller, w. of W. E.
    Oliver, Mar. 12, 1931
  Calvin, s. of Thomas and
    Mary Oliver, Apr. 11, 1844
  E. A. (Mrs.), d. of Rev.
    Simon Murfee, Aug. 31, 1871
  E. J., Feb. 15, 1877
  Edward Smyth, Jan. 30, 1890
  Elizabeth (Mrs.), Feb. 25,
    1864
  Emily W., w. of Reuben Oliver,
    June 26, 1879
  G. Y., May 29, 1924
  George H. (Rev.), Oct. 4, 11,
    and 18, Nov. 8, 1928
  George W., Jan. 30, 1879
  Harrison (Capt.), June 16,
    1887

* Possible inaccuracy in name, or spelling, but given as printed

OBITUARY NOTICES IN THE RELIGIOUS HERALD WITH DATES OF PUBLICATION

Isaac, Mar. 11, 1831
James A., Oct. 22, 1846
James W., Aug. 11, 1887
Jennie A., w. of Maj. G.
  Y. Oliver, Sept. 24, 1914
Johnnie T., s. of B. F.
  and E. D. Oliver, July 14,
  1887
Lucy (Mrs.), Jan. 27, 1927
Martha A., Jan. 6, 1870
Muscoe, child of William H.
  and Sallie Oliver, Feb. 1,
  1872
Philip H., Feb. 4, 1897
Reuben, Dec. 25, 1890
William A. (Capt.), Dec.
  29, 1864
William E. (Dr.), July 3,
  1930
William Fitzhugh, July
  26, 1928
William J., Feb. 8, 1934
OLLIVER
  Lucy, w. of J. D. Olliver,
  Nov. 3, 1927
OMAHUNDRO
  Mary D., w. of E. P.
  Omahundro, July 17, 1879
OMOHONDRO
  Mary, w. of Capt. T. W.
  Omohondro, May 22, 1856*
OMOHUNDRO
  (Mrs.), w. of Capt. T. W.
  Omohundro, Feb. 20, 1829*
  Charles F., May 8, 1913
  E. B., Mar. 12, 1857
  Edward B., Jan. 15, Mar.
  12, 1857
  Elizabeth (Mrs.), June 22,
  1854
  Elizabeth Jane, d. of Allen
  C. Omohundro, Oct. 12,
  1848
  Gillie, w. of John K. Omo-
  hundro, d. of William H.
  Sadler, Apr. 15, 1880
  Ida M., d. of R. Omohundro,
  Dec. 7, 1871
  J. Austin, s. of Sarah Anne
  Omohundro, June 4, 1885
  John, Aug. 28, 1845
  John J., s. of John W.
  Omohundro, Aug. 9, 1839
  Lucy B., w. of George C.
  Omohundro, Aug. 19, 1858
  Richard F., July 22, 1841
  Robert Lilly, s. of William
  C. Omohundro, gr.s.
  of Elder Robert Lilly,
  Nov. 8, 1866
  Sarah A. T., w. of Capt.
  John F. Omohundro, Jan.
  13, 1881
  Sarah Anne, June 4, 1885
  Sidney A., d. of R. Omo-
  hundro, Feb. 8, 1872
  Thomas W. (Capt.), Feb.
  22, 1855
  Thomas W., s. of William
  C. Omohundro, Aug. 24,
  1871
  William, Oct. 6, 1881
  William J. G., s. of
  William C. Omohundro,
  Apr. 6, 1854
O'NEILL
  Philip, Oct. 31, 1828
ORCUTT
  Joseph E., July 12, 1934
ORGAN
  Edmond W., s. of William
  Organ, Sept. 6, 1849
ORRILL
  Robert T., s. of Joseph
  and Frances Orrill,
  May 7, 1891
ORRISON
  Mary W., d. of Jonah Orri-
  son, June 7, 1855
OSBERN
  Bettie, w. of William
  Osbern, Sept. 4, 1862
OSBORNE
  Mary D. (Mrs.), d. of
  Elder A. A. Baldwin,
  July 16, 1863
  N. E. (Mrs.), Jan. 17,
  1924
OSTERBINE
  Andrew B., Jan. 28, 1937

* Possible inaccuracy in name, or spelling, but given as printed

OBITUARY NOTICES IN THE RELIGIOUS HERALD WITH DATES OF PUBLICATION

OTEY
    Austin, s. of James W.
      and Mary A. Otey, Nov.
      29, Dec. 6, 1855
    C. C. (Col.), June 19,
      1862
    Ellen Slater, w. of John
      O. Otey, May 8, 1902
    Ethel May, d. of John B.
      and Mary Snelling Otey,
      Sept. 16, 1909
    Isaac, Dec. 5, 1839
    James, Mar. 31, 1853
    Mary Elizabeth, d. of W. C.
      Otey, Sept. 24, 1891
    Mary Louisa, w. of Dr. James
      Otey, d. of Maj. James R.
      Kent, Oct. 13, 1892
    Ophelia M., w. of John O.
      Otey, Feb. 11, 1869
    Virginia H. (Mrs.), d. of
      Richard and Kitty Frayser,
      May 13, Dec. 3 and 23, 1897
OTLEY
    Emma (Mrs.), Oct. 1, 1891
    J. Arthur, Aug. 31, 1933
    J. G. (Mrs.), Oct. 1, 1891
    James G., Jan. 21, 1892
OUTTEN
    Ann Scarbraugh, w. of G. F.
      Outten, d. of William
      Nottingham, Feb. 25,
      1875
    Jesse Thomas, July 2, 1936
    Mary P., d. of Shadrach W.
      Outten, May 15, 1852
OUTWATER
    Theron (Rev.), May 13,
      1915
OVERBEY
    Anderson, Dec. 21, 1876
    Elisha, d. of Warren and
      Nannie Overbey, Sept. 2,
      1858
    Martha, w. of Henry Overbey,
      Oct. 17, 1889
    Sallie A., Aug. 18, 1870
OVERBY
    Adelia (Mrs.), July 28,
      1904
    Ann E., w. of Isaac Overby,
      Mar. 1, 1839
    Anna, d. of R. C. Overby,
      Sept. 2, 1897
    Isaac, June 20, 1872
    Jechonias, Dec. 23, 1836
    Matilda B., w. of James M.
      Overby, d. of Capt. Thomas
      Marshall, June 4, 1840
    Nannie F., w. of W. Overby,
      d. of Elisha Betts, Aug.
      9, 1860
    Robert Y., Aug. 29, 1872
    William J., Nov. 28, 1872
OVERHOLT
    Mary G. (Mrs.), d. of Will-
      iam and Sallie Yarbrough,
      Oct. 29, 1863
OVERSTREET
    Cornelius R., Aug. 15, 1861;
      Feb. 13, 1862
    Elizabeth, Dec. 18, 1913
    Glenn McLeod, s. of M. L.
      Overstreet, Jan. 5, 1922
    Jennie Hiter, w. of James
      Overstreet, Dec. 25, 1890
    John H., Dec. 24, 1885
    M. L., Apr. 2, 1931
    Martha A. (Mrs.), Jan. 3,
      1878
OVERTON
    Aton, s. of Rev. S.
      B. Overton, Jan. 31, 1907
    Elizabeth E., w. of William
      S. Overton, Nov. 4, 1852
    Goodrich, Feb. 28, 1907
    S. B. (Mrs.), Oct. 15, 1931
    S. J., w. of James J. Over-
      ton, d. of Rev. S. J.
      Atkins, Jan. 11, 1912
    Sarah J., w. of Richard J.
      Overton, Aug. 20, 1868
    William S., July 29, 1841
OWEN
    Augustine, June 8, 1843
    Augustine A., Jan. 5, 1865
    Aurelius Fabius, Feb. 13,
      1930
    Austin E. (Rev.), May 10,
      1906

OBITUARY NOTICES IN THE RELIGIOUS HERALD WITH DATES OF PUBLICATION

Carrie E., Mar. 8, 1923
Charlie, May 10, 1894
Edward J., Apr. 14, 1870
Eva (Mrs.), Mar. 25, 1926
Geneva A. (Mrs.), Sept. 17, 1936
Ida (Mrs.), Mar. 1, 1934
Isaac Payne, s. of John M. and Ellen Owen, Dec. 19, 1878
John, June 17, 1858
John Abner, Sept. 20, 1928
John G. (Mrs.), Nov. 26, 1925
John S., May 28, 1885
Kitty, w. of John Owen, Jan. 1, 1830
Louise Andrews, d. of Rev. A. E. and Ettie M. Owen, Aug. 28, 1879
Mary E. (Mrs.), Sept. 4, 1930
Mary R., d. of George Owen, Nov. 28, 1844
Myrtle Belle, d. of Rev. A. E. and Ettie M. Owen, Sept. 2, 1869
R. A. (Mrs.), Nov. 4, 1920
Sallie, Dec. 18, 1851
Sallie Ellen, d. of William

Owen, June 27, 1861
Thomas (Rev.), Aug. 9, 1877
Wilby, Oct. 28, 1897

OWENS
  Catherine (Mrs.), Jan. 27, 1859
  Cornelia L., d. of Rev. W. Owens, Nov. 21, 1872
  Fannie, w. of Rev. Reuben R. Owens, Feb. 15, 1906
  Nancy (Mrs.), Apr. 20, 1871
  Olive J. PARR (Mrs.), Dec. 31, 1896
  Putnam (Rev.), May 24, June 7, 1877
  H. R., s. of Rev. Putnam Owens, Mar. 21, 1901
  Reuben R. (Rev.), June 4, 1891
  S. H., Mar. 16, 1899
  W. B., Feb. 15, 1872
  Warren (Elder), Jan. 22, 1874
  Willie Virginia (Mrs.), Aug. 10, 1922
  Z. A. (Rev.), Nov. 9, 1882

OZLIN
  Thomas W. (Mrs.), May 1, 1924

P

PACA
  Ernest Greenleaf, s. of John P. and Ella G. Paca, June 25, 1874
PACE
  David, Mar. 5, 1863
  Elizabeth F. J., d. of James M. Pace, Oct. 22, 1857
  Elizabeth L., w. of George D. Pace, Feb. 10, 1859
  G. T., Oct. 10, 1878
  Harriet W., d. of James M. Pace, Oct. 22, 1857
  Henderson, Mar. 5, 1863
  Henry, Nov. 14, 1834
  J. W. (Mrs.), Mar. 20, 1890
  Langston Mosby, s. of Henry and Susan Pace, Feb. 3, 1832
  Lucy, w. of William Pace, Nov. 15, 1860
  Lucy, May 18, 1893
  M. Fannie, w. of George R. Pace, d. of John Wesley and Frances S. Pace, Feb. 20, 1896
  Muscoe Russell, Jr., Aug. 24, 1905
  Sarah F., Mar. 16, 1876
  Susan M., d. of James M. Pace, Oct. 22, 1857
  William F., s. of James M. Pace, Oct. 22, 1857
PACK
  Charles Henry, Jan. 12, 1911
  Martha C. (Mrs.), Dec. 4, 1884
PADGET
  Albert (Mrs.), Nov. 4, 1886
  P. P., Apr. 18, 1918
  Sallie (Mrs.), July 3, 1890
PADGETT
  A. M. (Rev.), Sept. 20, 1934
  Elizabeth (Mrs.), Nov. 19, 1857
  Mary (Mrs.), Aug. 5, 1836
  Presley Broadus, s. of M. R. Padgett, Feb. 21, 1918*
PAGE
  Barnette Marion, Dec. 11, 1924
  George W., Sept. 25, 1862
  John W., s. of William Page, Oct. 9, 1862
  Judith R., Dec. 10, 1840
  Martha A., w. of John W. Page, d. of W. W. Groome, Jan. 26, 1871
  Martha A., w. of Carter Page, Sept. 28, 1882
  Mary Jane, w. of Edmond Page, Feb. 23, 1843
  N. M. (Mrs.), Apr. 14, 1892
  Nicholas M., Mar. 20, 1902
  Nicholas M., Dec. 16, 1937
  Richard L. (Gen.), Aug. 15, 1901
  S. M., May 5, 1921
  William, May 1, 1862
  William Byrd, Sept. 12, 1828
PAINE
  Thomas, Mar. 4, 1875
PAINTER
  Anderson, Apr. 24, 1851
  Jennie, Oct. 11, 1888
  Sarah (Mrs.), Oct. 9, 1862
PALMER
  Alfred, Feb. 16, 1888
  Alpheus (Mrs.), d. of Abram B. Bailey, Jan. 10, 1866
  Bettie, Nov. 29, 1900
  Fannie R., w. of Dr. Philip Palmer, d. of G. Y. Nichols, Sr., Apr. 8, 1869
  John (Capt.), May 19, 1842
  John, s. of Edwin Palmer, Aug. 17, 1843
  John L., June 25, 1854
  Martha Jane, w. of Lewis Palmer Jan. 12, 1865
  Mary (Mrs.), Aug. 15, 1828
  Mary J., w. of John W. Palmer, Nov. 23, 1854
  Matilda, w. of Alfred Palmer, Mar. 23, 1854
  Rebecca E. J. (Mrs.), Jan. 18, 1872

* Possible inaccuracy in name, or spelling, but given as printed

OBITUARY NOTICES IN THE RELIGIOUS HERALD WITH DATES OF PUBLICATION

Sarah C., w. of G. W. Palmer, Nov. 21, 1844
Susanna J. (Mrs.), May 1, 1919
PALMORE
  A. W., Dec. 28, 1893
  Abner, Apr. 15, 1858
  Benjamin, June 28, 1849
  Charles, Mar. 21, 1850
  Elizabeth, Mar. 7, 1850
  L. A. R., w. of A. W. Palmore, Aug. 13, 1857
  M. E., w. of Thomas W. Palmore, July 28, 1870
  Mary, w. of W. F. Palmore, May 6, 1920
  Nora Lewis, w. of E. R. Palmore, d. of T. J. and Alice F. Cowman, Mar. 19, 1896
  Spencer C. (Mrs.), Aug. 12, 1869
  Spencer C., Jan. 30, 1896
PAMPLIN
  Ella, Mar. 23, 1882
  George Henry, s. of William H. and Mary V. Pamplin, Jan. 29, 1863
  Maria Alice, d. of William H. and Mary V. Pamplin, Jan. 29, 1863
PANKEY
  Christopher C., s. of James E. Pankey, Jan. 29, 1857
  Fannie A., Mar. 28, 1918
  Mandeville, d. of John and Frances Pankey, Apr. 23, 1840
  Thomas S., May 28, 1903
  Willie, s. of William T. Pankey, Sept. 10, 1874
  Young, May 31, 1833
PANNELL
  Maggie E., d. of Joseph Pannell, Apr. 22, 1880
  Maria C., d. of Rev. William Pannell, May 7, 1874
PANNILL
  Morton, Jan. 6, 1859
  William (Elder), May 7, 1874
PANSON
  J. Thornton, Nov. 5, 1874
PARHAM
  J. R., May 8, 1890
PARIS
  Josiah, July 27, 1843
PARISH
  Perkins, Oct. 30, 1862
  Samuel, Jan. 16, 1840
PARISHER
  A. (Mrs.), May 26, 1892
PARKER
  C. D. (Mrs.), June 27, 1918
  C. J. D., Oct. 3 and 17, 1935; Jan. 9, Feb. 27, 1936
  Duncan T., May 8, 1890
  George M. (Mrs.), Feb. 1, 1917
  Helen, d. of Rev. C. J. D. Parker, Dec. 10, 1914
  Jane, w. of W. Parker, July 29, 1831
  Joseph (Elder), Oct. 9, 1879
  Lucy (Mrs.), May 5, 1859
  M. A., June 30, 1904
  M. C. (Mrs.), Oct. 30, 1913
  Margaret (Mrs.), Oct. 27, 1837
  Martha A., w. of James W. Parker, June 4, 1857
  Mary F., Apr. 13, 1916
  Nell Carter (Mrs.), Feb. 8, 1923
  Richard (Judge), Sept. 24, 1840
  Robert (Mrs.), Nov. 19, 1885
  Sally R., w. of John N. Parker, July 15, 1858
  Stella May, d. of William T. and Sallie F. McGhee Parker, May 22, 1879
  Susan W., Nov. 19, 1885
  T. C., Nov. 8, 1928
  W., Sept. 26, 1912
  W. W. (Dr.), Aug. 10, 1899
  Waller J., Apr. 28, 1921
  William A., Nov. 18, 1915
  William A. (Mrs.), d. of Rev. R. W. Cridlin, May 7, 1936
PARKINSON
  Albert T., Dec. 1, 1892
  Ann Eliza, w. of Albert T. Parkinson, May 2, 1895
  Hannah D., w. of James F.

OBITUARY NOTICES IN THE RELIGIOUS HERALD WITH DATES OF PUBLICATION

Parkinson, Dec. 21, 1854
Maria Louisa (Mrs.), Feb. 23, 1893
PARKS
F. O., July 30, 1925
Louisa F., w. of Col. W. C. Parks, d. of William Porter, Aug. 5, 1858
Susan P., July 26, 1906
William Carroll (Rev.), Sept. 1, 1892
PARLEIRE
Raymond, June 27, 1929
PARNETT
E. J., May 7, 1868
PARR
Elizabeth (Mrs.), Jan. 13, 1837
Elizabeth, w. of W. W. Parr, July 17, 1879
John, Sept. 4, 1890
Lucy, Feb. 4, 1926
Susan, d. of William Parr, Feb. 21, 1861
PARRAMORE
Sarah A. (Mrs.), Mar. 29, 1877
PARRAN
Cordelia, Feb. 22, 1894
PARRISH
Ada, d. of F. M. and Martha S. Parrish, June 17, 1858
Alice Maud, d. of John G. Parrish, Oct. 11, 1877
Calvin H., Apr. 20, May 18, 1922
Carroll E., s. of Walter and Georgie Parrish, July 22, 1915
Elizabeth V., w. of Royal Parrish, July 15, 1841
Garland N., Feb. 23, 1905
George M., Feb. 9, 1865
James, July 19, 1855
Lewis N., Aug. 3, 1848
Madison E. (Rev.), June 23, July 7, 1910
Margaret, w. of Woodson Parrish, July 25, 1828
Marrion, s. of E. M. Parrish, July 13, 1911
Martha M., w. of William S. Parrish, Sept. 10, 1846

Mary (Mrs.), Oct. 8, 1860
N. A., w. of Elder William S. Parrish, Nov. 13, 1884
Sallie A., d. of Tarlton and Susan Parrish, Aug. 22, 1861
Susan G., w. of Elder John G. Parrish, Oct. 22, 1868
Susanah, w. of Capt. Abram Parrish, Aug. 21, 1856
William S., Jr., s. of Rev. William S. Parrish, Sept. 3, 1874
PARRON
Emma Derieux (Mrs.), d. of Peter I. Derieux, Mar. 22, 1906
PARROTT
Mary R., (Mrs.), July 28, 1842
PARSLEY
Martha Ann, d. of Ulysses and Sarah Parsley, Dec. 29, 1842
PARSONS
Anne S., w. of Z. Parsons, Sept. 25, 1919
Caroline H. (Mrs.), Feb. 2, 1854
Christiana, w. of J. L. Parsons, Oct. 15, 1863
Mary E., w. of Henry S. Parsons, Jan. 31, 1884
Melissa Ann, w. of Z. Parsons, Nov. 13, 1856
William E., s. of Mary A. Parsons, Mar. 25, 1863
Woodson, Jan. 4, 1883
Z., Oct. 31, 1901
PARTLOW
Edmonia Jones (Mrs.), Dec. 14, 1922
John, s. of Capt. L. and Mary A. Partlow, June 25, 1885
PARTRIDGE
George, Aug. 15, 1828
PATES
Lucy M., w. of Chandler Pates, July 27, 1848
PATRICK
J. M., May 27, 1869

OBITUARY NOTICES IN THE RELIGIOUS HERALD WITH DATES OF PUBLICATION

John, s. of J. W. Patrick,
Sept. 13, 1860
John, Sept. 8, 1887
Lavinia, w. of J. M. Patrick,
Mar. 11, 1869
PATTERSON
A. W. (Mrs.), Oct. 13, 1932
Ann E., w. of Cornelius
Patterson, Sept. 1, 1892
B. G. (Capt.), Mar. 15, 1900
Caroline Virginia, d. of John
B. and Mary J. Patterson,
Jan. 17, 1861
Carrie Brown, d. of Rev. J. B.
T. and Mary M. Patterson,
Feb. 16, 1871
Carroll W., Mar. 16, 1893
Catherine M., July 5, 1906
J. B. T. (Rev.), Nov. 2 and 9, 1882
John L. (Dr.), Apr. 30, 1868
John Watson, Sept. 18, 1913
Mollie R., d. of James L.
and Martha A. Patterson,
Nov. 5, 1863
R. A. (Dr.), Apr. 11, 1912
Richard Fuller, s. of Dr. R.
A. Patterson, Feb. 15, 1917
Sarah (Mrs.), Sept. 3, 1840
Sophia C., w. of John M.
Patterson, Oct. 3, 1867
Thomas, Nov. 21, 1834
Thomas Neale, Feb. 24, 1887
W. C. (Mrs.), July 5, 1917
PATTESON
Alexander F., Aug. 23, 1883
Augustine M., May 21, 1863
David, Oct. 22, 1857
Lucy M. (Mrs.), Dec. 4, 1884
Maria G., Jan. 10, 1884
Mary G., Jan. 15, 1925
Peter R., Dec. 4, 1884
Samuel (Dr.), July 23, 1830
Sarah, w. of David Patteson,
Aug. 2, 1855
Susan F., w. of James Patteson,
d. of J. Shipman, Apr. 30, 1857

PATTISON
T. Harwood (Dr.), Feb. 25, 1904
PATTILLO
Edward, s. of Edward M. and
Mary J. Pattillo, May 21, 1863
Ella D., d. of Edward M. and
Mary J. Pattillo, May 21, 1863
Samuel T., s. of Edward M.
and Mary J. Pattillo, May 21, 1863
Walter P., s. of Edward M.
and Mary J. Pattillo, May 21, 1863
PATTON
Burley M., Apr. 5, 1923
John M. (Col.), Nov. 30, 1899
Lucinda R., w. of H. M.
Patton, Apr. 30, 1857
Robert, Nov. 7, 1828
PAUL
Luke, Feb. 26, 1863
PAULETT
Martha Jane, w. of J. M.
Paulett, d. of Dennis R.
Fielder, Apr. 27, 1854
PAULETTE
Thomas B., June 4, 1863
PAXTON
Isabella, d. of Capt. Alexander Paxton, Oct. 19, 1843
Samuel, Apr. 15, 1841
PAYNE
Ann M., d. of Col. Barrett
G. Payne, July 23, 1840
Anna, w. of G. A. Payne, Aug. 31, 1838
Annie Eliza, d. of T. Lee
and Anna C. Payne, Oct. 6, 1870
Barrett G. (Col.), Sept. 8, 1853
Caroline Victoria, w. of
John Walter Payne, May 18, 1882
Ellen, w. of Dr. Alexander
Payne, Jan. 28, 1886
Elma Maud, d. of William B.

OBITUARY NOTICES IN THE RELIGIOUS HERALD WITH DATES OF PUBLICATION

and Mary J. Payne, May 20, 1858
Euphemia L., w. of E. W. Payne, d. of W. J. C. Moody, May 14 and 21, 1891
Francis, Apr. 28, 1859
Gertrude Alexander, w. of Rev. G. H. Payne, Nov. 14, 1918
Harry W., Feb. 17, 1910
Heningham Watkins, w. of Joseph A. Payne, d. of B. W. Seay, Oct. 22, 1857
J. S., s. of Capt. William Overton Payne, Oct. 5, 1916
James A. (Rev.), Nov. 7, 1844
John R., Jr., Mar. 25, 1937
Joseph, Sept. 6, 1894
L. Price, child of Luther R. and Mollie V. Payne, July 9, 1963
Lewis, Aug. 29, 1901
Louisa Catharine, w. of John H. Payne, d. of Frederick and Miranda Shelton, May 13, 1915
Louisa S., w. of Lewis Payne, Mar. 8, 1900
Luther R., Oct. 8, 1885
Margaret S., July 2, 1840
Martha, w. of William A. Payne, Sept. 26, 1872
Martha Ann Mosby, w. of Capt. William Overton Payne, Feb. 11, 1897
Martha Susan (Mrs.), July 16, 1896
Mary C., d. of Dr. B. F. Payne, Feb. 17, 1876
Meredith E., July 28, 1842
Minora Evaline, d. of Col. W. B. and Mary J. Payne, Apr. 27, 1854
Mollie, d. of William A. and Martha Payne, Jan. 17, 1867
Mollie V. (Mrs.), Jan. 13, 1898
Nannie, w. of J. J. Payne, Apr. 1, 1920
Pattie Anne, d. of Capt. William O. Payne, May 18, 1922
Reva, Jan. 22, 1885
Robert A., s. of Robert B. and Franky Payne, May 6, 1897
Robert B., June 10, 1875
Robert Mosby, s. of Capt. W. O. and M. A. Mosby, Nov. 28, 1895
Sallie, Apr. 28, 1904
Samuel, June 26, 1862
Samuel Barrett, s. of Col. William B. and Mary J. Payne, Apr. 27, 1854
Sarah Pannill, w. of Robert G. Payne, d. of Samuel T. and Fannie E. Miller, Apr. 22, 1915
Susan Ann, d. of Col. William B. and Mary J. Payne, Apr. 27, 1854
Thomas Payne, May 15, 1873
William G., Feb. 7, 1924
William H., Oct. 26, 1882
William J., s. of Samuel Payne, Feb. 18, 1858
Woodson B., Sept. 8, 1853

PAYTON
William W., s. of Minor Payton, Jan. 24, 1861

PEACE
C. Ridley, d. of Samuel M. and Mary E. Peace, Dec. 15, 1892; Jan. 5, 1893

PEAK
Agnes A. (Mrs.), Mar. 14, 1861
Alonzo B., Nov. 16, 1876
L., (Mrs.), d. of Dr. A. B. Conrad, Mar. 6, 1930

PEAKE
Louise J. (Mrs.), Dec. 30, 1896
Mary Abell, d. of William and Mary E. Peake, July 24, 1873
William B., Mar. 22, 1866
William Benjamin, s. of J. B. Peake, July 17, 1862
William Vernon, s. of William and Mary E. Peake, gr.s. of J. Ralls Abell, Oct. 31, 1878

PEALE

OBITUARY NOTICES IN THE RELIGIOUS HERALD WITH DATES OF PUBLICATION

S. J., w. of A. N. Peale, d. of Henry and Martha Bushnell, Jan. 17, 1878

PEARCE
  Augustus Newell, Mar. 10, 1921
  Helen Zimina L., d. of O. F. and Fanny Pearce, Nov. 10, 1864
  Junius, July 22, 1920
  Nathaniel C., Aug. 21, 1829
  Robert W., July 19, 1855
  Willie A. (Mrs.), July 6, 1892

PEaRCEY
  Rebecca, w. of Nicholas Pearcey, Aug. 9, 1849

PEARCY
  David, s. of Rev. George and F. M. Pearcy, Dec. 1, 1870
  Frances, w. of Rev. George Pearcy, d. of Samuel Miller, Dec. 31, 1903
  George (Rev.), s. of Nicholas Pearcy, Nov. 25, Dec. 2, 1875
  Isham, June 6, 1878
  John Hardy (Rev.), June 18, July 16, 1936
  Rebecca, d. of Rev. George and F. M. Pearcy, Dec. 1, 1870
  Thomas, May 6, 1858

PEARSON
  Alice, Oct. 10, 1929
  Alice Ann, w. of J. W. Pearson, d. of Joseph A. Dunnaway, May 20, 1886
  Ann Elizabeth, d. of Charles Grandison and Sarah Elizabeth Pearson, Dec. 4, 1873
  C. G., May 11, 1893
  Elizabeth (Mrs.), Mar. 2, 1882
  Ella, w. of W. L. Pearson, Sept. 28, 1911
  Ennis, s. of Addison and Mary Pearson, Aug. 15, 1878
  Mary, w. of Rev. William A. Pearson, July 30, 1908
  Minnie Boyce, d. of G. B. and S. L. Pearson, July 29, 1869
  S. A. (Miss), Aug. 7, 1884
  Sarah Elizabeth Christian, w. of Charles Grandison Pearson, Dec. 4, 1873
  W. A. (Rev.), Jan. 1, June 17, 1920
  William Grandison, s. of Charles Grandison Pearson, Mar. 14, 1878

PEASELEY
  Caroline, w. of G. B. Peasley, Mar. 27, 1884
  Judith (Mrs.), Feb. 1, 1849
  Nancy Linton, w. of Gabriel B. Peaseley, Aug. 2, 1833
  Thomas Sanderson, s. of G. B. and Caroline Peaseley, July 18, 1844

PEASLEY
  Thomas B., July 29, 1926

PEATROSS
  Amy (Mrs.), Jan. 8, 1830
  George W., Feb. 24, 1887
  Samuel D., July 26, 1866
  Sarah Ellen, w. of W. T. Peatross, d. of Col. Mordecai Abraham, Feb. 25, 1875
  Sarah P., w. of S. D. Peatross, Aug. 4, 1842
  Selina E., d. of Samuel D. Peatross, Feb. 5, 1852

PEAY
  Austin, Aug. 19, 1852
  Helen, Nov. 22, 1855
  James H., Mar. 15, 1838
  Mildred (Mrs.), July 30, 1832

PECK
  Harriet, Sept. 9, 1875

PECOR
  Lily, w. of E. C. Pecor, Oct. 28, 1875

PEDDIE
  John (Rev.), Feb. 5, 1891

PEDIGO
  William B. (Rev.), June 4, 1891

PEEBLES
  Harrison E., s. of Rev. J. D. Peebles, June 17, 1926

OBITUARY NOTICES IN THE RELIGIOUS HERALD WITH DATES OF PUBLICATION

PEED
   Edmonia Custis, w. of A. J.
     Peed, d. of Mrs. Lucy B.
     Alderson, Apr. 27, May
     11, 1882
   F. H. (Mrs.), May 13, 1920
   John Gordon, s. of R. A. and
     Hattie L. Peed, gr.s. of
     Rev. J. H. Newbill, Dec.
     24, 1908
   John N., Mar. 14, 1935
   L. A. (Miss), May 2, 1878
   R. A., Nov. 4, 1926
   Vidy, d. of J. C. and
     Mary C. Peed, Aug. 22,
     1878
PEELE
   (Brother), m. Addie Evans,
     Dec. 11, 1930
PEERS
   Annie Belle, d. of George
     T. and Jennie C. Peers,
     June 24, 1869
   George T., Dec. 3,
     1908
   Martha L., May 15, 1829
   William J., Dec. 27,
     1900
   Willie, Aug. 9, 1900
PEGRAM
   John (Gen.), Apr. 15,
     1831
   Robert G. (Capt.), Nov. 1,
     1894
PEIRCE
   Anne, w. of Ransdell Peirce,
     Mar. 18, 1847
   Ransdell, Mar. 31, 1853
PEMBERTON
   Addie Belle, w. of Judson F.
     Pemberton, d. of Frank
     McWhirt, Nov. 15, 1900
   Charles Samuel, s. of W. R.
     and M. F. Pemberton,
     July 7, 1892
   Henrietta Burruss, d. of W. R.
     and Malvina F. Pemberton
     July 8, 1880
   Jane, Mar. 20, 1862
   Malvina F., w. of W. R.
     Pemberton, Aug. 4, 1887
   Margaret W., w. of John
     Pemberton, Mar. 11, 1880
   Mary Ann (Mrs.), June 8, 1843
   Reuben, May 5, 1853
   Susan, w. of Thomas Pemberton,
     May 11, 1882
PENDELL
   Mildred R. (Mrs.), Sept. 17,
     1885
PENDER
   Minnie, d. of Joshua C. and
     Katie Pender, Oct. 7, 1875
PENDLETON
   Amanda Bailey, w. of A. S.
     Pendleton, July 28, 1870
   Benjamin F., s. of George M.
     and Catharine Pendleton,
     Mar. 9, 1865
   Catherine, May 29, 1856
   David H. (Dr.), Mar. 31, 1859
   Dulcie, w. of Jackson Pendleton,
     d. of William Landrum, May
     31, 1888
   Edmund (Col.), Aug. 3, 1899
   Elizabeth (Mrs.), Nov. 24, 1837
   Elizabeth (Mrs.), Sept. 17,
     1846
   Fanny, Feb. 27, 1862
   J. M. (Rev.), Mar. 12, 1891
   John Thomas, s. of Joseph H.
     and Sarah M. Pendleton, Feb.
     4, 1841
   Margaret Esther, w. of Jerome
     B. Pendleton, Mar. 6, 1890
   Mary, w. of Richard Pendleton,
     Nov. 18, 1847
   Mary B. (Mrs.), Oct. 9, 1835
   Mary C. (Mrs.), Nov. 29, 1855
   Micajah, Apr. 18, 1844
   Mollie Eliza, d. of John Edmund
     Pendleton, Sept. 7, 1916
   Robert S., Aug. 11, 1887
   Samuella T. (Mrs.), Aug. 11,
     1887
   Sarah Louisa, d. of Col. Edmund
     Pendleton, Apr. 11, 1844
   Virginia, Apr. 22, 1858
PENICK
   Bettie Tarpley Martin, w. of

OBITUARY NOTICES IN THE RELIGIOUS HERALD WITH DATES OF PUBLICATION

Rev. William Sydnor Penick,
  d. of Dr. Chesley Martin,
  Aug. 8, 1918
J. B., Jan. 6, 1876
Jane E., w. of Capt. N. Penick,
  d. of Thomas H. Averett,
  June 21, 1883
M. B. (Miss), July 24, 1890
Nannie Bland, w. of G. A.
  Penick, d. of J. D. McGill,
  July 31, 1873
Nattie Wise, s. of G. A. and
  A. B. Penick, Mar. 28, 1872
T. R. (Mrs.), Sept. 8, 1859
Veva, d. of Rev. W. S. Penick,
  Nov. 14, 1889
Werta, w. of. Nathan
  Penick, Nov. 19, 1885
William, Aug. 13, 1874
PENN
  George L., Feb. 22, 1877
  Lucy M., w. of Nathan Penn,
    d. of Nathan Multiply, Feb.
    5, 1903
PENNEY*
  Julia E., d. of E. M. C. and
    Sophia J. Penney, May 29,
    1863
  S. J., w. of E. M. C. Penney,
    Jan. 11, 1883
PENNINGTON
  Agatha P. (Mrs.), Mar. 3, 1881
  Polly (Mrs.), Aug. 19, 1858
  Sallie E. (Mrs.), Mar. 15, 1877
PENNY
  Cornelius C., s. of E. M. C.
    Penny, Feb. 27, 1862*
  Elizabeth A. (Mrs.), Mar. 2,
    1865
PENTECOST
  Elizabeth (Mrs.), Oct. 20, 1927
  George Bedford, May 10, 1855
  Jane, w. of George Pentecost,
    Sept. 22, 1864
  Lucy Virginia, d. of Richard
    and Mary A. Pentecost, Feb.
    23, 1860
  R. B., June 12, 1924
  Sarah Fannie, d. of William
    Pentecost, Sept. 22, 1864
  Sarah Jane, d. of Richard J.
    and Mary A. Pentecost, Feb.
    28, 1861
PERCIVAL
  E. C. (Mrs.), Mar. 18, 1909
  M. Z., Jan. 19, 1933
  Mildred Anne, w. of Maurice
    Langborne Percival, May
    13, 1909
PERDUE
  Bartholomew, Aug. 20, 1840
  Benjamin Joseph, July 16, 1931
  Elizabeth A. J., w. of Samuel
    R. Perdue, July 29, 1858
  Esther D., d. of Bartholomew
    Perdue, Apr. 12, 1855
  J. B., June 18, 1936; Apr. 15,
    1937
  James A., s. of N. D. Perdue,
    Feb. 28, 1901
  Sidney (Mrs.), d. of Samuel
    Pleasant and Martha Wilkin-
    son Goode, Feb. 24, 1938
PEREGOY
  James Edgar, s. of James F.
    Peregoy, Mar. 1, 1877
PEREOR
  Nancy L. (Mrs.), Dec. 17, 1925
PERKINS
  A., Apr. 26, 1923
  Ada C., Aug. 7, 1930
  Ann J., w. of Andrew J. Perkins
    May 1, 1873
  Archelaus (Maj.), June 14, 1849
  Catherine S. M., w. of Dabney
    N. Perkins, May 1, 1844
  Charlie, s. of John W. and Mary
    Perkins, Feb. 9, 1860
  Dabney M., Dec. 9, 1886
  Edgar Taylor, s. of J. C. and
    Elizabeth Jane Perkins, June
    18, 1863
  Elizabeth Jane, w. of Rev.
    Jesse Clopton Perkins, Sept.
    8, 1910
  Emily, w. of John N. Perkins,
    Feb. 5, 1852
  Fannie P., w. of Col. T.
    Perkins, June 18, 1857
  Frederick A. (Dr.), s. of Dr.

* Possible inaccuracy in name, or spelling, but given as printed

OBITUARY NOTICES IN THE RELIGIOUS HERALD WITH DATES OF PUBLICATION

Thomas H. Perkins, Aug. 9, 1877
G., w. of Archer Perkins, Mar. 26, 1857
Garland A., May 24, 1855
I. O., Mar. 13, 1913
Isaac O., Aug. 14, 1862
J. M., Feb. 19, 1925
J. O., June 26, 1862
Jesse C. (Rev.), Sept. 23, Nov. 25, 1886
John, Apr. 20, 1848
John A. A., s. of William M. Perkins, July 24, 1873
John Nicholas, Jan. 3, 1907
Joseph Dabney, s. of Dabney M. and Catharine S. M. Perkins, May 1, 1844
Joseph S., Aug. 13, 1874
Lewis W., s. of Dr. Thomas H. Perkins, Apr. 12, 1877
Louisiana, w. of J. O. Perkins, July 2, 1863
Martha, w. of Capt. Archer Perkins, Feb. 17, 1916
Martha M., Jun. 7, 1892
Mary M., w. of John Perkins, July 8, 1886
Mattie, w. of Stephen Joseph Perkins, May 22, 1913
Nancy, w. of Joseph S. Perkins, Aug. 13, 1874
Nathaniel, s. of Isaac Perkins, Feb. 16, 1865
Rebecca T., w. of Knight B. Perkins, Oct. 20, 1853
Rosalie, d. of Dr. A. H. Perkins, June 18, 1857
Sallie, d. of John N. and Mary Perkins, Apr. 18, 1872
Sally Ann (Mrs.), Jan. 15, 1850
Samuel Henry, Dec. 28, 1933
Sarah, d. of Dr. A. H. Perkins, June 18, 1857
Stephen Joseph, May 22, 1913
Susan, w. of Dabney M. Perkins, Mar. 21, 1850
T. H., Aug. 28, 1924
Tabitha G., d. of Knight B. Perkins, Sept. 20, 1833
Thomas O. F., Apr. 30, 1857
W. J., July 26, 1900
William, Feb. 16, 1854
William C., s. of Isaac O. Perkins, July 22, 1858
William C., s. of Elder J. C. Perkins, June 25, 1874
William Henry, s. of Augustus M. and Winefred E. Perkins, Aug. 24, 1854
Willie B., Sept. 26, 1889

PERKINSON
Edward F., May 29, 1863
Elizabeth L., w. of Beverly B. Perkinson, d. of H. Q. Stephens, July 28, 1853
George W. (Dr.), June 26, 1829
Thomas N. (Mrs.), Aug. 4, 1864
Vera Elam (Mrs.), Nov. 8, 1934
Virginia H., d. of T. N. and Frances Perkinson, Dec. 31, 1846

PERKS
M. L., w. of Thornton Perks, d. of Benjamin T. and Sallie Clift Wharton, May 17, 1900

PERRIN
E. J. (Mrs.), June 14, 1923
E. M., Jan. 25, 1912
Elizabeth (Mrs.), Oct. 6, 1881
Eula, d. of J. V. and M. A. Perrin, Apr. 18, 1878
James Herndon, s. of James Vaiden and Mary Ann Perrin, Mar. 23, Apr. 13, 1933
James Vaiden, May 18, 1905
M. A. (Mrs.), Nov. 29, 1923
Mary Ann (Mrs.), Nov. 29, 1923

PERROW
William E., May 21, 1863

PERRY
Alice, d. of Elder William S. Perry, Dec. 31, 1863
Charles W., s. of Rev. W. S. and Elizabeth M. Perry, June 13, 1861
Edward Hiram Woods, s. of John, Jr., and Ella S. Perry, Mar. 25, 1897
Elizabeth (Mrs.), Sept. 27,

OBITUARY NOTICES IN THE RELIGIOUS HERALD WITH DATES OF PUBLICATION

1839
Elizabeth, w. of Rev. W. S.
Perry, d. of Dr. Richard
Winfield, June 13, 1861
Ellen Terrill (Mrs.), June
25, 1891
Frank B. (Dr.), Mar. 18, 1937
J. M. (Rev.), Aug. 11, 1904
John Pollard, s. of John, Jr.,
and Ella S. Perry, Aug. 21,
1879
Julia, Feb. 3, 1898
L. L., Jan. 23, 1890
Lovey, w. of Peter Perry, June
25, 1846
Marvin Archibald, s. of Mrs. L.
L. Perry, Aug. 13, 1891
Mary P. (Mrs.), Dec. 13, 1877
Virginia V., w. of John H.
Perry, Dec. 4, 1856
Warren A., May 5, 1898
PERRYMAN
George W. (Dr.), Jan. 6, 1916
PERSINGER
Elizabeth C. (Mrs.), Mar. 12,
1863
William (Capt.), Oct. 29, 1863
PERSONS
Lucy, July 22, 1841
PETER
Arthur (Mrs.), Apr. 17, 1902
Arthur (Dr.), Jan. 15, 1903
PETERKIN
Rebecca, d. of Dr. Joshua
Peterkin, July 30, 1891
PETERS
Amanda M., w. of B. F. Peters,
Mar. 7, 1844
Barbara, w. of Jacob Peters,
Apr. 8, 1869
Eleanor, d. of Rev. T. E.
Peters, July 5, 1934
Elizabeth (Mrs.), June 10, 1847
Mary S., w. of James E. Peters,
July 21, 1859
William E. (Col.), Mar. 29, 1906
PETTAWAY
John, Apr. 30, 1868
PETTIGREW
Allan N., Sept. 23, 1937

PETTIS
Eliza (Mrs.), Oct. 27, 1870
PETTIT
Angelina F., w. of Edward
Pettit, June 2, 1853
E. A., July 12, 1883
Early, child of W. W. and
M. E. Pettit, Oct. 31, 1872
George W. (Col.), Apr. 12, 1883
O. F., June 27, 1861
William, July 23, 1891
PETTRY
Zephner Lewis, s. of John and
Pattie Pettry, May 5, 1859
PETTUS
A. E. (Mrs.), Mar. 31, 1887
C. H., Oct. 17, 1867
Elizabeth, w. of George W.
Pettus, Jan. 6, 1842
Elizabeth H., w. of John O.
Pettus, Feb. 4, 1858
Emma Turner, w. of John C.
Pettus, July 14, 1904
H. F. (Mrs.), Jan. 19, 1860
Mary A. B., w. of Cephas H.
Pettus, May 17, 1883
Mary Coleman, w. of T. F.
Pettus, Jan. 10, 1901
Mary J. (Mrs.), Feb. 5, 1880
Susan, w. of Stephen Pettus,
Mar. 13, 1845
Susan, d. of Cephas H. and M.
B. Pettus, Feb. 17, 1853
T. Taylor (Mrs.), d. of Richard
Clauselle Puryear, June 2,
1904
Thomas F., Jan. 7, 1909
W. H., Jr., Feb. 20, 1936
William, Nov. 11, 1841
PETTY
Ann (Mrs.), May 24, 1860
Anna V. (Mrs.), Nov. 28, 1929
Caroline Elvenia, d. of Daniel
and Dorothy Petty, Apr. 14,
1857
Cornelia, Aug. 28, 1902
Fannie W. (Mrs.), d. of George
W. Baldwin, Dec. 23, 1869
George (Elder), Feb. 19, 1852
H. E. (Mrs.), Apr. 20, 1911

OBITUARY NOTICES IN THE RELIGIOUS HERALD WITH DATES OF PUBLICATION

Henry (Rev.), July 28, 1904
Herbert St. Clair, s. of
   William O. Petty, Apr. 12,
   1883
John, Nov. 21, 1872
L. Kate, Oct. 2, 1884
Mary Virginia, d. of Charles S.
   and Ellen Petty, Dec. 5,
   1867
P. M. (Rev.), Jan. 27, 1921
Philip Marshal (Rev.), Mar. 9,
   1933
Thomas Ezra, s. of W. R. Petty,
   Apr. 8, 1852
W. C. (Mrs.), Mar. 22, 1934
William Oscar, Dec. 23, 1926
PEYTON
Bernard Taylor, s. of Oscar
   C. and Annie M. Peyton,
   Aug. 29, 1889
Eliza H., w. of Dr. E. O.
   Peyton, d. of John T.
   Anderson, Mar. 22, 1888
Ella Isabella, w. of Col. J.
   B. Peyton, Jan. 17, 1901
George H., Oct. 27, 1842
George W., Feb. 28, 1889
Henry, Sept. 17, 1891
Imogene, d. of James F. and
   Maria C. Peyton, Aug. 21,
   1879
Katie, d. of Rev. A. and Annie
   W. Peyton, July 26, 1866
Lydia Newman, d. of John W.
   and Alice G. Peyton, Feb. 4,
   1892
Malinda C., w. of W. H. Peyton,
   Apr. 4, June 13, 1907
Pauli, s. of James F. and Maria
   C. Peyton, Oct. 9, 1879
Rosalie F., d. of Col. George
   L. Peyton, Mar. 13, 1884
Virginia Price, w. of Thomas
   P. Peyton, May 8, 1862
Waller Lewis, s. of George Q.
   and Huldah L. Peyton, Oct.
   2, 1873
William H. (Col.), June 4, July
   2, 1891
Willie Ann, w. of William S.
Peyton, d. of William Newman,
   May 14, 1891
PHAUP
Eudora, d. of Richard and Lucy
   A. Phaup, Mar. 14, 1878
Fannie, d. of Richard and Lucy
   A. Phaup, Sept. 4, 1862
Julia B. (Mrs.), Jan. 13, 1832
Olivia, d. of Richard and Lucy
   A. Phaup, Feb. 21, 1861
Susanna, w. of William Phaup,
   Sept. 18, 1845
PHELPS
Charles, Nov. 24, 1884
G. Lee (Rev.), Nov. 24, 1938
George W., Dec. 31, 1857
Jane, w. of Hector Phelps, Feb.
   16, 1888
Martha, w. of James E. Phelps,
   d. of P. A. Blackwell, Apr.
   23, 1863
Pattie A., w. of John W. Phelps,
   Nov. 7, 1889
PHENIX
Cora R., d. of J. P. and Cora
   A. Phenix, Nov. 30, 1893
Octavia (Mrs.), July 21, 1904
PHILIPS
Bernard (Elder), Apr. 21, 1870
Clementina, w. of William
   Philips, Dec. 25, 1835
George L., Sept. 24, 1857
James, Jan. 14, 1847
John D., Dec. 13, 1860
Nannie V., w. of W. S. Phil-
   ips, Aug. 26, 1858
Samuel W., June 14, 1860
Sarah, w. of Elder B. Phil-
   ips, Feb. 7, 1861
PHILLIPS
(Sister), June 12, 1856
A. J., w. of J. W. Phil-
   lips, June 3, 1869
Ada M., d. of William and Ellen
   M. Phillips, Nov. 8, 1860
Alice (Mrs.), Dec. 21, 1916
Alonzo (Gen.), Nov. 4 and 25,
   1909
Babel, Mar. 15, 1894
Baxter Ballard, Dec. 5, 1907

OBITUARY NOTICES IN THE RELIGIOUS HERALD WITH DATES OF PUBLICATION

Betsy, Apr. 2, 1874
Christopher Coplon, Sept. 1, 1892
Emma Smithson (Mrs.), Aug. 21 and 28, 1919
Eslie Roland, Sept. 26, 1935
Fanny, May 31, 1849
Fleming, father of Gen. A. L. Phillips, Dec. 14, 1899
Florence E., w. of R. A. Phillips, May 1, 1913
George W., May 17, June 21, 1866
H. H. (Mrs.), June 29, 1905
Hattie H., w. of Capt. John B. Phillips, Dec. 1, 1921
J. F. (Dr.), Apr. 14, 1881
J. Watson, Sept. 25, 1924
J. Wilton, Dec. 21, 1916
John Christopher, s. of W. T. Phillips, Dec. 5, 1907
Joseph Pendleton, Feb. 2, 1882
Joseph R., s. of Rev. Bernard Phillips, July 4, 1867
Joseph W., July 3, 1890
Josephine PECK, w. of Dr. J. R. Phillips, July 8, 1880
Kate, July 9, 1891
Maggie (Mrs.), Mar. 9, 1916
Malvina (Mrs.), Apr. 5, 1923
Margarette Elsie, d. of H. H. Phillips, Apr. 4, 1907
Maria (Mrs.), Mar. 20, May 1, 1924
Mollie, d. of J. W. and N. P. Phillips, Jan. 20, 1887
Rebecca, d. of Elder Bernard and Sarah Phillips, Apr. 17, 1845
Richard D., Mar. 10, 1881
Ruth (Mrs.), Jan. 31, 1935
S. Wortley, w. of John B. Phillips, d. of Col. J. A. Abrahams, Dec. 2, 1869
Samuel E., May 20, 1897
Samuel Everett, July 14, 1932
Sarah A., w. of Samuel W. Phillips, Feb. 10, 1870
Susie R. (Mrs.), May 23, 1935
Thomas Dodson, s. of Elder Barnard Phillips, July 8, 1841
Vincent W., May 12, 1887
W. T., Apr. 10, 1924

PHILPOT
Dianna, w. of David Philpot, d. of John and Dianna Cahill, Nov. 1, 1855

PHIPPEN
Ann Lownes, d. of George and Hannah P. Phippen, Dec. 30, 1847
Eliza Rhodes, d. of George and Hannah P. Phippen, Oct. 8, 1846
William, s. of Rev. George Phippen, Jan. 16, 1845

PHIPPS
Columbus, Sept. 17, 1936
Julia A. (Mrs.), Sept. 27, 1888
Temperance (Mrs.), June 12, 1873
Thomas Wingfield, Apr. 3, 1930
Winfield, May 31, 1860

PICKET
Sarah, Jan. 29, 1830

PICKETT
Ann, w. of Capt. James S. Pickett, June 7, 1860
Charles (Maj.), brother of Gen. George E. Pickett, Mar. 30, 1899
John Sanford (Rev.), Jan. 18, 1877
Julia, Dec. 21, 1865
M. A., w. of A. J. Pickett, d. of Solomon Siler, Nov. 19, 1868
Reuben (Elder), July 15, 1875
Willie Herndon, s. of John and Sarah A. Pickett, Feb. 14, 1856

PIERCE
Bettie, w. of Micajah Pierce, Feb. 16, 1922
Copeland, Sept. 1, 1842
E. S. (Rev.), June 14 and 28, July 5, 12, and 26, 1923
Elizabeth S., w. of Felix Pierce, Oct. 7, 1852

OBITUARY NOTICES IN THE RELIGIOUS HERALD WITH DATES OF PUBLICATION

Ellie, July 26, 1928
Ettie Puryear, w. of Rev. E. S.
  Pierce, Dec. 23, 1915
J. Newton, July 16, 1903
Laura V. (Mrs.), Mar. 21, 1935
Martha A., w. of Thomas J.
  Pierce, July 22, 1886
Martha Susan, w. of J. Newton
  Pierce, July 28, 1904
Mary Elizabeth, w. of William
  W. Pierce, d. of William E.
  Clopton, June 25, 1885
Pamela (Mrs.), Aug. 29, 1850
R. S., July 22, 1915
Richard W., Aug. 11, 1892
Thelma O., Aug. 5, 1897
Washington, s. of John Pierce,
  June 21, 1855
William, May 22, 1879
PIGG
  Louisa J. (Mrs.), Mar. 22, 1855
PILCHER
  Anthea Parsons, d. of John A.
    and Elizabeth Ann Pilcher,
    Dec. 20, 1849
  Charles Manly, s. of John M.
    and M. Lucy Pilcher, July
    27, 1876
  Edith, Aug. 28, Sept. 11, 1902
  Edwin Mason, s. of Rev. John M.
    Pilcher, Jan. 23, Feb. 13,
    1913
  J. M. (Mrs.), w. of Dr. J. M.
    Pilcher, Oct. 27, 1904
  Rebecca Spratley, w. of John
    Alsop Pilcher, d. of Robert
    and Rebecca Jane Judkins,
    Apr. 12, 1906
  W. S., Feb. 11, 1892
PILLOW
  William Thomas, Apr. 30, 1931
PINCHAM
  Onitia M. (Mrs.), Mar. 20,
    1862
PINCHBECK
  Henry Ernest, Dec. 4, 1930
  Martha M., d. of William
    Pinchbeck, Feb. 21, 1861
PINKARD
  Elizabeth, w. of Spencer
    Pinkard, Mar. 26, 1863
PIPER
  R. R., Apr. 26, 1866
PITMAN
  Edwin (Capt.), Nov. 8, 1877
  G. H., July 15, 1926
  Lucy A. (Mrs.), Jan. 25, 1872
  Maria, Dec. 24, 1896
PITT
  A. Taylor, Dec. 12, 1935
  Annie C., w. of Dr. R. H. Pitt,
    Aug. 3 and 17, 1933
  Douglas Hatcher, s. of Rev. R.
    H. Pitt, Aug. 13, 1885
  Frances, d. of Albert L. and
    Fanny Pitt, Oct. 23, 1884
  Richard T., s. of Dr. Richard
    G. Pitt, Aug. 13, 1874
  Walter J., Apr. 23, 1931
  William Horace, Nov. 5, 1891
PITTARD
  W. G., Feb. 25, Apr. 1, 1937
PITTMAN
  Ashton, Mar. 10, 1921
  John H., Feb. 1, 1855
  Robert L., Feb. 25, 1875
PITTS
  Andrew J., Dec. 24, 1874
  Elizabeth, w. of Thomas C.
    Pitts, May 14, 1908
  Ettie B., Nov. 30, 1893
  John H., Jan. 1, 1863
  Kate H., Nov. 16, 1871
  Lillie M., June 23, 1921
  Lucy Elizabeth, d. of Capt.
    R. L. Pitts, Oct. 30, 1835
  Mahalia, w. of Willis Pitts,
    Sept. 14, 1882
  Martha Ellen, w. of Philip B.
    Pitts, Apr. 19, 1894
  Mary Everitt, d. of V. Y.
    Pitts, Sept. 26, 1912
  Mary Hyter (Mrs.), Dec. 25,
    1890
  Myrtle, d. of O. D. and Mary
    H. Pitts, Apr. 4, 1872
  Pearl Broaddus, d. of Philip
    B. Pitts, Oct. 1, 1885
  Philip B., Oct. 19, 1893
  Robert S., Feb. 7, 1878

OBITUARY NOTICES IN THE RELIGIOUS HERALD WITH DATES OF PUBLICATION

Thomas (Maj.), Aug. 5, 1841
Thomas C., Jan. 23, 1902
William Dorroh, s. of J. D.
  and Phebe Pitts, Mar. 19,
  1874
Willis, June 28, 1877
Wilton W., Jan. 1, 1863
PLANK
  Allie Lavinia (Mrs.), Mar.
  21, 1935
PLANT
  A. E. (Miss), Aug. 15, 1844
  Elizabeth (Mrs.), d. of William Phelps, Feb. 1, 1849
PLEASANT
  Louella Hughes, Jan. 17,
  1929
PLEASANTS
  Benjamin J., Nov. 20, 1913
  Edwin C., s. of Samuel
    Pleasants, Feb. 26, 1891
  Elizabeth (Mrs.), June 19,
    1862
  James, May 1, 1873
  James E., s. of Thomas W. and
    Susan Pleasants, Feb. 6,
    1840
  Jane (Mrs.), May 11, 1848
  John H., Mar. 5, 1846
  John S. (Capt.), July 16, 1857
  Joseph (Capt.), Feb. 2, 1860
  Julia Logan, d. of Joseph B.
    and Rosa Pleasants, June 2,
    1859
  Keziah F., w. of W. H. Pleasants, June 19, 1851
  Margaret, w. of Dr. Samuel
    Pleasants, Jan. 13, 1837
  Maria Antoinette, w. of J.
    Hampden Pleasants, May 3,
    1917*
  Martha M., Mar. 10, 1898
  Martha Rebecca, w. of R. T.
    Pleasants, Feb. 11, 1909
  Mary C., w. of Benjamin B.
    Pleasants, d. of Thomas
    Carter, Sept. 30, 1886
  Mary E., d. of Thomas W. and
    Susan Pleasants, Feb. 6,
    1840
  Mildred Ann, d. of Mrs.
    Kesiah Pleasants, Oct. 12,
    1848*
  Pattie Goodwin, w. of Joseph
    Pleasants, Feb. 9, 1905
  Philip, Mar. 11, 1831
  Polly, d. of Tarlton W. Pleasants, Nov. 4, 1869
  Sallie H., w. of Robert Thaddeus Pleasants, Sept. 2,
    1847
  Susan H., w. of Thomas H.
    Pleasants, Feb. 6, 1840
  Thomas W., Nov. 3, 1859
  Walter H., Mar. 2, 1838
  William H., July 26, 1900
PLUMER
  William S. (Dr.), Oct. 28,
    1880
PLUMMER
  Albert Gallatin (Col.), July
    8, 1836
PLUNKET
  William H. (Rev.), Jan. 24,
    1884*
PLUNKETT
  Eugene C., s. of N. N. Plunkett, Sept. 30, 1926
  Hattie E. Z., w. of Willis A.
    Plunkett, d. of Capt. A. B.
    Baker, Jan. 31, 1884
  William H. (Rev.), Mar. 13,
    1884*
POARCH
  Blanche, Mar. 19, 1903
  John H., Apr. 9, 1931
  Ruth, d. of Garland Poarch,
    Feb. 14, 1924
POATES
  Elizabeth M., w. of Lewis L.
    Poates, Apr. 13, 1838
POE
  Clara, Sept. 5, 1828
  Mary, Mar. 20, 1829
POINDEXTER
  A. M. (Rev.), May 16 and 23,
    1872
  A. M. (Mrs.), Oct. 10, 1912
  A. W. (Capt.), Sept. 8, 1864
  Ann (Mrs.), Mar. 26, 1840

* Possible inaccuracy in name, or spelling, but given as printed

OBITUARY NOTICES IN THE RELIGIOUS HERALD WITH DATES OF PUBLICATION

Boudeville, Mar. 5, 1846
Eliza, w. of A. M. Poindexter, d. of Maj. John Wimbush, Oct. 10, 1867
Frances, w. of Edward Poindexter, Aug. 15, 1828
Frances, w. of Rev. Richard Poindexter, d. of Abram and Prudence Maer, June 29, 1843
Harriet B., w. of A. V. Poindexter, Nov. 13, 1873
James (Col.), Dec. 26, 1839
Julia, w. of William A. Poindexter, Oct. 21, 1875
Margaret, w. of Rev. John Poindexter, Aug. 22, 1850
Mary A. (Mrs.), Mar. 24, 1881
R. L., Jan. 30, 1896
Sarah Burnley, d. of William H. and Sarah W. Poindexter, Dec. 25, 1845
Thomas F. (Capt.), Oct. 22, 1885
Virginia Frances, d. of Lewis D. Poindexter, Dec. 8, 1842

POINT
Charles, s. of Charles J. and Mary Point, Apr. 5, 1849
Mary A., Apr. 15, 1852

POINTER
Kate, w. of Archibald Pointer, May 5, 1892

POLKINHORN
Harriet Godwin (Mrs.), Apr. 29, 1926

POLLARD
Bessie, d. of J. M. and E. C. Pollard, Nov. 23, 1893
Charlotte H., w. of George W. Pollard, Jan. 12, 1838
Edward Bagby, July 21, 1927
Elisha (Capt.), Nov. 21, 1844
Elizabeth, w. of Capt. Francis Pollard, Aug. 23, 1833
Elizabeth M. (Mrs.), Jan. 7, 1892
Ella, d. of Thornton and Elizabeth Pollard, Oct. 15, 1891
Ella Cabiness (Mrs.), d. of
John T. Gale, Oct. 11, 1917
Francis (Capt.), May 24, 1860
Frederick Gresham, s. of Henry R. Pollard, July 29, 1915
George D., Mar. 12, 1885
H. R., Jr., Apr. 28, 1932
Hannah (Mrs.), Mar. 16, 1871
Harriet C., w. of H. G. Pollard, Oct. 31, 1901
Henry Robinson, Aug. 16 and 23, 1923
Hezekiah G., July 27, 1899
James, Sept. 22, 1898
James J., July 16, 1931
John (Col.), Oct. 4 and 18, 1877
John, Jr., s. of John Garland Pollard, May 3, 1900
John (Dr.), Sept. 28, 1911
John (Mrs.), w. of Dr. John Pollard, May 2, 1918
John Garland, July 20, 1911
John Garland, May 6, 1937.
John Newton, s. of R. H. and Jessie Pollard, Apr. 27, 1871
Joseph, Jr., Feb. 1, 1849
Joseph Thomas, Apr. 3, 1924
Juliet, w. of Col. John Pollard, d. of Thomas Jefferies, Oct. 22, 1874
Mary (Mrs.), May 14, 1840
Mary A. (Mrs.), Mar. 8, 1894
Mary Ann, d. of Henry and Mary Pollard, Sept. 1, 1837
Mattie E., w. of R. N. Pollard, d. of John and Hannah Gresham, May 31, 1917; June 7, 1939
Mildred, w. of E. Pollard, Feb. 27. 1851
Nathan, Dec. 23, 1836
Patsy (Sister), Mar. 21, 1867
R. Peyton, Dec. 22, 1881
R. T. (Dr.), Feb. 3 and 10, 1938
Rebecca Ann, w. of Elisha Pollard, Aug. 25, 1837
Robert Nelson, Sept. 9, 1926

OBITUARY NOTICES IN THE RELIGIOUS HERALD WITH DATES OF PUBLICATION

Sallie B., d. of Joseph L.
and Martha E. Pollard,
June 16, 1892
Sarah (Mrs.), Apr. 9, 1857
Susie, d. of Dr. John Pollard,
Sept. 20, 1906
Susie May, d. of James and
Susie Pollard, Jan. 18,
1877
Susie Virginia, d. of John
and Virginia Bagby Pollard,
Jan. 31, 1907
Thomas, s. of Col. John
Pollard, Dec. 9, 1852
Thomas F., Apr. 23, 1903
POLLOCK
Charles Lee, gr.s. of Charles
Lee, Attorney General under
President Washington, Apr.
19, 1888
Maria W., d. of Dr. T. Pollock, May 3, 1855
Robert (Rev.), Sept. 12, 1828
POMFREY
Margaret A. (Mrs.), Feb. 9, 1882
POND
Abigail C. (Mrs.), Dec. 13,
1883
Anna F. (Mrs.), Sept. 11,
Oct. 2, 1902
Norfleet L., June 3, 1875
PONTON
George Edward, Mar. 21, 1929
POOL
Frances W., w. of William P.
Pool, June 26, 1856
L., Dec. 13, 1888
Nannie H. P., Jan. 30, 1896
Nannie Lou, d. of Thomas C. P.
Pool, Dec. 9, 1880
Thomas C. P., Nov. 2, 1905
William P., June 29, 1893
POOR
A., July 1, 1858
Elizabeth Henry, d. of Capt.
Edward H. Poor, Mar. 8, 1833
Frances, w. of Thomas Poor,
Dec. 14, 1832
Martha W., d. of Abram Poor,
June 27, 1844

Rebecca B., w. of James E.
Poor, d. of N. W. and
Sallie T. Ware, July 21,
1864
Thomas, Sept. 18, 1845
Thomas Jackson, s. of Capt.
James Poor, Mar. 8, 1833
William Bonaparte, s. of Capt.
James Poor, Mar. 8, 1833
POORE
Livinia, w. of Maj. James
Poore, Mar. 31, 1853
POPE
Caroline R. (Mrs.), Aug. 8,
1895
Charles King, Oct. 9, Nov.
13, 1890
John W., s. of E. S. Pope,
Mar. 2, 1911
T. H. (Rev.), July 22, 1875
POPHAM
John M. (Col.), Aug. 17, 1854
POPKINS
George W. (Rev.), Feb. 26,
PORTER
Amanda, Nov. 10, 1921
Amelia S., Jan. 15, 1880
Ann F., July 13, 1838
Ebenezer (Rev.), Apr. 18,
1834
Elizabeth A., Mar. 3, 1853
Estelle Rudd (Mrs.), Mar. 16,
1916
Henry Duncan, Aug. 20, 1896
J. J., Aug. 2, 1888
James, Aug. 7, 1862
Jeremiah (Rev.), Apr. 19,
1866
Kate, d. of C. W. and Bettie
Porter, May 1, 1862
Mary W., w. of John Porter,
Jan. 19, 1838
P. P. (Dr.), May 13, 1858
Peter (Mrs.), June 5, 1862
Samuel Judson, Mar. 14, 1935
Victoria, Nov. 27, 1856
William (Capt.), Nov. 4,
1858
William D., s. of Rev. Jeremiah Porter, Sept. 30, 1869

OBITUARY NOTICES IN THE RELIGIOUS HERALD WITH DATES OF PUBLICATION

PORTWOOD
 Edward L., s. of George W. Portwood, Oct. 7, 1852
POSEY
 Grace Ann (Mrs.), Aug. 4, 1859
POTEAT
 Edwin McNeill (Dr.), s. of James and Julia A. McNeill Poteat, July 8, 1937
 J. E. (Mrs.), June 13, 1929
POTTER
 Nelson, May 7, 1925
POTTS
 Ann Louisa, w. of John F. C. Potts, June 23, 1853
 Bettie, w. of Dr. Richard Potts, Mar. 19, 1874
 David G. (Col.), Feb. 3 and 17, 1887
 Eliza A., w. of Edward D. Potts, Sept. 27, 1883
 Elizabeth F., Oct. 4, 1883
 Elizabeth G., w. of Col. David G. Potts, Nov. 11, 1841
 John T., s. of Capt. John W. Potts, July 28, 1853
 John W. (Capt.), Dec. 19, 1878
 Louisa F., Oct. 4, 1883
 Lucretia A., w. of Rev. Ramsey D. Potts, June 27, 1850
 Martha J. (Mrs.), d. of Samuel Dinkle, Mar. 23, 1871
 Mary Chambliss, d. of John W. and Caroline Potts, May 20, 1858
 Morton W., Feb. 5, 1885
 S. T., May 19, 1938
 Thomas W., s. of Capt. John W. Potts, July 28, 1853
 Virginia, w. of Charles G. Potts, June 22, 1848
 Virginia W., d. of J. N. and Maggie A. Potts, Nov. 2, 1876
POUND
 Eliza Y., w. of Richard Pound, Nov. 25, 1858
POWEL
 Thomas (Dr.), Aug. 2, 1877
POWELL
 (Mrs.), d. of John Adams, Mar. 25, 1836
 Ann Eliza, w. of William Powell, Oct. 15, 1846
 Anna E. (Mrs.), d. of George W. Sutler, Nov. 15, 1877
 Bettie A. KIRK (Mrs.), Mar. 28, 1912
 C. G. (Dr.), Aug. 3, 1882
 Earnest Linwood, s. of William A. and Patty Powell, Apr. 25, 1889
 Edwin D., Aug. 25, 1864
 Elizabeth, w. of William Powell, May 11, 1854
 Ellen, Jan. 18, 1872
 F. F., m. Mary Frances Gentry, Aug. 22, 1901
 Grace, d. of Joshua H. Powell, May 26, 1904
 Ira M., Sept. 18, 1829
 J. E. (Rev.), Aug. 9, 1928
 J. Harvey, Dec. 29, 1887
 J. L. (Elder), Mar. 17, 1870
 James H., Feb. 22, 1844
 James R., Sr., Oct. 29, 1914
 Jefferson, Oct. 10, 1850
 John G., May 29, June 5, 1890
 John L., Sept. 24, 1863
 Julia A., w. of A. W. Powell, Feb. 28, 1884
 Julia T., w. of Rev. James L. Powell, Aug. 31, 1893
 Laura F. (Mrs.), July 31, 1902
 Lewis, Sept. 19, 1872
 Littleton Green, May 8, 1890
 Lucy (Mrs.), Apr. 24, 1902
 Lucy DeLoatche, w. of F. M. Powell, Aug. 22, 1918
 Maria L., w. of John Leven Powell, d. of Dr. Edward Grady, Mar. 19, 1891
 Martha, w. of Benjamin H. Powell, July 15, 1836

OBITUARY NOTICES IN THE RELIGIOUS HERALD WITH DATES OF PUBLICATION

Mary, w. of William C. Powell,
  Mar. 26, 1840
Mary (Mrs.), d. of Joseph R.
  Woodson, Jan. 10, 1850
Mary F., w. of G. W. Powell,
  Mar. 11, 1886
Mary S., w. of Elder William
  R. Powell, Mar. 1, 1877
Nicholas, Mar. 22, 1866
Paul J., Dec. 4, 1930
Peter T., Nov. 28, 1907;
  Feb. 20, 1908
R. J. (Dr.), Sept. 20, 1883
Richard H., Feb, 5, 1880
Rosa J., w. of Thomas B.
  Powell, Jan. 24, 1895
Sue Willhoit, w. of Charles
  G. Powell, June 2, 1892
William D. (Dr.), May 31, 1934
POWER
  Catherine Mary Cary, w. of
    James F. Power, d. of Miles
    and Ariana Cary, June 4,
    1903
  Frederick W., Jr., s. of
    Frederick W. and Medora B.
    Power, Oct. 2, 1884
  John W., Aug. 17, 1916
POWERS
  Alice, w. of William Powers,
    June 19, 1851
  Ellen, Jan. 1, 1852
  J. Pike (Mrs.), w. of Rev.
    J. Pike Powers, June 14,
    1923
  John, Aug. 3, 1854
  John A. (Rev.), Nov. 11, 1886
  Lona Reeder (Mrs.), Jan. 3,
    1935
  Nancy (Mrs.), July 23, 1891
  Roxie, d. of W. L. and Cor-
    delia Powers, Dec. 15, 1892
  Thomas H., Feb. 19, 1863
  William Alpheus, s. of James
    D. and Mildred Powers,
    Nov. 27, 1851
  William J., Aug. 24, 1893
  Willard S., s. of Logan W.
    and Louisa I. Powers, Dec.
    22, 1881

  Willie B., w. of William J.
    Powers, Aug. 24, 1893
PRATT
  William, Sept. 25, 1856
PRESSON
  Emma F., Feb. 9, 1911
  James H., June 21, 1877
  Joel C., s. of James H.
    and M. I. Presson, Sept.
    29, 1859
  Martha Alice, w. of J. C.
    Presson, Dec. 20, 1883
  Mary, w. of William Presson,
    Dec. 10, 1830
  Pattie J., w. of James H.
    Presson, Mar. 6, 1862
  Sallie A., d. of James H. and
    Mollie Presson, Oct. 17,
    1872
PRESTON
  Benjamin T. (Col.), June 5,
    1862
  Elizabeth S., w. of John
    Preston, Feb. 19, 1863
  John S. (Col.), May 12, 1881
  William S., June 20, 1828
PRESTRIDGE
  J. N. (Dr.), Nov. 6, 1913
PRIBBLE
  Samuel Ethelbert (Dr.), Apr.
    6, 1882
PRICE
  Ann Overton, d. of Capt.
    Joseph Farrell Price, Sept.
    24, 1830
  Anna (Mrs.), June 8, 1843
  B. E. (Mrs.), d. of Joel B.
    and Eliza Lemon, Aug. 30,
    Dec. 6, 1906
  Barbara, w. of Capt. Thomas
    Price, June 17, 1831
  Caleb, s. of Francis M. and
    Sibba Price, Apr. 3, 1873
  Cyrus, s. of G. W. Price,
    June 11, 1903
  Eliza F.,w. of Capt. Joseph
    F. Price, d. of Col. John
    Winston, Jan. 13, 1853
  Elizabeth (Mrs.), July 12,
    1888

OBITUARY NOTICES IN THE RELIGIOUS HERALD WITH DATES OF PUBLICATION

Ellen Maria, w. of Dr. Lucien B. Price, d. of Capt. Joseph F. Winston, Feb. 8, 1883
Emma Taylor (Mrs.), Apr. 29, 1909
G. W., Jr., Aug. 26, 1858
George Cook (Capt.), Sept. 6, 1888
George W., Feb. 16, 1905
Glover V., s. of Dr. R. N. and E. B. Price, July 2, 1868
Harvey Lee, s. of Benjamin F. and Mary Price, Sept. 8, 1887
Henry George, Jan. 27, 1898
J. M., Aug. 11, 1921
Jane B., Jan. 20, 1848
Joseph Ferrell (Capt.), s. of Capt. Thomas Price, Dec. 4, 1862
Joseph J., Mar. 20, 1873
Lottie, Feb. 8, 1917
Lucien B., s. of Dr. Lucien B. Price, May 29, 1851
Lucien B. (Dr.), Jan. 31, 1889
Martha, w. of Abner B. Price, Mar. 6, 1845
Richard, Jr., May 22, 1879
Rosalie Lewis, d. of Dr. Richard N. and Eliza B. Price, Nov. 17, 1859
S. W. (Rev.), Nov. 16, 1876
Sally, w. of Capt. Barnett Price, Aug. 5, 1852
Sophronia J., w. of Albert Price, June 27, 1878
Sue, June 15, 1899
Thomas Ferrille, s. of Lucien and Ellen Price, Sept. 4, 1835
Tommie, child of Francis M. and Sibba Price, Apr. 3, 1873
W. A. (Mrs.), Dec. 21, 1911
William M., s. of Joseph F. Price, Nov. 28, 1834
William M., Aug. 20, 1846

PRICHARD

Annie Judson, d. of Rev. John L. Prichard, gr.d. of Rev. James B. Taylor, Apr. 2, May 7, 1874
Clarissa (Mrs.), Feb. 18, 1864
Ernest Duggan, s. of George T. and Lou W. Prichard, Aug. 8, 1889
George Taylor, Dec. 13, 1934
James Taylor, s. of Rev. J. L. and Jane E. Prichard, Aug. 21, 1856
Jane E., w. of Rev. J. L. Prichard, d. of Rev. James B. Taylor, Feb. 12, 1874
John L., s. of Rev. J. L. Prichard, July 12, 1877
Lou Waters, w. of George Taylor Prichard, d. of Rev. Waters, Aug. 5, 1915
Lydia, w. of Rev. John L. Prichard, Nov. 26, 1868
Mary Banks, w. of Elder John L. Prichard, Jan. 10, 1850
Robert S., s. of Rev. J. L. Prichard, Feb. 1, 1872; Mar. 27, 1873
Robert Samuel, Apr. 23, 1925

PRIDDY

Catharine, Oct. 20, 1853
Charles M., s. of William H. and Nancy Priddy, Sept. 25, 1845
John Robert, Jan. 26, 1928
Margaret Ann, d. of W. H. and Nancy Priddy, Sept. 25, 1845

PRIEST

Filmore, s. of John M. Priest, Mar. 26, 1863
Lucie Fannie, w. of Job M. Priest, d. of John Holland, Mar. 26, 1863
Mary Ann, w. of James Priest, Sept. 27, 1877
Mary E., w. of John M. Priest, Nov. 17, 1853; Jan. 26,

OBITUARY NOTICES IN THE RELIGIOUS HERALD WITH DATES OF PUBLICATION

1854
PRINCE
  Annie (Mrs.), Apr. 19, 1934
  Bettie T., d. of J. H. and
    E. B. Prince, Apr. 10, 1879
  Clara, d. of Mrs. N. B. Prince,
    Jan. 9, 1902
  Elizabeth B., w. of Capt.
    Joseph H. Prince, d. of
    Joseph Claud, Mar. 17, 1887
  George W., Feb. 28, Mar. 20,
    1924
  Harry Thomas (Mrs.), June 15,
    1931
  James, Apr. 19, 1860
  Jessie M., d. of Joseph H. and
    Elizabeth B. Prince, July
    3, 1856
  John (Col.), Nov. 9, 1899
  Joel, Nov. 30, 1854
  Joseph H. (Capt.), Dec. 18,
    1884; Jan. 15, May 14, 1885
  Martha, w. of Benjamin Prince,
    Feb. 2, 1871
  Martha Frances, w. of Judge
    J. B. Prince, July 9 and 23,
    1896
  Raymond, Aug. 4, 1898
  Rebecca C., June 16, July 7,
    1859
  Richard (Capt.), Aug. 15, 1850
  Sarah Jane (Mrs.), Mar. 27, 1924
  Virginia Ann DUGGER, w. of Col.
    John Prince, June 4, 1896
PRINGLE
  Alice Goode, Aug. 15, 1872
  Cornelia Rebeka, w. of Capt.
    W. C. Pringle, d. of William D. and Rebeka Wade
    Wright, June 14, 1888*
  W. E., Jan. 30, 1896
  W. S. (Capt.), Mar. 12, 1891
  William, Mar. 5, 1857
PRITCHARD
  Helen, w. of J. P. Pritchard,
    d. of J. R. Walker, June 2,
    1881
  John L. (Rev.), June 4, July 9,
    1863
  Thomas Hume, Jan. 24, 1929

PRITCHETT
  Caroline E., w. of Ira A.
    Pritchett, Jan. 5, 1865
  Culbreth T. (Lt.), Feb. 12,
    1863
  Edgar Westley, s. of Joshua
    H. Pritchett, Nov. 7, 1918
  Emily H. (Mrs.), Oct. 14,
    1869
  Joshua Howard, Jan. 26, 1933
  Lucy S., Apr. 20, 1854
  Olivia B. (Mrs.), June 19,
    July 10, 1924
  Thomas, Dec. 27, 1849
  William P., Mar. 16, 1899
PROCTOR
  Harvey W., Nov. 12, 1925
PROFFIT
  Ann T., w. of Obadiah Proffit, Oct. 4, 1860
PROFFITT
  Sallie (Mrs.), Mar. 3, 1932
PROSSER
  John H., Mar. 20, 1873
PROVENCE
  Ethel, d. of Rev. S. M. and
    India Watkins Provence,
    July 11, 1889
  S. M. (Dr.), May 1, 1924
PRUDEN
  Edward Hughes (Rev.), Dec. 3,
    1936
  Johnnie Ryland Cox, s. of L.
    S. Pruden, Feb. 5, 1885
PRUITT
  C. W. (Mrs.), w. of Rev. C.
    W. Pruitt, Dec. 11, 1884
PRYOR
  Eliza A., w. of Gen. B. W.
    Pryor, Aug. 5, 1858
  Elizabeth, w. of John C.
    Pryor, July 3, 1845
  Lucy A. (Mrs.), July 27, 1882
  Nancy L., w. of Madison C.
    Pryor, May 13, 1847
  Richard T., Dec. 1, 1864
  Samuel, Feb. 28, 1878
  Sarah, w. of Col. John Pryor,
    May 1, 1845
PUCKET

* Possible inaccuracy in name, or spelling, but given as printed

OBITUARY NOTICES IN THE RELIGIOUS HERALD WITH DATES OF PUBLICATION

Elizabeth (Mrs.), Sept. 21, 1832
George W., Apr. 23, 1863
PUCKETT
   Martha A., May 14, 1903
   Rebecca, w. of Henry Puckett, June 30, 1859
PUGH
   A. T., July 27, 1922
   John Andrew, s. of Col. Thomas Pugh, June 17, 1847
   Lucy (Mrs.), June 2, 1921
   Lucy (Mrs.), Feb. 7, 1924
   Martha Jane, d. of Col. Thomas Pugh, Mar. 17, 1853
   Sallie, July 6, 1893
   Virginia R., w. of George Pugh, May 26, 1870
   William M., Feb. 7, 1861
PULLEN
   Henrietta, w. of Rev. John Pullen, Mar. 11, 1897
   John (Elder), Feb. 13, Mar. 12, 1868
   John (Rev.), Sept. 8, 1898
   Johnnie, s. of Thomas E. and Martha A. Pullen, gr.s. of Rev. John Pullen, Sept. 4, 1873
   Martha A., w. of Thomas E. Pullen, May 23, 1889
PULLER
   Ann G., d. of James T. and Martha E. Puller, Sept. 9, 1858
   Catherine (Mrs.), July 5, 1860
   Emily, w. of Maj. J. W. Puller, May 30, 1867
   James, June 7, 1849
   James T., Jan. 29, 1863
   John M., Jan. 29, 1863
   R. Ashly, s. of James E. and Kate E. Puller, Mar. 5, 1874
   R. T., Jan. 31, 1918
   Richard A., Mar. 25, 1869
   T. R., Feb. 23, 1922
   Thomas, June 3, 1831
   William, July 11, 1861
PULLEY
   Franklin Pierce, May 10, 1928
PULLIAM
   John R. (Maj.), Feb. 13, 1851
   M. P., Nov. 26, 1925
   Samuel G., Feb. 8, 1844
   William E., Jan. 4, 1877
PULLING
   Thomas, Sept. 25, 1829
PULLUM
   Permelia P., w. of James B. Pullum, d. of Edward L. and Harriet D. Pugh, July 3, 1851
PUMPHREY
   Elizabeth, Dec. 25, 1845
PURCELL
   James R., June 5, 1862
   John, July 5, 1894
   L. Mortimer, Nov. 3, 1870
   McDaniel, s. of C. W. and M. A. Purcell, Feb. 26, 1891
PURDIE
   John Robinson (Dr.), Nov. 17, 1898
PURKINS
   Cornelia Burt, w. of William Purkins, Sept. 12, 1861
   Emma Kate, d. of James H. and Clementina Purkins, Feb. 3, 1859
   George Robert, s. of James H. and Clementina Purkins, Aug. 7, 1856
   John R., May 17, 1839
   Lucy Ann, June 21, 1883
   Thomas (Col.), July 5, 1855
   Thomas Edward, Jan. 25, 1912
   Washington H., Feb. 25, 1847
PURKS
   Nannie E., d. of P. B. and Nannie Purks, Sept. 5, 1878
   Thornton, June 19, 1851
PURVIS
   Edward D., s. of Winston Purvis, Feb. 26, 1863
PURYEAR
   Bennett, Apr. 2, 1914
   Cynthia, Sept. 3, 1829

OBITUARY NOTICES IN THE RELIGIOUS HERALD WITH DATES OF PUBLICATION

Elizabeth, w. of Samuel Puryear, Nov. 15, 1833
Smith, July 22, 1831
Virginia C., w. of B. Puryear, Aug. 25, 1870
Willard, s. of Thomas J. and Eugenia E. Puryear, Aug. 16, 1888

PUTNEY
Lucy J., w. of Dr. William R. Putney, Dec. 3, 1885
Mary A., w. of Ellis W. Putney, Sr., Sept. 12, 1878
Samuel Ellis, s. of Ellis W. and Virginia A. Putney, June 14, 1888
Samuel F., Nov. 5, 1885
W. R. (Mrs.), Jan. 8, 1925
W. W., May 19, 1927
William L., s. of Dr. W. R. Putney, Nov. 7, 1889
William Pitt, Mar. 31, 1927
William R. (Dr.), Feb. 13, 1902

- Q -

QUARLES
Ann (Mrs.), Sept. 7, 1838
Ann (Mrs.), Sept. 23, 1858
Ann Rebecca, w. of Jesse L. Quarles, d. of John Otey, Jan. 12, 1860
B. L., Mar. 13, 1924
Bessie Lee, d. of Henry and Anna G. Quarles, Oct. 6, 1873
Charles (Dr.), Aug. 25, 1881
Clevears B., Oct. 19, 1838
David Benjamin, s. of Benjamin L. Quarles, Apr. 9, 1896
Dicy P., d. of A. D. and I. M. Quarles, Nov. 25, 1880
Edmund G., s. of John Quarles, Feb. 12, 1857
Ella, Aug. 14, 1890
Ellen V. HUNTER, w. of Elder Charles Quarles, Aug. 29, 1895
George Washington, Mar. 12, 1863
Gregory, s. of George W. and Rosa F. Quarles, Dec. 16, 1886
Henry Franklin, s. of Lemuel B. Quarles, Apr. 9, 1896
Henry Lewis (Rev.), Apr. 13 and 20, May 11, 1922
Jane McKenzie, w. of Lemuel Quarles, Apr. 17, 1913
John M., s. of Peter Quarles, June 22, 1848
John R. (Capt.), May 3, 1866
Johnnie, s. of John R. and Emma C. Quarles, Nov. 29, 1877
Letitia, w. of Capt. John R. Quarles, Dec. 12, 1850
Martha, w. of Washington Quarles, May 3, 1866
Mary Ann, d. of John R. and
Louisa D. Quarles, Oct. 19, 1858
Peter, May 19, 1859
Ralph, June 5, 1845
Robert F., July 28, 1842
Sarah, w. of P. M. John Quarles, Dec. 18, 1851
William W., Nov. 27, 1862
Wilson, June 27, 1850

QUESENBERRY
Mary (Mrs.), Mar. 27, 1851

QUICK
George W. (Mrs.), w. of Dr. G. W. Quick, Apr. 23, 1936
Sarah O., w. of J. V. Quick, June 4, 1903

QUILLEN
Ira D., Apr. 23, 1865
Louisa DAVIS, w. of Louis B. Quillen, Sept. 15, 1938

QUIN
M. (Elder), Oct. 25, 1839

QUINN
James C., July 27, 1882
Josephine, w. of S. J. Quinn, Sept. 2, 1897
Mary A. (Mrs.), Nov. 1, 1877
Sylvanus J. (Capt.), Dec. 22, 1910

QUISENBERRY
child of Carter Quisenberry, Sept. 29, 1837
Albert, Oct. 12, 1935
Albert Hill, Oct. 24, 1935
Alfred, s. of James Quisenberry, Nov. 10, 1864
Ernest L., Aug. 18, 1927
George, Oct. 28, 1897
Jane (Mrs.), Nov. 16, 1843
Jane H. (Mrs.), July 29, 1897
Lucy, w. of Elijah Quisenberry, Aug. 17, 1848
M. L., w. of N. Quisenberry, Nov. 9, 1843
Sallie C. (Mrs.), Dec. 16, 1909
William, Aug. 30, 1877

- R -

RABINEAU
  Ann H., d. of Dr. G. W.
    Rabineau, Nov. 13, 1845
  Bettie B., w. of George W.
    Rabineau, Aug. 7, 1884
  George W. (Dr.), Aug. 4, 1853
RADCLIFFE
  Ann Frances (Mrs.), Feb. 11,
    1847
RADY
  Charles P., Dec. 29, 1898
  Harriet, Mar. 21, 1907
RAE
  Bettie S., w. of Littleton V.
    Rae, Dec. 8, 1904
RAGLAND
  Alice T., w. of John F.
    Ragland, Nov. 7, 1901
  Ann P. (Mrs.), July 9, 1891
  Benjamin Nicholas, s. of H. D.
    and Araminta P. Ragland,
    Nov. 3, 1887*
  Bettie, Sept. 12, 1918
  Hugh Davis, s. of Rev. Hugh
    D. and Araminta M. Ragland,
    Apr. 27, 1871
  James A. (Dr.), Oct. 17, 1850
  Jennie C. (Mrs.), Feb. 2, 1893
  John B., July 21, 1842
  Luther, s. of Rev. Hugh D. and
    Araminta M. Ragland, Aug.
    20, 1868
  Mary (Mrs.), Dec. 9, 1841
  Mary M., d. of Mrs. Nathaniel
    H. Ragland, May 20, 1858
  Mary Sands (Mrs.), Feb. 14,
    1884
  N. H. Aug. 16, 1849
  Nancy, w. of John B. Ragland,
    July 21, 1842
  Rhoda (Mrs.), Sept. 25, 1858
  Sally (Mrs.), Jan. 14, 1869
  Thomas Finch, Jan. 13, 1870
RAIFORD
  Allie M., d. of Mrs. N. J.
    Raiford, Mar. 18, 1909
RAINES
  C. A. (Mrs.), Jan. 20, 1887
  Sarah J., w. of William Rains,
    Dec. 11, 1862
RALLS
  A. P., Oct. 23, 1862
RAMBO
  Martha S. (Mrs.), Aug. 15,
    1878
RAMOS
  John Jeter, s. of J. V. and
    Mariah H. Ramos, June 29,
    1854
RAMSBURG
  David L., Oct. 6, 1938
RAMSEY
  Annie (Mrs.), Dec. 20, 1928
  Helen Cain, d. of Dr. W. A.
    Ramsey, Sept. 25, 1873
  J. G., Nov. 21, 1918
  James P. (Mrs.), Sept. 6, 1934
  John M. (Mr. and Mrs.), Apr.
    28, 1932
  Nannie A., w. of W. E. Ramsey,
    Apr. 28, 1938
  Virginia, d. of Thomas Ramsey,
    Aug. 22, 1861
RANDOLPH
  Alice Bryan, w. of John Cary
    Randolph, Dec. 6, 1934
  Augusta, w. of Lt. Victor
    Moreau Randolph, Nov. 8, 1839
  Brett, Mar. 7, 1828
  Carrie S., w. of Dr. John
    Randolph, Oct. 30, 1879
  John T. (Mrs.), d. of Rev.
    William P. Farish, Mar. 17,
    1904
  John T. (Rev.), Dec. 14, 1905
  Mary, d. of Rev. J. T. and Ann
    E. Randolph, June 25, 1868
  Nancy Jane, d. of R. K. Ran-
    dolph, July 24, 1835
  Peyton, Jan. 2, 1829
  Richard K. (Dr.), Nov. 14,
    1834
  Thomas Mann, former Governor
    of Virginia, June 27, 1828

* Possible inaccuracy in name, or spelling, but given as printed

OBITUARY NOTICES IN THE RELIGIOUS HERALD WITH DATES OF PUBLICATION

RANGELY
  Imogene, w. of W. W. Rangely, Oct. 31, 1889
RANKIN
  Andrew, May 16, 1828
RANSOM
  L. A. (Mrs.), d. of Chastain Cocke, Jan. 20, 1887
RANSON
  Mary, d. of Rev. H. T. Ranson, Mar. 25, 1886
  Virginia, w. of Rev. H. T. Ranson, Dec. 4, 1884
  William Cleveland, s. of Rev. H. T. Ranson, Nov. 28, 1918
RANSONE
  Bettie, w. of H. W. Ransone, d. of William J. Meador, Mar. 5, 1903
  Everette Algeon, Jan. 17, 1924
  Rebecca Hamilton, d. of W. A. and Mary J. Ransone, July 31, 1890
RAPP
  Frederick, July 18, 1834
RATCLIFF
  Emma Jane (Mrs.), June 22, 1848
RATCLIFFE
  Ann M. (Mrs.), Jan. 28, 1915
  Carrie B., Oct. 20, 1932
  Mildred F. (Mrs.), June 19, 1924
  Virginia, Aug. 18, 1853
  Wellford C., s. of J. W. and A. M. Ratcliffe, July 30, 1868
  William B., Aug. 13, 1914
RAVENSCROFT
  John S. (Rev.), Mar. 19, 1830
RAVEY
  Elizabeth (Mrs.), Aug. 22, 1834
RAWLINGS
  Alice Gray Cole, d. of J. Boswell Rawlings, Apr. 21, May 12, 1932
  Anna Belle, w. of Richard H. Rawlings, d. of Capt. Z. H. Rawlings, Apr. 30, 1896
  Bettie B., w. of Z. H. Rawlings, d. of Absolom and Nancy Row, Apr. 19, 1888
  J. H. (Capt.), Nov. 9, 1916
  James, Feb. 23, 1838
  James B., July 27, 1882
  Judith Ann (Mrs.), d. of Lewis Johnson, May 26, 1910
  Lucy J. (Mrs.), Jan. 14, 1858
  Mary N., d. of Richard Rawlings, Aug. 28, 1879
  R. H., Aug. 31, 1905
RAWLINSON
  Frank (Mrs.), Feb. 8, 1917
RAWLS
  Gavin (Dr.), Oct. 26, 1922; Jan. 25, 1923
  John, Feb. 15, 1923
  Robert, Dec. 23, 1920
RAY
  Davie Jasper, w. of Dr. T. B. Ray, Dec. 13, 1923
  Lula Turpin, w. of J. Dudley Ray, d. of William H. Fleming, Apr. 5, 1888
  Mary Louisa, d. of Richard Henry and Sarah Catharine Ray, Sept. 29, 1859
  T. B. (Dr.), Jan. 25, 1934
RAYFIELD
  Frisby W., Jan. 24, 1884
RAYMOND
  Augusta, w. of Rev. Charles A. Raymond, Feb. 28, 1907
  Charles A. (Rev.), Mar. 14, 1895
  F. B. (Mrs.), Dec. 6, 1906
  John Egerton, Dec. 5, 1901
  Josephine Elizabeth, d. of George and Eliza Raymond, Aug. 4, 1842
  Maud, w. of Rev. Frank B. Raymond, Nov. 22, 1906
  Tamar Rebecka, d. of Mrs. E. A. Raymond, May 10, 1849
REA
  Bland, Aug. 20, 1868
  John, Jan. 26, 1893
  William T., May 12 and 19, 1910
READ

OBITUARY NOTICES IN THE RELIGIOUS HERALD WITH DATES OF PUBLICATION

Adalaide M. (Mrs.), Dec. 7, 1871
Adeline M., d. of Laudon U. and Adeline M. Read, Oct. 12, 1843
Alcinda, sister of Drs. A. W. and John Lafayette Read, Confed. surgeons, Mar. 29, 1900
Betsy (Mrs.), June 3, 1858
Callie, d. of Robert Read, Apr. 23, 1874
Charles H. (Rev.), Aug. 16, 1900
Elizabeth (Mrs.), Feb. 8, 1872
John, Oct. 29, 1857
John R. (Mrs.), Aug. 31, 1882
Manie Fisher, d. of W. A. and Samuella Owen Read, Apr. 17, 1890
Margaret L., w. of Dr. Calvin H. Read, Nov. 14, 1872
Mariah Ellen, w. of John R. Read, Mar. 17, 1859
Marshal (Rev.), Sept. 17, 1903
Richard Hall, Mar. 23, 1876
Samuella Crawford Owen, w. of William A. Read, Oct. 1, 1936
William S. (Dr.), Dec. 29, 1881
Winfrey (Mrs.), Mar. 28, 1889
REAEMY
Benjamin, Jan. 29, 1852
REAGUES
Helen E., w. of G. F. Reagues, d. of Thomas H. Johnson, Apr. 27, 1882
REAMEY
Mary, w. of John Reamey, Dec. 18, 1862
REAMS
Amanda M., w. of Jefferson Reams, Nov. 2, 1843
George P., Dec. 27, 1923
Mary, w. of Edward Reams, Apr. 20, 1854
Virgil Dudley, s. of W. B. and Alma Reams, June 30, 1898
REAMY
s. of Brother and Sister Reamy, Sept. 23, 1897

A. J. (Rev.), Jan. 2, 1936
Annie Terrell, Aug. 13, 1914
Frances (Mrs.), July 13, 1876
Harriet Margaret, w. of Thomas B. Reamy, Jan. 10, 1918
James, Aug. 22, 1861
James Samuel, s. of James and Sarah Colman Reamy, Oct. 22, 1931
Mabel Balderson, June 16, 1938
Susan, w. of Samuel T. Reamy, Aug. 23, 1883
Walter Lee, s. of Richard T. and Frances A. Reamy, Aug. 22, 1861
William, Oct. 12, 1854
REAVES
Jesse, July 3, 1873
REBMAN
William, Aug. 1, 1901
REBURN
Gracie Lee, d. of W. F. Reburn, Apr. 17, 1924
Mamie, Nov. 4, 1897
REDD
(Brother), Mar. 28, 1844
Caleb, Mar. 29, 1849
Elizabeth, w. of Temple Redd, Oct. 18, 1855
Elizabeth, w. of Samuel Redd, d. of Edmond Taylor, Jan. 20, 1859
Kate C., w. of James T., Oct. 28, 1880
Lewellyn Wentworth, Jan. 19, 1865
Louisiana, w. of John R. Redd, Aug. 22, 1872
Lucy, Edmonia, d. of James T. and Thomasia Redd, July 28, 1853
Lucy R., w. of John R. Redd, May 10, 1839
Mary A., w. of William Redd, Sept. 15, 1853
Samuel, Sept. 16, 1841
Samuel C. (Judge), Mar. 23, 1911
Sarah F., June 24, 1880
Temple, Feb. 25, 1872

OBITUARY NOTICES IN THE RELIGIOUS HERALD WITH DATES OF PUBLICATION

REDFORD
 Ann (Mrs.), Nov. 27, 1856
 Eliza (Mrs.), July 22, 1847
REDMAN
 John, Mar. 11, 1937
 John Cox, s. of John T. and
  Emma S. Redman, Apr. 5, 1855
REDWOOD
 Ann R., Feb. 11, 1858
 Elizabeth G. (Mrs.), May 16,
  1850
REED
 G. W. (Rev.), Oct. 17 and
  24, 1918
 Frances Miller HARDY, w. of
  John S. Reed, Dec. 5, 1918
 Laura Emma (Mrs.), d. of R. M.
  and S. F. Bragg, Jan. 15,
  1891
REEDY
 Eli W., Jan. 6, 1921
REES
 F. (Rev.), Jan. 4, 1855
REESE
 John R., Oct. 20, 1932
 Lucy Walker, d. of John E.
  and Sallie Reese, Nov.
  28, 1878
 M. C., w. of J. J. Reese, d.
  of Richard Blanks, Apr. 15,
  1880
 M. L. (Mrs.), May 23, 1918
 Mary (Mrs.), d. of Nicholas
  and Sarah Robertson, Nov.
  24, 1870
 S. L., Mar. 19, 1874
 Sallie Walker (Mrs.), Aug. 25,
  1898
 Walter J., Aug. 12, 1852
REEVE
 Samuel A., Feb. 21, 1856
REEVELY
 Sarah Virginia (Mrs.), May 19,
  1892
REEVES
 (Sister), Jan. 31, 1867
 J. (Rev.), Jan. 14, Feb. 4,
  1937
 Nancy, w. of Elijah Reeves,
  Feb. 27, 1890

 Peter May (Rev.), July 20, 1876
REID
 Alexander, July 19, 1855
 Alice (Mrs.), June 21, 1906
 Catharine Frances, d. of Col.
  John Reid, Jan. 13, 1842
 Charles, Jan. 26, 1899
 Edward Lewis, s. of H. C. and
  Eliza E. Reid, gr.s. of Rev.
  E. G. Shipp, Sept. 1, 1881
 Eliza Allen (Mrs.), June 24,
  1920
 Eliza Ann, w. of Dr. Mark
  Reid, May 20, 1841
 Florence, Sept. 27, 1906
 G. B. (Dr.), Sept. 10, 1891
 Harriet Louisa, Feb. 20, 1879
 Hiram C., Aug. 2, 1900
 John Fielding, s. of Dr. Mark
  and Eliza Reid, Oct. 22, 1840
 Mary Elizabeth, d. of Col. John
  Reid, Jan. 13, 1842
 Mary L. (Mrs.), Dec. 7, 1922
 Matilda Baker, Jan. 28, 1897
 Oliver W. (Dr.), May 21, 1888
 T. A., July 3, 1902
 Virginia M., d. of Alexander
  Reid, July 1, 1858
 Virginia P., d. of Dr. Mark
  Reid, Mar. 29, 1877
REILEY
 William, Dec. 3, 1891
REINS
 Jane F., June 5, 1851
 Mariann, w. of Charles Reins,
  Aug. 3, 1848
REITH
 Mary W., w. of H. J.Reith, d.
  of George Chambers, Mar.
  12, 1885
REMELY
 James (Rev.), Apr. 1, 1875
RENDLEMAN
 Bettie, w. of P. L. Rendleman,
  May 29, 1873
RENFROE
 J. J. D. (Rev.), June 14, 1888
RENNOLDS
 Bessie Goodrich, Oct. 26, 1916
 Martha D., w. of Capt. Stnrehle

OBITUARY NOTICES IN THE RELIGIOUS HERALD WITH DATES OF PUBLICATION

Rennolds, Nov. 30, 1832
Mary L., d. of Dr. B. G. Rennolds, Dec. 22, 1870
REPITON
   A. Paul (Rev.), Apr. 20, 1876
   Joseph A., July 5, 1833
REVERE
   E. H. (Corp.), Aug. 4, 1864
REYNOLD
   J. L. (Rev.), Dec. 27, 1877; Jan. 3, 1878
REYNOLDS
   Champe C., d. of O. J. and Caroline C. Reynolds, Sept. 25, 1873
   Charles J., June 12, 1930
   Hattie, d. of Judge John E. and Mattie Reynolds, Aug. 13, 1891
   James Corcoran, s. of Joseph and Mary L. Reynolds, Aug. 28, 1890
   James W., Jan. 21, 1874
   James W., Oct. 18, Nov. 8, 1928
   Jenetta, w. of William H. Reynolds, Apr. 9, 1874
   John Wirt, s. of Judge John O. Reynolds, Apr. 27, 1893
   Joseph D., Aug. 18, 1921
   Katharine, d. of Dr. James D. Reynolds, Apr. 18, 1907
   Mary, Oct. 10, 1872
   Mary E., w. of Washington S. Reynolds, Apr. 12, 1855
   Nancy (Mrs.), Mar. 4, 1836
   O. B. (Mrs.), May 15, 1890
   Powhatan W., June 14, 1934
   S. S., Jan. 31, 1867
   Sally, d. of James W. and Julia A. Reynolds, June 25, 1846
   Stokes Gregory, w. of G. A. Reynolds, d. of Dr. J. E. Gregory, Aug. 27, 1908
   T. E. (Mrs.), w. of Rev. T. E. Reynolds, July 23, 1903
   Taylor McCarthy, s. of R. L. and Narcissa E. Reynolds, Dec. 9, 1880
   W. J. (Rev.), July 21, Aug. 11, 1921
   W. W. (Rev.), Nov. 25, 1937
   William H., Mar. 17, 1864
RHEES
   Morgan J. (Rev.), Jan. 27, 1853
RHINE
   John B. H., Oct. 15, 1891
RHOADES
   A. R., d. of Robert Rhoades, June 9, 1870
   Susan, w. of John Rhoades, Mar. 1, 1860
RHODES
   Bennie, Aug. 17, 1893
   Mattie C., w. of William H. Rhodes, Apr. 18, 1918
   Mattie Gould, d. of William H. and Mattie C. Rhodes, Oct. 20, 1887*
   Maud Olivia, d. of William H. and Mattie Rhodes, Aug. 6, 1885
   Richard Gold, s. of W. H. and M. C. Rhodes, Aug. 15, 1889*
   Robert A., Apr. 2, 1925
   Samuel Oley, Dec. 21, 1893
   W. J., Nov. 30, 1933
   William H., June 11, 1908
RICE
   (Dr.), Sept. 16, 1831
   A. A. (Dr.), Dec. 25, 1902; Jan. 1 and Mar. 5, 1903
   A. B., s. of E. T. Rice, Jan. 25, 1866
   Ada Leigh, d. of Holman Rice, Dec. 18, 1856
   Adison Sanders, s. of Hampton A. and Lucie R. Rice, Mar. 15, 1877
   Charles Edgar, s. of Holman and Mary Rice, Dec. 18, 1856
   David, Aug. 8, 1878
   Dollie F., w. of Col. Evan Rice, Sept. 27, 1860
   E. T., Jan. 31, 1901
   Edna Moren, w. of C. Russel Rice, Sept. 16, 1926
   Elizabeth, w. of Tarlton Rice, Feb. 3, 1848

* Possible inaccuracy in name, or spelling, but given as printed

OBITUARY NOTICES IN THE RELIGIOUS HERALD WITH DATES OF PUBLICATION

Elizabeth, June 19, 1851
Frances M., w. of Stephen T. Rice, Jan. 28, 1847
George (Mrs.), Sept. 24, 1925
Harriet B., d. of Isham Rice, Oct. 3, 1834
J. J., July 12 and 19, 1866
James Stuart, Oct. 15, 1891
Jane Elizabeth, d. of William T. and Mary Rice, July 31, 1845
Jane S., Mar. 2, 1876
Jennie A., w. of J. V. Rice, Dec. 29, 1881
John H., Mar. 6, 1930
Lucinda W., w. of Dr. S. B. Rice, Oct. 12, 1854
Luther G. (Sgt.), Nov. 19, 1863
Margaret A. (Mrs.), Apr. 4, 1872
Mary Vaughan, w. of W. T. Rice, Mar. 20, 1890
Nancy (Mrs.), July 12, 1860
Nellie, d. of Rev. A. A. and M. C. Rice, Sept. 30, 1880
Nora Patterson (Mrs.), Jan. 22, 1920
Ruth Stuart, May 12, 1921
Sally B., d. of Dr. William T. Rice, May 4, 1854
Samuel Blair (Rev.), Feb. 18, 1886
Samuel D. (Capt.), Jan. 5, 1865
Thomas, Aug. 4, 1870
Thomas Burwell (Col.), May 1, 1873
Willianna, child of James J. and Frances A. Rice, Dec. 31, 1846

RICHARD
Ruth Wood (Mrs.), Jan. 24, 1878

RICHARDS
Alice Greer, w. of A. M. Richards, d. of Rev. T. W. Greer, Mar. 4, 1909
Ann Bedford, w. of Capt. John Y. Richards, Nov. 17, 1870
Betsy, w. of Rev. Nathaniel Richards, Aug. 17, 1905
Elisha, Apr. 16, 1830
Eliza, w. of John Richards, Dec. 21, 1832
John Y., s. of William Richards, Oct. 22, 1891
Julia Hawes DEJARNETTE (Mrs.), Feb. 2, 1899
Lelia Alice, d. of Capt. John Y. Richards, May 27, 1869
M. J. (Mrs.), d. of William W. Davis, Aug. 22, 1872
Nathaniel (Rev.), Apr. 19, 1923
Richard, Sr., Mar. 6, 1856
Richard, Sept. 9, 1875
Virginia, d. of Quintus and Florence M. Richards, Sept. 4, 1873
William (Elder), Aug. 18, 1837
Willie, Sept. 8, 1864

RICHARDSON
(Brother), June 10, 1920
Alexander, s. of Rev. J. C. Richardson, May 23, 1861
Ann (Sister), Nov. 8, 1860
Anzilia, Jan. 26, 1871
Bertheda Muir, w. of Rev. W. L. Richardson, Oct. 13, 1910
Caroline, d. of David Richardson, June 24, 1845
Carter, Mar. 5, 1908
Charles Henry, s. of W. S. Richardson, Oct. 12, 1848
David Philip, Feb. 12, 1925
David Philip (Mrs.), July 18, 1929
E. M., Jr. (Mrs.), Feb. 21, 1935
Eva Binford, d. of John A. and Arbela L. Richardson, Sept. 8, 1881
Fannie E. (Mrs.), Aug. 8, 1929
George, Mar. 17, 1910
George Nelson, s. of Rev. John A. Richardson, Mar. 5,

OBITUARY NOTICES IN THE RELIGIOUS HERALD WITH DATES OF PUBLICATION

1885
H. H. (Mrs.), Jan. 10, 1935
Ida Hundley (Mrs.), Mar. 3, 1921
J. Mason (Rev.), June 26, 1930
Jane M., w. of Henry W. Richardson, d. of Elder R. Lilly, July 29, 1831
John A. (Rev.), Mar. 22, 1900
John R., Aug. 25, 1864
Joseph Henry, s. of Henry W. Richardson, Aug. 15, 1834
Judith (Mrs.), Feb. 15, 1917
Lucinda M., w. of H. G. Richardson, Aug. 19, 1852
Lucy, w. of George E. Richardson, Apr. 29, 1858
Margaret (Mrs.), Oct. 26, 1871
Martha (Mrs.), June 15, 1832
Martha, w. of Henry W. Richardson, Oct. 3, 1850
Mary, Aug. 4, 1892
Mary A., w. of S. G. Richardson, Aug. 6, 1863
Mary E., d. of George P. Richardson, Apr. 29, 1858
Mary Elizabeth (Mrs.), Dec. 4, 1890
Mary Jane, June 24, 1845
Maud Augustine, d. of Willard H. and Bettie Richardson, Feb. 16, 1882
Norman B., Jan. 11, 1900
Rebecca, w. of Capt. John Richardson, Mar. 6, 1829
Robert Fuller, s. of John A. Richardson, May 20, 1886
Robert Samuel, s. of Henry W. Richardson, Mar. 4, 1831
Samuel G., Aug. 20, 1857
Susanna, d. of David Richardson, July 24, 1845
T. A., Nov. 29, 1923
W. F. (Dr.), July 19, 1888
W. W. (Dr.), Mar. 22, 1934
William R. (Capt.), Mar. 22, 1855

RICHERSON
Francis Buckner (Dr.), Mar. 9, 1865
Kate B., w. of J. R. Richerson, d. of Dr. John D. Butler, July 12, 1917
Reuben B., Dec. 21, 1882
Susan F., w. of R. B. Richerson, May 20, 1880
William A., Aug. 27, 1863

RICHESON
Alben S., May 31, 1849
Anne C. (Mrs.), Sept. 12, 1889
John E., s. of George Richeson, Nov. 23, 1838
Mary (Mrs.), July 3, 1890
Pittacus L. (Rev.), Sept. 22, 1870
Susan F., May 18, 1843
Willie A., s. of Col. William A. and Mary Richeson, Aug. 22, 1861

RICKARD
Eliza (Mrs.), Jan. 23, 1873
John J., Mar. 5, 1885

RICKMAN
E. H. (Mrs.), Sept. 2, 1847

RIDDELL
Susan Winston (Mrs.), Apr. 28, 1938

RIDDICK
James, s. of Dr. J. G. and Yates Riddick, Feb. 22, 1894
Julia, w. of Nathan Riddick, July 13, 1852

RIDDLE
Ida Thomas, d. of Mrs. Bettie A. Riddle, Aug. 29, 1867
Jane C., w. of Watkins P. Riddle, d. of Robert Daniel, July 10, 1856
Percy E., Feb. 9, 1899
Watkins P., Dec. 28, 1899

RIDER
Edward, Jan. 3, 1867

RIDLEY
John, Feb. 9, 1865

RIGGAN
George W., Apr. 23 and 30, May 14, 1885

OBITUARY NOTICES IN THE RELIGIOUS HERALD WITH DATES OF PUBLICATION

Sallie Garland, w. of George
W. Riggan, June 26, 1930
RIGGINS
Bennie, Aug. 11, 1921
Julian Dewitt, s. of J. B.
Riggins, Dec. 5, 1918
RILEY
E. S. (Mrs.), May 12, 1927
Otho B., Mar. 25, 1920
RINER
Elba, Dec. 27, 1900
Hettie B., d. of John Riner,
June 16, 1904
Lizzie, w. of E. E. Riner,
Oct. 20, 1898
RIPLEY
Dorothy, Jan. 20, 1832
H. J. (Rev.), June 3, 1875
RIPPETOE
Alexander Nicholas (Rev.),
Sept. 2, 1886
Jane, w. of Rev. A. N.
Rippetoe, d. of John Morris,
Mar. 3, 1904
RIPPON
Thomas, Dec. 25, 1890
RISER
Sidney T. (Rev.), May 31,
1888
RITCHEY
Mary, July 18, 1867
RITTENHOUSE
David C. (Rev.), June 8,
1899
H. J., Aug. 11, 1927
Henry, Sept. 10, 1857
Mary Virginia (Mrs.), Mar.
18, 1897
Sarah Jane Elsom, w. of H. E.
Rittenhouse, d. of Nelson
and Elizabeth Elsom, Jan.
15, 1885
RITTER
L. M., Feb. 1, 1906
Martha J., w. of George W.
Ritter, d. of James S. Jones,
Mar. 25, 1886
RIVERCOMB
Robert, Sept. 26, 1861
RIVES

Thomas P. (Dr.), Aug. 20,
1840
RIXEY
Ellen D., d. of Thomas C.
Rixey, Mar. 16, 1854
Mary P., w. of Capt. Samuel
Rixey, July 26, 1839
R. P. (Rev.), Feb. 18, 1932
Samuel (Mrs.), July 6, 1922
Tabitha, Oct. 4, 1866
Thomas C., Mar. 16, 1854
ROACH
Abner Whitfield, Aug. 14,
1845
Alma, d. of Thomas and Catherine Roach, Dec. 22, 1892
C. W. (Capt.), Oct. 7, 1875
Damaris Tuggle, w. of J. J.
Roach, May 5, 1859
E. W. (Rev.), July 26, Aug.
2 and 30, 1883
Henry H. (Capt.), Nov. 26,
1863
John Bryan, s. of John and
Frances Roach, Aug. 6, 1840
John W., June 23, 1842
Nancy A. (Mrs.), Oct. 4, 1839
Priscilla (Mrs.), May 7, 1863
ROADCAP
Lizzie, d. of D. L. and Nannie Roadcap, Apr. 23, 1868
ROANE
Bettie Brockenbrough, d. of
Dr. Samuel and Ann F.
Roane, Mar. 1, 1849
Birdie, Apr. 2, 1874
John M. (Rev.), Aug. 29, 1867
Mollie A., Dec. 25, 1879
Robert Ryland, Mar. 3, 1881
Samuel H., Aug. 28, 1862
Sarah A., w. of William H.
Roane, May 2, 1828
Warren G. (Rev.), Mar. 1 and
22, 1883
ROARK
Benjamin Cobb, Sept. 28, 1922
Elizabeth Ann, w. of John R.
Roark, Feb. 20, 1851
ROBERSON
Charles C., s. of W. E. and R. A

OBITUARY NOTICES IN THE RELIGIOUS HERALD WITH DATES OF PUBLICATION

Roberson, May 1, 1851
Rebecca, w. of W. E.
Roberson, Dec. 20,
1860
ROBERTS
A., Jan. 22, 1852
Alexander, Sept. 28,
1832
Anna, w. of Christopher
Roberts, Jan. 18, 1844
B. Georgia (Mrs.), Oct. 16,
1879
Benjamin F., May 13, 1841
Calvin, May 15, 1919
Caly Ann, d. of W. W. Roberts,
July 1, 1847
Christopher, Mar. 8, 1839
Eliza B., w. of H. D. Roberts,
d. of Nathan Landcroft,
Nov. 6, 1873
Eliza Blanche, w. of John M.
Roberts, July 8, 1920
Ella A. (Mrs.), May 2, 1878
Ella J., d. of Waddy W.
Roberts, Apr. 8, 1869
Elliott N., Sr., July 19, 1855
Frances A., d. of J. W.
Roberts, June 18, 1846
George E. (Mrs.), Sept. 30,
Nov. 25, 1920
James W., s. of James P. and
Elizabeth Roberts, Sept.
22, 1864
Jane C., w. of William C.
Roberts, Apr. 10, 1856
Janie V., w. of A. P. Roberts,
June 19, 1890
John A. (Mrs.), July 1, 1926
John E., July 1, 1847
Lucus T., s. of Henry H.
Roberts, June 23, 1859
Mary L., w. of William Roberts,
Jan. 15, 1836
Milton T., Mar. 28, 1844
Minnie P. (Mrs.), d. of Nathan
B. Clarke, Sept. 23, 1897
Richard, Feb. 25, 1841
Sarah N., July 30, 1840
Susan, w. of Joseph C. Roberts,
Apr. 12, 1855

T. W. (Rev.), Sept. 21, 1876
Tabitha A., d. of Enoch
Roberts, Aug. 10, 1832
Thomas Harris, Jr., s. of
T. H. and S. E. Roberts,
July 23, 1891
Waddy W. (Capt.), Feb. 25,
1875
William D., Apr. 8, 1841
ROBERTSON
(Rev.), May 26, 1932
A. T. (Dr.), July 9, 1914
Abram J., Oct. 2, 1862
Agnes C. LAND, w. of William Robertson, Jr., Feb.
17, 1848
Annie A., d. of Dr. R. H. and
Bettie Robertson, Nov.
2, 1893
Annis F., Dec. 31, 1914
Annis J., w. of A. J. Robertson, Dec. 8, 1859
Archalaus (Lt.), Sept. 22,
1864
Archer, July 10, 1856
B. M., Jan. 19, Mar. 2, 1882
Benjamin M., Jr., s. of Benjamin M. Robertson, Jan.
18, 1872
Bertha Estell (Mrs.), Sept.
7, 1893*
Bettie (Mrs.), Oct. 22, 1863
C. R., Jan. 14, 1932
Carrie, d. of J. C. and M.
E. Robertson, Jan. 19,
1865
Catharine, w. of William
Robertson, Nov. 6, 1845
Charles, May 5, 1892
Charlie Lee, s. of A. S.
Robertson, Aug. 7, 1873
Christopher C., July 16,
1863
E. W. (Mrs.), w. of Dr. E.
W. Robertson, Dec. 4, 1879
Eddie S., s. of A. S. and
L. G. Robertson, Dec. 2
and 23, 1875
Edgar W. (Dr.), Jan. 24,
1924

* Possible inaccuracy in name, or spelling, but given as printed

OBITUARY NOTICES IN THE RELIGIOUS HERALD WITH DATES OF PUBLICATION

Elisha W., Mar. 8, 1894
Eliza (Mrs.), July 22, 1897
Eliza Davis, w. of William D. Robertson, Jan. 25, 1900
Eliza T., w. of John C. Robertson, Aug. 12, 1847
Elizabeth, May 1, 1862
Ellen, w. of Frank H. Robertson, Dec. 16, 1886
Fannie M., d. of Benjamin M. Robertson, July 15, 1852
Fitzhugh, s. of John G. and Isabella Robertson, June 30, 1892
Francis H., Mar. 31, 1881
Francis Judson, s. of Francis H. and Mary E. Robertson, Oct. 13, 1842
Frank H., Feb. 13, 1919
Franklin Pierce, Oct. 20, 1927
Grayson Woods, Oct. 27, 1927
J., w. of William J. Robertson, Nov. 13, 1845
J. J., s. of F. H. Robertson, Sept. 19, 1918
J. P., Aug. 19, 1886
James, Jan. 31, 1867
James (Elder), s. of C. M. Robertson, Aug. 8, 1867
James, Feb. 27, 1873
James C. (Rev.), Sept. 19, 1867
James G., Mar. 26, 1874
James G. (Mrs.), d. of Rev. D. P. Bestor, July 13, 1882
Jane E. F., w. of Thomas L. Robertson, Aug. 4, 1859
John, Oct. 5, 1843
John (Capt.), Apr. 5, 1849
John (Judge), July 17, 1873
Joseph A. (Dr.), Oct. 27, 1842
Joseph H., Sept. 26, 1861
L. F. (Mrs.), Feb. 21, 1918
Leland, s. of Berta E. and W. E. Robertson, Dec. 25, 1890
Marcus W., Feb. 25, 1915
Maria E., w. of James G. Robertson, Mar. 10, 1853
Martha A., w. of Thomas Robertson, Apr. 28, 1864
Mary D. (Mrs.), Mar. 8, 1866
Mary H., w. of O. Robertson, Oct. 20, 1892
Mary Jane (Mrs.), Dec. 14, 1848
Mary S., Sept. 19, 1889
Mary Virginia, d. of Thomas N. and Lucy Robertson, Feb. 19, 1880
Matilda, w. of J. Robertson, Feb. 18, 1858
Nicholas, Nov. 9, 1848
R. H. (Dr.), Oct. 11, 1894
R. Hobson, July 7, 1921
Rebecca Jane (Mrs.), Dec. 19, 1929
Richard Gaines, May 1, 1919
Roxana, w. of John W. Robertson, June 17, 1915
Sabra M., d. of William and Mary Robertson, Mar. 8, 1866
Sallie Gaines, July 16, and 30, 1936
Stella Blanche, d. of L. P. and M. A. Robertson, Apr. 19, 1888
Susan, w. of C. M. Robertson, July 16, 1874
Susan F. (Mrs.), Mar. 11, 1875
Thomas Bolling, Oct. 17, 1828
W. E. (Rev.), Apr. 21, 1932
W. S. (Mrs.), Nov. 30, 1893
William A., s. of Elder John Robertson, Sept. 27, 1855
William D., May 20, 1897
Willis, s. of J. J. and Sallie L. Robertson, Aug. 29, 1889
Wilmonia Archer (Mrs.), Mar. 1, 1934

ROBEY
Mary R., Dec. 4, 1879

ROBINS
A. W., Jan. 31, 1878
Alexander Mebane, s. of W.

OBITUARY NOTICES IN THE RELIGIOUS HERALD WITH DATES OF PUBLICATION

B. and Bessie Robins, July 17, 1862
Amelia E., w. of Thomas C. Robins, May 28, 1885
Augustine Warner, July 13, 1876
Benjamin T. C., Feb. 1, 1872
Cornelius, Oct. 17, 1844
Frances Ann, Apr. 18, 1878
Janie F., w. of Albert H. Robins, d. of Robert S. and Nancy Heywood, Sept. 12, 1878
Nancy, w. of Thomas Robins, May 6, 1858
Olivia Harlow, d. of Thomas C. and Nannie Robins, June 8, 1882
Persis, s. of A. H. and J. F. Robins, Dec. 22, 1887
Robert C., s. of Thomas C. and Amelia Robins, Aug. 23, 1877
Robert Coleman, May 13, 1869
Virginia, w. of William Robins, Apr. 18, 1878

ROBINSON
(Mr.), Mar. 6, 1884
A. T. (Dr.), Sept. 27, 1934
Addie, d. of George J. and Mary A. Robinson, Apr. 12, 1866
Amanda Ann, w. of William Robinson, Jr., Nov. 21, 1850
Ann C., Jan. 1, 1880
Ann Eliza, w. of William Robinson, Nov. 16, 1854
Anna, Sept. 6, 1853
Annis (Mrs.), Dec. 1, 1859
Benjamin Hoomes, s. of Maj. Thomas and Mary S. Robinson, Jan. 20, 1887
Benjamin Parker, s. of William Robinson, June 24, 1847
C. C., June 1, 1876
Carrie Belle, d. of James A. Robinson, Feb. 25, 1886
Daniel C., s. of Mrs. Rebecca J. M. Robinson, Sept. 12, 1861

Elizabeth, w. of George Robinson, June 24, 1852
Elizabeth, w. of Col. Daniel Robinson, Dec. 12, 1867
Elizabeth Black (Mrs.), Apr. 19, 1923
Elizabeth C. (Mrs.), Dec. 31, 1885
Ella R. (Mrs.), d. of Hadrian A. and Mary A. Neaves, Oct. 4, 1900
Frances Isadore, d. of Howell A. and Josie Gresham Robinson, Aug. 23, 1900
Gregory B., June 8, 1843
Henry A., s. of Henry I. and Elizabeth C. Robinson, Nov. 19, 1857
Howell Allison, s. of H. A. and W. J. Robinson, June 2, 1892
Isadore M., Mar. 3, 1892
Jacob, Nov. 15, 1849
James, Jan. 28, 1858
John (Capt.), Aug. 12, 1847
John W. (Dr.), May 2, 1872
Julien Claiborne, s. of Maj. Thomas and Mary Susan Robinson, Oct. 21, 1880
Lillie Morton, d. of William and Indie Robinson, Apr. 28, 1864
Louisa B. (Mrs.), Mar. 15, 1849
Lucy Ann (Mrs.), Jan. 18, 1934
Luther, Sept. 10, 1931
M. R. (Mrs.), Sept. 23, 1847
Maria E., d. of Capt. James Robinson, Nov. 25, 1836
Mary Elizabeth, d. of William and Martha Robinson, Dec. 18, 1856
Mary Ellen, d. of Albert and Virginia F. Robinson,

OBITUARY NOTICES IN THE RELIGIOUS HERALD WITH DATES OF PUBLICATION

Nov. 17, 1881
Mary O., Apr. 21, 1904
Mary S., w. of Joseph Robinson, Oct. 17, 1889
Mary S. Hoomes (Mrs.), July 19, 1900
Mary Virginia (Mrs.), Mar. 8, 1894
Merritt M., July 25, 1828
Moncure, Nov. 19, 1891
Nannie B., w. of Capt. Sledge Robinson, d. of John and Eliza Wharton, Apr. 14, 1870
Parker Smith, Feb. 11, 1897
Rebecca J. M. (Mrs.), Nov. 7, 1878
Richard W., May 2, 1867
S. S. (Rev.), Sept. 3, 1931; Aug. 18, 1932
Susan (Mrs.), Aug. 20, 1868
Victor Cheek, s. of William and India Robinson, July 12, 1866
William, July 8, 1875
William Russell, s. of William and Martha Robinson, Dec. 18, 1856
William S., Jr., Aug. 12, 1847
William Thomas, s. of William P. and Blanche R. Robinson, Jan. 16, 1873

ROBSON
J. R., Mar. 18, 1875
W. T., Mar. 8, 1923

ROCK
A. J. (Mrs.), Oct. 29, 1908
Catharine, w. of L. C. Rock, July 6, 1848
Charles Hill, Jan. 31, 1861
Elizabeth (Mrs.), Mar. 15, 1877
Joseph (Elder), July 21, 1864
M. M. (Rev.), Oct. 17, 1850
Mary Ann, w. of A. D. Rock, Aug. 3, 1848
Virginia Key, d. of Elder Joseph Rock, Apr. 24, 1873
William Edward, s. of William Rock, Aug. 23, 1839

ROCKE
F. G. (Maj.), July 17, 1879
George Lee, Oct. 1, 1925

ROCKWELL
M. E. (Mrs.), Mar. 28, 1872

RODDEN
Henry W., s. of William S. and Nancy A. F. Rodden, Jan. 13, 1859
Sarah Ann Williams, d. of William S. and Nancy A. F. Rodden, Jan. 13, 1859
William T., s. of William S. and Nancy A. F. Rodden, Jan. 13, 1859

RODES
Charles, Nov. 10, 1859
Elizabeth (Mrs.), June 22, 1838
John, Feb. 13, 1868
John H., Oct. 11, 1855
William S., July 19, 1849

RODGERS
John Worsham, Apr. 27, 1922
Lucinda B., w. of Elder William M. Rodgers, May 2, 1872
Samuel E., June 19, 1856

RODMAN
William H., Dec. 30, 1920

ROEBUCK
Mary S., d. of Isaac Roebuck, July 26, 1866

ROGANNI
Joseph, s. of Gregory and Sarah F. Roganni, Oct. 1, 1840

ROGERS
A. E. (Rev.), Oct. 21, 1875
Alfred Benjamin Gunther, s. of Spencer F. Rogers, Apr. 12, 1917
Alice T. (Mrs.), Jan. 11 and 25, 1934
Amanda (Mrs.), Feb. 14, 1895
Andrew Broaddus, s. of Isaac N. and Amanda A. Rogers, May 29, 1863
Catherine, w. of John Rogers,

OBITUARY NOTICES IN THE RELIGIOUS HERALD WITH DATES OF PUBLICATION

Mar. 8, 1839
Eliza Jane, d. of Isaac Rogers, Oct. 13, 1887
Elmira S., w. of Thomas Rogers, Jan. 30, 1879
Emeline Roberta, d. of James Pendleton and Ellen McCance Rogers, June 3, 1875
Emma C., w. of J. T. Rogers, d. of Thomas P. Lide, July 18, 1872
Ferdinand A., Mar. 14, 1878
Finella H. (Mrs.), Feb. 23, 1888
Gertrude M., July 15, 1920
Hugh Gardner, s. of J. Pendleton and Ellen McCance Rogers, July 20, 1871
John Marshall, s. of Isaac Rogers, Oct. 13, 1887
Joseph Henry, Nov. 8, 1855
Lucia, w. of Maj. Henry J. Rogers, Aug. 9, 1877
Margaret (Mrs.), Jan. 8, 1885
Martha (Mrs.), May 19, 1927
Mary, w. of Hugh Rogers, Nov. 19, 1863
Mary J., w. of William H. Rogers, Jan. 26, 1871
Mary Roberta, d. of William H. and Mary Rogers, Nov. 23, 1843
P. Hamilton (Mrs.), Apr. 5, 1883
Patrick K. (Dr.), Aug. 15, 1828
Richard L., May 24 and 31, 1906
S. (Miss), Dec. 9, 1858
Samuel E., Sept. 22, 1921
Thacker, June 28, 1877
W. T., May 7, 1936
William Bird Giles, s. of Dr. R. and Elizabeth A. Rogers, July 26, 1839

ROLFE
Bettie (Mrs.), Jan. 28, 1915
Samuel D. (Col.), Sept. 22, 1859

ROLLAR
Roswell, July 5, 1866

ROLLER
Frank, s. of John B. and Sallie Easley Roller, July 21, 1898
John B., Sept. 9, 1909

ROLLINS
Austin, May 31, 1883
Samuel Brooke, s. of S. B. Rollins, Jan. 29, 1891
Tabitha A. (Mrs.), Apr. 15, 1886

ROLPH
Minerva P., w. of Reuben Rolph, Apr. 30, 1896
Reuben, Jan. 30, 1879

ROMERO
Margaret Gayle MARCHANT, w. of Dr. J. L. Romero, Mar. 1, 1906

ROOK
Squire, Jan. 17, 1878

ROOT
Erastus Colon (Rev.), Mar. 7, 1918
Madalene May, Dec. 12, 1918

ROPER
Amanda A., Nov. 20, 1835
Asenath, w. of John Roper, Dec. 29, 1837
Bartlett, Oct. 16, Nov. 6, 1913
Bettie A. (Mrs.), Dec. 26, 1912
Caroline Matilda, w. of Linsdale J. Roper, Mar. 15, 1906*
Emily Ann BARTLETT, w. of LeRoy Roper, Apr. 22, 1880
Emmett (Mrs.), June 19, 1879
George, Aug. 31, 1838
LeRoy, Aug. 28, 1884
Lonsdale J., June 6, 1907*
Marian O. (Mrs.), Mar. 25, 1858
Mary, w. of Elder David Roper, Sept. 26, 1844
Mary, w. of John Roper, Dec. 13, 1849
Nathaniel J., Jan. 23, 1840

* Possible inaccuracy in name, or spelling, but given as printed

OBITUARY NOTICES IN THE RELIGIOUS HERALD WITH DATES OF PUBLICATION

Rebecca, w. of John Roper,
   Apr. 1, 1858
Samuel C., Dec. 13, 1849
Virginia A., w. of Samuel C.
   Roper, May 19, 1842
RORABAUGH
   C. F. (Mrs.), Jan. 23, 1919
ROSE
   F. W., Sept. 25, 1924
   Richard, Dec. 21, 1843
   Robert N., Sept. 13, 1894
ROSEN
   Joseph A., Sept. 29, 1927
ROSENBAUM
   Sidney, Oct. 31, 1901
ROSS
   Annie Eanes (Mrs.), Aug. 26, 1926
   James, Sept. 1, 1859
   John D., s. of J. W. and Ann
      P. Ross, Sept. 11, 1856
   M. (Rev.), Feb. 29, 1828
   Martin (Elder), Jan. 2, 1829
   Mary, w. of George Ross,
      Oct. 16, 1845
   Nathaniel W., s. of J. and F.
      H. Ross, Apr. 30, 1863
ROSSER
   Charles Samuel, Oct. 30, 1873
   Elizabeth D., w. of George
      G. Rosser, d. of Samuel
      T. Miller, Feb. 25, 1886
   G. G., Apr, 19, 1900
   George Thomas, July 4, 1929
   Granville, s. of Joel Rosser,
      Aug. 20, 1863
   J. L. (Rev.), Apr. 23, June 4, 1914
   Kate (Mrs.), Mar. 31, 1927
   Reid Arnold (Dr.), Aug. 13, 1931
   S. S. (Mrs.), d. of Capt.
      Archibald Burnley Duke,
      Apr. 13, 1922
   Walter C., Apr. 15, 1926
ROSSON
   Nancy, w. of Reuben Rosson,
      July 20, 1838
ROTHWELL
   Ann, w. of A. Rothwell,
      Dec. 6, 1866
   Eleanor, d. of Andrew Rothwell, Feb. 20, 1851
   Eliza, d. of Paul and Sarah
      Rothwell, Mar. 1, 1894
   George W., s. of A. Rothwell, June 12, 1873
   William James, s. of Capt.
      J. B. Rothwell, Dec. 18, 1862
   William R. (Rev.), Jan. 26, 1899
ROUNDTREE
   Thomas, Dec. 7, 1843
ROUNTREY
   James, Nov. 29, 1877
ROUSE
   Mordecai B. (Mrs.), June 30, 1859
ROUTEN
   Samuel, s. of Samuel B.
      and Lucy Ann Routen, July 7, 1859
ROUTH
   Catherine, w. of Elder Asa
      Routh, Aug. 21, 1862
ROUTON
   Charles, Mar. 7, 1889
   Mary G., w. of Robert G.
      Routon, Dec. 30, 1880
ROUTT
   Ellen, w. of A. P. Routt,
      Mar. 27, 1851
   Nancy E., w. of William
      Routt, Apr. 9, 1863
ROUZIE
   John S., July 5, 1888
ROW*
   Absalom, Nov. 29, 1855
   Alice D., Dec. 30, 1852
   Fannie (Mrs.), Apr. 19, 1883
   Nancy, w. of Absalom Row,
      Apr. 24, 1873
   Sallie R., May 4, 1854
ROWE*
   A. P. (Maj.), June 7, 1900
   Benjamin, Sept. 6, 1888
   E. W. (Dr.), June 7, 1900
   Elizabeth, w. of James P.

* Possible inaccuracy in name, or spelling, but given as printed

OBITUARY NOTICES IN THE RELIGIOUS HERALD WITH DATES OF PUBLICATION

Rowe, Apr. 8, 1852
Elwood Blackford, s. of Absalom P. and Almedia F. Rowe, May 20, 1858
Fanny A., w. of Capt. Sterling Rowe, Sr., Apr. 11, 1889
John K., Feb. 23, 1854
Keeling, Aug. 19, 1869
Lucy, w. of Elder George Rowe, Apr. 23, 1863

ROWELL
E. E., July 22, 1937
Lucy Ann RICHARDSON (Mrs.), May 23, 1895
Nancy (Mrs.), Aug. 12, 1880

ROWLAND
A. J. (Dr.), Dec. 23, 1920
J. M. (Dr.), Aug. 25, 1938

ROWLES
Anna E., w. of Dr. B. F. Rowles, Sept. 15, 1892

ROWLET
Martha Ella, d. of G. A. and Mary H. Rowlet, Apr. 19, 1860

ROWLETT
Mary J., d. of Joseph P. and Mary C. Rowlett, Nov. 13, 1845

ROY
A. G. D. (Dr.), May 28, 1874
Elizabeth P. Todd, w. of R. B. Roy, Oct. 29, 1874
Ella F. P., d. of L. P. T. F. and R. B. Roy, Nov. 28, 1872
G. G. (Dr.), father of Dr. Dunbar Roy, Oct. 24, 1901
Jennie T., d. of Dr. G. G. and Flora Roy, July 4, 1878
Lucy E., Apr. 15, 1880
Mary A. E., d. of Mrs. Catherine Pendleton, Apr. 11, 1834
Mary C. (Mrs.), May 2, 1828
R. B., Oct. 29, 1874
Rosa Garnett, d. of G. G. and Flora Roy, Aug. 22, 1878
Susan E., w. of Dr. Beverly D. Roy, Mar. 14, 1850
William A. (Rev.), July 26, 1849

ROYAL
Jane (Mrs.), Apr. 13, 1922
W. H., July 20, 1893

ROYSTER
George, s. of G. W. and Mary Royster, Jan. 31, 1850
Jane C. (Mrs.), Aug. 29, 1901
John W. (Dr.), Apr. 14, 1842
L. S., Aug. 10, 1922
Lawrence, s. of Dr. John Woodson and Susan Bacon Wilkinson Royster, Nov. 12, 1908
Lizzie, July 14, 1870
Lucy C., d. of Mrs. Nancy Royster, Aug. 5, 1852
Percy Claire, May 14, 1925
Sallie Lewis, w. of William T. Royster, d. of Charles L. and Sarah Ann Brown, Apr. 11, 1918
Susan B., w. of Dr. John W. Royster, Mar. 16, 1871

RUCKER
Alexander, s. of J. Harvey Rucker, Mar. 19, 1896
C. A., d. of Elder R. D. Rucker, Oct. 27, 1853
Elizabeth, Jan. 17, 1834
Ellen, w. of J. H. Rucker, Mar. 25, 1915
Eugene C., Dec. 12, 1918
George H., Nov. 13, 1919
James Monroe, Aug. 1, 1878
Laura Eleanor Burton, w. of Wallace M. Rucker, July 13, 1893
Lelia Vixella, Aug. 1, 1878
Lizzie (Mrs.), Feb. 1, 1900
Mary (Mrs.), Mar. 6, 1884
Mary Ann D., w. of William B. Rucker, Apr. 16, 1863
Sallie F. Parker (Mrs.), Apr. 16, 1925
Wallace M., Aug. 18, Sept.

OBITUARY NOTICES IN THE RELIGIOUS HERALD WITH DATES OF PUBLICATION

  29, Oct. 20, Dec. 22,
   1938
  William B., Feb. 20, 1862
RUCKLES
  L. L., Nov. 8, 1894
RUCKS
  C. H. (Mrs.), Jan. 27, 1938
RUDASILL
  William G. (Mrs.), Mar. 10,
   1910
RUDASILLA
  George W., s. of Jacob and
   Eleanor M. Rudasilla, Mar.
   30, 1843
RUDD
  Alfred A., Feb. 13, Mar. 27,
   1902
  George Malcom, s. of R. T.
   Rudd, Feb. 7, 1901
  Harris, s. of A. Barton and
   Mary Rudd, Sept. 14, 1893
  Indie E. (Mrs.), Feb. 26,
   1914
  John J., s. of John Rudd,
   Oct. 13, 1853
  Letitia, Mar. 12, 1914
  Martha A., Jan. 5, 1865
  May Bagby (Mrs.), Nov. 18,
   1937
  Rachel, d. of Rev. A. B. and
   May Bagby Rudd, Nov. 2,
   1899
  Sarah Alice (Mrs.), Mar. 17,
   1938
RUFFIN
  William, Nov. 17, 1842
RUGGLES
  William, Sept. 20, 1877
RUNKLE
  Bertha Cora Frances, d. of
   Col. M. D. L. and Berta
   A. Runkle, May 3, 1883
RUPERT
  Laviro (Rev.), Nov. 4, 1880
RUSE
  John, Nov. 6, 1829
RUSH
  Mary Susan, w. of Peter Rush,
   Nov. 11, 1880
RUSHER

  Flavius Josephus, s. of
   Jordan P. Rusher, Mar. 13,
   1862
RUSSELL
  Mary B., w. of P. C. Russell,
   July 16, 1891
  Ragland, d. of C. A. Russell,
   Mar. 25, 1920
  Sarah (Mrs.), Aug. 1, 1828
  Simon P., Feb. 4, 1869
RUST
  Abigail L., s. of Thomas A.
   Rust, Oct. 20, 1837
  Angelina, w. of Dr. Bushrod
   Rust, July 20, 1905
  Bushrod (Dr.), Apr. 11, 1867
  Elizabeth, w. of Capt. George
   Rust, Feb. 8, 1844
  Elvira J., w. of Youel S.
   Rust, July 8, 1841*
  John, Jan. 28, 1847
  John (Mrs.), June 25, 1857
  Julie, w. of Dr. J. B. Rust,
   June 9, 1859
  Margaret, w. of Dr. Bushrod
   Rust, Sept. 8, 1864
  Mary Ann, w. of Charles B.
   Rust, May 10, 1883
  Mary Frances, d. of Thomas
   A. Rust, May 29, 1829
  Thomas A., Feb. 2, 1882
RUTHERFORD
  Constance Massie, w. of
   Thomas Rutherford, d. of
   Joel and Susan Thomas,
   Jan. 23, 1873
  Henry W., s. of Thomas and
   Connie M. Rutherford, Aug.
   2, 1906
  Lizzie M., Feb. 28, 1884
  Marie Louise, w. of Rev.
   William Rutherford, Aug.
   29, 1912
  Robert Wilmon, s. of John
   and Bettie Rutherford,
   Nov. 20, 1873
  Thomas J., Feb. 28, 1884
  Walter L., Feb. 28, 1884
RUTLEGE
  John Andrew, s. of A. and

* Possible inaccuracy in name, or spelling, but given as printed

OBITUARY NOTICES IN THE RELIGIOUS HERALD WITH DATES OF PUBLICATION

Ozelia Miles Rutlege, Jan. 6, 1876
RYALS
 Martha W., d. of V. C. Ryals, Feb. 27, 1851
 W. H. (Rev.), Feb. 3, 1927
RYAN
 Fannie Lee, w. of Capt. Joseph Ryan, d. of Charles Wilson, Apr. 29, 1875
 Maria, w. of William H. Ryan, June 21, 1849
 Nancy P., w. of Philip H. Ryan, Feb. 16, 1860
 P. H., Jan. 16, 1879
RYLAND
 Alice Garnett, w. of Dr. Charles Ryland, June 4, July 23, 1931
 Ann, Feb. 13, Mar. 13, 1913
 Ann Peachy, d. of Elder Robert Ryland, Nov. 2, 1832
 Anna M., w. of John N. Ryland, d. of Col. Reuben M. Garnett, Jan. 1, 1852
 C. P. (Rev.), July 12 and 26, 1934
 Callie V., w. of Josiah Ryland, d. of Archibald Thomas, July 30, 1868
 Catharine, w. of Josiah Ryland, d. of Samuel and Catharine Peachy, Sept. 30, 1858
 Catharine Gaines, w. of Samuel P. Ryland, d. of Robert Hill, Apr. 14 and 28, 1881
 Charles H. (Dr.), Aug. 6 and 20, 1914
 Charles H., Jr., s. of Charles H. Ryland, Oct. 4, 1917
 Dora, Nov. 14, 1907; Jan. 16, 1908
 Eunice Fox, w. of Rev. C. P. Ryland, Feb. 16, Mar. 2, 1933
 Helen, d. of Rev. J. and Anna Murdock Ryland, July 20, 1905
 Henry Pendleton, s. of John N. Ryland, July 29, 1852
 James Robert, Apr. 16, 1891
 John Newton, Apr. 12 and 26, 1906
 John Rollins, s. of Robert Ryland, Jan. 19, 1838
 John S., s. of John and Mary Ryland, Nov. 25, Dec. 23, 1926
 John W. (Rev.), Mar. 30, 1905
 Joseph, Oct. 24, 1872
 Joseph Addison, s. of J. S. and Lelia C. Ryland, July 19, 1900
 Joseph G., father of Rev. C. P. Ryland, Jan. 18, 1906
 Josephine, w. of Elder Robert Ryland, d. of Thomas and Ann Norvell, Nov. 5, 1846; Mar. 4, 1847
 Josiah, June 20, 1850
 Josiah, Jr., Oct. 18, 1900
 Josiah, s. of Samuel P. Ryland, June 4, 1903
 Lavinia Ann, w. of John Newton Ryland, Aug. 27, 1914
 Lucy F. (Mrs.), Mar. 24, 1921
 Lucy White, w. of Josiah Ryland, Jr., Jan. 18, 1900
 Margaret Baylor, d. of Robert S. and M. H. Ryland, July 9, 1891
 Mary B., July 23, 1896
 Mary Lane Wade, w. of Dr. Robert Hill Ryland, d. of Judge William C. and Olivia Ruffin Lane, Jan. 7, 1909
 Priscilla, w. of Joseph Ryland, d. of John Bagby, Mar. 29, 1888
 Richard Houston, May 27, 1920
 Robert (Dr.), Apr. 27, 1899
 Robert (Mrs.), June 29, 1905

OBITUARY NOTICES IN THE RELIGIOUS HERALD WITH DATES OF PUBLICATION

Robert H. (Dr.), Aug. 30, 1883
Robert Hall, June 26, 1835
Robert S. (Mrs.), July 16, 1914
Roberta, d. of Elder Robert Ryland, Dec. 22, 1842
Sallie Browne, d. of William Temple Ryland, Oct. 10, 1907
Samuel P., July 8 and 22, Aug. 5, Sept. 30, 1886
Susan, w. of William S. Ryland, Sept. 29, 1887; Jan. 26, 1888
Thomas M., s. of Samuel P. and Catharine G. Ryland, Oct. 13, 1870
William Morton, s. of Rev. W. S. and Mary E. Ryland, Dec. 22, 1881
William S., Jan. 31, Feb. 28, 1861
William S. (Dr.), Jan. 18, 1906

RYON
Margaret, d. of John Ryon, Oct. 18, 1860

S

SACRA
  Elizabeth Elva, w. of William Sacra, Jan. 10, 1907
  William, June 30, 1887
SADLER
  Elizabeth W., w. of John W. Sadler, Oct. 19, 1832
  Elizabeth W., w. of Wesley Sadler, Aug. 30, 1849
  Emma Cleveland, w. of William J. Sadler, Dec. 12, 1895
  Fannie Muse (Mrs.), Feb. 19, 1920
  H. W., father of W. H. Sadler, Jan. 10, Feb. 7, 1901
  J. E. (Mrs.), May 10, 1923
  J. H. (Mrs.), Aug. 7, 1930
  James Edwin, Feb. 2, 1905
  Jennie Perkins, w. of John W. Sadler, Mar. 28, 1895
  John A., Feb. 4, 1875
  John A., Mar. 10, 1881
  Lois, d. of William B. and Fannie Sadler, Nov. 5, 1885
  M. B. (Mrs.), Apr. 6, 1893
  Martha E., d. of John Sadler, Mar. 4, 1852
  Mildred, w. of John Sadler, Aug. 6, 1846
  R. S., Jan. 24, 1884
  Rachel, w. of William Sadler, Jan. 28, 1858
  Rebecca Jane, d. of John Sadler, May 6, 1841
  Samuel H., Oct. 23, 1856
  Sue (Mrs.), Oct. 18, 1923
  Virginia, w. of F. M. Sadler, July 27, 1933
  W. B., Apr. 16, 1931
  W. J. (Mrs.), July 11, 1935
  William H., June 5, 1884
  William Joseph (Rev.), Apr. 28, 1938
  Willie, s. of H. W. and P. J. Sadler, Sept. 19, 1861
ST. CLAIR
  Ada Florence (Mrs.), Mar. 5, 1936
ST. JOHN
  G. R. (Mrs.), May 31, 1923
  J. Baxter (Mrs.), Aug. 19, 1937
  John, Sept. 3, 1840
  Robert, Aug. 25, 1938
SAKREY
  Susan, July 30, 1857
SALE
  Albert G., Mar. 9, 1865
  Amanda F., w. of Moore Fauntleroy Sale, July 28, 1853
  Bettie R., d. of Mrs. J. A. Sale, July 20, 1854
  Catherine, w. of Capt. John Sale, Apr. 22, 1858
  Catherine S., w. of Robert R. Sale, May 29, 1862
  Elizabeth, w. of Thomas B. Sale, May 2, 1861
  Fanny (Mrs.), Dec. 4, 1856
  John, Dec. 18, 1829
  John Overton, Feb. 12, 1914
  Julia A., w. of Woodford Sale, Oct. 25, 1866
  Lucy J. (Mrs.), Jan. 26, 1871
  Lydia, d. of J. O. and Amanda Sale, Sept. 19, 1872
  Martha L., w. of Dr. R. A. Sale, May 16, 1861
  Mary A., w. of Capt. A. G. Sale, d. of Col. Ben Pollard, Oct. 12, 1876
  Mary E., w. of Dandridge Sale, Oct. 2, 1851
  Mildred D. (Mrs.), June 27, 1850
  Moore F., June 14, 1860
  Robert R., Oct. 14, 1869
  S. O. (Mrs.), Dec. 12, 1918
  Sallie V., w. of Julius C. Sale, d. of Dr. C. C. and A. L. Broaddus, July 6, 1882
  Sally (Mrs.), Aug. 22, 1861
  Sally B., May 23, 1872
  Silas B., s. of Rev. R. Sale, Jan. 1, 1857
  Thomas R., Dec. 25, 1851

OBITUARY NOTICES IN THE RELIGIOUS HERALD WITH DATES OF PUBLICATION

SALLADE
    William R., June 1, 1905
    Jacob (Rev.), July 28, 1910
SALLE
    Sarah, w. of Dr. Anderson
        Salle, Jan. 30, 1829
SALLEE
    Eugene W. (Rev.), June 18,
        1931
SALLINGS
    Lucy W., Mar. 15, 1866
SALMON
    Nannie Lewis, May 2, 1912
    Willie A., s. of William L.
        and Kate Salmon, Feb. 13,
        1873
SALMONS
    James E., Nov. 8, 1855
    John L., s. of George and
        Huldah Salmons, Sept. 25,
        1862
SALUSBURY
    Lewis, Mar. 2, 1876
SANDERS
    William A., July 31, 1856
SAMPEY
    Annie Renfree, w. of Dr.
        John R. Sampey, Feb. 5,
        1925
SAMPSON
    Frank K., Aug. 2, 1934
    Jane E., w. of George L.
        Sampson, Mar. 11, 1831
    Julia, d. of Stephen Sampson,
        Feb. 12, 1863
    Mehetabel M., w. of Rev. A.
        Sampson, July 17, 1845
    Robert, Sept. 5, 1828
    W. H., Sr., Dec. 1, 1921
SAMSON
    Sarah E., d. of Richard
        Samson, May 18, 1854
    Sarah Jane, w. of John W.
        Samson, d. of John Gwin,
        June 1, 1848
SAMUEL
    Andrew B., Sept. 1, 1842
    Ann (Mrs.), Feb. 13, 1873
    Bettie Frances, d. of T. E.
        Samuel, Jan. 3, 1861
    Clarence, s. of Garland Samuel,
        Aug. 27, 1863
    Elizabeth F. (Mrs.), d. of
        James Coleman, Oct. 1, 1857
    Fannie, w. of T. L. Samuel,
        Oct. 14, 1909
    Garland, Nov. 4, 1880
    George R., Feb. 28, 1855
    John R., Feb. 26, 1891
    Julian M., Aug. 18, 1921
    Leonard, Aug. 25, 1859
    Lizzie, d. of W. G. and Emily
        Samuel, Dec. 19, 1878
    Luther, s. of Mrs. Ann Samuel,
        Jan. 19, Feb. 2, 1848
    M. Gertrude, w. of George W.
        Samuel, Apr. 21, 1881
    Martha A. (Mrs.), Aug. 30,
        1849
    Mary A., d. of Peter D. Samuel,
        May 19, 1853
    Mary Louise, w. of William T.
        Samuel, Aug. 5, 1847
    Mary Walker, d. of W. G. and
        Emily Samuel, Dec. 19, 1878
    P., Dec. 5, 1878
    Philip C., Sept. 8, 1892
    Robert, Feb. 10, 1859
    Sarah, w. of Reuben Samuel,
        May 12, 1853
    Sarah W. (Mrs.), Mar. 11, 1886
    Susan D., w. of B. Samuel,
        July 20, 1871
    Virginia N., w. of George
        Samuel, July 10, 1851
SANDERLIN
    Nannie Eliza Wooten, d. of
        Rev. George W. and Eliza
        W. Sanderlin, Oct. 28, 1875
SANDERS
    Ida T., w. of Rev. C. E. Sanders, June 30, 1921
    John, Dec. 4, 1856
    John Ashton, s. of John A.
        Sanders, July 6, 1876
    Julia A., w. of Romulus Sanders, d. of Dr. Flippo,
        Dec. 20, 1894
    Mary A., w. of John R. Sanders, June 13, 1901

OBITUARY NOTICES IN THE RELIGIOUS HERALD WITH DATES OF PUBLICATION

Ruth Helen, d. of Thomas
and Hopy Sanders, July
28, 1837*
W. S. (Mrs.), Oct. 26, 1876;
July 19, 1877
William Henry, Feb. 13, 1873
SANDERSON
Ann E. (Mrs.), Feb. 3, 1870
Lucy W., w. of John Sanderson,
Sept. 13, 1855
Mary, w. of Thomas B. Sanderson, May 13, 1847
Susan, Aug. 22, 1861
Thomas B., Dec. 1, 1870
Willis Lynch, Aug. 2, 1906
SANDIDGE
Anne D., d. of William and
Callie C. Sandidge, May
21, 1863
M. Benjie, s. of William and
Callie C. Sandidge, May 21,
1863
Malinda J., w. of Valentine
F. Sandidge, d. of Solomon
Tanner, Jan. 16, 1873
Robert H., s. of William and
Callie C. Sandidge, May 21,
1863
Seaton B., s. of D. Sandidge,
Nov. 18, 1858
Willie, s. of William and
Callie C. Sandidge, May 21,
1863
SANDIGE
Ellen S., d. of Joseph and
Francis Sandige, Sept. 2,
1858
SANDRIDGE
Sallie Jennings, w. of Henry
A. Sandridge, Aug. 23, 1923
SANDS
A. H. (Rev.), Dec. 29, 1887
Alexander H. (Mrs.), Aug. 31,
1905
Emily, w. of John Sands, Nov.
10, 1842
John, Feb. 27, 1829
Mary Ellen, d. of William and
Ann Sands, May 13, 1831
Rosalia A., w. of Johnson Sands,
May 4, 1899
Wellington, s. of A. H.
and Ella V. Sands, July
7, 1853
William, Sept. 3 and 24,
1868; Apr. 14, 1870
William G., Oct. 3, 1844
SANDY
Henry, Dec. 10, 1857
Louisa M. (Mrs.), July 18,
1907
Philip Augustus (Capt.),
Apr. 11, 1895
Thomas Oldham, July 10,
1919
Virginia Lee, Oct. 3, 1872
William Philip, s. of Capt.
P. A. and L. M. Sandy,
Dec. 6, 1888
SANDYS
Edwin (Rev.), Dec. 7, 1876
William Sewall, s. of Edwin
and Elizabeth Sandys, May
19, 1859
SANFORD
Alverta Callahan, w. of Rev.
Robert Bailey Sanford,
Dec. 25, 1924
Bland, s. of Rev. M. F. and
Nellie R. Sanford, May
17, 1888
Carrie Ellyson, d. of Rev.
M. F. and E. R. Sanford,
Apr. 31, 1892
Claudia, d. of R. B. Sanford,
Sept. 17, 1891
Hartwell Stewart, s. of W.
H. and E. G. Sanford, Jan.
29, 1891
Margaret, w. of Dr. Ryland
Sanford, June 25, July
9 and 23, 1936
R. B. (Rev.), s. of Rev. J.
H. and Susan Bailey Sanford,
Feb. 5, Apr. 7, 1910
T. Ryland (Rev.), Mar. 18,
Apr. 9, 1908
SARGEANT
Alice Ann, w. of Barksdale R.
Sargeant, May 19, 1859

* Possible inaccuracy in name, or spelling, but given as printed

OBITUARY NOTICES IN THE RELIGIOUS HERALD WITH DATES OF PUBLICATION

SATTERLEE
  A. B. (Rev.), Oct. 23, 1856
SATTERWHITE
  Annie L., Mar. 3, 1881
  Eliza Hercelia (Mrs.), d. of John S. Laughton, Apr. 8, 1915
  Eliza R., w. of Henry Satterwhite, Sept. 15, 1853
  Frank M. (Rev.), Dec. 14, 1911
  Henry (Rev.), Nov. 29, 1877
  Mary Lankford, w. of Rev. F. M. Satterwhite, July 30, 1908
  William, Dec. 20, 1883
SAUL
  Curry, s. of J. P. Saul, Mar. 24, 1904
  John Peter, July 24, 1930
  Lula J., w. of John Peter Saul, Dec. 24, 1931
SAUNDERS
  A. Lee (Mrs.), Mar. 12, 1925
  Adelaide (Mrs.), Dec. 27, 1923
  Albin G., July 11, 1861
  Anderson H., July 6, Sept. 7, 1922
  Angeline L., w. of Julius Saunders, d. of Col. Lewis C. Arthur, Sept. 10, 1863
  Ann A., w. of J. G. Saunders, Oct. 31, 1895
  Ann C. (Mrs.), Aug. 1, 1850
  Ann E., w. of David C. Saunders, Apr. 4, 1861
  Ashton Woodward, s. of John A. and Olivia J. Saunders, July 27, 1876
  Carter Almond, m. Lucy Hill, Apr. 13, 1905
  Carter Almond (Mrs.), d. of Thomas Hill, Apr. 2, 1908
  Catharine, Sept. 7, 1893
  Charles P., May 9, 1889
  Charles S., July 12, 1888
  D. P., Feb. 27, 1868
  David J., June 26, Sept. 11, 1873
  E., Sept. 30, 1858
  Elizabeth (Mrs.), Mar. 1, 1839
  Elizabeth W. (Mrs.), July 11, 1889
  Emeline, w. of William A. Saunders, Mar. 5, 1874
  Etta Kathryn, d. of John A. and Olivia Jane Saunders, Dec. 9, 1920
  Eugenia, d. of Reuben Saunders, Feb. 20, 1862
  Fannie A., Mar. 10, 1921
  Fannie B. (Mrs.), Feb. 16, 1928
  Frances A., w. of John J. R. Saunders, Feb. 15, 1849
  Frances Agnes, d. of David Saunders, Sept. 9, 1920
  George M., s. of J. J. R. Saunders, May 10, 1849
  George M., Sept. 5, 1861
  Griffin F., Jan. 1, 1885
  Guilford D., s. of A. G. Saunders, July 19, 1849
  Harriet (Mrs.), Feb. 17, 1870
  Henry Clay, s. of Reuben and Lavinia Saunders, Feb. 23, 1843
  Hopy Angeline, d. of Thomas and Hopy Ann Saunders, June 30, 1837*
  Isaac J., July 9, 1863
  Isaac S., July 6, 1838
  J. S., Apr. 24, 1873
  James G. (Maj.), Oct. 28, 1880
  James H., s. of John Saunders, May 9, 1872
  John F., s. of D. J. Saunders, Sept. 29, 1870
  John J. R., June 3, 1852
  John R. (Col.), Mar. 22, 1934
  Joseph Pleasants, s. of W. H. Saunders, May 8, 1890

* Possible inaccuracy in name, or spelling, but given as printed

OBITUARY NOTICES IN THE RELIGIOUS HERALD WITH DATES OF PUBLICATION

Lewis Lunsford, Sept. 30, 1915
Lucy B., w. of Turner Saunders, Aug. 25, 1859
Maria, Jan. 1, 1885
Maria C., w. of David J. Saunders, Dec. 21, 1876
Martha, w. of James Saunders, Jan. 1, 1880
Martha F., d. of David J. and Maria C. Saunders, June 28, 1855
Martha Frances, d. of John J. and Frances A. Saunders, Nov. 12, 1840
Mary (Mrs.), mother of Rev. Samuel Saunders, Feb. 15, 1877
Mary A. (Mrs.), Dec. 5, 1878
Mary E., d. of Richard Saunders, Sept. 10, 1830
Mildred H., w. of John Saunders, Sept. 30, 1852
Mosely F., s. of Mrs. Lavinia Saunders, Nov. 28, 1876
Olivia J. (Mrs.), May 18, Oct. 12, 1911
Reuben, Dec. 29, 1864.
Richard, Sept. 13, 1839
Richard, Aug. 8, 1839
Sarah (Mrs.), Feb. 27, 1835
Sarah E., d. of John J. R. Saunders, Apr. 19, 1849
Thomas Alonza, Apr. 14, 1932
William, May 12, 1842
William H., Jan. 23, 1873
SAVAGE
Ann S., w. of Dr. William R. Savage, Mar. 1, 1894
Edward W., Sept. 15, 1898
Elizabeth Sheppard, Sept. 13, 1928
Eliza Fosque, d. of George S. Savage, Jan. 22, 1857
George Jeter, s. of L. W. and S. A. Savage, Aug. 23, 1877
George S., May 22, 1873
Josephine, w. of Edward Savage, Apr. 25, 1912
Kendal, May 12, 1842
Lizzie S., June 21, 1928
Martha C. (Mrs.), Mar. 4, 1909
Nancy H., w. of J. Savage, Feb. 19, 1863
O. B. (Dr.), Nov. 4, 1869
Robert, s. of Simon and Mary J. Savage, Oct. 27, 1892
Susannah S., Nov. 20, 1856
William R. (Dr.), Sept. 1, 1853
William V. (Rev.), Aug. 6, 1931.
William Vann (Rev.), June 2, 1938
Zarabable H., s. of George Savage, Apr. 5, 1855
SAVEDGE
Martha (Mrs.), Sept. 20, 1923
Mary A., w. of Anselm Savedge, Oct. 22, 1896
Ruth Ellis, w. of A. M. Savedge, Feb. 2, Mar. 9, 1933
Samuel S., July 20, 1871
SAWYER
Lillie Bell, w. of T. B. Sawyer, d. of Robert J. and Lydia Bell, Jan. 14, Mar. 25, 1926
SCAIFE
Eloise Robert, w. of Elder C. T. Scaife, d. of Elder W. H. Robert, May 2, 1872
SCANLAND
Sophronia (Mrs.), w. of John Scanland, Jan. 29, 1874
SCARBOROUGH
Charles W., Dec. 14, 1922
SCEA
John (Mrs.), w. of John

OBITUARY NOTICES IN THE RELIGIOUS HERALD WITH DATES OF PUBLICATION

Scea, Aug. 8, 1828
SCHAFFNER
  Henrietta (Mrs.), Apr. 20, 1876
SCHARVAWOLD
  Mary E., Apr. 22, 1858
SCHERER
  Philip Valentine, Feb. 16, 1922
SCHLEISER
  Martha (Mrs.), Apr. 26, 1906
SCHMELTZ
  George A., Jan. 26, 1911*
SCHMELZ
  Angeline (Mrs.), Apr. 15, 1886
  George A. (Mrs.), Dec. 23, 1909; Mar. 3; 1910*
  H. L. (Mrs.), Oct. 1, 1896
  Henry L., Oct. 22, 1914
  Myrtle, d, of Mrs. George A. Schmelz, Feb. 25, 1904*
SCHOFIELD
  Addison H., June 10, 1869
  Henry Thomas, Mar. 24, 1881
  Thomas, Dec. 19, 1878
  William W., Oct. 13, 1859
SCHOOLER
  Malcolm N., s. of Samuel Schooler, July 22, 1875
  Mary Eliza (Mrs.), Jan. 28, 1904
  May, d. of W. R. Schooler, Dec. 13, 1877
  Rice W., Dec. 29, 1853
  Susan E., w. of A. L. Schooler, Dec. 29, 1887
SCHOOLFIELD
  (Mrs.), Mar. 13, 1829
  John Howard, Feb. 10, 1837
  Joseph (Dr.), Oct. 24, 1850
  L. C., May 27, 1897
  Mary, w. of Dr. Joseph Schoolfield, Feb. 5, 1863
  Mary Slade, w. of Dr. Joseph N. Schoolfield, d. of David English, Nov. 23, 1865

SCHOOLS
  George (Elder), Dec. 16, 1836
SCLATER
  Martha Virginia, w. of R. C. Sclater, June 16, 1904
  Robert Walton, July 27, 1893
SCOTT
  A. F. (Rev.), Nov. 11, 1897
  Anna P., July 18, 1929
  Charles Lewis, Nov. 15, 1888
  Charles P., Aug. 22, 1895
  Charles P. (Dr.), Apr. 5, 12, and 26, June 7, 1934
  Charles W., Mar. 12, 1891
  E. Haseltine (Mrs.), July 13, 1876
  Eliza Catherine, d. of Alexander and Adeline Scott Nov. 14, 1867
  Elizabeth, w. of John L. Scott, d. of Dr. William H. Hening, Dec. 29, 1904
  Ellen C., Apr. 7, 1904
  Frances Mallory, d. of Rev. J. H. Scott, Nov. 19, 1846
  Green (Rev.), Sept. 26, 1861
  Hillery Erbie, s. of J. R. D. and Nannie B. Scott, May 9, 1872
  J. A., Feb. 2, Apr. 27, 1911
  J. M. G. (Rev.), Apr. 9, 1891
  James H., s. of Rolley Scott, Apr. 27, 1843
  James Morton, s. of W. L. and Rosa E. Scott, Mar. 14, 1901
  John, June 10, 1869
  John G., July 30, 1863
  John T., June 17, 1886
  Joseph (Capt.), May 16, 1828
  Joseph, May 6, 1880
  Lizzie R., d. of John W. and Ella H. Scott, July 7, 1853
  Lucy V., d. of W. B. and Callie Scott, Oct. 2, 1879
  Maggie Holt, d. of Rev. A. F. Scott, Dec. 13, 1883
  Margaret Elizabeth, w. of Elder

* Possible inaccuracy in name, or spelling, but given as printed

OBITUARY NOTICES IN THE RELIGIOUS HERALD WITH DATES OF PUBLICATION

A. Francis Scott, July 17, 1879
Martha Virginia Farish, d. of Rev. J. R. Scott, Mar. 25, 1858
Mary Ann, d. of John T. Scott, Jan. 15 and 29, 1857
Mary E., w. of William H. Scott, Jan. 5, 1882
Mary E. (Mrs.), June 28, 1888
Mary L. (Mrs.), mother of Rev. C. P. Scott, July 19, 1900
Mildred F., d. of Thomas and Sarah Scott, May 21, 1868
R. M., July 29, 1886
Sarah, w. of George H. Scott, Apr. 14, 1892
Sidney (Capt.), Oct. 8, 1908
Susan A. (Mrs.), May 14, 1925
Thomas, Nov. 12, 1885
Virginia O., w. of Thomas Scott, d. of Edward Henshaw, Apr. 10, 1879
Walter, s. of J. V. and S. A. Scott, Nov. 3, 1870
William F., s. of J. W. and Ella H. Scott, Nov. 12, 1857
Willie Coles, s. of John and Ella H. Scott, Aug. 26, 1886

SCRIMINGER
J. H., Mar. 25, 1926

SCRINAGER
Lilly A., w. of James Scrinager, June 14, 1860

SCRIPTURE
Violet, w. of Norman C. Scripture, July 9, 1914

SCRUGGS
Adaline, w. of J. H. Scruggs, June 9, 1887
Addie (Mrs.), Apr. 7, 1927
C. Scott, s. of Joseph Scruggs, Feb. 26, 1863
Eugenia Taylor, w. of A. E. T. Scruggs, June 3, 1886
George, Nov. 22, 1849
Joseph C., Feb. 20, 1879
Luke, s. of L. A. Scruggs, Nov. 18, 1920
Nelson E., Nov. 15, 1860
Samuel S., Mar. 5, 1863
Sarah Jane, d. of W. L. and S. A. Scruggs, June 14, 1860
William, Mar. 5, 1857

SCRUGS
Theophilus, Feb. 13, 1868

SEARES
John A., July 22, 1926

SEARGEANT
Elizabeth, July 30, 1846
Lou Rutherford (Mrs.), July 10, 1913

SEARS
Barnas (Rev.), July 15 and 22, 1880
E. M. (Mrs.), Aug. 10, 1911
Henry, s. of Robert T. and Lulie Sears, Nov. 12, 1868
John H. (Dr.), Dec. 19, 1901
Marguiritte Roffer, d. of J. E. and Janie Evans Sears, May 3, 1906
R. E. L., s. of J. L. Sears, Jan. 19, 1888
Sue A. C., June 15, 1905
Willie Ann, w. of John A. Sears, Aug. 4, 1898

SEASHOALS
Joseph Servetus Creath, s. of Dr. John and Lucretia J. Seashoals, Sept. 14, 1854

SEATON
Clarence A., Sept. 8, 1927

SEAWELL
E. M. (Mrs.), May 26, 1921
M. B., Aug. 19, 1886

SEAY
Adam P., Nov. 24, 1921
Anna Elizabeth, d. of Joseph M. Seay, July 28, 1853

OBITUARY NOTICES IN THE RELIGIOUS HERALD WITH DATES OF PUBLICATION

Austin, Sr., Feb. 26, 1836
Benjamin, Aug. 4, 1859
Bernard Chappell, Nov. 3, 1921
Bettie A. (Mrs.), d. of William D. Loving, May 3, 1894
Burrel, Apr. 23, 1866*
Burwell Warren, Jr., s. of Burwell W. and Catherine P. Seay, Oct. 22, Nov. 19, 1857
Caroline R., w. of R. W. Seay, Nov. 17, 1859
Carr W., Oct. 11, 1860
Clement Rush Fountain, s. of Peter H. and Nancy Seay, Mar. 24, 1881
Dudley, Nov. 27, 1835
Elizabeth (Mrs.), May 8, 1862
Elizabeth F. (Mrs.), July 15 and 22, 1926
Elizabeth G., Nov. 1, 1855
Elizabeth Y., Sept. 28, 1911
Ellen (Mrs.), Jan. 26, 1854
Francis Bledsoe, Sept. 1, 1927
George N. (Capt.), June 16, 1887
H. H., June 15, 1933
Harry Hamilton, s. of P. G. Seay, Aug. 11, 1910
Henningham Watkins Payne, d. of Burwell W. and Catharine P. Seay, Nov. 19, 1857
Jemima Gertrude, d. of Andrew J. and Josephine Seay, June 6, 1878
John E., May 5, 1921
Joseph M., Nov. 26, 1891
Joseph Motin, Sept. 23, 1915
Josephine (Mrs.), Dec. 14, 1933
Lucie C., w. of Andrew J.
Seay, d. of J. W. and Lucie Price Saunders, Oct. 13, 1881
Lucinda Rebecca Patton, d. of Burwell and Catharine P. Seay, Nov. 19, 1857
Margaret Anderson (Mrs.), Mar. 17, 1938
Martha Bruce, w. of Meredith F. Seay, Mar. 30, 1916
Mildred Ann, w. of Reuben Seay, Oct. 19, 1832
Patrick Henry, s. of Reuben and Mary Seay, Sept. 1, 1842
Petronilla L., w. of Capt. George N. Seay, July 27, 1876
Salina, d. of Joseph M. Seay, July 28, 1853
Sallie, w. of James W. Seay, d. of Thomas Barber, Dec. 2, 1858
Walter L., s. of C. R. F. and Mary A. Seay, Apr. 4, 1878

SEAYRES
Frances E. R. A., d. of Robert B. Seayres, May 19, 1842

SEBRELL
Annie Lee, d. of Thomas E. and Ella F. Sebrell, May 29, 1890
Fannie Maie, d. of Thomas E. and Ella F. Sebrell, May 29, 1890

SECRIST
child of Barkley Secrist, Dec. 11, 1862

SEDWICK
Eliza, w. of Rev. George C. Sedwick, June 2, 1859
Ellen Jane, w. of Rev. R. H. Sedwick, Aug. 27, 1840

SEGAR

* Possible inaccuracy in name, or spelling, but given as printed

OBITUARY NOTICES IN THE RELIGIOUS HERALD WITH DATES OF PUBLICATION

Agnes Pollard (Mrs.), Feb. 16, 1882
Artamesia, w. of John Segar, Apr. 6, 1848
Emma E., w. of John A. Segar, May 26, 1887
Frances (Mrs.), Sept. 23, 1847
Henry G. (Elder), Mar. 26, 1840
John F. (Capt.), s. of Joseph Segar, June 29, 1882
Lizzie C. (Mrs.), Jan. 8, 1880
Mary E., w. of Joseph Segar, Aug. 26, 1886
Priscilla, w. of Rev. Henry G. Segar, July 13, 1876
R. B. (Mrs.), Jan. 28, 1932
Sue Winder (Mrs.), Oct. 18, 1923
Virginia Simkins, d. of Joseph Segar, Apr. 2, 1914

SELDEN
Charles C. s. of E. B. and Sarah Selden, Aug. 7, 1845
Charles Douglas, s. of Mrs. Sarah A. Selden, Sept. 15, 1857

SELF
Mary G., w. of John E. Self, Mar. 7, 1834

SELLERS
L. W., w. of H. F. Sellers, May 27, 1920

SELPH
John R., s. of James Semple,

SEMPLE
Ann L., Dec. 13, 1900
James, Aug. 16, 1860
John R., s. of James Semple, Oct. 26, 1848
Mary P. (Mrs.), Aug. 9, 1855

SENTER
Mary Elizabeth Matthews, w. of J. M. Senter, d. of William and Permelia Matthews, Apr. 23, 1874

SERVANT
Olivia A., w. of R. B. Servant, Oct. 25, 1883
Richard Melville, s. of Richard B. and Olivia A. Servant, Aug. 15, 1872

SESSOMS
J. O., Jan. 7, 1892
L. V., w. of Rev. J. O. Sessoms, Sept. 8, 1898

SETZLER
L. M., May 1, 1873

SETTLE
Alice Morgan, d. of Joseph and Judie Settle, July 19, 1860
Diana T., Dec. 27, 1883
Frank (Mrs.), Feb. 6, Mar. 20, 1919
Laura P., Feb. 27, 1879
Lizzie, d. of R. H. Settle, Dec. 29, 1881
Lucy B., w. of Dr. James W. Settle, Mar. 22, 1860
Lucy F., May 6, 1886
Mary E., w. of Rev. J. J. Settle, Sept. 20, 1855
Mossie, Feb. 3, 1881
Sallie, d. of Joseph and Judie Settle, July 19, 1860
Willie A. (Mrs.), d. of William R. Claughton, May 8, 1890

SEWARD
A. H., May 20, 1880
Addie R. (Mrs.), Nov. 15, 1924
Ann Eliza, w. of James Seward, May 22, 1879
Anna E., w. of John E. Seward, Apr. 24, 1845
Catharine C., w. of Capt. Lewis B. Seward, Nov. 18, 1847
E. W. (Lt.), Aug. 4, 1864
Frances J., w. of John H. Seward, Mar. 21, 1850
George Lewis, s. of Lewis B.

OBITUARY NOTICES IN THE RELIGIOUS HERALD WITH DATES OF PUBLICATION

Seward, Feb. 7, 1861
James Dudley, s. of Albert
  Seward, Mar. 1, 1928
John W., s. of Lewis Seward,
  Oct. 4, 1839
Lewis, July 26, 1839
Lucy A., July 15, 1926
Mary Wallace, d. of James
  R. and Ann Eliza Seward,
  Mar. 14, 1878
Nancy D. (Mrs.), Oct. 24,
  1889
Nannie, May 2, 1901
R. Lee (Dr.), Feb. 10,
  May 26, Aug. 4, 1938
Roxie G., d. of James R.
  and Ann Eliza Seward,
  Mar. 14, 1878
Sarah V., w. of A. H.
  Seward, Mar. 22, 1877
Simon, Apr. 11, 1912
Simon (Mrs.), Aug. 27, 1936
William Thomas, June 13,
  1929
Willie J., s. of A. H.
  Seward, Nov. 20, 1879
SEYMOUR
  C. H. (Mrs.), Nov. 2, 1933
  J. H., Aug. 5, 1909
  William Butler, s. of Dr.
    William J. and Sallie
    Ann Seymour, Oct. 13,
    1853
SHACKELFORD
  Frances Everline, w. of
    John M. Shackelford,
    June 25, 1908
  John M., Mar. 11, 1909
  Lucinda, w. of Lunsford W.
    Shackelford, Oct. 7, 1858
  Sarah J., w. of James D.
    Shackelford, Apr. 6, 1876
SHACKFORD
  W. H. (Dr.), Nov. 1, 1906
SHACKLEFORD
  Bettie M., d. of Daniel
    Shackleford, July 27, 1854
  Hannah E. (Mrs.), Apr. 19,
    1833
  Margaret (Mrs.), Oct. 9, 1835

Nannie Byrd (Mrs.), Jan. 15,
  1931
Sarah (Mrs.), d. of William
  Cleveland, Feb. 27, 1851
Zachariah, Apr. 22, 1852
SHACKLETON
  Blanche Ida, d. of Samuel R.
    Shackleton, Apr. 8, 1875
  Mary A. R., w. of R. L.
    Shackleton, Jan. 30, 1890
  Nancy, w. of T. T. Shackleton,
    Mar. 14, 1872
SHADDOCK
  Edward M., Dec. 19, 1839
  James, May 25, 1843
  Lizzie C. (Mrs.), Mar. 27,
    1875
  William M., Aug. 19, 1841
SHADWELL
  Blanche Delaney (Mrs.), d.
    of J. M. Delaney, May 2,
    1929
SHADWICK
  Catharine, w. of James T.
    Shadwick, May 15, 1862
SHAPARD
  John Washington, Nov. 15,
    1928
  Robert, Jan. 2, 1829
  Rosey G., w. of Samuel V.
    Shapard, Mar. 24, 1864
SHARP
  Elizabeth Bell (Mrs.), Nov.
    11, 1875
  John (Capt.), Nov. 1, 1866
  Margaret H. (Mrs.), Dec. 13,
    1877
  Mary Bell, d. of Joshua
    Sharp, Mar. 26, 1868
  Mattie L., d. of C. R. and
    Pattie E. Sharp, Dec. 16,
    1880
  Sarah, w. of Thomas Sharp,
    Sept. 25, 1879
  Thomas, Feb. 7, 1856
SHARPE
  Ann, w. of Peter Sharpe,
    June 19, 1845
  Lizzie O. (Mrs.), Jan. 13,
    1870

OBITUARY NOTICES IN THE RELIGIOUS HERALD WITH DATES OF PUBLICATION

SHAVER
  David, Jan. 16, 1902
  Frances, d. of George
    Shaver, Sept. 26, 1912
  Letitia Elizabeth, d. of
    David and Lucy Catherine
    Shaver, July 17, 1862
  Michael, May 5, 1859
  Oscar (Rev.), Oct. 22, 1857
SHAW
  Anna, d. of Oliver A.
    Shaw, Jan. 4, 1849
  Norman L. (Mrs.), Nov. 13,
    Dec. 4, 1913
SHAWVER
  Lucy, w. of Thomas H. S.
    Shawver, Feb. 14, 1861
SHCKELFORD*
  Adline E., Jan. 1, 1857
SHEFFIELD
  David, Nov. 16, 1854
SHELL
  Anna, d. of John R. and
    Anna Shell, Oct. 15, 1891
  Anna Jones, w. of J. R. Shell,
    Jan. 30, Feb. 6, 1913
  Gray, s. of John R. Shell,
    July 11, Oct. 3, 1901
  John Henderson, s. of William and Eliza J. Shell,
    Feb. 12, 1863
  Rosa J., w. of Charles A.
    Shell, d. of Charles F.
    Beasley, Nov. 26, 1874
SHELTON
  Alice Belle, Feb. 16, 1888
  Ann M., w. of David Shelton,
    July 28, 1870
  Arthur M., s. of H. M. and
    N. B. Shelton, Nov. 30,
    1916
  Bettie Ann, d. of Joseph H.
    and Judith Shelton, June
    30, 1853
  Carson, s. of Claud Shelton,
    Jan. 15, 1925
  Creed, s. of Capt. Thomas L.
    Shelton, Oct. 11, 1849
  Jannette Frost, d. of Dr. T.
    W. Shelton, Apr. 12, 1883
    L., Sept. 27, 1906
  Langston C., Dec. 7, 1882
  Laura, d. of J. H. and Judith
    Shelton, Apr. 25, 1861
  Lena, d. of Dr. T. W. Shelton,
    Mar. 21, 1889
  Magdalene Dupuy (Mrs.), Aug.
    25, 1887
  Martha A., d. of S. Shelton,
    Nov. 11, 1858
  Mary, w. of John Shelton,
    May 16, 1828
  Mary, d. of H. H. and M. M.
    Shelton, July 28, 1870
  Mary Bettie, d. of A. G. and
    Louisa Shelton, Dec. 25, 1873
  Mary H., w. of Dr. John M.
    Shelton, May 31, 1855
  Mary Leigh, w. of Abram C.
    Shelton, Aug. 26, 1836
  Mary Louise, w. of J. H.
    Shelton, d. of Nathaniel
    B. Land, Mar. 31, 1904
  Missouri A., w. of William
    C. Shelton, May 15, 1862
  Nannie E., Feb. 4, 1886
  Roberta, w. of F. A. Shelton,
    July 26, 1923
  Sallie E. (Mrs.), Mar. 18,
    1897
  Susan R. (Mrs.), Mar. 28, 1872
  Thomas S., Jan. 27, 1859
  William Vincent, s. of William
    C. and Missouri A. Shelton,
    July 10, 1862
SHEPARD
  John M., Apr. 8, 1858
  Julia J., d. of Capt.
    Carrol M. Shepard, July
    9, 1857
  Mildred (Mrs.), Nov. 29,
    1855
  P. P., Dec. 25, 1879
SHEPHERD
  Albin L., Mar. 5, 1896
  Angeline T., July 15, 1858
  Austin, Aug. 26, 1836
  Bennie, s. of Frank and
    Lucie Shepherd, Sept. 25,
    1873

* Possible inaccuracy in name, or spelling, but given as printed

OBITUARY NOTICES IN THE RELIGIOUS HERALD WITH DATES OF PUBLICATION

Bettie, d. of Burwell Shepherd, Nov. 1, 1855
Bettie M., w. of Albert J. Shepherd, d. of Nelson W. Elsom, Nov. 2, 1905
Charlie Washington, s. of John A. and Evaline S. Shepherd, Aug. 18, 1853
Cora, d. of John F. and Lucie Shepherd, Nov. 16, 1882*
Cora Clayton, Mar. 4, 1897
Daniel A., May 10, 1877
David (Capt.), June 11, 1868
E. Catherine, w. of David Shepherd, d. of Elder Robert Lilly, June 14, 1877
E. F. (Mrs.), Mar. 12, 1885
Eliza A. L., w. of Capt. William M. Shepherd, June 6, 1844
Ella Claudine, Dec. 1, 1864
Ella Rogers, w. of T. B. Shepherd, Mar. 22, Apr. 5, 1900
Fannie Irene, d. of John F. and Lucy Shepherd, Oct. 1 and 15, 1874*
Frank W., Apr. 30, 1931
G. Littleton, Mar. 26, 1863
Ida Cleveland, w. of Jeter C. Shepherd, Feb. 8, 1923
Isabella, w. of William Shepherd, July 20, 1838
James, Sr., Jan. 2, 1840
James, Aug. 22, 1861
Jane R., w. of Holeman R. Shepherd, Feb. 12, 1863
John, Nov. 9, 1838
John B., s. of John N. and Fannie J. Shepherd, July 29, 1858
John F., July 2, 1896
John M., s. of Garland A. Shepherd, May 13, 1858
John Newton, Sept. 27, 1866
John Newton, brother of Rev. T. B. Shepherd, Jan. 23, 1896
John S., Apr. 24, 1884
Joseph Benjamin, s. of Christopher H. and Lucinda Shepherd, Mar. 3, 1837
Littleton, s. of Garland and Elizabeth Shepherd, Jan. 1, 1863
Lucy Duval, w. of William S. Shepherd, Aug. 19, 1897
Martha, w. of Thomas L. Shepherd, Aug. 26, 1858
Martin B., July 26, Aug. 22, 188
Mary, w. of John Shepherd, Sr., Feb. 15, 1859
Mary Cassie, w. of Smith Shepherd, d. of George and Louisa Cook, July 14, 1887
Mary J. Ashbey, w. of Robert G. T. Shepherd, Dec. 8, 1881
Mary K., w. of M. B. Shepherd, Apr. 15, 1869
Mary Otey, d. of Thomas J. and Sallie N. Shepherd, Mar. 5, 1863
Nancy Ann (Mrs.), Jan. 23, 1840
Rachel S., w. of James Shepherd, July 17, 1845
Richard Henry, s. of Col. William and Isabella Shepherd, Aug. 19, 1852
Sallie Leftwich, w. of T. J. Shepherd, Nov. 2, 1911
Sarah E., Nov. 20, 1851
Sarah T., w. of Thomas Shepherd, Jan. 19, 1838
Stevie M., Dec. 15, 1910
T. H., Feb. 16, July 26, 1928
Thomas Benton, May 24, 1906
Thomas J., May 14, 1874
Thomas J. (Mrs.), d. of Milton McLaurine, Sept. 21, 1933
William (Col.), July 1, 1836
William James, s. of Christopher and Lucinda Shepherd, Aug. 6, 1863

SHEPP

Susie T. NASH (Mrs.), May 31, 1917

* Possible inaccuracy in name, or spelling, but given as printed

OBITUARY NOTICES IN THE RELIGIOUS HERALD WITH DATES OF PUBLICATION

SHEPPARD
   Cordelia E. FORD (Mrs.), May 10, 1877
   George W., May 3, 1928
   M. G. C., w. of Mosby Sheppard, Aug. 14, 1851
   Nathaniel, May 2, 1828
   William B., Nov. 10, 1859
   Willie D., Sept. 4, 1862

SHERIFF
   George M. (Rev.), July 7, 1927
   Laura O. (Mrs.), May 29, 1913

SHERMAN
   Cecilia, w. of Thomas Sherman, Sept. 25, 1851
   Nancy, June 25, 1857

SHERRILL
   Z. V. (Mrs.), Dec. 12, 1918

SHERWOOD
   Adiel (Rev.), Aug. 28, Sept. 4, 1879
   R. H. (Corp.), s. of Elder S. Sherwood, Oct. 3, 1861
   Smith (Elder), July 19, 1839

SHIELDS
   Marion (Mrs.), d. of S. S. Hogge, Dec. 26, 1907

SHIFLETT
   Angie L., w. of L. R. Shiflett, Feb. 1, 1883
   Thomas G., Jan. 23, 1868

SHIP
   Edward A., s. of Rev. E. G. Ship, May 20, 1858
   Edward G. (Elder), May 7, 1863
   Harriet A., w. of Rev. Edward G. Ship, Jan. 15, 1857
   John (Capt.), Dec. 28, 1848
   John M., s. of Rev. Edward G. and Harriet Maury Ship, Oct. 20, 1921
   Mary Elizabeth, d. of Rev. Edward G. and Harriet Ship, Jan. 25, 1849

SHIPMAN
   Alexander M., Sept. 18, 1890
   Anna, d. of John, Jr., and Sallie A. Shipman, June 7, July 19, 1860
   Charles H., Jan. 19, 1865
   John, Sr., Apr. 8, 1852
   John, Jr., Feb. 4, 1858
   Lee, Jan. 12, 1905
   Miles T., brother of Rev. W. J. Shipman, Oct. 19, 1893
   Sarah Louise Johnson, w. of Rev. William J. Shipman, d. of Rev. Thomas N. Johnson, July 10, 17, and 24, 1913
   Thomas J. (Rev.), July 5, 1917
   W. J. (Dr.), Aug. 26, Sept. 2, Dec. 9, 1915
   William J. (Rev.), Apr. 11, 1889
   William M., s. of M. T. and Sallie A. Shipman, Jan. 26, 1865

SHIPP
   Leonard L., Feb. 3, 1927
   N. H., w. of Rev. E. G. Shipp, Mar. 28, July 4, 1878
   Susan M. (Mrs.), Dec. 16, 1926

SHIVERS
   Theodore Williams, s. of Dr. Offa and Catharine O. Shivers, Aug. 27, 1846

SHORE
   J. Edwin, s. of John E. and Lelia Shore, Nov. 16, 1871

SHORT
   Bernice Elizabeth, d. of O. C. Short, Sept. 24, 1903
   Lucy Ashton, w. of A. F. Short, d. of Col. D. G. Potts, Jan. 7, 1885
   Mary Sue (Mrs.), Sept. 17, 1936
   Ophelia (Mrs.), July 17, 1930
   Richard T., Jan. 3, 1895
   Samuel T., May 15, 1902

SHOTWELL
   James, Aug. 17, 1871
   James T., Feb. 11, 1875

OBITUARY NOTICES IN THE RELIGIOUS HERALD WITH DATES OF PUBLICATION

SHRADER
  Lucy (Mrs.), Jan. 24, 1929
SHREVES
  Dorothea (Mrs.), Nov. 14, 1918
SHUCK
  Carrie Trotti, d. of Rev. J. Lewis and Annie Trotti Shuck, June 25, 1863
  Gasper Trotti, s. of Rev. Lewis H. and Gassie T. Shuck, May 31, 1866
  Gassie T., w. of Dr. L. H. Shuck, Feb. 25, 1909
  J. Lewis (Rev.), Nov. 26, 1863
  Mollie Tobey, d. of Dr. L. H. Shuck, July 1, 1886
SHUMAN
  Callie O., Oct. 20, 1892
  Charles A., Nov. 28, 1918
  E. O., w. of C. A. Shuman, July 10, 1890
  Eliza H., w. of George Shuman, Mar. 3, 1881
  Estelle, d. of George and Eliza Shuman, Jan. 2, 1873
  Martin Grimes, s. of Rev. W. H. and M. E. Shuman, Nov. 6, 1873
  Sarah G. (Mrs.), July 30, 1936
SHUMATE
  Adelaide Rackett, Feb. 19 and 26, Mar. 26, 1914
  Andrew, Sept. 2, 1880
  William J., s. of James P. Shumate, Aug. 25, 1870
SHUTE
  Jennie K., w. of Rev. S. M. Shute, d. of Daniel Kerfoot, Mar. 21, 1895
SIBLEY
  George H., Feb. 2, 1871
SIDDONS
  Sarah A. E., d. of William H. and C. Siddons, Feb. 7, 1867
SIEG
  Mary Woolfolk, w. of George D. Sieg, d. of Robert and Josephine Goodwin Woolfolk, Mar. 8, 1923
SIEGFRIED
  Addie Childrey (Mrs.), Apr. 17, 1902
SILCOX
  Joseph Broadhead, Oct. 2, 1879
SILER
  Sarah, w. of Joseph M. Siler, Mar. 24, 1859
SILLS
  Mary P. (Mrs.), June 29, 1916
  Sarah T., w. of J. Benson Sills, Dec. 17, 1885
SIMKINS
  Margaret S. (Mrs.), June 29, 1876
SIMMONDS
  Laura Irene, w. of Percy Simmonds, Dec. 10, 1891
SIMMONS
  J. Dallas (Rev.), May 9, 1907
  J. W. (Mrs.), w. of Rev. J. W. Simmons, Jan. 31, 1935
  Jehu, July 6, 1854
  Mary, Sept. 2, 1909
SIMMS
  (Mrs.), d. of Peter and Sallie Cary Nelson, Feb. 14, 1907
  A. M. (Rev.), Aug. 15, 1918
  Albert G., July 4, 1872
  John, Aug. 5, 1852
  Lucie R., w. of Thomas H. Simms, Aug. 1, 1878
  Roy Ducker, s. of B. W. N. and Florence D. Simms, July 13, 1882
  Sallie M., w. of J. M. Simms, Feb. 15, 1872
  Salome B. (Mrs.), Feb. 1, 1877
  Sarah Isabella, d. of Albert G. Simms, Aug. 29, Sept. 12, 1878
SIMONS
  E. (Miss), Mar. 2, 1905
SIMPKINS
  Maggie, d. of John and Peggie

OBITUARY NOTICES IN THE RELIGIOUS HERALD WITH DATES OF PUBLICATION

Simpkins, Nov. 24, 1859
William J., Mar. 14, 1828
SIMPSON
  French, July 12, 1855
  George W., Feb. 27, 1896
  J. L. (Miss), Jan. 16, 1873
  John (Mrs.), June 28, 1883
  Kate, d. of James Harvey and Fannie Cornelia Simpson, Mar. 8, 1860
  Sarah A. (Mrs.), Mar. 30, 1832
  Sarah F., w. of William T. Simpson, Nov. 3, 1853
  Sarah Frances, w. of W. C. Simpson, June 8, 1911
SIMS
  Anna, w. of James P. Sims, Dec. 30, 1841; Jan. 13, 1842
  Emmett Reese, s. of Dr. A. L. and Hannah Sims, Dec. 21, 1882
  James Alexander, s. of Jordon G. and Ann G. Sims, Sept. 18, 1829
  John, Apr. 14, 1881
  Lily Helen, d. of Oliver C. and Lydia A. Sims, Nov. 16, 1876
  Lizzie A., w. of H. Clifford Sims, d. of A. A. and Indie Rudd, Nov. 24, 1881
  Miriam Virginia, d. of Fleming Sims, June 23, 1921
  Nancy, w. of Jordon G. Sims, Feb. 5, 1830
  Ollie Coleman, d. of Oliver C. and Rosa B. Sims, May 5, 1870
  Rosa Belle, w. of O. Sims, Jan. 9 and 23, 1873
  Ruby Ethel, Oct. 30, 1930
  William N., s. of William N. Sims, July 22, 1858
SINCLAIR
  Charles Anderson, s. of Charles and Willie Sinclair, Feb. 2, 1882
  W. B., s. of C. G. Sinclair, Mar. 16, 1893
SINCOE
  Catharine, July 9, 1857
  Elizabeth, w. of Brookes Sincoe, Sept. 16, 1858
SINGER
  Isaac Merritt, Aug. 5, 1875
SINGLETON
  Eliza Ann, w. of Temple Singleton, June 23, 1842
  Fanny, w. of R. A. Singleton, d. of Rev. Thomas King, Feb. 28, 1889
  John H., Aug. 7, 1862
  Julian West (Lt.), June 4, 1863
  Mary A., w. of Julian W. Singleton, Aug. 4, 1859
  Nannie, w. of R. A. Singleton, Aug. 17, 1882
  Rhoda Peter (Mrs.), June 29, 1882
SIRLES
  Lucy Anne, Aug. 25, 1938
SISSON
  Maria J., d. of John T. and Anna E. Sisson, June 4, 1868
  Wattie, s. of Warner and Bettie Sisson, Sept. 23, 1880
  William, Mar. 20, 1919
  Willie, s. of Warner and Bettie Sisson, Sept. 23, 1880
SIZER
  Ann H., w. of James Sizer, July 10, 1862
  Ann M., w. of John T. Sizer, Jan. 16, 1851
  Bettie Herndon (Mrs.), Apr. 12, 1900
  Edward C., s. of John T. and Ann Sizer, Apr. 10, 1851
  Elizabeth Lee, d. of John T. and Ann M. Sizer, Dec. 23, 1847
  Ellen, w. of Mordecai Sizer, d. of Lewis C. Montague, Aug. 30, 1860
  Geils Elizabeth, d. of Rev.

OBITUARY NOTICES IN THE RELIGIOUS HERALD WITH DATES OF PUBLICATION

J. M. Sizer, June 8, 1905
Hannah C., w. of John Sizer,
  June 2, 1870
James, July 11, 1867
James Mortimer, Mar. 9, 1922
John, Jan. 31, 1861
Kate Herndon, Dec. 19, 1878
Linda Ragland, w. of Robert
  F. Sizer, d. of Gideon
  Ragland, Mar. 20, 1879
Susan S., w. of Capt. Mordecai Sizer, Apr. 5, 1839
William, Jan. 20, 1832
William James, s. of John T.
  and Ann M. Sizer, Mar. 25,
  1841
SKAGGS
  Oliver, Dec. 20, 1877
  William, Oct. 10, 1861
SKELTON
  Henry (Dr.), Dec. 3, 1896
SKINKER
  B. M. (Mrs.), Feb. 12, 1920
  Ellen B., Nov. 30, 1871
  James B., Feb. 16, 1871
  M. Jane, w. of James B.
    Skinker, Mar. 17, Apr.
    14, 1910
  Nellie Blanche, Dec. 7,
    1871
SKINNER
  B. F., Oct. 21, 1926
  Benjamin F., Jan. 21, Feb.
    11, 1937
  Emmett (Mrs.), Feb. 28, 1924
  Florence Burnett, w. of Rev.
    T. Claggett Skinner, July
    12, 1928
  James, June 18, 1863
  Janie Smith (Mrs.), Oct. 8,
    1936
  Julia N., w. of James Skinner, d. of Edmond George
    Skinner, June 18, 1863
  Ludwell Jackson, Feb. 5,
    1920
  S., w. of Rev. J. T. Skinner,
    Aug. 7, 1884
  Thomas Claggett (Rev.), Feb.
    8, 1934

SLABEY
  Andrew, Sr. (Rev.), Jan. 10,
    1892
SLADE
  J. J., June 20, 1895
SLATE
  Martha, w. of William
    Slate, May 6, 1852
  S., Sept. 9, 1858
SLATER
  Amanda M., Sept. 11, 1856
  Ann Eliza, d. of John T.
    Slater, Jan. 2, 1851
  Beverly (Mrs.), Nov. 13,
    1890
  John, Feb. 2, 1838
  Mary Louisa, d. of Paris
    and Virginia Slater,
    Nov. 21, 1844
  Meredith, Dec. 15, 1837
  Sally, Feb. 7, 1878
  William, June 29, 1871
SLAUGHTER
  Carter Braxton, s. of J.
    Warren Slaughter, Feb.
    14, 1861
  E. T. (Mrs.), May 15, 1930
  Edmonia M. (Mrs.), d. of
    William H. Rogers, Nov.
    24, 1870
  Emily, w. of Reuben Slaughter, July 23, 1874
  Emily V., w. of Col. John
    Slaughter, Oct. 19, 1854
  F. L. (Mrs.), Dec. 31, 1925
  Harriet (Mrs.), Nov. 3, 1881
  J. J., Oct. 30, 1919
  J. Warren, Oct. 4, 1866
  Jane A., May 22, 1862
  Letitia, w. of Daniel F.
    Slaughter, d. of Gen.
    Madison, Mar. 7, 1828
  Marcellus, s. of T. J.
    Slaughter, Jan. 26, 1860
  Mary Camm, Nov. 20, 1884
  Matilda, w. of Philip Slaughter, Aug. 19, 1836
  Reuben, Nov. 22, 1860
  Sallie Moore, w. of J. Warren
    Slaughter, Aug. 11, 1881

OBITUARY NOTICES IN THE RELIGIOUS HERALD WITH DATES OF PUBLICATION

Thomas Jefferson, Dec. 25, 1873
William, s. of Col. John Slaughter, July 19, 1866
William Fielding Braxton, s. of Warren and Sally Moore Braxton Slaughter, Dec. 8, 1904

SLEDGE
Merit Franklin, s. of Merit P. and Rebecca Sledge, Aug. 14, 1856
W. A., Apr. 19, 1894

SLOCUMB
Blanche (Mrs.), Oct. 1, 1925

SLOVER
J. A. (Mrs.), May 21, 1863

SMALL
Annie Winston, d. of T. F. and Mary T. Small, May 25, 1876
Christian (Mrs.), Feb. 25, 1841

SMAW
Ann M. (Mrs.), d. of Rev. J. T. Elliot, Jan. 20, 1887

SMETHIE
Sallie Ann (Mrs.), Aug. 8, 1901

SMITH
A. B. (Rev.), Dec. 20, 1877
A. H. (Mrs.), Nov. 27, 1902
Abram, May 24, 1906
Ada Parr (Mrs.), Nov. 28, 1918
Alexander, Jan. 27, 1887
Alexander M., Jan. 28, Feb. 25, 1904
Alice Dix, d. of M. Smith, Apr. 28, 1887
Alice P., w. of Edward B. Smith, Oct. 25, 1917
Ann, w. of Capt. Presley Smith, July 12, 1860
Ann Eliza, d. of James Smith, Oct. 27, 1853
Anna (Mrs.), May 28, 1925
Anna L., July 26, 1883
Anne D. (Mrs.), Sept. 1, 1881
B. F., Sept. 11, 1873
Benjamin, Aug. 31, 1838
Benjamin E., Mar. 6, 1913
Benjamin Wilson, Aug. 4 and 11, 1887
Bettie Johnston (Mrs.), May 3, 1888
Bettie K., May 6, 1880
Bettie Mauldin, w. of D. T. Smith, Oct. 29, 1874
C. R. (Mrs.), Mar. 5, 1936
Caroline Ann, w. of Frank Smith, Mar. 6, 1873
Carrie, Jan. 16, 1873
Charles, Dec. 8, 1842
Charles Dickinson, s. of R. L. and D. N. Smith, Apr. 28, 1881
Christiana, w. of John A. Smith, Sept. 11, 1862
Clementine PRICE, w. of W. L. Smith, July 18, 1907
Cornelia Davis (Mrs.), July 1, 1926
Cornelius, Nov. 29, 1888
Dalrymple, June 25, 1830
Daniel, Aug. 29, 1844
David G., Feb. 27, 1879
David H., Nov. 22, 1894
Delia, July 14, 1853
Dorothy, w. of Joseph B. Smith, Sept. 20, 1839
Douglas M., s. of Frank and Caroline Smith, Oct. 24, 1867
Drury A., Mar. 7, 1861
E. J. (Mrs.), mother of Rev. L. W. Smith, Mar. 6, 1916
E. M. (Mrs.), July 2, 1891
Eddie O., s. of John H. and Sarah J. Smith, Mar. 14, 1901
Edgar A., June 25, 1885
Edward A., July 31, 1862
Edward B., Aug. 7 and 14, Dec. 4, 1890
Edward H., Aug 11 and 25, 1864
Elias (Rev.), Aug. 6, 1846
Elizabeth, d. of Charles Smith, May 13, 1831

OBITUARY NOTICES IN THE RELIGIOUS HERALD WITH DATES OF PUBLICATION

Elizabeth, w. of Capt. William Smith, Dec. 12, 1839
Elizabeth, w. of Alexander Smith, Sept. 3, 1846
Elizabeth (Mrs.), Jan. 7, 1858
Elizabeth Winn, d. of Rev. A. B. and S. W. Smith, Apr. 29, 1869
Ella Meacham, Mar. 25, June 17, 1937
Emmett Valvin, s. of John P. and Martha A. Smith, Dec. 30, 1886
Ernest Harrison, Feb. 13, 1879
Eva H., d. of A. C. Smith, July 1, 1920
Evie V., w. of Richard Walker Smith, d. of Lamech Jones, Feb. 9, 1899
Frances B., Aug. 29, 1844
Frances Osgood, w. of John Wesley Smith, d. of Sewell and Frances Courtney Osgood, Feb. 26, 1903
Frank A., Aug. 16, 1928
G. B. (Elder), s. of Elder A. B. Smith, Oct. 18, 1866
George, May 15, 1856
George, s. of Abijah Smith, Feb. 25, 1858
George H., May 12, 1921
George W., Aug. 13, 1925
George William (Dr.), May 1, 1856
Gilbert Clinton, Nov. 16 and 30, 1933; Feb. 1, 1934
Green Clay, July 4, 1895
H. E., Aug. 26, 1909
Hannah Baldwin, Apr. 20, 1882
Henley W., s. of Francis A. Smith, Aug. 5, 1852
Henry F. (Rev.), Feb. 24, 1887
Hezekiah H., s. of Robert A. and Lucy E. Smith, Apr. 13 and 20, 1876
Hugh C. (Rev.), Feb. 5, 19, and 26, Mar. 19, 1931
Hugh Mercer, May 27, 1897

Isaac T. (Mrs.), Nov. 15, 1877
J. A. W., Feb. 10, 1921
J. B. (Rev.), June 8, 1876
J. Lawrence (Dr.), Oct. 25, 1883
Jacob, July 16, 1830
Jacob H., Oct. 30, 1862
James, Dec. 29, 1859
James, Apr. 3, 1890
James H., May 23, 1935
James Henry, s. of Thomas D. Smith, Feb. 7, 1856
James L., Feb.. 8, 1923
James Walker, Mar. 21, 1857
Jane, w. of Drewry A. Smith, Mar. 26, 1857
Jane M., Jan. 10, 1884
Joel, s. of Charles Smith, Mar. 25, 1841
John A., s. of Jeremiah M. and Frances A. Smith, July 11, 1861
John A., Sept. 24, 1863
John Holliday, Dec. 27, 1883
John Lawrence, July 30, 1885
John M. (Capt.), Apr. 20, 1843
John Massie, Oct. 21, 1909
John W. (Mrs.), Aug. 1, 1929
Joseph (Dr.), July 9, 1846
Julana, Sept. 11, 1856*
Julius C. (Mrs.), sister of Rev. Basil and Charles Manly, Feb. 1, 1900
Langston Alexander, s. of John J. and Lucy J. Smith, Oct. 7, 1880
Lee J., Apr. 6, 1933
Leroy, Aug. 20, 1914
Leslie W., s. of Armistead and Louise Smith, Sept. 20, 1855
Lethe A. G., w. of Thomas D., Jan. 20, 1848
Louisa, Mar. 31, 1881
Louisa Witt (Mrs.), d. of Rev. E. W. Roach, Feb. 28, 1907
Lucie A. (Mrs.), May 14, 1891

* Possible inaccuracy in name, or spelling, but given as printed

OBITUARY NOTICES IN THE RELIGIOUS HERALD WITH DATES OF PUBLICATION

Lucy A., w. of Samuel Smith, Sr., Apr. 16, 1874
Lucy E., d. of Robert A. and Lucy E. Smith, Mar. 17, 1859
Lucy Hill, d. of Anderson D. and Susan P. F. Smith, Nov. 23, 1854
Lucy M., w. of W. M. Smith, Apr. 16, 1874
Lucy M. (Mrs.), June 28, 1888
Lucy Mildred, w. of Cornelius Smith, Apr. 11, 1889
Margaret M., w. of Timoleon Smith, Apr. 5, 1860
Maria Louisa, d. of James Smith, Dec. 21, 1882
Martha (Mrs.), Dec. 19, 1844
Martha, Feb. 11, 1875
Martha Elizabeth, w. of James Smith, Feb. 25, 1841
Martha M. (Mrs.), Aug. 19, 1875
Martha T., w. of Dr. William Smith, Oct. 8, 1868
Mary (Mrs.), Nov. 29, 1849
Mary (Mrs.), Sept. 4, 1862
Mary, w. of Elder A. B. Smith, Mar. 2, 1865
Mary, w. of Robert Smith, May 20, 1880
Mary C., w. of William Smith, Mar. 17, 1864
Mary E., June 23, 1853
Mary Emma, w. of R. G. Smith, d. of Richard Lumpkin, May 29, 1919
Mary Frances, w. of Bartholomew, Oct. 8, 1840
Mary Jane, June 14, 1934
Mary M., w. of William Smith, May 7, 1874
Mary M. (Mrs.), Feb. 21, 1878
Mary Moseley, d. of Elder P. P. Smith, May 18, 1848
Mildred Gardner, w. of Stephen P. Smith, Jan. 7, 1909
Mildred T., w. of R. Smith, Jan. 4, 1844
Morgan (Col.), Aug. 28, 1884
Mortimer, Feb. 28, 1861
N. (Mrs.), Sept. 30, 1858
Nannie Legrand, d. of L. E. and Lena Smith, Apr. 27, 1899
Natilie Wood, d. of James E. and Willie Smith, Sept. 3, 1874
Nellie Timberlake, w. of J. Massie Smith, Apr. 2, 1874
P. P. (Elder), Nov. 20, 1845
Peter C., Mar. 11, 1840
Presley (Capt.), June 13, 1850
Priscilla B., w. of James Smith, Mar. 9, 1876
Priscilla Browne, d. of James Smith, Dec. 8, 1898
R. M., June 15, 1933
R. P. (Capt.), Aug. 10, 1893
Rebecca H. (Mrs.), Apr. 27, 1882
Richard L., Sept. 14, 1843
Robert (Capt.), Jan. 16 and 23, 1913
Robert H., Aug. 4, 1870
Robert Judson, s. of Thomas D. Smith, May 7, 1857
Robert L., Mar. 7, 1889
Robert S. (Dr.), s. of James Smith, Feb. 16, 1860
Robert Taylor, Mar. 29, 1923
Ruth (Mrs.), Feb. 5, 1830
Ruth Judson, d. of F. P. and Ella Smith, Jan. 21 and 28, 1886
S. A., w. of P. C. Smith, Nov. 21, 1889
S. F. (Rev.), Nov. 28, 1895
S. W., w. of Rev. A. B. Smith, Feb. 28, 1889
Sallie, Mar. 27, 1879
Sarah, w. of William Smith, Aug. 29, 1844
Sarah E. (Mrs.), Oct. 7, 1915
Sarah Frances (Mrs.), d. of Rev. Henry Keeling, Dec. 16,

OBITUARY NOTICES IN THE RELIGIOUS HERALD WITH DATES OF PUBLICATION

1869
Sarah J. P., d. of William and Lucy Ann Smith, Aug. 25, 1859
Sarah P., w. of A. Smith, Apr. 2, 1863
Sarah W. (Mrs.), Feb. 4, 1884
Susan, d. of Elder Poindexter P. Smith, Dec. 31, 1846
Susan F., w. of Edward W. Smith, Oct. 10, 1867
T. A., July 24, 1890
Tabitha, w. of Cornelius Smith, July 13, 1854
Thomas D., Oct. 23, Nov. 6, 1884
Thomas S., s. of Peter and Virginia A. Smith, Oct. 15, 1891
Thomas W. (Rev.), May 24, 1883
V., Nov. 1, 1833
Virginia A., w. of James M. Smith, Apr. 3, 1856
W. H., July 14, 1904
W. L., May 9, 1907
W. R. L. (Mrs.), Aug. 10 and 31, 1882
W. R. L. (Mrs.), July 2, 1931
Walter F., July 2, 1863
William, Aug. 18, 1853
William, June 25, 1863
William, Jan. 5, 1865
William, Dec. 6, 1866; Jan. 3, 1867
William Clinton, Apr. 26, 1894
William E., Apr. 1, 1858
William H., July 13, 1933
Willie A., s. of D. H. and J. L. Smith, Mar. 16, 1871
Willie Julia (Mrs.), d. of Mrs. Julia Ann Wilburne, Mar. 24, 1904
Zachary S., Aug. 16, 1888

SMITHER
Austin F., Oct. 9, 1924
Bettie, w. of Edward L. Smither, Feb. 26, 1874
Caroline M., Oct. 6, 1881
Eliza (Mrs.), Mar. 17, 1881
Fannie R. (Mrs.), July 14, 1938
George L., Jr., Jan. 15, 1920
John A., June 11, 1936
Joseph E., June 22, 1871
Julia A., w. of James Smither, Jan. 4, 1839
Mary Elizabeth (Mrs.), Dec. 19, 1929
Mary F. (Mrs.), Apr. 8, 1852
Rigbon M., Mar. 23, 1871
T. O., Mar. 10, 1921

SMITHSON
Elizabeth A., w. of Sterling T. Smithson, Jan. 28, 1864
Francis L., Mar. 18, 1869
Isabella C. (Mrs.), Dec. 10, 1891
Margaret (Mrs.), May 10, 1928
Margaret D. (Mrs.), July 4, 1861
Martha, June 16, July 21, 1842
Sterling C., May 18, 1871
Susan (Mrs.), d. of William Brume, Jan. 21, 1847
Willie Mabel (Mrs.), Apr. 27, 1922

SMOOT
Amanda A., Apr. 28, 1837
Elizabeth, w. of Samuel Smoot, Dec. 6, 1849
Frances, Nov. 4, 1841
Henry C., June 23, 1853
Joseph A., June 11, 1846
Mary E. (Mrs.), d. of Temple Redd, Dec. 2, 1858
Mary J. (Mrs.), d. of William and Gabriella Bosher, Oct. 28, 1886
Nanny Lee, d. of William and Siana M. Smoot, Jan. 22, 1857
Sallie Dean, d. of B. F. Smoot, Aug. 29, 1878

SNEAD
A. J. (Dr.), s. of Edwin Snead, Apr. 4, 1872
Albert (Dr.), Nov. 13, 1873

OBITUARY NOTICES IN THE RELIGIOUS HERALD WITH DATES OF PUBLICATION

B. W., Dec. 31, 1863
Bagwell W., Sept. 8, 1853
Benjamin W., July 30, 1868
Betty A., d. of John and Elizabeth Snead, Nov. 27, 1851
C. G. (Mrs.), July 30, 1925
Cornelius Pollard, May 8, 1913
Courtney, d. of Thomas N. and Fannie I. Snead, Mar. 30, 1882
Earl Newton, Feb. 16, 1933
Edloe G. (Mrs.), Dec. 11, 1924
Edward F. (Dr.), Mar. 18, Apr. 1, 1897
Ella C., Feb. 23, 1854
Ellen C., d. of Dr. Albert Snead, Oct. 1, 1868
Esther W., w. of Louis L. Snead, Mar. 11, 1880
George H., Sept. 29, 1870
George H. (Dr.), July 6, Aug. 17, 1911
George T., Dec. 15, 1892; Aug. 24, 1893
Georgie Tillman, July 1, 1915
Helen, w. of C. P. Snead, Mar. 23, 1899
Heningham W., s. of Thomas N. and Fannie I. Snead, Oct. 9, 1862
Lawrence, s. of Dr. E. F. Snead, Sept. 17, 1891
Lawrence Reynolds, s. of Dr. Albert and Margaret Ann Snead, Feb. 10, 1881
Lou Blanche, d. of Marcellus and Ann Judson Snead, July 1, 1897
Louisa Atkinson, w. of Edwin B. Snead, Dec. 24, 1885
M. Adella, w. of J. P. Snead, d. of J. S. and M. T. Yarbrough, Jan. 2, 1879
Marcellus, Oct. 23, 1913
Martha M., w. of Moses Snead, Mar. 6, 1845
Mary (Mrs.), Oct. 27, 1842
Maud Winston, d. of Willie Payne and W. F. Snead, May 27, 1886
Nancy (Mrs.), Nov. 18, 1875
R. N., Sept. 15, 1892
Robert J., s. of R. W. and Octavia Snead, May 1, 1862; July 2, 1863
Sally Miller (Mrs.), Jan. 19, 1871
Sophia J., d. of George T. and Martha A. Snead, Sept. 11, 1873
Susan R., w. of Charles Snead, Apr. 26, 1883
Virginia Perkins (Mrs.), Sept. 18, 1919
W. C., Sept. 15, 1892
William, Sept. 5, 1867
William Frank, s. of William P. and Henrietta Snead, July 18, 1912
William P., Mar. 24, 1904
William Winston (Dr.), Oct. 11, 1923

SNEED
Garnet, s. of Charlie and Fannie Sneed, Apr. 18, 1889
James A., s. of C. P. and Helen Winn Sneed, Aug. 19, 1937*
Lucy A., w. of Benjamin Sneed, Dec. 18, 1835
Mary F., w. of Alexander Sneed, Oct. 24, 1850
Sally C., w. of Charles Sneed, Sept. 8, 1842
Virginia J., w. of J. C. Sneed, Sr., May 16, 1889
William B., Mar. 31, 1870

SNELLINGS
Alexander, s. of Zaccheus Snellings, Sept. 9, 1852
Francis G. (Elder), July 18, 1844
Lemuel, Aug. 27, 1863
Mary Susan, d. of Elliott Chiles, gr.d. of Rev. Andrew Broaddus, Dec. 10,

---

* Possible inaccuracy in name, or spelling, but given as printed

OBITUARY NOTICES IN THE RELIGIOUS HERALD WITH DATES OF PUBLICATION

1868
Sarah F., w. of Lemuel Snellings, d. of Ralph Brown, Aug. 27, 1863
SNELSON
Sarah, w. of Nathaniel Snelson, July 15, 1847
SNODDY
Eliza A., w. of James C. Snoddy, June 9, 1853
F. L., Mar. 26, 1891
Mable Steger, May 13, 1937
Mary A., Feb. 12, 1863
Philip, Mar. 17, 1892
R. H., Feb. 6, 1890
Sally F., w. of Cornelius Snoddy, July 22, 1858
Susie Bersch, w. of Gratton Snoddy, Mar. 26, Apr. 2, 1925
SNODGRASS
Ella (Mrs.), Feb. 24, 1927
SNOW
Elizabeth R. (Mrs.), Mar. 24, 1842
Phillipp C. (Mrs.), May 30, 1918
SNYDER
J. O., s. of David H. and Sarah Ann Snyder, Dec. 11, 1873
Joseph, Jan. 6, 1881
W. A. (Mrs.), w. of Rev. W. A. Snyder, Mar. 29, 1900
Willoughby A., s. of John and Rochelle, July 13, 1933
SOMEVAIL
Alexander (Dr.), Dec. 19, 1839; Jan. 16, 1840
Maria, w. of Dr. Alexander Somervail, Aug. 6, 1830
SOMERVILLE
William M., Oct. 16, 1856
SOPER
John R., Dec. 16, 1897
SOREN
F. F. (Dr.), Oct. 26, 1933
SORRELL

Elsie Madison (Mrs.), Sept. 29, 1927
Susan (Mrs.), May 28, 1885
SORSBY
N. C., Aug. 4, 1864
SOUTH
Ann Maria, w. of Robert South, Dec. 14, 1854
SOUTHALL
M., w. of P. Southall, Mar. 7, 1828
SOUTHGATE
Anna S., June 21, 1839
Elizabeth Ann, w. of Capt. George M. Southgate, Sept. 19, 1834
SOUTHWARD
George Ella Byron (Mrs.), d. of Capt. G. B. P. Bowis, Mar. 7, 1889
SOUTHWOOD
Susan, w. of Rev. William Southwood, Sept. 19, 1872
SOUTHWORTH
Irine May, d. of J. W. and A. S. Southworth, Jan. 21, 1897*
Rebecca, w. of James L. Southworth, Dec. 10, 1857
SOWELL
Georgie A., Feb. 27, 1873
S. C., Jan. 11, 1934
SOWERS
Frances A., w. of David H. Sowers, d. of Nathaniel S. Oden, June 21, 1855
George K., Aug. 6, 1840
Hattie, June 23, 1927
James, Mar. 21, 1850
John W., Feb. 28, 1889
Mary Frances, Aug. 10, 1922
Mary Turner (Mrs.), Jan. 21, 1926
N. O. (Rev.), May 20, 1926
SOYARS
John O., July 9, 1908
P. O. (Rev.), s. of J. W. Soyars, Oct. 24, 1918
SOYERS
Jane (Mrs.), Jan. 6, 1859

* Possible inaccuracy in name, or spelling, but given as printed

OBITUARY NOTICES IN THE RELIGIOUS HERALD WITH DATES OF PUBLICATION

SPAIN
  Fannie K. (Mrs.), Mar. 6, 1924
SPAINE
  Eliza D. (Mrs.), June 27, 1878
SPANN
  Armstead, Feb. 2, 1899
SPARKS
  Daniel (Col.), May 14, 1868
  Elijah (Rev.), Aug. 11, 1859
  Fanny (Mrs.), Nov. 7, 1895
  Henry T., Nov. 26, 1891
  Jane, w. of Alexander Sparks, Apr. 27, 1871
  Lucy M. O'BANNON, w. of Henry T. Sparks, Nov. 8, 1888
  Nannie, d. of R. W. and N. C. Sparks, Sept. 17, 1891
  Nannie Catherine (Mrs.), June 15, 1916
SPARROW
  Mary S. (Mrs.), Dec. 5, 1895
SPAULDING
  Lucy Jane ROYALL, w. of Albert G. Spaulding, Sept. 5, 1867
SPEARS
  Julia A. (Mrs.), Dec. 27, 1855
  Rebecca P., w. of Capt. William Spears, Nov. 6, 1913
  Robert, Nov. 30, 1832
  Thomas E., s. of Thomas A. Spears, June 28, July 12, 1849
SPEIDEN
  Alice, d. of Edgar and Lucy L. Speiden, Aug. 25, 1887
  Edgar, Dec. 28, 1905
  Edith Mauzy, d. of Theodore and Rosalie M. Speiden, Aug. 5, 1886
  Marian, w. of William Speiden, d. of Clement T. and Mary Coote, Nov. 8, 1866
SPEIGHT
  Henry, May 31, 1888
  J. A. (Rev.), Mar. 31, 1881
  J. A. (Dr.), Sept. 18, Oct. 18, 1913

SPENCE
  Matier Lafayette, Feb. 13, 1919
SPENCER
  Branch W., June 4, 1904
  Charles, Sept. 15, 1859
  James Emmet, s. of William T. and Nannie M. Spencer, Jan. 31, 1867
  John (Elder), Feb. 24, 1859
  John (Rev.), Nov. 28, 1889
  John Paulette, June 3, 1926
  Licetta Ann, d. of Robert Spencer, Feb. 8, 1855
  Maggie Walker, d. of B. W. and E. R. Spencer, Mar. 18, 1869
  Mary, w. of Dr. Lake Spencer, Feb. 21, 1850
  Mary E., Dec. 19, 1878
  Minitree D., June 6, 1851
  R. H. (Capt.), s. of Col. Robert Spencer, June 27, 1907
  Rebecca (Mrs.), Jan. 30, 1896
  Robert M. (Col.), June 28, 1860
  Virginia B., w. of Capt. R. H. Spencer, July 3, 1873
  Virginia Roy, d. of Capt. R. H. Spencer, Oct. 30, 1873
  William, Mar. 9, 1848
SPICER
  Joseph C., June 15, 1843
  Sallie W., w. of W. C. Spicer, d. of John B. and Elizabeth Baker, Jan. 3, 1878
SPIERS
  B. J., Dec. 25, 1890
  J. W., Oct. 14, 1897
  Lena, w. of Robert C. Spiers, Aug. 25, 1887
  Susie Elmerine, d. of Robert and Lena Spiers, Sept. 25, 1873
SPIGHT

OBITUARY NOTICES IN THE RELIGIOUS HERALD WITH DATES OF PUBLICATION

Thomas, May 6, 1920
SPILLER
  Robert Augustus, d. of W.
  A. and Bettie F. Spiller,
  July 6, 1854
  W. H. (Capt.), Mar. 31, 1837
SPILLMAN
  Alexander H. (Rev.), Apr. 29,
  July 22, 1875
SPILMAN
  Allen Lester, s. of Luther
  R. and Josephine Spilman,
  Sept. 14, 1876
  Clara F., d. of John A. and
  Susan R. Spilman, Feb. 13
  and 20, 1913
  Conway, Mar. 21, 1861
  Ella Marion, w. of S. Fisher
  Spilman, d. of Mann Stickler
  and Mary Jane Graves,
  July 20, 1933
  John Armistead, Apr. 11, 1889
  Mary Conway, d. of Luther R.,
  and Lucy T. Spilman, Apr. 2,
  1857
  Nancy, w. of Capt. Conway
  Spilman, Jan. 23, 1835
  Robert B., June 7, 1917
  Robert Coleman, s. of Luther
  R. and Lucy T. Spilman
  Apr. 2, 1857
  Susan R., w. of John A. Spilman, Apr. 2, 1874
  Telula Bayne, w. of R. B.
  Spilman, Dec. 6, 1900
SPINDLE
  B. T., Sept. 29, 1910
  Elizabeth C., w. of William
  Spindle, Apr. 12, 1860
  Ellen E., w. of Benjamin
  Spindle, Aug. 21, 1851
  F. M. (Mrs.), Sept. 30, 1852
  Sally (Mrs.), May 18, 1848
SPINNER
  Ann Elizabeth, Nov. 23,
  1899
SPIVEY
  Nancy, w. of Eley Spivey,
  Nov. 21, 1872
SPIVY
  Gilbert A., s. of Jeremiah
  Spivy, Aug. 21, 1862
SPODY
  Denard (Mrs.), Nov. 1, 1928
SPOTTS
  Austin P. (Mrs.), Mar. 20,
  1919
  Ephraim, Nov. 16, 1871
  James Campbell, s. of James
  C. and Mattie L. Spotts,
  Feb. 21, 1861
  James G., June 25, July 2,
  1857
  Nannie E., d. of James C.
  Spotts, July 25, 1878
SPOTTSWOOD
  Alexander Dandridge (Mrs.),
  Mar. 15, 1923
  Alfred R., s. of Dr. Norborne
  Spottswood, Mar. 15, 1833
SPOUSE
  Willanna Frances, Aug. 12, 1920
SPRAGGINS
  Thomas, May 11, 1854
SPRAGINGS
  Thomas L. (Capt.), June 18,
  1863
SPRAGINS
  Fayette B. (Dr.), Apr. 29, 1852
SPRATLEY
  Edward Stith, s. of William
  D. and Virginia Spratley,
  Oct. 3, 1878
  M. E., w. of E. W. Spratley,
  July 22, 1875
  William, Nov. 11, 1836
  William Davis, June 13, 1935
SPRINGER
  Job, Dec. 24, 1874
SPRUCE
  Ada Shields (Mrs.), June 21,
  1928
SPRUILL
  Johnnie, s. of William and
  Ellen Spruill, Jan. 16,
  1873
SPURZHEIM
  Gaspard (Dr.), Nov. 23, 1832
SQUAIR
  Isabella (Mrs.), Feb. 7, 1844

OBITUARY NOTICES IN THE RELIGIOUS HERALD WITH DATES OF PUBLICATION

STAINBACK
　Mary C. (Mrs.), Feb. 3, 1832
STALEY
　Martha Ann (Mrs.), June 16, 1910
STALLINGS
　Grace Mason (Mrs.), June 14, 1923
STAMPER
　Martha P., d. of Mrs. Martha J. Stamper, Feb. 17, 1859
STAMPS
　Thomas, May 8, 1835
STANARD
　Champe, Sept. 27, 1883
　Eloiza C., Mar. 8, 1866
　Jane Stith, d. of John Champe and Sarah Taliaferro Thornton Stanard, Mar. 22, 1917
　Mary, w. of William H. Stanard, Feb. 18, 1831
　P. B. (Maj.), May 2, 1878
STANFORD
　John (Mrs.), w. of John Stanford, May 2, 1834
　Sarah (Mrs.), Aug. 25, 1842
STANLEY
　Andrew Boyer, Aug. 5, 1915
　Eliza (Mrs.), Feb. 12, 1891
STANTON
　Antoinette, Feb. 14, 1834
STAPLES
　Eliza R., May 24, 1923
　J. C. (Mrs.), Dec. 16, 1909
　James Lawrence, s. of J. C. Staples, Sept. 23, 1897
　Jesse, May 13, 1836
　Martha Ann, w. of John T. Staples, Dec. 7, 1871
　Roxanna E., d. of William A. Staples, Sept. 17, 1857
　Sallie W., w. of Robert L. Staples, d. of P. Woolfolk, July 4, 1867
STARBUCK
　Almira, Jan. 10, 1924
STARK
　Edward, s. of Capt. J. and E. Stark, Mar. 10, 1864
　Edwin, July 16, 1830
　Mary Fannie, d. of Henry M. and Bettie C. Stark, Aug. 17, 1876
　Mary Louisa, June 27, 1878
STARKE
　A. A. (Mrs.), June 26, 1902
　Amanda, w. of Burwell Starke, July 21, 1837
　Americus Hatchett, s. of Burwell and Fanny L. Starke, Jan. 8, 1891
　Ann Baylor, w. of Burwell Starke, Apr. 24, 1851
　Bowling W. (Judge), s. of Bowling and Eliza G. Starke, July 25, Aug. 1, 1901
　Eliza G., w. of Col. Bowling Starke, Nov. 18, 1852
　Elizabeth, w. of John Starke, Nov. 21, 1837
　Fannie Lewis, w. of Burwell Starke, d. of Rev. William Hatchett, Sept. 24, 1891
　Gideon, Feb. 9, 1888
　J. Laprade, s. of T. J. and S. J. Starke, Apr. 9, 1863
　James (Capt.), July 20, 1871
　John, Jan. 9, 1829
　Joseph (Rev.), Aug. 11, 1853
　Kate Pleasants, d. of Gideon and Adaline A. Starke, Nov. 20, 1856
　Lucie E., June 28, 1877
　Marcella B. (Mrs.), Sept. 12, 1878
　Mary (Mrs.), June 9, 1859
　Patrick Henry, Dec. 29, 1881
　Sarah J., w. of Thomas J. Starke, Feb. 25, 1897
　Susan Laprad, w. of Col. William Starke, Dec. 16, 1875 *
　Thomas Benton, s. of Bowling and Eliza G. Starke, Mar. 9, 1838
　Thomas J., Mar. 1, 1888
STARLING

* Possible inaccuracy in name, or spelling, but given as printed

OBITUARY NOTICES IN THE RELIGIOUS HERALD WITH DATES OF PUBLICATION

Mary E. (Mrs.), Aug. 20, 1857
Richard, Apr. 22, 1875
STAUGHTON
   William (Rev.), Dec. 18, 1829
STEARNES
   Tempe, s. of T. F. Stearnes,
     June 9, 1898
STEARNS
   Emma F., Dec. 25, 1845
STEEL
   Araminta (Mrs.), Oct. 7, 1831
   Bettie Scott, w. of Dr. George
     B. Steel, d. of Rev. Thomas
     W. Sydnor, May 1, 1873
   Betty Winfree, d. of George
     and Ann W. Steel, Oct. 4,
     1866
   C. L. (Dr.), July 14, 1904
   David (Dr.), Apr. 1, 1886
   Edith Gwathmey, d. of Dr.
     George B. and Mollie Garnett Steel, June 11, 1896
   Elizabeth, w. of George Steel,
     Mar. 31, 1842
   George, Nov. 20, 1856
   George B. (Mrs.), w. of Dr.
     George B. Steel, d. of Rev.
     T. W. Sydnor, Apr. 3, 1873
   George B., s. of Dr. George
     B. and Mollie Steel, June
     28, 1877
   Joseph D., May 3, 1860
   Mary Ann, w. of Dr. George
     B. Steel, Oct. 15, 1863
   Mary Catherine, w. of Dr.
     David Steel, d. of Baker
     Mann, Dec. 25, 1856
   Mary J., w. of Dr. George
     B. Steel, d. of George
     and Mary L. Garnett, Feb.
     4 and 11, 1897
   Mattie Ryland, w. of Dr. G.
     B. Steel, d. of James
     Robert Fleet, June 15, 1871
   Mattie Ryland, d. of Dr. G.
     B. and Mattie R. Steel,
     June 15, 1871
   Mollie E., d. of George B.
     and Mary A. Steel, Nov. 24,
     1859

STEGER
   I. T., June 27, 1901
   Jeannette J., July 31, 1924
   John H. (Maj.), Sept. 6,
     1860
   Oscar S., May 27, 1886
STEIN
   H., June 25, 1857
   Robert Anton, s. of Henry
     and Mary A. Stein, Oct.
     17, 1844
STEMBRIDGE
   Bettie M., w. of James B.
     Stembridge, Mar. 11, 1886
STEPHEN
   Robert, Dec. 17, 1936
STEPHENS
   Fannie, May 4, 1882
   Henry C., Oct. 26, 1882
   Lizzie T., Sept. 29, 1881
   Maggie Carric (Mrs.), Oct. 19,
     1922
   Mary E. (Mrs.), Feb. 18,
     1897
   Mary F. (Mrs.), Sept. 27,
     1906
   Russell T., s. of J. W.
     Stephens, Mar. 8, 1894
   Theodosia W., w. of George
     Stephens, d. of Capt. James
     Early, Apr. 22, 1880
   Thomas H., June 5, 1856
   William (Mrs.), d. of
     Robert Harris, Nov. 16,
     1871
STEPHENSON
   d. of W. G. Stephenson,
     July 15, 1858
   Adoniram J., Mar. 21 and 28,
     1907
   Amanda (Mrs.), May 8, 1902
   Aurelia Alice (Mrs.), Oct. 17,
     1929
   Belle Holmes, w. of A. J.
     Stephenson, Sept. 5, 1895
   Charles W., Oct. 19, 1876
   Elizabeth L., w. of Levi W.
     Stephenson, Feb. 26, 1903
   Fannie (Mrs.), Feb. 27, 1890
   J. W. (Dr.), Apr. 25, 1889

-320-

OBITUARY NOTICES IN THE RELIGIOUS HERALD WITH DATES OF PUBLICATION

James A., s. of Allen and L. Stephenson, Dec. 23, 1858
Lavinia, w. of Allen Stephenson, Dec. 23, 1858
R. E., Apr. 15, 1886
Robert J., s. of William G. Stephenson, Apr. 19, 1860
Sophronia (Mrs.), d. of Solomon and Elizabeth Butler, Apr. 4, 1918
Virginia E., d. of Levi W. and Elizabeth L. Stephenson, Aug. 26, 1858
William H., Sept. 1 and 15, 1921

STEPTOE
S. P. (Mrs.), sister of William L. Goggin, gr.d. of Rev. William Leftwich, Sept. 22, 1870

STEVENS
E. J., May 31, 1883
John (Rev.), May 10, 1877
Mary (Mrs.), Sept. 7, 1848
Mary Lou, d. of M. L. and P. M. Stevens, gr.d. of Rev. Iverson L. Brookes, Feb. 25, 1875
Mary Thomas, d. of Mrs. Nancy Stevens, Jan. 15, 1857

STEVENSON
Carrie, Mar. 24, 1927
R. D., Aug. 28, 1924

STEWART
Anna Florentine, Oct. 11, 1877
Emma L. (Mrs.), Dec. 29, 1887
F. C. (Mrs.), Mar. 5, 1936
Fannie, w. of Dr. James Stewart, July 4, 1850
George W., Mar. 17, 1938
Lavinia L., w. of J. W. Stewart, June 4, 1868
Lucy, w. of James Stewart, Nov. 21, 1844
Martha Ann HEDGE, w. of Robert Stewart, Dec. 10, 1885
Mary Susan, w. of Samuel Dabney Stewart, Dec. 22, 1927
Robert, May 26, 1887
Virginia C. (Mrs.), Sept. 20, 1866

STICKLEMAN
E. G. (Mrs.), Mar. 1, 1888

STICKLER
Newman, s. of James Stickler, Mar. 19, 1874

STICKLEY
Philip, June 29, 1843

STICKNEY
William S., s. of William Stickney, Aug. 5, 1880

STIFF
Fannie Alice (Mrs.), Jan. 8, 1931
John W., Mar. 26, 1857
Madison, Aug. 9, 1860
Sarah, Oct. 17, 1834

STIFLER
J. M. (Dr.), Dec. 25, 1902; Jan. 1, 1903

STIGLER
Mary Torrey, w. of Col. James Stigler, Jan. 23, 1868

STILES
Sallie C., w. of Rev. C. A. Stiles, d. of R. Miles and M. A. Whaler, Nov. 19, 1874

STILL
Lucy, Mar. 2, 1922
Nancy, w. of Henry Still, Jan. 21, 1869

STINSON
John F., Mar. 1, 1934

STOCKDELL
Pascal R., Feb. 3, 1853
Philip, Sept. 10, 1840

STOKES
Annie B., w. of Terry Stokes, Sept. 10, 1885
Margaret (Mrs.), June 8, 1838

STONE
Charles Edwin, s. of Charles B. and Callie Stone, Nov. 14, 1918
Daniel, July 13, 1854

OBITUARY NOTICES IN THE RELIGIOUS HERALD WITH DATES OF PUBLICATION

Elizabeth Holmes, w. of S.
R. Stone, d. of Jacob Hubbard, May 6, 1886
Elizabeth M. (Mrs.), June 7, 1888
Emily Lucille, d. of John D. and Anna E. Stone, Feb. 1, 1883
Forest Creath, s. of R. R. and M. E. Stone, Nov. 10, 1892
Frances, Sept. 8, 1853
Harriet N., w. of R. J. Stone, Mar. 2, 1899
James A., s. of Rev. R. H. Stone, Apr. 15, 1915
Jane, Feb. 19, 1852
John, Jan. 12, 1922
John D., Apr. 3, 1884
Margaret Johnston (Mrs.), June 28, 1934
Mary R. (Mrs.), Apr. 2, 1931
Richard Barton, Oct. 11, 1923
Samuel, Sr., July 5, 1934
Samuel M., July 28, 1881
Sarah (Mrs.), July 20, 1838
Sarah, Oct. 1, 1857
Susan C. Broadus, d. of A. J. and C. F. Stone, Sept. 8 and 15, 1870
Susan J., w. of Rev. R. H. Stone, d. of James G. and Elizabeth Broaddus, Feb. 5, 1903
Tiberius G., Mar. 1, 1883
Walter Haskins, s. of R. R. and M. E. Stone, Nov. 10, 1892

STORKE
Betty Washington, d. of Seymour H. and Mary E. A. Storke, Oct. 1, 1846

STOTT
Elizabeth W., d. of Thaddeus Stott, Mar. 11, 1858
Elmonia A., Dec. 4, 1856
Jane (Mrs.), Dec. 2, 1841

STOUT
Elizabeth, Mar. 20, 1835
Elizabeth (Mrs.), May 19, 1842
Isaiah, Dec. 8, 1859
J. B. (Capt.), Jan. 1, 1857
Jacob, Aug. 14, 1851
Jane M., d. of J. Stout, Jr., May 19, 1837
Mary E., w. of John L. Stout, mother of Rev. Thomas Stout, Mar. 22, 1866
W. C. (Mrs.), d. of W. W. and Ann O. Davis, Jan. 20, 1916

STOVALL
George Quincy, Dec. 31, 1885
Virginia Tennessee, d. of Jonithan B. and Elizabeth M. W. Stovall, Aug. 30, 1855*

STRACHAN
John A. (Elder), Nov. 5, 1874
Robert A., s. of Rev. J. A. Strachan, Jan. 6, 1859
Thomas B., s. of Rev. J. A. Strachan, Dec. 31, 1891

STRALEY
D. A. (Mrs.), June 14, 1888
H. W., Sr., Mar. 16, 1905

STRANGE
A. P., Sept. 20, 1866
Ann A., w. of A. P. Strange, July 21, 1864
Annie, June 5, 1858
James Alloway, s. of John B. and Agnes Strange, Mar. 26, 1857
Mary Ann, w. of Abner W. Strange, Feb. 3, 1848
Mildred A. (Mrs.), July 14, 1837
William C. A., Sept. 30, 1841

STRATFORD
A. L. (Mrs.), d. of Rev. Richard Herndon, July 18, 1918
Lizzie Cooper, d. of Dr. A. Lafayette and Tillie Herndon Stratford, Sept. 15, 1892

STRATON
John Roach (Dr.), Nov. 7, 1929

STRATTON
Ann E., w. of R. H. Stratton,

* Possible inaccuracy in name, or spelling, but given as printed

OBITUARY NOTICES IN THE RELIGIOUS HERALD WITH DATES OF PUBLICATION

Sr., Feb. 17, 1887
Bethenia Ann, w. of William P. Stratton, Dec. 21, 1848
Carrie, June 16, 1892
David C., s. of David Stratton, May 22, June 19, 1862
George, s. of R. H. Stratton, Mar. 10, 1881
James A., Dec. 18, 1884
John Myers, s. of S. C. and Lena Myers, June 10, 1897
Joseph, Apr. 19, 1860
L. B., Jan. 29, 1891
Lorenzo D., s. of Richard B. and Martha Stratton, June 9, 1853
Margaret, w. of John Stratton, May 12, 1853
Martha A., w. of Richard B. Stratton, Mar. 24, 1870
Mary Diuguid, w. of W. M. Stratton, Aug. 23, 1900
Nancy, Sept. 6, 1849
Nora Belle, d. of Robert Arthur and Rosa Lee Stratton, Dec. 24, 1885
Rosa L., w. of R. A. Stratton, Jan. 5, 1899
T. J. (Mrs.), Nov. 22, 1917
Thomas J., Mar. 28, Apr. 18, 1918
William, Nov. 29, 1849
William P., July 18, 1850

STRAUGHAN
Alfred Nathaniel, June 17, 1852
Ann Catharine, June 17, 1852
Benjamin Walker, June 17, 1852
David (Capt.), Feb. 25, 1904
Lucy Mary, June 17, 1852
Marion L., w. of Judge S. L. Straughan, Mar. 12, 1885
Martha A., d. of Col. S. L. Straughan, Sept. 2, 1858
Nathaniel, June 17, 1852
Samuel L., Aug. 6, 1874

STREET
(Mrs.), mother of Rev. J. M. Street, Mar. 16, 1911
Ada Marion, d. of A. H. and N. B. Street, Aug. 16, 1860
Amelia H., w. of Capt. N. B. Street, Aug. 9, 1894
Annie Lee, d. of Dr. John W. and Virginia Street, Apr. 1, 1886
Elizabeth (Mrs.), Apr. 28, 1859
Elizabeth, w. of Thomas Street, Mar. 21, 1861
Fannie Augusta, w. of Capt. W. A. Street, d. of William Hundley, Sept. 24, 1863
Frances (Mrs.), May 21, 1863
Frances (Mrs.), Feb. 15, 1866
George (Maj.), Oct. 21, 1831
H. H., Nov. 24, 1927
Henry, Sr., Sept. 25, 1835
J. M., Jr., June 30, 1927
J. M. (Rev.), July 18, 1929
J. W. (Dr.), May 1, 1873
Lizzie E., d. of Dr. John W. and Virginia Street, Sept. 12, 1872
Mary (Mrs.), Feb. 5, 1927
Nancy (Mrs.), July 5, 1845
Thomas, Sept. 3, 1868
W. A. (Rev.), Aug. 30, 1900

STRIBLING
James H. (Rev.), Aug. 4, 1881

STRICKLAND
Edward C., May 8, 1862

STRICKLER
Fannie V. (Mrs.), Dec. 20, 1917
Isaac H., Dec. 10, 1885
Manuel C., May 27, 1897
Mary J., w. of M. C. Strickler, d. of Asa and Sarah Kirtley Graves, Apr. 9, 1908

STRINGER
John A., Jan. 13, 1881

STRINGFELLOW
Adoniram J., s. of Rev. Thornton Stringfellow, Mar. 4, 1841

OBITUARY NOTICES IN THE RELIGIOUS HERALD WITH DATES OF PUBLICATION

Amelia J., d. of Elder Thornton Stringfellow, Sept. 5, 1844
Anne, w. of Elder Thornton Stringfellow, Oct. 13, 1842
Annie, d. of B. W. and S. T. Stringfellow, Jan. 25, 1877
Bruce W., Dec. 17, 1908
Elizabeth, w. of Rev. Thornton Stringfellow, Feb. 27, 1868
Emily, w. of Rev. Thornton Stringfellow, Aug. 27, 1874
Mary Eliza (Mrs.), Aug. 1, 1895
Robert Henry, s. of Rev. Thornton Stringfellow, Dec. 1, 1837
Sally Judson, Apr. 20, 1899
Thornton (Rev.), Mar. 18, 1869
STRONG
   A. H. (Dr.), Dec. 29, 1921
STROTHER
   Elizabeth (Mrs.), Feb. 21, 1878
STUART
   C. E. (Rev.), Dec. 1, 1910
   J. H., Feb. 28, 1929
   J. P. (Dr.), Mar. 29, 1917
   Jemima, Dec. 21, 1843
   R. H. (Rev.), father of Rev. C. E. Stuart, Jan. 27, 1898
   Sarah Quarles, mother of Rev. C. E. Stuart, July 22, 1909
   Susan, Mar. 11, 1858
STUBBLEFIELD
   Fannie, Dec. 5, 1872
   Lillian Wiatt, d. of Russell and Minnie Stubblefield, Mar. 9, 1899
   Lucy F., w. of Emanuel Stubblefield, June 8, 1871
   Mary (Mrs.), May 5, 1892
STUBBS
   Jane W., w. of Elder Robert F. Stubbs, Apr. 15, May 6, 1852
   Robert F., s. of Rev. Robert F. and Susan E. Stubbs, June 16, 1881
STULL
   Alice Geneva, Mar. 31, 1921
STUMP
   John (Rev.), May 19, 1898
   Josephine Ragland, d. of Rev. John S. and Lillie Stump, Apr. 12, 1906
SUBLETT
   Benjamin, Apr. 15, 1897
   James A., s. of Benjamin B. Sublett, Nov. 27, 1862
   Nancy, w. of B. B. Sublett, Oct. 10, 1861
   Richard T., s. of Benjamin B. Sublett, Nov. 27, 1862
SUDDITH
   Elizabeth C. (Mrs.), Nov. 21, 1872
   Eugene B., Feb. 4, 1869
   Inman H., June 4 and 25, 1891
SULLAVAN
   Mary Elizabeth, w. of John L. Sullavan, June 3, 1880
SULLENS
   Helena A., w. of Thaddeus Sullens, May 16, 1918
SULLIVAN
   C. W., Oct. 21, 1886
   George Bailey (Dr.), Apr. 6, 1854
   Hattie Blake (Mrs.), Mar. 5, 1931
SUMMERS
   E. H., June 5, 1873
   Maria Antoinette (Mrs.), Feb. 3, 1853
   R. E., Mar. 18, 1937
   William S. (Mrs.), Oct. 20, 1887
SUMMERSON
   Harriet, w. of William Summerson, Aug. 6, 1830
SUMNER
   Elizabeth, d. of Rev. Samuel S. and Julia Bowen Sumner, Sept. 29, 1842
   George Russell, s. of George J.

OBITUARY NOTICES IN THE RELIGIOUS HERALD WITH DATES OF PUBLICATION

and Lucy Sumner, July 9, 1857
Georgie S., d. of Rev. M. T. Sumner, Aug. 31, 1871
John Marshall, s. of George J. Sumner, Feb. 17, 1876
L. M., w. of George J. Sumner, Nov. 28, 1867
Lute, child of George J. Sumner, Sept. 24, 1868
M. T. (Rev.), Aug. 50, 1883
SURBOUGH
David, June 26, 1873
SURFACE
J. Frank, Feb. 21, 1924
William Nicholas, s. of Henry and Mildred Hambrick Surface, Mar. 26, 1925
SUTHERLAND
Addie R., d. of W. H. and M. J. Sutherland, July 20, 1871
Alice V. (Mrs.), Feb. 15, 1923
Ann W., Feb. 11, 1858
Ella E., w. of W. H. Sutherland, Apr. 6, 1916
John Winston, Sept. 9, 1937
Joseph, Feb. 14, 1861
R. A., June 21, 1923
SUTHERLIN
Bird J., s. of Christopher T. Sutherlin, May 15, 1862
C. T., Jr., Apr. 4, 1935
Christopher Thomas, s. of John and Sarah Sutherlin, July 24, 1890
Edwin J., s. of C. T. Sutherlin, Dec. 29, 1864
Eliza Ann, d. of C. T. and Eliza Ann Sutherlin, Nov. 8, 1860
George Marshall, s. of C. T. and Eliza A. Sutherlin, Sept. 26, 1867
Henry Clay, s. of Christopher T. and Eliza Ann Sutherlin, Jan. 27, 1859
Nathaniel A. (Lt.), Mar. 26, 1863
Nathaniel J., s. of Christopher T. Sutherlin, Aug. 20, 1857
SUTLER
Frances Underwood, w. of G. W. Sutler, d. of John Underwood, Feb. 2, 1893
SUTTLE
Mary Ann, w. of Capt. A. B. Suttle, Mar. 12, 1857
SUTTON
Elvira M., July 23, 1857
SWAN
Allie Wilkerson (Mrs.), Oct. 17, 1929
SWANN
Ann, w. of Philip Swann, June 16, 1859
Elizabeth, July 14, 1837
George, Aug. 7, 1862
George B., Apr. 29, 1852
John, June 13, 1850
Kate E., d. of Thomas and Sarah A. Swann, July 30, 1896
Lillie Rogers, w. of George Swann, Aug. 1, 1907
Lucy F., w. of Edmund W. Swann, d. of John B. and E. A. Wood, Aug. 28, 1873
Martha B. (Mrs.), June 7, 1880
Mary, July 3, 1924
Mildred S., w. of T. T. Swann, June 23, 1842
Porterfield (Mrs.), Oct. 19, 1911
Rebecca H., d. of George Swann, Mar. 3, 1860
Sarah P. (Mrs.), Aug. 21, 1851
Victoria A., w. of John R. Swann, June 5, 1835
William H., s. of R. William Swann, Mar. 28, 1872
SWANSON
Elizabeth, w. of Col. William Swanson, Aug. 5, 1836
W. T. (Mrs.), May 12, 1921
SWART
Annie E., w. of Hugh T. Swart, May 22, 1856

OBITUARY NOTICES IN THE RELIGIOUS HERALD WITH DATES OF PUBLICATION

Hugh Thomas, Sept. 13, 1894
SWEENEY
  C. M. (Mrs.), Jan. 14, 1904
  Harriet Cary, w. of Elder J.
    A. Sweeney, d. of Rev. P.
    M. Cary, Feb. 12, 1874
SWEET
  America E., Nov. 10, 1859
  G. H. (Mrs.), Mar. 9, 1933
  Jennie (Mrs.), Feb. 16,
    1933
SWIFT
  Andrew Broaddus (Col.), s.
    of Timothy T. Swift,
    Nov. 13, 1856
  Charles Pemberton (Mrs.),
    Mar. 20, 1913
  Emerson L. (Rev.), Dec. 10,
    1931
  Judith, w. of Timothy T.
    Swift, Aug. 5, 1858
  Luther P., Oct. 25, 1883
  Mary E., d. of Joseph H.
    Swift, Dec. 17, 1857
  Timothy T. (Elder), June 5,
    1851
SWOOPE
  G. W. (Lt.), May 21, 1863
SWOPE
  Jonathan, May 2, 1872
SYDNOR
  child of William B. Sydnor,
    Aug. 22, 1850
  Edward Garland, s. of Rev. T.
    W. Sydnor, gr.s. of Dr.
    Stephen Chapin, Oct. 23,
    1862
  Elizabeth Garland, d. of William B. and Sarah Sydnor,
    Aug. 25, 1837
  G. Barrett, May 26, 1939
  J. S. (Col.), Sept. 23, 1869
  James McClanahan, s. of Thomas
    W. and Blanch W. Sydnor
    Dec. 13, 1860
  Margaret, w. of Edward Sydnor,
    Sept. 13, 1833
  Mary Lily COOK, w. of Walton
    Sydnor, Mar. 31, 1898
  Peter Barksdale, s. of William
    Sydnor, Mar. 13, 1862
  R. D. B. (Lt.), s. of Thomas
    Sydnor, Sept. 4, 1862
  Sallie, w. of R. L. Sydnor,
    Aug. 13, 1885
  Sally White, d. of Thomas W.
    and Blanch W. Sydnor, Dec. 13,
    1860
  Sarah, w. of Edward G. Sydnor,
    Nov. 29, 1855
  Sarah L. M., w. of Rev. Thomas
    W. Sydnor, May 25, 1843
  Sarah T., w. of William B.
    Sydnor, Sept. 18, 1879
  Stephen Chapin, s. of Thomas
    W. and Sarah L. M. Sydnor,
    Nov. 10, 1842
  Thomas L. (Dr.), June 11, 1931
  Thomas S., Nov. 18, 1852
  Thomas W. (Dr.), May 8, June 12,
    Aug. 7, 1890
  W. J., Mar. 16, 1911
  Walter, Nov. 24, 1927
  William A., May 10 and 17,
    1877
SYKES
  Ann J. (Mrs.), Apr. 1, 1869
  Annie Summerell, d. of Dr.
    Joseph H. and Laura S.
    Sykes, July 20, 1876
  Edward A., s. of Michael
    Sykes, May 14, 1857
  G. A. (Mrs.), w. of G. A.
    Sykes, Sept. 4 and 25,
    1879
  James P. (Mrs.), Mar. 19,
    1914
  John, Aug. 22, 1861
  Lelia J., w. of Solon Sykes,
    Aug. 5, 1809
  Margaret E., w. of G. A.
    Sykes, Mar. 2, 1854
SYME
  Frances, w. of John M. Syme,
    Feb. 29, 1828
SYMMES
  John Cleves (Capt.), June 12,
    1829
SZYMANSKI
  Louisa (Mrs.), Feb. 11, 1858

T

TABB
 Bruce Warden, s. of Dr.
   R. B. and Elizabeth
   Warden Tabb, May 2, 1889
 Charles, Aug. 22, 1872
 Diana W., w. of Augustin
   Tabb, Nov. 7, 1844
 Elizabeth A., w. of Dr. R.
   B. Tabb, May 21, 1891
 Elizabeth Cunningham, d. of
   Charles and Huldah Tabb,
   Mar. 28, 1872
 Frances, w. of John Tabb,
   May 2, 1828
 Grace, d. of Henry A. Tabb,
   May 17, 1883
 John, Feb. 7, 1861
 John N., Mar. 24, 1859
 Joseph P., Dec. 17, 1857
 Laura O., w. of Theodore K.
   Tabb, May 1, 1930
 Lewis Philip, Apr. 24, 1919
 Robert Morris, s. of Dr,
   R. B. and Elizabeth Tabb,
   Aug. 23, 1877
 Theodore K., May 17, 1883
 Thomas (Col.), Oct. 23,
   1902
 William S., Jan. 30, 1879
TAFF
 Thomas F., Dec. 24, 1885
TALBOT
 George A., Oct. 16, 1829
 John W., Dec. 4, 1862
 Martha R., Feb. 20, 1868
 Nannie Gertrude, Apr. 29,
   1926
 Thomas E., Dec. 4, 1862
TALBOTT
 Willie W., Jan. 25, 1883
TALIAFERO
 Benjamin (Dr.), Nov. 29,
   1855*
 Cicelia H., Mar. 10, 1859
 Jane L., w. of James F.
   Taliafero, d. of Col. P.
   Rose, Nov. 29, 1855*

 Louisa R., d. of James
   F. Taliafero, Nov. 29,
   1855
TALIAFERRO
 Benjamin (Capt.), June 18,
   1846
 Bettie, w. of Thomas J.
   Taliaferro, Aug. 4, 1853
 Catherine (Mrs.), Dec. 23,
   1869
 Charles B., Mar. 24, 1864
 Charles C., Dec. 10, 1846
 Elizabeth Fanny, w. of C.
   W. Taliaferro, July 16,
   1830
 Emuella, w. of Thomas J.
   Taliaferro, Feb. 22, 1894
 Fannie Walker, June 5, 1873
 Frances Cornelia, d. of
   John Seymour Taliaferro,
   Sept. 20, Oct. 11, 1906
 J. P. (Mrs.), Aug. 28, 1919
 James Edwin, s. of William
   F. and Mary Taliaferro,
   Dec. 23, 1847
 Jane L., w. of James F.
   Taliaferro, Mar. 10, 1853*
 John S., June 1, 1830
 Josie, d. of Dr. William
   Taliaferro, July 11, 1889
 Lewis T. (Dr.), Apr. 13, 1848
 Lucy A., w. of Capt. Talia-
   ferro, d. of Mrs. Judith
   Allen, Nov. 12, 1840
 Mary (Mrs.), Mar. 22, 1883
 Mary Courtenay, w. of Dr.
   Frank Taliaferro, d. of J. B.
   and E. B. Watkins, Mar. 21,
   1889*
 Mattie, d. of Dr. James M.
   Taliaferro, Nov. 11, 1886
 Nettie Garrett, w. of J. P.
   Taliaferro, Nov. 20, 1919
 Philip (Rev.), July 20,
   Aug. 17, 1848
 Thomas, Aug. 2, 1839
 William (Elder), June 18, 1857

* Possible inaccuracy in name, or spelling, but given as printed

OBITUARY NOTICES IN THE RELIGIOUS HERALD WITH DATES OF PUBLICATION

William Thomas, s. of William F. and Mary A. Taliaferro, June 8, 1848
Willie Allen, s. of Edward F. and Eliza P. Taliaferro, Mar. 12, 1863
TALLEY
child of George R. Talley, Oct. 26, 1854
Annie I., w. of Robert H. Talley, July 15, 1915
Anthony, s. of Elder Charles Talley, July 5, 1833
Catherine, w. of Elkanah Talley, Apr. 14, 1870
Clementine, w. of A. W. Talley, May 22, 1862
Coley, Nov. 2, 1843
Dibdall, Sept. 27, 1839
Dicy Ann, w. of Carey J. Talley, Oct. 19, 1854
Edmund, s. of Anderson and Maria L. Talley, Aug. 17, 1848
Elizabeth (Mrs.), Nov. 4, 1841
George R., Apr. 25, 1861
Harriett Theressa, w. of Rev. William E. Talley, Jan. 27, 1887
James, Sr., Oct. 30, 1829
James M., Oct. 20, 1898
Joseph, s. of Anderson and Maria L. Talley, Aug. 17, 1848
Lucy A. (Mrs.), June 28, 1860
Mary Ann V., d. of Elkanah Talley, July 26, 1866
Mary Christian (Mrs.), May 26, 1938
Mattie V., w. of G. Thaddeus Talley, d. of Benjamin B. Pleasants, Apr. 16, 1891
Mollie E. (Mrs.), May 22, 1902
Nelson, Jan. 7, 1892
Robert James, s. of James and Anne Talley, Sept. 4, 1856
S. J. (Mrs.), June 12, 1904
Sally, w. of Nelson Talley, Oct. 27, 1910
Sarah Jane, d. of Nelson and Sarah Talley, Dec. 31, 1846
Susannah Eliza, May 17, 1894
Thomas, Feb. 18, 1847
William, Mar. 14, 1834
William E. (Rev.), s. of Dr. Ezekiel S. Talley, July 23, 1908
Williamson, s. of L. W. Talley, July 4, 1861
Williamson, Mar. 23, 1871
Willie, Dec. 17, 1925
TALLY
Frances Emily, Apr. 3, 1862
Martha A. (Mrs.), Nov. 15, 1849
Mary Ann, w. of James B. Tally, Nov. 5, 1885
Nancy, July 21, 1842
Rosa Belle, Feb. 27, 1873
W., June 10, 1897
TALMAGE
T. Dewitt (Dr.), Apr. 17, 1902
TALMAN
Elizabeth Ann Royal, d. of Henry and Elizabeth Talman, Aug. 27, 1840
TANEY
Ann Eliza, w. of George W. Taney, d. of D. W. and Mary J. Blunt, July 3, 1890
TANNER
Albert A., Apr. 13, 1843
Harriet L., w. of John F. Tanner, July 6, 1882
John F., father of Col. William E. Tanner, Sept. 8 and 15, 1881
Martha Ann, w. of Charles Hubbard Tanner, July 22, 1897
Mary, w. of Elam Tanner,

OBITUARY NOTICES IN THE RELIGIOUS HERALD WITH DATES OF PUBLICATION

Dec. 27, 1833
William E., Oct. 11, 1855
William E. (Col.), Aug. 11, 1898
TAPSCOTT
Ella C. (Mrs.), Jan. 12, 1865
John Henry, s. of Henry and Elizabeth Tapscott, Mar. 13, 1873
Mary, w. of George N. Tapscott, Dec. 27, 1888
William (Mrs.), Dec. 20, 1883
TATE
A. C., Jan. 6, 1881
Maria Louise, w. of Capt. William C. Tate, d. of James Richard and Eliza Whitehead, Oct. 7, 1915
Preston, June 13, 1901
Waddy, s. of Henry Tate, July 8, 1852
William Carrington, Mar. 23, 1922
William Irvine, s. of W. C. and M. L. Tate, Mar. 26, 1891
TATEM
Cordelia (Mrs.), Feb. 15, 1923
TATUM
Martha G., w. of N. Tatum, Sept. 9, 1858
Mary Armstrong, w. of William H. Tatum, d. of Rev. William J. Armstrong, Oct. 6, 1870
TAURMAN
J. G., Oct. 17, 1889
Maria, w. of John Taurman, July 9, 1885
Mary H. (Mrs.), May 12, 1864
Sally E., d. of Thomas Taurman, June 1, 1854
William, June 2, 1842
TAYLOE
John, Mar. 7, 1828

TAYLOR
child of Joseph H. Taylor, Sept. 6, 1849
Abraham Poindexter, s. of Dr. J. B. Taylor, Nov. 12, 1914
Albert S., m. Jane A. Cridlin, Mar. 2, 1899
Alice Keaton, June 26, 1919
Amanda J., w. of Blagrove Taylor, d. of W. S. Ligon, Jan. 14, 1886
Andrew J., June 2, 1881
Anne Custis (Mrs.), Jan. 2, 1851
Aphrey (Mrs.), w. of Threshley Taylor, Oct. 26, 1871
Barbara O., w. of Robert Taylor, May 21, 1857
Barney, Mar. 14, Apr. 4, 1872
Beryl S., d. of William F. and Mollie Taylor, Mar. 16, 1911
Bessie Peyton, d. of Rev. George B. and Susan Spottswood Taylor, July 14, 1859
Betty, d. of Dr. J. Spottswood and Louise Taylor, Feb. 7, 1907
Blagrove, Apr. 25, 1861
Brooken, June 23, 1853
Carter Braxton, s. of Rev. George B. and Susan S. Taylor, July 29, 1869
Cate, d. of William B. and Elizabeth Taylor, Oct. 13, 1842
Charles E. (Mrs.), w. of Dr. Charles E. Taylor, d. of Rev. John L. Prichard, Aug. 16, 1906
Charles T. (Rev.), May 24 and 31, June 14, July 5, 1934
Christiana, w. of George Taylor, Aug. 27, 1846
Daniel Gray, May 8, 1890
Daniel T., Aug. 26, 1836
Drucillia (Mrs.), Jan. 31, 1935

OBITUARY NOTICES IN THE RELIGIOUS HERALD WITH DATES OF PUBLICATION

E. E. L. (Rev.), Sept. 3, 1874
E. L. (Mrs.), May 1, 1919
E. M., June 20, 1907
E. S. (Rev.), May 13 and 20, June 10, July 15, 1886
Edward Augustus, July 5, 1923
Edward B., Dec. 5, 1889
Edward W., s. of Rev. J. B. and Fannie P. Taylor, Sept. 2, 1869
Eleanor (Mrs.), Apr. 15, 1858
Eliza Ann, Jan. 22, 1846
Elizabeth B. (Mrs.), Apr. 19, 1894
Elizabeth S., w. of Judge Hezekiah Taylor, Apr. 19 and 26, 1894
Emma Z., Apr. 27, 1871
Esther, d. of Dr. W. C. Taylor, Oct. 24. 1918
Fannie, w. of Rev. J. B. Taylor, d. of Rev. A. M. Poindexter, Nov. 10 and 24, 1870
Fanny, d. of B. F. Taylor, Nov. 25, 1869
Frances Elizabeth (Mrs.), Jan. 22, 1925
Frank Seaford, s. of J. W. amd E. M. Taylor, July 30, 1868
George, Aug. 11, 1853
George, Dec. 29, 1853
George B. (Mrs.), Apr. 3, May 15, 1884
George Boardman (Dr.), Oct. 3, 1907
Grace, d. of Rev. George B. and Susan S. Taylor, Aug. 28, 1862
H. C., Apr. 5, 1923
H. Vernon, June 4, 1937
Henry Clay, June 8, 1922
Hezekiah, Feb. 25, 1892
J. B., Oct. 8, 1908
J. I., Apr. 6, 1911
J. J. (Dr.), Feb. 6, 1930

J. R. (Rev.), Aug. 17, Oct. 12, 1933
James B. (Rev.), Jan. 4 and 18, Feb. 1, 8, and 22, 1872
James B. (Dr.), Sept. 28, 1911
James Spottswood (Dr.), Oct. 5, 1922
Jane, May 16, 1889
Jessie Cabell (Mrs.), Sept. 21, 1893
John H. (Rev.), Mar. 30, May 4, 1916
John Lee (Rev.), May 29, 1924
John M. (Capt.), May 2, 1872
John R., s. of B. T. and Etheline Taylor, Apr. 26, 1888
John William, Nov. 7, 1889
Joshua, Apr. 10, 1879
Lefronia C., w. of R. M. Taylor, July 7, 1859
Lois Young, d. of Rev. C. T. Taylor, Mar. 22, 1928
Lucy E., w. of Richard E. Taylor, Sept. 23, 1869
Maria Augusta (Mrs.), d. of Judge Joseph Christian, July 24, 1890
Martha A. (Mrs.), June 25, 1896
Martha King, w. of Rev. Daniel G. Taylor, May 10, 1906
Mary A., June 6, 1895
Mary Argyle, Jan. 30, Feb. 13, 1930
Mary F., d. of Admire H. and Mary Taylor, July 1, 1847
Mary W., w. of Rev. James B. Taylor, Nov. 16, Dec. 7, 1876
Mary Woodson, w. of Rev. William H. Taylor, July 24, 1890
Mollie Burnley, w. of W.

OBITUARY NOTICES IN THE RELIGIOUS HERALD WITH DATES OF PUBLICATION

Robinson Taylor, d. of Hardin Burnley, Jan. 19, 1899
Nancy G., w. of Rev. Samuel Taylor, May 21, 1868
Nolie, s. of Roy and Annie E. Taylor, Aug. 20, 1903
Orina L. (Mrs.), June 30, 1853
R., child of Rev. D. G. Taylor, Feb. 26, 1857
R. E., Mar. 25, 1858
R. R., May 26, 1887
Raymond M., Mar. 21, 1901
Richard S., Oct. 2, 1873
Robert Manson (Rev.), Jan. 6, Feb. 24, Mar. 3, 1927
Robert S., Apr. 20, 1882
Robert Walker, Jan. 27, 1938
Rosena C., d. of Elder Samuel Taylor, Aug. 27, 1857
Ruth E., May 16, 1918
Samuel (Rev.), June 24, 1875
Samuel Frank (Rev.), Dec. 24, 1936
Sarah Ann, Aug. 26, 1869
Sarah Catharine, w. of Rev. J. H. Taylor, June 18, 1874
Susan, w. of Daniel Taylor, July 13, 1832
Susan Rice (Mrs.), Dec. 4, 1890
Susan Spotswood (Mrs.), d. of Carter and Elizabeth Mayo Braxton, Apr. 17, 1884
Temple H., Dec. 23, 1909
Theodorick, Mar. 27, 1873
Thomas A. (Dr.), Dec. 5, 1828
Thomas A., s. of Robert Taylor, Oct. 26, 1871
Threshley, Oct. 26, 1871
William F., Mar. 25, 1880
William Harris (Rev.), Jan. 30, 1890
Willie, Aug. 27, 1874
Willie, s. of Roy and Annie E. Taylor, July 9, 1903
Willie J., w. of John W. Taylor, Nov. 3, 1881

TEASDALE
Bettie B., July 28, 1892
Martha J., w. of Martin C. Teasdale, Oct. 5, 1876

TEBBS
Maria E. (Mrs.), mother of Dr. Robert H. Tebbs, Oct. 24, 1844

TEBO
Sarah, w. of William Tebo, July 16, 1830

TED
Charles (Col.), Jan. 20, 1832

TEEL
Elizabeth, d. of Capt. Lewis and M. Teel, Dec. 27, 1833
Lewis (Capt.), Aug. 25, 1864
Melinda, w. of Capt. Lewis Teel, Mar. 10, 1859

TEMPLE
Baylor, s. of Rev. Roy Temple, Oct. 6, 1892
Eliza H. (Mrs.), Mar. 25, 1869
Frances A., w. of James Harvey Temple, Mar. 5, 1857
Margaret, w. of Andrew Temple, Jan. 7, 1892
Roy (Rev.), July 6, 1922

TEMPLEMAN
Albin Dunkum, s. of Dr. J. H. Templeman, Aug. 15, 1872*
Catherine, w. of Elder Samuel Templeman, Feb. 27, 1840
Lucie Dunkum, w. of Dr. J. H. Templeman, Apr. 18, 1872*
Samuel (Elder), Dec. 24, 1840

TENSER
Edmonia, Nov. 9, 1933

* Possible inaccuracy in name, or spelling, but given as printed

OBITUARY NOTICES IN THE RELIGIOUS HERALD WITH DATES OF PUBLICATION

TERRANT
 Mary E., d. of Frank M. and
  Sarah A. Terrant, Mar. 11,
  1880
TERRELL
 child of Albert J. Terrell,
  July 27, 1854
 Agnes Lee, d. of William
  D. Terrell, Dec. 2, 1875
 Agnes W., w. of Dr. A. L.
  Terrell, d. of Rev. Rufus
  Chandler, July 30, 1868
 Ann Louise, d. of Dr. Albert
  J. Terrell, Aug. 19, 1852
 Etha, w. of W. D. Terrell,
  July 12, 1877
 Lucy, w. of Pleasant Terrell,
  Jan. 8, 1852
 M. S., w. of Capt. John
  M. Terrell, Apr. 25, 1935
 Mariah H. W., w. of J. P.
  Terrell, May 27, 1858
 Mildred, d. of Christopher
  Terrell, Apr. 8, 1841
 Mollie J. W., w. of James
  H. Terrell, Dec. 17, 1908
 Pleasant, Apr. 22, 1847
 Pleasant M., s. of Pleasant
  Terrell, Sept. 27, 1839
 Robert, Feb. 27, 1845
 Sue (Mrs.), June 28, 1906
TERRIER
 Margaret S., w. of John E.
  Terrier, d. of Ralph W.
  Armistead, Oct. 13, 1910
TERRILL
 Elizabeth, w. of William H.
  Terrill, May 6, 1858
 Frank Frazer, s. of Lucy
  M. and Oliver Towles,
  Terrill, May 30, 1918
 Jane, w. of Dr. Uriel Terrill,
  Mar. 10, 1870
 John (Capt.), Sept. 25,
  1873
 L. L., May 5, 1892
 Lucy Frazer (Mrs.), Sept.
  22, 1932
 Mollie C., Apr. 7, 1881
 Robertine Duerson, d. of
  Joseph P. and Jane Terrill,
  Dec. 15, 1859
 William Kincaid, s. of
  Joseph W. Terrill, Feb.
  9, 1854
TERRY
 Amanda M. D., May 31,
  1849
 C. G., s. of Thomad J.
  Terry, Aug. 2, 1855
 George, July 9, 1857
 George A. (Dr.), Aug. 2,
  1855
 James (Capt.), Jan. 30,
  1896
 James Nathaniel, Apr. 10,
  1919
 John H., Mar. 3, 1859
 Lizzie E. (Mrs.), Oct. 3,
  1935
 Lucinda J., w. of Stephen
  Terry, Dec. 10, 1896
 Mary, w. of Capt. James
  Terry, Mar. 3, 1904
 Myrl Ray, Aug. 14, 1930
 N. J. (Dr.), Apr. 29, 1897
 Nathaniel J., Mar. 27, 1862
 Nellie R. (Mrs.), Aug. 24,
  1922
 O. L. (Rev.), Aug. 28, 1930
 Patrick Henry, Apr. 29,
  1926
 Paulina, Aug. 28, 1851
 R. C. (Dr.), Apr. 7, 1881
 Sallie B. H., w. of Abner
  R. Terry, Aug. 31, 1854
 Sarah C., w. of Capt.
  William C. Terry, Oct.
  19, 1854
 Sarah Elizabeth (Mrs.), Apr.
  18, 1907
 Thomas W., June 26, 1856
TEWES
 Edward A., June 4,
  1896
 May Harris, Dec. 22, 1892
THACKER
 Catherine, w. of Henry Thacker
  June 9, 1859
 Elizabeth (Mrs.), July 6,

OBITUARY NOTICES IN THE RELIGIOUS HERALD WITH DATES OF PUBLICATION

1871
G. M., Sept. 29, 1921
Lewis, Oct. 11, 1877
William Montgomery, s. of
  William Thacker, Jr.,
  May 23, 1844
THAMES
  (Dr.), Mar. 5, 1914
THAXTON
  Fannie E. (Mrs.), Apr. 27,
    1932
  William H., Aug. 6, 1874
THOM
  Emma Mutius, w. of William
    Thom, Apr. 26, 1883
THOMAS
  A. J. S. (Dr.), Apr. 6, 1911
  A. W. (Rev.), Aug. 13, 1896
  Alven (Rev.), May 23, 1901
  Ann Eliza, d. of John W. and
    Julia Thomas, June 30, 1859
  Ann J., w. of M. E. Thomas,
    d. of James S. Pickett,
    Apr. 4, 1861
  Archibald, May 23, 1861
  Archibald Judson, s. of
    Archibald and Catherine
    E. Thomas, Sept. 17, 1846
  B. W., June 29, 1893
  Brantley Pollard, s. of
    Charles S. and Ella E.
    Thomas, July 14, 1887
  Catherine E., w. of Archibald
    Thomas, Apr. 29, June 17,
    1880
  Catlett, Jan. 6, 1848
  David Cornelius, Apr. 22, 1880
  Delia M., w. of Person S.
    Thomas, Sept. 13, 1906
  E. M. P. (Rev.), s. of Elder
    Edward Thomas, Mar. 15,
    1855
  Elias, Jan. 24, 1878
  Elias Burnett, s. of Elias
    and Mary H. Thomas, Mar. 24,
    1864
  Elizabeth, w. of Benjamin
    Thomas, May 4, 1838
  Elizabeth, w. of James Thomas,
    Sr., May 11, 1848
  Elizabeth E., July 22,
    1852
  Ella Marshall, d. of Dr.
    William A. Thomas, July
    25, Oct. 10, 1929
  Ellen Alsentine, d. of
    Alsen and Virginia Thomas,
    Dec. 14, 1854
  Emma Ridley (Mrs.), Jan. 27,
    1927
  Fannie, w. of B. W. Thomas,
    July 23, Oct. 8 and 22,
    1891
  Fannie C. (Mrs.), Nov. 7,
    1878
  Fayetta J., w. of David H.
    Thomas, Aug. 22, 1861
  George S., Feb. 2, 1899
  Griff E., July 22, 1841
  H. A., Feb. 12, 1857
  J. R. (Rev.), July 2,
    1914
  Jacob, Aug. 10, 1899
  James, Sr., Feb. 26, 1852
  James, Jr., Oct. 12, 1882
  James, Jr., Sept. 29,
    1897
  James, Jr., (Mrs.), Oct.
    14, 1897
  James M., Jr., Oct. 13,
    1870
  James M., May 24, 1888
  James M. (Mrs.), June 3,
    1897
  James M., Jan. 17, 1935
  James Turner (Lt.), Sept.
    18, 1862
  James W., Apr. 20, 1871
  Joe (Mrs.), Oct. 27,
    1910
  John, Jr., Sept. 9, 1858
  Joseph E., Sept. 4, 1862
  Julian P., Jr., May 5,
    1910
  Lavena, d. of Mrs. W. D.
    Thomas, Apr. 5, 1906
  Lily Denny, w. of Rev. W.
    S. O. Thomas, June 9,
    1921
  Lucy Nelson, w. of Wesley

OBITUARY NOTICES IN THE RELIGIOUS HERALD WITH DATES OF PUBLICATION

Thomas, Apr. 30, 1863
M. L. (Mrs.), Aug. 8, 1912
Maria J., d. of William P. Thomas, Feb. 14, 1884
Maria Levena, Nov. 15, 1906
Marion, s. of Mrs. Permelia Thomas, Jan. 17, 1865
Martha Susan, d. of George and Elizabeth Thomas, Mar. 18, 1847
Mary Wortham, w. of James Thomas, Jr., Oct. 21, 1897
Nancy (Mrs.), d. of Benjamin Thomas, May 14, 1863
Oliver, Apr. 25, 1895
Philip E., Apr. 18, 1901
Pinkey, d. of Lewis and Martha Thomas, Dec. 23, 1858
Reuben B., s. of David C. Thomas, Sept. 4, 1862
Rhoda, w. of Benejah Thomas, Feb. 3, 1859
Robert, Sept. 30, 1847
Robert Wilton, s. of Dr. J. R. Thomas, Sept. 26, 1918
S. C., w. of M. E. Thomas, d. of James Pickett, May 1, 1856
Sallie Ann, d. of James and Mary W. Thomas, Apr. 14, 1853
Sallie E. (Mrs.), Jan. 12, 1928
Sallie Richard, d. of George L. and Mollie E. Thomas, June 16, 1859
Sarah, w. of Archibald F. Thomas, June 28, 1839
Sarah A. E., w. of William J. Thomas, d. of David J. Saunders, Feb. 21, 1878
Sarah Francis, w. of C. H. Thomas, Mar. 10, 1927
Serena Byron, w. of David Cornelius Thomas, Apr. 22, 1880
Sula, Aug. 14, 1913

Thomas Benjamine, Sept. 11, 1924
Vera Clarke, w. of Rev. C. A. Thomas, d. of John W. Clarke, Aug. 30, 1888
W. D. (Mrs.), June 21, 1888
W. S. O. (Mrs.), Aug. 18, 1921
W. S. O. (Rev.), Apr. 23, 1925
William (Rev.), June 13, 1872
William D. (Mrs.), July 12, 1888
William D. (Dr.), May 23, July 18, 1901
William F., Dec. 29, 1853
William R., s. of Dr. William D. Thomas, Feb. 13, 1913
THOMASON
 Eugenia, w. of James Thomason, Oct. 4, 1860
 Jane L. (Mrs.), Oct. 21, 1875
THOMASSON
 James H., Nov. 4, 1920
THOMMASON
 John, Apr. 23, 1840
THOMPKIES
 Augustus J., Jan. 19, 1905
THOMPKINS
 Mary E., d. of E. G. and Sarah Thompkins, July 1, 1858
THOMPSON
 Ann E., w. of Nicholas Thompson, Sept. 19, 1872
 David, Sept. 4, 1884
 Fannie Hatchett (Mrs.), d. of Americus Hatchett, Jan. 17, 1889
 Fannie R., w. of Edward J. Thompson, Sept. 20, 1860
 Flora, d. of Rev. S. H. Thompson, Aug. 6, Sept. 3, 1908
 Frances Maria, Dec. 29, 1853
 George, Oct. 2, 1829
 George B., Aug. 4, 1864

OBITUARY NOTICES IN THE RELIGIOUS HERALD WITH DATES OF PUBLICATION

George W., s. of Washington Thompson, Mar. 27, 1829
Georgie Annie Wilson, d. of W. J. and Mary Ann Thompson, Dec. 29, 1864
Henry, July 12, 1855
J. J. (Mrs.), Nov. 2, 1916
James, Feb. 29, 1844
James Algie, Dec. 16, 1909
James H., s. of William and Nannie Thompson, Apr. 22, 1869
Jane W., d. of John G. Thompson, Oct. 11, 1860
Jennings C. (Dr.), Dec. 27, 1860
Jeremiah, Dec. 17, 1863
John, Apr. 4, 1929
John R., May 15 and 22, 1873
Josephine, May 18, 1922
Luther, Apr. 2, 1874
M. J., Oct. 7, 1886
Marina, d. of Reuben Thompson, Aug. 21, 1862
Martha (Mrs.), May 8, 1856
Martha A., Sept. 25, 1890
Mary, Feb. 20, 1890
Mary Lizzie, w. of S. H. Thompson, May 25, 1899
Montgomery, s. of Capt. Charles Thompson, Oct. 17, 1844
N. T., June 17, 1897
Nancy, w. of James Thompson, Feb. 20, 1834
Ola Rucker, Apr. 3, 1924
Pattie J. (Mrs.), d. of Jefferson Adams, Mar. 19, 1936
Quarles, s. of William and Nannie Thompson, Apr. 22, 1869
R. W., Dec. 1, 1921
Raleigh S., Apr. 12, 1877
S. H. (Rev.), Feb. 15, 1912
S. H. (Mrs.), w. of Rev. S. H. Thompson, Oct. 28, 1937
Sarah, Apr. 5, 1849
Sarah S., Nov. 19, 1857
Sylvester A., Apr. 21, 1921
Thelma Estelle, d. of S. A. Thompson, Dec. 12, 1918
William (Rev.), Feb. 1, 1872
William S., Jan. 2, 1873

THORNE
Levi (Rev.), Mar. 20, 1879

THORNHILL
Adeline (Mrs.), July 4, 1889
Emma S., Dec. 29, 1927
Francis Walker, s. of William and Ellen V. Thornhill, Aug. 20, 1868
George W. (Dr.), Jan. 12, 1893
Jesse, s. of Thomas Thornhill, Nov. 12, 1857
Joshua T. (Rev.), June 14, 1906
L. R., Feb. 12, 1931
Lucy Jane, July 7, 1842
Mary, w. of John Thornhill, Mar. 20, 1851
Thomas J., Jan. 22, 1931
W. D., July 5, 1917
William, Nov. 12, 1857

THORNLEY
C. C. (Mrs.), d. of Jesse M. K. White, June 22, 1876
John Willie, s. of William and Mattie Thornley, Feb. 1, 1872
Mary Maria, Oct. 9, 1856
Mattie Williams (Mrs.), Dec. 21, 1876
Winnifred (Mrs.), Sept. 1, 1842

THORNTON
Ann H., w. of Thomas G. Thornton, May 27, 1841
Ann R., w. of Anthony Thornton, Jan. 3, 1867
Anna Eliza, d. of John A. B. Thornton, July 7, 1859

OBITUARY NOTICES IN THE RELIGIOUS HERALD WITH DATES OF PUBLICATION

Anthony, Apr. 5, 1855
Anthony, May 21, 1885
Anthony R., Feb. 8, 1828
C. A. (Mrs.), d. of Spencer Adkins, July 4, 1918
Cabel A., Mar. 29, 1934
Charlotte E., w. of Edmond T. Thornton, July 1, 1858
Fannie E., w. of William T. Thornton, Dec. 5, 1878
Fanny Milly, d. of Col. James B. Thornton, Nov. 7, 1867
Francis, June 6, 1895
Francis H., Nov. 21, 1872
George (Dr.), s. of Thomas S. Thornton, Mar. 9, 1843
George (Dr.), Mar. 1, 1860
Harriet S., Sept. 14, 1832
Henry L., June 21, 1860
James B. (Mrs.), Sept. 23, 1852
James B., Jan. 8, 1863
James B. (Col.), Nov. 7, 1867
James Rudd, May 7, 1931
John (Capt.), Apr. 3, 1829
Laura C., w. of J. R. Thornton, Aug. 15, 1901
M. K. (Dr.), Dec. 16, 1937
Maria S., Oct. 18, 1866
Marie Russell, Oct. 11, 1923
Mary, w. of Edmond T. Thornton, Dec. 21, 1848
Mary, Mar. 1, 1860
Mary, w. of Francis H. Thornton, Jan. 12, 1865
Mary Ella, d. of Edmond T. Thornton, Apr. 12, 1855
Mildred, w. of James B. Thornton, June 5, 1845
Nannie (Mrs.), Apr. 26, 1860
Peter, Mar. 15, 1928
Pleasant L., Aug. 14, 1862
S. E., w. of John A. B. Thornton, d. of Col. Joel Hayes, June 29, 1893
Sarah E., Apr. 22, 1920
Sarah J., w. of Pleasant L. Thornton, Nov. 1, 1860
Sarah T. (Mrs.), Aug. 16, 1839
Susan (Mrs.), Feb. 6, 1651
William A., s. of Henry L. Thornton, Nov. 8, 1860
William L., Aug. 17, 1854

THORP
S. J., w. of M. A. Thorp, d. of R. F. Harris, May 17, 1894

THRASHER
Frank, s. of George C. and Amanda Thrasher, Apr. 17, 1862
George C. (Mrs.), Aug. 21, 1873
Louise Obenshain (Mrs.), July 2, 1925
Robert, s. of Rev. George and Amanda Thrasher, Apr. 17, 1862
Robert I., Mar. 26, 1863
S. F., w. of J. Q. A. Thrasher, Jan. 29, 1891

THRESHER
Ebenezer (Rev.), Jan. 28, 1886

THRIFT
Margaret, w. of Robert T. Thrift, Oct. 4, 1839
William I., July 3, 1845 55

THROCKMORTON
A. C., Jan. 22, 1925
Lewis B., Apr. 10, 1884
Mary (Mrs.), Jan. 11, 1906

THROCKMOTON
Mary F., w. of Col. John A. Throckmoton, d. of W. Crittenden, Dec. 14, 1905

THROGMORTON
Elijah, Aug. 9, 1855
Elizabeth F., w. of Elijah Throgmorton, Feb. 3, 1859

THROM
Mary S. (Mrs.), Feb. 4, 1892

THRUSTON
Anna Courtney (Mrs.), Apr. 21, 1932

OBITUARY NOTICES IN THE RELIGIOUS HERALD WITH DATES OF PUBLICATION

Catherine (Mrs.), Oct. 18, 1860
E. J., May 24, 1883
J. H., s. of Wilton and Anna Thruston, Apr. 29, 1897
William R., Sept. 13, 1855
Wilton, Aug. 11, 1910

THUFT
Frances, w. of Dr. George N. Thuft, Mar. 7, 1834
Robert, s. of George and Frances Thuft, Mar. 7, 1834

THURMAN
Estelle, d. of George P. Thurman, Jan. 16, 1873
Philip, June 29, 1871

THURMON
Lucy (Mrs.), Aug. 15, 1828
Lucy A. (Mrs.), Apr. 23, 1857

THURMOND
Bettie, w. of J. S. Thurmond, d. of A. N. Rippetoe, Dec. 6, 1900
Charles Thomas, s. of Philip and Mary Thurmond, Apr. 3, 1856
Rosa, July 15, 1926
Sarah Jane, w. of Capt. W. D. Thurmond, Nov. 2, 1899

THURSTON
James H., s. of Wilson and Anna Thurston, Oct. 15, 1896
John H., July 1, 1875
Lemira, w. of Lemuel Thurston, Mar. 4, 1831

TIBBS
Nancy, May 19, 1892

TICHENOR
Eppie, w. of Rev. I. T. Tichenor, d. of Walker and Hannah E. Reynolds, Apr. 4, 1878

TIGNOR
Elizabeth F., w. of Elijah Tignor, Dec. 10, 1885
John Gilmer, Dec. 15, 1932
Mary L., w. of William J. Tignor, Feb. 29, 1872
Miles Brantley, s. of James C. and B. B. Tignor, July 10, 1884
Septimus S., Feb. 4, 1875

TILLER
Mary Ida, d. of A. F. and Mary S. Tiller, May 27, 1858

TILLMAN
Kate, d. of Capt. John Tillman, May 4, 1905

TILMAN
Mary E., d. of W. B. Tilman, Jan. 18, 1894
Mollie Rae, w. of W. B. Tilman, June 7, 1894
P. L., Apr. 28, 1938

TIMBERLAKE
Alcinda (Mrs.), May 4, 1876
Amelia H. (Mrs.), Aug. 29, 1844
Elizabeth, w. of Franklin Timberlake, June 5, 1873
Elizabeth G., Apr. 20, 1871
Emuella, d. of Reuben and Elizabeth Timberlake, Sept. 12, Oct. 3, 1844
Henry (Col.), May 31, 1849
J. C., May 31, 1888
Mary Clements (Mrs.), d. of Thomas W. Clements, Sept. 13, 1928
Mary E., w. of William L. Timberlake, d. of Thomas G. Crittendon, Jan. 14, 1864
Mary Winn, w. of D. A. Timberlake, d. of Mrs. William B. Sydnor, Oct. 18 and 25, 1917
Mattie Floyd, Oct. 31, 1918
Peggy L., Dec. 5, 1872
Reuben, Dec. 31, 1846
Willietta A., w. of Alpheus R., Feb. 1, 1883

OBITUARY NOTICES IN THE RELIGIOUS HERALD WITH DATES OF PUBLICATION

TINDER
　　Eleanor, w. of David Tinder,
　　　Mar. 18, 1858
　　Ephraim A., Mar. 14, 1850
　　Estelle Irene (Mrs.), June
　　　22, 1911
　　George W., Feb. 26, 1885
　　John A., Feb. 6, 1873
　　Permelia F. (Mrs.), Mar.
　　　13, 1862
TINNELL
　　M. F., Feb. 15, 1934
　　Rosa A., w. of Marcellus
　　　F. Tinnell, d. of George
　　　M. Bell, Oct. 19, 1922
TINSLEY
　　Ann (Mrs.), July 29, 1836
　　Barbara Garland, w. of
　　　Joshua Tinsley, Apr. 10,
　　　1890
　　Benjamin T., Jan. 15, 1880
　　Cassandra D., w. of Addison
　　　Tinsley, Nov. 14, 1867
　　Charles C., May 1, 1862
　　Charles E., Apr. 1, 1926
　　Clarence Bell, s. of B. T.
　　　and E. S. Tinsley, Oct.
　　　22, 1863
　　Elizabeth (Mrs.), Aug. 12,
　　　1852
　　Elizabeth, Dec. 14, 1854
　　Elizabeth M., w. of Elder
　　　W. Tinsley, d. of Thomas and
　　　Phoebe M. Miles, Aug. 4,
　　　1864
　　Ella Walker, d. of B. T.
　　　and E. S. Tinsley, Oct. 22,
　　　1863
　　Emiline S. (Mrs.), July 21,
　　　1892
　　Etta Gilmer, w. of Richard W.
　　　Tinsley, Nov. 19, 1914
　　Fanny Peyton, July 27, 1871
　　Frances, Nov. 9, 1843
　　Isaac S., Dec. 15, 1881
　　J. Walter, Oct. 1, 1914
　　James W., s. of James H.
　　　and Frances Tinsley, Dec.
　　　27, 1855
　　John, Dec. 25, 1862

　　Leanna Catherine Bethel,
　　　w. of J. H. Tinsley,
　　　Feb. 17, 1921
　　Louella Delta, d. of H.
　　　C. and E. D. Tinsley,
　　　Apr. 7, 1881
　　Mary Ann E. (Mrs.), Feb.
　　　27, Mar. 13, 1913
　　Mary Covington, w. of
　　　Charles H. Tinsley,
　　　July 14, Aug. 4, 1938
　　Mary Park, d. of C. C.
　　　Tinsley, Mar. 22, 1833
　　Mary Winfree, d. of M. W.
　　　and Mary Tinsley, Sept.
　　　26, 1878
　　Sarah Ann, w. of Elder
　　　Isaac Tinsley, Dec. 2,
　　　1836
　　Tipton L., s. of James H.
　　　and Frances Tinsley, Dec.
　　　27, 1855
TIPPET
　　John W., Aug. 10, 1848
TISCHENDORF
　　(Dr.), Jan. 7 and 28, 1875
TISDALE
　　Joseph D., s. of Rev. Robert
　　　Tisdale, July 1, 1847
　　Lula V. (Mrs.), Apr. 20,
　　　1882
　　Robert (Elder), s. of John
　　　Tisdale, Dec. 25, 1856
　　Sarah, w. of Rev. Robert
　　　Tisdale, Nov. 24, 1842
TITUS
　　Tunis, June 22, 1899
TOBEY
　　Isabella H., w. of Rev.
　　　Thomas W. Tobey, Oct. 15,
　　　Dec. 17, 1857
　　T. W. (Rev.), Feb. 26, 1885
TOD
　　Columbia, Sept. 24, 1896
　　George, s. of Lovell Tod,
　　　May 7, 1863
　　Virginia Bird, Dec. 14, 1905
TODD
　　Clemenza L., w. of John
　　　B. Todd, Feb. 6, 1840

OBITUARY NOTICES IN THE RELIGIOUS HERALD WITH DATES OF PUBLICATION

Eliza, w. of Thomas Todd, June 3, 1831
Eliza A., w. of William S. Todd, d. of Col. Thomas Hudgins, Oct. 5, 1854
George M., Sept. 28, 1858
George T., May 19, 1859
H. G., Apr. 20, 1922
Joseph, Feb. 2, 1854
Julia, w. of Rev. William B. Todd, Nov. 15, 1900
Louisa (Mrs.), July 6, 1882
Lovell P., Apr. 23, 1874
Maria Louisa, d. of William B. Todd, Nov. 16, 1843
Mary Catherine, w. of Dr. William B. Todd, July 13, 1832
Mattie W., w. of Thomas J. Todd, d. of Rev. William T. Lindsay, Mar. 30, 1899
Mollie, d. of Lovell P. and Fanny Todd, Feb. 14, 1861
O. B., Apr. 20, 1899
Richard B., Jan. 30, 1919
Sallie Milton, w. of S. D. Todd, Aug. 31, 1882
Sarah E., w. of Bernard Todd, Apr. 19, 1860

TOLER
Annie, Dec. 30, 1880
Elizabeth B. (Mrs.), June 28, 1888
Hannah, w. of William Toler, Feb. 8, 1840
Richard, Mar. 14, 1844
Richard H., May 18, 1848
Sallie, w. of William L. Toler, Mar. 14, 1872
Susan, w. of Henry Toler, Oct. 29, 1896
Virginia M., w. of John T. Toler, Dec. 15, 1870
W. H., June 21, 1906
William B., s. of Matthew and Jane A. Toler, Sept. 3, 1840

TOLIN
Mary F., d. of Thomas U. and Mary C. Tolin, Apr. 1, 1858

TOLLEY
Evelyne Milton, d. of James M. and Mary A. Tolley, Dec. 29, 1859

TOMBES
Elizabeth Ann, w. of J. B. Tombes, d. of Joseph C. and Margaret B. Averett, Dec. 22, 1853

TOMKIES
Edgar Thornton, s. of Rev. C. W. and V. S. Tomkies, Dec. 3, 1885
Edward M., Sept. 21, 1882
Elizabeth, w. of Joseph Tomkies, d. of John Thornton, Sr., July 23, 1857
Elizabeth T., Sept. 30, 1880
Gertrude Thruston, d. of E. M. and Mary D. Tomkies, June 16, 1859
J. H. (Rev.), Sept. 26, 1878
Joseph T., s. of Edward M. Tomkies, Dec. 25, 1856

TOMPKINS
John S. (Dr.), Aug. 11, 1887
Mary D., w. of Edward W. Tompkins, Sept. 7, 1854
Moses (Rev.), July 13, 1849
Rebecca, w. of C. H. Tompkins, May 14, 1863
Rebecca McLaurine, d. of Christopher Tompkins, July 7, 1870

TOMS
Willie E., Oct. 17, 1929

TONEY
Ann E. (Mrs.), Dec. 19, 1907
Charles T., Oct. 3, 1850
George W., s. of William A. Toney, Feb. 18, 1847
John, s. of R. C. and M. S. Toney, Oct. 13, 1887
Mary, w. of John Toney, Sept. 27, 1839
William Judson, s. of John and Mary Toney, Sept. 27, 1839

TOONE

OBITUARY NOTICES IN THE RELIGIOUS HERALD WITH DATES OF PUBLICATION

A. Jackson, Dec. 16, 1886
Mary Ann, w. of William R.
  Toone, Apr. 27, 1893
Mildred (Mrs.), Apr. 19, 1849
TOPPING
  J. Warren, Oct. 3, 1935
  Keziah MEARS (Mrs.), June 13, 1889
TORIAN
  Carrie Lea, d. of J. T. Torian, Mar. 13, 1913
TOTTY
  Lallie J., w. of Robert B. Totty, Apr. 1, 1880
  Thomas T., Nov. 28, 1872
TOWILL
  Elizabeth E., w. of Capt. M. W. Towill, Dec. 22, 1842
  Mark W. (Elder), Jan. 26, 1888
  Mary F., Feb. 13, 1913
  Richard Judson (Rev.), Dec. 23, 1875
TOWLER
  Edward, s. of Simeon and Nancy Towler, Mar. 16, 1848
TOWLES
  Elizabeth Sidney (Mrs.), Apr. 30, 1914
TOWN
  V. (Miss), Sept. 2, 1869
TOWNES
  Bessie Sloan, d. of A. S. and L. B. Townes, Aug. 14, 1873
  Catherine H., w. of Capt. Stephen C. Townes, June 23, 1859
  Judith R., w. of Allen Townes, Sept. 4, 1856
TOWNLEY
  Elizabeth, w. of John Townley, Jan. 16, 1845
  William, July 14, 1859
TOWNSEND
  Henry C. (Rev.), Aug. 18, Sept. 29, Nov. 3, 1870
TOY
  Crawford Howell, June 26, 1919

Thomas D., June 26, 1879
TRABUE
  Frances, w. of Macon Trabue, Apr. 13, 1832
  Frances Ann, d. of Macon Trabue, Sept. 7, 1848
  John, Apr. 18, 1828
  Mary, w. of William Trabue, Apr. 7, 1842
TRACEWELL
  Alice R., w. of James T. Tracewell, d. of Daniel Updike, Mar. 5, 1903
TRAINHAM
  A. J. (Mrs.), mother of Rev. C. Wirt Trainham, Dec. 29, 1898
  Charles Wirt (Mrs.), w. of Rev. Charles Wirt Trainham, Mar. 17, May 26, 1932
  Julia A. (Mrs.), Jan. 9, 1902
  Sallie A., w. of Z. L. Trainham, d. of Rev. William S. Parrish, Oct. 31, 1872
  William H., Aug. 9, 1894
TRANT
  Edward L., s. of George R. Trant, Dec. 19, 1889
  James L., s. of Lawrence Trant, Jan. 16, 1879
  Lawrence, Apr. 18, 1872
  Mildred B. (Mrs.), Apr. 9, 1891
TRAVILLIAN
  A. J., Apr. 8, 1858
  Elizabeth, w. of Charles G. Travillian, Sept. 23, 1847
  H., w. of Rev. G. C. Travillian, Apr. 9, 1857
  Sarah E., d. of G. C. Travillian, Apr. 9, 1857
TRAVIS
  James, Oct. 17, 1872
TRAYLOR
  Alice, d. of Elder Boswell and Elizabeth Traylor, Apr. 11, 1861
  Benjamin F., July 10, 1862
  Boswell (Rev.), Jan. 25, 1877

OBITUARY NOTICES IN THE RELIGIOUS HERALD WITH DATES OF PUBLICATION

James J., s. of Boswell
  Traylor, July 28, 1837
Jane, w. of J. B. Taylor,
  Feb. 12, 1857
Robert A., Feb. 5, 1857
TRAYNHAM
  Bettie, w. of Thomas Traynham, Aug. 15, 1867
  Bettie S., July 17, 1862
  David P., Mar. 28, 1867
  Jeffrey P., Jan. 3, 1884
  R. C., Mar. 24, 1870
TREAKLE
  Alexena Wilson, d. of James C. and Maggie I. Treakle, Jan. 25, 1883
  Mary Jane, w. of Thornton B. Treakle, Sept. 26, 1895
TREBLE*
  Martha L., d. of George and Angelina Treble, Jan. 31, 1861
TREDWAY
  Chestley M., s. of Capt. William M. and Rebecca C. Tredway, May 13, 1909
  Janie B., d. of James L. and Almeyda Tredway, Sept. 22, 1881
  Rawley F. (Rev.), Feb. 13, 1913
  William M., Jr. (Capt.), May 28, 1885
TRENT
  Eliza, Nov. 21, 1935
  Martha D., w. of Capt. Thomas Trent, July 4, 1850
  Nancy R., w. of Dr. Joseph Trent, Apr. 18, 1828
  O. H., Nov. 8, 1866
  Thomas W., Feb. 26, 1903
TREVETT
  Nina A., w. of E. J. Trevett, June 19, July 3, 1913
TREVILIAN
  Susannah, w. of Thomas Trevilian, Nov. 25, 1831
TREVILLIAN
  A. J., Mar. 18, 1858
  E. C. (Rev.), Apr. 3, 1902

G. C. (Rev.), Apr. 12, 1877
Garrett C. (Rev.), May 1, 1873
Gideon (Rev.), Feb. 1, 1877
Lurene Austin, Feb. 6, 1936
Mary Martin, w. of G. A. Trevillian, Feb. 27, 1902
TRIBBLE
  Angelina (Mrs.), July 16, 1896*
  Estelle C., w. of Henry Wise Tribble, Feb. 25, 1926
  George L., Mar. 17, 1892*
  Henry Wise (Rev.), Feb. 15, 1912
  Luther Ward, s. of Rev. H. C. and Nancy Tribble, Jan. 17, 1878
  M. A. FULCHER (Mrs.), Feb. 14, 1895
  Mary Ann (Mrs.), Jan. 27, 1887
TRIBLE
  Penelope (Mrs.), d. of Rev. Philip Montague, Dec. 22, 1881
TRICE
  Amelia, d. of James and Ann Trice, Oct. 18, 1855
  Benjamin F., s. of George W. Trice, Mar. 1, 1860
  Edmonia L., d. of George W. Trice, Mar. 1, 1860
  Elizabeth D. (Mrs.), May 12, 1881
  Fannie B., d. of James and Ann Trice, Oct. 27, 1870
  G. W. (Elder), Mar. 12 and 26, 1868
  G. W., Sept. 13 and 20, 1906
  George W. (Elder), Dec. 29, 1837
  Ida, Feb. 18, 1937
  James, Jan. 25, Feb. 15, 1872
  James C., Nov. 15, 1888
  Jane W., w. of Rev. George W. Trice, Apr. 29, 1909
  Judith, w. of Elder George Trice, Nov. 2, 1843
  Leolia A., d. of Maj. Benjamin F. and Virginia Trice, Mar. 24, 1864
  Leroy, s. of George W. Trice,

* Possible inaccuracy in name, or spelling, but given as printed

OBITUARY NOTICES IN THE RELIGIOUS HERALD WITH DATES OF PUBLICATION

Jan. 20, 1842
Lucy A., d. of Dr. B. F.
  Trice, Oct. 11, 1855
M. G. (Miss), May 3, 1923
Mariah, w. of Elder George W.
  Trice, Feb. 15, 1839
Martha (Mrs.), July 12, 1849
Mary Evelyn, d. of Elder G.
  W. and Jane W. Trice,
  July 18, 1850
Mary Jane, d. of Col. Robert
  N. Trice, Dec. 1, 1864
Mary T., w. of Col. Robert
  N. Trice, Apr. 20, 1876
Pattie A., d. of Richard A.
  Trice, Dec. 27, 1855
Peggy (Mrs.), Dec. 29, 1842
Robert M., Feb. 27, 1908
Robert Minor, s. of Robert N.
  and Lucy J. Trice, Dec. 27,
  1849
Robert N. (Col.), Dec. 1, 1864
Sextine, Feb. 21, 1884
Virginia Minor, d. of R. N.
  and L. J. Trice, Aug. 27,
  1857
TRIGG
  Amanda, w. of Joseph W. Trigg,
    Sept. 29, 1859
  Matilda, July 21, 1859
TRIMMER
  C. C., June 15, 1922
TRIPLETT
  Mary Irwin, d. of G. S. R.
    and Carrie S. Triplett,
    Dec. 7, 1871
TROUPE
  M. E., w. of Samuel E.
    Troupe, d. of Mrs. Susan
    Wiast, Sept. 14, 1876
TROUT
  George Edward, Jr., s. of
    G. E. Trout, July 24, 1930
  Willie A. B., s. of William
    Trout, Nov. 15, 1860
TRUEHEART
  B. (Mrs.), June 20, 1918
TRUETT
  George E. (Rev.), June 11,
    1936

  Rebecca Kinsey, w. of C. L.
    Truett. Aug. 24, 1911
TRUMAN
  J. L. (Rev.), Feb. 6, 1890
TUBBY
  E. P. (Mrs.), June 4, 1863
TUCK
  Anderson, June 11, 1885
  Bennett, Aug. 11, 1881
  Catherine, w. of Glover Tuck,
    May 23, 1861
  Elizabeth, w. of Bennett
    Tuck, June 2, 1870
  Ellen, Nov. 7, 1889
  Fanny (Mrs.), Apr. 22, 1858
  Hannah (Mrs.), Feb. 28, 1895
  Maria Louisa, w. of Bennett
    Tuck, June 28, 1860
  Samuel R., s. of George P. and
    M. E. Tuck, Mar. 6, 1873
TUCKER
  Ambrosia, July 22, 1858
  Ann B., w. of Henry Tucker,
    Oct. 12, 1843
  Bernice, d. of Dr. D. W.
    Tucker, Dec. 5, 1901
  C. S., Dec. 16, 1897
  Charles W., s. of Edmond P.
    Tucker, Nov. 29, 1855
  Coleman, Aug. 21, 1856
  Daniel W., Dec. 29, 1904
  Elizabeth, w. of Martin
    Tucker, Jr., Oct. 23, 1835
  Elizabeth (Mrs.), Apr. 11,
    1901
  Elizabeth Ann (Mrs.), Apr.
    17, 1851
  Elizabeth C. (Mrs.), Oct. 11,
    1860
  Fannie, w. of Frederick
    Tucker, Apr. 28, 1864
  Harriet A. (Mrs.), Mar. 8,
    1860
  Hartwell, Sept. 6, 1849
  Harwood B., Apr. 6, 1848
  Henry, May 26, 1859
  Henry William (Dr.), Feb.
    22, 1828
  Hinton G., s. of John G.
    and Mary Tucker, July 31,

OBITUARY NOTICES IN THE RELIGIOUS HERALD WITH DATES OF PUBLICATION

1862
James Coleman, Sept. 11, 1884
James W. (Dr.), May 11, 1916
Jesse T., Dec. 21, 1891; Jan.
 7, 1892
John, Sr., Apr. 6, 1848
John C., June 17, 1926
L. B. (Mrs.), Aug. 1, 1935
Martha, w. of Colman Tucker,
 Aug. 19, 1847*
Martin, Jan. 14, 1864
Mary Green WILLIAMS (Mrs.),
 July 31, 1902
Matilda M. (Mrs.), Apr. 24, 1851
Mollie, June 5, 1873
Nancy, w. of William Tucker,
 Aug. 29, 1861
P. Hill, Apr. 8, 1937
Paulina J., w. of John D.
 Tucker, May 17, 1877
Peyton, Feb. 21, 1856
R. Atwell (Rev.), May 21,
 Aug. 13, 1903
Rachel (Mrs.), Nov. 15, 1888
Richard G., Aug. 6, 1857;
 Jan. 7, 1858
Sallie Bettie, d. of Edmond
 P. Tucker, Nov. 29, 1855
Sally, w. of William Tucker,
 Apr. 15, 1847
Susan Wilsher, Apr. 30, 1914
Willie W., w. of Rev. William H. Tucker, d. of W. W.
 Dabney, Feb. 13, 1879
TUGGLE
 Drusilla F., Apr. 9, 1857
TUGGLES
 Martha (Mrs.), Feb. 15, 1872
TULL
 Elizabeth (Mrs.), Dec. 5,
  1918
TUNE
 Nannie J., d. of Anthony
  Tune, Jan. 19, 1860
TUNSTALL
 Agnes W., Apr. 7, 1870
 Anne E., d. of Miles C.
  Tunstall, Mar. 26, 1857
 Ann Eliza, w. of Miles C.
  Tunstall, June 25, 1854

Betty F., Nov. 3, 1842
Jane G. (Mrs.), Aug. 10,
 1882
Mary Elsden, d. of Miles and
 Frances Tunstall, Dec. 19,
 1878
Richard G., June 1, 1876
Roberta V., w. of Samuel
 Tunstall, Oct. 9,
 1851
Samuel, Sept. 21, 1876
Thomas C., Aug. 10, 1832
Thomas R., s. of Miles C.
 Tunstall, Apr. 26, 1855
William Richard, Feb. 21,
 1878
TUPMAN
 J. H. (Lt.), Sept. 22, 1864
 Paul Micou (Dr.), Dec. 3,
  1863
TUPPER
 Eliza Yoer (Mrs.), July 21,
  1887
 Furman, June 23, 1887
 Henry Allen (Dr.), Apr. 3,
  1902
 Henry Allen, Jr. (Mrs.),
  w. of Dr. Henry Allen
  Tupper, Jr., June 30,
  1921
 Henry Allen (Mrs.), Jan. 29,
  1925
 Kate Lord, d. of Rev. H. A.
  Tupper, July 3, 1873
 Kerr Boyce, child of Rev. K.
  B. Tupper, June 20, 1878
TURLINGTON
 W. H., Feb. 18, 1904
TURNELL
 Sarah Jane, w. of J. Scott
  Turnell, d. of L. C. and M.
  T. Dowdy, Sept. 8, 1859
TURNER
 A. H., Oct. 27, 1927
 A. M., w. of H. M. Turner,
  Mar. 7, 1889
 Adie, d. of Hardaway and
  Sophia Turner, Apr. 9,
  1863
 Agrippa, July 27, 1854

* Possible inaccuracy in name, or spelling, but given as printed

-343-

OBITUARY NOTICES IN THE RELIGIOUS HERALD WITH DATES OF PUBLICATION

Alice (Mrs.), d. of
  Mrs. G. D. Blanks, Feb.
  14, 1907
Ann J., w. of Capt. James
  Turner, May 26, 1859
Atwood Wash, s. of W. W.
  Turner, Dec. 10, 1891
Austin D., Mar. 11, 1886
Barbary B. (Mrs.), Dec. 4,
  1873
Belinda, w. of J. M. Turner,
  Mar. 18, 1880
Benjamin W., s. of William
  M. Turner, May 13, 1875
Carrie Downey (Mrs.), Apr.
  7, 1927
Charly Bride, s. of R. D.
  and Lucy E. Turner, July
  4, 1878
Charles Clifton, s. of W. W.
  Turner, Dec. 10, 1891
Edward, s. of George Turner,
  Oct. 14, 1831
Edward, s. of Joseph and
  Mary Turner, Aug. 31, 1838
Edward Fuller, s. of Austin
  and Emily Turner, Nov. 30,
  1848
Elizabeth (Mrs.), Jan. 11,
  1828
Elizabeth, w. of John Turner,
  Feb. 20, 1862
Elizabeth A., w. of J. C.
  Turner, May 26, 1904
Ellen (Mrs.), Apr. 22, 1869
Emily J., w. of Austin D.
  Turner, Mar. 11, 1886
Eugenia Lawson, d. of C.
  Beverly Turner, Oct. 26,
  1882
Fannie Bacon, d. of W. W.
  Turner, Dec. 10, 1891
Floyd, s. of R. M. Turner,
  Nov. 1, 1877
Frances, Sept. 8, 1859
G. G. (Rev.), July 15, 1926
George (Maj.), Oct. 2, 1829
George Henry, s. of Thomas
  C. Turner, July 28, 1853
George S., Sept. 17, 1891

George W., Nov. 2, 1899
George W. (Mrs.), Nov. 2,
  1899
Gideon, May 16, 1889
Harry Eugene, s. of G. M.
  and Annie L. Turner, Mar.
  4, 1880
Henrietta, d. of Andrew Tur-
  ner, July 27, 1905
Henry (Maj.), Nov. 6, 1829
Huldah, May 2, 1850
Indie (Mrs.), Oct. 3, 1872
James, Nov. 22, 1849
James N., Mar. 15, 1928
James W., Aug. 28, 1850
Jennie Snow (Mrs.), Feb. 9,
  1922
Jesse Hurd (Mrs.), Oct. 1,
  1931
John, June 24, 1847
John (Elder), July 30, 1874
John P. (Rev.), Aug. 29,
  1872
Joseph A., May 16, 1878
Judith (Mrs.), June 11, 1830
Junius Walker, s. of Joseph
  H. and Eliza A. P. Turner,
  Aug. 31, 1838
Lawson C., Aug. 12, 1880
Lelia Virginia (Mrs.),
  d. of Dr. Charles L.
  Cocke, Oct. 26, Nov. 9,
  1899
Louisa B. KEMP, w. of Rev.
  John P. Turner, Oct. 22,
  1885
Lucy A., d. of Edward C. and
  Caroline T. Turner, Feb.
  26, 1863
Luther Rice, Feb. 3, 1848
Lydia Ann Judson, Feb. 3,
  1848
Mary (Mrs.), Sept. 20, 1860
Mary Ann, June 24, 1847
Mary Hansford, Feb. 3, 1848
Mary James, w. of Job
  Turner, Jan. 23, 1873
Mary Letitia, w. of John Will-
  iam Turner, d. of Fendall
  Chiles, June 25, 1885

OBITUARY NOTICES IN THE RELIGIOUS HERALD WITH DATES OF PUBLICATION

Mary P. (Mrs.), Oct. 12, 1876
Nancy C. (Mrs.), Apr. 14, 1881
Nannie J., w. of John W. Turner, d. of Joseph J. Pleasants, Dec. 2, 1875
Robert T., Aug. 25, 1870
Sallie A., w. of John R. Turner, d. of John S. and Jane Armstrong, Apr. 26, 1888
Sallie Frances, d. of Rev. W. G. and Susan A. Turner, Sept. 11, 1856
Sarah, Jan. 3, 1856
Sarah Ann, d. of Thomas C. Turner, Sr., Aug. 13, 1863
Susan Ann, w. of Elder William G. Turner, Oct. 20, 1859
Susanna, w. of William Turner, Jan. 22, 1836
Thomas, Mar. 25, 1926
Thomas C., Aug. 29, 1861
Thomas C., Apr. 9, 1863
Virginia, w. of J. S. Turner, Feb. 2, 1871
W. M., July 15, 1886
W. W., Sept. 7, 1911
William, Nov. 6, 1829
William Admire, s. of Hardaway and Sophia Turner, Apr. 9, 1863
William F. (Capt.), Oct. 2, 1884
William George, s. of William D. Turner, Nov. 7, 1850
William L., s. of John M. Turner, Oct. 1, 1863
William W., s. of Austin D. and Emily J. Turner, Mar. 11, 1886
Wilson, Feb. 6, 1845
Zephaniah (Capt.), July 13, 1848

TURNLEY
Alfred L., gr.s. of Edmond Turnley, July 23, 1857
Ira P. (Mrs.), d. of Rev. James L. Powell, Oct. 31, Nov. 21, 1895
Nelson Goodman, Oct. 17, 1872

TURPIN
(Mrs.), mother of Rev. J. B. Turpin, Aug. 18, 1887
A. H., Sept. 2, 1858
Cleopatra A., w. of Thomas M. Turpin, May 7, 1874
David, s. of Thomas Turpin, Jan. 11, 1855
Edward Gwathmey, s. of J. O. and M. B. Turpin, Aug. 21, 1856
Elizabeth (Mrs.), Oct. 6, 1837
Emmeline, d. of John Turpin, Aug. 31, 1832
Frances J. (Mrs.), Dec. 4, 1851
Henry, Nov. 30, 1843
Ida J., Aug. 30, 1928
James G., Jun. 13, 1853
John, June 16, 1870
John O. (Rev.), Mar. 13, Apr. 10 and 17, June 19, 1884
John O., Sept. 19, 1912
Lawrence R., Jan. 16, 1890
Lewis Morris, s. of George W. Turpin, Dec. 30, 1847
Loula Buford, d. of R. G. and Dora Turpin, Nov. 26, 1891
Malinda B., w. of George W. Turpin, d. of Wiley Dickinson, Mar. 8, 1855
Martha (Mrs.), w. of John O. Turpin, d. of Archie Brown, Apr. 19, 1894
Mary F., w. of Thomas Turpin, Mar. 4, 1875
Mildred H., d. of Elder Miles Turpin, Aug. 18, 1837
Mildred Jane, w. of H. H. Turpin, Dec. 19, 1850
Miles (Elder), Aug. 16, 1833
Miles, s. of Elder J. O.

OBITUARY NOTICES IN THE RELIGIOUS HERALD WITH DATES OF PUBLICATION

Turpin, Feb. 10, 1853
Miles, Feb. 9, Apr. 27, 1893
Philip (Dr.), May 16, 1828
Rebecca, w. of Miles Turpin,
  Sept. 15, 1904
Robert, s. of Rev. John O.
  Turpin, Dec. 4, 1884
Robert Lucian, s. of R. G.
  and Dora Turpin, Dec. 9,
  1886
Susan Bruce, w. of John
  Turpin, July 22, 1852
Susan H., w. of William H.
  Turpin, June 29, 1854
Susan Lamar, w. of Rev. John
  B. Turpin, d. of Rev. J. L.
  M. Curry, Jan. 13 and 27,
  1881
T. L., Jan. 4, 1883
Thomas, Sept. 24, 1857
W. H. (Mrs.), w. of William
  H. Turpin, Jan. 1, 1903
William H. (Dr.), Mar. 1, 1866
William Henry, Sept. 2, 1880
William L., June 28, 1900
William M. (Judge), s. of
  William H. Turpin, June 28,
  1917
TUTT
  Mildred, w. of Capt. Richard
  I. Tutt, June 2, 1837
TUTTLE
  Lena Jeter, d. of J. F. and
  India M. Tuttle, Oct. 13,
  1881
TUTWILER
  Amanda, Oct. 1, 1891
  M. M. (Miss), Mar. 18, 1897
TWEEDY
  Beatrice, w. of Allen
  Tweedy, May 30, 1918
  Elizabeth, Apr. 20, 1916
  G. Dabney, s. of Albert
  Tweedy, Aug. 20, 1863
  M. L. (Mrs.), May 9, 1907
  Martha J., July 26, 1917
  Mary Sue, d. of C. S. and
  R. B. Tweedy, Mar. 21,
  Apr. 4, 1907
TWITTY
  Allie W. WALTHALL, w. of
  Dr. S. G. Twitty, Nov. 12,
  1885
TWYMAN
  Ann, w. of George Twyman,
  Feb. 28, 1850
  Augusta, Oct. 28, 1920
  Edna Lillian (Mrs.), d. of
  E. H. and L. R. Benton,
  Feb. 5, 1925
  Eliza A. HILL (Mrs.), June
  13, 1901
  Emily Ann, d. of Thornel and
  Sarah K. Twyman, Feb. 28,
  1850
  Emma Joe (Mrs.), Oct. 27,
  1932
  Francis H., w. of Dr. W. H.
  Twyman, Jan. 21, 1864
  George, Mar. 22, 1833
  George, Sr., Oct. 12, 1848
  Laura S., w. of Barton
  Twyman, Sept. 29, Oct. 13,
  1892
  Mabel Booker, d. of Dr.
  Iverson S. and Martha E.
  Twyman, Jan. 23, 1896[*]
  Martha Elizabeth, Mar. 10,
  1904
  Samuel R., s. of Dr. Iverson
  Lewis and Martha E. Aus-
  tin Twyman, Oct. 22, 1925[*]
  Sarah, w. of William Twyman,
  Feb. 23, 1858
  Sarah K., w. of Thornel
  Twyman, Feb. 28, 1850
  Thornel, s. of George and
  Ann Twyman, Feb. 28, 1850
  Walker G., s. of Joseph and
  Elizabeth Twyman, Apr. 2,
  1863
TYACK
  Ann S., w. of Samuel Tyack,
  d. of Mrs. Sarah T. Wilkins,
  July 13, 1848
TYGA
  Frances A (Mrs.), Mar. 22,
  1855
TYLER
  Edna, w. of Richard Fountain

* Possible inaccuracy in name, or spelling, but given as printed

OBITUARY NOTICES IN THE RELIGIOUS HERALD WITH DATES OF PUBLICATION

Tyler, June 7, 1855
Fanny Beal, d. of R. B. and
  Lucy J. Tyler, Mar. 17,
  1853
George (Capt.), Feb. 8, 1835
J. H., Jr. (Mrs.), Oct. 23,
  1924
J. L., July 20, 1893
James E., May 16, 1918
Jane C. (Mrs.), May 14, 1857
John, Jan. 23, 1868
John M., s. of Elder John
  Tyler, July 22, 1852
Mary (Mrs.), July 1,
  1847
Mary E., d. of R. F. Tyler,
  July 22, 1858
Mary E., w. of Capt. H. W.
  Tyler, Jan. 19, 1882
Mary G., w. of John Tyler,
  Apr. 4, 1872
Mary T., w. of James O.
  Tyler, Jan. 19, 1888
Mary Virginia, d. of James
  P. Tyler, July 5, 1866
Millicent, w. of Capt. Hiram
  W. Tyler, Feb. 6, 1845
R. F., July 11, 1889
W. B. (Rev.), Sept. 7, 1933
William Thompson, s. of
  Thompson and Emily Tyler,
  July 7, 1842

TYNES
Frances Mary Tate, w. of Rev.
  W. E. Tynes, May 19, 1881

TYREE
Ann H., w. of William Tyree,
  Mar. 17, 1837
Cornelius (Mrs.), Mar. 20,
  1884
Cornelius (Mrs.), w. of Dr.
  Cornelius Tyree, June 16,
  1892
Eugenia C., d. of William
  and Martha Tyree, Oct.
  18, 1866
Frances, Apr. 18, 1861
James, May 25, 1843
Laura, Aug. 2, 1934
Martha Elizabeth, w. of
  William Tyree, d. of
  John West, Sr., Jan. 1,
  1885
Mary, w. of William M.
  Tyree, May 26, 1842
Robert Henry, s. of William
  and Martha E. Tyree, Oct.
  6, 1842
Rosa, May 15, 1890
Sallie, d. of R. T. and Mary
  Tyree, Oct. 27, 1870
Susan Barksdale, w. of Rev.
  William A. Tyree, Mar. 6,
  1902
William, Apr. 20, 1876
William A. (Rev.), Dec. 25,
  1884
William Cornelius (Rev.),
  Feb. 7, Mar. 14, 1929
William Howard, s. of Will-
  iam and Martha E. Tyree,
  Sept. 10, 1846

TYRON
W. M. (Elder), Dec. 16,
  1847

TYUS
James Edward, Jan. 30,
  1913

- U V -

UNDERWOOD
   Charles, s. of Rev. L. B.
     Underwood, Oct. 5, 1893
   John M., Oct. 30, 1930
   L. B. (Rev.), Feb. 1, 1934
   Roberta A. (Mrs.), Mar. 24, 1927
UPCHURCH
   J. W., July 31, 1930
UPDIKE
   Grafton (Mrs.), Feb. 12, 1925
   Ruth, w. of Daniel Updike, Sr., Oct. 22, 1840
UPSHUR
   Mary Elizabeth, w. of T. W. Upshur, June 24, 1869
UPTON
   Florence, d. of B. and L. Upton, May 13, 1880
URNER
   Charles H., Aug. 11 and 18, 1932
URQUHART
   Howard, s. of J. J. Urquhart, May 14, 1903
UTTERBACK
   Mary P. (Mrs.), Apr. 23, 1857
   Willie D., child of Bryant and Susan Utterback, Apr. 7, 1870
UZZELL
   Cattie Gardner, Mar. 20, 1919
   James, Jan. 13, 1887

VADEN
   C. F., Aug. 4, 1921
   Ella K., d. of R. W. and Mary R. Vaden, Aug. 13, 1874
   Giles H., Feb. 25, 1926
   Robert W., Mar. 11, 1875
VAIDEN
   Aubrey, July 27, 1871*
   Bettie Lucy, w. of H. B. Vaiden, May 22, 1873

   I. B. (Maj.), Sept. 23, 1886
   J. M., Dec. 13, 1883
   John Bolling, Sept. 13, 1917
   John M., s. of Galba and Lou Vaiden, Sept. 25, 1879
   John P., Jan. 11, 1855
   Joseph, May 25, 1848
   Mary Fielding (Mrs.), Oct. 24, 1889
   Mary Lucy, w. of Capt. Melville Vaiden, Sept. 27, 1855
   Myra Y., w. of John Bolling Vaiden, Feb. 25, 1937
   Sallie E., Mar. 9, 1911
   Victoria, w. of Rev. Vulosko Vaiden, Mar. 5, 1903
   William Aubry, s. of William and Bettie Lucy Vaiden, July 6 and 27, 1871*
VALENTINE
   Ann (Mrs.), Sept. 11, 1829
   C., Sept. 11, 1879
   Edward, Apr. 19, 1855
   Edward V., Oct. 23, 1930
   Jane F., Jan. 13, 1853
   Jane H., w. of J. B. Valentine, Nov. 22, 1860
   John B., Dec. 6, 1866
   Malinda A. (Mrs.), June 26, 1890
   Mary, Aug. 26, 1852
   T. C. (Mrs.), Sept. 1, 1938
VAN BUREN
   Mary Coleman, d. of B. B. and Mary E. Van Buren, Mar. 26, 1874
VANCLEVE
   Eliza (Mrs.), d. of Samuel Roberts and Naomi Van Meter Mar. 13, 1884
   Fannie N., w. of W. M. Vancleve, Mar. 25, 1880
   William M., July 15, 1886
VAN DERLIP
   Grace Rankin, w. of Rev. G. M. Van Derlip, Aug. 26, 1886

---

* Possible inaccuracy in name, or spelling, but given as printed

OBITUARY NOTICES IN THE RELIGIOUS HERALD WITH DATES OF PUBLICATION

VANDERSON
　William Lee, Dec. 25, 1862
VAN DEVENTER
　S. Lutie, d. of Guilford Gregg Van Deventer, Feb. 17, 1927
VAN DUZER
　Harriet Mildred BALL, w. of Benjamin Van Duzer, Feb. 5, 1874
VANHOOK
　C. L. (Mrs.), July 1, 1937
VAN HUSAN
　Caleb, Sept. 4, 1884
VAN LANDINGHAM
　Henry Asa, June 11, 1914
VANLANDINGHAM
　William B., Mar. 12, 1925
VANN
　L. L. (Mrs.), Sept. 2, 1926
VANNAME
　H. H. (Mrs.), Mar. 26, 1908
VAN NESS
　Rosie M., d. of W. P. and A. J. Van Ness, Sept. 7, 1871
VANSICKLER
　Lola Frances, Dec. 29, 1898
VASHON
　Eliza F., Oct. 1, 1846
VASON
　D. A. (Mrs.), Feb. 17, 1870
VASS
　Henry, Sept. 10, 1896
　Lucy (Mrs.), June 27, 1878
　Sarah E., May 20, 1897
VAUGHAN
　child of Rev. W. R. Vaughan, Apr. 22, 1875
　A. J., Mar. 27, 1924
　Alexander B., s. of Benjamin Vaughan, Oct. 7, 1852
　Ariadne, w. of James M. Vaughan, Mar. 2, 1854
　Benjamin, Mar. 7, 1861
　Benjamin Franklin, Aug. 2, 1917
　Catharine (Mrs.), Jan. 12, 1882
　Charles J., s. of James C. and Elizabeth Vaughan, Sept. 23, 1880
　Charlotte H., Apr. 24, 1873
　Dora (Mrs.), Apr. 3, 1930
　Elizabeth A., w. of Benjamin Vaughan, July 13, 1876
　Frances A., w. of Bolling Vaughan, June 24, 1847
　Franky, Aug. 17, 1838
　G. R., s. of Joseph and Catharine Vaughan, Mar. 12, 1857
　George, s. of Dr. W. R. and Mary Vaughan, May 8, 1890
　H. M. (Col.), Mar. 9, 1865
　Hallie Ruby, w. of Luther B. Vaughan, July 15, 1886
　Harriet (Mrs.), Apr. 24, 1873
　J. L., Dec. 2, 1858
　James M., Nov. 28, 1850
　James William, July 28, 1881
　John Meriwether, Nov. 27, 1913
　John R. F., May 14, 1925
　John W., Nov. 20, 1924
　Joseph, Oct. 25, 1849
　Joseph, Nov. 29, 1860
　Joseph H., Oct. 11, 1855
　Julia A., Oct. 26, 1893
　Kitty S. (Mrs.), Feb. 16, 1882
　Martha, w. of W. H. Vaughan, Apr. 22, 1886
　Mary B., w. of Joseph Vaughan, Mar. 6, 1856
　Mary Sclater (Mrs.), d. of John and Mary Jones, May 5, 1892
　Nancy (Mrs.), Sept. 8, 1881
　Nancy, w. of William Vaughan, Mar. 21, 1895
　Robert H. (Capt.), Mar. 17, 1864
　Robert Howell, s. of William R. and Mary E. Vaughan, Apr. 17, 1862
　Samuel, Oct. 8, 1857
　Sarah R., w. of Robert V.

OBITUARY NOTICES IN THE RELIGIOUS HERALD WITH DATES OF PUBLICATION

Vaughan, Oct. 31, 1872
Simon, Oct. 11, 1855
Stephen Noah, s. of B. F.
  and L. D. Vaughan, June 28,
  1894
Susie B., Oct. 16, 1930
Virginia, d. of Joseph
  Vaughan, Oct. 28, 1852
W. (Rev.), Apr. 19, 1877
William, Aug. 6, 1891
VAUGHN
  Cornelius, Mar. 29, 1855
  Francis W., Feb. 20, 1913
  J. M., Aug. 14, 1913
  Lucy E., w. of William H.
    Vaughn, July 5, 1906
  Mary E., Jan. 2, 1845
  William H., Jan. 31, 1889
VENABLE
  Rebecca A., w. of Samuel
    D. Venable, June 14, 1849*
  Rebekah A., w. of Samuel
    D. Venable, Apr. 18, 1850*
  Sarah (Mrs.), July 27, 1876
VERNON
  Mary Anna, w. of Rev. J.
    H. Vernon, July 19, 1888
VERSER
  Paulina S. (Mrs.), d. of
    George C. Poindexter,
    Jan. 14, 1847
VEST
  Jeannette Fleet, w. of Dr.
    Richard S. Vest, d. of
    Dr. William T. and Maria

    S. Fleet, Oct. 28, 1920
  Martha J., w. of Dr. R. S.
    Vest, d. of James M.
    Binford, Apr. 6, 1882
  Martha Snead, w. of James
    M. Vest, d. of Henry and
    Nancy Barnley, Jan. 7,
    Mar. 3, 1892
  Mary E. (Mrs.), Nov. 25, 1897
  Richard S. (Dr.), Feb. 6, 1902
  Susan, w. of G. Vest, July 4,
    1844
  W. B., Sept. 25, 1924
VEVERS
  John, July 13, 1838
VIARS
  Ann (Mrs.), May 21, 1840
VINCENT
  Amy D., w. of Nathan Vincent,
    Aug. 20, 1857
VINES
  Annie (Mrs.), Apr. 28, May
    5, 1921
VOGT
  A. M., Feb. 19, 1880
VOSS
  Mahala (Mrs.), Apr. 9, 1885
VOUGHT
  Laura Hepler, w. of Glen
    G. Vought, Mar. 25, 1926
VOWLES
  J. S., Jan. 3, 1918
  Lucy A. (Mrs.), June 11, 1885
  Sarah M. W. (Mrs.), Feb. 9,
    1893

* Possible inaccuracy in name, or spelling, but given as printed

W

WADDEL
William H., Sept. 24, 1863

WADDELL
Ann Rebecca, w. of James A. Waddell, Apr. 8, 1869
E. W., Aug. 3, 1916
Littleton, May 27, 1886

WADDILL
Clara (Mrs.), Oct. 15, 1925
Edmund (Judge), Aug. 27, 1931
Mary H., w. of William W. Waddill, May 1, 1873
Mary L., w. of E. Waddill, Apr. 19, 1860
Paschal, Jan. 10, 1878
Walter Wood, s. of William H. Waddill, Oct. 6, 1904

WADDLE
Laura Virginia, d. of Mrs. Mary A. Waddle, Nov. 10, 1853

WADDY
John P., Mar. 2, 1838
Marcia Scott, d. of G. T. Waddy, May 23, 1850
Robbie M., Jan. 6, 1876
Robert B., Mar. 12, 1868
Thomas O., Feb. 21, 1861
William K. (Dr.), Mar. 14, 1872

WADE
Ann, w. of R. Wade, Nov. 17, 1892
Emiline P., w. of Robert H. Wade, Feb. 28, 1850
Indiana, d. of Mrs. Sallie Wade, Dec. 29, 1859
J. Monroe, Sr. (Mrs.), Aug. 19, 1937
James M. (Dr.), Jan. 7, 1858
James M., s. of William M. and Martha M. Wade, Feb. 19, 1863
Lucy C., Dec. 27, 1855
Mary Ann, w. of Michael Wade, Sept. 27, 1839
Mary M., d. of Jefferson and Mary J. Wade, June 12, 1873
Nancy, w. of Archibald Wade, Sr., d. of Elder Alderson Weeks, Dec. 27, 1850
Octavia, w. of Elijah B. Wade, Dec. 27, 1855
Robert Lee, s. of Jefferson and Mary J. Wade, Sept. 26, 1867
T. J., Apr. 28, 1938
William C., Oct. 27, 1842
William M., Feb. 26, 1863

WAGELEY
Bernadine, Mar. 14, 1918

WAGER
H. E. (Mrs.), July 18, 1901
W. D., s. of James and Harriet Wager, Oct. 17, 1895

WAGGENER
John Pendleton, s. of Leslie and Fannie P. Waggener, Apr. 13, 1876

WAGSTAFF
Alice Young (Mrs.), Oct. 6, 1921
Christopher, May 13, 1875
George B., Feb. 4, 1892
H. C. (Mrs.), July 6, 1882
Ida Lee, Aug. 9, 1923
James Kemper, s. of John W. Wagstaff, Mar. 15, 1877
Rebecca, July 25, 1867
Zora Young, d. of J. W. and M. B. Wagstaff, July 2, 1874

WAID
James William, s. of Rev. John and Nannie A. Waid, Oct. 4, 1880
John Judson, s. of Rev. John

OBITUARY NOTICES IN THE RELIGIOUS HERALD WITH DATES OF PUBLICATION

and Nancy Waid, Apr. 28, 1864
Nannie A., w. of Rev. John Waid, d. of Rev. J. P. Corron, Feb. 13, 1868
WAIT
Maria, w. of Benjamin Wait, June 29, 1843
WAITE
George T. (Dr.), May 21 and 28, June 11, Nov. 12, 1936
Julia Francis, w. of Maj. Charles Waite, Aug. 8, 1901
Manlius Fillmore, Dec. 12 and 26, 1918
WALDEN
Edward, Apr. 4, 1895
Elizabeth, w. of Richard Walden, May 30, 1850
Elizabeth, Sept. 9, 1852
Fannie, w. of Edward Walden, June 10, 1909
George A., Feb. 9, 1860
Mary F., d. of Moses H. Walden, Dec. 31, 1857
Paulina A., w. of G. A. Walden, Mar. 13, 1856
Walker, d. of Nathan A. and Mary Walden, Jan. 3, 1901
William, Sept. 13, 1883
WALDER
Martha E., w. of James Walder, Jan. 25, 1900
WALDO
John (Elder), Feb. 25, 1841
WALDRON
Labán, Jan. 26, 1888
WALDROP
Ann Marietta, d. of William J. and Ann Waldrop, July 12, 1855
Ann Marsella, w. of William J. Waldrop, d. of William Tyree, Apr. 26, 1855
Archibald D., s. of Martin A. and Willianna A. Waldrop, May 2, 1872

Bird Young, s. of Capt. W. A. B. Waldrop, Dec. 7, 1871
Christopher, s. of William and Elizabeth Waldrop, Sept. 8, 1842
Lucian T., s. of Francis and Susan F. Waldrop, Nov. 13, 1856
Martin A., Mar. 1, 1906
Mary (Mrs.), May 25, 1848
Rebecca A., w. of Thomas Waldrop, Apr. 19, 1855
Richard N., s. of Thomas and Eudora Waldrop, Apr. 29, 1858
Samuella A., d. of Samuel Waldrop, June 5, 1835
Thomas A., Dec. 11, 1879
William, Jan. 6, 1842
William H., May 1, 1862
Willianna Anderson, w. of Martin A. Waldrop, Sept. 14, 1899
Willie H., s. of W. A. B. and Martha Waldrop, Jan. 3, 1856
WALDROPE
Mary, w. of Richard Waldrope, Jan. 26, 1854
WALK
Thomas (Mrs.), Nov. 28, 1844
WALKE
Lilly Barker, w. of Burfoot Walke, Dec. 26, 1929
Willie H., s. of J. C. and Nannie E. Walke, June 23, 1892
WALKER
(Mr.), June 13, 1828
Allen, Aug. 25, 1842
Ann Adelia, w. of L. B. Walker, July 1, 1886
Ann V. (Mrs.), Aug. 19, 1869
Aris (Capt.), July 8, 1852
Armistead, Jan. 19, 1860
Benjamin F., May 16, 1889
Bettie Lee, d. of E. and Virginia A. Putney Walker, June 5, 1884

OBITUARY NOTICES IN THE RELIGIOUS HERALD WITH DATES OF PUBLICATION

C. M., w. of John R. Walker, July 15, 1875
David, Jan. 29, 1852
Dulcibella, w. of W. Walker, Aug. 4, 1853
Eliza (Mrs.), Apr. 7, 1881
Elizabeth, July 7, 1853
Elizabeth, w. of John Walker, Aug. 22, 1861
Esther A. (Mrs.), Aug. 20, 1840
Fanny (Mrs.), Jan. 7, 1858
Frances A., w. of John H. Walker, Aug. 3, 1854
Georgie Hall, Oct. 19, 1933
Grizzelle J., w. of James W. Walker, Feb. 21, 1884
Helen, w. of John R. Walker, June 25, 1854
Henry Hiram, s. of Dr. H. H. and Bettie Walker, Sept. 12, 1878
Holland, Nov. 10, 1881
J. O. (Mrs.), Aug. 26, 1909
J. R., Aug. 29, 1895
James (Col.), July 25, 1828
James R. (Dr.), May 21, 1863
John, Aug. 19, 1852
John S., Mar. 23, 1922
Joseph (Rev.), Apr. 11, 1895
Judith C., w. of C. P. Walker, May 31, 1888
Julia Ryland, w. of Thomas N. Walker, Oct. 9, 1873
Kate T., w. of T. J. Walker, Aug. 14, 1879
L. B., Jan. 11, 1872
Lewis M., Aug. 11, 1881
Louisa, w. of Rev. Joseph Walker, d. of James Morrison, Apr. 4, 1872
Margaret J., w. of Rev. Joseph Walker, June 23, 1853
Maria Frances, w. of J. A. Walker, May 29, 1862
Maria Lipscomb, d. of J. A. and M. E. Walker, Aug. 24, 1871
Martha, w. of Henry Walker, Apr. 24, 1856
Martha A., w. of Dr. James R. Walker, Dec. 24, 1857
Martha E. F., w. of Dr. Benjamin J. Walker, Mar. 17, 1864
Martha S., Jan. 19, 1871
Martha T., d. of H. C. Walker, Nov. 2, 1882
Martin Franklin, Apr. 3, 1873
Mary, w. of James Walker, Dec. 1, 1837
Mary A., w. of Edwin C. Walker, May 30, 1878
Mary E., w. of John R. Walker, May 13, 1869
Mary Peachy, w. of Thomas N. Walker, d. of Samuel P. and Catherine G. Ryland, July 8, 1830
Mary Walker Samuel, w. of John L. Walker, Sept. 5, 1895
Perry (Judge), Jan. 6, 1881
Peter, Feb. 27, 1873
Rebecca (Mrs.), Sept. 25, 1873
Robert Albert, s. of Joshua A. and Mary E. Walker, July 3, 1873
Robin B., Jan. 29, 1874
Rosalie E., d. of Benjamin and Emma Walker, May 2, 1861
S., w. of Elder G. Walker, d. of Philip Peek, June 24, 1858
Sallie, w. of Baylor Walker, d. of John Craddock, Sept. 10, 1868
Sallie F. (Mrs.), Dec. 21, 1876
Sophia, w. of Daniel Walker, July 4, 1828
Susan T., d. of Maj. Humphrey Walker, May 5, 1842

OBITUARY NOTICES IN THE RELIGIOUS HERALD WITH DATES OF PUBLICATION

T. E. (Mrs.), Mar. 18, 1920
Thomas, Oct. 17, 1850
Thomas, s. of Thomas N. and Julia Ryland Walker, Sept. 5, 1867
Thomas Gibson, s. of Dr. John Walker, Jan. 4, 1906
W. A., May 18, 1911
William P., Aug. 7, 1873
William S., Dec. 16, 1841
WALL
  Sarah R. (Mrs.), Feb. 13, 1873
WALLACE
  A. F. (Mrs.), Jan. 24, 1861
  Ann (Mrs.), Feb. 23, 1893
  Bettie H., July 31, 1890
  Elizabeth S. (Mrs.), Apr. 26, 1917
  Emily T., w. of Gustavus B. Wallace, Aug. 5, 1869
  I. T. (Rev.), July 23, 1891
  J. R. (Mrs.), Aug. 26, 1926
  John Pilson, Apr. 24, 1902
  Margaret S., d. of Rev. I. T. and Emily J. Wallace, Nov. 7, 1867
  Martha A., w. of Thomas Wallace, Apr. 19, 1883
  Minnie May, Oct. 11, 1906
  O. C. S. (Mrs.), w. of Rev. O. C. S. Wallace, May 31, 1917
  Samuel, Nov. 4, 1869
  Samuel B., Nov. 15, 1888
  Susan (Mrs.), Nov. 25, 1880
  Thomas, June 11, 1868
  William, Sept. 19, 1872
  William B., Sept. 14, 1876
WALLER
  Absalom C., Dec. 30, 1831
  Annie WADDY, w. of Jordan Waller, Oct. 28, 1886
  B. (Capt.), Aug. 30, 1839
  Benjamin, Nov. 4, 1847
  Benjamin Franklin, Apr. 11, 1861
  Hannah C., Oct. 14, 1847
  Lizzie (Mrs.), Sept. 7, 1893
  Lucy, w. of Benjamin Waller, May 26, 1842
  Martha P., w. of Col. Mercer Waller, Jan. 1, 1857
  Mary Hampton DEJARNETTE, w. of Dr. N. S. Waller, Oct. 3, 1901
  Mildred Jane, d. of Rev. Absalom Waller, May 16, 1889
  Nannie, d. of Dr. N. S. and M. H. Waller, Mar. 2, 1899
  Nelson S. (Dr.), s. of Rev. Absalom Waller, Apr. 29, 1869
  Philadelphia Chew (Mrs.), Dec. 16, 1852
  Robert A., s. of R. B. and N. S. Waller, Jan. 27, 1887
  Vidillia A., w. of W. E. Waller, Mar. 28, 1907
  William Judson Carey (Dr.), Mar. 17, 1892
WALTERS
  Azariah G. (Capt.), Sept. 28, 1899
  Bettie B., w. of W. T. Walters, d. of A. A. Davidson, Feb. 7, 1856
  Eliza Jane, Feb. 4, 1904
  John, July 19, 1849
  Lucy, Feb. 23, 1854
  Malina, w. of Jacob Walters, Mar. 4, 1836
  Spires, Dec. 22, 1859
WALTHAL
  Burfoot Madison, s. of Joseph S. and Matilda E. Walthal, July 16, 1846
WALTHALL
  A. B. (Rev.), June 15, 1882
  Benjamin S., s. of Rev. Joseph S. Walthall, Apr. 11, 1872

OBITUARY NOTICES IN THE RELIGIOUS HERALD WITH DATES OF PUBLICATION

Christopher J., Jan. 19, 1865
Elizabeth A., w. of James D. Walthall, Oct. 21, 1847
Ella L., w. of Josephus Walthall, Nov. 2, 1893
Joe Clyde, s. of Josephus and Ella Walthall, Nov. 2, 1893
John Henry, Apr. 20, 1876
Joseph Stevens, June 9, 1870
Lindsay B., Aug. 8, 1912
Lucy James, d. of Christopher and Sarah Ann Walthall, June 4, 1840
Madison, Aug. 13, 1868
Matilda E., w. of Joseph S. Walthall, d. of Col. Lawson Burfoot, Oct. 2, 1873
Sally (Mrs.), Nov. 12, 1863
Sarah Ann, w. of Christopher Walthall, Sr., d. of Johnson Eubank, Sept. 11, 1884

WALTON
Ann (Mrs.), May 2, 1854
Clarence, s. of Carrington Walton, Jan. 5, 1905
Elizabeth Emeline, w. of Jesse W. Walton, May 11, 1848
Henry C., Oct. 21, 1909
J. C., Sept. 20, 1860
L. H. (Rev.), Dec. 28, 1922
Lavertt, d. of Robert D. and Adelia H. Walton, Oct. 6, 1881
Louisa A., w. of Josiah H. Walton, Jan. 30, 1845
Lucius E., s. of William G. and S. E. Walton, Mar. 10, 1864
M. A. (Mrs.), Sept. 20, 1906
Marion, May 4, 1911
Priscilla (Mrs.), Dec. 22, 1881
Rebecca J., w. of James B. Walton, Nov. 18, 1847

S. T. (Lt. Col.), Dec. 17, 1863
Sarah, w. of Sidney Walton, Apr. 26, 1860
Simeon, Jan. 18, 1839
Sydney Eugene, Nov. 26, 1874
Thomas A., Dec. 13, 1934
William Branch, Dec. 10, 1936

WALTZ
Meeky M., w. of Thomas H. Waltz, Apr. 14, 1881

WAMACK
Mary C., w. of L. A. Wammack, d. of Jordan Taylor, June 9, 1870

WAMBLE
Sarah N., Oct. 4, 1888

WAMMICK
Nannie Cabell, Mar. 9, 1916

WAPLES
Alice Woodward, d. of John S. and Lizzie Waples, Jan. 19, 1899
Anna Drummond (Mrs.), d. of John R. and Eleshea Drummond, May 27, 1915
Edward B. (Capt.), s. of Lt. Samuel Waples, Nov. 28, 1912
Martha W., d. of Samuel and Sabra P. Waples, Apr. 11, 1867
Sarah A., w. of Capt. E. B. Waples, July 15, 1886
Sarah T., Dec. 22, 1870

WARD
Daniel, Mar. 26, 1868
Dorothy B., Sept. 18, 1913; Apr. 2, 1914
Eliza, Sept. 17, 1885
Granville L., Aug. 29, 1834
John Wyatt (Rev.), Dec. 14, 1905
Judith E., w. of Col. Robert G. Ward, Aug. 26, 1841
Lucy A. C., w. of Rev. John Wyatt Ward, d. of Robert

OBITUARY NOTICES IN THE RELIGIOUS HERALD WITH DATES OF PUBLICATION

T. and Lucy A. Jones,
May 4, 1916
Marie L., w. of William B.
Ward, Sept. 8, 1864
Mary, w. of Col. Daniel
Ward, Dec. 28, 1854
Mary C. (Mrs.), Mar. 22,
1849
Sallie, d. of Rev. John F.
Ward, June 19, 1919
Susan (Mrs.), May 19, 1881
Susan Frances, d. of Mrs.
Amanda W. Ward, Mar. 15,
1860
W. L. (Dr.), July 19, 1917
WARDEN
Isabella (Mrs.), Dec. 13,
1888
Lydia (Mrs.), Jan. 30,
1840
WARDLAW
Lizzie, w. of John
B. Wardlaw, Jr., d. of
W. B. and Mary P. Davidson, Dec. 23, 1880
William W. (Dr.), s. of Dr.
Wardlaw, Mar. 25, 1831
WARDWELL
Clarence B., s. of Burnham
and S. J. Wardwell,
Aug. 12, 1858
WARE
Eliza (Mrs.), d. of James
B. Mahone, Apr. 21, 1859
Ellen E., w. of P. M. Ware,
Feb. 9, 1911
George E., June 4, 1908
Letitia P. (Mrs.), July 24,
1879
Margaret J., w. of A. G.
Ware, Oct. 3, 1872
T. M., June 21, 1900
Thomas, Jan. 8, 1852
Walter W., July 19, 1934
WARINER
Mary Susan, Nov. 30, 1865
WARING
Ann C., d. of R. P. Waring,
Dec. 11, 1856
Ann Catherine, w. of William
D. Waring, d. of Dr. M.
G. Fauntleroy, June 8,
1838
Arthur (Rev.), Oct. 18,
1866
Bettie F., w. of Robert P.
Waring, Jan. 7, 1869
Colston M. (Rev.), Dec. 26,
1834
Elton Ann, w. of Robert
Waring, June 17, 1847
Horace, Feb. 17, 1832
Lucia S. (Mrs.), Jan. 13,
1887
Martha A., w. of Robert P.
Waring, June 27, 1861
Mary M., w. of William L.
Waring, Feb. 3, 1842
William L. (Capt.), July 1,
1841
WARINNER
Martha (Mrs.), Mar. 5,
1846
WARNER
Elizabeth, w. of George
C. Warner, Jan. 27, 1859
Samuel C. (Dr.), Dec. 8,
1898
WARREN
Ann, w. of William Warren,
Aug. 5, 1858
Atla Virginia, d. of George
H. and Sue Latimer Warren,
Sept. 15, 1892
Bettie D., d. of Elder P.
T. and M. A. Warren,
Nov. 7, 1872
Elizabeth, d. of William
Warren, Dec. 3, 1844
Elizabeth, w. of Patrick
Warren, Feb. 6, 1851
Elizabeth, w. of Rev. P.
Warren, Sr., Sept. 4, 1884
Elizabeth A., w. of Rev.
Patrick Warren, July 10,
Sept. 4, 1884
George, s. of Elder P. T.
and Mollie A. Warren,
Dec. 22, 1870
George H. (Mrs.), July 16,

OBITUARY NOTICES IN THE RELIGIOUS HERALD WITH DATES OF PUBLICATION

1914
James Allen, s. of William
  A. Warren, Sept. 18,
  1879
Jane, d. of William Warren,
  Jan. 2, 1840
John J., May 7, 1896
Luther Rice, Sept. 9, 1915
Marshall S., s. of John and
  Mary Warren, Jan. 20, 1853
Mary, w. of William Warren,
  Jr., d. of Alexander Walker,
  July 16, 1874
Mary E., w. of B. B. Warren,
  d. of Rev. George F.
  Adams, May 11, 1871
Mattie A., Sept. 11, 1879
P. (Rev.), Mar. 23, Apr. 20,
  1871
Patrick, Jan. 12, 1854
Patrick Thomas (Rev.), s.
  of Rev. Patrick Thomas and
  Elizabeth Scott Warren,
  June 13, 1912
Robert, Sept. 26, 1834
Rosanna (Mrs.), Oct. 18, 1923
Sue Latimer, w. of George
  H. Warren, Dec. 3,
  1914
Thomas, May 31, 1855
Thomas G., Feb. 11, 1864
Thomas P., Nov. 8, 1894
Washington W., Sept. 9,
  1852
William, Dec. 23, 1852
William, Jr., Dec. 20, 1900
William Edward, Dec. 4,
  1930
WARRINER
  John W., Oct. 18, 1855
  Joseph Samuel Chancey,
    Sept. 24, 1857
WARWICK
  P. C. (Maj.), Jan. 4,
    1900
WASH
  A. A., June 28, 1883
  Andrew Melville, May 22,
    1930
  Annie E., Nov. 1, 1923
  George H., Sept. 12, 1918
  J. C., June 28, 1883
  Thomas A., s. of Atwood
    Wash, Aug. 26, 1858
WASHBURN
  William, May 23, 1872
WASHINGTON
  Ann E., w. of Capt. William
    Washington, May 5, 1842
  Anna Ratcliffe, w. of Boyd
    Washington, d. of William
    W. Thornton, June 4,
    1891
  B. G., June 8, 1893
  Fannie P., d. of John and
    Roberta B. Washington,
    June 15, 1911
  George B., Sept. 29, 1932
  John, Dec. 29, 1887
  L. A. (Mrs.), May 23, 1901
  Mary A., d. of John Washing-
    ton, May 11, 1876
  Robert B., w. of John Washing-
    ton, Oct. 18, 1888
WATERFIELD
  Amos, s. of Calvin and
    Iaca Waterfield, Nov. 14,
    1889
WATERS
  Jonathan, Nov. 11, 1852
  Robert, Apr. 9, 1857
  W. T., Mar. 13, 1879
WATKINS
  Ann T., w. of John Watkins,
    May 20, 1831
  Benjamin (Elder), July 22,
    Dec. 23, 1831
  Benjamin, May 17, 1855
  Benjamin C., Aug. 4, 1898
  Bettie Blair, d. of J. B.
    and B. S. Watkins,
    July 21, 1856
  Callie Hartwell, Oct. 31,
    1935
  Charles B., Dec. 18, 1862
  Charles H., Oct. 30, 1862
  David, Sr., Sept. 1, 1842
  Drury Myrvin, s. of James
    J. Watkins, Mar. 27, 1902
  E. A., May 28, 1936

OBITUARY NOTICES IN THE RELIGIOUS HERALD WITH DATES OF PUBLICATION

Eliza (Mrs.), Apr. 30, 1855
Elizabeth Cabell, d. of Henry Temple and Lura Cleveland Watkins, July 6, 1911
Elizabeth Leigh, d. of John Watkins, Feb. 5, 1857
Fannie, d. of Joel B. and Bettie S. Watkins, Dec. 18, 1862
Fannie B. (Mrs.), d. of Rev. J. W. and Susan Woodfin Fussell, Feb. 12, 1914
Frances W. (Mrs.), Aug. 3, 1838
George W., Dec. 12, 1834
Haddon S. (Mrs.), Aug. 31, 1916
Haddon S., May 3, 1928
Harriet A. Dupuy, w. of Ptolemy L. Watkins, June 5, 1873
Henry, June 17, 1836
Henry W. (Rev.), Mar. 28, 1872
Henry Walthall, s. of John and Susanna Watkins, July 10, 1851
J. B., Dec. 3, 1931
James E., Oct. 14, 1886
Jane M. (Mrs.), Mar. 13, 1873
Joel, Mar. 31, 1859
John, Apr. 3, 1862
John G., Oct. 9, 1890
Judith F., w. of Rev. H. W. Watkins, Dec. 25, 1879
L. M. (Mrs.), Feb. 23, 1933
Lucy Ann, w. of John Watkins, Apr. 14, 1837
Ludloe, Aug. 23, Sept. 13, 1917
Marcellus Lee, Dec. 28, 1933
Martha J., w. of Samuel P. Watkins, Aug. 4, 1859
Martha Sarah, w. of R. L. Watkins, Oct. 26, 1916
Mary, w. of Capt. Samuel Watkins, Aug. 10, 1838
Miller M., Mar. 7, 1861
Minnie Stuart, d. of Joel B. and Bettie S. Watkins, Dec. 18, 1862
Morton Witt, s. of Thomas G. and Susan E. Watkins, Feb. 12, 1863
N. T., Sept. 17, 1891
Nancy Wilson, w. of John Watkins, d. of Capt. Peter Wilson, Oct. 19, 1854
Philip, Nov. 6, 1829
Samuel (Mrs.), July 19, 1928
Selina, d. of Mansfield Watkins, Oct. 8, 1830
Stephen, Mar. 8, 1849
Susan F., w. of Thomas G. Watkins, Jan. 28, 1915
Thomas J., July 13, 1854
Virginia E., d. of N. T. Watkins, Nov. 4, 1869
Willis, s. of Milton Watkins, Sept. 10, 1914
Willis F., Mar. 20, 1879

WATKINSON
M. R. (Rev.), Oct. 4 and 11, 1877

WATLINGTON
Ann M., w. of J. O. W. Watlington, Oct. 30, 1862
Frances S. (Mrs.), July 30, 1874
T. R., Nov. 21, 1899

WATSON
Alma, d. of Thomas H. and Sallie Watson, May 3, 1860
Ann E. (Mrs.), Aug. 4, 1821
Bettie F., Feb. 20, 1890
Charles H. (Dr.), Sept. 3, 1931
E. H. (Mrs.), Feb. 10, 1938
Edward F., May 29, 1845
Edwin A., Aug. 14, 1890
Emma Lewis, d. of Joseph S. and Ella S. Watson, Nov. 12, 1863

OBITUARY NOTICES IN THE RELIGIOUS HERALD WITH DATES OF PUBLICATION

Florence S., July 18, 1895
John D. (Mrs.), Oct. 27, 1932
John E., Feb. 20, 1873
John T., Apr. 22, 1869
Joseph A. (Mrs.), Apr. 22, 1869
Joseph T., Mar. 31, 1892
Martha, w. of Capt. William Watson, Aug. 29, 1895
Mollie A., Apr. 22, 1869
Mollie Washington, d. of Joseph S. and Ella S. Watson, Sept. 22, 1859
Samuel, Jan. 12, 1871
Samuel Dayton, s. of W. J. and M. D. Watson, Nov. 4, 1869
W. A., Sr., Nov. 21, 1935
W. F. (Dr.), Aug. 5, 1920
Willie T., child of William J. and Martha D. Watson, Oct. 2, 1862

WATT
Cornelia Walker, w. of Capt. George Watt, Nov. 4, 1841
Malvina Tabitha, w. of George Watt, Jr., Apr. 20, 1848

WATTS
Annie McIver, w. of Capt. Josiah Turner Watts, Jan. 7, 1926
Corinda, w. of Thomas D. Watts, Feb. 9, 1865
Edna, d. of William B. Watts, July 27, 1899
Hugh T., s. of George A. and Mary A. Watts, July 29, 1880
J. A. (Dr.), Feb. 26, 1857
John (Col.), June 18, 1830
Martha A. V. ALLEN (Mrs.), Mar. 27, 1872
T. J. (Mrs.), Sept. 7, 1933

WAUGH
A. J., Aug. 20, 1936
Nicholas, Oct. 1, 1868
V. C. (Dr.), Jan. 28, 1909

WAY
James, Nov. 12, 1846

WAYLAND
Francis (Rev.), Oct. 19, 1865
Georgie H., s. of Henry and Mary Wayland, Nov. 8, 1860

WAYMAN
J. T. (Dr.), Sept. 28, 1933

WAYNE
Dwight, Jan. 14, 1926
Joseph W., Jan. 5, 1865

WAYT
Cynthia K., w. of Dr. John G. Wayt, Dec. 21, 1848
J. Howard, Feb. 21, 1901
Mary, w. of Twyman Wayt, June 13, 1844
William (Mrs.), Feb. 2, 1843
William, July 11, 1844
William W., Sept. 26, 1929

WAYTS
W. L. (Rev.), Jan. 13, 1938

WEALTHY
Newton C., Apr. 2, 1914

WEATHERFORD
John (Rev.), Mar. 15, 1833
John, May 26, 1859
John, Jan. 22, 1874
Mary E. (Mrs.), Feb. 27, 1873
Nancy H., w. of John W. Weatherford, Sept. 2, 1858
V. E., w. of A. W. Weatherford, Jan. 20, 1887
William, s. of John Weatherford, May 5, 1853

WEATHERS
Elizabeth (Mrs.), Mar. 24, 1842

WEAVER
Charles, Jan. 26, 1922
Esther Cotton (Mrs.), Oct. 19, 1922
James E., Jan. 13, 1938
Kate E., Mar. 21, 1929
Lulie, Nov. 3, 1881
Margaret A., w. of Charles A. Weaver, July 29, 1858

OBITUARY NOTICES IN THE RELIGIOUS HERALD WITH DATES OF PUBLICATION

Mary Ann (Mrs.), d. of Rev.
 Nathan Healy, Nov. 18, 1915
Thomas Boldridge, s. of J.
 Luther and Nannie D.
 Weaver, Aug. 28, 1913
William, May 3, 1888
William J., Feb. 15, 1912

WEBB
 Andrew S., Feb. 6, 1902
 C. T., Sept. 10, 1868
 Charles Shepherd (Dr.),
  Dec. 12, 1935
 Ella F., w. of Dr. Charles
  S. Webb, Feb. 16, 1899
 Flora McLauren, Aug. 26,
  1886
 Florence Bertha, June 29,
  1876
 James, Mar. 2, 1832
 James H., May 21, 1863
 Lula, Apr. 5, 1894
 Mary, w. of D. T. Webb,
  Feb. 1, 1900
 Merry, May 27, 1858
 Minor S., Feb. 7, 1850
 Pattie Cornelia (Mrs.),
  Jan. 29, 1920
 Polly (Mrs.), Dec. 4,
  1873
 Rosa V., d. of Dr. Charles
  S. Webb, Dec. 13, 1883
 Ruby, d. of D. Y. Webb,
  Oct. 12, 1899
 Sarah (Mrs.), Oct. 3, 1918
 Silas (Dr.), Apr. 18, 1850
 Theodosia (Mrs.), Nov. 11,
  1831
 William A., May 21, 1863
 William Henry, s. of William
  Webb, Sept. 17, 1874

WEBBER
 Susan, w. of Elder W. Webber,
  Aug. 19, 1831

WEBER
 child of Marseiles and
  Olie Weber, Nov. 22,
  1906
 James B., Apr. 20, 1899

WEDDELL
 Daniel, May 25, 1871
 Florence Lee, d. of John
  and Edmonia Weddell,
  May 25, 1871
 George H., s. of John and
  Edmonia Weddell, May 25,
  1871

WEDDLE
 Emmett N., Dec. 5, 1929

WEEBER
 Joseph S., s. of W. B. and
  Eliza C. Weeber, July 17,
  1862

WEEKS
 Catherine, Jan. 16, 1840
 Silas D. (Rev.), Nov. 5,
  1931
 W. W. (Dr.), June 21, 1928

WEISHAMPEL
 John F., May 19, 1904

WEISIGER
 Elizabeth, w. of Jacob
  Weisiger, Aug. 1,
  1834

WELCH
 Alphonso Ewart, Apr. 17,
  May 1, 1924
 Ann M., d. of Rev. O.
  Welch, Oct. 29, 1840
 B. T. (Dr.), Dec. 22, 1870
 Bartholomew (Rev.), Jan. 12,
  1871
 Eliza P., w. of Thomas Welch,
  Dec. 24, 1840
 John Mallory, s. of Rev.
  Oliver Welch, Sept. 23,
  1847
 M. M. (Mrs.), Feb. 2, 1911
 Teresa, w. of Rev. C.
  Welch, Nov. 19, 1840
 Uriah, s. of Elder Oliver
  Welch, Jan. 24, 1834
 Virinda, w. of Col. N.
  Welch, Jan. 19, 1882

WELLBORN
 M. J. (Rev.), Oct. 29, 1874

WELLFORD
 Horace (Dr.), June 6, 1828

WELLS
 Belfied (Elder), Sept. 29,
  1859

OBITUARY NOTICES IN THE RELIGIOUS HERALD WITH DATES OF PUBLICATION

E. W., Apr. 1, 1937
Florence Leslie (Mrs.),
  Sept. 3, 1931
George, Apr. 26, 1923
J. J., Jan. 31, 1929
J. Morgan, Dec. 10, 1896
John, Nov. 1, 1923
John S., Jan. 31, 1924
Lois Whitlow, July 12,
  1923
Margaret A., d. of William
  Wells, Oct. 16, 1851
S. P., Oct. 13, 1898
Simon Carson, Dec. 13,
  1900
Susie M., w. of W. W.
  Wells, July 1,
  1886
WELSH
  J. Elwood (Dr.), Feb. 28,
    1929
  R. P. (Mrs.), Dec. 7, 1933
WELTON
  Mary, d. of C. N. Welton,
    Jan. 25, 1894
WERTENBAKER
  Charles Hansford, s. of
    Thomas J. and Mary F.
    Wertenbaker, Aug. 14,
    Nov. 6, 1862
  Rosalie Christian, d. of
    Thomas J. and Mary F.
    Wertenbaker, Aug. 14,
    1862
  Willie Douglas, s. of
    Thomas J. and Mary F.
    Werntenbaker, Aug. 14,
    1862
WEST
  Beverly E. (Capt.),
    Jan. 26, 1865
  Carrie, Nov. 24, 1887
  Catharine, w. of John S.
    West, June 18, 1846
  E. E., Mar. 9, 1933
  Elizabeth (Mrs.), Apr. 6,
    1854
  Elizabeth Hope, d. of
    William H. and Anna
    E. West, Feb. 16, 1871

Elizabeth R., d. of Parker
  West, Apr. 15, 1886
Emma M., w. of A. L. West,
  Jan. 18, 1855
Eva Augusta (Mrs.), Mar. 10,
  1932
G. B., Mar. 22, 1917
Jane K., Dec. 27, 1855
John T., Sept. 8, 1887
Joseph E., Jan. 1, 1863
Mary J., w. of W. E. West,
  Oct. 7, 1858
N. S., Jan. 26, 1871
R. W. (Rev.), Aug. 2, 1866
Thomas P., Jan. 2, 1879
W. B., Feb. 7, 1907
William F., s. of W. E.
  and Mary J. West,
  Oct. 7, 1858
William H., Jr. (Dr.),
  Oct. 20, 1859
William M., Oct. 7, 1897
WESTCOTT
  Rosie, Nov. 18, 1875
WESTERMAN
  Fannie Katie, w. of F. B.
    Westerman, d. of Thomas
    Halligan, Sept. 11, 1890*
  Sallie Katie, w. of F. B.
    Westerman, d. of Thomas
    Halligan, Sept. 18,
    1890*
WESTMORELAND
  Robert, July 28, 1842
WESTON
  J. B., June 8, 1911
WESTWOOD
  W. J., Apr. 11, 1912
WETHERALL
  Leonard B., May 26,
    Aug. 4, 1887
WEYMOUTH
  William B., Mar. 1, 1866
WHARTON
  Charles Irvin, s. of Rev.
    M. B. and M. Belle Wharton,
    Aug. 2, 1866
  Henry Marvin (Rev.), June 28,
    1928
  James Ammon, Nov. 2, 1905

* Possible inaccuracy in name, or spelling, but given as printed

OBITUARY NOTICES IN THE RELIGIOUS HERALD WITH DATES OF PUBLICATION

John, Aug. 27, 1868
John S. (Rev.), Jan. 30, 1890
Julia, Oct. 31, 1878
WHATELY
  Richard, s. of Rev. Whately, Nov. 5, 1863
WHEAT
  Edna E. (Mrs.), d. of Capt. Fleming Bibb, Sept. 12, 1889
  Kate (Mrs.), May 10, 1928
WHEELER
  Agnes, Oct. 29, 1857
  Estelle, May 23, 1895
  Gabriel (Rev.), Dec. 19, 1907
  Janie Perkinson (Mrs.), July 24, 1924
  John, s. of Dr. S. J. Wheeler, Aug. 15, 1861; Feb. 13, 1862
  Mary, w. of Micajah Wheeler, Apr. 15, 1831
  Micajah, Feb. 8, 1855
  Nancy (Mrs.), May 7, 1857
  Sophia, d. of Mrs. Nancy Wheeler, May 7, 1857
  Wayne B., Sept. 15, 1927
WHEELEY
  Ann E. (Mrs.), Feb. 15, 1849
  Mary, Dec. 14, 1838
  Perfenda, child of Thomas and Mary Ann Wheeley, Aug. 5, 1838
WHILDEN
  Bayfield Waller (Mrs.), Dec. 16, 1875
  DeLeon, s. of B. W. Whilden, Nov. 23, 1876
  William G., June 10, 1897
WHITACRE
  Anthony, Mar. 14, 1828
WHITE
  Alice Sparrow (Mrs.), June 8, 15, and 22, 1922
  Amelia, w. of Dr. Aaron White, Dec. 28, 1848
  Anderson, Jan. 13, 1881

Angelina (Mrs.), Feb. 23, 1928
Ann, Aug. 28, 1873
Ann E., w. of David T. White, d. of Edwin Grubbs, Oct. 1, 1857
Ann P. DASHIELL (Mrs.), Aug. 5, 1880
Annis Simpson (Mrs.), Nov. 29, 1923
Augustus H., Mar. 5, 1908
Banister, Oct. 8, 1868
Benjamin Franklin, father of Rev. David F. White, Oct. 18, 1934
Beulah Owen (Mrs.), Feb. 21, Apr. 11, 1918
C. Oscar, s. of Gen. Thomas M. White, Sept. 8, Oct. 20, 1853
Catherine D. (Mrs.), May 12, 1921
Charles Dudley, s. of L. S. White, Jan. 31, 1907
Clyde, s. of W. C. White, Nov. 24, 1887
Diana H., w. of Banister White, Sept. 7, 1838
Diana H., d. of Banister White, Oct. 13, 1859
Edward Bouic, s. of S. R. and S. F. White, Aug. 20, 1874
Edward Thomas, Mar. 5, 1891
Elizabeth (Mrs.), mother of Col. William L. White, Dec. 10, 1840
Elizabeth, w. of James J. White, May 19, 1853
Elizabeth E., w. of James White, d. of Capt. Humphrey Bickley, Nov. 1, 1855
Elizabeth F., w. of John H. White, June 18, 1863
Elizabeth Winn, w. of Col. Thomas White, Feb. 10, 1842
Ellen, d. of Henry and Catherine White, Sept. 27, 1894
Emily Elizabeth, July 14, 1938
Ernest, July 28, 1892

-362-

OBITUARY NOTICES IN THE RELIGIOUS HERALD WITH DATES OF PUBLICATION

Eudora (Mrs.), d. of Baylor
  and Sarah Walker, Oct. 24,
  1867
G. Jefferson (Dr.), Aug. 3,
  1843
George B., s. of Thomas and
  Margaret White, Sept. 6,
  1849
George W. (Mrs.), Apr. 7,
  1927
Hannah Temple, w. of Elder
  Horace White, Mar. 14,
  1844
Harriet, w. of John White,
  Nov. 18, 1858
Henry, Aug. 20, 1868
Henry L., s. of John H.
  N. and Elizabeth White,
  Mar. 22, 1849
Horace (Rev.), Sept. 21,
  1854
Hugh R. (Capt.), Sept. 9,
  1875
Ira (Col.), June 19, 1856
Isaac, Sept. 20, 1855
Isabella Cora, d. of Samuel
  and Lovey White, Oct. 30,
  1873
J. J. (Mrs.), Jan. 19, 1911
James A., s. of David T. and
  A. E. White, Oct. 22,
  1863
James Archer, May 2, 1878
James G., Nov. 11 and 18,
  1897
James J., June 27, 1850
Jane Montague, d. of Pleasant
  and Jane D. White, Feb. 2,
  1843
Joanna, w. of Capt. John
  White, Mar. 22, 1849
John (Capt.), Aug. 17, 1843
John, Jan. 16, 1868
John B., Oct. 4, 1883
John E. (Dr.), July 30, Aug.
  6 and 13, 1931
John L., Sept. 3 and 10,
  1914
Judith, w. of Benjamin W.
  White, Dec. 25, 1845

Julia Temple, d. of James
  G. and Adeline W. White,
  June 30, 1870
Lawrence B. (Rev.), Feb. 21,
  1901
Leonora E., d. of E. B.
  and Sarah L. White, Aug. 15,
  1867
Logan Everette, s. of George
  W. and Pauline White,
  May 5, 1892
Louisa C. (Mrs.), Mar. 8,
  1894
Lucinda, w. of Anderson
  White, Sept. 13, 1883
Lucy Brooke, w. of P. L.
  White, Aug. 14, 1862
Lula, d. of Chastain and
  Lucy T. White, Oct. 4, 1883
M. C. (Mrs.), May 1, 1924
Margaret Ann, w. of Thomas
  W. White, Dec. 15, 1837
Marie C., d. of David H.
  and Bettie White, Sept. 23,
  1858
Martha (Mrs.), Mar. 16,
  1848
Martha B., w. of Henry P.
  White, May 14, 1874
Mary Eliza, w. of Dr. William
  A. White, d. of Capt.
  A. Mundy, June 4, 1857
Mildred, w. of Nathaniel
  White, May 10, 1839
Minnie Stone, w. of Harry
  White, d. of William
  and Susan Stone, June 9,
  1904
Mira Ann (Mrs.), Sept. 13,
  1860
Miranda (Mrs.), May 17, 1877
Mollie B., d. of William S.
  White, Feb. 1, 1866
Nancy, w. of Chapman White,
  May 6, 1847
Nathaniel, Apr. 29, 1836
R. E. (Rev.), Sept. 29, 1932
Rebecca, w. of David White,
  Oct. 28, 1852
Richard (Dr.), Dec. 26, 1889

OBITUARY NOTICES IN THE RELIGIOUS HERALD WITH DATES OF PUBLICATION

Robert W., June 1, 1876
Ruth E. (Mrs.), July 27, 1922
Ruth Hutchins (Mrs.), July 6, 1922
Sally, w. of James G. White, Feb. 8, 1894
Sarah E., d. of Col. M. M. White, Dec. 31, 1846
Sarah Elizabeth, d. of S. J. R. and Virginia M. White, Aug. 27, 1846
Sterling Y., Aug. 17, 1905
Susan Alice (Mrs.), d. of A. W. Sparrow, June 15, 1922
T. J., Feb. 1, 1872
Tarpley, s. of Col. Tarpley and Jane D. White, July 31, 1862
Tarpley (Col.), June 29, 1882
Thomas H., s. of Thomas W. White, Oct. 12, 1832
Virginia Eliza, d. of Thomas I. and Eliza A. White, June 6, 1834
Virginia M., w. of Smith J. R. White, May 20, 1847
W. S. (Rev.), Dec. 18, 1873
William A. ROTHWELL (Mrs.), Apr. 25, 1907
William C., Sept. 11, 1862
William E., s. of D. T. and A. E. White, Oct. 22, 1863
William Fuller, Feb. 25, 1932
William P., July 23, 1863
William Taylor, Feb. 5, 1852
William W., s. of Col. H. B. and A. E. White, June 5, 1873
Willie, child of William and Maria E. White, Mar. 15, 1855

WHITEAKER
Alexander, Apr. 14, 1898

WHITEHEAD
Benjamin, Apr. 25, 1861
E. A., w. of R. W. Whitehead, Aug. 6, 1857
Edgar, June 26, 1829
J. W., Mar. 13, 1919
James R., Dec. 1, 1859
Mildred C., d. of John C. and Catherine Whitehead, Feb. 15, 1855
Pencie J., May 1, 1913
Sallie (Mrs.), Mar. 16, 1911
V. G. (Mrs.), Mar. 31, 1887

WHITEHORN
Eugenia W., Dec. 6, 1860
F. P., June 25, 1863
Fannie Hinton (Mrs.), Feb. 1 and 15, 1923

WHITEHORNE
J. E., Dec. 17, 1914
J. W. (Mrs.), Oct. 29, 1908
O. W., June 22, 1916

WHITEHURST
Charlotte (Mrs.), Dec. 1, 1892
Margaret S. REW (Mrs.), mother of Rev. T. C. Whitehurst, Feb. 1, 1906
Mary E., w. of J. W. Whitehurst, Apr. 14, 1887
R. T., June 26, 1913
Robert W., Oct. 14, 1920
T. J., Oct. 20, 1887
W. L., Dec. 5, 1878
Washington, Jan. 25, 1877

WHITESCARVER
C. F. (Rev.), Oct. 29, Nov. 5, 1874
Edward Massie, s. of L. C. and M. A. Whitescarver, Mar. 3, 1887
Elizabeth (Mrs.), d. of Mrs. Gracy B. Griffin, Apr. 13, 1843
Fanny, d. of Rev. C. F. Whitescarver, Mar. 12, 1874
Frances, w. of Frederick Whitescarver, Sept. 27, 1855

OBITUARY NOTICES IN THE RELIGIOUS HERALD WITH DATES OF PUBLICATION

Frank Wayne, s. of Maj. L. C. and Margaret A. Whitescarver, Oct. 25, 1860
Frederick H., Feb. 17, 1853
Giles Kyle, s. of Rev. C. F. and Ellen Whitescarver, Mar. 25, 1869
W. A. (Rev.), Oct. 17, 1895
Willie, s. of Maj. L. C. and Margaret A. Whitescarver, Oct. 25, 1860

WHITFIELD
Emma Morefield, June 23, 1932
James H. (Rev.), Oct. 17, 1912
Mary (Mrs.), d. of Dr. T. P. Matthews, Nov. 5, 1908
Theodore (Dr.), May 31, 1894

WHITING
John R., Aug. 31, 1843
Louisa Randolph, d. of John R. and Louisa E. Whiting, Aug. 24, 1838
Mollie S., w. of H. C. Whiting, d. of James Segar, Jan. 1, 1885

WHITLATCH
Elijah, Jan. 11, 1894

WHITLEY
J. F. (Mrs.), Oct. 14, 1915
James F., Jan. 16, 1919
Jesse T., Sept. 8, 1927
Robert E., s. of Mrs. M. E. Whitley, July 1, 1858

WHITLOCK
Alma, d. of J. M. Whitlock, Dec. 11, 1884
Armistead, Oct. 1, 1863
Bettie, w. of George W. Whitlock, July 10, 1913
Bettie Alma, d. of James M. Whitlock, Feb. 5, 1885
Cornelius Tyree, s. of James M. Whitlock, Feb. 14, 1867
Etta Louise, d. of Junius E. and Nannie Pierce Whitlock, July 22, 1897
Frances E. (Mrs.), Nov. 26, 1874
James Buchanan, s. of John M. and Winney C. Whitlock, Jan. 27, 1876
John E., July 16, 1896
John Henry, s. of J. M. and Sarah E. Whitlock, Nov. 29, 1849
Julian Judson, s. of J. M. and Sarah E. Whitlock, Nov. 29, 1849
Mary, w. of Charles Whitlock, Dec. 21, 1865
Mary C., Apr. 28, 1864
Mary E., w. of James M. Whitlock, Nov. 1, 1906
Rosa E. (Mrs.), Nov. 5, 1885
Sarah, Apr. 13, 1832
Sarah Eliza, w. of James M. Whitlock, Nov. 29, 1849
Thaddeus, s. of John T. Whitlock, Oct. 17, 1889

WHITMAN
B. L. (Rev.), Jan. 4, 1912
Sarah Helen POWER (Mrs.), Jan. 30, 1879

WHITSITT
D. A. (Mrs.), mother of William H. Whitsitt, May 30, 1872

WHITTED
Hugh Sidney, s. of J. S. Whitted, Feb. 27, 1930

WHITTEMORE
Benjamin B., Aug. 14, 1829

WHITTLE
James M., Apr. 16, 1891

WHITWORTH
Cora A., July 9, 1891
Cynthia, Sept. 3, 1925

WIATT
Catharine A., w. of Elder T. Wiatt, d. of William Blackwell, Apr. 6, 1848
Catharine R., w. of William E. Wiatt, d. of M. D.

OBITUARY NOTICES IN THE RELIGIOUS HERALD WITH DATES OF PUBLICATION

Spencer, Dec. 20, 1849
Charles A., s. of Elder
William E. and Charlotte
L. Wiatt, Oct. 1, 1857
John Edward, s. of Elder
William E. Wiatt, June 27,
1918
Louisa Park, d. of William
E. and Catharine Wiatt,
Aug. 3, 1848
Mary Louisa, d. of A. V. and
Alice R. Wiatt, Nov. 17,
1859
Nannie, w. of Elder William E.
Wiatt, d. of Robert S.
and Nancy B. Heywood
Mar. 30, 1911
Samuel T. (Elder), Apr. 21,
1853; Jan. 12, 1854
William E. (Elder), Feb. 21,
Apr. 25, 1918
WICKER
Elizabeth. w. of Bentley
Wicker, June 9, 1859*
Martha A., w. of Bently
Wicker, Apr. 9, 1840*
Mary D., w. of William
Wicker, July 22, 1836
WICKHAM
John, Jan. 25, 1839
William C. (Gen.), July 26,
1888
WICKS
George D., Aug. 7, 1873
WIDGEON
Charlie, Feb. 7, 1924
WIDGEONS
Elizabeth, Feb. 9, 1911
WIDGIN
John T., Mar. 13, 1879
WIGGLESWORTH
Ann, w. of Joseph Wiggles-
worth, Sept. 25, 1845
Thomas, Jan. 2, 1829
WIGHTMAN
Eliza J., w. of John T.
Wightman, May 4, 1854
J. H., Jan. 8, 1931
John, Aug. 19, 1858
Martha, w. of John Wightman,
Aug. 19, 1858
WIGLESWORTH
Lucy L., w. of Warren A.
Wiglesworth, Nov. 23, 1843
Mary Ann, Apr. 21, 1859
Mary Helen, d. of Robert L.
Wiglesworth, June 3,
1852
WILBOURNE
John G., Sept. 27, 1877
WILBUNE
Julia Ann BAILEY, w. of
William Jones Wilbune,
Mar. 24, 1904
WILBUR
T. S., Dec. 12, 1929
WILBURN
E. A. (Mrs.), May 9, 1878
John Cabble, Jan. 30, 1890
Susan A. (Sister), June 29,1848
W. W., Nov. 20, 1924
WILBURNE
Julia F., w. of C. W.
Wilburne, Aug. 16, 1860
WILCHER
Permelia G., Jan. 26, 1865
Sallie Brown (Mrs.), Feb. 25,
1909
WILCOX
Emma, Oct. 19, 1911
Rebecca W., June 24, 1869
WILDER
John H. (Elder), Dec. 8,
1842
Mary A., d. of Elder John
H. Wilder, July 20, 1838
WILDMAN
J. W. (Rev.), Jan. 11, 1934
John W., father of Rev.
James W. Wildman, Jan. 29,
1891
Mary Alice (Mrs.), Feb. 4,
1937
WILES
(Mrs.), Apr. 19, 1866
WILEY
Edmonia Evelyn, d. of Dr.
Z. K. Wiley, Dec. 3,
1885
George H. (Rev.), Sept. 11,

* Possible inaccuracy in name, or spelling, but given as printed

OBITUARY NOTICES IN THE RELIGIOUS HERALD WITH DATES OF PUBLICATION

1930
Joseph G., Oct. 26, 1876
Oliver Benton, May 6,
1926
WILHOIT
  George H., May 7, 1868*
  John C., Oct. 30, 1862
  Milton, Mar. 15, 1894*
  Virginia Madison, d. of
    Curtis and Maria L.
    Wilhoit, Aug. 20, 1863
WILHOITE*
  Elizabeth Riddell, w. of
    Milton Wilhoite, Mar.
    12, 1868
WILKERSON
  Glenmore Buchanan, June
    25, 1931
  J. P., Nov. 28, 1929
  J. R. (Rev.), May 9, 1912
  Leah, d. of Richard H. and
    Deborah Wilkerson, June
    25, 1854
  Loulie Reed, d. of William
    C. and Virginia Wilkerson,
    Mar. 30, 1882
  Margaret, Apr. 8, 1852
WILKES
  John H., Jan. 26, 1865
  Laura E., Nov. 22, 1883
  Maria Louisa, w. of T.
    W. Wilkes, Feb. 16, 1854
  William D., s. of Banister
    and Lizzie Wilkes, July
    30, 1885
WILKINS
  Ednah LeMoyne, d. of Rev.
    Frank L. and Minnie B.
    Wilkins, Apr. 6, 1895
  Margaret, w. of Joakim Wilkins,
    Feb. 4, 1858
  Richard Williams, Oct. 22,
    1863
  Robert E., Mar. 13, 1879
  W. L. S., Aug. 1, 1878
WILKINSON
  Agnes M., June 14, 1906
  Ann C., w. of William Wilkinson, Aug. 27, 1840
  Augustus C., s. of J. B.
    Wilkinson, Sept. 20,
    1883
  Branch, Dec. 9, 1897
  Cary, s. of Dr. Cary
    Wilkinson, Dec. 14, 1832
  Catharine C., w. of John
    A. Wilkinson, May 15,
    1851
  E. H. (Mrs.), Dec. 27, 1917
  E. Thomas, Oct. 10, 1861
  Elishaba, w. of William Wilkinson, d. of Elder Edmond
    Goode, June 5, 1845
  Gracie Amanda, d. of Whitfield and Fannie Wilkinson, Oct. 14, 1886
  H., Sept. 19, 1878
  Lucy, w. of Alexandria
    Wilkinson, June 6, 1918
  Lucy Jones, w. of A. N.
    Wilkinson, Nov. 1, 1934
  Margaret H., w. of Dr.
    Cary Wilkinson, Apr.
    13, 1832
  Maria M. (Mrs.), June 22,
    1838
  Mary (Mrs.), Feb. 1, 1906
  Mary E. (Mrs.), Dec. 11,
    1862
  Mary E., w. of Thomas C.
    Wilkinson, Jan. 10, 1889
  Matilda, Mar. 21, 1861
  Mittie O., d. of Pleasant
    and Virginia Wilkinson,
    Feb. 16, 1865
  Nancy, June 7, 1855
  Robert E., s. of Pleasant
    Wilkinson, Oct. 30, 1862
  S. A. (Mrs.), Nov. 21, 1935
  Samuel, Sept. 23, 1883
  Sarah P., Apr. 28, 1853
  Susie, d. of William Wilkinson, Oct. 8, 1863
  Virginia (Mrs.), July 3, 1890
  Virginia Cadwell, w. of
    C. P. Wilkinson, d. of
    H. W. Cadwell, Aug. 22, 1901
  W. W., Nov. 5, 1896
  William Mark, s. of W. E.
    and Sallie Wilkinson, Sept.

Possible inaccuracy in name, or spelling, but given as printed

OBITUARY NOTICES IN THE RELIGIOUS HERALD WITH DATES OF PUBLICATION

8, 1910
Willie, child of William
Wilkinson, Oct. 8,
1863
WILLARD
   Cynthia H., June 29, 1893
   John A., Nov. 12, 1885
   Ruth E., w. of H.·C.
   Willard, June 9, 1887
WILLCOX
   Nancy (Mrs.), Dec. 15,
   1842
WILLETT
   John Henry, May 11, 1922
WILLETTE
   Kate (Mrs.), Aug. 30, 1894
WILLHOIT*
   George, May 7, 1840
WILLIAMS
   A. D., w. of Henry Williams
   Apr. 1, 1852
   Albert Woodfin, s. of Rev.
   G. F. and E. V. Williams,
   Oct. 12, 1882
   Alice Kennon, d. of Edwin
   A. and Lucy P. Williams,
   Jan. 29, Feb. 5, 1874
   Amanda, d. of Jesse Williams,
   July 30, 1830
   Ann (Mrs.), July 23, 1891
   Anna Louise, d. of Carter N.
   and Rosa H. Williams, Oct.
   8, 1891
   Annie L., Mar. 10, 1932
   Annie V., d. of Anderson Williams, Dec. 31, 1863
   Bettie, Aug. 1, 1878
   Bettie (Mrs.), d. of N. Burt,
   Feb. 2, 1888
   Carrie Budd, d. of Rev. W.
   H. Williams, Nov. 8, 1888
   Carter N., Feb. 26, 1914
   Cecilia Jones, d. of W.
   Hunter and S. Williams,
   Oct. 23, 1884
   Charles A., Jan. 17, 1856
   Charles Melville, s. of Jesse
   and Maria Williams, July 1,
   1847
   Charlie, s. of Charles P. and

   Sue M. Williams, Dec.
   18, 1856
   Charlie, s. of Rev. N.
   B. Williams, Sept.
   5, 1878
   Christina, w. of Jesse
   Williams, June 24,
   1836
   Cornelia, Oct. 16, 1862
   C. T., s. of A. J. and J.
   A. Williams, July 11, 1889
   Daniel A., Mar. 9, Apr.
   27, 1899
   Drury H., s. of Joseph
   G. Williams, Dec. 23,
   1852
   E. C., d. of W. H. and
   Mary A. Williams, Dec.
   21, 1876
   E. Calvin, Sept. 28, 1893
   E. L. (Elder), Dec. 13,
   1866
   Edward, father of Rev.
   J. W. Williams, Jan.
   12, 1854
   Edwin A. (Capt.), Nov.
   4 and 25, 1880
   Elijah, Oct. 3, 1872
   Elijah L. (Rev.), s. of
   Thomas Williams, Jan.
   10, 1867
   Elisha J., Feb. 28, 1867
   Elisha S. (Rev.), Mar. 6,
   1845
   Eliza Jane, w. of Robert
   M. Williams, d. of John
   Kerr Clayton, Aug. 13,
   1914
   Elizabeth T., w. of Samuel
   Williams, June 2, 1853
   Evan, s. of Evan R. and
   Thomasia M. Williams,
   Oct. 16, 1879
   Evan Robert, s. of E. R.
   and Thomasia Williams,
   Feb. 16, 1888
   Fannie L., Dec. 12, 1929
   Fanny, w. of G. K. Williams
   May 14, 1874
   Flora Belle, d. of T. N.

* Possible inaccuracy in name, or spelling, but given as printed

OBITUARY NOTICES IN THE RELIGIOUS HERALD WITH DATES OF PUBLICATION

and L. C. Williams
Feb. 19, 1863
Florence (Mrs.), Aug. 12, 1897
Frank, s. of Rev. G. F. Williams, Mar. 22, 1877
Frank (Mrs.), Mar. 15, 1894
G. F. (Rev.), June 22, 1893
G. F. (Mrs.), Sept. 15 and 22, Oct. 6, 1910
G. W. (Mrs.), Oct. 12, 1854
George F. (Rev.), Feb. 26, 1914
Georgianna, w. of C. H. Williams, Apr. 29, 1869
H. C. (Rev.), June 6, 1935
Indiana V., w. of Joseph Williams, May 10, 1860
J. D. (Rev.), Nov. 3, 1870
J. J., June 16, 1921
J. Watt, Apr. 18, 1918
James F., June 27, 1901
James M., Sept. 2, 1897
James W., Mar. 28, 1850
Jared J., Oct. 20, 1853
Jesse, father of Rev. W. H. Williams, Dec. 3 and 24, 1874
John Branch (Rev.), July 11, Aug. 22, 1929
John C., Dec. 15, 1910
John G. (Rev.), June 23, 1898
John J. (Col.), Oct. 19, 1899
John R. (Mrs.), Aug. 20, 1891
John T., Apr. 14, 1898
John W. M., s. of Rev. J. W. M. Williams, Apr. 14, 1853
Josephine, d. of Smith Williams, Aug. 18, 1904
Julia W., w. of Dr. E. F. Williams, Oct. 29, 1857
L. (Mrs.), May 23, 1878
L. E., w. of John B. Williams, Feb. 23, 1889
Lawrence Miller, s. of G. F. Williams, Aug. 5,*1886
Lewis Thomas, Aug. 6, 1914
Lizzie, d. of Evans and Thomasin Williams, Mar. 23, 1893*
Louise, Oct. 16, 1913
Lucy Page, w. of E. A. Williams, Feb. 16, 1893
Lucy Page, d. of Carter N. Williams, July 7, Aug. 11, 1910
Luritta, Aug. 9, 1849
M. E., w. of George W. Williams, d. of Julia A. and Richard F. West, Oct. 31, 1878
Macie M., w. of Evan R. Williams, Jan. 23, 1913
Margaret (Mrs.), Feb. 18, 1864
Maria, w. of Jesse Williams, Mar. 3, 1853
Marietta E. P., w. of R. M. Williams, Jan. 15, 1857
Martha A. (Mrs.), Apr. 24, 1902
Martha A. W., d. of Edward Williams, Sept. 27, 1877
Mary, w. of Lemuel W. Williams, July 31, 1856
Mary, w. of John Williams, Feb. 25, 1858
Mary Alice, w. of W. W. Williams, d. of G. W. Peatross, June 13, 1918
Mary Isabella, d. of John B. and Martha Williams, Apr. 24, 1862
Mary Jarman, w. of Dr. J. C. Williams, July 22,

* Possible inaccuracy in name, or spelling, but given as printed

OBITUARY NOTICES IN THE RELIGIOUS HERALD WITH DATES OF PUBLICATION

1875
Mary T., d. of John Williams, May 14,
1857
Maud (Mrs.), d. of G. M. Tuck, Dec. 18, 1902
Nancy C., w. of Charles Williams, Nov. 30, 1893
Nancy F. J., June 16, 1887
Norman Hill, Mar. 15, 1928
Orelia B., Sept. 3, 1936
Owen Lee, Apr. 22 and 29, 1926
Patsy (Mrs.), Mar. 22, 1849
Pattie, Oct. 16, 1862
Pheba M., d. of John B. and Martha A. Williams, Apr. 24, 1862
R. L., Mar. 21, 1907
R. S., Mar. 27, 1913
Rebecca (Mrs.), d. of Edward F. Baugh, Mar. 12, 1868
Rebecca, Dec. 5, 1878
Rebecca R., w. of Edmond Williams, Sept. 20, 1900
Reuben Edward, s. of D. A. Williams, Sept. 2, 1875
Robert H. (Capt.), Oct. 11, 1877
Robert M., Aug. 26, 1886
Roberta A. (Mrs.), Apr. 30, 1936
Rosa Haskins, w. of C. N. Williams, Feb. 1, 1912
Rosamond, w. of Joseph Williams, Feb. 21, 1861
S. E., w. of W. P. Williams, Mar. 7, 1901
S. H., w. of Dr. W. L. Williams, June 6, 1895
Sallie, d. of Ambrose R. and Sarah F. Williams, Feb. 1, 1900
Samuel, Oct. 10, 1834
Samuel C. (Capt.), Dec. 24,

1863
Sarah, w. of James Williams, June 18, 1863
Sarah Scott, d. of John B. and Martha Williams, Apr. 24, 1862
Susan, w. of John H. Williams, July 10, 1835
Susan H., w. of Dr. William L. Williams, June 27, 1895
T. C., Apr. 11, 1889
T. C., Jr., Feb. 21, 1929
T. DeWitt, child of J. Watts Williams, May 16, 1907
Thomas, Jr., June 20, 1828
Thomas, Mar. 27, 1829
Thomasia Mildred, d. of J. R. and A. E. Williams, Aug. 20, 1891
Tillie, w. of Rev. Harrison Williams, Aug. 3, 1905
W. A. (Mrs.), May 6, 1928
W. B. (Rev.), Apr. 8, 1886
William, Mar. 1 and 8, 1877
William Harrison (Rev.), Aug. 31, 1893
William L. (Mrs.), w. of Dr. William L. Williams, June 27, 1895
William Linsay, Dec. 17, 1863
William P., May 7, 1874
William R. (Dr.), Apr. 9, 1885
William Wallace, s. of Andrew and Pauline Jones Williams, Nov. 1, 1917
Willie Jessup Russell, w. of Norman H. Williams, Jan. 18, 1917

WILLIAMSON
Abel, June 17, 1875
Absalom, Sept. 20, 1888

OBITUARY NOTICES IN THE RELIGIOUS HERALD WITH DATES OF PUBLICATION

Ann F., w. of Benjamin T.
  Williamson, Jan. 30,
  1835
Benjamin T., Dec. 30,
  1831
Dabney (Capt.), Apr. 20,
  1848
Eliza (Mrs.), Apr. 12,
  1888
Elizabeth C., w. of Capt.
  William Williamson, July
  30, 1846
F., s. of Frank Williamson, Apr. 5, 1888
H. J., Jan. 14, 1932
Hartwell Judson, Oct. 8,
  1931
J. E., Sept. 14, 1922
James J., Nov. 14, 1901
John, Sept. 4, 1873
Lucy, w. of Capt. Dabney
  Williamson, July 28,
  1853
Mary, w. of Abel Williamson, Apr. 24, May 1,
  1873
Mary B., Dec. 30, 1886
Matoaka, w. of Rev. Robert
  Williamson, Aug. 14,
  1890
Richard, Oct. 1, 1885
Sallie D. (Mrs.), Apr.
  27, 1933
Sarah, d. of Rev. Robert
  Williamson, Mar. 4, 1875
Sarah, d. of Thomas Williamson, Sept. 6, 1888
Sarah Frances (Mrs.), Apr.
  1, 1926
Virginia F., Oct. 29, 1863
William W. (Capt.), Oct.
  27, 1853
WILLINGHAM
  A. B., May 23, 1907
  B. L., Feb. 24, 1898
  F. G. (Mrs.), Mar. 2,
    1905
  Mary Jane, w. of Allen
    Willingham, Apr. 22, 1852
  Mildred, d. of A. B. Willingham, July 7, 1904
  R. J. (Dr.), s. of Benjamin
    Lawton and Elizabeth
    Baynard Willingham, Dec. 24
    and 31, 1914
  Robert J., Sr. (Mrs.),
    June 5, 1930
WILLIS
  Abner W., Dec. 27, 1877
  Absalom Graves, Sept. 3,
    Nov. 5, 1903
  Alice V., Nov. 14, 1867
  Ann Eliza, d. of Larkin
    Willis, Nov. 18, 1847
  Ara A., Aug. 11, 1892
  Bessie Young, w. of Eugene
    H. Willis, d. of Hugh
    G. Hiter, May 17, 1923
  Betty K., w. of James
    Willis, Apr. 13, 1911
  E. J. (Mrs.), Jan. 28,
    1875
  E. J. (Rev.), Mar. 5,
    1891
  Eliza, w. of William H.
    Willis, Dec. 6, 1849
  Elizabeth (Mrs.), Nov. 8,
    1877
  Ella Virginia, d. of
    Edward J. and Virginia
    A. Willis, July 17, 1856
  Emily, w. of Robert Willis,
    Feb. 28, 1850
  Eugene H., May 17, 1917
  Evelyn Taylor (Mrs.),
    Apr. 14, 1904
  Frances E., d. of Thomas
    Hite and Elizabeth Ryland Willis, Apr. 26,
    1906
  H. A. (Rev.), Mar. 18,
    Apr. 8 and 29, 1937
  Hammond, s. of A. E. Willis,
    Sept. 29, 1892
  Isaac (Capt.), Jan. 2,
    1868
  J. Harrison, s. of A.
    G. Willis, May 17,
    1923
  J. M. (Rev.), June 17, 1909

OBITUARY NOTICES IN THE RELIGIOUS HERALD WITH DATES OF PUBLICATION

James, May 17, 1900
James Sydnor, Feb. 22, 1923
Jean Cochran, d. of E. O. and Sallie Hart Willis, Nov. 3, 1904
John, Mar. 23, 1848
John M. (Rev.), May 6, 1858
Josephine, d. of Thomas Hite Willis, Oct. 30, 1845
Juliet Pollard, Dec. 19, 1935
Larkin, July 17, 1856
Larkin, June 16, 1927
Lelia A., w. of Larkin Willis, d. of Miles Turpin, Feb. 8 and 22, 1917
Lucy Jane, w. of Washington Willis, Oct. 4, 1860
Lucy Taylor Gordon, w. of Marion G. Willis, Aug. 16, 1906
Marion G., Jr., Dec. 23, 1920; Mar. 3, 1921
Marshall G. H., Feb. 19, 1903
Mary, w. of Larkin Willis, Nov. 17, 1881
Mary, d. of J. M. Willis, Jan. 19, 1905
Mary Holman (Mrs.), Feb. 6, 1919
Miles Turpin, s. of Larkin Willis, May 22, 1884
Richard, s. of A. E. Willis, Sept. 29, 1892
Sarah (Mrs.), Sept. 17, 1830
Susan A. (Mrs.), Sept. 21, 1854
Vaiden, Mar. 31, 1853

WILLMARTH
Isaac Mason, father of Dr. James W. Willmarth, May 7, 1891

WILLOUGHBY
Elizabeth, w. of James F. Willoughby, Mar. 28, 1872
W. W., Apr. 15, 1886

WILLS
Carlton Bradley, s. of B. F. Wills, Mar. 25, 1897
Eliza, w. of James E. Wills, May 1, 1873
Frederick Miles, Jan. 16, 1913
Irvin Crop (Capt.), Mar. 7, 1912
J. E., Apr. 20, 1882
John M. (Dr.), July 19, 1855
L. P., Dec. 12, 1918
Rebecca M., w. of Miles C. Wills, May 8, 1890
Robert H., May 13, 1915

WILMER
Bradford T., Sept. 25, 1890

WILMORE
James C., Sept. 22, 1864

WILSHER
R. W., Oct. 16, 1862

WILSON
Alderson, Apr. 20, 1871
Ann (Mrs.), mother of Mrs. Martha F. Rowlett, Dec. 31, 1846
Anna (Mrs.), d. of Robert Sands, Jan. 5, 1838
Anna Eloise (Mrs.), d. of C. M. Carpenter, Mar. 19, 1908
Annie Maude, d. of Henry J. and Annie M. Wilson, Sept. 23, 1886
Benjamin, Mar. 18, 1847
Clara (Mrs.), Nov. 16, 1843
D. M., Feb. 20, 1873
E. C., w. of A. P. Wilson, Nov. 29, 1877
Elizabeth C., w. of C. J. Wilson, Aug. 23, 1855
Elizabeth Sarah, w. of

OBITUARY NOTICES IN THE RELIGIOUS HERALD WITH DATES OF PUBLICATION

James S. Wilson, June 13, 1850
Eula Lee, w. of F. C. Wilson, Oct. 15, 1891
Fannie H., d. of James A. Wilson, Aug. 5, 1880
Franklin (Rev.), June 9, 1898
Franklin Hamilton, s. of Rev. Franklin Wilson, May 19, 1892
Hypatia, w. of George N. Wilson, Aug. 5, 1869
J. W., Oct. 15, 1936
J. W. (Mrs.), May 19, 1938
James (Mrs.), May 13, 1869
James H., Aug. 4, 1938
John, Mar. 24, 1881
John Christopher, s. of John S. and Mollie Wilson, Mar. 24, 1881
Joseph B., s. of Henry C. Wilson, Jan. 20, 1859
Julia A., Apr. 29, 1875
Lee A., Jr., Jan. 22, 1931
Lillian Brooke, d. of J. S. and Mary E. Wilson, July 19, 1888
Lloyd T. (Dr.), Oct. 26, Nov. 9, 1933
M. A. (Rev.), Sept. 22, 1904
Magdaline (Mrs.), Dec. 29, 1864
Malvina, Feb. 25, 1841
Margaret Jane, w. of J. D. Wilson, Apr. 22, 1875
Martha, w. of Hudson Wilson, May 7, 1857
Mary, w. of Asa L. Wilson, Apr. 1, 1852
Mary Frances, w. of Frank Claiborne Wilson, d. of Maj. James and Angeline McGruder Hill, Dec. 2, 1920

Mary J., w. of Abraham Wilson, Nov. 21, 1844
Mary Jane, d. of Robert Wilson, Nov. 12, 1840
Mary W. (Mrs.), d. of William Lyne and Elizabeth Baylor, Aug. 4, 1870
N. W. (Rev.), Sept. 12 and 19, 1878
N. W. (Mrs.), Mar. 29, 1923
Nancy W., w. of John Wilson, Apr. 23, 1885
Nannie C., w. of Dr. E. A. Wilson, d. of Peter Burton, Mar. 30, 1865
Nell W. (Mrs.), d. of G. W. and B. C. Widgen, Mar. 1, 1900
Peter P., s. of Edward Wilson, Feb. 13, 1890
R. Milton, July 29, 1869
Robert F., s. of John Wilson, Apr. 16, 1863
Sallie W., d. of Capt. William Wilson, June 29, 1854
Samuel P., Nov. 29, 1894
Sarah W., w. of Solomon J. Wilson, Apr. 13, 1843
Serena Reubens, w. of Dr. John T. Wilson, d. of Alexander and Serena Hutcherson, Sept. 1, 1904
Stephen Glenn, s. of Andrew J. and Martha S. Wilson, July 18, 1872
T. G., brother of Rev. N. W. Wilson, Mar. 30, 1899
Virginia Appleton (Mrs.), Oct. 2 and 9, 1902
W. P. (Mrs.), Mar. 15, 1906
William (Capt.), July 3, 1862

-373-

OBITUARY NOTICES IN THE RELIGIOUS HERALD WITH DATES OF PUBLICATION

William Alexander, Mar. 10, 1927
William E., s. of Edwin Wilson, Mar. 14, 1878
William L., Oct. 25, 1900
WILT
  William, Aug. 4 and 11, 1921
WILTSE
  Leonidas, child of H. C. and Sallie R. Wiltse, Nov. 23, 1876
WILTSHIRE
  Bettie M., Mar. 11, 1926
  J. H. (Rev.), Apr. 15 and 29, 1915
  J. P. Ennis, May 10, 1906; Mar. 7, 1907
  Joseph A., Oct. 20, 1927
  Melinda, w. of Weedon Wiltshire, Dec. 2, 1915
  Nancy Brooks (Mrs.), May 10, 1923
  Mannie L. (Mrs.), Dec. 28, 1922
  Sarah (Mrs.), Dec. 6, 1849
  W. B., Mar. 16, 1911
  William F., Apr. 28, 1853
WIMBISH
  Eliza H., w. of E. Y. Wimbish, July 22, 1852
  Nancy (Mrs.), Apr. 8, 1836
WINDER
  Annie E., w. of Levin T. Winder, Dec. 6, 1860; Jan. 10, 1861
  Cornelia, Dec. 5, 1929
  Edmond, Sr., Jan. 30, 1879
  John R., Mar. 14, 1895
  Levin Y., Dec. 18, 1879
  Louisa Anna, d. of J. H. Winder, May 5, 1864
  Mary H., w. of Dr. George Winder, Mar. 20, 1845
  Mary L., Nov. 14, 1867
  Otis Fielding, s. of William H. and Maria J. Winder, Oct. 9, 1856
WINEGAR

  John J., June 11, 1936
WINFRE
  Peter, Sept. 9, 1852
WINFREE
  Ada B., d. of William A. Winfree, Nov. 13, 1884; Apr. 30, 1885
  Bettie Sue (Mrs.), Aug. 18, 1910
  David B., s. of W. A. and Julia Winfree, Dec. 14, 1871
  David B. (Rev.), Dec. 20, 1888; Jan. 3, 1889; May 15, 1890
  Douglas Goode, s. of Rev. Robert Winfree, Apr. 12, 1900
  Holland, s. of Rev. Robert H. Winfree, Jan. 20, 1910
  John M., Oct. 18, 1866
  John T., May 11, 1843
  Julia, w. of William A. Winfree, d. of Joseph Nuckols, Dec. 14, 1905
  Lorena, d. of W. A. and Julia Winfree, Dec. 14, 1871
  Maria L., w. of Rowlett Winfree, May 20, 1852
  Mary (Mrs.), Apr. 29, 1831
  Mary Elizabeth, w. of Rev. David Winfree, Aug. 29, 1850
  Matthew, May 24, 1849
  Robert Holland, s. of Rev. R. H. Winfree, Mar. 24, 1910
  Rosa C., d. of William A. and Julia Winfree, June 11, 1857
  William H., May 25, 1843
WINFREY
  E. W., Jan. 16, 1890
  Egbert Bolling, June 4, 1891; Apr. 21, 1892
  Elisha W., Apr. 2 and 9, 1931

OBITUARY NOTICES IN THE RELIGIOUS HERALD WITH DATES OF PUBLICATION

George Hill, s. of William
H. and Sarah Yancey Holman Winfrey, Feb. 28,
1918
Judith C., w. of George H.
Winfrey, d. of Elisha
and Mary Maxey Robertson, Dec. 23, 1915
Mattie Woodson (Mrs.), Mar.
22, 1928
Roberta Jones LAYNE, w. of
E. W. Winfrey, Aug. 28,
1913
WINGATE
Washington Manly (Rev.), Mar.
13, 1879
WINGFIELD
Bettie, d. of B. F. Wingfield, Sept. 11, 1856
G. C. N. (Rev.), Dec. 28,
1916
George (Rev.), Apr. 12,
1917
Ida Vest (Mrs.), Feb. 27,
1930
Jane H., July 3, 1835
John H., Oct. 16, 1862
Judith Hughes, w. of Rev.
George Wingfield, Mar.
8, 1917
Lucie, d. of Dr. C. L.
and Virginia Wingfield,
Apr. 15, 1858
R. C., Jan. 30, 1896
Thomas, Sr., Aug. 27,
1830
W. Tupper (Rev.), July 19,
Oct. 25, 1923
WINGO
Alice Virginia, w. of
James Polk Wingo, July
11, 1935
Charles E. (Capt.), Mar.
23, 1911
George Edward, s. of William A. and Nannie Wingo,
July 19, 1849
Henry, Aug. 31, 1876
James Polk, Feb. 5, 1931
Junius F., Feb. 9, 1905

Maria F., w. of William W.
Wingo, Dec. 29, 1837
Martha Anne, w. of Samuel
B. Wingo, Oct. 31, 1907
Samuel B. (Maj.), Oct. 11,
1906
Sarah A., w. of W. E. Wingo,
Apr. 25, 1878
T. R. (Dr.), Nov. 12, 1914
William Atkins, Feb. 10,
1859
WINKLER
E. T. (Dr.), Nov. 15, 1883
Lucy, Oct. 5, 1882
WINN
Eliza, w. of Jesse Winn,
Nov. 24, 1842
Jane Frances, d. of Jesse
Winn, Mar. 14, 1834
John (Capt.), Nov. 14, 1844
Lucy, w. of Capt. John Winn,
Mar. 7, 1850
Lucy, w. of John Winn,
July 28, 1859
Lucy Archer, Jan. 5, 1933
Mary Bowles, d. of Jesse
Winn, Mar. 14, 1834
W. H., Aug. 11, 1864
WINSLOW
Ann (Mrs.), Jan. 9, 1851
Claude, s. of J. B. and
C. W. Winslow, Nov. 1,
1866
Columbia C., Aug. 3, 1854
Cordelia W. (Mrs.), d. of
Rev. Thomas Binford, Feb.
8, 1877
J. M. (Col.), Aug. 30, 1894
WINSTON
Alfred Irvin, s. of Alfred
and Isabella Winston, Apr.
11, 1878
Alice B., w. of Thomas Winston, June 1, 1876
Alma (Mrs.), Mar. 24, 1910
Beverly C., child of S. C.
and Ella Winston, Sept.
22, 1870
Blair, s. of James B. Winston, Jan. 27, 1887

OBITUARY NOTICES IN THE RELIGIOUS HERALD WITH DATES OF PUBLICATION

Blanche, d. of Alfred and Aphra M. Winston, May 9, 1872
Charles H., May 2, 1918
Collins J., Apr. 16, 1863
Dorothea, w. of Judge Edward Winston, Mar. 4, 1831*
Edward Alonso, s. of Peter Winston, Aug. 21, 1835
Eliza Jane, Aug. 25, 1842
Elizabeth S., w. of Major William D. Winston, Nov. 26, 1857
Elizabeth Shepherd, d. of Alfred Winston, Mar. 3, 1853
Ella McTyre, Aug. 25, 1932
F. V. (Mrs.), Apr. 10, 1913
Henry L., s. of Capt. Joseph Winston, Sept. 2, 1836
I. Cary (Capt.), June 19, 1919
James B. (Mrs.), Sept. 16, 1909
Jane (Mrs.), d. of Capt. James Doswell, Mar. 6, 1835
Joanna E., Aug. 7, 1845
John T., s. of Alfred and Lucy Winston, Dec. 3, 1840
Judith, w. of John B. Winston, Dec. 3, 1840
Julia Isabella (Mrs.), Jan. 3, 1918
Kate, d. of Charles H. Winston, Jan. 17, 1929
M. (Rev.), May 10, 1866
Martha, w. of Isaac Winston, Feb. 9, 1860
Mary Fanny, w. of James J. Winston, May 20, 1858
Mary Susan, Jan. 23, 1913
Mattie, d. of Cary and Ella Winston, Nov. 13, 1873
Mollie Rice (Mrs.), Oct. 4, 1934
Peter (Dr.), Feb. 26, 1920
Rebecca (Mrs.), June 6, 1861
Richard F., s. of Edmond Winston, June 21, 1860
Sally Ann, w. of Edmond Winston, Dec. 5, 1872
Sarah (Mrs.), Mar. 13, 1851
Sue Nelson, d. of O. M. and Nannie D. Winston, Sept. 28, 1854
Thomas, s. of Peter and Eliza Ann Winston, June 14, 1839
Virginia, w. of James B. Winston, Nov. 18, 1909
W. B., July 6, 1854
William D. (Maj.), Dec. 23, 1858
Willie Y., w. of Edmond P. Winston, July 2, 1868

WIRT
William, Feb. 28, 1834
William (Mrs.), Feb. 5, 1857

WISE
Andrew J., May 1, 1862
Ann (Mrs.), Jan. 27, 1859
Barton Haxall, gr.s. of former Governor Henry A. Wise, Feb. 9, 1899
Catherine McGill, w. of Dr. Theo. N. Wise, Apr. 14, 1904
Fannie Crozier, w. of William F. Wise, Sept. 1, 1904
Mary F., Oct. 5, 1905
Mildred, w. of T. P. Wise, July 23, 1840

WISMAN
Clarke, June 25, 1908

WITHERS
Chloe, w. of James Withers, Sept. 29, 1837
Michael Wilson, July 9, 1863

WITT
Alice, sister of Rev. Jesse and Daniel Witt, Jan. 31, 1878
Chastaine Eggleston, s. of

---

* Mrs. Winston was formerly married to the Revolutionary leader,

OBITUARY NOTICES IN THE RELIGIOUS HERALD WITH DATES OF PUBLICATION

Elder Jesse and Susan
  Witt, Sept. 25, 1845
Daniel, Jr., s. of Jesse
  Witt, Sept. 18, 1851
Daniel, Nov. 25, 1871;
  Feb. 29, Mar. 14, 1872
David, July 13, 1899
Dennis, June 11, 1840
Harriet N., d. of Elder
  J. Witt, May 13, 1847
Henry Jeter, s. of Rev.
  D. Witt, July 3, 1862
Ida, w. of William Witt,
  Mar. 5, 1863
James D., Nov. 1 and 22,
  1860
Mary A., w. of Rev. Daniel
  Witt, Nov. 10, 1842
Mary E. (Mrs.), Mar. 27,
  1835
Mary Ellen, w. of Rev.
  Daniel Witt, Sept. 28,
  1882
Mary Ida, d. of David and
  Elizabeth Witt, May 31,
  July 19, 1860
Mary Lewis, w. of James D.
  Witt, May 12, 1859
Samuel Brown (Judge),
  Aug. 1, 1912
Thomas, Apr. 19, 1833
WITTE
  Burgess, Apr. 24, 1873
WOHLFORD
  Frances Ann, d. of Joseph
    and Margaret Wohlford,
    Jan. 3, 1861
WOLFE
  Lizzie T., w. of Daniel
    N. Wolfe, Jan. 22, 1925
WOLLARD
  Austin G. (Dr.), Dec. 3,
    1891
WOLTZ
  Mollie G., Oct. 11, 1883
WOMACK
  Benjamin T., Feb. 11, 1864
  Francis Marian, s. of Jesse
    and Elizabeth Womack,
    Aug. 2, 1877*

Jesse, Apr. 22, Aug. 12,
  1880
Nannie M., d. of Edward and
  Virginia B. Womack,
  Oct. 29, 1857
Rose Ann, w. of Rev. Jesse
  Womack, July 12, 1860
WOMBLE
  James Dixie, Feb. 13, 1902
WOMBEWELL
  Martha, w. of Rev. Joseph
    H. Wombwell, May 1,
    1856
WOOD
  Alice V., w. of Frank Wood,
    d. of J. G. and M. E. Hew-
    lett, July 27, 1882
  Amanda A., d. of Job Wood,
    Aug. 16, 1855
  Andrew J., Nov. 16, 1933
  B. J., Sept. 19, 1929
  Burwell K., Oct. 31, 1844
  C. Dudley, June 3, 1926
  Caroline A., w. of Jackson
    B. Wood, d. of Peter
    Burns, Apr. 30, May 28,
    1885
  Charles C., s. of Muscow
    Wood, Dec. 22, 1842
  Columbia L., w. of Pollard
    Wood, May 26, 1904*
  Daniel Pollard, Jan. 1, 1925
  Dora Columbia, d. of Pollard
    and Columbia S. C. Wood,
    Aug. 18, 1870*
  Eliza, d. of Lewis Wood,
    July 9, 1840
  Elizabeth Ann, w. of John
    B. Wood, Jan. 14, 1858
  Emily E., d. of John and Cas-
    sandria Wood, Aug. 16,
    1855*
  Emma L., d. of Matthew Wood,
    May 18, 1893
  F. (Col.), Apr. 4, 1878
  George, Sept. 15, 1870
  George S. (Rev.), Jan. 3,
    1884
  Granville, s. of W. N. and
    Nannie Wood, June 18, 1874

* Possible inaccuracy in name, or spelling, but given as printed

OBITUARY NOTICES IN THE RELIGIOUS HERALD WITH DATES OF PUBLICATION

Henry H., s. of Elder William Wood, Jan. 22, 1874
J. B. (Maj.), Mar. 14, 1929
James, Sr. (Capt.), Dec. 6, 1894
Jane (Mrs.), July 14, 1887
Jimmie, s. of Charles B. and Marie E. Wood, July 24, 1873
John, Aug. 16, 1855
John B., s. of Rev. William Wood, July 20, 1882
John Wise, Oct. 24, 1935
Joseph (Dr.), Apr. 12, 1888
Laura Cornelia (Mrs.), d. of Isaac L. Graves, Jan. 5, 1882
Lizzie, d. of Capt. William H. Wood, Sept. 30, 1869
Lizzie, Nov. 9, 1922
Louise E., d. of Christopher and Martha J. Wood, Aug. 12, 1858
Lucy Ann, d. of William Wood, June 1, 1871
Lucy J., w. of Joseph T. Wood, Oct. 26, 1876
M. L. (Rev.), June 16, 1932
M. M. (Mrs.), Oct. 28, 1875
Maria Catherine, w. of Rev. W. W. Wood, Sept. 25, 1924
Martha J. C., w. of Christopher Wood, Apr. 15, Aug. 12, 1858
Mary A., w. of Green Wood, June 25, 1846
Mary A., w. of William W. Wood, Jan. 21, 1869
Mary A., w. of J. N. Wood, Sept. 17, 1891
Mary A. R., w. of John Wood, Aug. 19, 1875
Mary Annie, July 1, 1920
Mary F., w. of H. H. Wood, Nov. 5, 1885
Mary Jane Frances, d. of Silas and Eliza J. Wood, July 15, 1852
Mollie, July 29, 1926
Nannie E., w. of James P. Wood, Aug. 2, 1888
Pollard, father of Rev. W. W. and D. J. Wood, May 31, 1888
Polly (Mrs.), July 10, 1890
Rebecca (Mrs.), Sept. 30, 1869
Rebecca A., w. of J. H. Wood, Aug. 5, 1852
Reuben, Apr. 4, 1872
Richard Clement, May 31, 1917
Robbie, s. of George W. and Lucie M. Wood, Oct. 18, 1877
T., June 21, 1866
Thomas, Sr., Dec. 18, 1856
Thomas F., s. of M. B. Wood, Nov. 19, 1857
Thomas G. (Rev.), s. of Mrs. Sophia Wood, Apr. 30, 1914
W. A., July 14, 1904
W. H. (Mrs.), Feb. 21, 1901
W. N., Mar. 11, 1909
William E. (Dr.), Feb. 21, 1884
William F., Oct. 13, 1892
William H. s. of T. A. and F. H. Wood, Apr. 14, 1887
Willis, Dec. 26, 1889

WOODCOCK
Ursula (Mrs.), Oct. 2, 1835

WOODDY
Arrena Harriet, w. of Capt. James P. Woody, d. of James and Catherine Sale Andrews, Oct. 11, 1900
James P., s. of Robert C. and Mary Corey Wooddy, July 21, 1910
Mary S., w. of Robert Wooddy, Dec. 4, 1835
Robert C., Aug. 7, 1873

WOODFIN
A. B. (Mrs.), w. of A. B. Woodfin, Sept. 30, 1915

OBITUARY NOTICES IN THE RELIGIOUS HERALD WITH DATES OF PUBLICATION

Amanda M. (Mrs.), Nov. 12, 1863
Annie Dudley, w. of Thomas E. Woodfin, Feb. 8, 1906
Augustus B., s. of Rev. A. B. and M. Belle Woodfin, June 23, 1870
Catherine, w. of James Woodfin, May 4, 1871
David, Dec. 25, 1862
Elisha, Sr., May 3, 1855
Elisha, Aug. 25, 1859
Eliza A., w. of John N. Woodfin, June 16, 1859
Florence Peyton, d. of Rev. A. B. and M. B. Woodfin, Jan. 16, 1879
Frances Ann, w. of George Woodfin, Feb. 16, 1838
George, Sept. 22, 1864
Helen Susan, w. of William G. Woodfin, June 27, 1872
James, Sr., Oct. 26, 1854
James, June 30, 1859
James E., Jan. 22, 1863
John N., July 29, 1880
Joseph, Oct. 30, 1862
Judith R. (Mrs.), Mar. 25, 1858
Lucy C., d. of E. B. and L. C. Woodfin, June 5, 1854
Lucy C., w. of E. B. Woodfin, June 13, 1861
Marcella M., d. of James B. and Catherine Woodfin, Aug. 18, 1859
Martha A., Nov. 5, Dec. 24, 1868
Mary W., d. of Edmond Woodfin, Oct. 11, 1860
Samuel (Elder), Feb. 3, 1832
Susan, d. of William G. Woodfin, Oct. 17, 1872
William Beverly, s. of Rev. A. Peyton and Anna L. Woodfin, Aug. 4, 1870

WOODFORD
Caroline F., w. of William Woodford, Mar. 3, 1859

WOODING
Mary Kent, w. of Robert T. Wooding, May 6, 1875
Mattie S., d. of Thomas H. and Olivia Gilliam Wooding, Dec. 26, 1895
Nathaniel, Oct. 28, 1875
Olivia F., w. of Thomas H. Wooding, Feb. 14, 1907
S. Josie (Mrs.), Nov. 2, 1876
Samuel, Sept. 2, 1915
Thomas Hill, Dec. 14, 1922
William Tazewell, Mar. 16, 1922

WOODINGTON
Mabel, Oct. 14, 1886

WOODRUFF
A. B. (Mrs.), July 31, 1890

WOODS
John J. (Sgt.), Nov. 12, 1863
Micajah, Sept. 8, 1837
William P., Aug. 30, 1900

WOODSON
A. R., Apr. 5, 1888
Ann S., d. of John Woodson, Nov. 22, 1833
Charles Alexander (Rev.), Mar. 30, 1922
Drury A. (Rev.), Aug. 18, 1887
Drury W., Apr. 11, 1901
Edwin W. (Rev.), June 9, 1853
Elizabeth G., w. of John Woodson, Jan. 6, 1837
Emma C., w. of C. E. Woodson, July 8, 1880
Grandison L., s. of Elder Woodson, Nov. 19, 1863

OBITUARY NOTICES IN THE RELIGIOUS HERALD WITH DATES OF PUBLICATION

Harriet. E., w. of Rev. David M. Woodson, May 5, 1837
Jacob, May 25, 1848
James G. (Capt.), Sept. 8, 1864
Jane E., w. of Lineaus Woodson, Aug. 23, 1877
Joseph R., June 14, 1860
Julia (Mrs.), Sept. 13, 1860
M. B., May 9, 1901
M. Ellen, w. of J. Cary Woodson, Feb. 1, 1872
Mary Ellen SHINER, w. of George T. Woodson, June 7, 1928
Matthew, July 18, 1828
R. J., July 12, 1849
Richard S., Feb. 7, 1850
Sarah Jane (Mrs.), Aug. 2, 1849
Sidney J., s. of W. M. Woodson, Jan. 27, 1881
Susan M., w. of F. Augustus Woodson, Feb. 25, 1875
Thomas, Sr., Apr. 23, 1857
Thomas A., Sept. 13, Oct. 18, 1928
William James, s. of James G. Woodson, Aug. 22, 1861

WOODWARD
Anne, d. of Samuel B. and Mary E. Woodward, Apr. 23, 1857
Bessie Jeter, w. of J. B. Woodward, Sept. 14, 1882
Catharine (Mrs.), Dec. 11, 1851
David A. (Capt.), July 11, 1834
E. B. (Mrs.), Dec. 9, 1858
Elizabeth B. (Mrs.), d. of Dudley Ragland, Jan. 27, 1859
Jeremiah, Nov. 19, 1863
Jeremiah Clifford, s. of Richard B. and Elizabeth A. Woodward, Aug. 3, 1871
John E. (Dr.), Oct. 23, 1879
Juliet, d. of Philemon T. Woodward, Jan. 3, 1856
Juliet, Aug. 23, 1923
Marietta, w. of J. F. Woodward, July 6, 1876
Mary Ann (Mrs.), Feb. 22, Mar. 22, 1894
Mary Elizabeth, w. of Philemon T. Woodward, Mar. 29, 1900
Mary Jane, Aug. 30, 1860
Philemon Taylor, Feb. 18, 1892
Richard B., Jun. 29, Apr. 16, June 25, 1891
Richard L., s. of John P. L. and Mary M. Woodward, Oct. 31, 1878
Samuel Benjamin, Mar. 31, 1859
Selena, w. of William H. Woodward, Jan. 25, 1849
Susan Elizabeth, d. of William H. and Alice P. Woodward, July 10, 1856
Theophilus H., May 30, 1889
Virginia Franklin, w. of Wyatt F. Woodward, July 22, 1886
William Wallace, s. of J. B. and Norma O. Woodard, July 30, 1896

WOODY
Adeline, Oct. 24, 1834
Eloise R., d. of Samuel Woody, Nov. 27, 1835
James H., July 23, 1874
James P. (Capt.), June 30, 1910

WOODYARD
Rachel, w. of Levi S. Woodyard, Aug. 21, 1930

WOOLDRIDGE
Caren, w. of Elder John Wooldridge, Apr. 8, 1841

OBITUARY NOTICES IN THE RELIGIOUS HERALD WITH DATES OF PUBLICATION

Charlotte T. (Mrs.), May 22, 1856
George, s. of John and Agnes Wooldridge, July 23, 1857
John (Rev.), May 12, 1859
Katie (Mrs.), Jan. 24, 1878
Martha, w. of Elder John Wooldridge, Oct. 28, 1831
Mary Susan, w. of R. W. Wooldridge, Oct. 8, 1945

WOOLFOLK
Charles, s. of Elder Spillsbee Woolfolk, Dec. 23, 1858
Elizabeth, w. of Capt. Thomas Woolfolk, Mar. 26, 1840
John (Col.), Feb. 10, 1859
Virginia H., w. of Robert Woolfolk, Apr. 23, 1874
William W., Jan. 28, 1897

WOOLRIDGE
P. R. Jr., s. of P. R. and M. E. Wooldridge, Feb. 1, 1900

WOOTEN
Eliza, Apr. 26, 1906

WOOTTON
Mary L., Oct. 11, 1860
W. W. (Mrs.), June 11 and 25, 1908

WORD
Benjamin, June 2, 1892
Benjamin Heath, s. of Benjamin F. and Catherine A. Word, Nov. 6, 1856
Catherine, d. of John L. and Elizabeth Word, Jan. 9, 1845
J. Nelson, s. of J. H. and M. A. Word, Oct. 18, 1866
John Washington, s. of William Cary Word, June 28, 1855
Louisa, w. of Benjamin Word, d. of Henry Mason, Sept. 1882
Nannie (Mrs.), Mar. 19, 1903

WORMACH
Bettie, w. of Logan Wormach, June 15, 1933

WORSHAM
Edmonia, w. of Samuel Worsham, Sept. 17, 1903
Harriet G., Jan. 25, 1866
Hessie, child of Charles D. and Arie Branch Worsham, Aug. 29, 1872
James Thomas, s. of William C. and Julia A. Worsham, Oct. 22, 1857
Martha A., w. of Thomas D. Worsham, Jan. 25, 1866

WORTHAM
A. G. (Dr.), Dec. 4, 1873
Albert Carr, s. of Charles T. Wortham, Sept. 14, 1848
Ann E., w. of Dr. Edwin Wortham, Sept. 30, Oct. 14, 1880
Fanny, w. of Edwin Wortham, Apr. 4, 1844
Jane, w. of Charles Wortham, Nov. 19, 1830
Julia A., w. of Dr. A. G. Wortham, d. of Archibald Thomas, Apr. 29, 1897
Lewis Scott, s. of Dr. Robert and Mary F. Wortham, July 10, 1856
Mary C., w. of Samuel Wortham, Aug. 12, 1858
Mary Jane, w. of Charles T. Wortham, Apr. 21, 1859
Richard C., May 29, 1856
Richard Conway, s. of Samuel and Mary C. Wortham, Apr. 2, 1857
Samuel, s. of Samuel and

OBITUARY NOTICES IN THE RELIGIOUS HERALD WITH DATES OF PUBLICATION

Mary C. Wortham, Apr. 2, 1857
Samuel, Mar. 1, 1883
William, Mar. 28, 1844
Willie Dey, child of Charles E. and Mary F. Wortham, Apr. 7, 1859

WORTHINGTON
Virginia Lawrence, w. of James Worthington, May 19, 1904

WRAY
O. D. (Mrs.), June 13, 1907

WREN
Charles (Maj.), Apr. 28, 1837
Nannie M. (Mrs.), Apr. 22, 1915
Theodocia, w. of Capt. William D. Wren, Sept. 12, 1828
William H. (Mrs.), d. of M. B. Tate, July 2, 1891

WRENN
C. E. (Rev.), June 4, 1914
John E., Oct. 7, 1897
Thomas J., May 7, 1868

WRIGHT
Agnes Maxwell, Jan. 18, 1912
Alexander Eugene, Sept. 14, 1871
Ann A. (Mrs.), Nov. 7, 1844
Benjamin P. (Dr.), May 21, 1908
Bettie Johnson (Mrs.), Dec. 26, 1907
Catharine, w. of James Wright, Sept. 9, 1852
Charles, Jan. 29, 1830
Charles, Jan. 24, 1834
Cynthia Jane, d. of James and Eliza Ann Wright, June 2, 1842
D. B., w. of William T. Wright, Dec. 15, 1870
E. M. (Dr.), Jan. 13, 1881
Edward, Mar. 3, 1837
Eliza, w. of Richard H. Wright, July 20, 1876
Eliza A., w. of James Wright, Nov. 13, 1845
Ellsworth, Oct. 4, 1894
Emma C. (Mrs.), June 24, 1920
Emma Morris (Mrs.), Jan. 13, 1927
Fannie (Mrs.), Aug. 2, 1900
Florence (Mrs.), Oct. 9, 1930
Frances M., w. of Garland Wright, d. of Elder Lewis Chaudoin, June 24, Sept. 9, 1841
G. B., Nov. 3, 1881
Granville, Jan. 17, 1834
Guy Fitzgerald, Sept. 30, 1916
Harriet S., w. of Alsup Wright, d. of Nicholas and Nancy Pace, Oct. 13, 1910
Harvey B., s. of Isaac Wright, Oct. 14, 1858
Henry, Mar. 6, 1856
J. H. (Rev.), Feb. 4 and 18, 1892
James (Elder), Mar. 4, 1831
James D., Jr., s. of James D. Wright, Sept. 27, 1883
James Durrett, May 19, 1898
James H. (Rev.), Jan. 14, 1892
James J., Oct. 29, 1936
Joel, Mar. 11, 1875
John H. (Capt.), May 8, 1919
John Marshall, s. of James and Eliza Ann Wright, June 2, 1842
Julia A. (Mrs.), Sept. 8, 1864

OBITUARY NOTICES IN THE RELIGIOUS HERALD WITH DATES OF PUBLICATION

Julia P., d. of Joseph P. Wright, Jan. 8, 1863
Leonora, d. of Mrs. Annie J. Wright, May 30, 1850
Mamie Everett, d. of James H. and Mollie S. Wright, Dec. 25, 1890
Margaret, w. of Robert Wright, Nov. 15, 1855
Martha (Mrs.), Apr. 19, 1833
Martha A. (Mrs.), Mar. 11, 1897
Martha E., w. of William J. Wright, Aug. 13, 1846
Mary Ann, w. of Rev. William J. Wright, Mar. 29, 1855
Mary Ellen, w. of George A. Wright, Nov. 14, 1844
Mary Emily, w. of Daniel Wright, May 3, 1855
Mary M., w. of Granville T. Wright, Feb. 14, 1878
Mary S. (Mrs.), May 27, 1926
Mollie L., d. of John T. Wright, June 10, 1875
Neil C., s. of Mrs. N. C. Wright, Jan. 3, 1895
Nettie M. MOORE, w. of Rev. W. E. Wright, May 26, 1896
Paulina P., Apr. 16, 1863
Rebecca, w. of George B. Wright, June 26, 1851
Richard Lewis, s. of Garland and Frances M. Wright, June 24, 1841
Robert, Sept. 9, 1836
Robert, Jan. 22, 1857
Robert P., Apr. 13, 1876
Roland Pierce, Oct. 16, 1930
S. Maggie (Mrs.), Sept. 25, 1890
Sallie Witt, w. of Roland Pierce Wright, May 14, 1936
Sarah (Mrs.), Sept. 15, 1837

Sarah, w. of Capt. John Wright, Nov. 9, 1838
Sarah Rebecca, w. of Benjamin E. Wright, Nov. 8, 1849
Sidney, s. of John S. and Elizabeth Wright, Sept. 23, 1880
Silas, Apr. 16, 1925
Silas Alonzo, s. of John S. and Lizzie Wright, Jan. 20, 1887
Starke, Apr. 13, 1838
Sue A., w. of R. G. Wright, Dec. 24, 1874
Susan F., w. of Col. George Wright, Dec. 1, 1842
Susan Matilda, Jan. 28, 1841
T. J. (Capt.), July 26, 1900
Thomas, Nov. 26, 1840
Thomas, Apr. 3, 1856
W. L. (Dr.), Oct. 4, 1900
William, Mar. 15, 1833
William, June 1, 1838
William, June 8, 1893
William B., Jan. 2, 1930
William Edward (Rev.), June 5 and 26, 1924
William H., Jan. 4, 1855
William J., Dec. 24, 1874
Winifred, w. of Col. William Wright, Mar. 2, 1843

WYATT
Adella May, d. of West Wyatt, Sept. 16, 1852
Alexander, s. of William Preston Wyatt, Aug. 12, 1875
Charlotte Rebecca, d. of Silas and Almeda R. Wyatt, May 21, 1868
Elizabeth B., Apr. 27, 1899
Ida, d. of W. Wyatt, Oct. 17, 1901
John W., July 9, 1891
Julia Ann, w. of Joshua G. Wyatt, Mar. 20, 1856
Louisa C., w. of Dr. William

OBITUARY NOTICES IN THE RELIGIOUS HERALD WITH DATES OF PUBLICATION

G. Wyatt, Nov. 4, 1847
Lucy, w. of Silas Wyatt, Oct. 11, 1849
Lucy Almeda, d. of Silas Wyatt, July 22, 1852
Mary E., w. of William G. Wyatt, d. of Rev. William Hackett, Nov. 25, 1852
Mary Lora, w. of West Wyatt, Sept. 2, 1847
Matthew Thomas, June 29, 1876
Peter Deforest, s. of West and Mary Wyatt, Aug. 6. 1840
Richard Watson, Aug. 4, 1881
Spivey (Maj.), Jan. 22, 1836
Thomas, Mar. 22, 1849
Virginia A. (Mrs.), Mar. 2, 1911
West, July 25, 1867
WYER
  H. H. (Mrs.), w. of Rev. H. H. Wyer, Feb. 23, 1905
  Henry H. (Rev.), Feb. 28, 1901
  Henry Otis, s. of Elder Henry H. and A. E. Wyer, June 9, 1859
WYNKOOP
  Joseph Thomas, July 31, 1919
WYNN
  Maria I. (Mrs.), Jan. 31, 1884

- XYZ -

XANDRY
  Frederick, July 21, 1864
  George Lewis, s. of Frederick
    and Mary F. Xandry, July
    26, 1866

YAGER
  David F., Sept. 18, 1862
  Eliza, w. of Mordecai Yager,
    May 4, 1843
  Elma, d. of Thomas and Lucy
    Yager, Aug. 26, 1858
  G. W., July 18, 1895
  Lucy Ann, w. of Waller Yager,
    June 9, 1837

YANCEY
  Cornelia, July 26, 1860
  Gazena Watkins (Mrs.),
    Feb. 8, 1912
  Jane Lovell, w. of J. W.
    Yancey, d. of Dr. Ter-
    rill, Aug. 16, Sept. 20,
    1888
  Mary Ann, w. of James P.
    Yancey, July 7, 1859
  Melvina (Mrs.), Sept. 24,
    1857
  Robert, Mar. 17, 1892
  Robert J., May 14, 1863
  Susan T., May 30, 1850

YANCY
  Jannet, d. of John W. and
    Jane E. Yancy, July 10,
    1856
  Lucy, w. of John F. Yancy,
    Dec. 13, 1888
  Sarah M., w. of John W.
    Yancy, May 24, 1849

YARBROUGH
  Ann Worthin, d. of William
    Yarbrough, Nov. 19, 1830
  Anna Maria, d. of Charles B.
    and Laura E. Yarbrough,
    Aug. 20, 1874
  Johnnie Walton, s. of George
    W. and Bettie H. Yarbrough,
    Aug. 31, 1876

  Mary Harriet, d. of George
    W. and Bettie H. Yarbrough,
    Mar. 19, 1874
  Sarah, w. of William Yar-
    brough, d. of Joseph Tally,
    June 4, 1857
  W. T. (Rev.), Apr. 5, 1900
  William Baptist, s. of Elisha
    and Mary F. Yarbrough,
    Sept. 19, 1834

YARRINGTON
  John L., July 6, 1911
  Martha Ann, w. of John B.
    Yarrington, May 16, 1834

YATES
  A. J. (Mrs.), Jan. 14, 1926
  Betty, Jan. 27, 1837
  Boswell P., June 4, 1857
  C. A. (Mrs.), d. of J. H.
    Yates, Oct. 10, 1867
  Charles William, d. of
    Charles and Fanny Yates,
    May 13, 1847
  Eliza Moring (Mrs.), May
    17, 1894
  Joseph A. (Capt.), Aug. 11,
    1853
  Kate L. (Mrs.), Apr. 21,
    1892
  L. E. (Mrs.), Nov. 2, 1933
  M. T. (Dr.), Mar. 22, 1888
  Mary (Mrs.), Jan. 30, 1890
  Mary C., d. of J. H. Yates,
    Oct. 10, 1867
  P. L. (Mrs.), Jan. 23 and
    30, 1913
  Rosa T. (Mrs.), Feb. 10,
    1881
  Sallie E., w. of A. R.
    Yates, d. of Robert Hud-
    son, July 2, 1903
  T. A., s. of A. R. Yates,
    Mar. 27, 1902
  Thomas C., Apr. 25, 1861

YEAMAN
  James A., May 19, 1921
  Mary Sue (Mrs.), Feb. 18, 1937

OBITUARY NOTICES IN THE RELIGIOUS HERALD WITH DATES OF PUBLICATION

YEARICK
  John G., Sept. 21, 1882
YEATMAN
  Edward, s. of S. M. Yeatman, Oct. 24, 1895
  J. T., July 1, 1886
  Julia Booth (Mrs.), May 6, 1920
  Marinda Alice, d. of John H. Yeatman, Jan. 11, 1917
  Mary, w. of J. H. Yeatman, Sr., Sept. 11, 1873
  Mary, d. of Mrs. J. H. Yeatman, Sept. 6, 1883
  Robert W. S., s. of J. H. Yeatman, Feb. 23, 1854
YERBY
  Frances Louisa, w. of William H. Yerby, June 14, 1849
  Sarah C., May 28, 1857
  William H., Aug. 12, 1869
YOCUM
  J. Franklin, Mar. 6, 1879
  Maggie, d. of Edmund P. G. and S. D. Yocum, gr. d. of Rev. Israel R. Deacon, Mar. 4, 1875
YOUNG
  Abner G., Feb. 10, 1853
  Arthur (Rev.), Apr. 25, 1828
  Ellen (Mrs.), Aug. 12, 1869
  James, June 9, 1853
  John W. (Capt.), Oct. 18, 1888
  Jonathan B., Aug. 11, 1864
  M. C., d. of Charles O. Young, Mar. 18, 1926
  Maria S. (Mrs.), Nov. 26, 1857
  Mary A., w. of John W. Young, Nov. 30, 1871
  Mollie Bettie, d. of William and Ann B. Young, Oct. 14, 1858
  P. E., Dec. 24, 1863
  Susan (Mrs.), July 2, 1874
  William, Jan. 4, 1833
  William M. (Rev.), Mar. 6 and 13, 1879
YOUNGER
  Annie M., w. of Francis A. Younger, d. of Benjamin Bowles, Sept. 11, 1879
  Grace Gilliam, w. of Dr. E. F. Younger, July 18, 1912
  John T., s. of S. W. Younger, Nov. 29, 1877
  Mary Ellen, d. of Fleming S. and Susan C. Younger, Feb. 25, 1864
YOWELL
  R. F., Mar. 2, 1916
  Rufus F., July 30, 1908

ZIMMERMAN
  Mary, w. of George Zimmerman, Jan. 31, 1834
  Virginia L., d. of Matilda Zimmerman, Oct. 7, 1841
ZION
  Ann McNeil, Jan. 4, 1912
  Ann McNiel, Nov. 16, 1911*

* Possible inaccuracy in name, or spelling, but given as printed

PREVIOUS PUBLICATIONS OF THE HISTORICAL RECORDS SURVEY
OF VIRGINIA

INVENTORY OF THE COUNTY ARCHIVES OF VIRGINIA:

AMELIA COUNTY, No. 4, Richmond, Virginia, February 1940;
CHESTERFIELD COUNTY, No. 21, Charlottesville, Virginia, August 1939;
DINWIDDIE COUNTY, No. 27, Richmond, Virginia, July 1939;
ISLE OF WIGHT COUNTY, No. 47, Richmond, Virginia, April 1940;
MIDDLESEX COUNTY, No. 60, Richmond, Virginia, May 1939;
POWHATAN COUNTY, No. 73, Richmond, Virginia, August 1939; and
SOUTHAMPTON COUNTY, No. 88, Richmond, Virginia, March 1940.

INVENTORY OF CHURCH ARCHIVES OF VIRGINIA:

DOVER BAPTIST ASSOCIATION, Richmond, Virginia, December 1939; and
NEGRO BAPTIST CHURCHES IN RICHMOND, Richmond, Virginia, June 1940.

INVENTORY OF FEDERAL ARCHIVES IN THE STATES:

DEPARTMENT OF JUSTICE, NO. 45, VIRGINIA, Richmond, Virginia, December 1940

www.ingramcontent.com/pod-product-compliance
Lightning Source LLC
Chambersburg PA
CBHW071238300426
44116CB00008B/1089